"A word to the wise is enough."
—Poor Richard

The model for *Poor Charlie's Almanack* is, of course, Ben Franklin's *Poor Richard's Almanack*. Franklin, as many know, was a polymath. Born in Boston and a leader of the American Revolution, he was a journalist, publisher, author, philanthropist, abolitionist, public servant, scientist, librarian, diplomat, and inventor.

Using the pseudonym of "Poor Richard," Franklin published his *Almanack* from 1733 to 1758. Its content varied, including not only many Franklin aphorisms that became famous but also calendars, weather forecasts, astronomical information, and astrological data. The *Almanack* was hugely popular in the American colonies, selling about 10,000 copies per year.

Poor Richard's maxims ranged widely in topic and were typically laced with humor. Some samples include:

- *"No nation was ever ruined by trade."*
- *"Drive thy Business, or it will drive thee."*
- *"He that falls in love with himself will have no rivals."*
- *"Where there's Marriage without Love, there will be Love without Marriage."*
- *"Necessity never made a good bargain."*
- *"Three may keep a secret, if two of them are dead."*
- *"There is no little enemy."*
- *"It's difficult for an empty sack to stand upright."*

Poor Charlie's

Almanack

Poor Charlie's

Almanack

—Expanded Second Edition—

The Wit and Wisdom of

CHARLES T. MUNGER

Foreword By ***WARREN E. BUFFETT***

Edited by Peter D. Kaufman

Abridged edition 2005
Second abridged printing 2006
Expanded second edition 2006

For information write:
The Donning Company Publishers
184 Business Park Drive, Suite 206
Virginia Beach, VA 23462

Dwight Tompkins, Project Director
Steve Mull, General Manager
Pamela Koch, Editor
Scott Rule, Designer

Original illustrations and caricatures by Ed Wexler

Library of Congress
Cataloging-in-Publication Data

Poor Charlie's almanack : the wit and wisdom of Charles T. Munger / edited by Peter D. Kaufman.
p. cm.
Includes index.
ISBN 1-57864-303-1 (original hardcover : alk. paper)
ISBN-10 1-57864-366-X (expanded second edition)
ISBN-13 978-1-57864-366-0 (expanded second edition)
1. Investments--Decision making. 2. Investments--Humor. 3. Berkshire Hathaway Inc.--History. 4. Munger, Charles T., 1924- I. Kaufman, Peter D. II. Title.
HG4515.M86 2005
332.6'02'07--dc22
2005000483

Printed in the United States of America
by Walsworth Publishing Company
Marceline, Missouri

For additional copies of *Poor Charlie's Almanack: The Wit and Wisdom of Charles T. Munger*, go online to:
www.poorcharliesalmanack.com

For Charles T. Munger

who, in his own words, would tell you:

"Acquire worldly wisdom and adjust your behavior accordingly. If your new behavior gives you a little temporary unpopularity with your peer group... then to hell with them."

Contents

Appendixes

Index

Acknowledgments

This book is a survey of Charles T. Munger: his approach to learning, decision making, investing, his speeches, his "zingers," and more. The impetus for the book came from the many people who, over the years, have said they wished one existed—and have done so with ever-increasing vigor at Berkshire and Wesco shareholder meetings, at dinner parties, on message boards, and many other places. Hearing this clamor, your editor, Peter Kaufman, suggested to Warren Buffett that a book be done and was encouraged to take it upon himself to make it happen. What you are about to read is the result.

Illustrator and caricature artist Ed Wexler has made caricature drawings of each contributor to the project and has also produced several dozen other illustrations throughout the book. We hope you enjoy all of his work as much as we do. Special recognition is also due Whitney Tilson, who compiled the Mungerisms section; Michael Broggie, the author of our biographical portrait of Charlie; and Carol Loomis, who edited certain sections of the book (and on multiple occasions saved the editor from himself.)

The production team included, from left to right (back row), Travis Gallup, Carl Foote, Scott Rule, Dwight Tompkins, Michael Broggie, Steve Mull, (middle row) Pamela Koch, Eric Hartman-Birge, Paul Hartman, Charles Belser, Ed Wexler, (front row) Whitney Tilson, Marcus Kaufman, Peter Kaufman, Carol Loomis, Debbie Bosanek, and Doerthe Obert.

Finally, if you enjoy reading *Poor Charlie's Almanack* half as much as we enjoyed putting it together, we will consider our efforts a distinct success. In every respect, but particularly in our interactions with Charlie, his family, and the Mungers' wide circle of friends and associates, we have been favored with calm skies and smooth sailing in the production of this book. We hope our efforts have proven worthy of our subject, a good and admirable man.

Charles Helman Lea once said, “It will generally be admitted that the true test of all books is the influence they have upon the lives and conduct of their readers.” We hope our book passes this test, exerting a lasting influence on you.

Foreword: Buffett on Munger

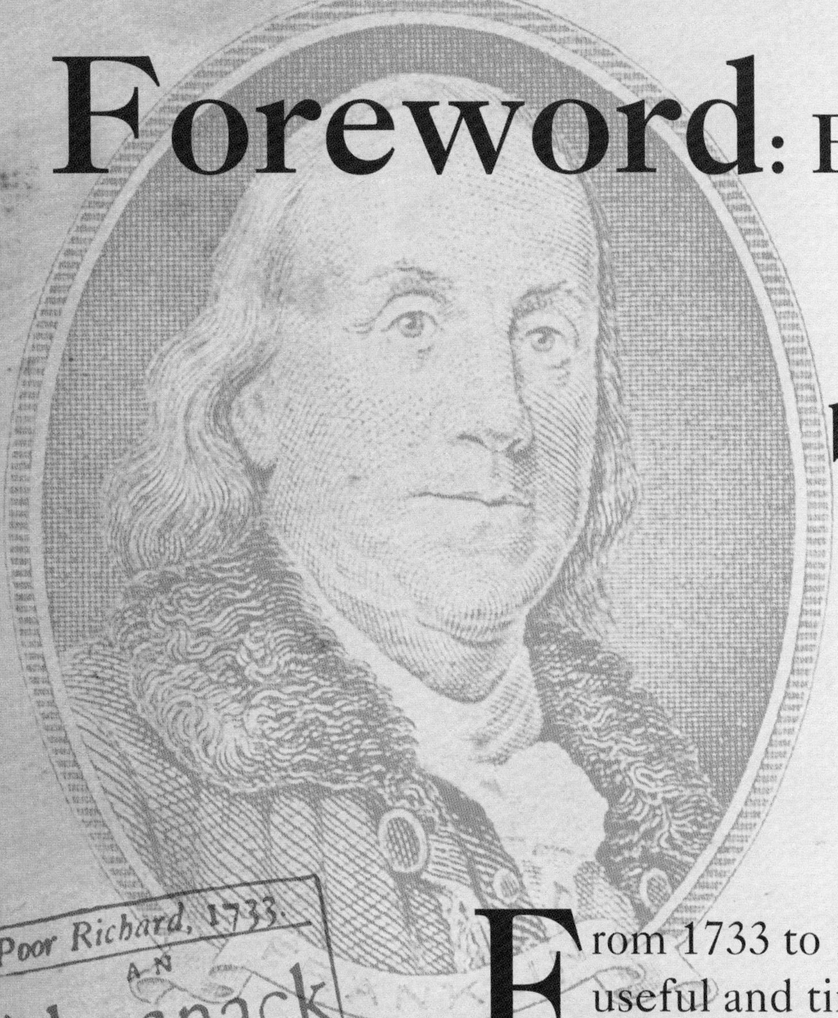

by Warren E. Buffett

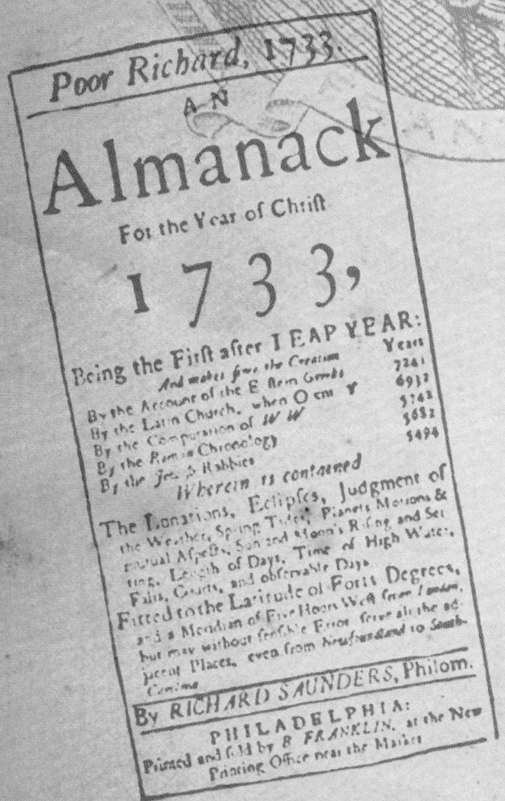

From 1733 to 1758, Ben Franklin dispensed useful and timeless advice through *Poor Richard's Almanack*. Among the virtues extolled were thrift, duty, hard work, and simplicity.

Subsequently, two centuries went by during which Ben's thoughts on these subjects were regarded as the last word. Then Charlie Munger stepped forth.

Initially a mere disciple of Ben's, Charlie was soon breaking new ground. What Ben had recommended, Charlie demanded. If Ben suggested saving pennies, Charlie raised the stakes. If Ben said be prompt, Charlie said be early. Life under Ben's rules began to look positively cushy compared with the rigor demanded by Munger.

Moreover, Charlie consistently practiced what he preached (and, oh, how he preached). Ben, in his will, created two small philanthropic funds that were designed to teach the magic of compound interest. Early on, Charlie decided

"PARTNERS"

that this was a subject far too important to be taught through some posthumous project. Instead, he opted to become a living lesson in compounding, eschewing frivolous (defined as "any") expenditures that might sap the power of his example. Consequently, the members of Charlie's family learned the joys of extended bus trips while their wealthy friends, imprisoned in private jets, missed these enriching experiences.

In certain areas, however, Charlie has not sought to improve on Ben's thinking. For example, Ben's "Advice on the Choice of a Mistress" essay has left Charlie in the "I have nothing to add" mode that is his trademark at Berkshire annual meetings.

There was only one partner who fit my bill of particulars in every way—Charlie.

"A partner who is not subservient, who is himself extremely logical, is one of the best mechanisms you can have."

—Buffett

As for myself, I'd like to offer some "Advice on the Choice of a Partner." Pay attention.

Look first for someone both smarter and wiser than you are. After locating him (or her), ask him not to flaunt his superiority so that you may enjoy acclaim for the many accomplishments that sprang from his thoughts and advice. Seek a partner who will never second-guess you nor sulk when you make expensive mistakes. Look also for a generous soul who will put up his own money and work for peanuts. Finally, join with someone who will constantly add to the fun as you travel a long road together.

All of the above is splendid advice. (I've never scored less than an A in self-graded exams.) In fact, it's so splendid that I set out in 1959 to follow it slavishly. And there was only one partner who fit my bill of particulars in every way—Charlie.

In Ben's famous essay, he says that only an older mistress makes sense, and he goes on to give eight very good reasons as to why this is so. His clincher: "…and, lastly, they are so grateful."

Charlie and I have now been partners for forty-five years. I'm not sure whether he had seven other reasons for selecting me. But I definitely meet Ben's eighth criterion. I couldn't be more grateful.

Rebuttal:

Munger on Buffett

I think there's some mythology in the idea that I've been this great enlightener of Warren. He hasn't needed much enlightenment. I frankly think I get more credit than I deserve. It is true that Warren had a touch of brain block from working under Ben Graham and making a ton of money. It's hard to switch from something that's worked so well. But if Charlie Munger had never lived, the Buffett record would still be pretty much what it is.

It's hard to believe that he's getting better with each passing year. It won't go on forever, but Warren is actually improving. It's remarkable: Most men in their seventies are not improving, but Warren is. Berkshire is drowning in money—we have great businesses pounding out money. When Warren is gone, the acquisition side of Berkshire will not do as well, but the rest will do well. And the acquisition side will do just fine.

I think the top guy won't be as smart as Warren. But it's silly to complain, "What kind of world is this that gives me Warren Buffett for forty years and then some bastard comes along who's worse?"

Charles T Munger

Introduction

by Peter D. Kaufman

You are about to embark on an extraordinary journey toward better investing and decision making. You may also arrive at a better understanding of life as well, all thanks to the wit, wisdom, speeches, and writings of Charlie Munger—this generation's answer to Benjamin Franklin. Charlie's unique worldview, what he calls his "multidisciplinary" approach, is a self-developed model for clear and simple thinking—yet his concepts and models are anything but simplistic. Notice how well Charlie's thinking stands the test of time: The earliest talk in this collection is almost twenty years old, yet it is as relevant today as the day he first delivered it. As you will soon discover, Charlie's observations and conclusions are based on fundamental human nature, basic truths, and core principles from a wide range of disciplines.

L·O·L·L·A·P·A·L·O·O·Z·A

lol•la•pa•loo•za [ˌlälə-pə-ˈlü-zə] n. slang: 1. Something outstanding of its kind. 2. As personified by Charles Munger, the critical mass obtained via a combination of concentration, curiosity, perseverance, and self-criticism, applied through a prism of multidisciplinary mental models.

Throughout the book, Charlie reveals his intellect, wit, values, and no end of rhetorical flair. His encyclopedic knowledge allows him to cite references from classical orators to eighteenth- and nineteenth-century European literati to pop culture icons of the moment. Where else would you find Demosthenes and Cicero juxtaposed against Johnny Carson or today's investment managers set against Nietzsche, Galileo, and a "one-legged man in an ass-kicking contest"? Or how about Ben Franklin versus Bernie Cornfeld in a battle of worldly wisdom? Using self-deprecation and imagination to great effect, Charlie cheerfully compares himself to a counting horse, proposes "Glotz's sugared, caffeinated water" as a marketing-bereft label for Coca-Cola, and attests, "At least when I was young I wasn't a total klutz."

In one talk (Practical Thought About Practical Thought?), Charlie even takes on the challenge of building, from scratch, a two-trillion-dollar business, and then walks us through his diverse mental models to accomplish that mighty feat.

The quotes, talks, and speeches presented here are rooted in the old-fashioned Midwestern values for which Charlie has become known: lifelong learning, intellectual curiosity, sobriety, avoidance of envy and resentment, reliability, learning from the mistakes of others, perseverance, objectivity, willingness to test one's own beliefs, and many more. But his advice comes not in the form of stentorian admonishments; instead, Charlie uses humor, inversions (following the directive of the great algebraist, Jacobi, to "Invert, always invert"), and paradox to provide sage counsel about life's toughest challenges.

Charlie also employs historical and business case studies to great effect. In these presentations, he makes his points with subtlety and texture, often using a story-like context instead of abstract statements of theory. He regales his audience with humorous anecdotes and poignant tales, rather than with a blizzard of facts and figures. He well knows, and wisely exploits, the traditional role of the storyteller as purveyor of complex and detailed information. As a result, his lessons hang together in a coherent "latticework" of knowledge, available for recall and use when needed.

It is clear throughout these talks and speeches that Charlie places a premium on life decisions over investment decisions. His mental models, drawn from every discipline imaginable, recur repeatedly and, in no way, focus on "business portfolio strategy" or "beta" or "Cap M." Rather, they center on fundamental truth, human accomplishment, human foibles, and the arduous path to wisdom. Charlie once said, "I wanted to get rich so I could be independent, like Lord John Maynard Keynes." Independence is the end that wealth serves for Charlie, not the other way around.

About the Book:

We open with a "portrait" biography that chronicles Charlie's progress from a modest Omaha childhood to prodigious financial success. New to this edition, Charlie then offers us his reflections on aging, inspired by Cicero's *Discourse of Old Age*. Next, we summarize the Munger approach to life, learning, decision making, and investing. This section details both Charlie's unconventional way of thinking and his extraordinary work ethic—the twin fonts of his amazing success. Our "Mungerisms: Charlie Unscripted" section presents a collection of the trenchant remarks he has made at past Berkshire Hathaway and Wesco Financial annual meetings.

In the balance of the book, Charlie speaks to his audience via speeches and talks he gave over a twenty-year period. In this new edition, each Talk is followed by a brief Postscript written in 2006, in which Charlie reflects on his earlier work as he views it today. The "Ten Talks" cover a wide spectrum of Charlie's interests, ranging from how one acquires worldly wisdom, to how his "Multiple Mental Models" can be applied to business, to how the investment strategies used by charitable foundations can be improved. The tenth talk is a special rendition of "The Psychology of Human Misjudgment" that Charlie created especially for this book. Each talk is well worth your time not only for the enjoyment it will provide you, but also for what you can absorb from the rich assortment of ideas and practices that Charlie relies on. You will probably never find a better opportunity to learn from someone so smart—and so forthright. In his talks, Charlie simply opens up and tells it like it is. A special note: Charlie's redundancy in expressions and examples is purposeful: for the kind of deep "fluency" he advocates, he knows that repetition is the heart of instruction.

"If you skillfully follow the multidisciplinary path, you will never wish to come back. It would be like cutting off your hands."

A word about the style and layout of the book: Charlie is enormously curious about nearly everything he bumps into in life. Accordingly, as we ourselves bumped into people, places, and subjects mentioned by Charlie in his talks, we supplemented his text with related information, photographs, and other graphics. The "sidebars" peppered throughout the talks, for example, serve to explain concepts, add a supporting voice, or emphasize an important Munger idea. We hope these sidebars will not only inform, but also amuse and even encourage you to further pursue these subjects on your own.

I wish you good reading and an appreciation of the brightness and dry humor that those of us who know Charlie Munger have come to treasure and expect from him.

"I've gotten paid a lot over the years for reading through the newspapers." Awaiting luncheon on the Thames, 1996.

Chapter One

A Portrait of Charles T. Munger

By Michael Broggie

"The next thing most like living one's life over again seems to be a recollection of that life, and to make that recollection as durable as possible by putting it down in writing."

—Benjamin Franklin

"I sometimes tell my friends, 'I'm doing the best I can. But, I've never grown old before. I'm doing it for the first time. And I'm not sure that I'll do it right.'"

Behind the extraordinary story of Berkshire Hathaway are two financial geniuses: the widely acclaimed Warren Buffett and his "silent partner," Charlie Munger, who relishes his obscurity.

Charlie is Warren's friend, lawyer, advisor, devil's advocate (Warren once called him the "abominable no-man"), and one of the largest stockholders in one of the most successful publicly traded companies in American business history. Since 1964, when Warren, and some years later, Charlie, assumed management of Berkshire, its market value has increased an astonishing 13,500 times, from $10 million to roughly $135 billion, without much of an increase in outstanding shares. Such phenomenal growth is the singular achievement of these two unassuming Midwesterners, who combine their synergistic abilities to recognize and seize opportunities other businessmen consistently overlook.

Here's Charlie in a scene destined to be repeated countless times over the years: successful fishing in Cass Lake, Minnesota.

According to Charlie, his boss's staunch anti-socialist attitude was manifested in his rule requiring the boys to present two pennies at the end of their shifts to cover the cost of the new Social Security Act. In return, they received a $2 daily wage along with the admonition that socialism is inherently evil.

While Warren is one of the most admired and publicized business leaders in the country, Charlie has purposefully sidestepped the limelight, choosing relative anonymity instead. To better understand this complex and highly private businessman, we must start at the beginning. Charles Thomas Munger was born on January 1, 1924, in America's heartland, Omaha, Nebraska. Many notables share his Midwestern roots: Will Rogers, Henry Fonda, John Pershing, Harry Truman, Walt Disney, Ann Landers, Gerald Ford—and, of course, Warren Buffett.

Charlie initially crossed paths with the Buffett family during the formative years of his life when he worked at Buffett and Son, an upscale grocery store in Omaha, about six blocks from the Munger household. The boss and part-owner was Warren's grandfather, Ernest. A strict disciplinarian, he scheduled his young workers for twelve-hour shifts with no meals or breaks. According to Charlie, his boss's staunch

Charlie with wife Nancy aboard their catamaran, the *Channel Cat*, off the Santa Barbara coast.

anti-socialist attitude was manifested in his rule requiring the boys to present two pennies at the end of their shifts to cover their share of the cost of the new Social Security Act. In return, they received a $2 daily wage—along with a considerable lecture about the evils of socialism.

The arduous working conditions in the Buffett grocery store had a lasting influence on both Charlie and Warren. Warren, six years younger, served his hard times under Grandpa Ernest several years after his future business partner had moved on.

Charlie's formal education began at Dundee Elementary School where he and his younger sisters, Mary and Carol, were indoctrinated with ethical homilies. Charlie's teachers remember a smart kid who was also inclined to be a bit of a wiseacre. He enjoyed challenging the conventional wisdom of teachers and fellow students with his ever-increasing knowledge gained through voracious reading, particularly biographies. Today, he can't remember the first time he was exposed to the aphorisms of Ben Franklin, but they fueled an ineffaceable admiration for the eclectic and eccentric statesman/inventor. Charlie's parents, Al and Florence Munger, encouraged reading and gave each of their children several books at Christmas, usually devoured by that night.

At the nearby home of the Mungers' close friends, the Davises, Charlie often read the medical journals belonging to Dr. Ed Davis, who was both his father's best friend and a family physician. Charlie's early exposure to Dr. Davis's medical library spawned a lifelong interest in science. By the time he was fourteen, the precocious learner also became one of the doctor's best friends. Charlie became so interested in medicine that he watched motion pictures of Dr. Davis, a urologist, performing surgery and became fascinated with the statistical outcomes of similar procedures in the field.

"In my whole life, I have known no wise people (over a broad subject matter area) who didn't read all the time—none, zero. You'd be amazed at how much Warren reads—and at how much I read. My children laugh at me. They think I'm a book with a couple of legs sticking out."

Hamster breeder and trader

At home, Charlie developed a fondness for raising hamsters and periodically traded them with other children. Even at an early age, Charlie showed sagacious negotiating ability and usually gained a bigger specimen or one with unusual coloring. When his brood grew to thirty-five animals, his mother ordered an end to his hobby because of the pungent odor from his basement hamster farm. One of his sisters remembered years later that the family had to endure the incessant squeaking of hungry hamsters until Charlie arrived home from school to feed them.

Charlie attended Central High School, a very large public school that was recognized as a good college preparatory school. The teachers, mostly women, were dedicated to their work and to their students. The Central High curriculum provided a conventional classic education, in which Charlie naturally excelled because of his logically driven, inquiring mind.

Throughout elementary and secondary school, Charlie was younger and smaller than his classmates, having been moved ahead in elementary school after his mother taught him to read phonically. Too small to compete in regular high school sports, he joined the rifle team, earned a varsity letter, and eventually became team captain. His letterman's sweater ("a large letter on a very small chest" is Charlie's memory) attracted attention from coeds who wondered how such a scrawny kid could earn a varsity letter. Fortunately for Charlie, his father was an avid outdoorsman and duck hunter and took joy in his son's marksmanship.

Omaha was not spared the severity of the Great Depression. Charlie's immediate family was not dramatically affected, but some members of his extended family were.

Omaha in the 1920s was the proverbial melting pot; different races and religions mixed socially and commercially, and crime was practically unknown. Doors and vehicles were left unlocked, and a person's word was trusted implicitly. Kids played "Kick the Can" on warm summer evenings and went to Saturday matinees to see the latest "talkies," such as *King Kong*, a favorite of eight-year-old Charlie.

The 1930s brought hard times, and Omaha experienced the severity of the Great Depression. Charlie's observations of the plight of those less fortunate made lasting impressions. He saw hobos roaming the streets looking for handouts and others who were willing to sweep a driveway or porch in exchange for a sandwich. Thanks to family connections, Charlie landed a boring job counting passersby; it paid forty cents an hour. Charlie preferred this work to carrying heavy boxes of groceries.

Charlie learned that, by supporting each other, the Mungers weathered the worst economic collapse in the nation's history.

Charlie's grandfather was a respected federal judge, and his father followed in his footsteps to become a prosperous lawyer. Charlie's immediate family was not dramatically affected by the depression, but some members of Charlie's extended family were. This era provided real learning experiences for young Charlie. He witnessed the generosity and business acumen of his grandfather as he helped rescue a small bank in Stromsburg, Nebraska, that was owned by Charlie's Uncle Tom. Because of the miserable economy and drought-damaged crops, the bank's farm-based clients were defaulting on loans. Tom had rolled up $35,000 in uncollectible notes when he called upon Grandpa Munger for support. The judge risked nearly half of his assets by exchanging $35,000 in sound first mortgages for the bank's weak loans, thus enabling Tom to open his doors after Roosevelt's bank holiday. The judge eventually recovered most of his investment, but not until a great many years later.

Judge Munger also sent his daughter's husband, a musician, to pharmacy school and helped him buy a well-located pharmacy that had closed because of the depression. The business prospered and secured the future for Charlie's aunt. Charlie learned that, by supporting each other, the Mungers weathered the worst economic collapse in the nation's history.

"I had a brief immersion in elementary physics, prompted entirely by the unusual incentives provided by WWII. This immersion greatly improved my wisdom. What occurred was that I was given more models, so I was less like that 'man with a hammer.'"

Fortunately, Al Munger's law practice prospered during the depression and was given a boost when the United States Supreme Court agreed to review a tax case involving a small soap-making company he represented. Coincidently, the huge Colgate-Palmolive Company was also affected by the Court's decision. Concerned that the Midwestern attorney didn't have the requisite experience to argue successfully before the highest court, Colgate offered to pay Al liberally to step aside and allow a famous New York attorney to take his place. The big-city lawyer lost the case while Al pocketed a substantial fee. Later, he joked that he could have lost the case just as well for a much smaller fee. The amount of the fee has never been revealed, but it was enough, when combined with income Al earned from his other clients, to help keep the Mungers comfortable during the depression. Charlie also helped the family by working to earn his own spending money and thus learned first-hand the value of financial independence.

"I attended Caltech for only nine months, during WWII, courtesy of the Army Air Corps, which installed me in a meteorology program. Predicting weather in those early days was, even more than now, much like the use of horse-race data to predict horse-race outcomes, and my interest in meteorology, absent war pressure, was zero."

In 1941, as the war raged across the Atlantic, Charlie graduated from Central High School and left Omaha for the University of Michigan. There he chose mathematics as his major, drawn by the appeal of numerical logic and reason. He also discovered physics after enrolling in a basic course to fulfill an academic requirement for science. Charlie was fascinated by the power of physics and its boundless reach. In particular, he was impressed by the process followed by physicists, such as Albert Einstein, to address the unknown. Physics-like problem solving was to become a passion for Charlie and is a skill he considers helpful in framing the problems of life. He has often stated that anyone who wants to be successful should study physics because its concepts and formulas so beautifully demonstrate the powers of sound theory.

College-aged men were then in high demand for military service. Days after turning nineteen and completing his second year at Michigan, Charlie enlisted in the Army Air Corps in a program that would eventually make him a second lieutenant. He was sent to the Albuquerque campus of the University of New Mexico for studies in general science and engineering. Next he was shuffled to the prestigious California Institute of Technology in Pasadena, California. He was schooled in thermodynamics and the science of meteorology—then essential to flyers—and trained to become a meteorologist. After completing his studies at Caltech, Charlie was dispatched to a permanent duty station in Nome, Alaska.

Harvard Dean Roscoe Pound interceded to gain Charlie's admittance to Harvard.

While still in the service, he married Nancy Huggins, a young woman from Pasadena who was a good friend of his sister Mary at Scripps College. They were stationed in Albuquerque and then San Antonio until Charlie was discharged from the Army Air Corps in 1946. Soon Charlie and Nancy had their first child, a boy whom they named Teddy.

Although he had attended several universities, Charlie still did not have a bachelor's degree. Nevertheless, using the GI Bill, he applied to Harvard Law

School where his father had preceded him. His lack of an undergraduate degree threatened to derail him, but a family friend, former Harvard Law School Dean Roscoe Pound, interceded on Charlie's behalf. Charlie was admitted, despite the determination of the admissions office to first send him back to college.

As it turned out, Charlie had little trouble succeeding at Harvard though he annoyed a few people along the way.

"It's a sad thing, but not everybody loves me."

As it turned out, Charlie had little trouble succeeding at Harvard though he annoyed a few people along the way. Because of his intellect (the Army measured his I.Q. at the top of the curve), Charlie had a tendency to be abrupt, which was often interpreted as rudeness. Actually, Charlie was just in a hurry, and the customary pleasantries of the classroom were of little concern to him. Even so, he was liked by most of his peers and fully enjoyed the social aspects of student life in Cambridge.

Charlie graduated from Harvard Law School in 1948 and was one of twelve in his class of 335 to graduate magna cum laude. He considered joining his father's law practice, but, after a discussion with his father, both of them concluded that Charlie should try a larger city. He headed off to Southern California, a place he had liked while a student at Caltech. After passing the California bar exam, he joined the firm of Wright & Garrett, later renamed Musick, Peeler & Garrett. Charlie built a house, designed by his architect uncle, Frederick Stott, in South Pasadena where he and Nancy and their three children, Teddy, Molly, and Wendy, lived.

Charlie indulges his lifelong interest in architecture on the streets of London.

Despite outward appearances, all was not sunny in Charlie's world. His marriage was in trouble, and he and his wife finally divorced in 1953. Not long thereafter, Charlie learned that his adored son, Teddy, was terminally ill with leukemia. It was a significant burden for twenty-nine-year-old Charlie. In that era, before bone marrow transplants, there was no hope. A friend remembers that Charlie would visit his dying son in the hospital and then walk the streets of Pasadena crying.

During this sad time, his friend and law partner, Roy Tolles, arranged through a friend for Charlie to meet Nancy Barry Borthwick, who lived in Los Angeles. She was a Stanford graduate and had two small boys, close to the ages of his girls. Charlie and Nancy had much in common and had fun together, and after a few months of dating became engaged. They were married in a small family wedding in January 1956, and all four children, his girls and her boys, ages four to seven, attended the wedding.

Charlie and Nancy lived in her house in the hills of west Los Angeles for several years. Then, partly to shorten Charlie's daily commute, they moved to Hancock Park where they still reside. The house they built there was large enough for their ever-expanding family: three more boys and a girl for a total of eight. Fortunately, both liked children! They also liked golf, the beach, and social clubs. Charlie and Nancy were soon members of the University Club, the California Club, the Los Angeles Country Club, and the Beach Club.

Charlie marries Nancy Barry Borthwick, January 27, 1956.

With many new responsibilities, Charlie worked hard at his law practice. Even so, his earnings were unsatisfactory to him as they were based on a combination of billable hours and seniority. He wanted more than what a senior law partner would be able to earn. He sought to be like his firm's leading capitalist clients, in particular, the universally admired Harvey Mudd, later the founder of the college bearing his name. With Nancy's support, he turned to outside ventures and alternative ways to generate income. However, he never forgot the sound principles taught by his grandfather: to concentrate on the task immediately in front of him and to control spending.

Following this conservative approach, Charlie seized opportunities to build wealth. He began investing in stocks and acquired equity in one of his client's electronics businesses—a practice common among lawyers in the mid-1950s and 1960s. This investment was mutually beneficial: Charlie gained invaluable knowledge about business while his client enjoyed the proactive attention of a lawyer who knew more than just the law.

In 1961, Charlie tackled property development for the first time, in partnership with Otis Booth, a client and friend. The venture, building condominiums on land near Caltech, was a smashing success, and the partners earned a handsome profit of $300,000 on a $100,000 investment. Charlie and Otis then undertook other successful construction and development projects in Pasadena. Later, Charlie participated in similar projects in Alhambra, California. He sharpened his business acumen by handling the negotiations and contracts. In all cases, he left all of his profits in real estate ventures so that bigger and bigger projects became possible. When he stopped in 1964, he had a nest egg of $1.4 million from real estate projects alone.

"I think when you're buying jewelry for the woman you love, financial considerations probably shouldn't enter into it."

In February 1962, he joined four colleagues from Musick, Peeler & Garrett in establishing a new law firm. The original partners were Roy Tolles, Rod Hills, Dick Esbenshade, Fred Warder, and Charlie. They were joined by Rod's wife, Carla, and James T. Wood, a sole practitioner and friend of the Hills, and, importantly, who had a client. They named the firm Munger, Tolles & Hills. Over the years, the firm had

Charlie on attracting clients: "It's the work on your desk.... It's the work on your desk. Do well with what you already have and more will come in."

several names, always beginning with Munger, Tolles. With the addition of Ron Olson, it finally became Munger, Tolles & Olson, shortened as "Munger Tolles" or "MTO."

The successful practice of law was by then a backstop rather than an ending objective for Charlie. At about the time that he was launching his new law firm, he was carefully crafting his exit plan. Charlie set up an investment partnership with Jack Wheeler, and they were later joined by Al Marshall. The idea for this partnership arose a few years earlier when the death of Charlie's father required him to return to Omaha to administer the estate. To welcome him home, the children of Charlie's friend and medical mentor, Dr. Ed Davis, arranged for a dinner party. Both of the Davis boys, Eddie Jr. and Neil, were former childhood chums of Charlie and were now physicians while their sister Willa had married an Omaha businessman, Lee Seemann. The dinner party included Willa and Lee, Neil and his wife Joan, and a fellow named Warren Buffett.

The dinner party included Willa and Lee, Neil and his wife Joan, and a fellow named Warren Buffett.

Charlie's father,
Alfred C. Munger

It was Charlie's return home to Omaha to administer his father's estate that led to his meeting Warren Buffett.

Charlie recognized Warren's family name from his days at Buffett and Son, and Warren had heard of Charlie a few years earlier when he was raising investment capital in Omaha. At one point, Warren had met with Dr. Davis and his wife, Dorothy, to explain his investment philosophy, and they agreed to place a large part of their life savings—$100,000—with him. Why? The doctor explained that Warren reminded him of Charlie Munger. Warren didn't know Charlie but already had at least one good reason to like him.

During the homecoming dinner, Charlie and Warren realized they shared many ideas. It also became evident to the others at the table that this was going to be a two-way conversation. As the evening progressed, the two young men—Warren was twenty-nine and Charlie thirty-five—became engrossed in a wide-ranging dialogue

Q and A with Warren Buffett

OK, the first question is how, when, and where did you first meet Charlie Munger?

Well, I first met Charlie in 1959 when the Davis family got me together with him. Dr. Davis previously had often mistaken me for Charlie, and I wanted to find out whether that was a compliment or an insult. So, when Charlie came home to Omaha in 1959, the Davises arranged for us to go to dinner; in fact, I think we had a small little private room with a few Davises in attendance. Sometime during the evening, when Charlie started rolling on the floor laughing at his own jokes, I knew I had met a kindred spirit.

What was your first impression?

My first impression was that I had run into somebody that had a lot of similarities to me. I've been known to roll on the floor laughing at my own stuff, too, and to try to dominate the conversation. Charlie was a little more successful at that than I've ever been, but he's been great to study under.

This is great. Now, here's your big one. What are the secrets of his success?

Well, one time, some attractive woman sat next to Charlie and asked him what he owed his success to, and, unfortunately, she insisted on a one-word answer. He had a speech prepared that would have gone on for several hours. But, when forced to boil it down to one word, he said that he was "rational." You know, he comes equipped for rationality, and he applies it in business. He doesn't always apply it elsewhere, but he applies it in business, and that's made him a huge business success.

What other character traits do you think have contributed to his success?

I think actually it really does come out of Ben Franklin that he admires so much. I mean, there is honesty and integrity, and always doing more than his share and not complaining about what the other person does. We've been associated for forty years, and he's never second-guessed anything I've done. We've never had an argument. We've disagreed on things, but he's a perfect partner.

What would you say are his most unusual characteristics?

I would say everything about Charlie is unusual. I've been looking for the usual now for forty years, and I have yet to find it. Charlie marches to his own music, and it's music like virtually no one else is listening to. So, I would say that to try and typecast Charlie in terms of any other human that I can think of, no one would fit. He's got his own mold.

Last question, what effect do you think Nancy has had on his life?

I would have to say that Charlie is not looking for anyone to have an effect on him, but that Nancy has done a remarkable job in spite of that fact. I would hate to be a marriage broker with Charlie as a client.

Q and A with Susie Buffett

Tell us about Warren and Charlie first meeting one another.

The first night they met, Neil Davis had gotten them together at this restaurant, and I'm watching these two people and I thought, did Neil bring them together because he wanted to see what happened when these egos clashed? Because you have these two strong, verbose, brilliant guys. It was amazing to me to see Warren get quieter and let Charlie take the lead. I had never seen that before. Warren always took that role, and I'd never seen anybody take that away from him, and he relinquished it to Charlie that night. It was unique, I'll never forget that evening.

That was unusual?

Well, Warren is usually so much quicker, he's just so much faster and smarter than everybody. I mean, it can't be helped. And here was Charlie "taking off," you see. It was really fascinating to me. And then what happened after that is history.

I think Warren felt that Charlie was the smartest person he'd ever met, and Charlie felt Warren was the smartest person he'd ever met. And that was unique to each of them, and it's continued to be that way, and so their respect for each other's intelligence was I think the beginning. You know, when they see the integrity they have in common, and so forth. It's a match made in heaven.

It's exciting. It's like chemistry and I could see, always when they were together, I mean it's like combustion. It was really, really great. I think that Warren was an aberration in his family, Charlie perhaps was in his, and they just happened, luckily, to meet each other.

What effect do you think Nancy has had on Charlie's life?

I think it's obvious to everybody that Charlie's life is enhanced in every aspect because of Nancy. She does things with such grace and humor and dignity. I'm like everyone else that knows this wonderful woman—I just respect her, love her, and she's a phenomenal human being. I think if Charlie's had any good luck in his life, his ultimate luck was, and is, Nancy.

Wendy Munger conducted these interviews with Warren and Susan Buffett in November of 1998. Susan Buffett passed away in July 2004.

covering many aspects of business, finance, and history. Where one was knowledgeable, the other was just as excited to learn.

Warren was unenthusiastic about Charlie's continued practice of law. He said that while law might be a good hobby for Charlie, it was a far less promising business than what Warren was doing. Warren's logic helped Charlie to decide to quit law practice at the earliest point he could afford to do so.

When Charlie returned to Los Angeles, the conversations continued via telephone and via lengthy letters, sometimes as long as nine pages. It was evident to both that they were meant to be in business together. There was no formal partnership or contractual relationship—the bond was created by a handshake and backed by two Midwesterners who understood and respected the value of one's word.

There were many benefits to their partnership: friendship, investment opportunities, and the unique ability to grasp each other's ideas and observations. Later, the two organizations they headed were also beneficiaries. As Warren was investing in and acquiring companies, he sent business to Munger Tolles, a practice that allowed him over time to benefit from having one of the nation's top law firms at his disposal. Munger Tolles, meanwhile, not only got Buffett's legal fees, but also gained because his reputation attracted other blue-chip clients to the firm.

Munger Tolles is not just about money, though. Mirroring the way Charlie conducts his personal life, the firm has an enviable record of quietly providing pro bono assistance to support groups for impoverished and disadvantaged people in the Los Angeles community. To this day, Charlie continues to influence the

Too Much Alike?

The insightfulness of Charlie's "worrying" was evident in a 2005 interview with *Kiplinger Personal Finance Magazine:*

"How do Warren Buffett and you differ in your approach to investing and decision making?"

"Not much. And therein lies the problem: If something gets by one of us, it's likely to get by both of us."

There was no formal partnership or contractual relationship—the bond was created by a handshake and backed by two Midwesterners who understood and respected the value of one's word.

Munger, Tolles & Olson LLP

Munger, Tolles & Olson, founded in 1962 by Charlie Munger and six other partners, is today a leading business law firm with offices in Los Angeles and San Francisco. Its litigators and transactional lawyers focus on handling their clients' most important problems. Charlie's influence and simple maxims have had a deep and continuing impact on the firm, encouraging a relentless focus on understanding and solving the clients' problems. The firm largely eschews conventional law firm marketing, following Charlie's advice that "The best source of new legal work is the work on your desk." The firm's lawyers have worked closely with Warren and Charlie on matters for Berkshire Hathaway, with Ron Olson leading the negotiations that resolved Salomon Brothers' Treasury auction problems. Bob Denham left the firm in 1991 to be Salomon's general counsel (while Warren was interim chairman) and then became chairman and CEO of Salomon after Warren's departure. Denham returned to MTO in 1998 after selling Salomon to what is now Citigroup. The firm's lawyers continue to handle Berkshire's acquisitions and its relatively rare significant litigation.

"Charlie Munger has spent a professional lifetime studying lives that have worked well and others that have glitches or have experienced failures. This compilation illuminates what he has learned and makes plain why he remains for Munger, Tolles & Olson its most important mentor."

—Ronald Olson

—Robert E. Denham
Partner, Munger, Tolles & Olson
Wesco Financial director

—Ronald L. Olson
Partner, Munger, Tolles & Olson
Berkshire Hathaway director

firm's attorneys, reminding them, "You don't need to take the last dollar" and "Choose clients as you would friends." Though Charlie left the firm as an active partner in 1965 after only three years, his indelible influence remains, as indicated by the fact that his name still heads the listing of 175 attorneys. When he left, he didn't take his share of the firm's capital. Instead, he directed that his share go to the estate of his young partner, Fred Warder, who left behind a wife and children when he died of cancer.

To this day, Charlie continues to influence the firm's attorneys, reminding them, "You don't need to take the last dollar" and "Choose clients as you would friends."

Charlie's plan for financial independence was soon working with great success. He spent much time building the asset base of Wheeler, Munger & Co., his investment partnership with Jack Wheeler. He also spent time working on various real estate developments. All was going as planned, with no significant reverses. At Wheeler, Munger, Charlie was investing in stocks partly with his own money and partly with other people's money. Charlie concentrated more on putting his capital to work than in attracting new clients. Because Jack Wheeler held two seats on the Pacific Coast Stock Exchange, the partnership paid low trading commissions while Wheeler, Munger kept the overhead cost at close to zero.

FORBES 400

Charles Munger

$1.6 billion

Investments. *Los Angeles.*

80. Divorced, remarried; 8 children

Less lauded, far less wealthy partner of Warren Buffett, still plays integral role at Berkshire Hathaway. Vice chairman since 1978, demands intense number-crunching analysis of investments. Met Buffett in 1959; soon began investing in Berkshire. Other investments: substantial stakes in Costco Wholesale (discount retail), Daily Journal (legal news), Price Legacy (real estate investments). Education enthusiast funded new wing at Pasadena's Huntington Library; on board of Harvard-Westlake School.

Forbes, October 11, 2004

The Answer Man

Twenty thousand people attend the Berkshire annual meeting, and nearly five hundred gather at Wesco Financial. For roughly six hours at the Berkshire meeting and three at Wesco, without so much as a pencil and paper, and with no rehearsal or screening of the questions, Charlie responds to any and all queries. Case in point from the 2004 Wesco meeting:

Question: "I'll be hitting the Wall-Eye Opener next Friday night at Eagle Lake, Minnesota. Any recommendations concerning lures or bait?"

Charlie: "I stopped fishing for wall-eye; I've become a bass fisherman in my old age. But in my lake, they do better with wall-eye at night."

As time passed, Charlie and Warren kept up their frequent telephone conversations and letters, sharing ideas and investment concepts. Sometimes they would agree to invest in the same company. Other times they went different directions. In time, their independent portfolios had overlapping investments. Warren invested in the Blue Chip Stamp Co. and became the largest single shareholder. Charlie became the second largest shareholder, and, eventually, Berkshire Hathaway ended up acquiring the company.

Charlie built the Wheeler, Munger partnership from 1962 through 1975. It did exceptionally well for the first eleven years, compounding at 28.3 percent gross (20.0 percent net) vs. 6.7 percent for the Dow, without a single down year. But the partnership was hit hard in the vicious bear market of 1973 and 1974 when it fell 31.9 percent and 31.5 percent in back-to-back years, as the partnership's largest holdings, Blue Chip Stamps and New America Fund, fell sharply. This decline was despite, as Charlie puts it, "having its major investments virtually sure of eventually being saleable at prices higher than the quoted market prices." But the partnership rebounded strongly in 1975, rising 73.2 percent, bringing the overall record over fourteen years to 19.8 percent (13.7 percent net) compounded annual returns vs. 5.0 percent for the Dow.

After this difficult experience, Charlie followed Warren in concluding that he no longer wanted to manage funds directly for investors (Warren had closed his own partnerships in 1969). Instead, they resolved to build equity through stock ownership in a holding company. When Wheeler, Munger was liquidated, its stakeholders received shares in Blue Chip Stamps and Diversified Retailing. Later, these shares were converted into Berkshire Hathaway stock, which ended 1975 at $38. Today, each share is worth more than $85,000, making Charlie a member of the Forbes list of 400 wealthiest individuals. While he doesn't mind the wealth, he regrets having his name on any such list. Despite his healthy self-image, Charlie would prefer to be anonymous.

Charlie Munger Investment Partnership Results

"Table 5 is the record of a friend of mine who is a Harvard Law graduate, who set up a major law firm. I ran into him in about 1960 and told him the law was fine as a hobby but he could do better. He set up a partnership quite the opposite of Walter's (Walter J. Schloss, another superinvestor profiled in the article). His portfolio was concentrated in very few securities and, therefore, his record was much more volatile but it was based on the same discount-from-value approach. He was willing to accept greater peaks and valleys of performance, and he happens to be a fellow whose whole psyche goes toward concentration, with the results shown. Incidentally, this record belongs to Charlie Munger, my partner for a long time in the operation of Berkshire Hathaway. When he ran his partnership, however, his portfolio holdings were almost completely different from mine and the other fellows mentioned earlier."

[Excerpt from "The Superinvestors of Graham-and-Doddsville," by Warren E. Buffett]

Table 5 -- Charles Munger

Year	Mass. Inv. Trust (%)	Investors Stock (%)	Lehman (%)	Tri-Cont. (%)	Dow (%)	Over-all Partnership (%)	Limited Partners (%)
Yearly Results (1)							
1962	-9.8	-13.4	-14.4	-12.2	-7.6	30.1	20.1
1963	20.0	16.5	23.8	20.3	20.6	71.7	47.8
1964	15.9	14.3	13.6	13.3	18.7	49.7	33.1
1965	10.2	9.8	19.0	10.7	14.2	8.4	6.0
1966	-7.7	-9.9	-2.6	-6.9	-15.7	12.4	8.3
1967	20.0	22.8	28.0	25.4	19.0	56.2	37.5
1968	10.3	8.1	6.7	6.8	7.7	40.4	27.0
1969	-4.8	-7.9	-1.9	0.1	-11.6	28.3	21.3
1970	0.6	-4.1	-7.2	-1.0	8.7	-0.1	-0.1
1971	9.0	16.8	26.6	22.4	9.8	25.4	20.6
1972	11.0	15.2	23.7	21.4	18.2	8.3	7.3
1973	-12.5	-17.6	-14.3	-21.3	-13.1	-31.9	-31.9
1974	-25.5	-23.6	-30.3	-27.6	-23.1	-31.5	-31.5
1975	32.9	33.3	30.8	35.4	44.4	73.2	73.2
Compound Results (2)							
1962	-9.8	-13.4	-14.4	-12.2	-7.6	30.1	20.1
1962-3	8.2	0.9	6.0	5.6	11.5	123.4	77.5
1962-4	25.4	15.3	20.4	19.6	32.4	234.4	136.3
1962-5	38.2	26.6	43.3	32.4	51.2	262.5	150.3
1962-6	27.5	14.1	39.5	23.2	27.5	307.5	171.3
1962-7	53.0	40.1	78.5	54.5	51.8	536.5	273.0
1962-8	68.8	51.4	90.5	65.0	63.5	793.6	373.7
1962-9	60.7	39.4	86.9	65.2	44.5	1046.5	474.6
1962-70	61.7	33.7	73.4	63.5	57.1	1045.4	474.0
1962-71	76.3	56.2	119.5	100.1	72.5	1336.3	592.2
1962-72	95.7	79.9	171.5	142.9	103.9	1455.5	642.7
1962-73	71.2	48.2	132.7	91.2	77.2	959.3	405.8
1962-74	27.5	10.3	62.2	38.4	36.3	625.6	246.5
1962-75	69.4	47.0	112.2	87.4	96.8	1156.7	500.1
Average Annual Compounded Rate	**3.8**	**2.8**	**5.5**	**4.6**	**5.0**	**19.8**	**13.7**

Warren and Rick on "Commodore Charlie"

The *Channel Cat*, Santa Barbara, California

"Warren, why do you think Charlie built this enormous catamaran?"

"Well, that's the question that's been asked throughout the nautical world and, actually, there are two of us that know the answer to that. Rick Guerin and I had an experience in Minnesota where, on a totally calm day, not a ripple on the surface of the lake, Charlie managed to sink a boat with no outside help whatsoever. As Rick and I went down for the third time, we shouted out to Charlie that the next time he should get a boat with a little more stability to it. We've decided that Charlie, with 3,400 square feet of surface area on his *Channel Cat*, may have finally found a boat that he can pilot with only a moderate risk of sinking it single-handedly."

Rick Guerin adds: "As I came up for the first time, it just so happened that I was nose to nose with Warren. His eyes were as wide as saucers. It was only after I rescued him that I realized I had missed an enormous opportunity, namely, that the time to negotiate a reward for rescuing someone is before, not after, you save them. Who knows, with a little more presence of mind, maybe, just maybe, I would today be chairman of Berkshire Hathaway. By the way, I call Charlie's catamaran 'Munger's Folly.' It's the only completely irrational thing Charlie has ever done."

Charlie gets the last word: "The boat was fun to design and build. What's irrational about that?"

The story of Berkshire Hathaway's extraordinary success under Warren and Charlie's leadership has been told many times elsewhere, so the details won't be repeated here. To summarize, however, they have a spectacular track record of identifying undervalued companies and then either buying large stakes in the public markets or acquiring them outright. Regarding the latter, they have acquired a diverse assortment of businesses such as Johns Manville, the Buffalo Evening News, FlightSafety International, NetJets, Shaw Carpet, Benjamin Moore Paint, GEICO, and Dairy Queen. In addition, they have purchased meaningful stakes in public companies such as The Washington Post, Coca-Cola, Gillette, and American Express. For the most part, they have held their major investments for the long term—in fact, they still own almost every business they've ever acquired outright.

"That sounds funny, making friends among 'the eminent dead,' but if you go through life making friends with the eminent dead who had the right ideas, I think it will work better for you in life and work better in education. It's way better than just giving the basic concepts."

Charlie's affinity for Benjamin Franklin's expansive career in government, business, finance, and industry, can be found in his many speeches and whenever he holds an audience, large or small. At the seventy-fifth anniversary of See's Candy, Charlie said, "I am a biography nut myself. And I think when you're trying to teach the great concepts that work, it helps to tie them into the lives and personalities of the people who developed them. I think you learn economics better if you make Adam Smith your friend. That sounds funny, making friends among 'the eminent dead,' but if you go through life making friends with the eminent dead who had the right ideas, I think it will work better for you in life and work better in education. It's way better than just giving the basic concepts."

Charlie on Being a Partner

"A partner, ideally, is capable of working alone. You can be a dominant partner, subordinate partner, or an always collaborative equal partner. I've done all three.

People couldn't believe that I suddenly made myself a subordinate partner to Warren, but there are some people that it is okay to be a subordinate partner to. I didn't have the kind of ego that prevented it. There are always people who will be better at something than you are. You have to learn to be a follower before you become a leader. People should learn to play all roles."

Charlie Munger's Lesson in Philanthropy

At the end of his speech to a foundations financial officers group, entitled "Investment Practices of Leading Charitable Foundations" (1998), Charlie Munger speaks of

> . . . the current harmful trend in which ever more of the nation's ethical young brain power is attracted into lucrative money management and its attendant modern frictions, as distinguished from work providing much more value to others. . . . Early Charlie Munger [he says of himself] is a horrible career model for the young, because not enough was delivered to civilization in return for what was wrested from capitalism.

I can state from first-hand experience that "later" Charlie Munger has become an admirable model and has delivered much back to civilization. Nancy and Charlie Munger's philanthropy to educational and research institutions has always been steady and significant, if somewhat quiet, until they began to include in their giving the funding for construction of important new buildings, which made their generosity visible. They began with the science center at the Harvard-Westlake School in North Hollywood, California, where Charlie was a trustee. They have continued here at the Huntington Library with a new addition, named The Nancy and Charles Munger Research Center, and are continuing at Stanford University Law School with a new graduate residence that will house law, business, and other graduate students.

The Huntington is an independent research library located in San Marino, California, established by railroad magnate Henry E. Huntington in 1919. Its principal purpose is the support of advanced scholarship in the humanities and social sciences. The library's main collection strengths are British and American history and literature and the history of science, medicine, and technology. The collections number more than six million items, and the library hosts almost 1,800 postdoctoral scholars annually. Nancy Munger was a trustee for ten years and continues as Trustee Emerita. At the time of her active retirement, she and Charlie wanted to make a significant gift to the institution and decided upon the much-needed expansion of the research library's facilities.

The resulting building, dedicated in September and fully opened to scholars by mid-November of 2004, is a 90,000-square-foot building that adds significant space for collection growth, an enlarged reading room for use of rare materials, offices for scholars in residence, new conservation and photography laboratories, and a suite of offices for the institutional administration.

What a marvelous experience it was to work with the Mungers, and particularly Charlie, in the design and function of the Munger

Research Center. Charlie had specific ideas about the exterior design of the building, which has resulted in a neoclassical facade that references and complements the historical buildings on the Huntington grounds. Charlie left the internal function of the building, though, to my staff and me to develop. This was a complex process because we had the finite budget of their gift to manage and the existing library building to consider, which had already undergone five additions from 1929 through 1984. As the project progressed, I came to realize that Charlie had set a delicious mathematical problem before us to solve, and that like everything else he throws himself into, he was looking for measurable results. We worked with the Earl Corporation of Pasadena, a design/build company that Charlie had recommended to us, and the end result was a spacious, highly functional building that will serve our collections and scholars through the twenty-first century. We not only came in on time and slightly under budget, but also as the building took shape, some of the Mungers' friends and a few foundations made additional contributions toward its furnishing and operation. As a result, we have an elegant, fully furnished, functional research center and four years of operating expenses, which will give us time to raise endowment for its continued operation.

Another important part of the quotation from Charlie's speech above is " . . . work providing much more value to others." Nancy and Charlie Munger's gift to the Huntington for the Munger Research Center has allowed us to succeed and to provide, in turn, value to our scholars for this century. Value for one's money is as important in philanthropy as it is in investing. Thus endeth another important Charlie Munger lesson.

—David S. Zeidberg
R. Stanton Avery Director,
The Huntington Library

The Munger Research Center of the Huntington Library receives all net proceeds from the sale of this book.

2005 © www.AlanLevenson.com

"It is a grand mistake to think of being great without goodness and I pronounce it as certain that there was never a truly great man that was not at the same time truly virtuous."

—Benjamin Franklin

Franklin used his self-made wealth to achieve financial independence so he could concentrate on societal improvement. Charlie admires that trait in his mentor and strives to emulate Franklin. He has had long involvement with Good Samaritan Hospital and Harvard-Westlake School, both in Los Angeles, and has chaired the boards of each. He and Nancy have also long supported Stanford University and the Huntington Library, Art Collections, and Botanical Gardens in San Marino, California. They recently provided funding for a major expansion to the Huntington called the Munger Research Center (which will receive the net proceeds of this book). Although Charlie is a self-described conservative Republican, chief among his causes is Planned Parenthood. He believes that every child deserves to be born to a welcoming mother. He also supports efforts to improve the environment and the quality of education. As the father of eight and grandfather of sixteen, Charlie regards his legacy as helping future generations inherit a better world.

With his incisive wit and wisdom, Charlie Munger continues to be an invaluable partner to his best friend, Warren Buffett, and teacher to the broader business world. Together, they have built one of the most successful and widely admired companies in history.

Praising Old Age

Munger's Reflections on Aging, Inspired by Cicero's *Discourse of Old-Age*

In 1744, Ben Franklin was still a relatively unknown tradesman engaged in printing in Philadelphia. At that time, he published, as a non-commercial labor of love, a book containing the first American translation from Latin into English of Cicero's *de Senectute*. Cicero had written this work, praising old age, in roughly the sixtieth year of his life.

I first heard of this book in 2006 when I received from my friends, Angus and Lucy McBain, an exact reprint of Franklin's 1744 translation. It was entitled *Cicero, On a Life Well Spent* (2005, Levenger Press). I practically went into orbit upon seeing a work by Cicero that I could not recall ever having heard of, full of praise for old age. Perhaps the McBains figured I needed an authoritative book explaining the many opportunities and consolations still available to me at age 82. Whatever their motivations, the McBains inspired the following reflections.

I practically went into orbit upon seeing a work by Cicero...full of praise for old age.

When I first learned of Cicero while studying Latin at Omaha Central High at the tail-end of the Great Depression, it did not seem sad to me that Cicero had died shortly after the ending of the republican form of government he loved.

Marcus Tullus Cicero

Marcus Tullus Cicero lived to age 63, a long span for a Roman of his time. Then he was murdered in 43 B.C. by order of Marc Anthony for opposing continuation of the autocracy that had replaced Roman democracy a few years earlier, upon Caesar's becoming Emperor. Thus ended the life of Rome's greatest writer, orator and lawyer, who was also one of Rome's greatest statesmen.

Greco-Roman

The Getty Villa in Malibu, California is an example of classical Roman architectural style with Greek influences. Reopened in 2006, the Getty Villa showcases Greek, Roman and other antiquities.

"Greco-Roman" reflects the essential unity of the Mediterranean world at the time when those cultures flourished, between the 8th century B.C. and the 5th century A.D.

After all, he would have soon died from some other cause. And all around me I could see that in some important sense Cicero had not fully died. Indeed, it was plain that Cicero dead had favorably influenced many more people than Cicero living. This outcome was caused not by his martyrdom, but by the preserved words of so great an author.

Nor had his beloved republican form of government perished irretrievably. In fact, a form of government prescribed by Cicero surrounded me right there in Nebraska. Moreover, not only the form but also the trappings of Ciceronian government were present. The architecture and statuary of Central High were Greco-Roman in nature, reflecting the admirable desire of early Nebraskans to give due credit to ancient models responsible for present felicity.

His underlying philosophical view was one of deep and realistic cynicism about human nature...

The full merits of the peculiar form of government that Cicero had recommended and Nebraska had adopted did not come through to me well at Central High, where I did not have an opportunity to study the Cicero tract that explained it. But I later came to share Cicero's governmental views. What he recommended was a combination of aspects of limited-franchise democracy, oligarchy and temporary kingship formed into an elaborate system of checks and balances designed to prevent any one politician from causing unendurable damage. His underlying philosophical view was one of deep and realistic cynicism about human nature, including a distaste for pure mob rule and demagogues. This cynicism was of course counterbalanced by his belief that it was the duty of the citizenry, particularly its most eminent members, to serve the State and its values wisely and vigorously, even if that required a great sacrifice on the part of the servers. All ages have found that the duty part of this prescription is a hard sell. Indeed, Cicero in his own time found it necessary to invent the Latin word "moralis," root of our word moral, to help flog his fellow Romans in the right direction.

What moved me...was my recognition that in a value system like Cicero's I would be pretty likely to rise.

After I came to share Cicero's political views, I fancied many times that I had been converted out of concern for my fellow man. But now I believe that a man seldom fully knows his own motives. Accordingly, I now think that what moved me, in substantial part, was my recognition that in a value system like Cicero's I would be pretty likely to rise.

As it worked out, I got more out of life than I deserved. And the thought patterns that seem to be rewarded in one's life are usually those which end up as part of one's most intense convictions. And so I have come to like Cicero better and better as the years have rolled by. At one time I even skimmed Trollope's biography of Cicero in the course of deciding never to recommend it to anyone not already a Cicero addict.

Notwithstanding the McBains' questionable social tact in giving an old man a book on aging, their whole judgment was perfect. Cicero's talk would have done me no good at Omaha Central High, where my main ambition was to make a better impression on Shirley Smails. But in 2006 Cicero's discussion of old age met an enthusiastic reception.

For instance, the very first page lightened one of my main burdens. There Cicero reported that the "thoughts that flowed on me … in composing [this work] … proved so entertaining and delightful to me that … they have [made] Old Age [appear] … agreeable and comfortable." Here, obviously, spoke a man of my

Anthony Trollope
(1815 – 1882)

Anthony Trollope was one of the most successful, prolific and respected English novelists of the Victorian era. Trollope wrote penetrating novels on political, social, and intergender issues and conflicts of his day. He also occasionally veered–sometimes densely–into biography, addressing the lives of such as Cicero and Lord Palmerston. Trollope's popularity continues to this day.

own kind, automatically entranced and convinced by his own words. I had long believed that I had a social defect in my tendency to gain enthusiasm in the course of telling others what I thought they should know. After all, I often caused antipathy I could partially counteract only through being generous to an extent that was sometimes irksome. Happily, the great Cicero described this trait as a helpful virtue, easing the process of instructing the world. Precisely. But what are we to think of the high school that had this great man give me an extra paragraph or two on the Catiline conspiracy when he could have been telling me to become more confident about my own words? I suppose the answer is that Central High was a pretty good place for its era or that many of my fellow students were so strong in self-regard that they didn't have my youthful need for reassurance.

Catiline Conspiracy

Lucius Sergius Catilina (108 BC – 62 BC), known in English as Catiline, was a Roman politician best known for his attempt to overthrow the Roman Republic and in particular the power of the aristocratic Senate. Cicero, his most bitter political enemy, spared no denunciation in his "Catiline Orations." The Catiline conspiracy is one of the most famous events of the turbulent final decades of the Roman Republic.

Cicero's words also increased my personal satisfaction by supporting my long-standing rejection of a conventional point of view.

As I continued through Cicero's pages, I found much more material celebrating my way of life. As the years have passed, I have encountered more and more criticism from being lost in my own thoughts when others were talking to me. This behavior, too, is deemed a virtue by Cicero as he demonstrates in his appraisal of the astronomer Gallus and others like him: "How often did the rising sun surprise him, fixed on a calculation he began overnight … and how many others we have known in their old age [so] delighting themselves in their studies … ingenious and commendable?"

And Cicero's words also increased my personal satisfaction by supporting my long-standing rejection of a conventional point of view. I have always refused to accept one interpretation of the Parable of the Pharisee and the Publican in the Christian Bible. Under this interpretation, a learned, pious man, after a long life spent doing his duty, is criticized for rejoicing that he didn't end up like another man who behaved much worse and fell into a low moral and worldly condition. Cicero, like me, is totally against refraining from enjoyment of this sort of delightful contrast. To him, pride in a job well done is vastly constructive. For instance, it motivates good conduct in early life because, in remembrance, you can make yourself happier when old. To which, aided by modern knowledge, I would add "and, besides, as you pat yourself on the back for behaving well, you will improve your future conduct."

...as you pat yourself on the back for behaving well, you will improve your future conduct.

Luke 18:9-14 (King James Version)

And he spake this parable unto certain which trusted in themselves that they were righteous, and despised others:

Two men went up into the temple to pray; the one a Pharisee, and the other a publican. The Pharisee stood and prayed thus with himself, God, I thank thee, that I am not as other men are, extortioners, unjust, adulterers, or even as this publican. I fast twice in the week, I give tithes of all that I possess.

And the publican, standing afar off, would not lift up so much as his eyes unto heaven, but smote upon his breast, saying, God be merciful to me a sinner. I tell you, this man went down to his house justified rather than the other: for every one that exalteth himself shall be abased; and he that humbleth himself shall be exalted.

In praise of the potentialities of advanced age, Cicero, for pages and pages, recites great accomplishments of war, statecraft and literature by old and eminent men who are made happy by performing so well for so long. For example, he says of one of the great Scipios, "Had his life been protracted a hundred years, can you suppose it would ever have proved burdensome to him?"

In the course of describing these instances of success in old age, Cicero supplies interesting facts about the Roman political system. He has Cato say: "It was with great uneasiness to myself that, when Censor, I turned Lucius Flaminus out of the Senate, seven years after he had been consul. But I could not bear that his [killing a Gaul with his own hands merely to amuse his favorite prostitute who missed seeing gladiatorial deaths in Rome] should pass without public censure." Ah, those were the days! Given such Roman power, would not any wise person now approach the U.S. Senate with delight? And perhaps also publish a list of Senators under review?

Milo or Milon of Croton

(Late 6th century, B.C.)

A six-time Olympic victor in wrestling, and one of the most famous Greek athletes in antiquity, Milo kept on competing even well after what would have been considered a prime age for an Olympic athlete.

Ancient sources report Milo would demonstrate his strength by holding his arm out, fingers outstretched, and no man could bend even his little finger. Another legend maintains he would train in off years by carrying a newborn calf on his back every day. By the time the Olympics arrived, he was carrying a four-year-old cow.

Moreover, it is not enough for Cicero to praise the virtues of the old. He also criticizes the defects and follies of the young. In one case he attributes the destruction of a great government to the following cause: "A parcel of young, raw and ignorant orators started up who took upon them to act as statesmen and found means to insinuate themselves with and manage the People."

Cicero, learned man that he was, believed in self-imrovement so long as breath lasts.

Cicero generally weighs the normal advantages of youth as inferior to the normal advantages of age. To this end, he points out that Agamemnon in the war on Troy "never once wished for ten more men with the strength of Ajax but, instead, wanted ten more with the wisdom of Nestor."

The age preference of Cicero is clearly attributable to his valuing, most highly, strength of mind over strength of body. In one place he reports: "Milo is said to have entered into the Olympic field carrying an ox on his back. Now, if the choice were given you, would you prefer Milo's strength of body or Pythagoras' ability of mind?" To Cicero this is a rhetorical question with only one answer.

Cicero, learned man that he was, believed in self-improvement so long as breath lasts. He commends Socrates for learning to play the fiddle late in life and another Roman for mastering Greek when old. Indeed, according to Cicero, the deaths of others that hurt the most are the ones of people you are learning from. And so at one point he has Cato say of Quintus Fabius Maximus: "I was so fond of hearing him speak [that] I … feared that when he was taken from us, I should never find another [such] man to improve by." And Cicero twice quotes with relish what was often said of Solon, the great man of early Athens: "Daily learning something, he grew old."

Cicero counsels that the study of philosophy, in a life-long search for basic causes, is an ideal activity, usually serviceable for old people all the way to the grave.

His praise of this form of learning is unstinting: "We can never sufficiently admire the excellences of Philosophy; to whose Dictates whosoever submits, he will never fail to find himself [easy] in any stage or condition of life." When I reflected on Cicero's love of knowledge, as displayed above, I happened to remember what I regard as Cicero's wisest and most cutting critique of Rome, delivered without the need for a single word: When Cicero was Quaestor in Sicily he sought out the grave of Archimedes, by far the greatest mathematician of antiquity, and found it covered with thorns—a natural, defective outcome in a Roman civilization that had almost no interest in either mathematics or science.

Archimedes
(287? – 212 B.C.)

An ancient Greek mathematician, physicist, engineer, astronomer and philosopher, Archimedes had one of the greatest minds in antiquity. He discovered principles of density, buoyancy, optics, and, most famously, leverage. Of this last principle, Archimedes said, "Give me a lever long enough and a fulcrum on which to place it, and I shall move the world."

Cicero counsels that the study of philosophy... is an ideal activity, usually serviceable for old people all the way to the grave.

As might be expected in a work first published in America by Ben Franklin, Cicero's discourse often supplies recommendations regarding all sorts of conduct, sometimes supported pithily by reasons. For instance, Cicero argues against miserly conduct by the elderly rich: "Can anything be more senselessly absurd than that the nearer we are to our journey's end, we should still lay in more provision for it?"

And fear of death is silly and unacceptable for this Roman. He reasons that either (a) you are going to a perpetual, better afterlife, or (b) you won't retain any pain if there is no such outcome.

To Cicero it is unworthy that an old man would work to improve only what he would live to enjoy. For him the only life worth living is dedicated in substantial part to good outcomes one cannot possibly survive to see.

Pythagorean Philosophy

Pythagorean geometry resolved one of the great problems of the day, the duplication of the square. The solution is known as the theorem of the square on the hypotenuse, or the Pythagorean proposition. More germane to Cicero's discourse, Pythagorarean philosophy argues that there are three kinds of men: those who may be classified as lovers of wisdom, lovers of honor, and lovers of personal gain.

Early retirement is criticized by Cicero as virtually unthinkable. He cites the moral idea of Pythagoras that "no man should quit his post but at the command of his General; that is, of God himself."

In general, Cicero did not appraise the last part of life as inferior, constituting a poor residue of a better life when young. Not for Cicero is the attitude attributed to Lord Chesterfield who "having drunk the cup of life three quarters of the way to the bottom was now willing to share the dregs with some wealthy woman." To Cicero, if you live right, the inferior part of life is the early part.

To Cicero, if you live right, the inferior part of life is the early part.

Cicero believed in the display of great respect to elderly males. He thus had roughly the same good idea as Confucius. Moreover, he counsels old men to stand up for their rights: "Old age is ever honorable when it takes care to support its proper rights and gives them not weakly away but asserts them to the last."

Cicero is never in favor of complaining about personal misfortune, and he has reasons. For instance, he does not believe the old should complain about diminutions in sexual vigor. Instead, he thinks they should rejoice that they are now less likely to disgrace themselves or contract venereal diseases. Thus Cicero found benefits in age similar to those discovered by an old friend of mine, here called "Glotz." Just before he died at age 75, he said to me: "I used to be troubled by unwelcome, lustful thoughts about my friends' wives, but, by God, I finally licked it." However, Cicero is not content when everyone, at 75, is more like Glotz. Cicero, still in his early sixties, brags of his state in which "voluptuous enjoyments" seem inferior to "oratory … and the Practice of Pleading." In this the great man may have gone too far in extrapolating a personal preference. Being the greatest lawyer in the world, he may have been misled by his own balance of talents. Surely the rest of us, when still in our early sixties, will not very often prefer litigation as Cicero does.

As part of his opposition to complaining, Cicero points out how silly it is to complain of reaching old age. According to Cicero, the best a young person can hope for is to get old before he dies, and it is not fitting to complain about getting the best outcome you could have ever reasonably wanted.

Cato the Elder
(234 – 149 BC)

"Patience is the greatest of all virtues."

Marcus Porcius Cato was a Roman statesman, surnamed "The Censor," but known to history as "the Elder," to distinguish him from Cato the Younger (his great-grandson). He came from a noted family, established himself as a scholar and served in a number of governmental offices in Rome. As Censor to Rome, he revised with unsparing severity the lists of senators and knights, ejecting many whom he judged unworthy on moral grounds or for their lack of ability. The expulsion of L. Quinctius Flamininus for wanton cruelty was an example of his rigid justice.

Cicero, like Cato before him, concedes that, in moderation and meritorious company, the convivial imbibing of wine improves life. So also with stays at one's country place, well tended by others, a practice also favored by Jefferson, who shared Cicero's conviction that such stays fostered sound values.

There is a judge-like objective balance in Cicero that makes him shade some of his observations. He has someone ask Cato if his wonderful old age does not benefit from more than his moral attitude, to wit, if his old age has not been benefited by his great success. Cato replies that some benefit probably came from the success.

In reverse, while Cicero argues that handling a low worldly outcome with the right morality and diligence is just as admirable as handling a high outcome, he concedes that abject poverty, if it comes, is inevitably going to make aged life difficult.

According to Cicero, the best a young person can hope for is to get old before he dies.

But Cicero does not go so far as to concede that wealth will protect the weak and improvident from misery. According to Cicero, the wealthy are sure to suffer if they are lacking in moral and providential skill.

The most celebrated passage in *de Senectute* is probably the following grand summary: "The best Armour of Old Age is a well spent life preceding it;

Marc Antony
(83 BC - 30 BC)

Following Caesar's assassination on the Ides of March of 44 BC, Cicero and Marc Antony, Caesar's subordinate, became the leading men in Rome: Cicero as spokesman for the Senate, and Antony as consul and executor of Caesar's will. But the men had never been on friendly terms, and their relationship worsened after Cicero made it clear he felt Antony was taking unfair liberties in interpreting Caesar's wishes and intentions. Cicero, in a series of speeches called the "Philippics," attacked Antony and praised his rivals. Through the "Philippics" and his renowned wisdom, Cicero became a hugely popular leader. Eventually provoked into forming a militia, Antony hunted down Cicero and reclaimed Rome. Once in power, Antony proclaimed Cicero an enemy of the state and had him executed in 43 BC.

a Life employed in the Pursuit of useful Knowledge, in honourable Actions and the Practice of Virtue; in which he who labours to improve himself from his Youth, will in Age reap the happiest Fruits of them; not only because these never leave a Man, not even in the extreamest [sic] Old Age; but because a Conscience bearing Witness that our Life was well-spent, together with the Remembrance of past good Actions, yields an unspeakable Comfort to the Soul."

[Franklin] left behind a full record of an old age that was among the most constructive and happy ever lived...

Do all these prescriptions of Cicero, if followed pretty well, really improve life? Well, by a strange coincidence, Ben Franklin, the man who first published them in America, followed the prescriptions as well as he could. And he lived a very long life, eminent to the end, and left behind a full record of an old age that was among the most constructive and happy ever lived. And this happened despite many disadvantages he suffered, medical and otherwise.

As usual, Ben Franklin improved what he found. Not satisfied with mere cheerful acceptance of an aged state, Franklin *relished* the role of an old man and played it joyously to a fare-thee-well, while also laboring to help create what he could not possibly live to enjoy. Thus, these ideas of Cicero worked well for Franklin.

Marc Antony Roman Imperatorials

And, no doubt, they will still work well for quite a few others. So there is a special reason, apart from Cicero's contributions to political science, in keeping so many statues of Cicero in our public places. In this way Cicero is still being helpful more then two thousand years after Marc Anthony tried to rid the world of his influence.

Moreover, Warren Buffett, as a sort of modern baton carrier for a Ciceronian point of view, is now doing a good job in imitating Cicero and Franklin in old age. Not only does Buffett, much like Cato, stay in the arena with no plan to ever leave. He does so joyously and while providing good results for those who will trust him patiently. And from a pulpit built high by worldly success, he also imitates Cicero, Cato

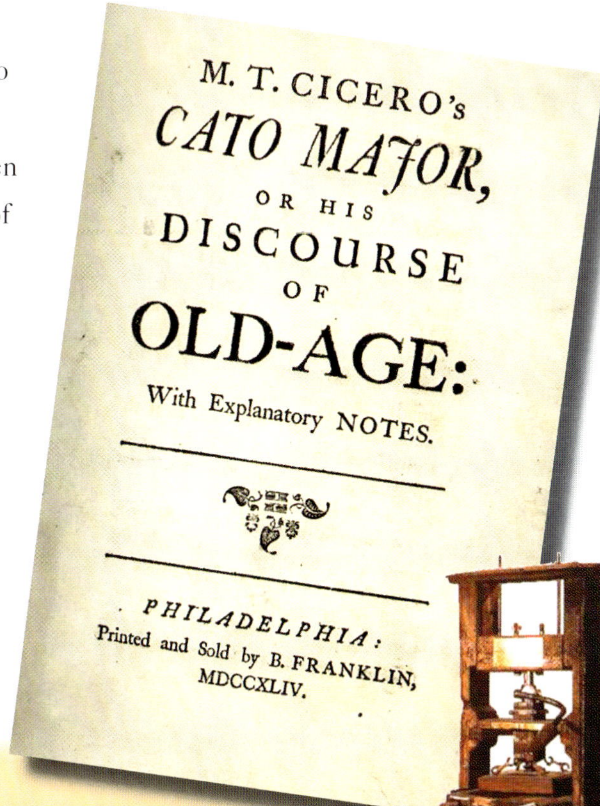
M. T. CICERO's
CATO MAJOR,
OR HIS
DISCOURSE
OF
OLD-AGE:
With Explanatory NOTES.

PHILADELPHIA:
Printed and Sold by B. FRANKLIN,
MDCCXLIV.

Franklin on Aging

"I guess I don't so much mind being old, as I mind being fat and old. I should have no objection to go over the same life from its beginning to the end: requesting only the advantage authors have, of correcting in a second edition the faults of the first. Life's Tragedy is that we get old too soon and wise too late. When you're finished changing, you're finished."

Franklin was noted for his curiosity, ingenuity and diversity of interests. He continued his career of inventing, writing, and statesmanship and more into old age, developing a phonetic alphabet at age 62. Five years later, he published two of his most celebrated pro-American satirical essays: "Rules by Which a Great Empire May Be Reduced to a Small One," and "An Edict by the King of Prussia." In 1776 at age 70, Franklin assisted in writing the Declaration of Independence, radically editing Jefferson's draft. Later that year, he was dispatched to France as commissioner for the United States and remained there until 1785. After his return, Franklin became an abolitionist, freeing both of his slaves and eventually becoming president of The Society for the Relief of Free Negroes Unlawfully Held in Bondage. At age 81, Franklin served as delegate to the 1787 meetings that would produce the United States Constitution to replace the Articles of Confederation. He is the only Founding Father who is a signatory of all three of the major documents of the founding of the United States: the Declaration of Independence, the Treaty of Paris and the United States Constitution. On April 17,1790, he died in his Philadelphia home at age 92, leaving his famous autobiography unfinished. Carried only up to the year 1757, it omitted many of the achievements for which he is best remembered.

and Franklin by communicating much that tells others what they should think and how they should behave. And his words are often made more acceptable through use of insightful humor.

This highly unusual case, I think, should not cause all others to push so hard as Buffett does to follow almost every prescription of Cicero. In the modern world, with its increased wealth and longevity, a great many people live into gross impairment, and others while still in great condition are forced away from high worldly power when they have much life ahead of them. Therefore, some cheerful, non-Buffett-like adjustment to a reduced worldly role is usually sensible for the old. And, finally, it is wise for most didactic people to heed the warning, timed to George Bernard Shaw's death, that the world rewards gadflies, but only a few, with those usually chosen because, like Shaw, they tempered morality with wit.

"The best Armour of Old Age is a well-spent life preceding it."

Charlie Munger on the Sacramento River, 2005

Remembering:

The Children on Charlie

From Charles T. Munger, Jr.

On the last day of a family ski vacation in Sun Valley when I was fifteen or so, my dad and I were driving back in the snow when he took a ten-minute detour to gas the red jeep we were driving. He was pressed for time to have our family catch the plane home, so I was surprised to notice as he pulled into the station that the tank was still half-full. I asked my dad why we had stopped when we had plenty of gas, and he admonished me: "Charlie, when you borrow a man's car, you always return it with a full tank of gas."

My freshman year at Stanford, an acquaintance lent me his car, more because friends we had in common twisted his arm than that he knew me all that well. The tank was half-full, and the Audi Fox was red. So I remembered the jeep and topped the tank before I brought the car back. He noticed. We've had a lot of good times since, and he stood as a groomsman at my wedding.

After Stanford, I learned that on that vacation we had been staying at Rick Guerin's house and driving Rick Guerin's jeep. Rick is one of my dad's friends who, on his return to Sun Valley, certainly wouldn't have been troubled, and was unlikely even to notice, if his jeep had less gas than when he left it. My dad still didn't skip a point of fairness and consideration. So I was taught that day not only how to get a good friend, but also how to keep one.

Family Values at the Munger Dinner Table By Wendy Munger

My dad often used the forum of the family dinner table to try to educate his children. His favorite educational tools were the Morality Tale, in which someone faced an ethical problem and chose the correct path, and the Downward Spiral Tale, in which someone made the wrong choice and suffered an inevitable series of catastrophic personal and professional losses.

His specialty was the Downward Spiral Tale. He could really warm to the topic of apocalyptic consequences. He used such extreme and horrific examples that we were often simultaneously groaning and laughing by the time he finished. He's in a league of his own when it comes to describing negative outcomes and the lessons to be learned from them.

His Morality Tales were more straightforward. I remember the story my dad told his kids, then ranging from age five to twenty-five, about a financial officer at one of his companies who made a mistake that resulted in the loss of hundreds of thousands of dollars to the company. As soon as this officer realized his mistake, he went immediately to the president of the company and told him about it. My dad told us that the president then said, "This was a terrible mistake, and we don't want you ever to make another one like it. But people make mistakes, and we can forgive that. You did the right thing, which was to admit your mistake. If you had tried to hide the mistake, or cover it up for even a short time, you would be out of this company. As it is, we'd like you to stay." I think back on this story every time I hear of yet another government official who chose the cover-up instead of the honest confession after making a mistake.

I don't know why I use the past tense in describing my dad's educational efforts at the dinner table. His oldest children are heading toward their sixties, the table is now crowded with grandchildren, and he's still using his distinctive style of storytelling to keep us on the side of the angels. We're very lucky to have him at the head of our table.

From William H. (Hal) Borthwick

It has been a fascinating and wonderful fifty years (nearly) since Charlie and my mother were married. There were many opportunities that I offered Charlie for formative education. Here are a couple:

1. Do the job right the first time.

This story goes back to Minnesota times. One of my jobs as a driving-age teen was to pick up and deliver the housekeeper from the town of Cass Lake. This wasn't just a drive down the street; the boat had to be driven across the lake to the marina where I would hop into the car to drive to town, and then the process was reversed. Part of the job in the morning was to pick up a newspaper while I was in town. Well, one day a big storm blew in—rain, waves, wind, etc., big-time.

The "Blue Viking"

With all the excitement and difficulty, I did get to town in the morning and returned with the maid, but forgot the paper. Charlie and I had a one-second or so discussion after I answered the question, "Where's my paper?" in the negative. "Go back and get the paper and never forget it again!" So, back I went through the storm to get the paper, bouncing in the waves with rain sheeting off the boat, thinking to myself that I wasn't going to allow anything like this ever to happen again.

2. Be responsible.

Charlie's mother drove herself from Omaha to Minnesota each summer. When she was there, we used her car for errands. There was but one set of keys, and while I was playing with friends in a sailing boat on the lake, the keys fell out of my pocket into five feet of murky water. I went home and confessed. Of course, in the Great North Woods, there aren't many locksmiths, and with Charlie, there wasn't patience for such stupidity. The solution, again in about a second, was: "Go out with your friends and keep diving till you get those keys, and don't come home without them." After about two hours of diving, with the sun sinking like a stone, the miraculous glint of metal in the weeds was before my eyes, and I could go home.

There are a lot of these gems from Minnesota because, in those days when Charlie worked so hard and so long, that was the only meaningful time we spent with him. During the work weeks, he was off before dawn and home about dinner time and then studied Standard & Poor's and, later, would spend a couple of hours on the phone with Warren.

From David Borthwick

Many years ago, Father decided our Minnesota lake cabin absolutely had to have a tennis ball practice machine for the court that had been built a few years earlier. While he certainly wanted the children to groove their groundstrokes, there was a bit more to it than that. For it was Father who was out on court more than anyone, with the machine positioned so he could endlessly practice-volley close by the net. Before long, he mastered the well-placed easy put-away volleys, the kind of shots everyone else instinctively tried to kill but usually hit into the net or ten feet out. By working on the tennis version of golf's short game, which few others could be bothered to practice, Father, as he's done throughout his life, gave himself a fair if maddening competitive advantage. I really dreaded playing against him, especially in doubles where the netplay really counts. Thank God it was tennis, not business.

Thinking about Father made me remember a long-ago humorous TV beer ad in which a smartly dressed man at a table is so engrossed in his glass of beer as to be oblivious to a rampaging bull charging a bullfighter right in front of him. He doesn't flinch even when the bull smashes the table into matchsticks. The announcer's tagline was "Try…beer for a truly unique experience," or something like that.

Take away the beer and substitute the financial market listings, architectural plans, or a scholarly biography of Keynes, and you have a dead-on comedic take on Father night after night in his favorite chair poring over something, all but deaf to the roughhousing younger children, a blaring TV, and Mom trying to summon him to dinner.

Even when not reading, Father was often so deep in contemplation that a routine drive to take Molly and Wendy back to Pasadena could have turned into an excursion to San Bernardino without Mom calling out the correct freeway turnoffs. Whatever was on his mind, it wasn't the outcome of a football game or a botched golf shot. Father's ability to Chinese wall off the most intrusive distractions from whatever mental task he was engaged in—a practice alternately amusing and irritating if you were trying to get his attention—accounts as much as anything else for his success.

From Molly Munger

When I went to college in 1966, I was very lucky to have been thoroughly steeped in Daddy's influence. In an angry and radical era, I would buy the *Wall Street Journal* or *Fortune* at the subway kiosk just outside the college gates, tuck it under my oxford cloth arm, and stride off to economics and business classes. People were occupying the dean's office, going to jail. I was in the basement of the Lamont Library learning how to read a balance sheet.

Daddy raised us to be skeptical, even contrarian, and that was a particularly helpful way of thinking to carry into the maelstrom of the late sixties. Over many years, sitting in the library at our house on June Street, he had told us often funny stories of people who either followed the group too blindly or lashed out too reflexively. "Crazy," "maladjusted," "pompous," "self-satisfied"—we knew from his adjectives what he thought we should avoid.

In Minnesota, he found a way to hard-wire the same message into our very bodies. He had arranged for the old Larsen Boat Works to make us an "aquaplane," a heavy wooden affair we stood on as he towed it behind the boat. He would make sharp turns to see if we could hold on, and the only way to avoid the disgrace of a fall was to keep shifting weight to compensate for the extreme angles. Then, and on into the future, I would always be viscerally terrified if it seemed any thought or activity was getting out of hand in one direction or another.

The Aquaplane

When I was in college, Daddy had seven other children to raise, worked in a seedy part of Spring Street, and owned but one company, a small, grimy outfit that made motor additive. But he saw these were unhinged times. He sent me the allowance of a much richer father, keeping me in professionally ironed shirts and making me feel sharp as a bandbox. From 3,000 miles away, he continued to help me keep my balance.

I could go on. Suffice it to say that our father has always known what he was doing, as a parent as in so much else. I appreciated it greatly. I still do.

From Emilie Ogden

"You have your father's hands," my husband remarked out of the blue, as we shared a glass of wine. I looked at him, a little stunned, not by the comparison, but by his telepathy. I had been devising a short piece about my father, and the very subject had been on my mind.

I had already noticed that my oldest son's hands are like his grandfather's, with fingertips slightly square, and nail beds shaped like teacups rather than ovals. But it's something about the way our hands take positions that first sparks the comparisons. My father, my son, and I all cross our hands behind us in the same distinct manner, the left hand holding the wrist of the right, as we walk, minds elsewhere.

"What is it about my hands, exactly, that reminds you of my father's?" I asked.

"It's in the 'U' where your index finger curves into your thumb," he said, showing me. "It's the way you hold things there."

My father is holding his hands out above me. His fingers are curled, and his thumbs are pointing at each other, like handles on a bike. I reach my girl arms up straight, and I grasp each of his thumbs as he lifts me off the ground. I hang on delighted until my strength is spent. And when one child is too big for "thumbs," there is always another, on down through the line of grandchildren.

Sometimes we'd get him to put down the *Wall Street Journal* and play "sandwich." As he sits in the green armchair in the library, we pile on like the bacon, lettuce, and tomato of a BLT, his hands squeezing us together in a multilayered hug.

My father holds a perfect chicken egg. We've won the father-daughter egg toss, earning me one of my favorite possessions: a marble cube sprouting gilt acanthus leaves, with a life-size golden replica of an egg on top. This trophy sits on my desk, reminding me of the sunny day when my dad was so present and so gentle as to keep a flying egg from breaking in either of our hands.

My father's hands know the tensile strength of different fishing lines by feel. They tie on a chartreuse jig or a plain old hook. His hands rise to his lips where he cinches his knots with his teeth and bites off the extra line. His hands get wet reaching into tin bait buckets. They pinch twisting black leeches or one of Leroy's famous minnows, "guaranteed to catch fish, or die trying." His hands hold yellow-green Zingers, pickles so spicy-hot a bite will bring a laugh, and peanut butter-mustard sandwiches.

My father's hands rise early, with the rest of him, and appear at the edges of the business pages. In Minnesota, he might crumple this newsprint into loose balls, build kindling pyramids, strike long hearth matches, and press spade-shaped wooden bellows. With the fire lit, he might cook blueberry buckwheat pancakes on the Ben Franklin wood stove, using an old wood-handled spatula with chipped red paint.

But if you play Password and give the clue "Charlie Munger's hands," anyone will first answer, "books." No matter where he is, his hands are always holding open a volume, typically a Ben Franklin biography, or the latest treatise on genetics. One might also answer "graph paper," for the buildings he's been designing.

When I think of my father's hands, I also see them up on stage, in front of thousands in Omaha every year. His fingers encircle a Diet Coke, pinch peanut brittle or the stick of a Dilly Bar, or try to search incognito through a See's Candies' box, zeroing in on the rum nougat. His hands are crossed in front of him, as he shakes his head saying, "I have nothing to add." Or they move to the rhythm of a longer philosophical answer, making all the hands in the stadium clap together.

My father's hands, gesturing alongside every colorful joke and guiding story, have molded me as surely as a sculptor's. I can be nothing but glad, and grateful, for the touch of my father's hands in mine, and in my son's.

From Barry Munger

Several years ago, I came across a book by Calvin Trillin called *Messages from My Father*, a memoir about Trillin's father, Abe, who was born in the Ukraine, grew up in Missouri, and spent much of his career operating neighborhood grocery stores in Kansas City. Abe Trillin regarded thrift as a moral virtue, paid his bills the day they arrived, and got up at four in the morning, six days a week, to pick the produce for his stores. A man of few words, he was nevertheless convivial, trenchantly funny, and spoke naturally to small children. He was skilled at cards. He was sardonic, but had an underlying optimism that one could get along in the world with the proper outlook and character.

The fact that my father shares many of these qualities, even if he's not known for his discernment about produce, does not fully explain my attachment to this light, deft, and anecdotal little book. Reading it somehow conjures my father for me, even though in the broad outlines of his life, my father has almost nothing in common with Abe Trillin, other than the fact that my father once worked part-time at a Midwestern grocery store, Buffett & Son in Omaha.

Like my father, Abe Trillin had a fundamental reserve, partially Midwestern in origin, that was at odds with his personable qualities. He did not regard a long drive in a car or a fishing outing as an opportunity to "catch up." He did not linger on the telephone. His son eventually came to marvel at "how much my father managed to get across to me without those heart-to-hearts that I've read about fathers and sons having in the study or in the rowboat or in the car." The title *Messages from My Father* comes from the author's surmise that his father must have been communicating his expectations through coded messages. "It's possible that my father had a code so subtle that I didn't know of its existence," he writes.

Anyone who knows my father knows that his manner of expression is not always subtle, but he has many ways of sending his messages. If he doesn't like the way his bridge partner plays out a hand, for example, he might say, "You played that like a plumber," but if he wants to offer serious counsel to one of his children, he is more likely to couch the message in an anecdote, preferably delivered in a group setting so that no one is singled out. In both instances, he appears blunt and avuncular—that inimitable Charlie—but at the card table, he uses a lack of indirection for harmless ribbing, and at the dinner table, he uses indirection to spare feelings. He's more subtle than he appears.

A friend of mine recently began an anecdote about my father by saying, "So your dad's sitting in his chair, like Rushmore...." I knew exactly what he meant. Not many people can summon up the image of a 5,700-foot granite mountain and the faces of four presidents simply by taking possession of an upholstered chair, but my father can. All of the Munger children have at one time or another approached Rushmore to make a request and felt like Dorothy approaching Oz, except that Oz was more voluble. Rushmore did not always respond. Sometimes my father made a low steady noise from somewhere around his larynx, as though Rushmore had gone volcanic, but that was not so easy to interpret. Can you be more subtle than silent?

Unlike Abe Trillin, perhaps, my father really does send messages, in the form of speeches he has written, letters he has received and sent, and articles from varied sources about social policy, psychology, business ethics, and law, among other topics. Many of them appear in this book. What doesn't appear is the note my father scrawled on the enclosure. The note is usually extremely brief, and often just a "send to" list, but every once in a while the note will have a wry fillip, like this one from 1996, which was appended to a long appreciative letter from a Berkshire Hathaway shareholder in Sweden. "I hope you find this amusing," my father wrote. "If only I had the influence with my wife and children that I have in some other quarters!"

When I finished the Trillin book, I sent it to my father. Even if he didn't recognize himself in it, I figured he would enjoy the book's Midwestern milieu, the immigrant striving of the Trillin family, and the humor. The book is written with so much affection that I thought I could even use it to communicate such feelings to my dad indirectly, which is the preferred route. At the very least, I thought the book might reassure my father that his messages were being received, even if they were not always heeded.

About a week later, the book came back, in a padded envelope, with an address label supplied by his secretary. There was no note, so I wasn't sure whether he had read the book or rejected it. It seemed untouched, so I concluded that my message had gone unreceived, loose pages tossed on Rushmore. Not much escapes my father, however. It turned out that he had simply instructed his secretary to send copies to the whole family.

From Philip Munger

Some of my most affectionate memories of my father are of shopping for clothes at Brooks Brothers and Marks and Spencer. Most people already know that Father is not a big fashion man. He once said that he was nonconformist enough in his behavior and opinions that it made sense to chart a very straight course in attire. His going along with normal social customs and his sense of humor, he said, were what allowed his otherwise sometimes prickly temperament to harmonize with other people.

I vividly recall going with my Father to Brooks Brothers, when it was still housed in that beautiful old wood-paneled building in downtown Los Angeles, to buy my first serious suit. I must have been about eleven or twelve. I can see those polished brass elevator doors opening. We looked through the racks. Father picked out a pin-striped charcoal grey suit. When I was sixteen, we went to buy another suit, this time a three-piece, which I wore religiously during my debate days. It kept the icy wind blowing off the lake at Northwestern, during a tournament, at bay. We bought, at the same time, a pair of wing-tip shoes for my summer stint at the *Daily Journal* (a coming of age ceremony required by Father for each boy), shoes which have lasted till this day. There is another theme here. When we bought a brown tweed coat at Marks and Spencer in London, Father said, "This will always keep its crease." He admired both stores because they were durable institutions and because their merchandise was, too, and fairly priced. Durability has always been a first-rate virtue in my father's view, along with ritual and tradition. He never had a desire to change his primary habits, sartorial or otherwise, once he had, like Franklin, acquired them.

I still shop at Brooks, partly because each year at Christmas Father gives every child a gift card, which is perfectly timed for the winter sale. But I always end up going more often than that. One year, I used his largess to purchase trousers with pleats. My father looked at them askance and said, "Do you want to look like a jazz drummer?" In New York, Brooks is still housed in its grand old building. I think of my father every time I go; I'm very attached to the place. When I went to study at Oxford, in winter 1988, he gave me an old Brooks coat of his, dating from the forties, of a sort of tannish-olive hue, I think, with a warm zip-in lining. As I walked home from the Bodleian Library each night, that nasty damp penetrating English cold would not get through. When I returned to the United States, I realized I had left the coat on a bus. I wept at the loss. Even now I wish I had that coat.

Celebrating their forty-fifth wedding anniversary with the family in August 2001 in Kent, England.

Friends Have Their Say: "Charlie's Smart, Curious, Focused...and a Little Absentminded."

"We all have our little quirks—my family and friends tell me I'm sometimes absentminded and opinionated. Maybe they're right."

—Charles T. Munger

Roy Tolles, friend and business associate since 1946

"Charlie has a desire to understand exactly what makes things happen. He wants to get to the bottom of everything, whether it's something of serious interest to him or not. Anything that comes to his attention, he wants to know more about it and understand it and figure out what makes it tick."

Glen Mitchel, friend since 1957

"He knows how to take all of his brains and all of his energy and all of his thought and focus exactly on a single problem, to the exclusion of anything else. People will come into the room and pat him on the back or offer him another cup of coffee or something, and he won't even acknowledge their presence because he is using one hundred percent of his huge intellect."

Bob Bird, President, Wesco Financial, friend and business associate since 1969

"When Charlie is in deep thought, he often loses track of a lot of what's going on around him, including social niceties. I remember that when we were negotiating with CenFed to have them take over our savings and loan business, Charlie and I went over to their offices to meet with their CEO, Tad Lowrey. We had a perfectly wonderful meeting—Charlie can put on the charm if he puts his mind to it—and we were winding things up very satisfactorily.

"Tad walked us to the elevator. Just as we got there, the elevator door opened, and Charlie walked directly inside. He never said goodbye, never shook hands, nothing. Tad and I were left standing there, smiling and speechless."

Warren Buffett, friend and partner since 1959

"I was in New York City with Charlie to attend a Salomon Brothers board meeting. We had come out of the building and were standing on the sidewalk, discussing what had transpired at the meeting. At least, that's what I thought we were doing, for suddenly I realized that I had been talking to myself for some time. I looked around for Charlie, only to see him climbing into the back of a taxicab, headed off to the airport. No goodbye, no nothing.

"People think it's Charlie's eyes that cause him to miss seeing things (Charlie lost his vision in one eye many years ago due to complications from cataract surgery). BUT IT'S NOT HIS EYES, IT'S HIS HEAD! I once sat through three sets of traffic lights, and plenty of honking behind us, as Charlie discussed some complex problem at an intersection."

Dick Esbenshade, friend and business associate since 1956

"When it comes to being curious and focused, when Charlie gets interested in something, he REALLY gets interested in it. I remember three talks he prepared and presented to our law firm on some of what he referred to as 'the eminent dead' he had encountered through his extensive reading: Isaac Newton, Albert Einstein, and Simon Marks. In particular, I remember the central message of the talk on Simon Marks (of retailer Marks and Spencer): 'Find out what you're best at and keep pounding away at it.' This, of course, has always been Charlie's basic approach to life."

Howard Buffett, son of Warren Buffett and friend of Charlie's since 1959

"For years, I would see Charlie at our Southern California beach house. I remember having 'conversations' that were essentially one-sided, feeling like I should have a dictionary at my side to look up all the words I didn't understand. I remember not saying much, being scared to ask a question and appearing stupid. He's so darned smart, like my father, in the stratosphere.

"I've been quoted in the past (out of context, of course) as saying my father is the second smartest person I've ever known, Charlie being the first. To keep peace in my family, I have no comment on such reports."

And Bill Gates Has His Say:

"Ben Franklin once said, 'I cannot conceive otherwise than that He, the Infinite Father, expects or requires no worship or praise from us, but that He is even infinitely above it.'

"I think the same can be said of Charlie Munger—despite any accolades from me or others in this book he will still be his own best critic as well as the person who appreciates his own jokes the most.

"Warren told me before I met Charlie that he was the most amazing business partner a man could have. He also warned me not to expect to get a word in edgewise when talking to Charlie because even at a cocktail party Charlie would hold his hand up to prevent others from starting to speak while he took a drink.

"He also warned me that Charlie might not be the best person to choose as a boat captain, relating a story where he managed to sink a boat in a totally calm lake with no other traffic by going full speed in reverse with a low transom on the stern.

"Charlie exceeded even the high expectations that Warren set. He is truly the broadest thinker I have ever encountered. From business principles to economic principles to the design of student dormitories to the design of a catamaran he has no equal.

"Our most memorable correspondence was about stock options and their power to distort business results. Our longest correspondence was a detailed discussion on the mating habits of naked mole rats and what the human species might learn from them.

"Charlie has the ability to capture knowledge with simple descriptions. When discussing the intelligence of offspring, he refers to the 'genetic lottery.' When discussing venture capitalists who defend stock options, he deems them 'no better than the piano player in a whorehouse.' When discussing the deleterious effects on efficiency of cost-plus contracts, he likes to say 'even the mule knew to slow down.'

"This book capturing Charlie's wisdom is long overdue."

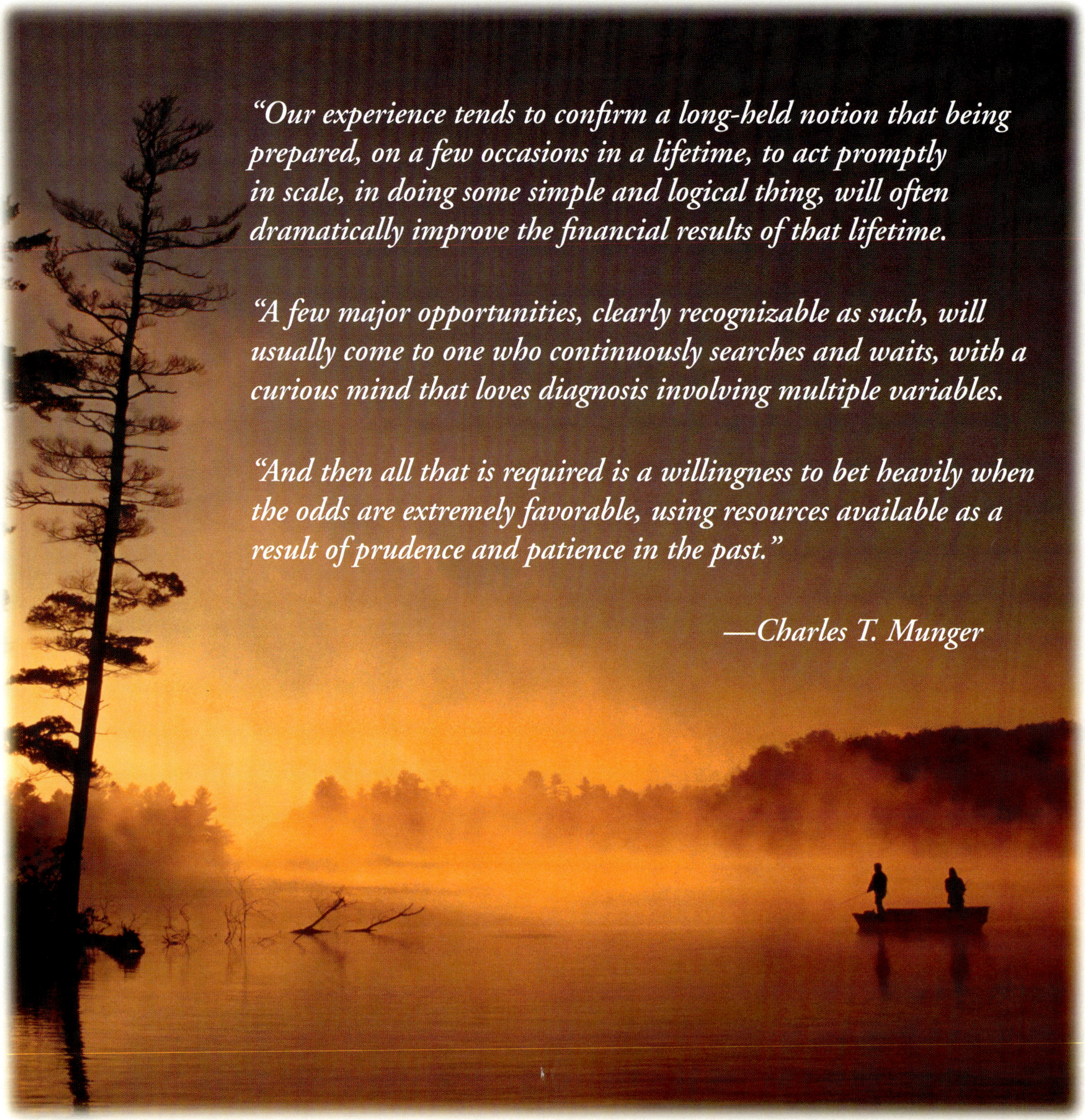

"Our experience tends to confirm a long-held notion that being prepared, on a few occasions in a lifetime, to act promptly in scale, in doing some simple and logical thing, will often dramatically improve the financial results of that lifetime.

"A few major opportunities, clearly recognizable as such, will usually come to one who continuously searches and waits, with a curious mind that loves diagnosis involving multiple variables.

"And then all that is required is a willingness to bet heavily when the odds are extremely favorable, using resources available as a result of prudence and patience in the past."

—Charles T. Munger

Chapter Two

The Munger Approach to Life, Learning, and Decision Making

"Take a simple idea and take it seriously."
—Munger

Despite being largely self-taught, Ben Franklin was spectacularly successful in such diverse fields as journalism, publishing, printing, philanthropy, public service, science, diplomacy, and inventing. Much of Franklin's success was due to the essential nature of the man—most especially his appetite for hard work but also his insatiable curiosity and patient demeanor. Above all, he possessed a quick and willing mind that enabled him to easily master each new field of endeavor he chose to undertake. It is not surprising that Charlie Munger considers Franklin his greatest hero, for Munger is also largely self-taught and shares many of Franklin's unique characteristics. Like Franklin, Charlie has made himself into a grandmaster of preparation, patience, discipline, and objectivity. He has parlayed these attributes into great success in both his personal and business endeavors, especially in his investing.

Business as an Ecosystem

"When we try to pick out anything by itself, we find it hitched to everything else in the universe."
—John Muir

"I find it quite useful to think of a free market economy—or partly free market economy—as sort of the equivalent of an ecosystem. Just as animals flourish in niches, people who specialize in some narrow niche can do very well.

"This is a very unfashionable way of thinking because early in the days after Darwin came along, people like the robber barons assumed that the doctrine of the survival of the fittest authenticated them as deserving power. But the truth is that it is a lot like an ecosystem. And you get many of the same results.

"In business we often find that the winning system goes almost ridiculously far in maximizing and/or minimizing one or a few variables—like the discount warehouses of Costco."

To Charlie, successful investing is simply a byproduct of his carefully organized and focused approach to life. Warren Buffett once said, "Charlie can analyze and evaluate any kind of deal faster and more accurately than any man alive. He sees any valid weakness in sixty seconds. He is a perfect partner." Why does Buffett proffer such high praise? The answer lies in the markedly original approach Munger applies to life, learning, and decision making—the principal subject of this overview.

A word to the wise before we begin: Given the complexity of Charlie's approach, what follows is not intended as a "how-to" lesson for the aspiring investor. Instead, it is a general overview of "how he seems to do it." Our goal here is to present the basic outline of Charlie's approach to prepare you for the voluminous details that follow in the rest of the book. If you are anxious to get to the heart of the matter, the "Mungerisms: Charlie Unscripted" and "Ten Talks" sections—presented verbatim in Charlie's own words—are the best source for exacting "how-to" advice on a broad range of topics. Here we will content ourselves with a presentation of the general thought processes Charlie employs when considering an investment, followed by an outline of his guiding investment principles.

Munger's "Multiple Mental Models" Approach to Business Analysis and Assessment

"You must know the big ideas in the big disciplines and use them routinely—all of them, not just a few. Most people are trained in one model—economics, for example—and try to solve all problems in one way. You know the old saying: 'To the man with a hammer, the world looks like a nail.' This is a dumb way of handling problems."

Charlie's approach to investing is quite different from the more rudimentary systems used by most investors. Instead of making a superficial stand-alone assessment of a company's financial information, Charlie conducts a comprehensive analysis of both the internal workings of the investment candidate as well as the larger, integrated "ecosystem" in which it operates. He calls the tools he uses to conduct this review "Multiple Mental Models." These models, discussed at length in several of the Talks (especially numbers Two, Three, and Four), serve as a framework for gathering, processing, and acting on information. They borrow from and neatly stitch together the analytical tools, methods, and formulas from such

"You have to realize the truth of biologist Julian Huxley's idea that, 'Life is just one damn relatedness after another.' So you must have the models, and you must see the relatedness and the effects from the relatedness."

traditional disciplines as history, psychology, physiology, mathematics, engineering, biology, physics, chemistry, statistics, economics, and so on. The unassailable logic of Charlie's "ecosystem" approach to investment analysis: *Just as multiple factors shape almost every system, multiple models from a variety of disciplines, applied with fluency, are needed to understand that system.* As John Muir observed about the interconnectedness of nature, "When we try to pick out anything by itself, we find it hitched to everything else in the universe."

A Latticework of Mental Models

"Simplicity is the end result of long, hard work, not the starting point."
—Frederick Maitland

"I've long believed that a certain system—which almost any intelligent person can learn—works way better than the systems that most people use. What you need is a latticework of mental models in your head. And, with that system, things gradually get to fit together in a way that enhances cognition.

"However, my particular approach seldom seems to get through, even to people of immense ability. Things usually die after going to the 'Too-Hard' pile."
—Munger

Charlie seeks to discover the universe hitched to each of his investment candidates by gaining a firm grasp on all, or at least most, of the relevant factors comprising both its internal and external environment. When properly collected and organized, his Multiple Mental Models (about one hundred in number, he estimates) provide a context or "latticework" that leads to remarkable insights as to the purpose and nature of life. More pertinent to our purpose here, his models supply the analytical structure that enables him to reduce the inherent chaos and confusion of a complex investment problem into a clarified set of fundamentals. Especially important examples of these models include the redundancy/backup system model from engineering, the compound interest model from mathematics, the breakpoint/tipping-moment/autocatalysis models from physics and chemistry, the modern Darwinian synthesis model from biology, and cognitive misjudgment models from psychology.

Famously willing to change his mind, Thomas Alva Edison (1847–1931) found "10,000 ways that won't work" in his ultimately successful pursuit of the incandescent bulb.

The net result of this broad-spectrum analysis is a heightened understanding for how the many factors affecting an investment candidate blend and link to one another. Sometimes this understanding reveals the existence of second order, "ripple," or "spillover" effects. Other times the factors employed combine to create enormous "*lollapalooza-level results*," good or bad. By applying this framework,

A Willingness to Change His Mind

"Faced with the choice between changing one's mind and proving there is no need to do so, almost everyone gets busy on the proof."

—John Kenneth Galbraith

Charlie has developed an unusual additional attribute—a willingness, even an eagerness, to identify and acknowledge his own mistakes and learn from them. As he once said, "If Berkshire has made a modest progress, a good deal of it is because Warren and I are very good at destroying our own best-loved ideas. Any year that you don't destroy one of your best-loved ideas is probably a wasted year."

Charlie likes the analogy of looking at one's ideas and approaches as "tools." "When a better tool (idea or approach) comes along, what could be better than to swap it for your old, less useful tool? Warren and I routinely do this, but most people, as Galbraith says, forever cling to their old, less useful tools."

T·H·E L·O·L·L·A·P·A·L·O·O·Z·A E·F·F·E·C·T

"Of course, the term Munger has coined for factors which reinforce and greatly amplify each other is 'Lollapalooza Effect.'"
—Henry Emerson, Editor, *Outstanding Investor Digest*

"The most important thing to keep in mind is the idea that especially big forces often come out of these one hundred models. When several models combine, you get lollapalooza effects; this is when two, three, or four forces are all operating in the same direction. And, frequently, you don't get simple addition. It's often like a critical mass in physics where you get a nuclear explosion if you get to a certain point of mass—and you don't get anything much worth seeing if you don't reach the mass. Sometimes the forces just add like ordinary quantities and sometimes they combine on a breakpoint or critical-mass basis.

"More commonly, the forces coming out of these one hundred models are conflicting to some extent. And you get huge, miserable tradeoffs. But if you can't think in terms of tradeoffs and recognize tradeoffs in what you're dealing with, you're a horse's patoot. You clearly are a danger to the rest of the people when serious thinking is being done. You have to recognize how these things combine. And you have to realize the truth of biologist Julian Huxley's idea that 'Life is just one damn relatedness after another.' So you must have the models, and you must see the relatedness and the effects from the relatedness."

—*Outstanding Investor Digest,* December 29, 1997

Multiple Mental Models

"I'll Do It Myself"

"When my friend Buffett and I left our respective graduate schools, we found huge predictable patterns of obvious extreme irrationality in the business world. This irrationality was grossly important in what we were trying to do, yet it had never been mentioned by our professors. Our solution, one we learned at a very early age in the nursery: '"Then I'll do it myself," said the Little Red Hen.'

"So if your professors won't give you an appropriate multidisciplinary approach, if each wants to overuse his own models and underuse the important models in other disciplines, you can correct that folly yourself."

Wisdom Reaffirmed

Munger and Buffett aren't the only elite investors who use nonbusiness models to superb success. Legendary fixed income expert Bill Gross (PIMCO) once told the students of the UCLA Anderson School of Business: "The book that rests on my library coffee table is not Peter Lynch's *Beating the Street* or even my own, but several books by historian Paul Johnson on the makings of the nineteenth and twentieth centuries.

"There is no better teacher than history in determining the future.... There are answers worth billions of dollars in a $30 history book."

Particularly in Talks Two, Three, and Four, Charlie lectures on the value and importance of using multiple models in business. He explains where he found his unique models and how he mastered them, and he cites specific examples of their application in real-world analysis and decision making.

Charlie lives in a different world from most investors when it comes to investment analysis. His approach accepts the reality that investment problems are inherently complex, and in a manner more in keeping with the rigors of scientific inquiry than conventional "investing," he attacks them with a staggering degree of preparation and broad-based research.

Charlie's "Big Ideas from the Big Disciplines" approach to investment evaluation is certainly unique in the business world—as is its origin. Not finding any existing approach adequate to the task, Charlie painstakingly created his own largely self-taught system. The "self-taught" statement is no exaggeration; he once said, "To this day, I have never taken any course, anywhere, in chemistry, economics, psychology, or business." And yet these disciplines—especially psychology—form the foundation upon which his system is built.

It is this signature approach, backed by Charlie's formidable intellect, temperament, and decades of relevant experience, that have made him the virtuoso of business pattern recognition so valued by Buffett. Like a chess grandmaster, through logic, instinct, and intuition, he determines the most promising investment "moves," all the while projecting the illusion that the insight came easily, even simply. But make no mistake: This "simplicity" comes only at the end of a long journey toward understanding—not at the beginning. His clarity is hard won: the product of a lifetime of studying the patterns of human behavior, business systems, and a myriad of other scientific disciplines.

Charlie counts preparation, patience, discipline, and objectivity among his most fundamental guiding principles. He will not deviate from these principles, regardless of group dynamics, emotional itches, or popular wisdom that "this time

An Acceptance for Reality

"I'm afraid that's the way it is. If there are twenty factors and they interact some, you'll just have to learn to handle it—because that's the way the world is. But you won't find it that hard if you go at it Darwin-like, step by step with curious persistence. You'll be amazed at how good you can get."

—Munger

"Perhaps the most valuable result of all education is the ability to make yourself do the thing you have to do, when it ought to be done, whether you like it or not. It is the first lesson that ought to be learned and however early a man's training begins, it is probably the last lesson that he learns thoroughly."

—Thomas Henry Huxley
Darwin's self-appointed
advocate or "bulldog"

Patience Escalier, 1888, Van Gogh

Patience: The Art of "Waiting Without Tiring of Waiting"

"Look at those hedge funds—you think they can wait? They don't know how to wait! In my personal portfolio, I have sat for years at a time with $10 to $12 million in treasuries or municipals, just waiting, waiting....

"As Jesse Livermore said, 'The big money is not in the buying and selling...but in the waiting.'"

around it's different." When faithfully adhered to, these traits result in one of the best-known Munger characteristics: *not buying or selling very often*. Munger, like Buffett, believes a successful investment career boils down to only a handful of decisions. So when Charlie likes a business, he makes a very large bet and typically holds the position for a long period (see Warren Buffett's analysis of the original 1962–1975 Munger partnership on page 21). Charlie calls it "sit on your ass investing" and cites its benefits: "You're paying less to brokers, you're listening to less nonsense, and if it works, the tax system gives you an extra one, two, or three percentage points per annum." In his view, a portfolio of three companies is plenty of diversification. Accordingly, Charlie is willing to commit uncommonly high percentages of his investment capital to individual "focused" opportunities. Find a Wall Street organization, financial advisor, or mutual fund manager willing to make that statement!

Given Charlie's record of success, not to mention Buffett's endorsement, why aren't his investment practices more routinely emulated by others? Perhaps the answer is that, for most people, Charlie's multidisciplinary approach is simply too hard. Further, few investors share Charlie's willingness to appear foolish by not following "the herd." Religious in his objectivity, Charlie is content to swim imperturbably against the tide of popular

LEMMING
(*Dicrostonyx groenlandicus*)

Discipline and Patience

Ted Williams' Seventy-Seven-Cell Strike Zone

"It takes character to sit there with all that cash and do nothing.
I didn't get to where I am by going after mediocre opportunities."
—Munger

"In making investments, I have always believed that you must act with discipline whenever you see something you truly like. To explain this philosophy, Buffett/Munger like to use a baseball analogy that I find particularly illuminating, though I myself am not at all a baseball expert. Ted Williams is the only baseball player who had a .400 single-season hitting record in the last seven decades. In the *Science of Hitting*, he explained his technique. He divided the strike zone into seventy-seven cells, each representing the size of a baseball. He would insist on swinging only at balls in his 'best' cells, even at the risk of striking out, because reaching for the 'worst' spots would seriously reduce his chances of success. As a securities investor, you can watch all sorts of business propositions in the form of security prices thrown at you all the time. For the most part, you don't have to do a thing other than be amused. Once in a while, you will find a 'fat pitch' that is slow, straight, and right in the middle of your sweet spot. Then you swing hard. This way, no matter what natural ability you start with, you will substantially increase your hitting average. One common problem for investors is that they tend to swing too often. This is true for both individuals and for professional investors operating under institutional imperatives, one version of which drove me out of the conventional long/short hedge fund operation. However, the opposite problem is equally harmful to long-term results: You discover a 'fat pitch' but are unable to swing with the full weight of your capital."

—Li Lu of LL Investment Partners

opinion—indefinitely, if necessary—which is a rare attribute in the average investor. And while this behavior can at times appear simply stubborn or contrarian, that is not the defining characteristic. Charlie is simply content to trust his own judgment even when it runs counter to the wisdom of the herd. This "lone-wolf" aspect of Charlie's temperament is a rarely appreciated reason why he consistently outperforms the larger investment community. Indeed, if temperament chiefly arises from inborn tendencies, it may be that hard work, intellect, and experience, regardless of their intensity, are by themselves insufficient to make a great investor like Charlie Munger. As we shall witness throughout the remainder of this book, the right kind of genetically predetermined "wiring" is needed as well.

At the 2004 Berkshire Hathaway annual meeting, a young shareholder asked Buffett how to succeed in life. After Buffett shared his thoughts, Charlie chimed

"When Warren lectures at business schools, he says, 'I could improve your ultimate financial welfare by giving you a ticket with only twenty slots in it so that you had twenty punches—representing all the investments that you get to make in a lifetime. And once you'd punched through the card, you couldn't make any more investments at all. Under those rules, you'd really think carefully about what you did, and you'd be forced to load up on what you'd really thought about. So you'd do so much better.'"

The Influence of Phil Fisher

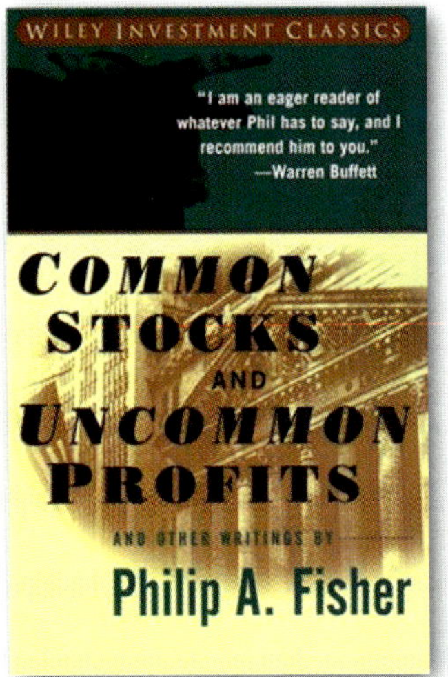

"I always like it when someone attractive to me agrees with me, so I have fond memories of Phil Fisher."

Philip Fisher (1907–2004), author of *Common Stocks and Uncommon Profits*, among many other books, began his investment career in 1931. Like Ben Graham, he achieved impressive results over his lifetime, but Fisher did it with a markedly different approach. Unlike Graham, who typically invested in statistically cheap "cigar-butts" (with the notable exception of GEICO), Fisher preferred to buy and hold the stocks of high-quality companies that could, "grow and grow and grow."

in: "Don't do cocaine. Don't race trains. And avoid AIDS situations." Many would dismiss his seemingly flippant answer as merely humorous (which it certainly was), but in fact it faithfully reflects both his general views on avoiding trouble in life and his particular method for avoiding missteps in investing.

Often, as in this case, Charlie generally focuses first on what to avoid—that is, on what NOT to do—before he considers the affirmative steps he will take in a given situation. "All I want to know is where I'm going to die, so I'll never go there" is one of his favorite quips. In business as in life, Charlie gains enormous advantage by summarily eliminating the unpromising portions of "the chess board," freeing his time and attention for the more productive regions. Charlie strives to reduce complex situations to their most basic, unemotional fundamentals. Yet, within this pursuit of rationality and simplicity, he is careful to avoid what he calls "physics envy," the common human craving to reduce enormously complex systems (such as those in economics) to one-size-fits-all Newtonian formulas. Instead, he faithfully honors Albert Einstein's admonition, "A scientific theory should be as simple as possible, but no simpler." Or in his own words, "What I'm against is being very confident and feeling that you know, for sure, that your particular action will do more good than harm. You're dealing with highly complex systems wherein everything is interacting with everything else."

Another Benjamin—Graham, not Franklin—played a significant role in forming Charlie's investing outlook. One of the most enduring concepts in Graham's *The Intelligent Investor* is Mr. Market. Usually, Mr. Market is a temperate and reasonable fellow, but some days he is gripped by irrational fear or greed. Graham cautioned the investor to carefully use his own, unemotional judgment of value instead of relying on the often manic-depressive behavior of the financial markets. Similarly, Charlie recognizes that even among the most competent and motivated of people, decisions are not always made on a purely rational basis. For this reason, he considers the psychological factors of human misjudgment some of the most important mental models that can be applied to an investment opportunity:

"Personally, I've gotten so that I now use a kind of two-track analysis. First, what are the factors that really govern the interests involved, rationally considered? And second, what

The Influence of Ben Graham

Mr. Market

"In the short run, the market is a voting machine. But in the long run, it is a weighing machine."

Valuation

"Investment is most successful when it is most businesslike."

"Investors should purchase stocks like they purchase groceries—not like they purchase perfume."

—Ben Graham

Paradox

"It's not the bad ideas that do you in, it's the good ideas. And you may say, 'That can't be so. That's paradoxical.' What he [Graham] meant was that if a thing is a bad idea, it's hard to overdo. But where there is a good idea with a core of essential and important truth, you can't ignore it. And then it's so easy to overdo it. So the good ideas are a wonderful way to suffer terribly if you overdo them."

—Munger

are the subconscious influences where the brain at a subconscious level is automatically forming conclusions in various ways—which, by and large, are useful—but which often malfunction? One approach is rationality—the way you'd work out a bridge problem, by evaluating the real interest, the real probabilities, and so forth. And the other is to evaluate the psychological factors that cause subconscious conclusions—many of which are wrong." (For more specifics on this topic see Talk Ten, in which Charlie applies mental models from the field of psychology to illustrate twenty-five common causes of human misjudgment.)

Obviously, the methods described to this point can't be learned in a university classroom or on Wall Street. They were developed by Charlie, from scratch, to satisfy his own exacting requirements. They probably deserve a title of their own, something like: "Quickly Eliminate the Big Universe of What Not to Do, Follow Up with a Fluent, Multidisciplinary Attack on What Remains, Then Act Decisively When, and Only When, the Right Circumstances Appear." Is it worth the effort to develop and adhere to such an approach? Charlie seems to think so: "It's kind of fun to sit there and outthink people who are way smarter than you are because you've trained yourself to be more objective and more multidisciplinary. Furthermore, there is a lot of money in it, as I can testify from my own personal experience."

Jeremiah Lamenting the Destruction of Jerusalem, 1630, Rembrandt

The Two-Track Analysis

"Generally, stocks are valued in two ways. One is the way that wheat is valued—in terms of its perceived practical utility to the user of the wheat. The second way is the way that Rembrandts are valued. And to some extent, Rembrandts are valued highly because they've gone up in price in the past."

"To us, investing is the equivalent of going out and betting against the pari-mutuel system. We look for a horse with one chance in two of winning and which pays you three to one. You're looking for a mispriced gamble. That's what investing is. And you have to know enough to know whether the gamble is mispriced. That's value investing."

Swimming Against the Current

"We're emphasizing the knowable by predicting how certain people and companies will swim against the current. We're not predicting the fluctuation in the current." (Photo: The Alcatraz Sharkfest Swim pits experienced swimmers against brutal currents and frigid water temperatures).

Munger's Investment Evaluation Process

"The number one idea is to view a stock as an ownership of the business and to judge the staying quality of the business in terms of its competitive advantage. Look for more value in terms of discounted future cash-flow than you are paying for. Move only when you have an advantage. It's very basic. You have to understand the odds and have the discipline to bet only when the odds are in your favor. We just keep our heads down and handle the headwinds and tailwinds as best we can, and take the result after a period of years."

As we've noted, Charlie doesn't make a lot of investments. His approach is perhaps best summarized by Thomas Watson Sr., the founder of IBM: *"I'm no genius. I'm smart in spots, and I stay around those spots."* If Charlie knows anything, he knows his "spots": his carefully identified circles of competence. To stay within these circles, he first applies a basic, overall screen, designed to limit his investment field to only "simple, understandable candidates." As he says, "We have three baskets for investing: yes, no, and too tough to understand." To identify potential "yes" candidates, Charlie looks for an easy to understand, dominant business franchise that can sustain itself and thrive in all market environments. Understandably, few companies survive this first cut. Many investor favorites such as pharmaceuticals and technology, for example, go straight to the "too tough to understand" basket. Heavily promoted "deals" and IPOs earn immediate "no's." Those that do survive this first winnowing are subjected to the screens and filters of Charlie's mental model approach. The process is intense and Darwinian, but also efficient. Charlie detests "placer mining," the process of sifting through piles of sand for specks of gold. Instead, he applies his "Big Ideas from the Big Disciplines" to find the large, unrecognized nuggets of gold that sometimes lie in plain sight on the ground.

Throughout his exhaustive evaluation, Charlie is no slave to a database: He takes into account all relevant aspects, both internal and external to the company

Circles of Competence

"If we have a strength, it is in recognizing when we are operating well within our circle of competence and when we are approaching the perimeter."
—Warren Buffett

"If you have competence, you pretty much know its boundaries already. To ask the question [of whether you are past the boundary] is to answer it."
—Munger

"I'm no genius. I'm smart in spots, and I stay around those spots."
—Thomas Watson Sr.

Identifying Your Circle of Competence

In Talk Nine (page 400), Charlie tells the apocryphal story of Max Planck and the chauffeur who drove him to the public lectures he gave throughout Germany. On one occasion the chauffeur, who by this time knew the lecture by heart, suggested that he and Planck switch places. At the conclusion of the chauffeur's flawless recitation of the lecture, a physicist stood up and posed a very difficult question. The chauffeur, ready for the situation, replied, "I'm surprised that a citizen of an advanced city like Munich is asking so elementary a question, so I'm going to ask my chauffeur to respond."

In the real world, it is critical to distinguish when you are "Max Planck," and when you are the "chauffeur." It you cannot respond legitimately to the *next* question, you lack true mastery and are likely outside your "Circle of Competence."

and its industry, even if they are difficult to identify, measure, or reduce to numbers. His thoroughness, however, does not cause him to forget his overall "ecosystem" theme: Sometimes the maximization or minimization of a single factor (notably specialization, as he likes to point out regarding Costco's discount warehouses) can make that single factor disproportionately important.

Charlie treats financial reports and their underlying accounting with a Midwestern dose of skepticism. At best, they are merely the beginning of a proper calculation of intrinsic valuation, not the end. The list of additional factors he examines is seemingly endless and includes such things as the current and prospective regulatory climate; state of labor, supplier, and customer relations; potential impact of changes in technology; competitive strengths and vulnerabilities; pricing power; scalability; environmental issues; and, notably, the presence of hidden exposures (Charlie knows that there is no such thing as a riskless investment candidate; he's searching for those with few risks that are easily understandable). He recasts all financial statement figures to fit his own view of reality, including the actual free or "owners" cash being produced, inventory and other working capital

Warren and Charlie on "Moats"

Buffett: "So we think in terms of that moat and the ability to keep its width and its impossibility of being crossed as the primary criterion of a great business. And we tell our managers we want the moat widened every year. That doesn't necessarily mean the profit will be more this year than it was last year because it won't be sometimes. However, if the moat is widened every year, the business will do very well. When we see a moat that's tenuous in any way—it's just too risky. We don't know how to evaluate that. And, therefore, we leave it alone. We think that all of our businesses—or virtually all of our businesses—have pretty darned good moats. And we think the managers are widening them. Charlie?"

Munger: "How could you say it better?"

Buffett: "Sure. Have some peanut brittle on that one."

—From the 2000 Berkshire Hathaway annual meeting

assets, fixed assets, and such frequently overstated intangible assets as goodwill. He also completes an assessment of the true impact, current and future, of the cost of stock options, pension plans, and retiree medical benefits. He applies equal scrutiny to the liability side of the balance sheet. For example, under the right circumstances, he might view an obligation such as insurance float—premium income that may not be paid out in claims for many years—more properly as an asset. He especially assesses a company's management well beyond conventional number crunching—in particular, the degree to which they are "able, trustworthy, and owner-oriented." For example, how do they deploy cash? Do they allocate it intelligently on behalf of the owners, or do they overcompensate themselves, or pursue ego-oriented growth for growth's sake?

Above all, he attempts to assess and understand competitive advantage in every respect—products, markets, trademarks, employees, distribution channels, societal trends, and so on—and the durability of that advantage. Charlie refers to a company's competitive advantage as its "moat": the virtual physical barrier it presents against incursions. Superior companies have deep moats that are continuously widened to provide enduring protection. In this vein, Charlie carefully considers "competitive destruction" forces that, over the long term, lay siege to most companies. *Munger and Buffett are laser-focused on this issue: Over their long business careers they have learned, sometimes painfully, that few businesses survive over multiple generations.* Accordingly, they strive to identify and buy only those businesses with a good chance of beating these tough odds.

Finally, Charlie seeks to calculate the intrinsic value of the whole business and, with allowance for potential dilution, etc., to determine an approximate value per share to compare to market prices. *This latter comparison is the fundamental purpose of the whole process—comparing value (what you get) with price (what you pay).* On this subject he is famous for his viewpoint that "*a great business at a fair price is superior to*

Independent Thinking

"You are neither right or wrong because the crowd disagrees with you. You are right because your data and reasoning are right."

—Benjamin Graham

"The most difficult thing in business is first getting yourself to thinking and then getting others to thinking."

—Harvey Firestone

"Apply logic to help avoid fooling yourself. Charlie will not accept anything I say just because I say it, although most of the world will."

—Warren Buffett

"Never fool yourself, and remember that you are the easiest person to fool."

—Richard P. Feynman

Margin of Safety

"The margin of safety is always dependent on the price paid. It will be large at one price, small at some other price, and nonexistent at some higher price."

—Benjamin Graham

(With respect to margin of safety, Charlie frequently suggests that investors can benefit from following the "Big Idea Model" of redundancy from engineering. Bridges are designed with backup systems and extra capacity to prevent failures—so too should investing strategies.)

a fair business at a great price." Warren Buffett often credits Charlie with convincing him of the wisdom of this approach: "Charlie understood this early. I was a slow learner." Charlie's insight helped Buffett move from pure Benjamin Graham–style investing to focusing on great businesses such as The Washington Post, GEICO, Coca-Cola, Gillette, and others.

Though extremely thorough, Charlie is able to ignore insignificant detail and the distractions to which others sometimes fall victim. Investment variables, just like all other variables, go through their own process of elimination. By the time he is finished with his analysis, he has reduced the candidate to its most salient elements and achieved a remarkable degree of confidence about whether or not to act. *The*

"Charlie shoved me in the direction of not just buying bargains, as Ben Graham had taught me. This was the real impact Charlie had on me. It took a powerful force to move me on from Graham's limiting views. It was the power of Charlie's mind. He expanded my horizons."

— Warren Buffett

evaluation, finally, becomes not so much mathematical as philosophical. Ultimately "a feel" emerges, a function of both the analysis itself and Charlie's lifetime of accumulated experience and skill in recognizing patterns.

At this point, only an exceptionally superior investment candidate will still be in the running. But Charlie does not immediately rush out and buy it. Knowing that a necessary companion to proper valuation is proper timing, he applies yet a finer screen, a "prior to pulling the trigger" checklist, which is especially useful in evaluating what he refers to as "close calls." The checklist includes such items as: What are current price, volume, and trading considerations? What disclosure timing or other sensitivities exist? Do contingent exit strategies exist? Are better uses of capital currently or potentially available? Is sufficient liquid capital currently on hand or must it be borrowed? What is the opportunity cost of that capital? And so on.

Charlie's exhaustive screening process requires considerable self-discipline and

Fluency and Perspective

"You need to have a passionate interest in why things are happening. That cast of mind, kept over long periods, gradually improves your ability to focus on reality. If you don't have the cast of mind, you're destined for failure even if you have a high I.Q."

"The deep structure of the human mind requires that the way to full-scope competency of virtually any kind is learn it all to fluency, like it or not."

—Munger

"I notice that when all a man's information is confined to the field in which he is working, the work is never as good as it ought to be. A man has to get perspective, and he can get it from books or from people—preferably from both."

—Harvey Firestone

Properly Playing the Hand

"The right way to think is the way Zeckhauser plays bridge. It's just that simple."

"Most players gain pleasure from feeling accepted or belonging to the group. The good player, however, gains pleasure from his ability to cope with the realities of the game."

—John Finn

"In investing, just as in baseball, to put runs on the scoreboard, one must watch the playing field, not the scoreboard."

—Warren Buffett

results in long periods of apparent "inactivity." But as Charlie says, "Hard work is an essential element in tracking down and perfecting a strategy or in executing it." For Charlie and Warren, the hard work is continuous, whether it results in current investing activity or not—and usually it does not. *This habit of committing far more time to learning and thinking than to doing is no accident.* It is the blend of discipline and patience exhibited by true masters of a craft: an uncompromising commitment to "properly playing the hand." Like world-class bridge player Richard Zeckhauser, Charlie scores himself not so much on whether he won the hand, but rather on how well he played it. *While poor outcomes are excusable in the Munger/Buffett world—given the fact that some outcomes are outside of their control—sloppy preparation and decision making are never excusable because they ARE controllable.*

On those relatively few occasions when all the circumstances are just right and Charlie does invest, he will likely make a large, decisive bet. He does not pick around the edges, take "initial positions," or make "small, speculative investments."

Such behavior implies uncertainty, and Charlie's moves, few as they are, are anything but uncertain. As he says, he practices "extreme patience combined with extreme decisiveness." Charlie's self-confidence is based not on who, or how many, agree or disagree with him, but on his ability to objectively view and measure himself. This self-mastery affords him rare objectivity in gauging his actual knowledge, experience, and correctness of thought. Again, we see the important role played by the right kinds of temperamental qualities: self-discipline, patience, calm, independence. *Charlie's level of investment performance is arguably impossible without them.*

Okay, it's a good company. But is the price low enough? Is the management made up of people Munger and Buffett are comfortable with? If it is cheap enough to buy, is it cheap for the wrong reason or the right reason? What's the flip side? What can go wrong that I haven't seen?

What makes a great business model for Charlie? His recommended reading materials (see Appendix) provide some guidance. *Guns, Germs, and Steel*, *The Selfish Gene*, *Ice Age*, and *Darwin's Blind Spot* all have a certain theme: a focus on the aforementioned issue of "competitive destruction" and an examination of why some entities are nevertheless able to adapt, survive, and even dominate over time. When this theme is extrapolated into investment selection, the preferred Munger business emerges: Some thrive by outcompeting (a la *Selfish Gene*) and others by outcooperating (*Darwin's Blind Spot*). Once again, we see Charlie's rich fluency across a broad range of disciplines at work: How many investors ever consider, as Charlie routinely does, such a broad and sophisticated spectrum of factors? To name but a few, he routinely considers factors such as *conversion*, i.e., how the laws of thermodynamics intersect with laws of economics (for instance how paper and

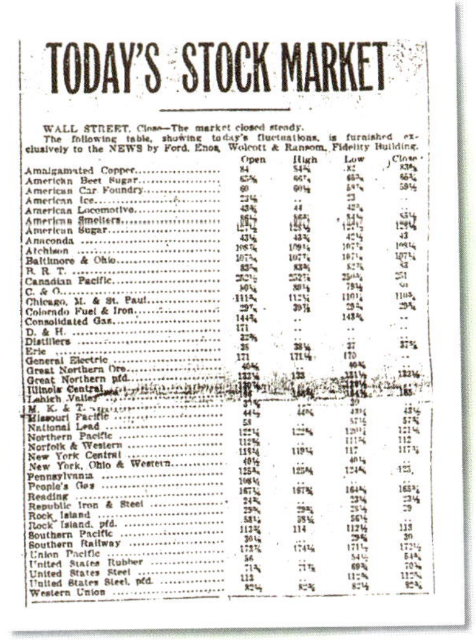
TODAY'S STOCK MARKET

WALL STREET, Close—The market closed steady.

The following table, showing today's fluctuations, is furnished exclusively to the NEWS by Ford, Enos, Wolcott & Ransom, Fidelity Building.

	Open	High	Low	Close
Amalgamated Copper	84	[illegible]	82	[illegible]
American Beet Sugar	[illegible]	[illegible]	[illegible]	[illegible]
American Car Foundry	60	[illegible]	[illegible]	[illegible]
American Ice	[illegible]	..	23	..
American Locomotive	[illegible]	44	[illegible]	..
American Smelters	[illegible]	[illegible]	[illegible]	[illegible]
American Sugar	[illegible]	[illegible]	[illegible]	[illegible]
Anaconda	[illegible]	[illegible]	[illegible]	43
Atchison	[illegible]	[illegible]	[illegible]	[illegible]
Baltimore & Ohio	[illegible]	[illegible]	[illegible]	[illegible]
B. R. T.	[illegible]	[illegible]	[illegible]	[illegible]
Canadian Pacific	[illegible]	[illegible]	[illegible]	251
C. & O.	[illegible]	[illegible]	[illegible]	[illegible]
Chicago, M. & St. Paul	[illegible]	[illegible]	[illegible]	[illegible]
Colorado Fuel & Iron	[illegible]	[illegible]	[illegible]	[illegible]
Consolidated Gas	[illegible]	..	[illegible]	..
D. & H.	171	..	..	..
Distillers	[illegible]	..	..	..
Erie	[illegible]	[illegible]	37	[illegible]
General Electric	171	[illegible]	170	..
Great Northern Ore	[illegible]	..	[illegible]	..
Great Northern pfd.	[illegible]	133	[illegible]	[illegible]
Illinois Central	[illegible]	[illegible]	[illegible]	[illegible]
Lehigh Valley	[illegible]	[illegible]	[illegible]	[illegible]
M. K. & T.	[illegible]	[illegible]	30	..
Missouri Pacific	[illegible]	[illegible]	[illegible]	[illegible]
National Lead	53	..	[illegible]	[illegible]
Northern Pacific	[illegible]	[illegible]	[illegible]	[illegible]
Norfolk & Western	[illegible]	..	[illegible]	112
New York Central	[illegible]	[illegible]	117	[illegible]
New York, Ohio & Western	[illegible]	..	[illegible]	..
Pennsylvania	[illegible]	[illegible]	[illegible]	[illegible]
People's Gas	[illegible]	..	..	..
Reading	[illegible]	[illegible]	[illegible]	[illegible]
Republic Iron & Steel	[illegible]	..	[illegible]	[illegible]
Rock Island	[illegible]	[illegible]	[illegible]	[illegible]
Rock Island, pfd.	[illegible]	[illegible]	[illegible]	..
Southern Pacific	[illegible]	114	[illegible]	113
Southern Railway	[illegible]	..	[illegible]	30
Union Pacific	[illegible]	[illegible]	[illegible]	[illegible]
United States Rubber	56	..	[illegible]	[illegible]
United States Steel	[illegible]	[illegible]	[illegible]	[illegible]
United States Steel, pfd.	113	..	[illegible]	[illegible]
Western Union	[illegible]	[illegible]	[illegible]	[illegible]

"Competitive Destruction"

"I have a clipping from the 1911 *Buffalo Evening News* that lists the fifty most important stocks then actively traded on the New York Stock Exchange. Today only one, General Electric, remains in business as a large, independent company. That's how powerful the forces of competitive destruction are. Over the very long term, history shows that the chances of any business surviving in a manner agreeable to a company's owners are slim at best.

"It gets extra tough when a fanatical small competitor—like a Rose Blumkin, or a Les Schwab, or a Sam Walton—sets their sights on your particular marketplace. How do you compete against a true fanatic? You can only try to build the best possible moat and continuously attempt to widen it."

petroleum become a newspaper delivered to a front door), *psychological* tendencies and incentives (notably the extreme behavioral pressures they create, both good and bad), and fundamental *sustainability* over time (the constant and often deadly interplay between positive factors such as "moats" and the ravages of competitive destruction). *Charlie is possibly without peer when it comes to the checklist of atypical investment factors he considers and his deep fluency in the diverse disciplines from which they are drawn.*

"All intelligent investing is value investing—acquiring more than you are paying for. You must value the business in order to value the stock."

Price is What You Pay, Value is What You Get

On several occasions, incurring the skepticism that must often be borne by "value-style" investors, the United States has made astute territorial acquisitions. In 1803, Thomas Jefferson's administration completed the Louisiana Purchase from Napoleon's France for the sum of $15 million, which worked out to roughly 2.9 cents an acre. In 1867, in what at the time was known as "Seward's Folly," the US acquired the Territory of Alaska from Russia for the sum of $7.2 million in gold, or roughly 2.5 cents an acre. By way of comparison, the Alaska purchase price, in 2006 dollars, is the equivalent of $1.67 billion, certainly no folly in terms of the value of oil, minerals, and strategic advantages obtained.

The Limitations of Formulas

"People always want a formula—but it doesn't work that way. You have to estimate total cash generated from now to eternity, and discount it back to today. Yardsticks such as P/Es are not enough by themselves."

—Buffett

"You need a different checklist and different mental models for different companies. I can never make it easy by saying, 'Here are three things.' You have to derive it yourself to ingrain it in your head for the rest of your life."

—Munger

An Investing Principles Checklist

"No wise pilot, no matter how great his talent and experience, fails to use his checklist."

We have now examined Charlie's approach to thinking in general and to investing in particular. In keeping with our intent to observe "how he seems to do it," we will recap his approach by using the "checklist" methodology he advocates. (For Charlie's own words of wisdom on the value and importance of checklists, see Talk Five and page 320.) Note, however, that the following principles are most certainly not employed by Charlie in a one-by-one or one-time fashion as the checklist format might seem to imply. Nor can they necessarily be prioritized in terms of any apparent or relative importance. Rather, each must be considered as part of the complex whole or gestalt of the investment analysis process, in much the same way that an individual tile is integral to the larger mosaic in which it appears.

- Risk—All investment evaluations should begin by measuring risk, especially reputational
  - Incorporate an appropriate margin of safety
  - Avoid dealing with people of questionable character
  - Insist upon proper compensation for risk assumed
  - Always beware of inflation and interest rate exposures
  - Avoid big mistakes; shun permanent capital loss
- Independence—"Only in fairy tales are emperors told they are naked"
  - Objectivity and rationality require independence of thought
  - Remember that just because other people agree or disagree with you doesn't make you right or wrong—the only thing that matters is the correctness of your analysis and judgment
  - Mimicking the herd invites regression to the mean (merely average performance)

Compound Interest

"...'tis the stone that will turn all your lead into gold.... Remember that money is of a prolific generating nature. Money can beget money, and its offspring can beget more."

—Benjamin Franklin

"If you took our top fifteen decisions out, we'd have a pretty average record. It wasn't hyperactivity, but a hell of a lot of patience. You stuck to your principles and when opportunities came along, you pounced on them with vigor."

"There are worse situations than drowning in cash and sitting, sitting, sitting. I remember when I wasn't awash in cash—and I don't want to go back."

—Munger

Invert, Always Invert

Know What to Avoid

"The 'Munger System of Avoiding Dumb Stuff' will alone, strictly adhered to, allow you to prevail over your 'betters,' no matter how smart they are."

- Preparation—"The only way to win is to work, work, work, work, and hope to have a few insights"
  - Develop into a lifelong self-learner through voracious reading; cultivate curiosity and strive to become a little wiser every day
  - More important than the will to win is the will to prepare
  - Develop fluency in mental models from the major academic disciplines
  - If you want to get smart, the question you have to keep asking is "why, why, why?"
- Intellectual humility—Acknowledging what you don't know is the dawning of wisdom
  - Stay within a well-defined circle of competence
  - Identify and reconcile disconfirming evidence
  - Resist the craving for false precision, false certainties, etc.
  - Above all, never fool yourself, and remember that you are the easiest person to fool

"Understanding both the power of compound interest and the difficulty of getting it is the heart and soul of understanding a lot of things."

- Analytic rigor—Use of the scientific method and effective checklists minimizes errors and omissions
  - Determine value apart from price; progress apart from activity; wealth apart from size
  - It is better to remember the obvious than to grasp the esoteric

- Be a business analyst, not a market, macroeconomic, or security analyst
- Consider totality of risk and effect; look always at potential second order and higher level impacts
- Think forwards and backwards—Invert, always invert

■ Allocation—Proper allocation of capital is an investor's number one job

- Remember that highest and best use is always measured by the next best use (opportunity cost)
- Good ideas are rare—when the odds are greatly in your favor, bet (allocate) heavily
- Don't "fall in love" with an investment—be situation-dependent and opportunity-driven

■ Patience—Resist the natural human bias to act

- "Compound interest is the eighth wonder of the world" (Einstein); never interrupt it unnecessarily
- Avoid unnecessary transactional taxes and frictional costs; never take action for its own sake
- Be alert for the arrival of luck
- Enjoy the process along with the proceeds, because the process is where you live

■ Decisiveness—When proper circumstances present themselves, act with decisiveness and conviction

- Be fearful when others are greedy, and greedy when others are fearful
- Opportunity doesn't come often, so seize it when it does
- Opportunity meeting the prepared mind: that's the game

Mispriced Bets

"It's not given to human beings to have such talent that they can just know everything about everything all the time. But it is given to human beings who work hard at it—who look and sift the world for a misplaced bet—that they can occasionally find one."

Thomas Carlyle
(1795–1881)

"The task of a man is not to see what lies dimly in the distance, but to do what lies clearly at hand."

- Change—Live with change and accept unremovable complexity
    - Recognize and adapt to the true nature of the world around you; don't expect it to adapt to you
    - Continually challenge and willingly amend your "best-loved ideas"
    - Recognize reality even when you don't like it—especially when you don't like it
- Focus—Keep things simple and remember what you set out to do
    - Remember that reputation and integrity are your most valuable assets—and can be lost in a heartbeat
    - Guard against the effects of hubris and boredom
    - Don't overlook the obvious by drowning in minutiae
    - Be careful to exclude unneeded information or slop: "A small leak can sink a great ship"
    - Face your big troubles; don't sweep them under the rug

Since human beings began investing, they have been searching for a magic formula or easy recipe for instant wealth. As you can see, Charlie's superior performance doesn't come from a magic formula or some business-school-inspired system. It comes from what he calls his "constant search for better methods of thought," a willingness to "prepay" through rigorous preparation, and from the extraordinary outcomes of his multidisciplinary research model. *In the end, it comes down to Charlie's most basic guiding principles, his fundamental philosophy of life: Preparation. Discipline. Patience. Decisiveness.* Each attribute is in turn lost without the other, but together they form the dynamic critical mass for a cascading of positive effects for which Munger is famous (the "lollapalooza").

Charlie Sums It Up

"How do some people get wiser than other people? Partly it is inborn temperament. Some people do not have a good temperament for investing. They're too fretful; they worry too much. But if you've got a good temperament, which basically means being very patient, yet combine that with a vast aggression when you know enough to do something, then you just gradually learn the game, partly by doing, partly by studying. Obviously, the more hard lessons you can learn vicariously, instead of from your own terrible experiences, the better off you will be. I don't know anyone who did it with great rapidity. Warren Buffett has become one hell of a lot better investor since the day I met him, and so have I. If we had been frozen at any given stage, with the knowledge hand we had, the record would have been much worse than it is. So the game is to keep learning, and I don't think people are going to keep learning who don't like the learning process."

Finally, a word or two on why this overview of Charlie's investment philosophy has focused so much on the subject of "what to buy" and so little on "when to sell." The answer, in Charlie's own words, serves as a wonderful summation of the "Munger School" of highly-concentrated, focused investing described here:

"We're partial to putting out large amounts of money where we won't have to make another decision. If you buy something because it's undervalued, then you have to think about selling it when it approaches your calculation of its intrinsic value. That's hard. But, if you can buy a few great companies, then you can sit on your ass. That's a good thing."

Like his hero, Benjamin Franklin, Charlie Munger painstakingly developed and perfected unique approaches to personal and business endeavors. Through these methods, and the development and maintenance of sound, lifelong habits, he has achieved extraordinary success.

"And so these complex, aging prodigies carefully tend their compound interest machine, a joint creation of two exceptional personalities. Others may try to duplicate Berkshire Hathaway, but they won't be able to duplicate these two exceptional minds."

—Robert Lenzner and David S. Fondiller

Honesty Is the Best Policy

Bill Gross

Consistent with his Midwestern roots, honesty and integrity and Charles Munger have always been synonymous. As Charlie once said, "Doing the right thing can pay big dividends both personally and professionally." As a testimonial to just how deeply honesty and integrity are ingrained in Charlie, his daughter Wendy recalls the Watergate era and the sympathy she had for the daughters of Richard Nixon, as their father's ethical lapses became known. "I knew without a doubt that my dad would never put us in a similar situation. I can't tell you how wonderful that made me feel."

We asked legendary fixed-income expert Bill Gross of PIMCO to comment on Charlie and honesty. Here is what he had to say: "When the East and the West coasts fall into the sea, either through storm, earthquake, or a deterioration of values, there will still be Munger's Omaha. Charlie's ethical standards should be beamed by satellite to all global financial centers to prevent future Enrons and WorldComs.

"What fine examples and teachers Charlie and Warren are, especially for young people. As Albert Schweitzer said, 'Example is not the main thing in teaching—it is the only thing.' Charlie and Warren, in a lifetime business 'race,' have not only finished up front, but have never cut any corners along the way.

"One could not find more exemplary 'Honest Abes' in the financial world than Warren Buffett and Charlie Munger. Their annual reports are legend, and they contain not only words of bona fide investment wisdom, but self-recrimination when deemed necessary."

"I think track records are very important. If you start early trying to have a perfect one in some simple thing like honesty, you're well on your way to success in this world."

—Charles T. Munger

Rick Guerin, longtime friend and business associate adds: "On two occasions, I saw Charlie pay more than he needed to in business transactions. First, with two little old ladies who held notes in a business we were buying, which we could have easily redeemed at far less than face value—Charlie nevertheless paid them face value. Second, to raise some cash I needed for another investment, I offered to sell him my half of a venture we were in together, and he said to set a fair price—I said $130,000; he said, no, $230,000 was correct, and he paid me that. This also presented Charlie with the opportunity to use one of his favorite lines: 'I'm right, and you're smart, and sooner or later you'll see I'm right.' Of course, he was right on both scores—he had set a more accurate price, and I did eventually come to see it that way.

"Taking advantage of a cheap stock price on the stock exchange is one thing, but taking advantage of partners or old ladies is something else—something Charlie just doesn't do."

Rick Guerin

"Charlie just loves to use one of his favorite lines on me: 'I'm right, and you're smart, and sooner or later you'll see I'm right.'"

Charlie on Honesty:

2004 Wesco Meeting

"Ability will get you to the top, but it takes character to keep you there."

"Trickery and treachery are the practices of fools that have not the wits enough to be honest."

"Louis Vincenti, who used to sit in the chair I occupy today, used to say, 'If you tell the truth, you don't have to remember your lies.' So we try and keep it simple by telling it like it is at all times. Having so many longtime loyal shareholders means that we have never given a damn whether any quarter's earnings were up or down—at least we don't care in terms of their effect on shareholders. We prefer profits to losses, obviously. But we're not willing to manipulate in any way just to make some quarter look a little better. And that's a very different ethos from the standard.

"And in terms of intellectual content, I think this place tries harder to be rational than most places. And I think it tries harder than most places to be ethical—meaning to tell the truth and to not be abusive. Now with 175,000 employees, or something like that, at Berkshire, I'll bet as I sit here at least one of them is doing something that I would very much regret. However, despite the presence of some human failing, we've had an amazingly low amount of litigation or scandal or anything of that sort over a vast number of decades. And people notice that.

"We think there should be a huge area between what you're willing to do and what you can do without significant risk of suffering criminal penalty or causing losses. We believe you shouldn't go anywhere near that line. You ought to have an internal compass. So there should be all kinds of things you won't do even though they're perfectly legal. That's the way we try to operate.

"I don't think we deserve a lot of credit for that because we early understood that we'd make more money that way. And since we understood it so well, I'm not sure that we're entitled to credit for such morality as we have.

"Of course, it is hard to know your own motivations. But I'd like to believe that we'd all behave well even if it didn't work so well financially. And every once in a while, we get an opportunity to behave that way. But more often we've made extra money out of morality. Ben Franklin was right for us. He didn't say honesty was the best morals, he said it was the best policy."

Our First
I Have Nothing to Add...

On occasion, Charlie will pose a challenging question to his audience, or receive one, and leave it unanswered. By so doing, he says, he encourages his listeners to "reach" for the answers themselves and, as a result, better learn and retain the information they discover. Charlie says his father routinely used this same technique with him, with results that still benefit him today.

In keeping with the promise of this book to present the wit and wisdom of Charlie Munger, we consider it a responsibility and duty to once and for all provide answers to some of the riddles and questions Charlie has long left us "reaching" for, but never quite grasping.

We begin with this question from the talk Charlie gave at the Harvard Faculty Club, October 6, 1994, "The Psychology of Human Misjudgment":

Question: "You cite the Warren Buffett rule for outcry auctions: 'Don't go.' Then you say, 'We don't go to the closed bid auctions either, but for a different reason, one which Zeckhauser would understand.'"

Answer: "Zeckhauser—he's the Harvard professor who is also a great bridge player. The problem, a different one, with closed bid auctions is that they are frequently won by people making a technical mistake, as in the case of Shell paying double for Belridge Oil. You can't pay double the losing bid at an open outcry auction. You don't have that problem, you have different ones. But closed bid auctions invite a possibility for big mispricing errors."

Look for more "I Have Nothing to Add" moments sprinkled throughout the book.

2005 © www.AlanLevenson.com

Chapter Three

Mungerisms: Charlie Unscripted

Highlights from Recent Berkshire Hathaway and Wesco Financial Annual Meetings

By Whitney Tilson

"The wisdom of the wise, and the experience of ages, may be preserved by quotations."
—Isaac Disraeli

"It is a good thing for an uneducated man to read books of quotations."
—Sir Winston Churchill

Warren Buffett and Charlie Munger are undoubtedly the greatest investment duo ever, so any investor who fails to learn as much as possible about these two men and how they achieved their success is, to use one of Charlie's favorite words, "bonkers."

But the real joy of studying Warren and Charlie is not that one can learn a great deal about how to compound money at a high rate for an extended period—though this is certainly a nice side benefit! Rather, by absorbing their teachings, one will gain a far deeper understanding of the human condition, the state of the world, how to think rationally, and, most importantly, how to better lead a life of integrity, happiness, and kindness (here's a hint: these characteristics are intertwined).

Learning from Warren isn't hard—there are many books about him; he regularly gives speeches, writes articles, and makes public appearances; and he's published lengthy annual letters for decades (you can read the last twenty-eight of them for free at www.berkshirehathaway.com; if you haven't done so already, what are you waiting for?!). But Charlie is more private: There are only two books about him, and he is a far less prolific writer and speaker.

For this reason, many people fail to recognize that Charlie is a genius in his own right, and that he has had a profound effect on Warren's investment philosophy, which Warren freely acknowledges. The dynamic between them is pretty funny to watch. On stage at the Berkshire annual meeting, Warren generally takes the first stab at answering a question, but then usually turns and says, "Charlie?" Immobile and expressionless (they could easily substitute a mannequin for him, and no one would notice most of the time), Charlie typically replies, "I have nothing to add." Those five words have become a trademark of Charlie's that often delights both Warren and the audience. (In fact, at the special meeting for the Gen Re acquisition in September 1998, Warren actually showed up with a cardboard cutout of Charlie and a recording of Charlie saying, "I have nothing to add." According to one of my friends in attendance, "Warren would get that impish look each of the half dozen or so times he used it.") Those words also reflect both Charlie's abrupt, curmudgeonly nature—at least that's his public persona—and the "two-minds-as-one" relationship of brilliant partners joined in their thoughts.

But when Charlie *does* have something to add, it is often piercing and insightful, and he doesn't pull any punches. To use his own words, Charlie is a "cranky, old-

"Armed with this collection of Mungerisms, I plan to plagiarize Charlie more frequently and accurately than I have been able to in the past!"

—C. B. "Chuck" Thornton

fashioned" man and has never worried about being politically correct—he just calls it the way he sees it.

Since Warren does most of the talking at the Berkshire meeting, I always like to attend the Wesco annual meeting a few days later in Pasadena to hear Charlie's in-depth thinking (he is the chairman of Wesco Financial, a holding company with a structure similar to Berkshire's, which owns 80.1 percent of Wesco). One needn't even be a shareholder to attend; Charlie—as he and Warren do at the Berkshire meeting—welcomes all pilgrims to the church of Graham, Dodd, Buffett, and Munger. I've never regretted making the cross-country trip so soon after returning from Omaha, as Charlie's mind remains in peak form. During the 2003 meeting, as Charlie made one insightful observation after another, one of my friends leaned over and whispered to me, "This is one unbelievable eighty-year-old!" Indeed!

As a teacher and a thinker, Charlie is Warren's equal, and I've learned an enormous amount from him, which is why I was so delighted to hear that Peter Kaufman was pulling this book together—and why I immediately agreed to contribute!

A Cardboard Charlie "with Nothing to Add"

At the special Berkshire meeting for the Gen Re acquisition in September 1998, Warren actually showed up with a cardboard cutout of Charlie and a recording of Charlie saying, "I have nothing to add." According to one of my friends in attendance, "Warren would get that impish look each of the half-dozen or so times he used it."

This chapter is intended to complement Charlie's formal writings and speeches that appear elsewhere in this book. Drawn from my notes from the Berkshire and Wesco annual meetings over the past five years, this is a collection of the most insightful, provocative, spontaneous, funny things Charlie said at these meetings. Since almost all of his remarks are in response to questions from shareholders, he comments extensively on Berkshire Hathaway and many business- and investing-related topics.

To make Charlie's teachings more accessible, I've organized them by topic and also done some light editing, but the goal is to let him speak for himself. Enjoy!

"I have been associated for many years with a man legendary for good judgment, and it never ceases to amaze me to see how much territory can be grasped if one merely masters and consistently uses all the obvious and easily learned principles."

—Munger

Keys to Our Success

1) It is occasionally possible for a tortoise, content to assimilate proven insights of his best predecessors, to outrun hares that seek originality or don't wish to be left out of some crowd folly that ignores the best work of the past. This happens as the tortoise stumbles on some particularly effective way to apply the best previous work, or simply avoids standard calamities. We try more to profit from always remembering the obvious than from grasping the esoteric. It is remarkable how much long-term advantage people like us have gotten by trying to be consistently not stupid, instead of trying to be very intelligent.

2) We don't claim to have perfect morals, but at least we have a huge area of things that, while legal, are beneath us. We won't do them. Currently, there's a culture in America that says that anything that won't send you to prison is okay.

We believe there should be a huge area between everything you should do and everything you can do without getting into legal trouble. I don't think you should come anywhere near that line. We don't deserve much credit for this. It helps us make more money. I'd like to believe that we'd behave well even if it didn't work. But more often, we've made extra money from doing the right thing.

Remember Louis Vincenti's rule: Tell the truth, and you won't have to remember your lies. It's such a simple concept.

Comments on Berkshire Hathaway

Berkshire Is a Hell of a Business

NetJets, purchased by Berkshire in 1998, is one of the many successful businesses Warren and Charlie have added to Berkshire's portfolio. Capably run by Rich Santulli—inventor of fractional ownership—the company continues to expand internationally, as evidenced by the ad below in Arabic.

We're like the hedgehog that only knows one big thing: If you can generate float [cash from insurance premiums that Berkshire can invest before claims must be paid] at three percent and invest it in businesses that generate thirteen percent, that's a pretty good business.

The businesses that Berkshire has acquired will return thirteen percent pretax on what we paid for them, maybe more. With a cost of capital of three percent—generated via other people's money in the form of float—that's a hell of a business. That's the reason Berkshire shareholders needn't totally despair. Berkshire is not as good as it was in terms of percentage compounding [going forward], but it's still a hell of a business.

I hate to be an optimist, but we have really added a lot of wonderful businesses to Berkshire over the past few years.

Berkshire's Past Returns

Berkshire's past record has been almost ridiculous. If Berkshire had used even half the leverage of, say, Rupert Murdoch, it would be five times its current size.

Berkshire's Future Outlook

One of the smartest things a person can do is dampen investment expectations, especially with Berkshire. That would be mature and responsible. I like our model, and we should do nicely.

The future will be harder for Berkshire Hathaway for two reasons:

1) We're so big. It limits our investment options to more competitive areas that are examined by very smart people like Alice Schroeder [the insurance analyst from Paine Webber and then Morgan Stanley, who was sitting in the audience].

2) The current climate offers prospects in common stocks over the next fifteen to twenty years that are way less than we've experienced over the past fifteen to twenty years. Read Warren's *Fortune* article—I totally agree with it. ["Mr. Buffett on the Stock Market," 11/22/99]

Berkshire Hathaway's value will be higher in twenty years, but it is certain that the annual rate of percentage growth will be much lower.

But this is not a tragedy. We're content. Berkshire Hathaway and Wesco will accumulate cash every year, and we have a structure that gives us enormous flexibility. While we're too big to buy the stock of a small company, we have the advantage of having entire companies offered to us. Something has always turned up for us. I'm not discouraged, but I don't think your money here is going to do anything like what you're used to.

It's a finite and very competitive world. All large aggregations of capital eventually find it hell on earth to grow and thus find a lower rate of return.

Personally, I think Berkshire will be a lot bigger and stronger than it is. Whether the stock will be a good investment from today's price is another question. The one thing we've always guaranteed is that the future will be a lot worse than the past.

The Law of Large Numbers:
A Heavy Anchor

"Economic progressions, as they grow larger, forge their own mathematical anchors."

—Buffett

"We're not crying wolf at how hard it is to compound at the old rates—it can't be done. Look how tough it is to earn $100 million pretax doing anything; few ever accomplish it. Then $1 billion, then $5 billion, then $10 billion...."

—Munger

Andrew Carnegie (1835–1919) rose from penniless immigrant to become the wealthiest man on earth. Selling his steel empire for $500 million, he created schools, a peace endowment, New York's Carnegie Hall, and 2,811 free public libraries. He also paid for the acquisition and installation of 7,689 church organs. His vision was to create "an ideal state in which the surplus wealth of the few will become, in the best sense, the property of the many."

The future returns of Berkshire and Wesco won't be as good in the future as they have been in the past. [This is true of all large, successful companies.] The only difference is that we'll tell you.

Berkshire Hathaway's Culture

Our culture is very old-fashioned, like Ben Franklin's or Andrew Carnegie's. Can you imagine Carnegie hiring consultants?! It's amazing how well this approach still works. A lot of the businesses we buy are kind of cranky and old-fashioned like us.

For many of our shareholders, our stock is all they own, and we're acutely aware of that. Our culture [of conservatism] runs pretty deep.

This is an amazingly sound place. We are more disaster-resistant than most other places. We haven't pushed it as hard as other people would have pushed it.

I'm happy having ninety percent of my net worth in Berkshire stock. We're going to try to compound it at a reasonable rate without taking unreasonable risk or using leverage. If we can't do this, then that's just too damn bad.

Berkshire's and Wesco's Stock Prices

We like the stocks of both Berkshire and Wesco to trade within hailing distance of what we think of as intrinsic value. When it runs up, we try to talk it down. That's not at all common in Corporate America, but that's the way we act.

Go, or square one, from the Parker Brothers' classic board game, Monopoly. The game was created by Charles B. Darrow of Germantown, Pennsylvania, in 1934.

I don't want to go back to Go. I've been to Go. A lot of our shareholders have a majority of their net worth in Berkshire, and they don't want to go back to Go either.

Today, it seems to be regarded as the duty of CEOs to make the stock go up. This leads to all sorts of foolish behavior. We want to tell it like it is.

Berkshire Shareholders

We like our current shareholders and don't want to entice anyone to become one.

I think our reporting, considering the complexity of the enterprise, is better than that of any enterprise I know at giving shareholders the information they need. We do it conscientiously.

Berkshire's Acquisition Strategy

Two-thirds of acquisitions don't work. Ours work because we don't try to do acquisitions—we wait for no-brainers.

Competition for Acquisitions

We've had private equity competitors for a long time, but one way or another, we've managed to buy quite a few things.

The general assumption is that it must be easy to sit behind a desk and people will bring in one good opportunity after another—this was the attitude in venture capital until a few years ago. This was not the case at all for us—we scrounged around for companies to buy. For twenty years, we didn't buy more than one or two per year.

It's fair to say that we were rooting around. There were no commissioned salesmen. Anytime you sit there waiting for a deal to come by, you're in a very dangerous seat.

Otis Booth
Hand in Pocket

"I was a good investor myself, but I couldn't do what Warren and Charlie did so well—virtually never have any losers. The best investing decision I ever made was keeping my hands in my pockets for all these years and hanging on to my Berkshire position, letting those guys do it. I simply recognized they were better at it than I was."

—Otis Booth,
major Berkshire Hathaway shareholder,
real estate development partner, and
friend of Charlie's for over fifty years.

Managers of Acquired Companies

We've bought business after business because we admire the founders and what they've done with their lives. In almost all cases, they've stayed on, and our expectations have not been disappointed.

What matters most: passion or competence that was inborn? Berkshire is full of people who have a peculiar passion for their own business. I would argue passion is more important than brain power.

I don't think our managers who come to this meeting are picking up new tricks—they know all the tricks related to their business—but this is an interesting place and it gets more interesting every year and they like being part of it.

Managing Subsidiaries

By and large, we've chosen people we admire enormously to have the power beneath us. It's easy for us to get along with them on average because we love and admire them. And they create the culture for whatever invention and reality recognition is going on in their businesses. And included in that reality recognition is the recognition that previous conclusions were incorrect.

There are certain virtues that are common in all of Berkshire's subsidiaries. We don't create them—we select companies that have them already. We just don't screw it up. We have decentralized power to a point just short of total abdication.

It would help current shareholders to hear our CEOs [of the Berkshire operating subsidiaries], but we promised them they could spend one hundred percent of their time on their businesses. We place no impediments on them running their businesses. Many have expressed to me how happy they are that they don't have to spend twenty-five percent of their time on activities they don't like.

"If you ever want to sell your company, yet feel like you didn't sell it at all, talk to Warren and Charlie. All they want you to do is go out and run your business well, and, if you do that, they leave you completely alone. I don't feel like I sold FlightSafety; I just traded my FlightSafety stock certificate for a Berkshire certificate."

—Al Ueltschi,
founder and chairman,
FlightSafety International.

Synergies

The reason we avoid the word "synergy" is because people generally claim more synergistic benefits than will come. Yes, it exists, but there are so many false promises. Berkshire is full of synergies—we don't avoid synergies, just claims of synergies.

Making the Right Personnel Decisions

It's amazing how few times over the decades we've had to remove a person—far less than other companies. It's not that we're soft or foolish, it's that we're wiser and luckier. Most people would look back and say their worst mistake was not firing someone soon enough. [We don't say that.] Our record is fabulous. We're old-fashioned. For example, in the case of CORT Business Services [a furniture rental business that Wesco acquired], Warren said to me, "You're going to love Paul Arnold [CORT's CEO]." And he was right. Paul's been running the business since he was in law school and loves it.

Ajit Jain heads the National Indemnity reinsurance business of Berkshire Hathaway. Widely considered to have one of the most brilliant minds in the insurance field, he routinely finds significant new sources of low-cost float for redeployment by Warren and Charlie.

Warren regularly reminds shareholders of Ajit's contributions to their company, as in this tribute in the 2001 Annual Report:

"Ajit's business will ebb and flow—but his underwriting principles will not waiver. It's impossible to overstate his value to Berkshire."

Berkshire's Insurance Operations

Reinsurance is not as much of a commodity business as it might appear. There's such a huge time lag between when the policy is written and when it is paid that the customer has to evaluate the insurer's future willingness and ability to pay. We have a reputational advantage, though it's not as big as it should be.

I do think we get some advantage in reinsurance because people trust our willingness and ability to pay, so it's not a commodity. I think we have some special talents. That being said, I think it's dangerous to rely on special talents—it's better to own lots of monopolistic businesses with unregulated prices. But that's not the world today. We have made money exercising our talents and will continue to do so.

I'm glad we have insurance, though it's not a no-brainer, I'm warning you. We have to be smart to make this work.

The overall result is that we're going to do pretty well—meaning in the top ten percent [of the industry]—because we do different things and we're willing to do some unpleasant things.

Generally speaking, we're mildly optimistic about our insurance operations.

Growing float at a sizeable rate at low cost is almost impossible—but we intend to do it anyway.

I've been amazed by the growth and cost of our float. It's wonderful to generate billions of dollars of float at a cost way below Treasury notes.

Lumpy results and being willing to write less insurance business if market conditions are unfavorable…that is one of our advantages as an insurer—we don't give a damn about lumpy results. Everyone else is trying to please Wall Street. This is not a small advantage.

Wall Street's New York Stock Exchange is the world's leading and most technologically advanced equities market. On an average day, 1.46 billion shares, valued at $46.1 billion, trade on the NYSE.

Nobody else does it, but to me [not worrying about trying to please Wall Street] is obviously the only way to go. A lot about Berkshire is like this. Being controlling owners is key—it would be hard for a committee to make these kinds of decisions.

Berkshire Hathaway Repurchasing Shares

In the past, when Berkshire has gotten cheap, we've found other even cheaper stocks to buy. I'd always prefer this. It's no fun to have the company so lacking in repute that we can make money for some shareholders by buying out others.

Splitting Berkshire Stock to Create More Liquidity

I think the notion that liquidity of tradable common stock is a great contributor to capitalism is mostly twaddle. The liquidity gives us these crazy booms, so it has as many problems as virtues.

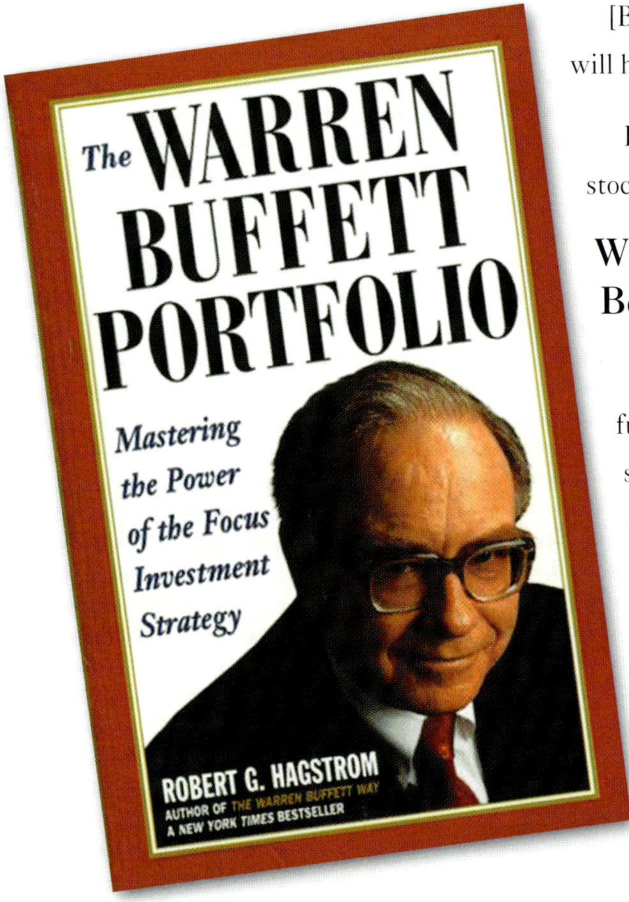

Robert Hagstrom's book, recommended by both Munger and Buffett, clearly lays out Berkshire Hathaway's successful approach for all to follow.

[Buffett: Berkshire trades $50 million of stock per day, so very few people will have a problem selling it.]

But we're trying to create more people who have the problem of owning stock worth so much that liquidity is an issue.

Why Don't More Companies and Investors Copy Berkshire Hathaway?

It's a good question. Our approach has worked for us. Look at the fun we, our managers, and our shareholders are having. More people should copy us. It's not difficult, but it looks difficult because it's unconventional—it isn't the way things are normally done. We have low overhead, don't have quarterly goals and budgets or a standard personnel system, and our investing is much more concentrated than is the average. It's simple and common sense.

I was recently speaking with Jack McDonald, who teaches a course on investing rooted in our principles at Stanford Business School. He said it's lonely—like he's the Maytag repairman.

The Maytag Repairman

Starting in 1967, actor Jesse White portrayed the appliance repairman who, because of the great reliability of Maytag products, becomes the "loneliest man in town." White maintained the role until 1989, when Gordon Jump took over. In 2003, Jump retired, and a former Mr. Goodwrench, Hardy Rawls, took over the role.

Comments on Buffett

It's hard to believe that he's getting better with each passing year. It won't go on forever, but Warren is actually improving. It's remarkable: Most seventy-two-year-old men are not improving, but Warren is.

Charlie's Influence on Warren

I think those authors give me more credit than I deserve. It is true that Warren had a touch of brain block from working under Ben Graham and making a ton of money—it's hard to switch from something that's worked so well. But if Charlie Munger had never lived, the Buffett record would still be pretty much what it is.

I think there's some mythology in this idea that I've been this great enlightener of Warren. He hasn't needed much enlightenment. But we know more now than five years ago.

"The main reason they have me up here, at age 80, is to make Warren look young."

—Charlie at 2004 Berkshire Hathaway annual meeting

What Happens When Buffett's Gone?

The key is having good businesses. There's a lot of momentum here. [However,] I don't think our successors will be as good as Warren at capital allocation.

Berkshire is drowning in money—we have great businesses pounding out money. If the stock went down, Berkshire could buy it back. There's no reason to think it will go to hell in a bucket, and I think there's reason to believe it could go on quite well. I'd be horrified if it isn't bigger and better over time, even after Warren dies.

Another Comment on Buffett

Marc Hamburg
CFO, Berkshire Hathaway

"What's it like to work with someone as brilliant as Warren Buffett?"

"Warren is remarkably easy to work with—the best I've ever encountered. It is wonderful to have someone with such a good feel for how results should come out (in fact, if the number is widely different from his, we suspect we've made a mistake). He has a remarkable ability to look at the same set of figures that everyone else is looking at and come up with original insights and perspectives. He does this all the time—comes up with great ideas that seem so simple after you hear them, but don't occur to anyone else."

When Warren is gone, the acquisition side of Berkshire will not do as well, but the rest will do well. And the acquisition side will do just fine. In any case, we've guaranteed you that the historical rate of growth will go down, and we wouldn't want to make a liar out of me.

I think the top guy won't be as smart as Warren. But it's silly to complain: "What kind of world is this that gives me Warren Buffett for forty years, and then some bastard comes along who's worse?"

If anyone would have a reason to worry, it would be me, but having known the Buffett family for decades, I say to you: "Don't worry about it. You should be so lucky."

What If Charlie Dies?

As you can tell, we're planning on immortality here. What do you need—sitting on a pile of money and Warren Buffett sitting at the parent corporation?

Charlie as the Abominable No-Man

Buffett: You just have to learn how to calibrate his answers. If you ask Charlie something and he says "no," then we put all of our money in it. If he says "that's the stupidest thing I've ever heard," then we make a more moderate investment. If you calibrate his answers, you'll get a lot of wisdom.

Charlie, the Abominable No-Man

Exchange at a recent Berkshire shareholders' meeting:

Warren: "Charlie, do you have any additional comment?"

Charlie: "No. I think you said 'no' perfectly."

The Abominable No-Man

Photo: Kiley Christian Cruse/ Omaha World-Herald

Chuck Rickershauser, former Munger Tolles partner and friend since 1964

"Warren told me a story once that, back in the early days of their relationship, when they had no financial connection and each had an investment partnership, Warren would frequently call up Charlie and say, 'I'm thinking of doing something' and describe it, and Charlie would say, 'My God, are you kidding? There's this risk and that risk.' They'd go right through all these risks that Charlie saw, and Warren would usually say, 'I think you're right.' But once in a while, he would say, 'Charlie, I've heard everything you said, but I think I'm going to go ahead.' Warren said that it wasn't until that instant that he'd learn what Charlie really thought because occasionally Charlie would respond, 'Warren, if you do it, could I have a percentage of it?' People often think of Charlie as identifying risks and saying, 'No,' but it was his ability to identify the times to ask for a percentage that was most valuable."

Otis Booth, friend and business associate since 1956

"Charlie realizes that it is difficult to find something that is really good. So, if you say 'No' ninety percent of the time, you're not missing much in the world."

Appreciation For Charlie

George Gillespie, longtime friend:

"Charlie is of the highest intellect and character, is devoted to his family, and is extremely considerate of his friends. To me, he is a man for all seasons."

Fred Stanback, longtime friend:

"Charlie has a great store of practical wisdom. I always learn something when I hear him or read his writings."

Brad Reed, longtime friend:

"I have found particularly helpful Charlie's suggestion to use ideas from distinct disciplines, his insistence on trying to ascertain the consequences of consequences (of consequences), his suggestion that issues be analyzed by asking how to produce undesired results, and his injunction to abandon—or at least rigorously challenge—one's most cherished ideas. For me, his most apt aphorism is that 'a thing not worth doing is not worth doing well.'"

Jeff Moore,
Principal, Ares Management:

"Charlie's investment genius stems not only from superior intellect and thorough analysis but, equally importantly, from patience and a steadfast application of his investment principles and philosophy. Both a student and a teacher, he is one of the titans of investing; a man worthy of study."

Investment Advice

The Importance of Temperament, Patience, and Curiosity

[One of the key elements to successful investing is having the right] temperament—most people are too fretful; they worry too much. Success means being very patient, but aggressive when it's time. And the more hard lessons you can learn vicariously rather than through your own hard experience, the better.

I think there's something to be said for developing the disposition to own stocks without fretting. [But] temperament alone won't do it. You need a lot of curiosity for a long, long time.

You need to have a passionate interest in why things are happening. That cast of mind, kept over long periods, gradually improves your ability to focus on reality. If you don't have that cast of mind, you're destined for failure even if you have a high I.Q.

Focus Investing

Our investment style has been given a name—focus investing—which implies ten holdings, not one hundred or four hundred.

Our game is to recognize a big idea when it comes along, when one doesn't come along very often. Opportunity comes to the prepared mind.

The idea that it is hard to find good investments, so concentrate in a few, seems to me to be an obviously good idea. But ninety-eight percent of the investment world doesn't think this way. It's been good for us—and you—that we've done this.

What's funny is that most big investment organizations don't think like this. They hire lots of people, evaluate Merck vs. Pfizer and every stock in the S&P 500, and think they can beat the market. You can't do it.

We have this investment discipline of waiting for a fat pitch.

If I was offered the chance to go into a business where people would measure me against benchmarks, force me to be fully invested, crawl around looking over my shoulder, etc., I would hate it. I would regard it as putting me into shackles.

Very few people have adopted our approach. Focus investing is growing somewhat, but what's really growing is the unlimited use of consultants to advise on asset allocation, to analyze other consultants, an so forth. Maybe two percent of people will come into our corner of the tent, and the rest of the ninety-eight percent will believe what they've been told [e.g., that markets are totally efficient].

Misteaching Investing

Beta and modern portfolio theory and the like—none of it makes any sense to me. We're trying to buy businesses with sustainable competitive advantages at a low, or even a fair, price.

How can professors spread this [nonsense that a stock's volatility is a measure of risk]? I've been waiting for this craziness to end for decades. It's been dented, but it's still out there.

Warren once said to me, "I'm probably misjudging academia generally [in thinking so poorly of it] because the people that interact with me have bonkers theories."

Waiting for a Fat Pitch

Harmon Killebrew (b. 1936) played for the Washington Senators, Minnesota Twins, and Kansas City Royals over his twenty-two-year career. Famous for his ability to put fat pitches deep into the bleachers, the Hall of Fame slugger hit 573 career home runs. At the time of his election to the Hall of Fame in 1984, he ranked fifth on the all-time home run list and was second only to Babe Ruth among American League players.

"Don't gamble. Take all your savings and buy some good stock and hold it till it goes up, then sell it. If it don't go up, don't buy it."

—Will Rogers

Diversification

The idea of excessive diversification is madness.

We don't believe that widespread diversification will yield a good result. We believe almost all good investments will involve relatively low diversification.

If you took our top fifteen decisions out, we'd have a pretty average record. It wasn't hyperactivity, but a hell of a lot of patience. You stuck to your principles, and when opportunities came along, you pounced on them with vigor.

Berkshire in its history has made money betting on sure things.

Sit-on-Your-Ass Investing

If you buy something because it's undervalued, then you have to think about selling it when it approaches your calculation of its intrinsic value. That's hard. But if you buy a few great companies, then you can sit on your ass. That's a good thing.

We're partial to putting out large amounts of money where we won't have to make another decision.

What Is a Better Business?

There are two kinds of businesses: The first earns twelve percent, and you can take the profits out at the end of the year. The second earns twelve percent, but all the excess cash must be reinvested—there's never any cash. It reminds me of the guy who sells construction equipment—he looks at his used machines, taken in as customers bought new ones, and says, "There's all of my profit, rusting in my yard." We hate that kind of business.

See's Candy: Case Study of a Better Business

If See's Candy [when we were buying it] had asked for $100,000 more [Buffett chimed in, "$10,000 more"], Warren and I would have walked—that's how dumb we were.

Ira Marshall said you guys are crazy—there are some things you should pay up for, like quality businesses and people. You are underestimating quality. We listened to the criticism and changed our mind. This is a good lesson for anyone: the ability to take criticism constructively and learn from it. If you take the indirect lessons we learned from See's, you could say Berkshire was built on constructive criticism.

Canadian Charles See came to Los Angeles in 1921 and, using his mother's recipes, started a high-quality confection business. An image of his mother, Mary See, also became the company's icon. See's grew from one shop to twelve by the mid-1920s—and then kept growing throughout California. In 1972, in a transaction initiated by Robert T. Flaherty (now a Wesco Financial director), See's was purchased by Blue Chip Stamps, now wholly-owned by Berkshire Hathaway. Today, See's Candies are sold in more than two hundred shops and in certain foreign locations, such as Hong Kong and Tokyo.

Mistakes

The most extreme mistakes in Berkshire's history have been mistakes of omission. We saw it, but didn't act on it. They're huge mistakes—we've lost billions. And we keep doing it. We're getting better at it. We never get over it.

There are two types of mistakes: 1) doing nothing, what Warren calls "sucking my thumb" and 2) buying with an eyedropper things we should be buying a lot of.

After nearly making a terrible mistake not buying See's, we've made similar mistakes many times. We are apparently slow learners. These opportunity costs don't show up on financial statements but have cost us many billions.

Since mistakes of omission [aren't visible], most people don't pay attention to them. We rub our noses in mistakes of omission—as we just did. [They had just discussed failing to buy Wal-Mart stock because it moved up a bit, a $10 billion mistake.]

Buying into Stock Declines

Over many decades, our usual practice is that if [the stock of] something we like goes down, we buy more and more. Sometimes something happens, you realize you're wrong, and you get out. But if you develop correct confidence in your judgment, buy more and take advantage of stock prices.

Attractive investment opportunities tend to be ephemeral.

Really good investment opportunities aren't going to come along too often and won't last too long, so you've got to be ready to act. Have a prepared mind.

Opportunities for Small Investors

If you have only a little capital and are young today, there are fewer opportunities than when I was young. Back then, we had just come out of a depression. Capitalism was a bad word.

There had been abuses in the 1920s. A joke going around then was the guy who said, "I bought stock for my old age and it worked—in six months, I feel like an old man!"

Seated Old Man was painted by Pablo Picasso (1881-1973) at the age of ninety, just two years prior to his death. The painting is currently displayed at Musée Picasso, Paris.

In 1963, Picasso said, "Everything can be explained scientifically today, except Art. You can go to the moon or walk under the sea, or anything else you like, but painting remains painting because it eludes such investigation. It remains there like a question. And it alone gives the answer."

It's tougher for you, but that doesn't mean you won't do well—it just may take more time. But what the heck, you may live longer.

I'd work with very small stocks, searching for unusual mispriced opportunities, but it's such a small world.

Short Selling

Being short and seeing a promoter take the stock up is very irritating. It's not worth it to have that much irritation in your life.

The foundation for Osaka Castle's formidable moat was laid in 1583. The main tower of the castle was struck by lightning in 1665 and burned to the ground. In 1931, the present iron and concrete reconstruction of the castle was undertaken; major repairs in 1997 restored much of the castle's original condition.

Moats and Sustainable Competitive Advantage

Old moats are getting filled in and new moats are harder to predict, so it's getting harder.

Learning Process

I don't know anyone who [learned to be a great investor] with great rapidity. Warren has gotten to be one hell of a lot better investor over the period I've known him, as have I. So the game is to keep learning. You gotta like the learning process.

I've watched Warren for decades. Warren has learned a lot, which has allowed him to [expand his circle of competence so he could invest in something like PetroChina].

"Modern civilization needs energy. Warren and I will be disappointed if there isn't [attractive investment] activity in this area."

If you're going to be an investor, you're going to make some investments where you don't have all the experience you need. But if you keep trying to get a little better over time, you'll start to make investments that are virtually certain to have a good outcome. The keys are discipline, hard work, and practice. It's like playing golf—you have to work on it.

If you don't keep learning, other people will pass you by.

Circle of Competence and Its Boundaries

There are a lot of things we pass on. We have three baskets: in, out, and too tough. We have to have a special insight, or we'll put it in the "too tough" basket. All you have to look for is a special area of competency and focus on that.

If you have competence, you know the edge. It wouldn't be a competence if you didn't know where the boundaries lie. [Asking whether you've passed the boundary is] a question that almost answers itself.

Cost of Capital and Opportunity Costs

[Buffett: Charlie and I don't know our cost of capital. It's taught at business schools, but we're skeptical. We just look to do the most intelligent thing we can with the capital that we have. We measure everything against our alternatives. I've never seen a cost-of-capital calculation that made sense to me. Have you, Charlie?]

Never. If you take the best text in economics by Mankiw, he says intelligent people make decisions based on opportunity costs—in other words, it's your alternatives that matter. That's how we make all of our decisions. The rest of the world has gone off on some kick—there's even a cost of equity capital. A perfectly amazing mental malfunction.

N. Gregory Mankiw, on the economics faculty at Harvard University, is also a research associate of the National Bureau of Economic Research and an adviser to the Federal Reserve Bank of Boston and the Congressional Budget Office. His popular textbooks have been translated into many other languages.

Obviously, consideration of costs is key, including opportunity costs. Of course, capital isn't free. It's easy to figure out your cost of borrowing, but theorists went bonkers on the cost of equity capital. They say that if you're generating a one hundred percent return on capital, then you shouldn't invest in something that generates an eighty percent return on capital. It's crazy.

Value of Forecasts

People have always had this craving to have someone tell them the future. Long ago, kings would hire people to read sheep guts. There's always been a market for people who pretend to know the future. Listening to today's forecasters is just as crazy as when the king hired the guy to look at the sheep guts. It happens over and over and over.

IPOs

It is entirely possible that you could use our mental models to find good IPOs to buy. There are countless IPOs every year, and I'm sure that there are a few cinches that you could jump on. But the average person is going to get creamed. So if you think you're talented, good luck.

IPOs are too small for us, or too high tech—we won't understand them. So, if Warren's looking at them, I don't know about it.

The once high-flying eToys built on its "successful" IPO to secure a market capitalization of almost $10 billion. The California-based company has since filed for bankruptcy. It closed its "brick-and-mortar-free" doors in 2001.

"The Greek orator was clearly right about an excess of optimism being the normal human condition, even when pain or the threat of pain is absent. Witness happy people buying lottery tickets or believing that credit-furnishing, delivery-making grocery stores were going to displace a great many superefficient cash-and-carry supermarkets."

—From Talk Ten: "The Psychology of Human Misjudgment"

Portrait of Hendrickje Stofells, Rembrandt van Rijn, 1659, oil on canvas, National Gallery in London

Comments on the Market

Stocks, Rembrandts, and Bubbles

Stocks are valued partly like bonds, based on roughly rational projections of producing future cash. But they are also valued partly like Rembrandt paintings, purchased mostly because their prices have gone up so far. This situation, combined with big "wealth effects," at first up and later down, can conceivably produce much mischief.

[April 2000] It's the most extreme in modern capitalism. In the 1930s, we had the worst depression in 600 years. Today is almost as extreme in the opposite way.... We use the phrase "wretched excess" because the consequences are wretched.

Bonds are much more rational. No one thinks a bond's value will soar to the moon.

Future Market Returns

[November 2000] If stocks compound at fifteen percent going forward, then it will be due to a big "Rembrandt effect." This is not good. Look at what happened in Japan, where stocks traded at fifty to sixty times earnings. This led to a ten-year depression. I think that was a special situation, though. My guess is that we won't get extreme "Rembrandtization," and the returns [thereafter] will be six percent. If I'm wrong, it could be for a bad reason. If stocks trade more like Rembrandts in the future, then stocks will rise, but they will have no anchors. In this case, it's hard to predict how far, how high, and how long it will last.

[April 2001] I think generally that American investors should reduce their expectations. People aren't being a little stupid, but massively stupid. No one has an interest in saying this though.

[May 2001] We are not in a hog-heaven period. The investment game is getting more and more competitive.

I don't know if we'll ever see stocks in general at the mouth-watering levels that we saw in 1973–74 or even in 1982. I think there's a very excellent chance that neither Warren or I will see those opportunities again, but that's not all bad. We'll just keep plugging away.

[Buffett: It's not out of [the realm of] possibility though. You can never predict what markets will do. In Japan, a ten-year bond is yielding five-eighths of one percent. Who could have ever imagined that?]

If that could happen in Japan, something much less bad could happen in the U.S. We could be in for a period in which the average fancy-paid investment advisor just won't do very well.

The relatively small island nation of Japan has a population of approximately 126 million, which gives it a population density roughly three times that of Europe and twelve times that of the U.S. With a culture skewed toward savings, Japan is the world's largest creditor nation. It has an estimated $1 trillion in net surplus external assets.

The temporary collapse in junk bonds [in late 2002], where they got to thirty-five to forty percent yields, was just a strange thing. There was absolute chaos at the bottom tick. Apply this behavior to stocks—it's not hard to imagine a big crunch coming along.

Current Outlook

[May 2004] In terms of the general climate, I think it's pretty miserable for anyone who likes easy, sure money. Common stocks may be reasonably fairly valued, but they are not overwhelming bargains.

Our cash is speaking for itself. If we had a lot of wonderful ideas, we wouldn't have so much cash.

Berkshire and Wesco are full of cash that we don't know what to do with. Berkshire has $70 billion if you count the bonds, and Wesco is drowning in cash. It's the most extreme it's ever been. In the past, we've just been patient, and we were able to put it to work.

"Nothing to Add" Number Two

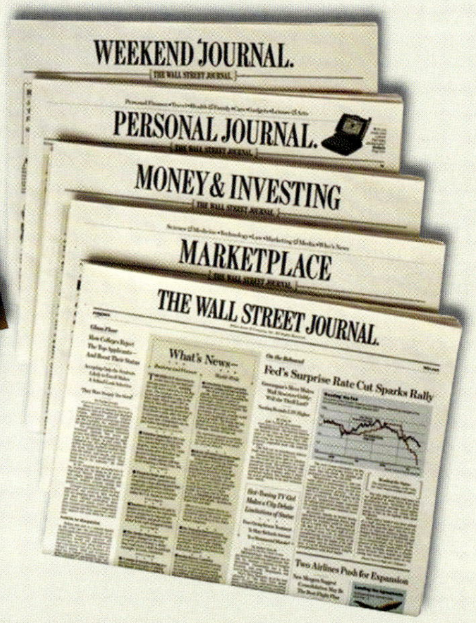

We continue with the question of how Charlie monitors broad economic trends and changes:

Question: "What macro statistics do you regularly monitor or find useful in your attempt to understand the broader economic landscape?"

Answer: "None. I find by staying abreast of our Berkshire subsidiaries and by regularly reading business newspapers and magazines, I am exposed to an enormous amount of material at the micro level. I find that what I see going on there pretty much informs me about what's happening at the macro level."

Critique on Corporate Management

Earnings Manipulation and Accounting Shenanigans

With so much money riding on reported numbers, human nature is to manipulate them. And with so many doing it, you get Serpico effects, where everyone rationalizes that it's okay because everyone else is doing it. It is always thus.

Now, it's chain-letter mechanics. Because it's mixed with legitimate activities like venture capital, it looks respectable. But we're mixing respectable activity with disrespectable activity—hence my comment at the Berkshire Hathaway annual meeting about if you mix raisins with turds, you've still got turds. There is nothing in accounting that can prevent unscrupulous managers from engaging in a chain-letter-type fraud.

Former Enron CEO Ken Lay is taken into federal court by law enforcement officers in Houston, Texas.

Spotting Crooked Managements

Bernie Ebbers and Ken Lay were caricatures—they were easy to spot. They were almost psychopaths. But it's much harder to spot problems at companies like Royal Dutch [Shell].

But we don't learn because I'd still expect that Exxon's figures are fair.

I want to make an apology. Last night, referring to some of our modern business tycoons I said that when they're talking, they're lying, and when they're quiet, they're stealing. This wasn't my witticism; it was used [long ago] to describe the robber barons.

Corporate America's Addiction to Extraordinary Charges

If it happens every year like clockwork, what's so extraordinary about it?

Corporate Governance

The cause of reform is hurt not helped when an activist makes an idiotic suggestion like saying that having Warren on the board of Coke is contrary to the interests of Coke. Nutty behavior undermines their cause.

Berkshire Hathaway and the Coca-Cola Company

Holding 200 million shares, Berkshire Hathaway is the largest shareholder of the Coca-Cola Company and has been so since the late 1980s. Berkshire's investment in Coca-Cola has a cost basis of $1.3 billion and a current market value of over $8 billion. The Coca-Cola Company began in 1886 as a soda fountain beverage seller and has evolved into one of the largest companies in the world.

Critique of the Money Management Business

Flawed Incentives

The general systems of money management [today] require people to pretend to do something they can't do and like something they don't. It's a terrible way to spend your life, but it's very well paid.

No Value Added

Mutual funds charge two percent per year and then brokers switch people between funds, costing another three to four percentage points. The poor guy in the general public is getting a terrible product from the professionals. I think it's disgusting. It's much better to be part of a system that delivers value to the people who buy the product. But if it makes money, we tend to do it in this country.

[It's] a funny business because on a net basis, the whole investment management business together gives no value added to all buyers combined. That's the way it has to work.

Stockbrokers vs. Index Funds

It's hard to sit here at this annual meeting, surrounded by smart, honorable stockbrokers who do well for their clients, and criticize them. But stockbrokers, in toto, will do so poorly that the index fund will do better.

The Wesco Annual Meeting

Carolyn Denham (left, wife of Wesco Director Robert Denham) and Carolyn Carlburg (right, Wesco Director since 1991) enjoy the proceedings at the standing-room-only 2004 annual meeting in Pasadena, California. Although much smaller in scale than the Berkshire meeting in Omaha (500 attendees vs. 20,000), the Wesco meeting offers a close-up opportunity to hear Charlie hold forth, solo, on just about any subject. Transcripts of these meetings have been available over the years from *Outstanding Investor Digest* and are highly recommended for your perusal.

I think indexing is a wiser choice for the average foundation than what it is now doing in unleveraged equity investment—and particularly so as its present total croupier costs exceed one percent of principal per annum. Indexing can't work well forever if almost everybody turns to it. But it will work all right for a long time.

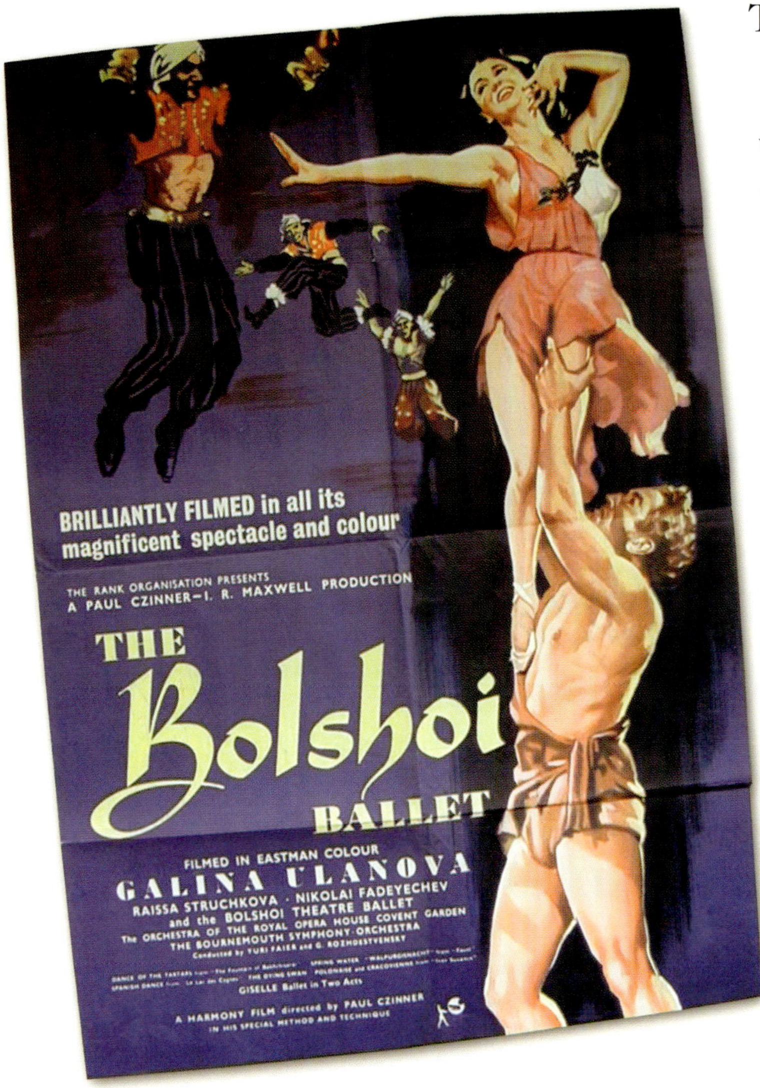

The Mutual Fund Scandal

The business of selecting investment managers was recently shown to be even harder by the revelation that a significant fraction of mutual fund managers took bribes to betray their own shareholders.

It was as if a man came up and said, "Why don't we kill your mother, and we'll split the insurance money?" And many people said, "Why, yes, I'd like some of that insurance money."

And many of them think what happened to them was unjust.

If mutual fund directors are independent, then I'm the lead character in the Bolshoi Ballet.

Critique of Wall Street

Wall Street's Lack of Ethics

The ethics of Wall Street will always average out to mediocre at best.... This doesn't mean there aren't some wonderful, intelligent people on Wall Street—there are, like those in this room—but everyone I know has to fight his own firm [to do the right thing].

The general culture of investment banking has deteriorated over the years. We did a $6 million deal years ago for Diversified Retailing, and we were rigorously and intelligently screened. The bankers cared and wanted to protect their clients.

The culture now is that anything that can be sold for a profit will be. "Can you sell it?" is the moral test, and that's not an adequate test.

Salomon Case Study

Robert Maxwell: "The Bouncing Czech"

It's amazing what goes on. Salomon was at least as disciplined and rational as other investment banks, but by the end, Salomon was begging for investment business from Robert Maxwell, whose nickname was "The Bouncing Czech." You'd think if this was his nickname, investment banks wouldn't be chasing his business.

[Buffett: The day they found him bobbing [in the water; he committed suicide as the scandal about his misdeeds broke], we [Salomon] sent money to him in exchange for money he was sending to us, but he didn't pay. So, we went to England to collect from his sons, and it was a mess. We got what we deserved.] [*Editor's Note: Unlike most creditors, Salomon did eventually get paid. As Charlie puts it, "It was a minor miracle—we didn't deserve to get it back."*]

An investment banker's earnings would be [increased in] a significant way if he wrote a few more tickets to Maxwell. You have to control this if guys can make money by bringing dubious things in the door.

Normandy America Case Study

[Warren and Charlie chuckled to themselves as they recalled Salomon doing business with another shady character they didn't name. At the 2002 annual meeting, however, Charlie identified the company as Normandy America Inc., whose IPO Salomon had to pull before money exchanged hands when they discovered the promoter had completely manufactured his record. According to a report on the SEC's website, "Normandy's stock commenced trading on the NASDAQ National Market System on August 15, 1995. One day later, Normandy withdrew its offering from the market and rescinded all trades."]

That was a wonderful experience [dripping with sarcasm]. Warren, Lou Simpson, and I were all on the board [of Salomon], we were the largest shareholders, and we said, "Don't do business with this guy." But they ignored us and said that the underwriting committee had approved it.

[Buffett: He had a neon sign on him saying "CROOK." He did go to jail. Incidentally, he claimed to have owned a lot of Berkshire stock and to have made a lot of money on it, but I checked the shareholder records and couldn't see it. It could have been in street name, but for a block that big, I think I would have found it (so he was probably lying about his Berkshire holdings).]

"For five years, I served with Charlie on the audit committee at Salomon. If I were in charge of drafting audit committee members for a public company, he would be my first choice. The mind of Charlie Munger is outstanding, off the curve. To have someone who can look at something and say the emperor has no clothes is extraordinarily valuable. He just hones right in on things."

—Lou Simpson,
President and CEO,
Capital Operations,
GEICO Corporation

Critique of Accountants

Demise of Ethics Among the Major Accounting Firms

When I was younger, the major accounting firms were quite ethical places, and nobody got filthy rich. But in the space of twenty-five years, they sold out to terrible behavior, one little step at a time. Once you start doing something bad, then it's easy to take the next step—and in the end, you're a moral sewer. The idea that the major accounting firms of the country would sell obviously fraudulent tax shelters....

Too many law and accounting firms get roped into shady things. For example, tax shelters, with their contingency fees and secrecy, are a total abomination.

You'll better understand the evil of top audit firms starting to sell fraudulent tax shelters when I tell you that one told me that they're better [than the others] because they only sold [the schemes] to their top twenty clients, so no one would notice.

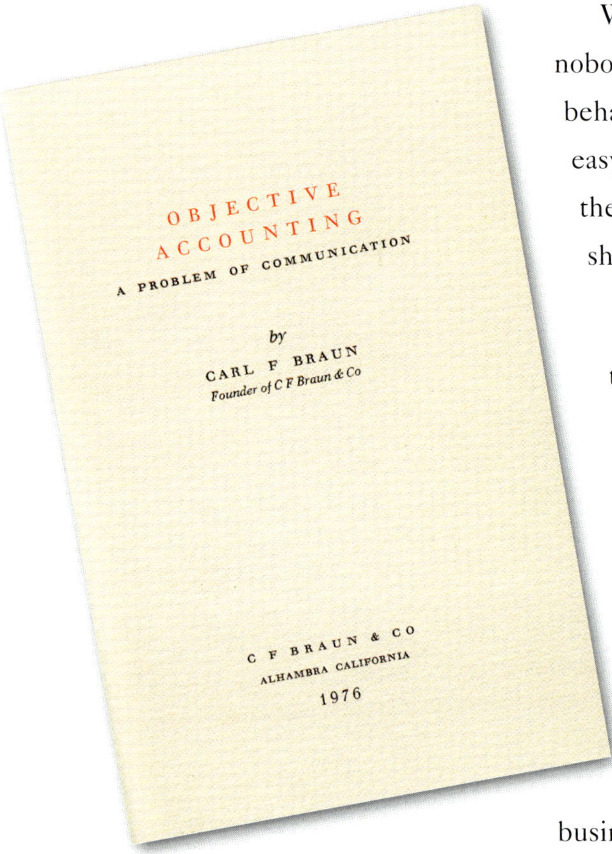

The Curse of Creative Accounting

"The fundamental thing that accountants must learn to realize, is that reports are not for the benefit of the report maker. The sole reason for a report is to serve the user. Remember that accounting reports are a measuring stick of performance. They will not serve the user well unless they have the qualities of a good measuring stick. They must be easy to read and to understand. They must be invariably consistent."

—C. F. Braun
(See pages 170-171)

Aggressive Accounting

We're so horrified by aggressive accounting [that is rampant in Corporate America] that we reach for ways to be conservative. It helps our business decisions and protects Berkshire. How did we get in situations where we're all so close to the line?

Creative accounting is an absolute curse to a civilization. One could argue that double-entry bookkeeping was one of history's great advances. Using accounting for fraud and folly is a disgrace. In a democracy, it often takes a scandal to trigger reform. Enron was the most obvious example of a business culture gone wrong in a long, long time.

Misuse of EBITDA

I think that, every time you see the word EBITDA [earnings before interest, taxes, depreciation, and amortization], you should substitute the words "bullshit earnings."

Arthur Andersen

I regard [what happened to the innocent employees of Arthur Andersen] as very unfair, but capitalism without failure is like religion without hell. When it gets this bad and there's a lack of systems for control—which Arthur Andersen didn't have—maybe a firm should just go down.

We couldn't do anything that would bring down Berkshire. Arthur Andersen was particularly vulnerable because it was a partnership. A partnership must be extra careful in its behavior, choosing clients, etc.

Unrealistic Assumptions

"Abraham Lincoln once asked: 'How many legs does a dog have if you call the tail a leg? Four. Calling a tail a leg doesn't make it a leg.' Likewise, just because an actuary says you can earn 9% on pension-plan assets, it doesn't magically alter the reality of your future liability."

—Buffett

The Scandal of American Pension Fund Accounting

The current practice [of using unrealistically high assumptions for pension plan returns] is a dumb and improper way to handle things. But if you talk to management, their eyes glaze over even before hostility comes.

Pension fund accounting is drifting into scandal by using unrealistic assumptions. It's human nature to extrapolate the recent past into the future, but it's terrible that managements go along with this.

IBM just raised its return expectations for its pension fund to ten percent. [Year 2000] Most companies are at nine percent. We think six percent is more realistic. [Company leaders] may believe it—they're honest people—but subconsciously they believe it because they want to believe it. It makes earnings good so they can promote the stock.

The reason accountants don't say anything is best summed up by the saying, "Whose bread I eat, his song I sing." I think you're getting very foolish numbers in American accounting. I don't think it's willful dishonesty, but it might as well be.

The Guitar Player, Vermeer, 1672, Kenwood House, London.

"Whose bread I eat, his song I sing."

Bad Accounting Leads to Immorality

People who have loose accounting standards are just inviting perfectly horrible behavior in other people. And it's a sin, it's an absolute sin. If you carry bushel baskets full of money through the ghetto, and made it easy to steal, that would be a considerable human sin because you'd be causing a lot of bad behavior, and the bad behavior would spread. Similarly, an institution that uses sloppy accounting commits a real human sin, and it's also a dumb way to do business.

Critique of Stock Options

Stock Options as Compensation

If you look at the impact of stock options, you'll see a lot of terrible behavior. To give a lot of options to a CEO who built the business and is in his sixties, to incent loyalty, is demented. Would the doctors at the Mayo Clinic or the lawyers at Cravath who are in their sixties work harder if they had options?

As our shareholders know, our system is different from most big corporations. We think it's less capricious. The stock option system may give extraordinary rewards to some people who did nothing, and give nothing to those who deserve a lot. Except where we inherit it [a stock option program], we don't use it.

A Proper Goal

"We are about building a good company and performing for the long term. I know everyone says that—that it sounds trite when I repeat it that way—but that is and has always been our attitude about our business. If we do the right things, the stock price will take care of itself and our shareholders will be rewarded."

—Jim Sinegal
CEO, Costco

Valuing Options and the Black-Scholes Model

Black-Scholes works for short-term options, but if it's a long-term option and you think you know something [about the underlying asset], it's insane to use Black-Scholes.

Black-Scholes is a know-nothing system. If you know nothing about value—only price—then Black-Scholes is a pretty good guess at what a ninety-day option might be worth. But the minute you get into longer periods of time, it's crazy to get into Black-Scholes.

For example, at Costco we issued stock options with strike prices of $30 and $60, and Black-Scholes valued the $60 ones higher. This is insane.

Accounting for Stock Options

The theory that options have no cost has contributed to a lot of excesses, which is bad for the country because corporate compensation is perceived as unfair.

I'm so tired of this subject. I've been on this topic for so long. It's such a rotten way to run a civilization to make the accounting wrong. It's like getting the engineering wrong when making a bridge. When perfectly reputable people say options shouldn't be expensed, it's outrageous.

A stock option is both an expense *and* dilution. To argue anything else is insane.

These people [the eighty-eight senators who voted to maintain the status quo of not expensing stock options] are stupid and dishonorable. They knew it was wrong and did it anyway.

The only thing that's consistent is that the whole thing is disgusting.

I'd rather make my money playing piano in a whore-house than account for options as recommended by John Doerr.

Warnings About Financial Institutions and Derivatives

Risks of Financial Institutions

The nature of a financial institution is that there are a lot of ways to go to hell in a bucket. You can push credit too far, do a dumb acquisition, leverage yourself excessively—it's not just derivatives [that can bring about your downfall].

Maybe it's unique to us, but we're quite sensitive to financial risks. Financial institutions make us nervous when they're trying to do well.

We're exceptionally goosey of leveraged financial institutions. If they start talking about how good risk management is, it makes us nervous.

We fret way earlier than other people. We've left a lot of money on the table through early fretting. It's the way we are—you'll just have to live with it.

Derivatives

The system is almost insanely irresponsible. And what people think are fixes aren't really fixes. It's so complicated I can't do it justice here—but you can't believe the trillions of dollars involved. You can't believe the complexity. You can't believe how difficult it is to do the accounting. You can't believe how big the incentives are to have wishful thinking about values and wishful thinking about ability to clear.

"LEMME SEE HIM, HUCK"

The Long Tail of Derivatives

"A man who carries a cat by the tail learns something he can learn in no other way."

—Mark Twain

It is the nature of many forms of derivatives, and insurance as well, to have "long tails" of exposure. Years can elapse before an actual day of reckoning occurs with respect to loss or gain on an individual transaction. Insurers or financial institutions that incorrectly assess their true exposure often experience the kind of painful lesson Twain refers to above.

Misuse of Derivatives: It's a Mad Hatter's Tea Party

"Take some more tea," the March Hare said to Alice, very earnestly.

"I've had nothing yet," Alice replied in an offended tone, "so I can't take more."

"You mean you can't take LESS," said the Hatter, "it's very easy to take MORE than nothing."

From Lewis Carroll's *Alice's Adventures in Wonderland*.

The Hatter, popularly known as the "The Mad Hatter" is an enigmatic character encountered at a tea party and later as a trial witness in Lewis Carroll's *Alice's Adventures in Wonderland.* The "real" Hatter is generally believed to be Theophilus Carter, inventor of an alarm-clock bed, exhibited at the Great Exhibition of 1851, that tipped out the sleeper at waking time. Carter later owned a furniture shop, and became known as the "Mad Hatter" from his habit of standing in the door of his shop wearing a top hat. Sir John Tenniel is reported to have come to Oxford for the express purpose of sketching Carter for one of his *Wonderland* illustrations.

People don't think about the consequences of the consequences. People start by trying to hedge against interest rate changes, which is very difficult and complicated. Then, the hedges make the [reported profits] lumpy. So then they use new derivatives to smooth this. Well, now you've morphed into lying. This turns into a Mad Hatter's Tea Party. This happens to vast, sophisticated corporations.

Somebody has to step in and say, "We're not going to do it—it's just too hard."

I think a good litmus test of the mental and moral quality at any large institution [with significant derivatives exposure] would be to ask them, "Do you really understand your derivatives book?" Anyone who says yes is either crazy or lying.

It's easy to see [the dangers] when you talk about [what happened with] the energy derivatives—they went kerflooey. When [the companies] reached for the assets that were on their books, the money wasn't there. When it comes to financial assets, we haven't had any such denouement, and the accounting hasn't changed, so the denouement is ahead of us.

Derivatives are full of clauses that say if one party's credit gets downgraded, then it has to put up collateral. It's like margin—you can go broke [just putting up more margin]. In attempting to protect themselves, they've introduced instability. Nobody seems to recognize what a disaster of a system they've created. It's a demented system.

In engineering, people have a big margin of safety. But in the financial world, people don't give a damn about safety. They let it balloon and balloon and balloon. It's aided by false accounting. I'm more pessimistic about this than Warren.

Accounting for Derivatives

I hate with a passion GAAP [Generally Accepted Accounting Principles] as applied to derivatives and swaps. JP Morgan sold out to this type of accounting to front-end revenues. I think it's a disgrace.

It's bonkers, and the accountants sold out. Everyone caved, adopted loose [accounting] standards, and created exotic derivatives linked to theoretical models. As a result, all kinds of earnings, blessed by accountants, are not really being earned. When you reach for the money, it melts away. It was never there.

It [accounting for derivatives] is just disgusting. It is a sewer, and if I'm right, there will be hell to pay in due course. All of you will have to prepare to deal with a blowup of derivative books.

To say accounting for derivatives in America is a sewer is an insult to sewage.

"Hey Dad, that sewer joke is your line!"
—Maggie Kaufman, age eighteen, with father Peter Kaufman at 2002 Berkshire Hathaway shareholders' meeting.

Likelihood of a Derivatives Blowup

We tried to sell Gen Re's derivatives operation and couldn't, so we started liquidating it. We had to take big markdowns. I would confidently predict that most of the derivative books of [this country's] major banks cannot be liquidated for anything like what they're carried on the books at. When the denouement will happen and how severe it will be, I don't know. But I fear the consequences could be fearsome. I think there are major problems, worse than in the energy field, and look at the destruction there.

I'll be amazed if we don't have some kind of significant [derivatives-related] blowup in the next five to ten years.

I think we're the only big corporation in America to be running off its derivative book.

It's a crazy idea for people who are already rich—like Berkshire—to be in this business. It's a crazy business for big banks to be in.

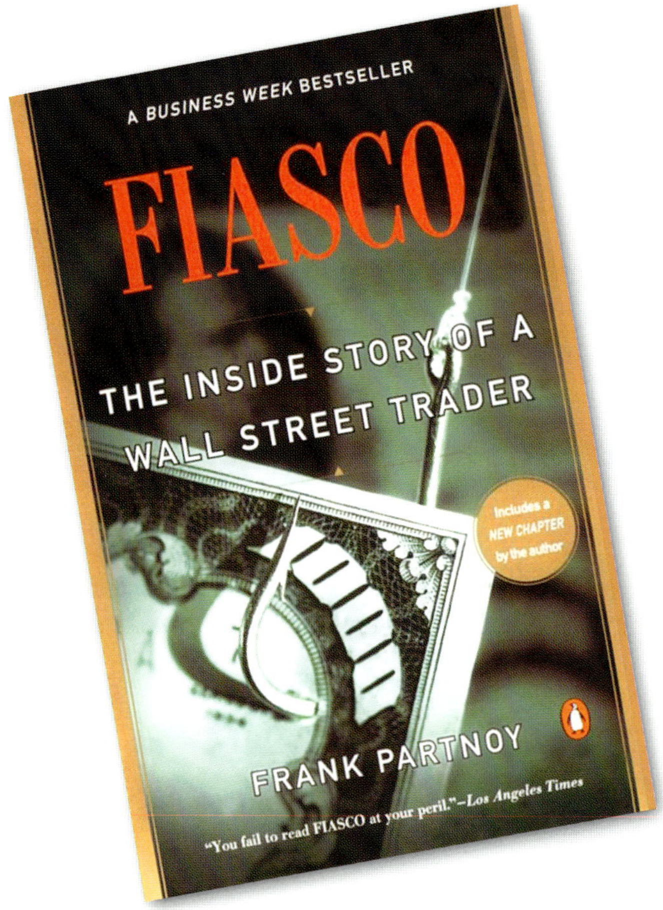

"You would be disgusted if you had a fair mind and spent a month really delving into a big derivative operation. You would think it was Lewis Carroll [author of *Alice's Adventures in Wonderland*]. You would think it was the Mad Hatter's Tea Party. And the false precision of these people is just unbelievable. They make the worst economics professors look like gods. Moreover, there is depravity augmenting the folly. Read the book *F.I.A.S.C.O.*, by law professor and former derivatives trader Frank Partnoy, an insider account of depravity in derivative trading at one of the biggest and best-regarded Wall Street firms. The book will turn your stomach."

Critique of Lawyers, Law Firms, and Litigation

Demise of Ethics Among Law Firms

I never have the slightest interest in defending miscreants and helping them misbehave. But the general view is that it's wonderful what Johnny Cochran did [getting O. J. Simpson off].

Lawyers Botched the Martha Stewart Case

What happened with Martha Stewart was that she heard some news, panicked, and sold the stock. It turns out that if she'd just told the truth, she'd have been okay. But because she had a vague idea that what she'd done was wrong, she had a totally phony story when the investigators came and she lied to them and that's a felony. And she did these acts *after* she'd hired highfalutin' lawyers! And I'm sure they charged her a lot. I do not invent these stories.

Were I her lawyer, I would have said, "You know, Martha, that's an interesting story, and I'm your lawyer, so I'm required to believe you, but nobody else will. So, you're going to have to come up with a different story, or you'll have to tell it through a different lawyer because I don't like losing cases." And it'll work. It's so simple. Literally, she went to prison for her behavior *after* she'd hired a lawyer!

The Tort System

What's particularly pernicious is the increasing political power of the plaintiffs' bar. State supreme court judges are generally on for life. The only thing that can jeopardize this is for them to really anger some important group—like the plaintiffs' bar. Thus, the judges allow junk science and the like.

Born and raised in Nutley, New Jersey, Martha Stewart personifies "gracious living." Her catering, publishing, and broadcasting empire includes her wildly popular syndicated television show, *Martha Stewart Living*. In 2004, in connection with an earlier sale of ImClone shares that she made, she was found guilty of obstructing justice and lying to investigators. She began serving her five-month prison sentence later that year.

Because of the tort system, there are whole areas for the already rich to avoid. For example, a company developed a new, safer, better police helmet but sold the product to a judgment-proof company [because the helmet-developer was afraid of liability]. It would be crazy for Berkshire to be in the business of providing security guards at airports. The system discourages the best companies from entering certain businesses.

Asbestos and Tort Reform

Asbestos has morphed into a situation with enormous amounts of fraud. People with serious injuries are being hurt [as more and more money flows to the plaintiffs' bar and to claimants with no current injuries]. The Supreme Court has practically invited Congress to step in, but Congress has refused due to the influence of the trial lawyers. I'd be surprised if there's a constructive solution in the next five years. I expect there will just be more of the current mess.

What's happened in asbestos is that a given group of people get mesothelioma—a horrible cancer that comes only from asbestos exposure and kills people. Then, there's another group of claimants who smoked two packs of cigarettes a day and have a spot on their lung. Then you get a lawyer who gets a doctor to testify that every spot is caused by asbestos. Once you effectively bribe a doctor, then you can get millions of people to sue on fears of getting cancer.

But there's not enough money [to pay all of the claimants], so people who are truly harmed don't get enough. In a southern state with a jury pool that hates all big companies [you get big judgments], but lawyers are stealing money from people who are hurt and giving it to people who aren't entitled. It's a bonkers system, but with federalism [states' rights], there's no way to stop it. The Supreme Court refused to step in.

Trying to buy people off is like trying to put out a fire by dousing it with gasoline. With word processors, lawyers can easily produce countless claimants. But only twenty-five percent of the money goes to claimants—the rest goes to the lawyers, doctors, etc.

If you want to be cynical, look at the perjury. There are only three solvent companies left [facing asbestos claims], so plaintiffs can only remember those three names [when recalling which products they were exposed to decades ago]. It's a case of perjury being suborned by practicing lawyers.

The only people who can fix it are the Supreme Court or Congress. The Supreme Court—some people would say rightly—refused to get involved, [but I say] they chickened out. And Congress, given the politics, has yet to step in.

There's an important lesson here: Once wrongdoers get rich, they get enormous political power and you can't stop it, so the key is to nip things like this in the bud.

It would be easy to fix the problem: The right way is to say we're not going to pay off all these little claims.

The Supreme Court consists of the Chief Justice of the United States and such number of associate judges as may be fixed by Congress, currently eight. As provided by the Judicial Act of 1799, the U.S. Supreme Court holds ultimate judicial power. It receives approximately 8,000 petitions each year.

The Government's Lawsuit Against Microsoft

[April 2000] Someone whose salary is paid by U.S. taxpayers is happy to dramatically weaken the one place where we're winning big?!

Every business tries to turn this year's success into next year's greater success. It's hard for me to see why Microsoft is sinful to do this. If it's a sin, then I hope all of Berkshire Hathaway's subsidiaries are sinners.

"I am one of the few people in America who constantly prays that Bill Gates achieves more success. I figure we former nerds have to stick together."

—Munger

Mental Models

The Importance of Multiple Mental Models

You must know the big ideas in the big disciplines and use them routinely—all of them, not just a few. Most people are trained in one model—economics, for example—and try to solve all problems in one way. You know the old saying: To the man with a hammer, the world looks like a nail. This is a dumb way of handling problems.

You need a different checklist and different mental models for different companies. I can never make it easy by saying, "Here are three things." You have to derive it yourself to ingrain it in your head for the rest of your life.

You can't learn those one hundred big ideas you really need the way many students do—where you learn 'em well enough to bang 'em back to the professor and get your grade, and then you empty them out as though you were emptying a bathtub so you can take in more water next time. If that's the way you learn the one hundred big models you're going to need, [you'll be] an "also ran" in the game of life. You have to learn the models so that they become part of your ever-used repertoire.

Charlie's oft-used diagnosis of narrow specialization:

"To the man with a hammer, the world looks like a nail."

By the way, there's no rule that you can't add another model or two even fairly late in life. In fact, I've clearly done that. I got most of the big ones quite early [however].

The happier mental realm I recommend is one from which no one willingly returns. A return would be like cutting off one's hands.

The Ethos of Not Fooling Yourself

It is ridiculous the way a lot of people cling to failed ideas. Keynes said, "It's not bringing in the new ideas that's so hard. It's getting rid of the old ones."

The Earth: Flat or Round?

As early as AD 140, Ptolemy produced a map that depicted the Earth as a globe. The Mediaeval church rejected the Greek idea, calling it heresy: the earth was flat—above the Earth was Heaven, below was Hell, and in between lived Man and Woman. For many hundreds of years sailors feared losing sight of land, and sea voyages hugged coastlines. But beginning in the 14th-century, exploration of the oceans began in earnest—islands, countries and continents were discovered. Many explorers completed voyages of discovery—Marco Polo, Christopher Columbus, and Vasco Da Gama. The known world expanded with every voyage until it became obvious to all who wanted to see it that the Earth was indeed a sphere. Finally the Victoria, the only surviving ship of Ferdinand Magellan's fleet, circumnavigated the world and put the issue to rest.

Provenance unknown, illustration from the dust-jacket, Daniel Boorstin's *The Discoverers*, attributed to a 16th century woodcut by the Bettmann Archive.

The ethos of not fooling yourself is one of the best you could possibly have. It's powerful because it's so rare.

Common (and Uncommon) Sense

Organized common (or uncommon) sense—very basic knowledge—is an enormously powerful tool. There are huge dangers with computers. People calculate too much and think too little.

Part of [having uncommon sense] is being able to tune out folly, as opposed to recognizing wisdom. If you bat away many things, you don't clutter yourself.

We read a lot. I don't know anyone who's wise who doesn't read a lot. But that's not enough: You have to have a temperament to grab ideas and do sensible things. Most people don't grab the right ideas or don't know what to do with them.

The more basic knowledge you have, the less new knowledge you have to get. The guy who plays chess blindfolded [a chess master comes to Omaha during Berkshire's annual meeting weekend and, in an exhibition, plays multiple players blindfolded]—he has a knowledge of the board, which allows him to do this.

Henry E. Singleton
(1916–1999)

Business and Chess Master

Singleton was co-founder of Teledyne, Inc. and chief executive of the Los Angeles-based conglomerate for three decades. He attended the Naval Academy, then transferred to MIT where he received Bachelor's, Master's, and Ph.D. degrees in Electrical Engineering. An enormously skilled chess player, he was only 100 points below the Grandmaster level and could play without looking at the board.

From 1963 to 1990, Teledyne returned an astounding 20.4 percent compound annual return to shareholders—a period in which the S&P 500 returned 8.0 percent. Adroitly repurchasing 90 percent of Teledyne's outstanding shares primarily between 1972 and 1984, Singleton built a record as a manager and capital allocator with few peers in modern business history.

Sharing Buffett's admiration for Henry E. Singleton, Charlie wonders, "Given the man's talent and record, have we learned enough from him?"

"Henry Singleton has the best operating and capital deployment record in American business...if one took the 100 top business school graduates and made a composite of their triumphs, their record would not be as good as Singleton's."

—Warren Buffett, 1980

Critique of Academia

Plato
(427 B.C. – 347 B.C.)

Credit for the Institution of Academia is generally ascribed to Plato. As an institution, academia is charged with stewardship for the body of knowledge, its ongoing exploration, and transmission to successive generations.

Fatal Unconnectedness

There's a lot wrong [with American universities]. I'd remove three-fourths of the faculty—everything but the hard sciences. But nobody's going to do that, so we'll have to live with the defects. It's amazing how wrongheaded [the teaching is]. There is fatal disconnectedness. You have these squirrelly people in each department who don't see the big picture.

I think liberal arts faculties at major universities have views that are not very sound, at least on public policy issues. [However,] they may know a lot of French.

Whitehead spoke of the fatal unconnectedness of academic disciplines, wherein each professor didn't even know the models of the other disciplines, much less try to synthesize those disciplines with his own. I think there's a modern name for this approach that Whitehead didn't like, and that name is bonkers.

How to Be Happy, Get Rich, and Other Advice

Tips on How to Be Happy and Successful

If all you succeed in doing in life is getting rich by buying little pieces of paper, it's a failed life. Life is more than being shrewd in wealth accumulation.

A lot of success in life and business comes from knowing what you want to avoid: early death, a bad marriage, etc.

Just avoid things like AIDs situations, racing trains to the crossing, and doing cocaine. Develop good mental habits.

Avoid evil, particularly if they're attractive members of the opposite sex.

Ulysses and the Sirens,
Herbert James Draper (British, 1863–1920), oil on canvas, private collection

If your new behavior earns you a little temporary unpopularity with your peer group, then the hell with them.

Be Satisfied with What You Have

Here's one truth that perhaps your typical investment counselor would disagree with: If you're comfortably rich and someone else is getting richer faster than you by, for example, investing in risky stocks, so what?! Someone will always be getting richer faster than you. This is not a tragedy.

Look at Stanley Druckenmiller [who ran one of George Soros' funds, which suffered large losses in speculative tech and biotech stocks]: He always had to be the best and couldn't stand that others were beating him by investing in these sectors.

Madwoman (Obsession of Envy), Theodore Gericault (1791–1824), oil on canvas, Musée des Beaux-Arts, Lyon, France

Soros couldn't bear to see others make money in the technology sector without him, and he got killed. It doesn't bother us at all [that others are making money in the tech sector].

Beware of Envy

The idea of caring that someone is making money faster [than you are] is one of the deadly sins. Envy is a really stupid sin because it's the only one you could never possibly have any fun at. There's a lot of pain and no fun. Why would you want to get on that trolley?

How to Get Rich

[A young shareholder asked Charlie how to follow in his footsteps, and Charlie brought down the house by saying:]

We get these questions a lot from the enterprising young. It's a very intelligent question: You look at some old guy who's rich and you ask, "How can I become like you, except faster?"

Spend each day trying to be a little wiser than you were when you woke up. Discharge your duties faithfully and well. Step by step you get ahead, but not necessarily in fast spurts. But you build discipline by preparing for fast spurts…. Slug it out one inch at a time, day by day. At the end of the day—if you live long enough—most people get what they deserve.

How to Find a Good Spouse

What's the best way to get a good spouse? The best single way is to deserve a good spouse because a good spouse is by definition not nuts.

The Importance of Reading

In my whole life, I have known no wise people (over a broad subject matter area) who didn't read all the time—none, zero. You'd be amazed at how much Warren reads—and at how much I read. My children laugh at me. They think I'm a book with a couple of legs sticking out.

I am a biography nut myself. And I think when you're trying to teach the great concepts that work, it helps to tie them into the lives and personalities of the people who developed them. I think you learn economics better if you make Adam Smith your friend. That sounds funny, making friends among the eminent dead, but if you go through life making friends with the eminent dead who had the right ideas, I think it will work better in life and work better in education. It's way better than just being given the basic concepts.

"I have always imagined that Paradise will be a kind of library."

—Jorge Luis Borges

Reduce Material Needs

Most people will see declining returns [due to inflation]. One of the great defenses if you're worried about inflation is not to have a lot of silly needs in your life—you don't need a lot of material goods.

Philanthropy

[Warren and I] feel that those of us who have been very fortunate have a duty to give back. Whether one gives a lot as one goes along as I do, or a little and then a lot [when one dies] as Warren does, is a matter of personal preference. I would hate to have people ask me for money all day long. Warren couldn't stand it.

Avoid Debt

Once you get into debt, it's hell to get out. Don't let credit card debt carry over. You can't get ahead paying eighteen percent.

The Decline of Public Schools

You could argue that [the decline of public schools] is one of the major disasters in our lifetime. We took one of the greatest successes in the history of the earth and turned it into one of the greatest disasters in the history of the earth.

Japan's Recession

Anyone has to be flabbergasted by Japan's recession, which has endured for ten years, despite interest rates below one percent. The government is playing all the monetary games, but it's not working. If you had described this situation to Harvard economists, they would have said it's impossible. Yet at the same time, there's an asset bubble in Hong Kong. *Why? Because Japan and China are two vastly different cultures. The Chinese are gamblers.*

This is a classic example of why, to be a successful investor, one must draw from many disciplines. Imagine an economist standing up at a meeting of economists and giving my explanation. It wouldn't be politically correct! But the tools of economics don't explain what's going on.

Humor

- I'd rather throw a viper down my shirt front than hire a compensation consultant.
- [When asked at a cocktail party whether he played the piano, Charlie replied,] "I don't know, I've never tried."
- I always like it when someone attractive to me agrees with me, so I have fond memories of Phil Fisher.
- It is, of course, normal for self-appraisal to be more positive than external appraisal. Indeed, a problem of this sort may have given you your speaker today.

When you mix raisins and turds, you've still got turds. [Comparing the benefits that the Internet and technology are providing to society versus the evils of stock speculation in these sectors.]

"I've always disliked that reference of Charlie's about the raisins. But it does no good for me to say anything; he's going to keep using it anyway."

—Nancy Munger

- In the corporate world, if you have analysts, due diligence, and no horse sense, you've just described hell.
- It's been so long since we've bought anything that [asking us about our market impact when we're trading] is like asking Rip Van Winkle about the past twenty years.
- When I first moved to California, there was a part-time legislature that was controlled by gambling interests, racetrack owners, and liquor distributors, who wined and dined the legislators, supplied them with prostitutes, etc. I think I prefer that to today's full-time legislature.

- [On the book *Deep Simplicity*], it's pretty hard to understand everything, but if you can't understand it, you can always give it to a more intelligent friend.

- If you rise in life, you have to behave in a certain way. You can go to a strip club if you're a beer-swilling sand shoveler, but if you're the bishop of Boston, you shouldn't go.

- I think the people who are attracted to be prison guards are not nature's noblemen to begin with.

- You don't want to be like the motion picture executive who had many people at his funeral, but they were there just to make sure he was dead. Or how about the guy who, at his funeral, the priest said, "Won't anyone stand up and say anything nice about the deceased?" and finally someone said, "Well, his brother was worse."

- [Responding to a question at the 1999 Berkshire Hathaway annual meeting about the year 2000 compliance issue, Munger replied:] I find it interesting that there is such a problem. You know, it was predictable that the year 2000 would come.

Ben Franklin was a very good ambassador, and whatever was wrong with him from John Adams' point of view [I'm sure] helped him with the French.

Simpson on Munger

When I first met Charlie Munger, I knew he was a unique individual, but I didn't realize just how unique until I knew him better. I have now known Charlie for twenty-five years and have had the opportunity to observe him under a wide range of circumstances, including the aftermath of the Salomon bond crisis of the early nineties where we were both serving on the board of directors.

I can attest that Charlie has a combination of characteristics that I have never seen in any other single individual. He has an extraordinary and deep intelligence across a broad range of interests, and he never seems to forget anything, no matter how arcane or trivial. On top of these attributes is his absolute commitment to honesty, ethics, and integrity—Charlie never "grabs" for himself and can be trusted without reservation. If that's not enough, he has a temperament toward investing that can only be described as ideal: unyielding patience, discipline, and self-control—Charlie just doesn't crack or compromise on his principles, no matter how stressful the situation.

How fortunate we have all been to have this duo of Charlie Munger and Warren Buffett as our partners, teachers, and role models for all these years. These are truly exceptional men.

Louis A. Simpson, President and CEO, Capital Operations, GEICO Corporation

Munger on Simpson

Lou Simpson is a highly intelligent and honorable man. I was pleased that in the annual letter to shareholders this year (2005), Warren printed Lou's twenty-five-year investment track record. It's not unheard of to beat the market averages for a couple of years, maybe even five or ten years. But, imagine beating the S&P 500 by an average annual gain of 6.8 percent over twenty-five years! This extraordinary track record speaks for itself—Lou has one of the greatest investment minds of our time. He is, as Warren says, "a shoo-in for the investment Hall of Fame."

I remember well the dot-com boom of the late nineties and how Lou handled it. You can't believe the pressure that he was under, year after year, as the world seemed to be reaping enormous gains while he, correctly, avoided the bubble altogether, staying true to fundamentals. Lou was a wonderful example in that period—intelligent, honorable, and true to his fundamentals.

Sinegal on Munger

I had the pleasure of meeting Charlie eight years ago when he agreed to have lunch with me in Los Angeles at the California Club. My purpose was to convince him to consider joining the Costco board of directors. I liked him from the moment we met when he told me how much he enjoyed shopping at Costco; and despite our being interrupted continuously by the other 500-plus people dining there that day, who all felt compelled to say hello to Charlie and whom Charlie identified by name in almost every instance, we managed to have a great conversation. First off, Charlie was astute enough to recognize what a great value Costco membership represented. Later, of course, I learned of Charlie's reputation for thriftiness, which clarified Costco's appeal, but, more importantly his straightforwardness and common sense business acumen came through loud and clear.

James D. Sinegal,
President and CEO,
Costco Wholesale Corporation

Later when he called to accept the position on the board, he referred to himself as a septuagenarian. Pretty fancy description to share with someone from the warehouse industry; I was flattered he thought I understood him.

Since then he has provided everything that can be expected from a director. His insight, questioning, and support have made Costco a better-governed and better-operated company.

As an extra bonus, we are treated to regular doses of the Munger wit—we're lucky people!

Munger on Sinegal

You just wouldn't believe how efficient and sophisticated Costco's warehouse operation is. Jim Sinegal is a fabulous business operator—like a Carnegie, Rockefeller, or James J. Hill. I consider him to be one of the top five retailers of the past century. He's that good.

He works eighty hours a week and sets a terrific example for his entire organization in terms of work ethic, integrity, loyalty, and selflessness. He's a moral leader as well as a practical leader. These are not minor virtues.

We have our own living, breathing Sam Walton at Costco.

Ten Talks

Charlie Munger is not the least bit shy when it comes to offering both frank criticism and constructive advice. When he sets his sights on an issue—be it a corrupt business practice, an academic failing, or a financial scandal—he lets loose with both barrels. Which is not to say he spends all his time focused on life's failings. He is equally at home discussing the values of lifelong learning or the joys of a successful marriage. But whatever the topic, Charlie is apt to tell it like it is, which is exactly what he has done in over two decades of public speaking. Here then are ten of Charlie's best talks, including a special compilation he has prepared exclusively for this book. Enjoy.

In a vow that students the world over may hope he renounces, Charlie delivered "the one and only graduation speech I will ever make" in 1986 at the Harvard School in Los Angeles. The occasion was the graduation of Philip Munger, the last of five Munger family sons to matriculate at this prep school (originally an all-boys institution and now the coeducational school called Harvard-Westlake).

Despite Charlie's self-effacing protestations about then lacking "significant public-speaking experience," he demonstrates imposing rhetorical talents in this short speech. We also get a good taste of both Charlie's value system and wit. Most graduation speakers choose to lay out a prescription for attaining a happy life. Charlie, using the inversion principle he recommends in the speech, compellingly makes the opposite case by setting forth what a graduate may do to reach a state of misery.

For those of you who want to remain unenlightened and mirthless, do not, under any circumstances, read this selection.

Harvard School Commencement Speech

June 13, 1986

Now that Headmaster Berrisford has selected one of the oldest and longest-serving trustees to make a commencement speech, it behooves the speaker to address two questions in every mind:

1) Why was such a selection made?

2) How long is the speech going to last?

I will answer the first question from long experience alongside Berrisford. He is seeking enhanced reputation for our school in the manner of the man who proudly displays his horse that can count to seven. The man knows that counting to seven is not much of a mathematical feat, but he expects approval because doing so is creditable, considering the performer is a horse.

The second question, regarding the length of the speech, I am not going to answer in advance. It would deprive your upturned faces of lively curiosity and obvious keen anticipation, which I prefer to retain, regardless of source.

Marcus Tullius Cicero
(106–43 BC)

A poet, philosopher, rhetorician, and humorist, Cicero was also one of Rome's great orators. Cicero viewed public service to be a Roman citizen's highest duty. He defended those unjustly accused by dictatorial leaders and brought down corrupt governments. Late in life, he led the Senate's unsuccessful battle against Antony, for which he paid with his life in 43 BC. The illustration is *Young Cicero Reading,* c. 1464, Vincenzo Foppa, Wallace Collection, London.

But I will tell you how my consideration of speech length created the subject matter of the speech itself. I was puffed up when invited to speak. While not having significant public-speaking experience, I do hold a black belt in chutzpah, and I immediately considered Demosthenes and Cicero as role models and anticipated trying to earn a compliment like Cicero gave when asked which was his favorite among the orations of Demosthenes. Cicero replied:

"The longest one."

However, fortunately for this audience, I also thought of Samuel Johnson's famous comment when he addressed Milton's poem *Paradise Lost* and correctly said, "No one ever wished it longer." And that made me consider which of all the twenty Harvard School graduation speeches I had heard that I had wished longer. There was only one such speech, given by Johnny Carson, specifying Carson's prescriptions for guaranteed misery in life. I, therefore, decided to repeat Carson's speech but in expanded form with some added prescriptions of my own. After all, I am much older than Carson was when he spoke and have failed and been miserable more often and in more ways than was possible for a charming humorist speaking at a younger age. I am plainly well qualified to expand on Carson's theme.

What Carson said was that he couldn't tell the graduating class how to be happy, but he could tell them from personal experience how to guarantee misery. Carson's prescription for sure misery included:

1. Ingesting chemicals in an effort to alter mood or perception;
2. Envy; and
3. Resentment.

I can still recall Carson's absolute conviction as he told how he had tried these things on occasion after occasion and had become miserable every time.

It is easy to understand Carson's first prescription for misery—ingesting chemicals. I add my voice. The four closest friends of my youth were highly intelligent, ethical, humorous types, favored in person and background. Two are long dead, with alcohol a contributing factor, and a third is a living alcoholic—if you call that living.

Carson said he couldn't tell the graduating class how to be happy, but he could tell them from personal experience how to guarantee misery.

While susceptibility varies, addiction can happen to any of us through a subtle process where the bonds of degradation are too light to be felt until they are too strong to be broken. And yet, I have yet to meet anyone, in over six decades of life, whose life was worsened by fear and avoidance of such a deceptive pathway to destruction.

Envy, of course, joins chemicals in winning some sort of quantity prize for causing misery. It was wreaking havoc long before it got a bad press in the laws of Moses. If you wish to retain the contribution of envy to misery, I recommend that you never read any of the biographies of that good Christian, Samuel Johnson, because his life demonstrates in an enticing way the possibility and advantage of transcending envy.

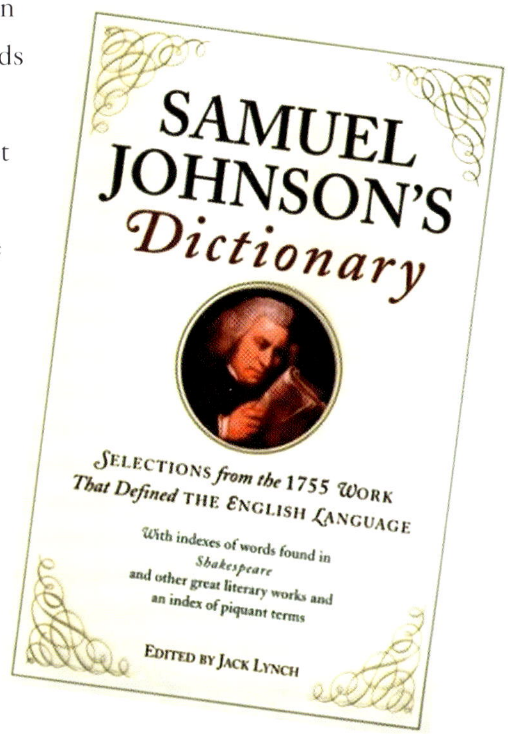

Samuel Johnson
(1709–1784)

Samuel Johnson, English author and the leading literary scholar and critic of his time, was celebrated for his brilliant and witty conversation. Johnson's first work of lasting importance, and the one that permanently established his reputation, was his *Dictionary of the English Language* (1755). James Boswell's famous biography of Johnson presents his life, his sharp comments, and wit in exhaustive and fascinating detail.

John Milton
(1608–1674)

One of the greatest poets of the English language, John Milton was best known for his epic poem *Paradise Lost* (1667). His powerful prose and the eloquence of his poetry had an immense influence, especially on eighteenth-century verse. Milton also published pamphlets defending civil and religious rights. To Samuel Johnson's point about Milton's long-windedness, *Paradise Lost* runs to twelve "books" and thousands of lines.

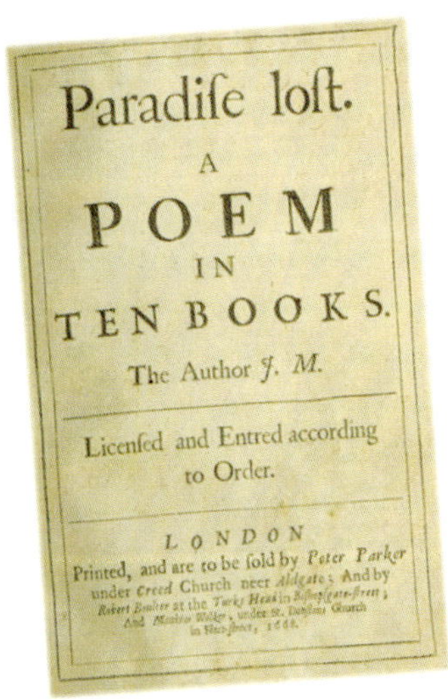

Paradiſe loſt.
A
POEM
IN
TEN BOOKS.
The Author *J. M.*

Licenſed and Entred according to Order.

LONDON
Printed, and are to be ſold by *Peter Parker* under *Creed* Church neer *Aldgate*; And by [illegible]

Resentment has always worked for me exactly as it worked for Carson. I cannot recommend it highly enough to you if you desire misery. Johnson spoke well when he said that life is hard enough to swallow without squeezing in the bitter rind of resentment.

Johnson spoke well when he said that life is hard enough to swallow without squeezing in the bitter rind of resentment.

For those of you who want misery, I also recommend refraining from practice of the Disraeli compromise, designed for people who find it impossible to quit resentment cold turkey. Disraeli, as he rose to become one of the greatest prime ministers, learned to give up vengeance as a motivation for action, but he did retain some outlet for resentment by putting the names of people who wronged him on pieces of paper in a drawer. Then, from time to time, he reviewed these names and took pleasure in noting the way the world had taken his enemies down without his assistance.

Addiction can happen to any of us through a subtle process where the bonds of degradation are too light to be felt until they are too strong to be broken.

Well, so much for Carson's three prescriptions. Here are four more prescriptions from Munger:

First, be unreliable. Do not faithfully do what you have engaged to do. If you will only master this one habit, you will more than counterbalance the combined effect of all your virtues, howsoever great. If you like being distrusted and excluded from the best human contribution and company, this prescription is for you. Master this one habit, and you will always play the role of the hare in the fable, except that instead of being outrun by one fine turtle, you will be outrun by hordes and hordes of mediocre turtles and even some mediocre turtles on crutches.

I must warn you that if you don't follow my first prescription, it may be hard to end up miserable even if you start disadvantaged. I had a roommate in college who was and is severely dyslexic. But he is perhaps the most reliable man I have ever known. He has had a wonderful life so far, outstanding wife and children, chief executive of a multibillion dollar corporation. If you want to avoid a conventional, main-culture, establishment result of this kind, you simply can't count on your other handicaps to hold you back if you persist in being reliable.

I cannot here pass by a reference to a life described as "wonderful so far," without reinforcing the "so far" aspects of the human condition by repeating the remark of Croesus, once the richest king in the world. Later, in ignominious captivity, as he prepared to be burned alive, he said: "Well now do I remember the words of the historian Solon: 'No man's life should be accounted a happy one until it is over.'"

Croesus
(about 546 BC)

Croesus, legendary for his huge wealth, was king of Lydia from 560 BC until his defeat by the Persians in about 547 BC. Upon capture, Croesus supposedly threw himself upon a funeral pyre.

My second prescription for misery is to learn everything you possibly can from your own experience, minimizing what you learn vicariously from the good and bad experience of others, living and dead. This prescription is a sure-shot producer of misery and second-rate achievement.

You can see the results of not learning from others' mistakes by simply looking about you. How little originality there is in the common disasters of mankind—drunk driving deaths, reckless driving maimings, incurable venereal diseases, conversion of bright college students into brainwashed zombies as members of destructive cults, business failures through repetition of obvious mistakes made by predecessors, various forms of crowd folly, and so on. I recommend as a memory clue to finding the way to real trouble from heedless, unoriginal error the modern saying: "If at first you don't succeed, well, so much for hang gliding."

The other aspect of avoiding vicarious wisdom is the rule for not learning from the best work done before yours. The prescription is to become as non-educated as you reasonably can.

Perhaps you will better see the type of nonmiserable result you can thus avoid if I render a short historical account. There once was a man who assiduously mastered the work of his best predecessors, despite a poor start and very tough time in analytical geometry. Eventually, his own work attracted wide attention, and he said of his work:

"If I have seen a little farther than other men, it is because I stood on the shoulders of giants."

The bones of that man lie buried now, in Westminster Abbey, under an unusual inscription:

Franklin on Vicarious Learning

"If you will not hear reason, she will surely rap your knuckles."

"They that won't be counseled, can't be helped."

"Experience keeps a dear school, but fools will learn in no other and scarce in that; for it is true, we may give advice, but we cannot give conduct."

Sir Isaac Newton
(1642–1727)

At birth in Lincolnshire, England, Newton was so tiny and frail that he was not expected to live. Yet he lived into his eighties. During his young adulthood, Newton made tremendous discoveries in general mathematics, algebra, geometry, calculus, optics, and celestial mechanics. Most famous among these discoveries was his description of gravity. The publication of his book *The Mathematical Principles of Natural Philosophy* in 1687 marked the peak of Newton's creative career.

"Here lie the remains of all that was mortal in Sir Isaac Newton."

My third prescription to you for misery is to go down and stay down when you get your first, second, or third severe reverse in the battle of life. Because there is so much adversity out there, even for the lucky and wise, this will guarantee that, in due course, you will be permanently mired in misery. Ignore at all cost the lesson contained in the accurate epitaph written for himself by Epictetus: "Here lies Epictetus, a slave, maimed in body, the ultimate in poverty, and favored by the gods."

"Invert, always invert," Jacobi said. He knew that it is in the nature of things that many hard problems are best solved when they are addressed backward.

My final prescription to you for a life of fuzzy thinking and infelicity is to ignore a story they told me when I was very young about a rustic who said, "I wish I knew where I was going to die, and then I'd never go there." Most people smile (as you did) at the rustic's ignorance and ignore his basic wisdom. If my experience is any guide, the rustic's approach is to be avoided at all cost by someone bent on misery. To help fail, you should discount as mere quirk, with no useful message, the method of the rustic, which is the same one used in Carson's speech.

What Carson did was to approach the study of how to create X by turning the question backward, that is, by studying how to create non-X. The great algebraist, Jacobi, had exactly the same approach as Carson and was known for his constant repetition of one phrase: "Invert, always invert." It is in the nature of things, as Jacobi knew, that many hard problems are best solved only when they are addressed backward. For instance, when almost everyone else was trying to revise the electromagnetic laws of Maxwell to be consistent with the motion laws of Newton, Einstein discovered special relativity as he made a 180-degree turn and revised Newton's laws to fit Maxwell's.

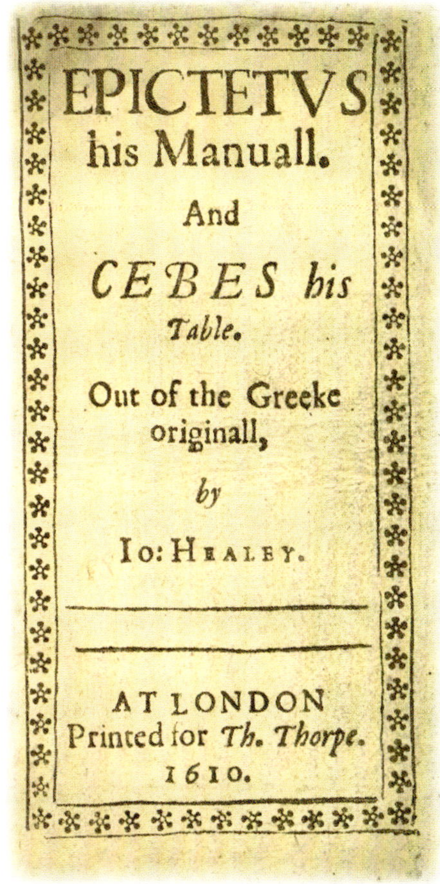

EPICTETVS
his Manuall.
And
CEBES his
Table.
Out of the Greeke
originall,
by
Io: HEALEY.

AT LONDON
Printed for Th. Thorpe.
1610.

Epictetus
(55–135)

Even though he was born a slave in Hierapolis and endured a permanent physical disability, Epictetus maintained that all human beings are perfectly free to control their own lives and to live in harmony with nature. After intense study of the traditional Stoic curriculum of logic, physics, and ethics, Epictetus spent his entire career teaching philosophy and promoting a daily regime of rigorous self-examination. He eventually gained his freedom but was exiled from Rome by Domitian in 89.

It is my opinion, as a certified biography nut, that Charles Robert Darwin would have ranked near the middle of the Harvard School graduating class of 1986. Yet he is now famous in the history of science. This is precisely the type of example you should learn nothing from if bent on minimizing your results from your own endowment.

Darwin's result was due in large measure to his working method, which violated all my rules for misery and particularly emphasized a backward twist in that he always gave priority attention to evidence tending to disconfirm whatever cherished and hard-won theory he already had. In contrast, most people early achieve and later intensify a tendency to process new and disconfirming information so that any original conclusion remains intact. They become people of whom Philip Wylie observed: "You couldn't squeeze a dime between what they already know and what they will never learn."

Charles Darwin
(1809–1882)

Charles Darwin was a British naturalist whose teachings on evolution by natural selection revolutionized the science of biology. His *On the Origin of Species* sold out immediately and was heavily attacked because it did not support the depiction of creation given in the Bible.

The life of Darwin demonstrates how a turtle may outrun the hares, aided by extreme objectivity, which helps the objective person end up like the only player without a blindfold in a game of Pin the Tail on the Donkey.

The life of Darwin demonstrates how a turtle may outrun a hare, aided by extreme objectivity, which helps the objective person end up like the only player without a blindfold in a game of Pin the Tail on the Donkey.

If you minimize objectivity, you ignore not only a lesson from Darwin but also one from Einstein. Einstein said that his successful theories came from "Curiosity, concentration, perseverance, and self-criticism." And by self-criticism, he meant the testing and destruction of his own well-loved ideas.

Finally, minimizing objectivity will help you lessen the compromises and burden of owning worldly goods because objectivity does not work only for great physicists and biologists. It also adds power to the work of a plumbing contractor in Bemidji. Therefore, if you interpret being true to yourself as requiring that you retain every notion of your youth, you will be safely underway, not only toward maximizing ignorance, but also toward whatever misery can be obtained through unpleasant experiences in business.

It is fitting that a backward sort of speech end with a backward sort of toast, inspired by Elihu Root's repeated accounts of how the dog went to Dover, "leg over leg." To the class of 1986:

Gentlemen, may each of you rise by spending each day of a long life aiming low.

Elihu Root
(1845–1937)

Elihu Root, born in New York and the son of a mathematics professor, became one of the most brilliant administrators in American history. By age thirty, he had established himself as a prominent lawyer specializing in corporate affairs. Shifting to public service, Root distinguished himself as secretary of war, secretary of state, U.S. senator, and ambassador to Russia. In the interest of worldwide peace, he originated many treaties of arbitration. He was awarded the Nobel Peace Prize in 1912.

Invitation Letter from Harvard School

This is the original letter from Headmaster Berrisford of the Harvard School inviting Charlie to speak at the graduation ceremony the following June. Note Charlie's reply at the bottom of the letter.

HARVARD SCHOOL
3700 Coldwater Canyon Road
Post Office Box 1037
North Hollywood, California 91604
Telephone 818 • 980-6692

Christopher Berrisford
Headmaster

September 13, 1985

Mr. Charles T. Munger
P.O. Box 55007
Los Angeles, California 90057

Dear Charlie:

We discovered last June that a Commencement Speaker who knew the School well, and who had a command of the language, was a much better contributor to our celebrations than a distinguished citizen with a mastery of platitudes.

Last year I spent time and energy chasing two or three distinguished politicians in the hope that their presence at our Commencement exercises would add a little luster to the proceedings. I was wrong. Nat Reynolds did us proud; the politicians were as evasive as you might suppose.

I am anxious to settle the issue for next year in good time and I believe that we should henceforth stay with those that know Harvard and should avoid outsiders. Since this year sees the last Munger (of the present generation, at least) graduating from Harvard School and since you must know more about Harvard than anyone who is not an alumnus - and probably more than most who are - I would like to invite you with as much persuasion as I can muster to be Harvard's Commencement Speaker for the Class of 1986.

Jim Maloney set a precedent when he spoke at Tom's graduation. Would you be kind enough to follow his lead and perform the same function for Philip's graduating class?

This invitation has been on my mind for awhile, but it was brought back to my immediate attention because, in sorting through papers left over from last year, I came across the Berkshire Hathaway Report to which you contributed. I re-read your section and what Warren Buffet had to say, envying the clarity of insight that you both show and the capacity you have to say what is on your mind succinctly, precisely and eloquently. What better credentials could there be for a Commencement Speaker?

My colleagues at the School enthusiastically support this invitation. We all hope you will accept.

Best wishes,

Chris

Christopher Berrisford

cc: Dr. Norman F.Sprague, III

Chris 9/16/85

Will do.

Charlie

BERKSHIRE HATHAWAY INC.

CHARLES T. MUNGER
VICE CHAIRMAN OF THE BOARD

July 7, 1986

Mr. Johnny Carson
NBC-National Broadcasting
Company, Inc.
3000 W. Alameda Avenue
Burbank, CA. 91523

Dear Mr. Carson:

This year at my son's graduation from Harvard School I repeated the graduation speech you made when your son graduated. There were some additions of my own, and I, of course, gave due credit to the Carson original.

I thought you might be amused by the educational influence you have had, on and through me, and I therefore enclose a copy of my expanded version of your speech.

I also enclose a copy of Berkshire Hathaway's 1986 annual report, which may possibly interest you because of our recent acquisition of a large stock position in the ABC television network, which, unfortunately, has no equivalent of Johnny Carson.

Best regards,

Charles T. Munger

CTM/mek
Enclosures
bcc: Warren E. Buffett
Thomas S. Murphy

P.O. BOX 55007, LOS ANGELES, CA 90055

August 6, 1986

Mr. Charles T. Munger
Berkshire Hathaway Inc.
P.O. Box 55007
Los Angeles, Ca. 90055

Dear Charles:

Thanks for your kind letter and the copy of your speech to the Harvard school graduates. I am happy I was able to furnish a small framework for you to expand on.

All Good Wishes,

Johnny Carson

JC/daw

Johnny (John William) Carson
(1925–2005)

Born in Corning, Iowa, Johnny Carson became famous as America's late-night king of comedy. He had a popular radio show in Omaha for years and claimed the city as his hometown. For thirty years, from 1962 to 1992, he entertained millions as host of NBC television's *The Tonight Show.* His show featured thousands of authors, filmmakers, actors, singers—and stand-up comedians, of course, many of whose careers he launched.

Talk One Revisited

As I review in 2006 this talk made in 1986, I would not revise a single idea. If anything, I now believe even more strongly that (1) reliability is essential for progress in life and (2) while quantum mechanics is unlearnable for a vast majority, reliability can be learned to great advantage by almost anyone.

Indeed, I have often made myself unpopular on elite college campuses pushing this reliability theme. What I say is that McDonald's is one of our most admirable institutions. Then, as signs of shock come to surrounding faces, I explain that McDonald's, providing first jobs to millions of teenagers, many troubled, over the years, has successfully taught most of them the one lesson they most need: to show up reliably for responsible work. Then I usually go on to say that if the elite campuses were as successful as McDonald's in teaching sensibly, we would have a better world.

If

Avoiding Life's Pitfalls a la Kipling

If you can keep your head when all about you
Are losing theirs and blaming it on you,
If you can trust yourself when all men doubt you
But make allowance for their doubting too,
If you can wait and not be tired by waiting,
Or being lied about, don't deal in lies,
Or being hated, don't give way to hating,
And yet don't look too good, nor talk too wise…

If you can talk with crowds and keep your virtue,
Or walk with kings—nor lose the common touch,
If neither foes nor loving friends can hurt you;
If all men count with you, but none too much,
If you can fill the unforgiving minute
With sixty seconds' worth of distance run,
Yours is the Earth and everything that's in it,
And—which is more—you'll be a Man, my son!

Excerpted from the poem "If,"
which Charlie has always admired.

Well-known because it was published in *Outstanding Investor Digest* (May 5, 1995), this talk was given in 1994 to Professor Guilford Babcock's business class at the University of Southern California. Charlie ranges in the talk from education systems to psychology to the importance of possessing both common and uncommon sense. Dissecting business management, he brilliantly describes psychological impacts that can damage or benefit a firm. He also presents an outstanding set of principles for investment, business management, and—most importantly from Charlie's perspective—decision making in everyday life.

Your time investment in reading this talk will be paid back quickly via the effect it will have on your own decision-making abilities.

A Lesson on Elementary, Worldly Wisdom as It Relates to Investment Management and Business

The University of Southern California Marshall School of Business, April 14, 1994

I am going to play a minor trick on you today—because the subject of my talk is the art of stock picking as a subdivision of the art of worldly wisdom. That enables me to start talking about worldly wisdom—a much broader topic that interests me because I think all too little of it is delivered by modern educational systems, at least in an effective way.

And, therefore, the talk is sort of along the lines that some behaviorist psychologists call "Grandma's Rule"—after the wisdom of Grandma when she said that you have to eat the carrots before you get the dessert.

Eat Your Carrots

The iron fist of "Grandma's Rule" dictates the course of Charlie's lecture on Worldly Wisdom and Investment Management at the Marshall School of Business, USC.

The carrot part of this talk is about the general subject of worldly wisdom, which is a pretty good way to start. After all, the theory of modern education is that you need a general education before you specialize. And I think, to some extent, before you're going to be a great stock picker, you need some general education.

The talk is sort of along the lines that some behaviorist psychologists call "Grandma's Rule"—after the wisdom of Grandma when she said that you have to eat the carrots before you get the dessert.

So, emphasizing what I sometimes waggishly call remedial worldly wisdom, I'm going to start by waltzing you through a few basic notions.

What is elementary, worldly wisdom? Well, the first rule is that you can't really know anything if you just remember isolated facts and try and bang 'em back. If the facts don't hang together on a latticework of theory, you don't have them in a usable form.

You've got to have models in your head. And you've got to array your experience—both vicarious and direct—on this latticework of models. You may have noticed students who just try to remember and pound back what is remembered. Well, they fail in school and fail in life. You've got to hang experience on a latticework of models in your head.

What are the models? Well, the first rule is that you've got to have multiple models—because if you have just one or two that you're using, the nature of human psychology is such that you'll torture reality so that it fits your models, or at least you'll think it does. You become the equivalent of a chiropractor, who, of course, is the great boob in medicine.

It's like the old saying, "To the man with only a hammer, every problem looks like a nail." And, of course, that's the way the chiropractor goes about practicing medicine. But that's a perfectly disastrous way to think and a perfectly disastrous way to operate in the world. So you've got to have multiple models.

And the models have to come from multiple disciplines—because all the wisdom of the world is not to be found in one little academic department. That's why poetry professors, by and large, are so unwise in a worldly sense. They don't have enough models in their heads. So you've got to have models across a fair array of disciplines.

You may say, "My God, this is already getting way too tough." But, fortunately, it isn't that tough—because eighty or ninety important models will carry about ninety percent of the freight in making you a worldly-wise person. And, of those, only a mere handful really carry very heavy freight.

Poetry professors, by and large, are so unwise in a worldly sense. They don't have enough models in their heads. So you've got to have models across a wide array of disciplines.

"There is no royal road to learning; no short cut to the acquirement of any art."

—Anthony Trollope

So let's briefly review what kind of models and techniques constitute this basic knowledge that everybody has to have before they proceed to being really good at a narrow art like stock picking.

Pierre de Fermat
and Blaise Pascal

Invited by French aristocrat Chevalier de Méré to help resolve a gambling dispute in the mid-seventeenth century, mathematicians Pierre de Fermat and Blaise Pascal laid the foundations for probability theory in a series of letters.

De Méré's question concerned bets on rolls of a die that at least one "6" would appear during four rolls. From experience, he knew he would win more often than lose at this game. As a diversion, he changed the game to a bet that he would get a total of 12, or a double "6," on twenty-four rolls of two dice. The new game was less profitable than the old one. He asked the mathematicians to determine why this change occurred.

First there's mathematics. Obviously, you've got to be able to handle numbers and quantities—basic arithmetic.

And the great useful model, after compound interest, is the elementary math of permutations and combinations. And that was taught in my day in the sophomore year in high school. I suppose by now, in great private schools, it's probably down to the eighth grade or so.

The basic neural network of the brain is there through broad genetic and cultural evolution. And it's not Fermat/Pascal. It uses a very crude, shortcut-type of approximation.

It's very simple algebra. And it was all worked out in the course of about one year in correspondence between Pascal and Fermat. They worked it out casually in a series of letters.

It's not that hard to learn. What is hard is to get so you use it routinely almost every day of your life. The Fermat/Pascal system is dramatically consonant with the way that the world works. And it's fundamental truth. So you simply have to have the technique.

Many educational institutions—although not nearly enough—have realized this. At Harvard Business School, the great quantitative thing that bonds the first-year class together is what they call "decision tree theory." All they do is take high school algebra and apply it to real life problems. And the students love it. They're amazed to find that high school algebra works in life.

By and large, as it works out, people can't naturally and automatically do this. If you understand elementary psychology, the reason they can't is really quite simple: The basic neural network of the brain is there through broad genetic and cultural evolution. And it's not Fermat/Pascal. It uses a very crude, shortcut-type of approximation. It's got elements of Fermat/Pascal in it. However, it's not good.

So you have to learn in a very usable way this very elementary math and use it routinely in life—just the way if you want to become a golfer, you can't use the natural swing that broad evolution gave you. You have to learn to have a certain grip and swing in a different way to realize your full potential as a golfer.

If you don't get...elementary probability into your repertoire...you go through a long life like a one-legged man in an ass-kicking contest.

If you don't get this elementary, but mildly unnatural, mathematics of elementary probability into your repertoire, then you go through a long life like a one-legged man in an ass-kicking contest. You're giving a huge advantage to everybody else.

One of the advantages of a fellow like Buffett, whom I've worked with all these years, is that he automatically thinks in terms of decision trees and the elementary math of permutations and combinations.

C. F. Braun Company

The C. F. Braun Company, a petrochemical engineering and construction firm, rose to prominence in the San Gabriel Valley in the early to mid-twentieth century. Along with competitors such as Fluor, Bechtel, and Parsons, Braun designed and built plants throughout the world. In the early 1980s, Braun was purchased by Santa Fe International, ably led by Ed Shannon.

Obviously, you have to know accounting. It's the language of practical business life. It was a very useful thing to deliver to civilization. I've heard it came to civilization through Venice, which, of course, was once the great commercial power in the Mediterranean. However, double-entry bookkeeping was a hell of an invention.

And it's not that hard to understand.

But you have to know enough about it to understand its limitations—because although accounting is the starting place, it's only a crude approximation. And it's not very hard to understand its limitations. For example, everyone can see that you have to more or less just guess at the useful life of a jet airplane or anything like that. Just because you express the depreciation rate in neat numbers doesn't make it anything you really know.

In terms of the limitations of accounting, one of my favorite stories involves a very great businessman named Carl Braun who created the C. F. Braun Engineering Company. It designed and built oil refineries—which is very hard to do. And Braun would get them to come in on time and not blow up and have efficiencies and so forth. This is a major art.

And Braun, being the thorough Teutonic type that he was, had a number of quirks. And one of them was that he took a look at standard accounting and the way it was applied to building oil refineries, and he said, "This is asinine."

So he threw all of his accountants out, and he took his engineers and said, "Now, we'll devise our own system of accounting to handle this process." And, in due time, accounting adopted a lot of Carl Braun's notions. So he was a formidably willful and talented man who demonstrated both the importance of accounting and the importance of knowing its limitations.

He had another rule, from psychology, which, if you're interested in wisdom, ought to be part of your repertoire—like the elementary mathematics of permutations and combinations.

His rule for all the Braun Company's communications was called the five Ws—you had to tell who was going to do what, where, when, and why. And if you wrote a letter or directive in the Braun Company telling somebody to do something, and you didn't tell him why, you could get fired. In fact, you *would* get fired if you did it twice.

You might ask why is that so important? Well, again, that's a rule of psychology. Just as you think better if you array knowledge on a bunch of models that are basically answers to the question, why, why, why, if you always tell people why, they'll understand it better, they'll consider it more important, and they'll be more likely to comply. Even if they don't understand your reason, they'll be more likely to comply.

If you always tell people why, they'll understand it better, they'll consider it more important, and they'll be more likely to comply.

So there's an iron rule that just as you want to start getting worldly wisdom by asking why, why, why in communicating with other people about everything, you want to include why, why, why. Even if it's obvious, it's wise to stick in the why.

Which models are the most reliable? Well, obviously, the models that come from hard science and engineering are the most reliable models on this Earth. And engineering quality control—at least the guts of it that matters to you and me and people who are not professional engineers—is very much based on the elementary mathematics of Fermat and Pascal.

It costs so much, and you get so much less likelihood of it breaking if you spend this much. It's all elementary high school mathematics. And an elaboration of that is what Deming brought to Japan for all of that quality-control stuff.

I don't think it's necessary for most people to be terribly facile in statistics. For example, I'm not sure that I can even pronounce the Gaussian distribution, although

W. Edwards Deming
(1900–1993)

Born in Iowa but raised in Wyoming from an early age, W. Edwards Deming grew up in a four-room tarpaper shack. A serious student despite his impoverishment, he earned a Ph.D. in mathematical physics from Yale. He took a job in the Department of Agriculture, but eventually developed a love for statistical analysis. During World War II, wanting to help the war effort, Deming sought to apply statistics to manufacturing. American companies essentially ignored his ideas. Following the war, Deming went to Japan to teach Japanese managers, engineers, and scientists how to build quality into their manufacturing. Only after Japanese manufacturing skill became apparent to the rest of the world (in the 1980s) did Deming gain fame in his home country. The Deming prize for quality was first awarded in Japan but is now recognized internationally. The Japanese poster reads "Factory Safety Leads to Efficiency."

I know what it looks like and I know that events and huge aspects of reality end up distributed that way. So I can do a rough calculation.

But if you ask me to work out something involving a Gaussian distribution to ten decimal points, I can't sit down and do the math. I'm like a poker player who's learned to play pretty well without mastering Pascal.

And, by the way, that works well enough. But you have to understand that bell-shaped curve at least roughly as well as I do.

And, of course, the engineering idea of a backup system is a very powerful idea. The engineering idea of breakpoints—that's a very powerful model, too. The notion of a critical mass—that comes out of physics—is a very powerful model.

All of these things have great utility in looking at ordinary reality. And all of this cost-benefit analysis—hell, that's all elementary high school algebra. It's just been dolled up a little bit with fancy lingo.

And you can demonstrate that point quite simply: There's not a person in this room viewing the work of a very ordinary professional magician who doesn't see a lot of things happening that aren't happening and not see a lot of things happening that are happening.

I suppose the next most reliable models are from biology/physiology because, after all, all of us are programmed by our genetic makeup to be much the same.

And then when you get into psychology, of course, it gets very much more complicated. But it's an ungodly important subject if you're going to have any worldly wisdom.

And the reason why is that the perceptual apparatus of man has shortcuts in it. The brain cannot have unlimited circuitry. So someone who knows how to take advantage of those shortcuts and cause the brain to miscalculate in certain ways can cause you to see things that aren't there.

Now you get into the cognitive function as distinguished from the perceptual function. And there, you are equally—more than equally in fact—likely to be misled. Again, your brain has a shortage of circuitry and so forth—and it's taking all kinds of little automatic shortcuts.

So when circumstances combine in certain ways—or more commonly, your fellow man starts acting like the magician and manipulates you on purpose by causing you cognitive dysfunction—you're a patsy.

And so just as a man working with a tool has to know its limitations, a man working with his cognitive apparatus has to know its limitations. And this knowledge, by the way, can be used to control and motivate other people.

The mind of man at one and the same time is both the glory and the shame of the universe.

"...all human beings, as we meet them, are commingled out of good and evil."

—Dr. Jekyll, reflecting on mankind, from Robert Louis Stevenson's *Dr. Jekyll and Mr. Hyde*

So the most useful and practical part of psychology—which I personally think can be taught to any intelligent person in a week—is ungodly important. And nobody taught it to me, by the way. I had to learn it later in life, one piece at a time. And it was fairly laborious. It's so elementary though that, when it was all over, I just felt like a total horse's ass.

And yeah, I'd been educated at Caltech and the Harvard Law School and so forth. So very eminent places miseducated people like you and me.

The elementary part of psychology—the psychology of misjudgment, as I call it—is a terribly important thing to learn. There are about twenty little principles.

Two Tracks of Another Kind

The famed James J. Hill Stone Arch Bridge, Minneapolis, Minnesota, is the only railway structure on which the legendary "empire-builder" Hill allowed his name to be inscribed. The $6.5 million span was completed in 1883 for Hill's Great Northern Railroad franchise, today the Burlington Northern Santa Fe. Your editor considers Hill, along with Andrew Carnegie, Harvey Firestone, and Les Schwab, to be among the best self-made operators who can be studied by young businesspeople.

And they interact, so it gets slightly complicated. But the guts of it is unbelievably important.

Terribly smart people make totally bonkers mistakes by failing to pay heed to it. In fact, I've done it several times during the last two or three years in a very important way. You never get totally over making silly mistakes.

There's another saying that comes from Pascal that I've always considered one of the really accurate observations in the history of thought. Pascal said, "The mind of man at one and the same time is both the glory and the shame of the universe."

And that's exactly right. It has this enormous power. However, it also has these standard misfunctions that often cause it to reach wrong conclusions. It also makes man extraordinarily subject to manipulation by others. For example, roughly half of the army of Adolf Hitler was composed of believing Catholics. Given enough clever psychological manipulation, what human beings will do is quite interesting.

I now use a kind of two-track analysis.

Personally, I've gotten so that I now use a kind of two-track analysis. First, what are the factors that really govern the interests involved, rationally considered? And second, what are the subconscious influences where the brain at a subconscious level is automatically doing these things—which, by and large, are useful but which often misfunction?

One approach is rationality—the way you'd work out a bridge problem: by evaluating the real interests, the real probabilities, and so forth. And the other is to evaluate the psychological factors that cause subconscious conclusions—many of which are wrong.

Now we come to another somewhat less reliable form of human wisdom—microeconomics. And here, I find it quite useful to think of a free market economy—or partly free market economy—as sort of the equivalent of an ecosystem.

Just as animals flourish in niches, similarly, people who specialize in the business world—and get very good because they specialize—frequently find good economics that they wouldn't get any other way.

The Pelican Flourishing for 40 Million Years

Fossil records for pelicans go back 40 million years, a track record endorsing their specialized feeding strategies of plunge-diving and group fishing. In group fishing, flocks employ the timeless value of teamwork, collaborating to drive schools of small fish into the shallows, where the pelicans then eat to their hearts' content.

This is a very unfashionable way of thinking because early in the days after Darwin came along, people like the robber barons assumed that the doctrine of the survival of the fittest authenticated them as deserving power—you know, "I'm the richest. Therefore, I'm the best. God's in his heaven, etc."

And that reaction of the robber barons was so irritating to people that it made it unfashionable to think of an economy as an ecosystem. But the truth is that it is a lot like an ecosystem. And you get many of the same results.

Just as in an ecosystem, people who narrowly specialize can get terribly good at occupying some little niche. Just as animals flourish in niches, similarly, people who specialize in the business world—and get very good because they specialize—frequently find good economics that they wouldn't get any other way.

And once we get into microeconomics, we get into the concept of advantages of scale. Now we're getting closer to investment analysis—because in terms of which businesses succeed and which businesses fail, advantages of scale are ungodly important.

For example, one great advantage of scale taught in all of the business schools of the world is cost reductions along the so-called experience curve. Just doing something complicated in more and more volume enables human beings, who are trying to improve and are motivated by the incentives of capitalism, to do it more and more efficiently.

In 1907, Henry Ford announced his goal for the Ford Motor Company: to create "a motor car for the great multitude." At that time, automobiles were expensive, custom-made machines. Ford installed the first moving assembly line in 1913, launching American industry mass production.

The very nature of things is that if you get a whole lot of volume through your operation, you get better at processing that volume. That's an enormous advantage.

The very nature of things is that if you get a whole lot of volume through your operation, you get better at processing that volume. That's an enormous advantage. And it has a lot to do with which businesses succeed and fail.

Let's go through a list—albeit an incomplete one—of possible advantages of scale. Some come from simple geometry. If you're building a great circular tank, obviously, as you build it bigger, the amount of steel you use in the surface goes up with the square and the cubic volume goes up with the cube. So as you increase the dimensions, you can hold a lot more volume per unit area of steel.

And there are all kinds of things like that where the simple geometry—the simple reality—gives you an advantage of scale.

For example, you can get advantages of scale from TV advertising. When TV advertising first arrived—when talking color pictures first came into our living rooms—it was an unbelievably powerful thing. And in the early days, we had three networks that had whatever it was—say ninety percent of the audience.

Am I going to take something I don't know and put it in my mouth—which is a pretty personal place, after all—for a lousy dime?

Well, if you were Procter & Gamble, you could afford to use this new method of advertising. You could afford the very expensive cost of network television because you were selling so damn many cans and bottles. Some little guy couldn't. And there was no way of buying it in part. Therefore, he couldn't use it. In effect, if you didn't have a big volume, you couldn't use network TV advertising—which was the most effective technique.

So when TV came in, the branded companies that were already big got a huge tailwind. Indeed, they prospered and prospered and prospered until some of them got fat and foolish, which happens with prosperity—at least to some people.

And your advantage of scale can be an informational advantage. If I go to some remote place, I may see Wrigley chewing gum alongside Glotz's chewing gum. Well, I know that Wrigley is a satisfactory product whereas I don't know anything about Glotz's. So if one is forty cents and the other is thirty cents, am I going to take something I don't know and put it in my mouth—which is a pretty personal place, after all—for a lousy dime?

Change: Friend or Foe of the Investor?

"Change, as in the case of the Internet, can be the friend of society. But it is the *absence* of change that is often the friend of the investor. While the Internet will change many things, it will not likely change the brand of gum people chew. Charlie and I like stable businesses like chewing gum and try to leave life's more unpredictable things to someone else."

—Buffett

Jack Welch on Management

Jack Welch
(b. 1935)

"From 1981 to 1995, we said we were going to be "the most competitive enterprise in the world" by being No. 1 or No. 2 in every market—fixing, selling, or closing every underperforming business that couldn't get there. There was no doubt what this mission meant or entailed."

"Before you are a leader, success is all about growing yourself. When you become a leader, success is all about growing others."

"What you measure is what you get. What you reward is what you get."

"The consistent lesson I've learned over the years is that I have been in many cases too cautious. Almost everything should have been done faster."

"Give a project visibility. Put great people on it and give them plenty of money. This continues to be the best formula for success."

"Finding great people happens in all kinds of ways, and I've always believed, 'Everyone you meet is another interview.'"

"A cardinal rule of business: never allow anyone to get between you and your customers or suppliers. Those relationships take too long to develop and are too valuable to lose."

"Don't kid yourself. It is the way it is."

So, in effect, Wrigley, simply by being so well known, has advantages of scale—what you might call an informational advantage.

Another advantage of scale comes from psychology. The psychologists use the term "social proof." We are all influenced—subconsciously and, to some extent, consciously—by what we see others do and approve. Therefore, if everybody's buying something, we think it's better. We don't like to be the one guy who's out of step.

Again, some of this is at a subconscious level, and some of it isn't. Sometimes, we consciously and rationally think, "Gee, I don't know much about this. They know more than I do. Therefore, why shouldn't I follow them?"

The social proof phenomenon, which comes right out of psychology, gives huge advantages to scale—for example, with very wide distribution, which of course is hard to get. One advantage of Coca-Cola is that it's available almost everywhere in the world.

Well, suppose you have a little soft drink. Exactly how do you make it available all over the Earth? The worldwide distribution setup—which is slowly won by a big enterprise—gets to be a huge advantage.... And if you think about it, once you get enough advantages of that type, it can become very hard for anybody to dislodge you.

There's another kind of advantage to scale. In some businesses, the very nature of things is to sort of cascade toward the overwhelming dominance of one firm. The most obvious one is daily newspapers. There's practically no city left in the United States, aside from a few very big ones, where there's more than one daily newspaper.

And, again, that's a scale thing. Once I get most of the circulation, I get most of the advertising. And once I get most of the advertising and circulation, why would anyone want the thinner paper with less information in it? So it tends to cascade to a winner-take-all situation. And that's a separate form of the advantages of scale phenomenon.

Similarly, all these huge advantages of scale allow greater specialization within the firm. Therefore, each person can be better at what he does.

And these advantages of scale are so great, for example, that when Jack Welch came into General Electric, he just said, "To hell with it. We're either going to be #1 or #2 in every field we're in or we're going to be out. I don't care how many people I have to fire and what I have to sell. We're going to be #1 or #2 or out."

The Saturday Evening Post *and all those things are gone. What we have now is* Motocross*—which is read by a bunch of nuts who like to participate in tournaments where they turn somersaults on their motorcycles.*

Brad Lackey wows the crowd with a feet-up, full-power slide at the Luxemburg Grand Prix, 1982. Lackey was the first American to win an international motocross championship. He was closely associated for many years with CZ, a premier Czechoslovakian motorcycle. (The editor of this book used to be one of these motocross nuts.)

That was a very tough-minded thing to do, but I think it was a very correct decision if you're thinking about maximizing shareholder wealth. And I don't think it's a bad thing to do for a civilization either, because I think that General Electric is stronger for having Jack Welch there.

And there are also disadvantages of scale. For example, we—by which I mean Berkshire Hathaway—are the largest shareholder in Capital Cities/ABC. And we had trade publications there that got murdered—where our competitors beat us. And the way they beat us was by going to a narrower specialization.

We'd have a travel magazine for business travel. So somebody would create one which was addressed solely at corporate travel departments. Like an ecosystem, you're getting a narrower and narrower specialization.

Well, they got much more efficient. They could tell more to the guys who ran corporate travel departments. Plus, they didn't have to waste the ink and paper mailing out stuff that corporate travel departments weren't interested in reading. It was a more efficient system. And they beat our brains out as we relied on our broader magazine.

That's what happened to the *Saturday Evening Post* and all those things. They're gone. What we have now is *Motocross*—which is read by a bunch of nuts who like to participate in tournaments where they turn somersaults on their motorcycles. But they care about it. For them, it's the principal purpose of life. A magazine called *Motocross* is a total necessity to those people. And its profit margins would make you salivate.

Just think of how narrowcast that kind of publishing is. So occasionally, scaling down and intensifying gives you the big advantage. Bigger is not always better.

The great defect of scale, of course, which makes the game interesting—so that the big people don't always win—is that as you get big, you get the bureaucracy. And with the bureaucracy comes the territoriality—which is again grounded in human nature.

The big people don't always win...as you get big, you get the bureaucracy.

Traditional Soviet Workers' Lament:

"They pretend to pay us, and we pretend to work."

And the incentives are perverse. For example, if you worked for AT&T in my day, it was a great bureaucracy. Who in the hell was really thinking about the shareholder or anything else? And in a bureaucracy, you think the work is done when it goes out of your in-basket into somebody else's in-basket. But, of course, it isn't. It's not done until AT&T delivers what it's supposed to deliver. So you get big, fat, dumb, unmotivated bureaucracies.

They also tend to become somewhat corrupt. In other words, if I've got a department and you've got a department and we kind of share power running this thing, there's sort of an unwritten rule: "If you won't bother me, I won't bother you, and we're both happy." So you get layers of management and associated costs that nobody needs. Then, while people are justifying all these layers, it takes forever to get anything done. They're too slow to make decisions, and nimbler people run circles around them.

Television was dominated by one network—CBS—in its early days.

During the 1960s, CBS was a formidable power in network television, boasting such popular weekly series as *The Wild, Wild West*, which aired 104 episodes from 1965 to 1969.

The constant curse of scale is that it leads to big, dumb bureaucracy—which, of course, reaches its highest and worst form in government where the incentives are really awful. That doesn't mean we don't need governments—because we do. But it's a terrible problem to get big bureaucracies to behave.

So people go to stratagems. They create little decentralized units and fancy motivation and training programs. For example, for a big company, General Electric has fought bureaucracy with amazing skill. But that's because they have a combination of a genius and a fanatic running it. And they put him in young enough so he gets a long run. Of course, that's Jack Welch.

But bureaucracy is terrible.... And as things get very powerful and very big, you can get some really dysfunctional behavior. Look at Westinghouse. They blew billions of dollars on a bunch of dumb loans to real estate developers. They put some guy who'd come up by some career path—I don't know exactly what it was, but it could have been refrigerators or something—and all of a sudden, he's loaning

Sam Walton. Mike Wimmer. 2005. Oil on canvas. 2nd floor near rotunda, Oklahoma State Senate. Sponsored by The Wal-Mart Foundation.

Walton on Learning

"It was a real blessing for me to be so green and ignorant, because it was from that experience that I learned a lesson which has stuck with me through all the years: *you can learn from everybody.* I didn't just learn from reading every retail publication I could get my hands on, I probably learned the most from studying what [my competitor] was doing across the street."

money to real estate developers building hotels. It's a very unequal contest. And, in due time, they lost all those billions of dollars.

CBS provides an interesting example of another rule of psychology—namely, Pavlovian association. If people tell you what you really don't want to hear—what's unpleasant—there's an almost automatic reaction of antipathy. You have to train yourself out of it. It isn't foredestined that you have to be this way. But you will tend to be this way if you don't think about it.

Television was dominated by one network—CBS—in its early days. And Paley was a god. But he didn't like to hear what he didn't like to hear, and people soon learned that. So they told Paley only what he liked to hear. Therefore, he was soon living in a little cocoon of unreality and everything else was corrupt—although it was a great business.

So the idiocy that crept into the system was carried along by this huge tide. It was a Mad Hatter's Tea Party the last ten years under Bill Paley.

And that is not the only example, by any means. You can get severe misfunction in the high ranks of business. And, of course, if you're investing, it can make a hell of a lot of difference. If you take all the acquisitions that CBS made under Paley after the acquisition of the network itself, with all his dumb advisors—his investment bankers, management consultants, and so forth, who were getting paid very handsomely—it was absolutely terrible.

So life is an everlasting battle between those two forces—to get these advantages of scale on one side and a tendency to get a lot like the U.S. Agriculture Department on the other side—where they just sit around and so forth. I don't know exactly what they do. However, I do know that they do very little useful work.

On the subject of advantages of economies of scale, I find chain stores quite interesting. Just think about it. The concept of a chain store was a fascinating invention. You get this huge purchasing power—which means that you have lower merchandise costs. You get a whole bunch of little laboratories out there in which you can conduct experiments. And you get specialization.

If one little guy is trying to buy across twenty-seven different merchandise categories influenced by traveling salesmen, he's going to make a lot of dumb decisions. But if your buying is done in headquarters for a huge bunch of stores, you can get very bright people that know a lot about refrigerators and so forth to do the buying.

The reverse is demonstrated by the little store where one guy is doing all the buying. It's like the old story about the little store with salt all over its walls. And a stranger comes in and says to the store owner, "You must sell a lot of salt." And he replies, "No, I don't. But you should see the guy who sells me salt."

So there are huge purchasing advantages. And then there are the slick systems of forcing everyone to do what works. So a chain store can be a fantastic enterprise.

How does a guy in Bentonville, Arkansas, with no money, blow right by Sears, Roebuck? And he does it in his own lifetime—in fact, during his own late lifetime because he was already pretty old by the time he started out with one little store....

It's quite interesting to think about Wal-Mart starting from a single store in Arkansas—against Sears, Roebuck with its name, reputation and all of its billions. How does a guy in Bentonville, Arkansas, with no money, blow right by Sears, Roebuck? And he does it in his own lifetime—in fact, during his own late lifetime because he was already pretty old by the time he started out with one little store....

He played the chain store game harder and better than anyone else. Walton invented practically nothing. But he copied everything anybody else ever did

Wal-Mart

Founded in 1962 by Sam Walton with just one store in Rogers, Arkansas, Wal-Mart expanded to twenty-four stores in only five years. In 1970, Wal-Mart moved its distribution center and corporate headquarters to Bentonville, Arkansas, its current home. Growth continued throughout the United States and abroad to today's Wal-Mart, which has well over one million employees, better than $250 billion in revenues, and a market capitalization that exceeds $200 billion. The company is well-known for its slavish dedication to offering low prices to customers.

that was smart—and he did it with more fanaticism and better employee manipulation. So he just blew right by them all.

He also had a very interesting competitive strategy in the early days. He was like a prize-fighter who wanted a great record so he could be in the finals and make a big TV hit. So what did he do? He went out and fought forty-two palookas. Right? And the result was knockout, knockout, knockout—forty-two times.

Walton, being as shrewd as he was, basically broke other small town merchants in the early days. With his more efficient system, he might not have been able to tackle some titan head-on at the time. But with his better system, he could sure as hell destroy those small town merchants. And he went around doing it time after time after time. Then, as he got bigger, he started destroying the big boys.

Well, that was a very, very shrewd strategy.

Juan Trippe and Pan Am

Juan Trippe (1899–1981) joined the Navy during World War I. Graduating from Yale in 1921, he sold bonds on Wall Street until launching Pan Am in 1927. Trippe developed routes and built the airline into an international travel provider. He did much to create demand for his industry, marketing "jet-set" glamour and making travel affordable for the common person.

You can say, "Is this a nice way to behave?" Well, capitalism is a pretty brutal place. But I personally think that the world is better for having Wal-Mart. I mean, you can idealize small town life. But I've spent a fair amount of time in small towns. And let me tell you—you shouldn't get too idealistic about all those businesses he destroyed.

Plus, a lot of people who work at Wal-Mart are very high-grade, bouncy people who are raising nice children. I have no feeling that an inferior culture destroyed a superior culture. I think that is nothing more than nostalgia and delusion. But, at any rate, it's an interesting model of how the scale of things and fanaticism combine to be very powerful.

And it's also an interesting model on the other side—how with all its great advantages, the disadvantages of bureaucracy did such terrible damage to Sears,

Roebuck. Sears had layers and layers of people it didn't need. It was very bureaucratic. It was slow to think. And there was an established way of thinking. If you poked your head up with a new thought, the system kind of turned against you. It was everything in the way of a dysfunctional big bureaucracy that you would expect.

In all fairness, there was also much that was good about it. But it just wasn't as lean and mean and shrewd and effective as Sam Walton. And, in due time, all Sears' advantages of scale were not enough to prevent it from losing heavily to Wal-Mart and other similar retailers.

The net amount of money that's been made by the shareholders of airlines since Kitty Hawk is now a negative figure.

Here's a model that we've had trouble with. Maybe you'll be able to figure it out better. Many markets get down to two or three big competitors—or five or six. And in some of those markets, nobody makes any money to speak of. But in others, everybody does very well.

Over the years, we've tried to figure out why the competition in some markets gets sort of rational from the investor's point of view so that the shareholders do well, while in other markets there's destructive competition that destroys shareholder wealth.

If it's a pure commodity like airline seats, you can understand why no one makes any money. As we sit here, just think of what airlines have given to the world—safe travel, greater experience, time with your loved ones, you name it. Yet, the net amount of money that's been made by the shareholders of airlines since Kitty Hawk is now a negative figure—a substantial negative figure. Competition was so intense that, once it was unleashed by deregulation, it ravaged shareholder wealth in the airline business.

Kill Devil Hills was the site of the Wright brothers' first heavier-than-air flight in 1903—and, hence, the birthplace of aviation. In the 1930s, workers planted hearty grasses on the dune to prevent erosion. The Wright Brothers Memorial, located on the apex of the hill, is visible for miles in the otherwise barren landscape.

Kellogg

Dr. John Harvey Kellogg and his brother, William, were experimenting with new, "healthy" food items for patients at their Battle Creek Sanitarium in 1894 when they found that, by running boiled wheat dough through rollers and baking the result, they produced cereal flakes. William eventually began production of the new cereal product and, by 1906, was selling 2,900 cases per day. He continued to create new products and expanded the company into a breakfast food empire. Today, sales exceed $9 billion annually.

Yet, in other fields—like cereals, for example—almost all the big boys make out. If you're some kind of a medium-grade cereal maker, you might make fifteen percent on your capital. And if you're really good, you might make forty percent. But why are cereals so profitable—despite the fact that it looks to me like they're competing like crazy with promotions, coupons, and everything else? I don't fully understand it.

Obviously, there's a brand identity factor in cereals that doesn't exist in airlines. That must be the main factor that accounts for it.

And maybe the cereal makers, by and large, have learned to be less crazy about fighting for market share—because if you get even one person who's hell-bent on gaining market share.... For example, if I were Kellogg and I decided that I had to have sixty percent of the market, I think I could take most of the profit out of cereals. I'd ruin Kellogg in the process. But I think I could do it.

In some businesses, the participants behave like a demented Kellogg. In other businesses, they don't. Unfortunately, I do not have a perfect model for predicting how that's going to happen.

For example, if you look around at bottler markets, you'll find many markets where bottlers of Pepsi and Coke both make a lot of money and many others where they destroy most of the profitability of the two franchises. That must get down to the peculiarities of individual adjustment to market capitalism. I think you'd have to know the people involved to fully understand what was happening.

In microeconomics, of course, you've got the concept of patents, trademarks, exclusive franchises, and so forth. Patents are quite interesting. When I was young, I think more money went into patents than came out. Judges tended to throw them out—based on arguments about what was really invented and what relied on prior art. That isn't altogether clear.

But they changed that. They didn't change the laws. They just changed the administration—so that it all goes to one patent court. And that court is now very much more pro-patent. So I think people are now starting to make a lot of money out of owning patents.

Patent, Trademark, Exclusive Franchise

Patent: A grant made by a government conferring upon the creator of an invention the sole right to make, use, and sell that invention for a set period of time. An invention protected by such a grant.

Trademark: A name, symbol, or other device identifying a product, officially registered and legally restricted to the use of the owner or manufacturer. A distinctive characteristic by which a person or thing comes to be known.

Exclusive franchise: A right or license that is granted solely to an individual or group to market a company's goods or services in a particular territory under the company's trademark, trade name, or service mark and that often involves the use of rules and procedures designed by the company and services (as advertising) and facilities provided by the company in return for fees, royalties, or other compensation; also, a business granted such a right or license.

Trademarks, of course, have always made people a lot of money. A trademark system is a wonderful thing for a big operation if it's well known.

The exclusive franchise can also be wonderful. If there were only three television channels awarded in a big city and you owned one of them, there were only so many hours a day that you could be on. So you had a natural position in an oligopoly in the pre-cable days.

When Technology is Going to Kill You:

In the *Terminator* series of science fiction films, Arnold Schwarzenegger portrays a chilling futuristic cyborg that kills without emotion.

And if you get the franchise for the only food stand in an airport, you have a captive clientele, and you have a small monopoly of a sort.

The great lesson in microeconomics is to discriminate between when technology is going to help you and when it's going to kill you. And most people do not get this straight in their heads. But a fellow like Buffett does.

The great lesson in microeconomics is to discriminate between when technology is going to help you and when it's going to kill you.

For example, when we were in the textile business, which is a terrible commodity business, we were making low-end textiles—which are a real commodity product. And one day, the people came to Warren and said, "They've invented a new loom that we think will do twice as much work as our old ones." And Warren said, "Gee, I hope this doesn't work—because if it does, I'm going to close the mill." And he meant it.

What was he thinking? He was thinking, "It's a lousy business. We're earning substandard returns and keeping it open just to be nice to the elderly workers. But we're not going to put huge amounts of new capital into a lousy business."

And he knew that the huge productivity increases that would come from a better machine introduced into the production of a commodity product would all go to the benefit of the buyers of the textiles. Nothing was going to stick to our ribs as owners.

"They've invented a new loom that we think will do twice as much work as our old ones."

They don't do the second step of the analysis—which is to determine how much is going to stay home and how much is going to flow through to the customer.

That's such an obvious concept—that there are all kinds of wonderful new inventions that give you nothing as owners except the opportunity to spend a lot more money in a business that's still going to be lousy. The money still won't come to you. All of the advantages from great improvements are going to flow through to the customers.

Conversely, if you own the only newspaper in Oshkosh and they were to invent more efficient ways of composing the whole newspaper, then when you got rid of the old technology and got new, fancy computers and so forth, all of the savings would come right through to the bottom line.

In all cases, the people who sell the machinery—and, by and large, even the internal bureaucrats urging you to buy the equipment—show you projections with

NCR factory floor c. 1900

the amount you'll save at current prices with the new technology. However, they don't do the second step of the analysis—which is to determine how much is going to stay home and how much is just going to flow through to the customer. I've never seen a single projection incorporating that second step in my life. And I see them all the time. Rather, they always read: "This capital outlay will save you so much money that it will pay for itself in three years."

So you keep buying things that will pay for themselves in three years. And after twenty years of doing it, somehow you've earned a return of only about four percent per annum. That's the textile business.

And it isn't that the machines weren't better. It's just that the savings didn't go to you. The cost reductions came through all right. But the benefit of the cost reductions didn't go to the guy who bought the equipment. It's such a simple idea. It's so basic. And yet it's so often forgotten.

Then there's another model from microeconomics that I find very interesting. When technology moves as fast as it does in a civilization like ours, you get a phenomenon that I call competitive destruction. You know, you have the finest buggy whip factory, and, all of a sudden, in comes this little horseless carriage. And before too many years go by, your buggy whip business is dead. You either get into a different business or you're dead—you're destroyed. It happens again and again and again.

The cash register was one of the great contributions to civilization.

And when these new businesses come in, there are huge advantages for the early birds. And when you're an early bird, there's a model that I call "surfing"—when a surfer gets up and catches the wave and just stays there, he can go a long, long time. But if he gets off the wave, he becomes mired in shallows.

But people get long runs when they're right on the edge of the wave, whether it's Microsoft or Intel or all kinds of people, including National Cash Register in the early days.

The cash register was one of the great contributions to civilization. It's a wonderful story. Patterson was a small retail merchant who didn't make any money. One day, somebody sold him a crude cash register, which he put into his retail operation. And it instantly changed from losing money to earning a profit because it made it so much harder for the employees to steal.

But Patterson, having the kind of mind that he did, didn't think, "Oh, good for my retail business." He thought, "I'm going into the cash register business." And, of course, he created National Cash Register.

And he "surfed." He got the best distribution system, the biggest collection of patents, and the best of everything. He was a fanatic about everything important as the technology developed. I have in my files an early National Cash Register Company report in which Patterson described his methods and objectives. And a well-educated orangutan could see that buying into partnership with Patterson in those early days, given his notions about the cash register business, was a total one hundred percent cinch.

And, of course, that's exactly what an investor should be looking for. In a long life, you can expect to profit heavily from at least a few of those opportunities if you develop the wisdom and will to seize them. At any rate, "surfing" is a very powerful model.

However, Berkshire Hathaway, by and large, does not invest in these people that are "surfing" on complicated technology. After all, we're cranky and idiosyncratic—as you may have noticed.

National Cash Register Company

In 1884, John H. Patterson founded the National Cash Register Company (NCR), maker of the first mechanical cash registers. Two decades later, NCR introduced the first cash register powered by an electric motor. In the early 1950s, NCR branched into computer manufacturing for aviation and business applications. In the late 1990s, the firm shifted from a hardware-only company to a "full-solution" business automation provider.

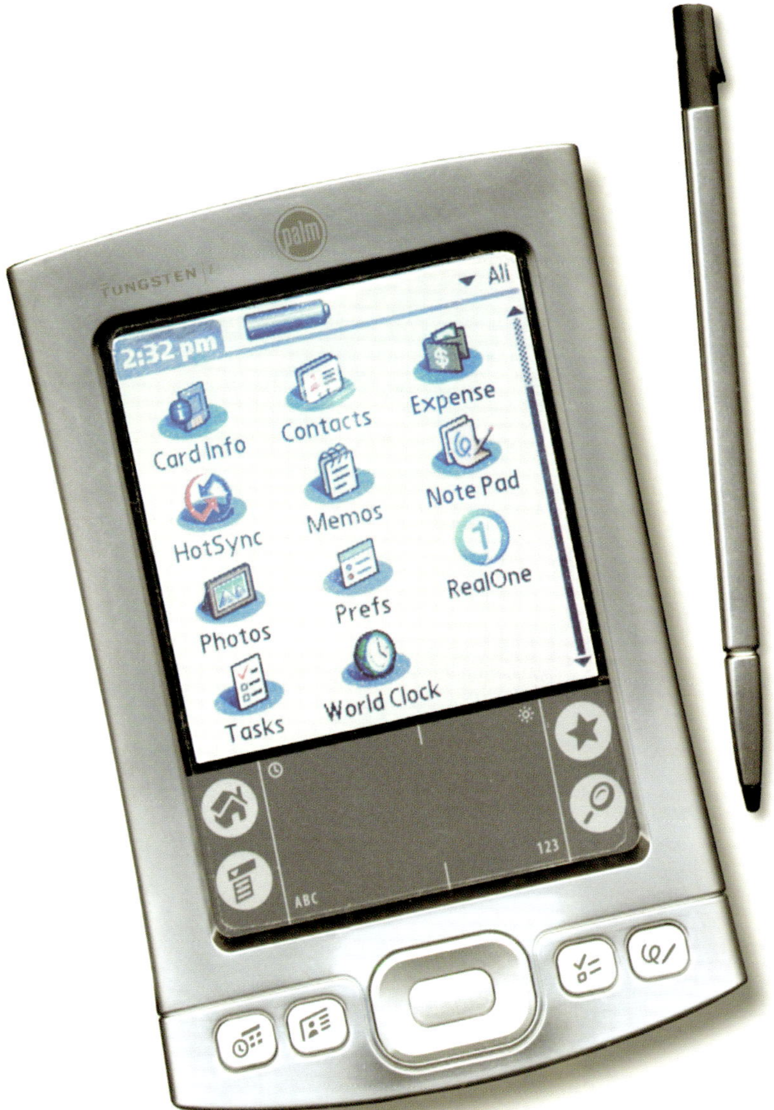

And Warren and I don't feel like we have any great advantage in the high-tech sector. In fact, we feel like we're at a big disadvantage in trying to understand the nature of technical developments in software, computer chips, or what have you. So we tend to avoid that stuff, based on our personal inadequacies.

Again, that is a very, very powerful idea. Every person is going to have a circle of competence. And it's going to be very hard to enlarge that circle. If I had to make my living as a musician.... I can't even think of a level low enough to describe where I would be sorted out to if music were the measuring standard of the civilization.

So you have to figure out what your own aptitudes are. If you play games where other people have the aptitudes and you don't, you're going to lose. And that's as close to certain as any prediction that you can make. You have to figure out where you've got an edge. And you've got to play within your own circle of competence.

Warren and I don't feel like we have any great advantage in the high-tech sector.

If you want to be the best tennis player in the world, you may start out trying and soon find out that it's hopeless—that other people blow right by you. However, if you want to become the best plumbing contractor in Bemidji, that is probably doable by two-thirds of you. It takes a will. It takes the intelligence. But after a while, you'd gradually know all about the plumbing business in Bemidji and master the art. That is an attainable objective, given enough discipline. And people who could never win a chess tournament or stand in center court in a respectable tennis tournament can rise quite high in life by slowly developing a circle of competence—which results partly from what they were born with and partly from what they slowly develop through work.

Paul and Babe, Bemidji, Minnesota. Paul Bunyan, of course, was the great lumberjack hero of storybook fame.

So some edges can be acquired. And the game of life to some extent for most of us is trying to be something like a good plumbing contractor in Bemidji. Very few of us are chosen to win the world's chess tournaments.

You have to figure out what your own aptitudes are. If you play games where other people have the aptitudes and you don't, you're going to lose.

Some of you may find opportunities "surfing" along in the new high-tech fields—the Intels, the Microsofts, and so on. The fact that we don't think we're very good at it and have pretty well stayed out of it doesn't mean that it's irrational for you to do it.

Well, so much for the basic microeconomic models, a little bit of psychology, a little bit of mathematics, helping create what I call the general substructure of worldly wisdom. Now, if you want to go on from carrots to dessert, I'll turn to stock picking—trying to draw on this general worldly wisdom as we go.

I don't want to get into emerging markets, bond arbitrage, and so forth. I'm talking about nothing but plain vanilla stock picking. That, believe me, is complicated enough. And I'm talking about common stock picking.

The first question is, "What is the nature of the stock market?" And that gets you directly to this efficient market theory that got to be the rage—a total rage—long after I graduated from law school.

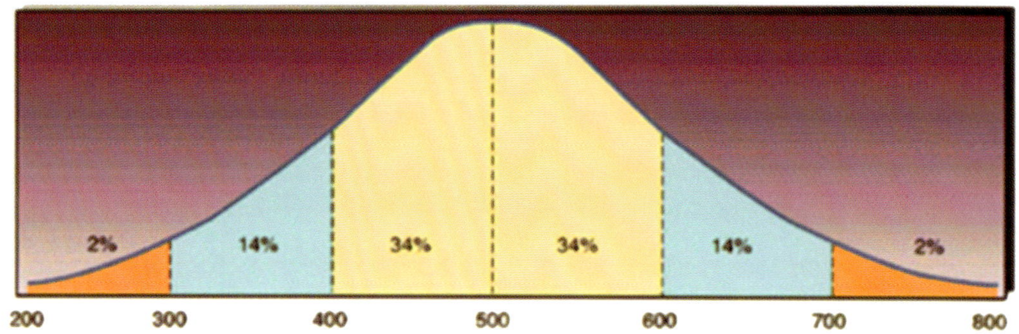

The iron rule of life is that only twenty percent of the people can be in the top fifth.

And it's rather interesting because one of the greatest economists of the world is a substantial shareholder in Berkshire Hathaway and has been from the very early days after Buffett was in control. His textbook always taught that the stock market was perfectly efficient and that nobody could beat it. But his own money went into Berkshire and made him wealthy. So, like Pascal in his famous wager, he hedged his bet.

Is the stock market so efficient that people can't beat it? Well, the efficient market theory is obviously roughly right—meaning that markets are quite efficient and it's quite hard for anybody to beat the market by significant margins as a stock picker by just being intelligent and working in a disciplined way.

Indeed, the average result has to be the average result. By definition, everybody can't beat the market. As I always say, the iron rule of life is that only twenty percent of the people can be in the top fifth. That's just the way it is. So the answer is that it's partly efficient and partly inefficient.

And, by the way, I have a name for people who went to the extreme efficient market theory—which is "bonkers." It was an intellectually consistent theory that enabled them to do pretty mathematics. So I understand its seductiveness to people with large mathematical gifts. It just had a difficulty in that the fundamental assumption did not tie properly to reality.

Again, to the man with a hammer, every problem looks like a nail. If you're good at manipulating higher mathematics in a consistent way, why not make an assumption that enables you to use your tool?

Thor's Hammer

Thor, an ancient Norse pagan deity, governed the atmosphere and environment. He was also the god of justice and law. Generally depicted as a well-built, red-bearded man with a fiery stare, Thor used a hammer that symbolized lightning, which, along with the thunderbolt, comprised his weapons against the enemies of heaven and earth. The hammer was also used in blessings, based on various important attributes—it could never be broken, it never missed its mark when thrown, it always returned to Thor's hand, and it could shrink in size so that Thor could conceal it in his shirt.

The model I like—to sort of simplify the notion of what goes on in a market for common stocks—is the pari-mutuel system at the race track. If you stop to think about it, a pari-mutuel system is a market. Everybody goes there and bets, and the odds change based on what's bet. That's what happens in the stock market.

Any damn fool can see that a horse carrying a light weight with a wonderful win rate and a good post position, etc., etc., is way more likely to win than a horse with a terrible record and extra weight and so on and so on. But if you look at the damn odds, the bad horse pays 100 to 1, whereas the good horse pays 3 to 2. Then, it's not clear which is statistically the best bet using the mathematics of Fermat and Pascal. The prices have changed in such a way that it's very hard to beat the system.

And then the track is taking seventeen percent off the top. So not only do you have to outwit all the other bettors, but you've got to outwit them by such a big margin that on average, you can afford to take seventeen percent of your gross bets off the top and give it to the house before the rest of your money can be put to work.

If you stop to think about it, a pari-mutuel system is a market. Everybody goes there and bets, and the odds change based on what's bet. That's what happens in the stock market.

Given those mathematics, is it possible to beat the horses using only one's intelligence? Intelligence should give some edge because lots of people who don't know anything go out and bet lucky numbers and so forth. Therefore, somebody who really thinks about nothing but horse performance and is shrewd and mathematical could have a very considerable edge, in the absence of the frictional cost caused by the house take.

Pari-mutuel System

A system of betting on races in which the winners divide the total amount bet, after deducting management expenses, in proportion to the sums they have wagered individually.

Unfortunately, what a shrewd horseplayer's edge does in most cases is to reduce his average loss over a season of betting from the seventeen percent that he would lose if he got the average result to maybe ten percent. However, there are actually a few people who can beat the game after paying the full seventeen percent.

I used to play poker, when I was young, with a guy who made a substantial living doing nothing but bet harness races. Now, harness racing is a relatively inefficient market. You don't have the depth of intelligence betting on harness races that you do on regular races. What my poker pal would do was to think about harness races as his main profession. And he would bet only occasionally when he saw some mispriced bet available. And by doing that, after paying the full handle to the house—which I presume was around seventeen percent—he made a substantial living.

You have to say that's rare. However, the market was not perfectly efficient. And if it weren't for that big seventeen percent handle, lots of people would regularly be beating lots of other people at the horse races. It's efficient, yes. But it's not perfectly efficient. And with enough shrewdness and fanaticism, some people will get better results than others.

The stock market is the same way—except that the house handle is so much lower. If you take transaction costs—the spread between the bid and the ask plus the commissions—and if you don't trade too actively, you're talking about fairly low transaction costs. So that, with enough fanaticism and enough discipline, some of the shrewd people are going to get way better results than average in the nature of things.

Gambling continues to be wildly popular throughout the world. Mah Jong is the preferred medium of gambling in much of Asia. The game resembles the card game of Rummy, and some people believe that playing cards were derived from Mah Jong tiles.

The one thing all those winning bettors in the whole history of people who've beaten the pari-mutuel system have is quite simple: they bet very seldom.

It is not a bit easy. And, of course, fifty percent will end up in the bottom half, and seventy percent will end up in the bottom seventy percent. But some people will have an advantage. And in a fairly low transaction cost operation, they will get better than average results in stock picking.

How do you get to be one of those who is a winner—in a relative sense—instead of a loser?

Here again, look at the pari-mutuel system. I had dinner last night by absolute accident with the president of Santa Anita. He says that there are two or three bettors who have a credit arrangement with the track, now that they have off-track

Morning, Leaving for Work. Vincent Van Gogh. 1890. Oil on canvas. Hermitage, St. Petersburg, Russia.

betting, who are actually beating the house. The track is sending money out net after the full handle—a lot of it to Las Vegas, by the way—to people who are actually winning slightly, net, after paying the full handle. They're that shrewd about something with as much unpredictability as horse racing.

It's not given to human beings to have such talent that they can just know everything about everything all the time. But it is given to human beings who work hard at it—who look and sift the world for a mispriced bet—that they can occasionally find one.

And the wise ones bet heavily when the world offers them that opportunity. They bet big when they have the odds. And the rest of the time, they don't. It's just that simple.

The way to win is to work, work, work, work, and hope to have a few insights.

That is a very simple concept. And to me it's obviously right—based on experience not only from the pari-mutuel system, but everywhere else.

And yet, in investment management, practically nobody operates that way. We operate that way—I'm talking about Buffett and Munger. And we're not alone in the world. But a huge majority of people have some other crazy construct in their heads. And instead of waiting for a near cinch and loading up, they apparently ascribe to the theory that if they work a little harder or hire more business school students, they'll come to know everything about everything all the time. To me, that's totally insane.

How many insights do you need? Well, I'd argue that you don't need many in a lifetime. If you look at Berkshire Hathaway and all of its accumulated billions, the top ten insights account for most of it. And that's with a very brilliant man—Warren's a lot more able than I am and very disciplined—devoting his lifetime to it. I don't mean to say that he's only had ten insights. I'm just saying that most of the money came from ten insights.

So you can get very remarkable investment results if you think more like a winning pari-mutuel player. Just think of it as a heavy odds against game full of bullshit and craziness with an occasional mispriced something or other. And you're probably not going to be smart enough to find thousands in a lifetime. And when you get a few, you really load up. It's just that simple.

When Warren lectures at business schools, he says, "I could improve your ultimate financial welfare by giving you a ticket with only twenty slots in it so that you had twenty punches—representing all the investments that you got to make in a lifetime. And once you'd punched through the card, you couldn't make any more investments at all."

He says, "Under those rules, you'd really think carefully about what you did, and you'd be forced to load up on what you'd really thought about. So you'd do so much better."

Again, this is a concept that seems perfectly obvious to me. And to Warren, it seems perfectly obvious. But this is one of the very few business classes in the United States where anybody will be saying so. It just isn't the conventional wisdom.

I asked him, "My God, they're purple and green. Do fish really take these lures?" And he said, "Mister, I don't sell to fish."

To me, it's obvious that the winner has to bet very selectively. It's been obvious to me since very early in life. I don't know why it's not obvious to very many other people.

I think the reason why we got into such idiocy in investment management is best illustrated by a story that I tell about the guy who sold fishing tackle. I asked him, "My God, they're purple and green. Do fish really take these lures?" And he said, "Mister, I don't sell to fish."

Investment managers are in the position of that fishing tackle salesman. They're like the guy who was selling salt to the guy who already had too much salt. And as long as the guy will buy salt, why, they'll sell salt. But that isn't what ordinarily works for the buyer of investment advice.

If you invested Berkshire Hathaway–style, it would be hard to get paid as an investment manager as well as they're currently paid—because you'd be holding a block of Wal-Mart and a block of Coca-Cola and a block of something else. You'd be sitting on your ass. And the client would be getting rich. And, after a while, the client would think, "Why am I paying this guy half-a-percent a year on my wonderful passive holdings?"

So what makes sense for the investor is different from what makes sense for the manager. And, as usual in human affairs, what determines the behavior are incentives for the decision maker.

As usual in human affairs, what determines the behavior are incentives for the decision maker, and "getting the incentives right" is a very, very important lesson.

Federal Express

Frederick W. Smith was a Yale undergraduate student in 1965 when he wrote a term paper about the passenger route systems used by most airfreight companies. He saw the need for a system designed specifically for airfreight to accommodate time-sensitive shipments. In 1971, Smith bought controlling interest in Arkansas Aviation Sales. Smith quickly witnessed the difficulty in getting packages and other airfreight delivered within one to two days. He did the research necessary to create a more efficient distribution system. The company officially began operating in 1973 with fourteen small aircraft based at Memphis International Airport; eventually, company headquarters moved to Memphis as well. Unprofitable until July 1975, FedEx soon became the premier carrier of high-priority goods in the marketplace and the standard setter for the industry it established.

From all business, my favorite case on incentives is Federal Express. The heart and soul of its system—which creates the integrity of the product—is having all its airplanes come to one place in the middle of the night and shift all the packages from plane to plane. If there are delays, the whole operation can't deliver a product full of integrity to Federal Express customers.

And it was always screwed up. They could never get it done on time. They tried everything—moral suasion, threats, you name it. And nothing worked.

Finally, somebody got the idea to pay all these people not so much an hour, but so much a shift—and when it's all done, they can all go home. Well, their problems cleared up overnight.

So getting the incentives right is a very, very important lesson. It was not obvious to Federal Express what the solution was. But maybe now, it will hereafter more often be obvious to you.

All right, we've now recognized that the market is efficient as a pari-mutuel system is efficient—with the favorite more likely than the long shot to do well in racing, but not necessarily give any betting advantage to those that bet on the favorite.

In the stock market, some railroad that's beset by better competitors and tough unions may be available at one-third of its book value. In contrast, IBM in its heyday might be selling at six times book value. So it's just like the pari-mutuel system. Any damn fool could plainly see that IBM had better business prospects than the railroad. But once you put the price into the formula, it wasn't so clear anymore what was going to work best for a buyer choosing between the stocks. So it's a lot like a pari-mutuel system. And, therefore, it gets very hard to beat.

IBM's signature office product, the "Selectric" typewriter, used a replaceable, ball-shaped typing element rather than traditional-type bars or moveable carriages. The Selectric became a popular piece of office equipment because of its ease of use and availability, largely replacing standard electric typewriters, as above.

What style should the investor use as a picker of common stocks in order to try to beat the market—in other words, to get an above average long-term result? A standard technique that appeals to a lot of people is called "sector rotation." You simply figure out when oils are going to outperform retailers, etc., etc., etc. You just kind of flit around being in the hot sector of the market making better choices than other people. And presumably, over a long period of time, you get ahead.

However, I know of no really rich sector rotator. Maybe some people can do it. I'm not saying they can't. All I know is that all the people I know who got rich—and I know a lot of them—did not do it that way.

The second basic approach is the one that Ben Graham used—much admired by Warren and me. As one factor, Graham had this concept of value to a private owner—what the whole enterprise would sell for if it were available. And that was calculable in many cases.

Then, if you could take the stock price and multiply it by the number of shares and get something that was one-third or less of sellout value, he would say that you've got a lot of edge going for you. Even with an elderly alcoholic running a stodgy business, this significant excess of real value per share working for you means that all kinds of good things can happen to you. You had a huge margin of safety—as he put it—by having this big excess value going for you.

But he was, by and large, operating when the world was in shell-shock from the 1930s—which was the worst contraction in the English-speaking world in about 600 years. Wheat in Liverpool, I believe, got down to something like a 600-year low, adjusted for inflation. People were so shell-shocked for a long time thereafter that Ben Graham could run his Geiger counter over this detritus from the collapse of the 1930s and find things selling below their working capital per share and so on.

And in those days, working capital actually belonged to the shareholders. If the employees were no longer useful, you just sacked them all, took the working capital, and stuck it in the owners' pockets. That was the way capitalism then worked.

Nowadays, of course, the accounting is not realistic—because the minute the business starts contracting, significant assets are not there. Under social norms and the new legal rules of the civilization, so much is owed to the employees, that the minute the enterprise goes into reverse, some of the assets on the balance sheet aren't there anymore.

Now, that might not be true if you run a little auto dealership yourself. You may be able to run it in a way that there's no health plan and this and that so that if the business gets lousy, you can take your working capital and go home. But IBM can't or at least didn't. Just look at what disappeared from its balance sheet when it decided that it had to change size both because the world had changed technologically and because its market position had deteriorated.

And in terms of blowing it, IBM is some example. Those were brilliant, disciplined people. But there was enough turmoil in technological change that IBM

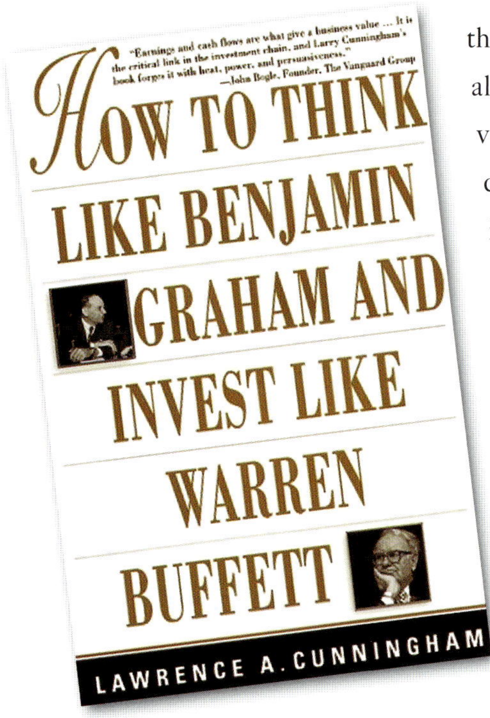

Benjamin Graham
(1894–1976)

Born in London, Benjamin Graham migrated with his family to America when he was very young. His father opened an importing business that quickly failed. Despite the challenges of poverty, Graham attended and graduated from Columbia University. He took a job as a chalker on Wall Street with Newburger, Henderson, and Loeb. His intelligence and capability were soon apparent, and by age twenty-five, he was a partner at the firm. The 1929 market crash almost wiped out Graham, but he learned valuable lessons about investing. In the 1930s, Graham published a series of books on investing that became classics. Among these impressive titles are *Security Analysis* and *The Intelligent Investor.* Graham introduced the concept of "intrinsic value" and the wisdom of buying stocks at a discount to that value.

got bounced off the wave after "surfing" successfully for sixty years. And that was some collapse—an object lesson in the difficulties of technology and one of the reasons why Buffett and Munger don't like technology very much. We don't think we're any good at it, and strange things can happen.

At any rate, the trouble with what I call the classic Ben Graham concept is that gradually the world wised up, and those real obvious bargains disappeared. You could run your Geiger counter over the rubble, and it wouldn't click.

But such is the nature of people who have a hammer—to whom, as I mentioned, every problem looks like a nail—that the Ben Graham followers responded by changing the calibration on their Geiger counters. In effect, they started defining a bargain in a different way. And they kept changing the definition so that they could keep doing what they'd always done. And it still worked pretty well. So the Ben Graham intellectual system was a very good one.

Perhaps the Soviets had this German proverb in mind when they selected the hammer for their revolutionary symbol:

"One must either be the hammer... or the anvil."

Of course, the best part of it all was his concept of "Mr. Market." Instead of thinking the market was efficient, Graham treated it as a manic-depressive who comes by every day. And some days "Mr. Market" says, "I'll sell you some of my interest for way less than you think it's worth." And other days, he comes by and says, "I'll buy your interest at a price that's way higher than you think it's worth." And you get the option of deciding whether you want to buy more, sell part of what you already have, or do nothing at all.

To Graham, it was a blessing to be in business with a manic-depressive who gave you this series of options all the time. That was a very significant mental construct. And it's been very useful to Buffett, for instance, over his whole adult lifetime.

However, if we'd stayed with classic Graham the way Ben Graham did it, we would never have had the record we have. And that's because Graham wasn't trying to do what we did.

For example, Graham didn't want to ever talk to management. And his reason was that, like the best sort of professor aiming his teaching at a mass audience, he was trying to invent a system that anybody could use. And he didn't feel that the man in the street could run around and talk to management and learn things. He also had a concept that management would often couch the information very shrewdly to mislead. Therefore, it was very difficult. And that is still true, of course—human nature being what it is.

And so having started out as Grahamites—which, by the way, worked fine—we gradually got what I would call better insights. And we realized that some company that was selling at two or three times book value could still be a hell of a bargain because of momentums implicit in its position, sometimes combined with an unusual managerial skill plainly present in some individual or other, or some system or other.

And once we'd gotten over the hurdle of recognizing that a thing could be a bargain based on quantitative measures that would have horrified Graham, we started thinking about better businesses.

Trump's signature message: "You're fired!"

Photo by Bill Davila/Reuters

And, by the way, the bulk of the billions in Berkshire Hathaway has come from the better businesses. Much of the first $200 or $300 million came from scrambling around with our Geiger counter. But the great bulk of the money has come from the great businesses.

Most investment managers are in a game where the clients expect them to know a lot about a lot of things. We didn't have any clients who could fire us at Berkshire Hathaway.

And even some of the early money was made by being temporarily present in great businesses. Buffett Partnership, for example, owned American Express and Disney when they got pounded down.

[Most investment managers are] in a game where the clients expect them to know a lot about a lot of things. We didn't have any clients who could fire us at Berkshire Hathaway. So we didn't have to be governed by any such construct. And we came to this notion of finding a mispriced bet and loading up when we were very confident that we were right. So we're way less diversified. And I think our system is miles better.

However, in all fairness, I don't think [a lot of money managers] could successfully sell their services if they used our system. But if you're investing for forty years in some pension fund, what difference does it make if the path from start to finish is a little more bumpy or a little different than everybody else's so long as it's all going to work out well in the end? So what if there's a little extra volatility.

In investment management today, everybody wants not only to win, but to have the path never diverge very much from a standard path except on the upside. Well, that is a very artificial, crazy construct. That's the equivalent in investment management to the custom of binding the feet of the Chinese women. It's the equivalent of what Nietzsche meant when he criticized the man who had a lame leg and was proud of it.

That is really hobbling yourself. Now, investment managers would say, "We have to be that way. That's how we're measured." And they may be right in terms of the way the business is now constructed. But from the viewpoint of a rational consumer, the whole system's "bonkers" and draws a lot of talented people into socially useless activity.

Professor Lucifer Gorgonzola Butts, pushing the limits of feasibility in this classic Rube Goldberg "machine." Goldberg's invention cartoons were influenced by the "machine age" at the beginning of the century and by the complex new mechanisms invented to simplify life. Charlie, like so many Americans, recalls enjoying the wacky creations of Goldberg's imaginative mind.

You're much more likely to do well if you start out to do something feasible instead of something that isn't feasible. Isn't that perfectly obvious?

And the Berkshire system is not "bonkers." It's so damned elementary that even bright people are going to have limited, really valuable insights in a very competitive world when they're fighting against other very bright, hardworking people.

And it makes sense to load up on the very few good insights you have instead of pretending to know everything about everything at all times. You're much more likely to do well if you start out to do something feasible instead of something that isn't feasible. Isn't that perfectly obvious?

How many of you have fifty-six brilliant insights in which you have equal confidence? Raise your hands, please. How many of you have two or three insights that you have some confidence in? I rest my case.

Adaptation

"It is not the strongest of the species that survives, nor the most intelligent, but the one most responsive to change."
—Charles Darwin

The Warbler Finch (*Certhidea olivacea*) is one of fourteen finch species Darwin discovered in the Galapagos Islands. In honor of his ground-breaking research, these species were given the name of Darwin's Finches.

I'd say that Berkshire Hathaway's system is adapting to the nature of the investment problem as it really is.

We've really made the money out of high-quality businesses. In some cases, we bought the whole business. And in some cases, we just bought a big block of stock. But when you analyze what happened, the big money's been made in the high-quality businesses. And most of the other people who've made a lot of money have done so in high-quality businesses.

Over the long term, it's hard for a stock to earn a much better return than the business which underlies it earns. If the business earns six percent on capital over forty years and you hold it for that forty years, you're not going to make much different than a six percent return—even if you originally buy it at a huge discount. Conversely, if a business earns eighteen percent on capital over twenty or thirty years, even if you pay an expensive looking price, you'll end up with one hell of a result.

So the trick is getting into better businesses. And that involves all of these advantages of scale that you could consider momentum effects.

How do you get into these great companies? One method is what I'd call the method of finding them small—get 'em when they're little. For example, buy Wal-Mart when Sam Walton first goes public and so forth. And a lot of people try to do just that. And it's a very beguiling idea. If I were a young man, I might actually go into it.

But it doesn't work for Berkshire Hathaway anymore because we've got too much money. We can't find anything that fits our size parameter that way. Besides, we're set in our ways. But I regard finding them small as a perfectly intelligent approach for somebody to try with discipline. It's just not something that I've done.

Finding 'em big obviously is very hard because of the competition. So far, Berkshire's managed to do it. But can we continue to do it? What's the next Coca-Cola investment for us? Well, the answer to that is I don't know. I think it gets harder for us all the time.

And ideally—and we've done a lot of this—you get into a great business which also has a great manager because management matters. For example, it's made a hell of a difference to General Electric that Jack Welch came in instead of the guy who took over Westinghouse—one hell of a difference. So management matters, too.

And some of it is predictable. I do not think it takes a genius to understand that Jack Welch was a more insightful person and a better manager than his peers in other companies. Nor do I think it took tremendous genius to understand that Disney had basic momentums in place that are very powerful and that Eisner and Wells were very unusual managers.

So you do get an occasional opportunity to get into a wonderful business that's being run by a wonderful manager. And, of course, that's hog heaven day. If you don't load up when you get those opportunities, it's a big mistake.

Occasionally, you'll find a human being who's so talented that he can do things that ordinary skilled mortals can't. I would argue that Simon Marks—who was second generation in Marks & Spencer of England—was such a man. Patterson was such a man at National Cash Register. And Sam Walton was such a man.

These people do come along—and, in many cases, they're not all that hard to identify. If they've got a reasonable hand—with the

Simon Marks
(1888–1964)

Born in Leeds, England, to Polish immigrant parents, Simon Marks spent his formative years roaming around his father's retail store, Marks and Spencer. Following graduation from the rigorous local grammar school (the equivalent of high school today), Marks went into the family business. At age twenty-eight, he was appointed chairman and led the Marks and Spencer Company into many retailing innovations and considerable financial success. Outside of his company obligations, Marks worked passionately for the re-establishment of a Jewish state.

fanaticism and intelligence and so on that these people generally bring to the party—then management can matter much.

However, averaged out, betting on the quality of a business is better than betting on the quality of management. In other words, if you have to choose one, bet on the business momentum, not the brilliance of the manager.

But, very rarely, you find a manager who's so good that you're wise to follow him into what looks like a mediocre business.

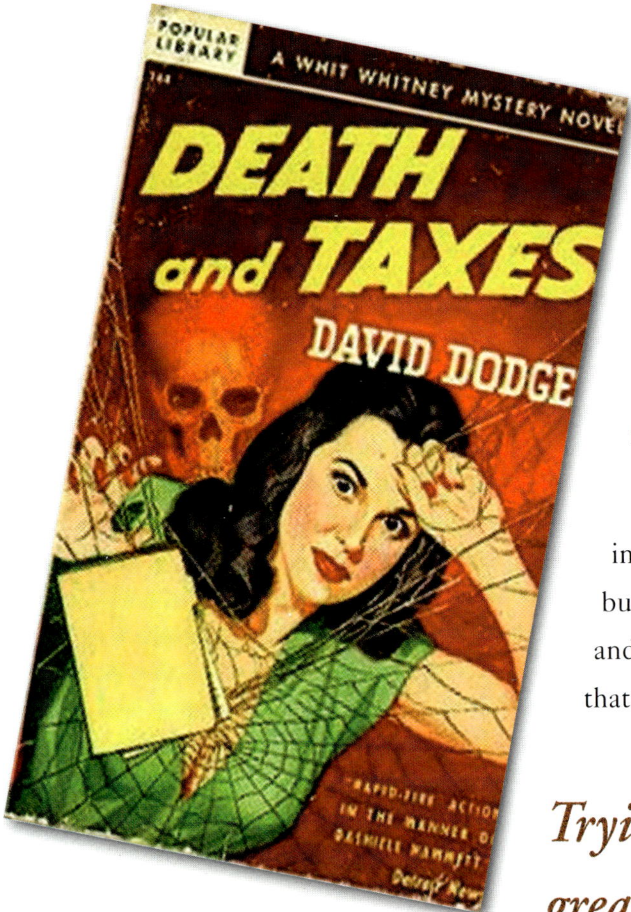

Another very simple effect I very seldom see discussed either by investment managers or anybody else is the effect of taxes. If you're going to buy something that compounds for thirty years at fifteen percent per annum and you pay one thirty-five percent tax at the very end, the way that works out is that after taxes, you keep 13.3 percent per annum.

Trying to minimize taxes too much is one of the great standard causes of really dumb mistakes.

In contrast, if you bought the same investment but had to pay taxes every year of thirty-five percent out of the fifteen percent that you earned, then your return would be fifteen percent minus thirty-five percent of fifteen percent—or only 9.75 percent per year compounded. So the difference there is over 3.5 percent. And what 3.5 percent does to the numbers over long holding periods like thirty years is truly eye-opening. If you sit on your ass for long, long stretches in great companies, you can get a huge edge from nothing but the way income taxes work.

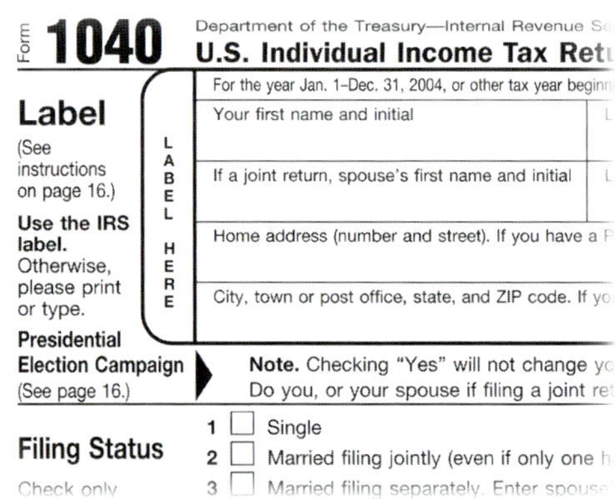
Form 1040 Department of the Treasury—Internal Revenue S
U.S. Individual Income Tax Ret
For the year Jan. 1–Dec. 31, 2004, or other tax year begin
Label (See instructions on page 16.) Use the IRS label. Otherwise, please print or type.
LABEL HERE
Your first name and initial
If a joint return, spouse's first name and initial
Home address (number and street). If you have a
City, town or post office, state, and ZIP code. If yo
Presidential Election Campaign (See page 16.)
Note. Checking "Yes" will not change yo
Do you, or your spouse if filing a joint re
Filing Status
Check only
1 Single
2 Married filing jointly (even if only one h
3 Married filing separately. Enter spouse

Even with a ten percent per annum investment, paying a thirty-five percent tax at the end gives you 8.3 percent after taxes as an annual compounded result after thirty years. In contrast, if you pay the thirty-five percent each year instead of at the end, your annual result goes down to 6.5 percent. So you add nearly two percent of after-tax return per annum if you only achieve an average return by historical standards from common stock investments in companies with low dividend payout ratios.

But in terms of business mistakes that I've seen over a long lifetime, I would say that trying to minimize taxes too much is one of the great standard causes of really dumb mistakes. I see terrible mistakes from people being overly motivated by tax considerations.

Warren and I personally don't drill oil wells. We pay our taxes. And we've done pretty well, so far. Anytime somebody offers you a tax shelter from here on in life, my advice would be don't buy it.

In fact, anytime anybody offers you anything with a big commission and a 200-page prospectus, don't buy it. Occasionally, you'll be wrong if you adopt "Munger's Rule." However, over a lifetime, you'll be a long way ahead—and you will miss a lot of unhappy experiences that might otherwise reduce your love for your fellow man.

There are huge advantages for an individual to get into a position where you make a few great investments and just sit on your ass: You're paying less to brokers. You're listening to less nonsense. And if it works, the governmental tax system gives you an extra one, two, or three percentage points per annum compounded.

And you think that most of you are going to get that much advantage by hiring investment counselors and paying them one percent to run around, incurring a lot of taxes on your behalf? Lots of luck.

Are there any dangers in this philosophy? Yes. Everything in life has dangers. Since it's so obvious that investing in great companies works, it gets horribly overdone from time to time. In the Nifty-Fifty days, everybody could tell which companies were the great ones. So they got up to fifty, sixty, and seventy times

"We Pay Our Taxes"

"Berkshire's Christmas present for Uncle Sam: On my right, Berkshire's 2004 Federal tax return—10,249 pages and $3,131,473,650 total tax. In my left hand, the tax return I filed at age 13 showing a total tax of $7."

—Buffett

"Warren and I personally don't drill oil wells. We pay our taxes. And we've done pretty well, so far. Anytime somebody offers you a tax shelter from here on in life, my advice would be don't buy it."

—Munger

The successful Disney franchise includes not only theme parks and motion pictures, but also books, comics, and lucrative video sales.

earnings. And just as IBM fell off the wave, other companies did, too. Thus, a large investment disaster resulted from too high prices. And you've got to be aware of that danger.

So there are risks. Nothing is automatic and easy. But if you can find some fairly priced great company and buy it and sit, that tends to work out very, very well indeed—especially for an individual.

Within the growth stock model, there's a sub-position: There are actually businesses that you will find a few times in a lifetime where any manager could raise the return enormously just by raising prices—and yet they haven't done it. So they have huge untapped pricing power that they're not using. That is the ultimate no-brainer.

That existed in Disney. It's such a unique experience to take your grandchild to Disneyland. You're not doing it that often. And there are lots of people in the country. And Disney found that it could raise those prices a lot, and the attendance stayed right up.

So a lot of the great record of Eisner and Wells was utter brilliance but the rest came from just raising prices at Disneyland and Disneyworld and through video cassette sales of classic animated movies.

At Berkshire Hathaway, Warren and I raised the prices of See's Candy a little faster than others might have. And, of course, we invested in Coca-Cola—which had some untapped pricing power. And it also had brilliant management. So a Goizueta and Keough could do much more than raise prices. It was perfect.

You will get a few opportunities to profit from finding underpricing. There are actually people out there who don't price everything as high as the market will easily stand. And once you figure that out, it's like finding money in the street—if you have the courage of your convictions.

If you look at Berkshire's investments where a lot of the money's been made and you look for the models, you can see that we twice bought into two-newspaper towns which have since become one-newspaper towns. So we made a bet to some extent.

We faced a situation where you had both the top hand in a game that was clearly going to end up with one winner and a management with a lot of integrity and intelligence. It was a dream—an absolute, damn dream.

The Washington Post

In 1877, Stilson Hutchins launched *The Washington Post.* Three years later, the *Post* became the first daily newspaper in Washington to publish seven times a week. In 1946, Philip Graham became publisher; he moved up to president of the paper in 1959. The *Post* acquired *Newsweek Magazine* and established a joint news service with the *Los Angeles Times* in the early 1960s.

In one of those—the *Washington Post*—we bought it at about twenty percent of the value to a private owner. So we bought it on a Ben Graham–style basis—at one-fifth of obvious value—and, in addition, we faced a situation where you had both the top hand in a game that was clearly going to end up with one winner and a management with a lot of integrity and intelligence. That one was a real dream. They're very high class people—the Katharine Graham family. That's why it was a dream—an absolute, damn dream.

Of course, that came about back in '73–'74. And that was almost like 1932. That was probably a once-in-forty-years-type denouement in the markets. That investment's up about fifty times over our cost. If I were you, I wouldn't count on getting any investment in your lifetime quite as good as the *Washington Post* was in '73 and '74.

Let me mention another model. Of course, Gillette and Coke make fairly low-priced items and have a tremendous marketing advantage all over the world. And in Gillette's case, they keep "surfing" along new technology, which is fairly simple by the standards of microchips. But it's hard for competitors to do.

So they've been able to stay constantly near the edge of improvements in shaving. There are whole countries where Gillette has more than ninety percent of the shaving market.

GEICO is a very interesting model. It's another one of the one hundred or so models you ought to have in your head. I've had many friends in the sick-business-fix game over a long lifetime. And they practically all use the following formula—I call it the cancer surgery formula:

> They look at this mess. And they figure out if there's anything sound left that can live on its own if they cut away everything else. And if they find anything sound, they just cut away everything else. Of course, if that doesn't work, they liquidate the business. But it frequently does work.

History of the Disposable Razor

King C. Gillette (1855-1932), a traveling hardware salesman who enjoyed improving the products he sold, learned early that disposable items made for big sales. In 1895, Gillette had a revelation: if he could put a sharp edge on a small square of sheet steel, he could market an economical razor blade that could be thrown away and replaced when it grew dull. In 1901, Gillette and William Emery Nickerson formed the American Safety Razor Company (soon thereafter renamed for Gillette himself). For the first time, razor blades were sold in multiple packages, with the razor handle a one-time purchase. Production began in 1903; Gillette won a patent for his product the next year.

And GEICO had a perfectly magnificent business—submerged in a mess, but still working. Misled by success, GEICO had done some foolish things. They got to thinking that, because they were making a lot of money, they knew everything. And they suffered huge losses.

All they had to do was to cut out all the folly and go back to the perfectly wonderful business that was lying there. And when you think about it, that's a very simple model. And it's repeated over and over again.

And, in GEICO's case, think about all the money we passively made. It was a wonderful business combined with a bunch of foolishness that could easily be cut out. And people were coming in who were temperamentally and intellectually designed so they were going to cut it out. That is a model you want to look for.

And you may find one or two or three in a long lifetime that are very good. And you may find twenty or thirty that are good enough to be quite useful.

Finally, I'd like to once again talk about investment management. That is a funny business—because on a net basis, the whole investment management business together gives no value added to all buyers combined. That's the way it has to work.

On a net basis, the whole investment management business together gives no value added to all buyers combined. That's the way it has to work.

GEICO

Leo and Lillian Goodwin started the Government Employees Insurance Company (GEICO) during the depths of the Great Depression in 1936. Their strategy of direct marketing allowed the company to charge lower premiums while earning a profit. The company grew quickly, even though it focused at first primarily on federal employees and military officers. GEICO soon expanded its market to the general public. In 1951, Warren Buffett purchased his first shares of the company. He kept acquiring stock through the years until, in 1996, GEICO became a wholly owned subsidiary of Berkshire Hathaway.

Of course, that isn't true of plumbing, and it isn't true of medicine. If you're going to make your careers in the investment management business, you face a very peculiar situation. And most investment managers handle it with psychological denial—just like a chiropractor. That is the standard method of handling the limitations of the investment management process. But if you want to live the best sort of life, I would urge each of you not to use the psychological denial mode.

I think a select few—a small percentage of the investment managers—can deliver value added. But I don't think brilliance alone is enough to do it. I think that you have to have a little of this discipline of calling your shots and loading up—if you want to maximize your chances of becoming one who provides above average real returns for clients over the long pull.

But I'm just talking about investment managers engaged in common stock picking. I am agnostic elsewhere. I think there may well be people who are so shrewd about currencies and this, that, and the other thing that they can achieve good long-term records operating on a pretty big scale in that way. But that doesn't happen to be my milieu. I'm talking about stock picking in American stocks.

I think it's hard to provide a lot of value added to the investment management client, but it's not impossible.

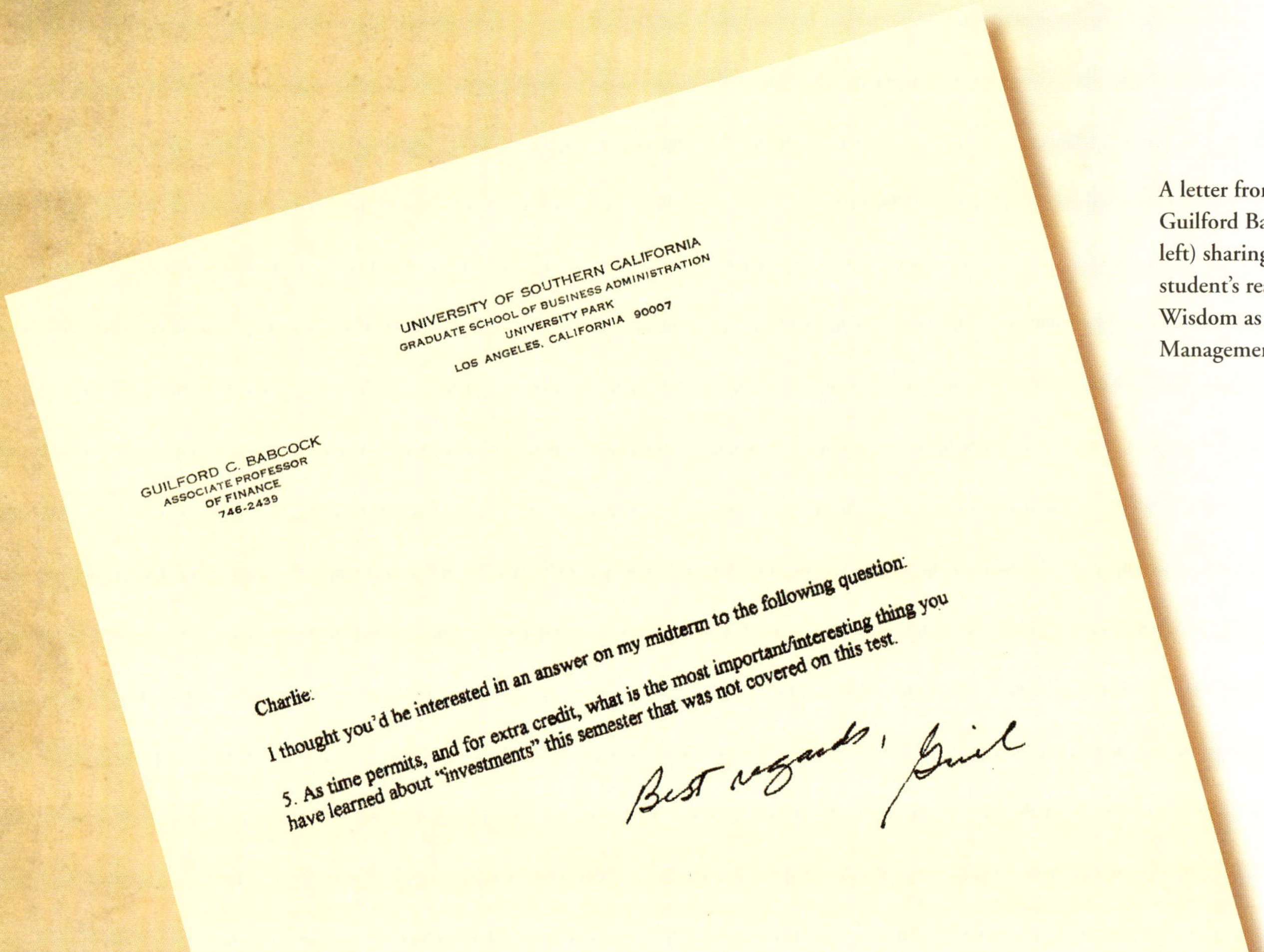

UNIVERSITY OF SOUTHERN CALIFORNIA
GRADUATE SCHOOL OF BUSINESS ADMINISTRATION
UNIVERSITY PARK
LOS ANGELES, CALIFORNIA 90007

GUILFORD C. BABCOCK
ASSOCIATE PROFESSOR
OF FINANCE
746-2439

Charlie:

I thought you'd be interested in an answer on my midterm to the following question:

5. As time permits, and for extra credit, what is the most important/interesting thing you have learned about "investments" this semester that was not covered on this test.

Best regards, Guil

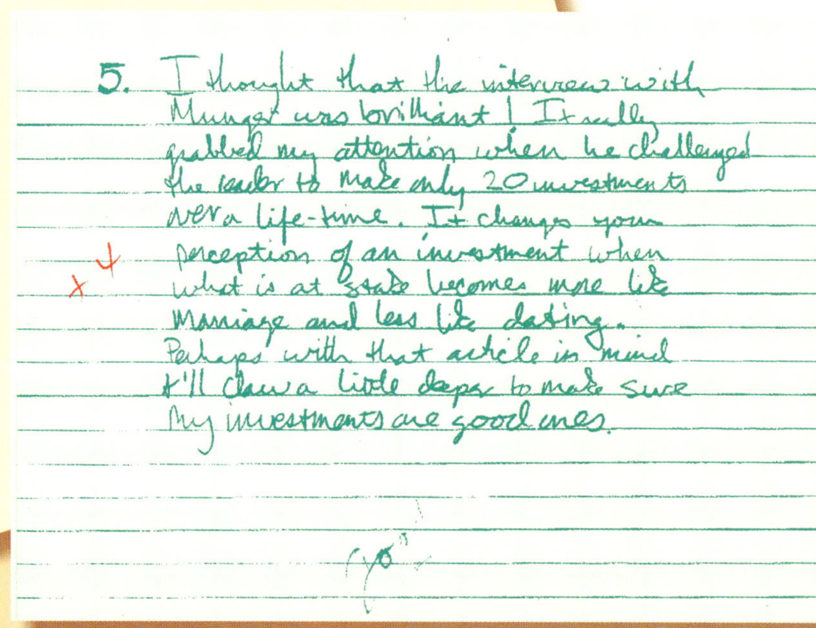

5. I thought that the interviews with Munger was brilliant! It really grabbed my attention when he challenged the reader to make only 20 investments over a life-time. It changes your perception of an investment when what is at stake becomes more like marriage and less like dating. Perhaps with that article in mind I'll dig a little deeper to make sure my investments are good ones.

A letter from USC finance professor Guilford Babcock (shown below and left) sharing with Charlie one of his student's reactions to the talk, "Worldly Wisdom as It Relates to Investment Management and Business."

"Nothing to Add" Number Three

We continue with this question occasioned by countless questions over the years at cocktail parties, etc.

Question: "All kinds of people ask me for some foolproof system for achieving financial security or saving for their retirement. I try to dodge those questions." [Editor: "But this time, Charlie, we're not going to let you dodge it."]

Answer: "Spend less than you make; always be saving something. Put it into a tax-deferred account. Over time, it will begin to amount to something. THIS IS SUCH A NO-BRAINER."

Talk Two Revisited

As I reviewed Talk Two in 2006, I thought it would be improved by adding (1) an attempt to explain the extreme investment success of Harvard and Yale in recent years, plus (2) a prediction about outcomes for the many pools of capital that will now try to duplicate the past success of Harvard and Yale by copying or continuing their methods, plus (3) a brief comment about implications for the efficient market hypothesis as demonstrated in a 2005 book, *Fortune's Formula*, by William Poundstone.

To me, it seems likely that, as Harvard and Yale de-emphasized conventional unleveraged holding of diversified U.S. common stocks, their investment success was boosted by factors including the four described below:

(1) By investing in LBO funds, Harvard and Yale, introduced leverage into their results from owning interests in U.S. businesses. And the LBO fund structure gave them a way to make their leveraged business investments in a manner safer than is possible in a normal margin account, prone during panics to forced sales. Decent comparative results often followed in markets with tolerable general outcomes. And this happened even when net-after-cost results from investments in the LBO funds were no better than would have occurred through only slightly leveraged investment in an index of U.S. stocks.

(2) In category after category, Harvard and Yale selected or directly employed investment managers who were way above average in ability, providing additional evidence that investment markets are not perfectly efficient and that some good investment results come from abnormal skill or other abnormal advantage. As one example, Harvard and Yale, by reason of their own prestige, were able to get into some of the most profitable high-tech venture-capital funds, not available to all other

investors. These funds, using momentum provided by their own past success, had an opportunity advantage over less well established venture capital operations, in that the best entrepreneurs, quite logically, made early presentations to the best-regarded funds.

(3) Harvard and Yale wisely and opportunistically imitated investment banking firms by going into several activities that were then non-traditional, like investing in distressed U.S. corporate bonds and high-coupon foreign bonds and leveraged "fixed income arbitrage," during a period when many good opportunities were available to skilled operators in the activities chosen.

(4) Finally, the benefits that came to Harvard and Yale in recent years through leverage and unconventionality were often, of course, given a large tailwind by a happy combination of declining interest rates and rising price-earnings ratios for stocks.

"Founded in 1636, Harvard is of course the oldest institution of higher learning in the United States. Its Latin motto translates simply as 'truth.' Not to be outdone, Yale University, founded years later in 1701, went them one better by adding 'light' to the equation."

—Munger

Thales of Miletus
620s BC - 546 BC

Aristotle identified Thales as the first person to investigate the idea of a basic originating substance of matter, a distinction making him the founder of the school of natural philosophy. Thales was interested in almost everything: philosophy, history, science, mathematics, engineering, geography, and politics. He proposed theories to explain many of the events of nature and the cause of change. His questioning approach to the understanding of heavenly phenomena was the beginning of Greek astronomy. He founded the Milesian school of natural philosophy and developed the scientific method.

The extreme investment success of Harvard and Yale gives me both pleasure and pain. My pleasure comes from this demonstration that academic skill is often useful in worldly affairs. People like me who were attracted by academia, yet have gone into business, naturally respond to such worldly achievement much like the many modern scientists who relish the example of Thales of Miletus. This scientist of antiquity made a large profit by leasing most of the olive presses in his area just before the occurrence of a particularly bountiful harvest.

My pain comes from (1) foreseeing a lot of future adversity for other worthy institutions, driven by envy and salesmen into enthusiastic imitation of Harvard and Yale and (2) disapproval of the conduct of many of the salesmen likely to succeed in pushing the imitation. Something similar to what I fear happened near the end of the high-tech bubble. At that time envy of successful early-stage, high-tech venture-capital investors like Stanford, plus dubious sales methods of many venture capitalists, caused about $90 billion to rush into low-quality, imitative early-stage ventures that by now may have created as much as $45 billion in net losses for late-coming investors.

Moreover, Harvard and Yale may now need new displays of unconventional wisdom that are different from their last displays. It is quite counter-intuitive to decrease that part of one's activity that has recently worked best. But this is often a good idea. And so also with reducing one's perception of one's needs, instead of increasing risks in an attempt to satisfy perceived needs.

Talk Two was made in 1994, about twelve years before this addendum was written. And during that twelve years much useful thought and data collection has supported the idea that neither securities markets nor pari-mutuel betting systems at race tracks prevent some venturers from gaining highly satisfactory, way-above-average results through unusual skill. William Poundstone's book, *Fortune's Formula*, collects much of the modern evidence on this point in a highly entertaining way. Moreover, the book contains an account of the lollapalooza investment record of Claude Shannon, pioneer scientist in information theory, that makes Shannon's methods look much like those of Charlie Munger.

Worldly Wisdom Updated: Q and A with Charlie

How do you and Warren evaluate an acquisition candidate?

"We're light on financial yardsticks; we apply lots of subjective criteria: Can we trust management? Can it harm our reputation? What can go wrong? Do we understand the business? Does it require capital infusions to keep it going? What is the expected cash flow? We don't expect linear growth; cyclicality is fine with us as long as the price is appropriate."

"You don't have to be brilliant, only a little bit wiser than the other guys, on average, for a long, long time."

—Munger

What should a young person look for in a career?

"I have three basic rules. Meeting all three is nearly impossible, but you should try anyway:

- Don't sell anything you wouldn't buy yourself.
- Don't work for anyone you don't respect and admire.
- Work only with people you enjoy.

I have been incredibly fortunate in my life: with Warren I had all three."

What overall life advice do you have for young people?

"Spend each day trying to be a little wiser than you were when you woke up. Discharge your duties faithfully and well. Step-by-step you get ahead, but not necessarily in fast spurts. But you build discipline by preparing for fast spurts. Slug it out one inch at a time, day-by-day, and at the end of the day—if you live long enough—like most people, you will get out of life what you deserve.

Life and its various passages can be hard, brutally hard. The three things I have found helpful in coping with its challenges are:

- Have low expectations.
- Have a sense of humor.
- Surround yourself with the love of friends and family.

Above all, live with change and adapt to it. If the world didn't change, I'd still have a twelve handicap."

This talk was given in 1996 to the students of Professor William C. Lazier, who was the Nancy and Charles Munger professor of business at Stanford University Law School. Because this talk—published in *Outstanding Investor Digest* on December 29, 1997, and March 13, 1998—repeats many of the ideas and much of the language included in other talks, particularly "Practical Thought About Practical Thought?" your editor has abridged certain passages and added comments to maintain the logic and flow of the speech. Even with the abridgments, this talk includes many unique ideas as well as familiar ones expressed in novel ways.

A Lesson on Elementary, Worldly Wisdom, Revisited

Stanford Law School

April 19, 1996

Hoover Tower, Stanford University

What I'm going to try to do today is to extend the remarks I made two years ago at the U.S.C. Business School.... You were assigned a transcript of my U.S.C. talk. And there's nothing I said then that I wouldn't repeat today. But I want to amplify what I said then.

[It's] perfectly clear ... that if Warren Buffett had never learned anything new after graduating from the Columbia Business School, Berkshire would be a pale shadow of its present self. Warren would have gotten rich—because what he learned from Ben Graham at Columbia was enough to make anybody rich. But he wouldn't have the kind of enterprise Berkshire Hathaway is if he hadn't kept learning.

How do you get worldly wisdom? What system do you use to rise into the tiny top percentage of the world in terms of having sort of an elementary practical wisdom?

A Pioneer in Multidisciplinary Thinking:
Sir William Osler
(1849–1919)

Sir William Osler, a Canadian physician, has been called "The Father of Modern Medicine." An outspoken advocate of "pluralism," like Charlie, he constantly warned of the dangers of specialization: "The incessant concentration of thought upon one subject, however interesting, tethers a man's mind in a narrow field."

Osler studied and taught at McGill University in Montreal, Quebec, where he obtained his medical degree. Later he became the first Professor of Medicine at Johns Hopkins University in Baltimore. A physician who made himself into a literary man, Osler was a voracious reader, a prolific author, and a great collector of books (at his death, his personal library numbered 8,000 volumes). His most famous work is the *Principles and Practice of Medicine*, which appeared in many editions and translations for over fifty years. His brilliance in reducing complex ideas to simpler forms is evidenced in one of Charlie's favorite Osler quotes:

"The very first step towards success in any occupation is to become interested in it."

I've long believed that a certain system—which almost any intelligent person can learn—works way better than the systems that most people use. As I said at the U.S.C. Business School, what you need is a latticework of mental models in your head. And you hang your actual experience and your vicarious experience (that you get from reading and so forth) on this latticework of powerful models. And, with that system, things gradually get to fit together in a way that enhances cognition.

[Charlie discusses several of the specific mental models elaborated in other talks.]

Your assigned reading for today included the latest annual letters from Jack Welch and Warren Buffett relating to General Electric and Berkshire Hathaway, respectively. Jack Welch has a Ph.D. in engineering. And Warren plainly could have gotten a Ph.D. in any field he wanted to pursue. And both gentlemen are inveterate teachers.

Worldly wisdom is quite academic when you get right down to it. Look at what General Electric has achieved—and, for that matter, what Berkshire Hathaway has achieved.

Of course, Warren had a professor/mentor—Ben Graham—for whom he had a great affection. Graham was so academic that when he graduated from Columbia, three different academic departments invited him into their Ph.D. programs and asked him to start teaching immediately as part of the Ph.D. program: [those three departments being] literature, Greek and Latin classics, and mathematics.

Graham had a very academic personality. I knew him. He was a lot like Adam Smith—very preoccupied, very brilliant. He even looked like an academic. And he was a good one. And Graham, without ever really trying to maximize the gaining of wealth, died rich—even though he was always generous and spent thirty years teaching at Columbia and authored or coauthored the best textbooks in his field.

So I would argue that academia has a lot to teach about worldly wisdom and that the best academic values really work.

Of course, when I urge a multidisciplinary approach—that you've got to have the main models from a broad array of disciplines and you've got to use them all—I'm really asking you to ignore jurisdictional boundaries.

And the world isn't organized that way. It discourages the jumping of jurisdictional boundaries. Big bureaucratic businesses discourage it. And, of course, academia itself discourages it. All I can say there is that, in that respect, academia is horribly wrong and dysfunctional.

And some of the worst dysfunctions in businesses come from the fact that they balkanize reality into little individual departments with territoriality and turf protection and so forth. So if you want to be a good thinker, you must develop a mind that can jump the jurisdictional boundaries.

You don't have to know it all. Just take in the best big ideas from all these disciplines. And it's not that hard to do.

I might try and demonstrate that point by [using the analogy of] the card game of contract bridge. Suppose you want to be good at declarer play in contract bridge. Well, you know the contract—you know what you have to achieve. And you can count up the sure winners you have by laying down your high cards and your invincible trumps.

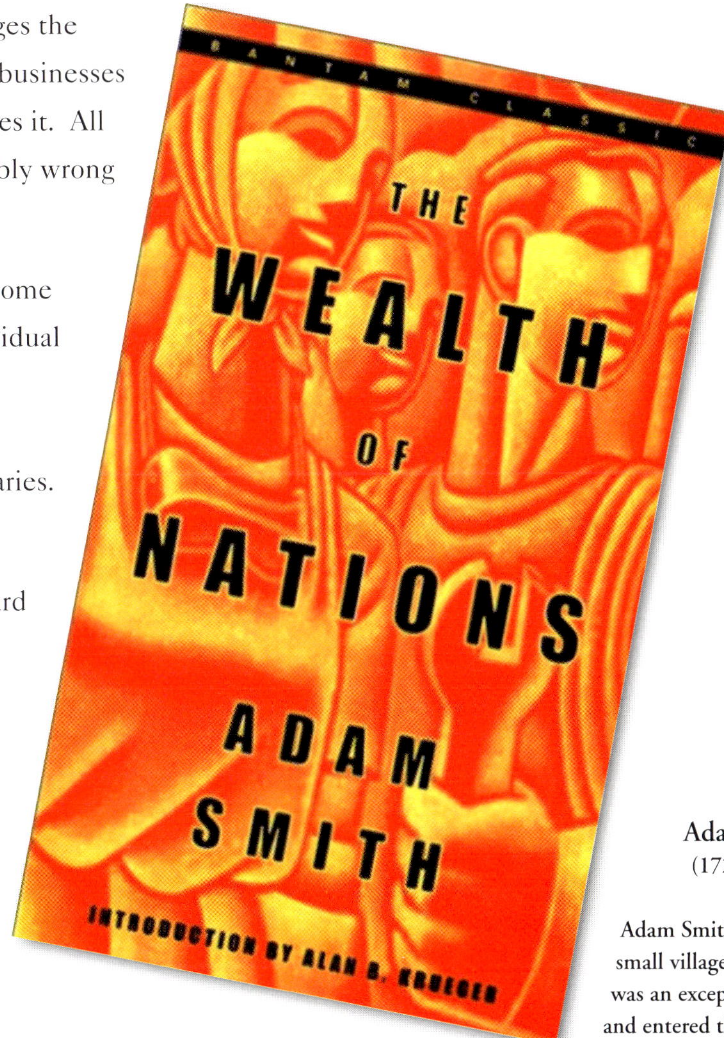

Adam Smith
(1723–1790)

Adam Smith, born in a small village in Scotland, was an exceptional student and entered the University of Glasgow at age fourteen. He later attended Oxford, returned home to Glasgow, and began an academic career in logic and moral philosophy. His seminal work, *The Wealth of Nations*, remains the fountainhead of contemporary economic thought. Smith's explanation of how rational self-interest drives a free-market economy greatly influenced thinkers and economists in his own day and in the generations that followed. His work forms the basis of classical economics.

But if you're a trick or two short, how are you going to get the other needed tricks? Well, there are only six or so different, standard methods. You've got long suit establishment. You've got finesses. You've got throw-in plays. You've got crossruffs. You've got squeezes. And you've got various ways of misleading the defense into making errors. So it's a very limited number of models.

But if you only know one or two of those models, then you're going to be a horse's patoot in declarer play.

Furthermore, these things interact. Therefore, you have to know how the models interact. Otherwise, you can't play the hand right.

Similarly, I've told you to think forward and backward. Well, great declarers in bridge think, "How can I take the necessary winners?" But they think it through backwards, [too. They also think,] "What could possibly go wrong that could cause me to have too many losers? And both methods of thinking are useful. So [to win in] the game of life, get the needed models into your head and think it through forward and backward. What works in bridge will work in life.

The *Little Red Hen* is a classic fable teaching the value of self-reliance in connection with important things. Charlie's advice on self-learning is reminiscent of Mark Twain's classic line, "I have never let my schooling interfere with my education."

That contract bridge is so out of vogue in your generation is a tragedy. China is way smarter than we are about bridge. They're teaching bridge in grade school now. And God knows the Chinese do well enough when introduced to capitalist civilization. If we compete with a bunch of people that really know how to play bridge when our people don't, it'll be just one more disadvantage we don't need.

Since your academic structure, by and large, doesn't encourage minds jumping jurisdictional boundaries, you're at a disadvantage because, in that one sense, even though academia's very useful to you, you've been mistaught.

My solution for you is one that I got at a very early age from the nursery: the story of the Little Red Hen. The punch line, of course, is, "'Then I'll do it myself,' said the Little Red Hen."

"'Then I'll do it myself,' said the Little Red Hen."

So if your professors won't give you an appropriate multidisciplinary approach—if each wants to overuse his own models and underuse the important models in other disciplines—you can correct that folly yourself. Just because he's a horse's patoot, you don't have to be one, too. You can reach out and grasp the model that better solves the overall problem. All you have to do is know it and develop the right mental habits.

And it's kind of fun to sit there and outthink people who are way smarter than you are because you've trained yourself to be more objective and multidisciplinary....

Furthermore, there's a lot of money in it—as I can testify from my own personal experience.

Hershey Food Corporation

Raised in rural central Pennsylvania and possessed of little formal education, Milton S. Hershey (1857–1945) became one of America's wealthiest individuals. He started his own candy business, Lancaster Caramel Company, in 1876 and failed after only six years. Undaunted, he tried again and had great success. In 1893, he learned the art of chocolate making and started the Hershey Chocolate Company. As the company expanded into other food products, Hershey began to build the Pennsylvania town that bears his name. Hershey's utopian ideas and principles continue to influence the company and the town.

[Charlie begins the Coca-Cola business case detailed in Talk Four, "Practical Thought About Practical Thought," and discusses the importance of flavor.]

One of my favorite business stories comes from Hershey. They get their flavor because they make their cocoa butter in old stone grinders that they started with in the 1800s in Pennsylvania. And a little bit of the husk of the cocoa bean winds up in the chocolate. Therefore, they get that odd flavor that people like in Hershey's chocolate.

Hershey knew enough when they wanted to expand into Canada to know they shouldn't change their winning flavor.

Hershey knew enough when they wanted to expand into Canada to know they shouldn't change their winning flavor. Therefore, they copied their stone grinders. Well, it took them five years to duplicate their own flavor. As you can see, flavors can be quite tricky.

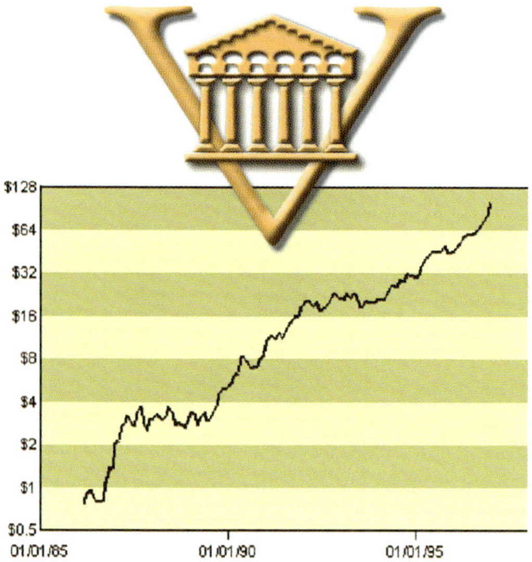

Value Line

Value Line's mission is "to help investors get the most accurate and independently created research information available, in any format they choose, and teach them how to use it to meet their financial objectives." In operation since 1931, Value Line has a solid reputation for reliability, objectivity, independence, and accuracy. Best known for the *Value Line Investment Survey*, the company publishes dozens of print and electronic research products.

Even today, there's a company called International Flavors and Fragrances. It's the only company I know that does something on which you can't get a copyright or a patent, but which nevertheless receives a permanent royalty. They manage to do that by helping companies develop flavors and aromas in their trademarked products—like shaving cream. The slight aroma of shaving cream is very important to consumption. So all of this stuff is terribly important.

[Continuing the Coca-Cola case study, Charlie explains how our understanding of graphic depictions of mathematical ideas are rooted in biology.]

My friend, Dr. Nat Myhrvold, who's the chief technology officer at Microsoft, is bothered by this. He's a Ph.D. physicist and knows a lot of math. And it disturbs him that biology could create a neural apparatus that could do automatic differential equations at fast speed—and, yet, everywhere he looks, people are total klutzes at dealing with ordinary probabilities and ordinary numbers.

By the way, I think Myhrvold's wrong to be amazed by that. The so-called fitness landscape of our ancestors forced them to know how to throw spears, run around, turn corners, and what have you long before they had to think correctly like Myhrvold. So I don't think he should be so surprised. However, the difference is so extreme that I can understand how he finds it incongruous.

Mankind invented a system to cope with the fact that we are so intrinsically lousy at manipulating numbers. It's called the graph.

At any rate, mankind invented a system to cope with the fact that we are so intrinsically lousy at manipulating numbers. It's called the graph. Oddly enough, it came out of the Middle Ages. And it's the only intellectual invention of the monks during the Middle Ages I know of that's worth a damn. The graph puts numbers in a form that looks like motion. So it's using some of this primitive neural stuff in your system in a way that helps you understand it. So the Value Line graphs are very useful.

The graph I've distributed is on log paper—which is based on the natural table of logarithms. And that's based on the elementary mathematics of compound interest—which is one of the most important models there is on earth. So there's a reason why that graph is in that form.

And if you draw a straight line through data points on a graph on log paper, it will tell you the rate at which compound interest is working for you. So these graphs are marvelously useful....

I don't use Value Line's predictions because our system works better for us than theirs—in fact, a lot better. But I can't imagine not having their graphs and their data. It's a marvelous, marvelous product....

[Charlie discusses the importance of trademarks to Coca-Cola's success and carries it over to a discussion of food products and Carnation.]

Carnation Company

In 1899, grocer E. A. Stuart founded the Pacific Coast Condensed Milk Company in the state of Washington based on the relatively new process of evaporation. Using a local tobacconist's store name, Carnation, he had a brand for his new milk product. Through attention to processes and clever marketing, Carnation became associated with its "Contented Cows" and high-quality milk products. In 1985, the company was acquired by Nestle.

Now, when Carnation tried to make a deal for its trademark, there was this one guy who sold Carnation Fish. So help me God, that was his trade name. Don't ask me why. And every time they'd say, "We'll pay you $250,000," he'd say, "I want $400,000." And, then, four years later, they'd say, "We'll give you $1 million," and he'd say, "I want $2 million." And they just kept doing that all the way through. And they never did buy the trademark—at least, they hadn't bought it the last time I looked.

In the end, Carnation came to him sheepfacedly and said, "We'd like to put our quality control inspectors into your fish plants to make sure that your fish are perfect; and we'll pay all the costs"—which he quickly and smirkily allowed. So he got free quality control in his fish plants—courtesy of the Carnation Company.

This history shows the enormous incentive you create if you give a guy a trademark [he can protect]. And this incentive is very useful to the wider civilization. As you see, Carnation got so that it was protecting products that it didn't even own.

That sort of outcome is very, very desirable [for society]. So there are some very fundamental microeconomic reasons why even communist countries should protect trademarks. They don't all do it, but there are very powerful reasons why they should. And, by and large, averaged out around the world, trademark protection's been pretty good.

[Charlie applies various mental models to Coca-Cola.]

However, if you don't have the basic models and the basic mental methods for dealing with the models, then all you can do is to sit there twiddling your thumbs as you look at the Value Line graph. But you don't have to twiddle your thumbs. You've got to learn one hundred models and a few mental tricks and keep doing it all of your life. It's not that hard.

And the beauty of it is that most people won't do it—partly because they've been miseducated. And I'm here trying to help you avoid some of the perils that might otherwise result from that miseducation.

OK. We've been through some of the general ideas in the search for worldly wisdom. And now I want to turn to something even more extreme and peculiar than the talk I've already given you. Of all the models that people ought to have in useful form and don't, perhaps the most important lie in the area of psychology....

I recently had an instructive experience: I just returned from Hong Kong. I have a pal there who's a headmaster of one of the leading schools. He gave me this book called *The Language Instinct*, written by Steven Pinker. Well, Pinker is a semanticist professor who rose in the shadow of Noam Chomsky—Linguistics Institute Professor at M.I.T.—who is probably the greatest semanticist who ever lived.

Steven Pinker
(b. 1954)

Born in Montreal, Steven Pinker earned a degree in experimental psychology at McGill University and then moved on to Harvard for his doctorate. He has taught at Harvard and MIT at various times and is currently the Johnstone Family Professor in the Department of Psychology at Harvard. Pinker is interested in language and the mind, including the field of visual cognition. That field encompasses the ability to imagine shapes and recognize faces and objects. He specializes in language development in children and has written many important papers and books on this and other topics.

And Pinker says that human language ability is not just learned—it's deeply buried, to a considerable extent, in the genome. It's not in the genome of the other animals, including the chimpanzee, to any really useful extent. It's a gift that came to humans. And Pinker proves his point pretty well.

Of course, Chomsky's already proven it. You have to be pretty ignorant not to realize that a good deal of language ability is right there in the human genome. And even though you have to work like hell to improve it through education, you start with a big leg up in your genes.

Pinker can't understand why Chomsky—who, again, is such a genius—takes the position that the jury's still out about why this ability is in the human genome. Pinker, in effect, says: "Like hell, the jury is still out! The language instinct got into humans in exactly the same way that everything else got there—through Darwinian natural selection."

"The language instinct got into humans in exactly the same way that everything else got there—through Darwinian natural selection."

Young Charles Darwin was the unpaid "official naturalist" aboard the *H.M.S. Beagle* during its 1831–1836 around-the-world surveying voyage. The amazing differentiation of species among the Galapagos Islands off South America inspired Darwin to remark, "This appears to be one of those admirable provisions of Infinite Wisdom by which each created thing is adapted to the place for which it was intended."

Well, the junior professor is clearly right—and Chomsky's hesitation is a little daft.

But if the junior professor and I are right, how has a genius like Chomsky made an obvious misjudgment? The answer's quite clear to me—Chomsky is passionately ideological. He is an extreme egalitarian leftist who happens to be a genius. And he's so smart that he realized that if he concedes this particular Darwinian point, the implications threaten his leftist ideology. So he naturally has his conclusion affected by his ideological bias.

And that gets into another lesson in worldly wisdom: If ideology can screw up the head of Chomsky, imagine what it does to people like you and me.

Heavy ideology is one of the most extreme distorters of human cognition. Look at these Islamic fundamentalists who just gunned down a bunch of Greek tourists shouting, "God's work!"

"I wear the chains I forged in life," quoth Jacob Marley's ghost in Dickens' *A Christmas Carol.*

Ideology does some strange things and distorts cognition terribly. If you get a lot of heavy ideology young—and then you start expressing it—you are really locking your brain into a very unfortunate pattern. And you are going to distort your general cognition.

If you get a lot of heavy ideology young—and then you start expressing it—you are really locking your brain into a very unfortunate pattern.

There's a very interesting history if you take Warren Buffett as an example of worldly wisdom: Warren adored his father—who was a wonderful man. But Warren's father was a very heavy ideologue (right wing, it happened to be), who hung around with other very heavy ideologues (right wing, naturally).

Warren observed this as a kid. And he decided that ideology was dangerous—and that he was going to stay a long way away from it. And he has throughout his whole life. That has enormously helped the accuracy of his cognition.

I learned the same lesson in a different way. My father hated ideology. Therefore, all I had to do was imitate my father and, thereby, stay on what I regard as the right path. People like Dornan on the right or Nader on the left have obviously gone a little daft. They're extreme examples of what ideology will do to you—particularly violently expressed ideology. Since it pounds ideas in better than it convinces out, it's a very dangerous thing to do.

Therefore, in a system of multiple models across multiple disciplines, I should add as an extra rule that you should be very wary of heavy ideology.

You can have heavy ideology in favor of accuracy, diligence, and objectivity. But a heavy ideology that makes you absolutely sure that the minimum wage should be raised or that it shouldn't—and it's kind of a holy construct where you know you're right—makes you a bit nuts.

This is a very complicated system. And life is one damn relatedness after another. It's all right to think that, on balance, you suspect that civilization is better if it lowers the minimum wage or raises it. Either position is OK. But being totally sure on issues like that with a strong, violent ideology, in my opinion, turns you into a lousy thinker. So beware of ideology-based mental misfunctions.

[Charlie laments how poorly the field of psychology deals with incentive-caused bias.]

Another reason that I mentioned Pinker, the semanticist who wrote the book that I told you about earlier, is that at the end of his book, he says (roughly), "I've read the psychology textbooks. And they're daft." He says, "This whole subject is misorganized and mistaught."

Well, I have far less in the way of qualifications than Pinker. In fact, I've never taken a single course in psychology. However, I've come to exactly the same conclusion—that the psychology texts, while they are wonderful in part, are also significantly daft.

In fact, just take simple psychological denial. About three centuries before the birth of Christ, Demosthenes said, "What a man wishes, that also will he believe." Well, Demosthenes was right.

About three centuries before the birth of Christ, Demosthenes said, "What a man wishes, that also will he believe."

Michael Faraday
(1791–1867)

Famous for his investigations of physics, chemistry, and electricity, Michael Faraday's wisdom includes:

> "Nothing is too wonderful to be true."
>
> "Work. Finish. Publish." (his advice to the young William Crookes, later a famous chemist and physicist in his own right)
>
> "The five essential entrepreneurial skills for success are concentration, discrimination, organization, innovation, and communication."
>
> "Why, sir, there is every possibility that you will soon be able to tax it!" (to Prime Minister William Gladstone, on the usefulness of electricity)

I had a family acquaintance whose much-loved son—who was brilliant and a star football player—flew off over the ocean and never came back. Well, his mother thought he was still alive. The mind will sometimes flip so that the wish becomes the belief. It will do so at various levels. Individuals vary in how much psychological denial they get. But miscognition from denial overwhelmingly pervades the reality that you're going to have to deal with. And yet, you won't find an adequate treatment of simple psychological denial in psychology texts.

So you can't learn psychology the way your professors teach it. You've got to learn everything they teach. But you've got to learn a lot more that they don't teach—because they don't handle their own subject correctly.

Psychology to me, as currently organized, is like electromagnetism after Faraday, but before Maxwell—a lot has been discovered, but no one mind has put it all together in proper form. And it should be done because it wouldn't be that hard to do—and it's enormously important.

Just open a psychology text, turn to the index, and look up envy. Well, envy made it into one or two or three of the Ten Commandments. Moses knew all about envy. The old Jews, when they were herding sheep, knew all about envy. It's just that psychology professors don't know about envy.

Books that thick are teaching a psychology course without envy?! And with no simple psychological denial?! And no incentive-caused bias?!

And psychological texts don't deal adequately with combinations of factors. I told you earlier to be aware of the lollapalooza effect when two or three or more forces are operating in the same direction.

Well, the single most publicized psychology experiment ever done is the Milgram experiment—where they asked people to apply what they had every reason to believe was heavy electrical torture on innocent fellow human beings. And they manipulated most of these decent volunteers into doing the torture.

So you can't learn psychology the way your professors teach it. You've got to learn everything they teach. But you've got to learn a lot more that they don't teach—because they don't handle their own subject correctly.

Milgram performed the experiment right after Hitler had gotten a bunch of believing Lutherans, Catholics, and so forth to perform unholy acts they should have known were wrong. He was trying to find out how much authority could be used to manipulate high-grade people into doing things that were clearly and grossly wrong.

And he got a very dramatic effect. He managed to get high-grade people to do many awful things.

But for years, it was in the psychology books as a demonstration of authority—how authority could be used to persuade people to do awful things.

Of course, that's mere first-conclusion bias. That's not the complete and correct explanation. Authority is part of it. However, there were also quite a few other

Stanley Milgram
Experiments on Authority

Stanley Milgram, born in 1933 in New York, grew up during World War II when Nazi atrocities became well known to the world. He earned a political science degree from Queens College and went on to Harvard for a Ph.D. in social relations. He took a faculty position at Yale, where he conducted a classic experiment that pitted the subject's moral beliefs against the demands of authority.

His experiment found that sixty-five percent of his subjects, ordinary residents of New Haven, were willing to give apparently harmful electric shocks to a pitifully protesting victim, simply because a scientific authority commanded them to, despite the fact that the victim did nothing to deserve punishment. Milgram's results have been used as partial explanation for the German atrocities of World War II.

psychological principles, all operating in the same direction, that achieved that lollapalooza effect precisely because they acted in combination toward the same end.

People have gradually figured that out. And if you read the recent psychology texts at a place like Stanford, you'll see that they've now managed to get it about two-thirds right. However, here's the main experiment in all of psychology. And even at Stanford, they still leave out some of the important causes of Milgram's results.

How can smart people be so wrong? Well, the answer is that they don't do what I'm telling you to do—which is to take all the main models from psychology and use them as a checklist in reviewing outcomes in complex systems.

No pilot takes off without going through his checklist: A, B, C, D.... And no bridge player who needs two extra tricks plays a hand without going down his checklist and figuring out how to do it.

But these psychology professors think they're so smart that they don't need a checklist. But they aren't that smart. Almost nobody is. Or, maybe, nobody is.

No pilot takes off without going through his checklist: A, B, C, D.... But these psychology professors think they're so smart that they don't need a checklist.

If they used a checklist, they'd realize the Milgram experiment harnesses six psychological principles, at least—not three. All they'd have to do is to go down the checklist to see the ones that they missed.

Similarly, without this system of getting the main models and using them together in a multimodular way, you'll screw up time after time after time, too.

Portrait of Ivan Pavlov, Mikhail Nesterov, 1935, The Tretyakov Gallery, Moscow

One reason psychology professors so screw up denial is that it's hard to do demonstrative experiments without conduct forbidden by ethics. To demonstrate how misery creates mental disfunction in people, think of what you'd have to do to your fellow human beings. And you'd have to do it without telling them about the injury to come. So, clearly, there are ethical reasons why it's practically impossible to do the experiments necessary to best lay out the ways human misery creates human mental misfunction.

Most professors solve this problem, in effect, by assuming, "If I can't demonstrate it with my experiments, then it doesn't exist." However, obviously, that's asinine. If something is very important but can't be perfectly and precisely demonstrated because of ethical constraints, you can't just treat it like it doesn't exist. You have to do the best you can with it—with such evidence as is available.

Pavlov himself spent the last ten years of his life torturing dogs. And he published. Thus, we have a vast amount of data about misery-caused mental misfunction in dogs—and its correction. Yet, it's in no introductory psychology book that you'll ever see.

I don't know whether they don't like the fact that Pavlov tortured dogs or whether B. F. Skinner, by overclaiming when he lapsed into his literary mode, made the drawing of implications from animal behavior into human behavior unpopular. However, for some crazy reason or other, the psychology books are grossly inadequate in dealing with misery-caused mental misfunction.

You may say, "What difference does all this psychological ignorance make?" Well, if I'm right, you need these models that are blanked out by this ignorance. And, furthermore, you need them in a form whereby, if there are twenty constructs, you have all twenty. In other words, you shouldn't be operating with ten. And you need to use them as a checklist. So you have to go back and put in your own head what I'd call the psychology of misjudgment in a form whereby you have all of the important models and you can use them.

And you especially need them when four or five forces from these models come together to operate in the same direction. In such cases, you often get lollapalooza effects—which can make you rich or they can kill you. So it's essential that you beware of lollapalooza effects.

There's only one right way to do it: You have to get the main doctrines together and use them as a checklist. And, to repeat for emphasis, you have to pay special attention to combinatorial effects that create lollapalooza consequences.

[Charlie discusses the lack of multidisciplinary teaching in the professions, especially how the field of psychology is virtually ignored in academia.]

The game of persuasion, the disreputable sort.

Elmer Gantry, a novel by Sinclair Lewis (1927) and later a film starring Burt Lancaster (1960), is a satiric depiction of a loud, overbearing huckster. Later he becomes a successful but greedy, shallow, and philandering minister to a large congregation.

You can also learn when you're playing the game of persuasion—for a reputable reason [I hope]—to combine these forces in a way that makes you more effective.

Let me give you an example of that—of wise psychology of yore. In Captain Cook's day, he took these long voyages. At the time, scurvy was the dread of the long voyage. And in scurvy, your living gums putrefy in your mouth—after which the disease gets unpleasant and kills you.

And being on a primitive sailing ship with a bunch of dying sailors is a very awkward business. So everybody was terribly interested in scurvy, but they didn't know about vitamin C. Well, Captain Cook, being a smart man with a multiple-model kind of approach, noticed that Dutch ships had less scurvy than English ships on long voyages. So he said, "What are the Dutch doing that's different?"

And he noticed they had all these barrels of sauerkraut. So he thought, "I'm going on these long voyages. And it's very dangerous. Sauerkraut may help." So he laid in all this sauerkraut, which, incidentally, happens to contain a trace of vitamin C.

But English sailors were a tough, cranky, and dangerous bunch in that day. They hated "krauts." And they were used to their standard food and booze. So how do you get such English sailors to eat sauerkraut?

Well, Cook didn't want to tell 'em that he was doing it in the hope it would prevent scurvy—because they might mutiny and take over the ship if they thought that he was taking them on a voyage so long that scurvy was likely.

So here's what he did: Officers ate one place where the men could observe them. And for a long time, he served sauerkraut to the officers, but not to the men. And, then, finally, Captain Cook said, "Well, the men can have it one day a week."

In due course, he had the whole crew eating sauerkraut. I regard that as a very constructive use of elementary psychology. It may have saved God knows how many lives and caused God knows how much achievement. However, if you don't know the right techniques, you can't use them.

[Charlie discusses psychological effects in play in marketing of consumer items, such as Coca-Cola, Procter & Gamble products, Tupperware, etc.]

Captain James Cook
(1728–1779)

Born in Marton, England, James Cook developed an early fascination for the sea and taught himself cartography. He served in the Royal Navy, participating in the siege of Quebec City and showing a talent for surveying and cartography. He mapped much of the entrance to the Saint Lawrence River during the siege. Later, he mapped the coast of Newfoundland, which brought him to the attention of the Royal Society, sponsor of many of his great voyages. In addition to having first-class cartographic skills, Cook developed excellent seamanship and displayed great courage in exploring dangerous locations. His voyages are chronicled in books that were extremely popular in his day and remain so today.

Serpico
(1973)

Serpico was a popular film directed by Sidney Lumet, based on the book by journalist Peter Maas of a "true story." The plot concerns undercover police officer Frank Serpico who does his best arresting criminals of all types, but especially drug dealers, despite working in a corrupt police department. Serpico refuses to accept bribes and becomes sufficiently appalled at his shady colleagues that he testifies against them, thus placing his life in jeopardy. Set in the early 1970s, the film makes several references to "hippie" culture and thus appears somewhat dated to current viewers. Al Pacino appeared in the title role and earned an Academy Award nomination for his acting. The film was also nominated for a screenwriting Oscar.

Worldly wisdom is mostly very, very simple. And what I'm urging on you is not that hard to do if you have the will to plow through and do it. And the rewards are awesome—absolutely awesome.

But maybe you aren't interested in awesome rewards or avoiding a lot of misery or being more able to serve everything you love in life. And, if that's your attitude, then don't pay attention to what I've been trying to tell you—because you're already on the right track.

It can't be emphasized too much that issues of morality are deeply entwined with worldly wisdom considerations involving psychology. For example, take the issue of stealing. A very significant fraction of the people in the world will steal if (A) it's very easy to do and (B) there's practically no chance of being caught.

And once they start stealing, the consistency principle—which is a big part of human psychology—will soon combine with operant conditioning to make stealing habitual. So if you run a business where it's easy to steal because of your methods, you're working a great moral injury on the people who work for you.

It can't be emphasized too much that issues of morality are deeply entwined with worldly wisdom considerations involving psychology.

Again, that's obvious. It's very, very important to create human systems that are hard to cheat. Otherwise, you're ruining your civilization because these big incentives will create incentive-caused bias and people will rationalize that bad behavior is OK.

Then, if somebody else does it, now you've got at least two psychological principles: incentive-caused bias plus social proof. Not only that, but you get Serpico effects: If enough people are profiting in a general social climate of doing wrong, then they'll turn on you and become dangerous enemies if you try and blow the whistle.

It's very dangerous to ignore these principles and let slop creep in. Powerful psychological forces are at work for evil.

How does this relate to the law business? Well, people graduate from places like Stanford Law School and go into the legislatures of our nation and, with the best of motives, pass laws that are easily used by people to cheat. Well, there could hardly be a worse thing you could do.

Let's say you have a desire to do public service. As a natural part of your planning, you think in reverse and ask, "What can I do to ruin our civilization?" That's easy. If what you want to do is to ruin your civilization, just go to the legislature and pass laws that create systems wherein people can easily cheat. It will work perfectly.

Take the workers' compensation system in California. Stress is real. And its misery can be real. So you want to compensate people for their stress in the workplace. It seems like a noble thing to do.

But the trouble with such a compensation practice is that it's practically impossible to delete huge cheating. And once you reward cheating, you get crooked lawyers, crooked doctors, crooked unions, etc., participating in referral schemes. You get a total miasma of disastrous behavior. And the behavior makes all the people doing it worse as they do it. So you were trying to help your civilization. But what you did was create enormous damage, net.

So it's much better to let some things go uncompensated—to let life be hard—than to create systems that are easy to cheat.

Let me give you an example: I have a friend who made an industrial product at a plant in Texas not far from the border. He was in a low-margin, tough business. He got massive fraud in the workers' compensation system—to the point that his premiums reached double-digit percentages of payroll. And it was not that dangerous to produce his product. It's not like he was a demolition contractor or something.

When the Incentives are Wrong: What a Pain!

Employee fraud in medical disability cases is often an outgrowth of hard-to-diagnose complaints such as ever-popular "back pain." But disability fraud extends as well to scams perpetrated by medical practitioners, including phantom treatments, double billing, unnecessary care, and unneeded tests. Charlie's point is that the system as designed invites cheating and that human beings are psychologically predisposed to commit fraud when available incentives overwhelm structural checks and balances. As he puts it, "If you want to change behaviors, you have to change motivations."

So he pleaded with the union, "You've got to stop this. There's not enough money in making this product to cover all of this fraud."

But, by then, everyone's used to it. "It's extra income. It's extra money. Everybody does it. It can't be that wrong. Eminent lawyers, eminent doctors, eminent chiropractors—if there are any such things—are cheating."

The importance of honesty was amplified by the Mormon Apostle Mark E. Petersen when he said:

"Honesty is a principle of salvation in the kingdom of God. Just as no man or woman can be saved without baptism, so no one can be saved without honesty."

And no one could tell them, "You can't do it anymore." Incidentally, that's Pavlovian mere association, too. When people get bad news, they hate the messenger. Therefore, it was very hard for the union representative to tell all of these people that the easy money was about to stop. That is not the way to advance as a union representative.

So my friend closed his plant and moved the work to Utah among a community of believing Mormons.

So my friend closed his plant and moved the work to Utah among a community of believing Mormons. Well, the Mormons aren't into workers' compensation fraud—at least they aren't in my friend's plant. And guess what his workers' compensation expense is today? It's two percent of payroll [—down from double-digits.]

This sort of tragedy is caused by letting the slop run. You must stop slop early. It's very hard to stop slop and moral failure if you let it run for a while.

[Charlie describes his notion of "deprival super-reaction syndrome" as it relates to gambling and the New Coke debacle of the mid-1980s.]

Of course, as I said before, there is one big consideration that needs huge and special attention as part of any use of techniques deliberately harnessing elementary psychological forces: And that is that once you know how to do it, there are real moral limits regarding how much you should do it. Not all of what you know how to do should you use to manipulate people.

Also, if you're willing to transcend the moral limits and the person you're trying to manipulate realizes what you're doing because he also understands the psychology, he'll hate you. There is wonderfully persuasive evidence of this effect taken from labor relations—some in Israel. So not only are there moral objections, but there are also practical objections—big ones in some cases....

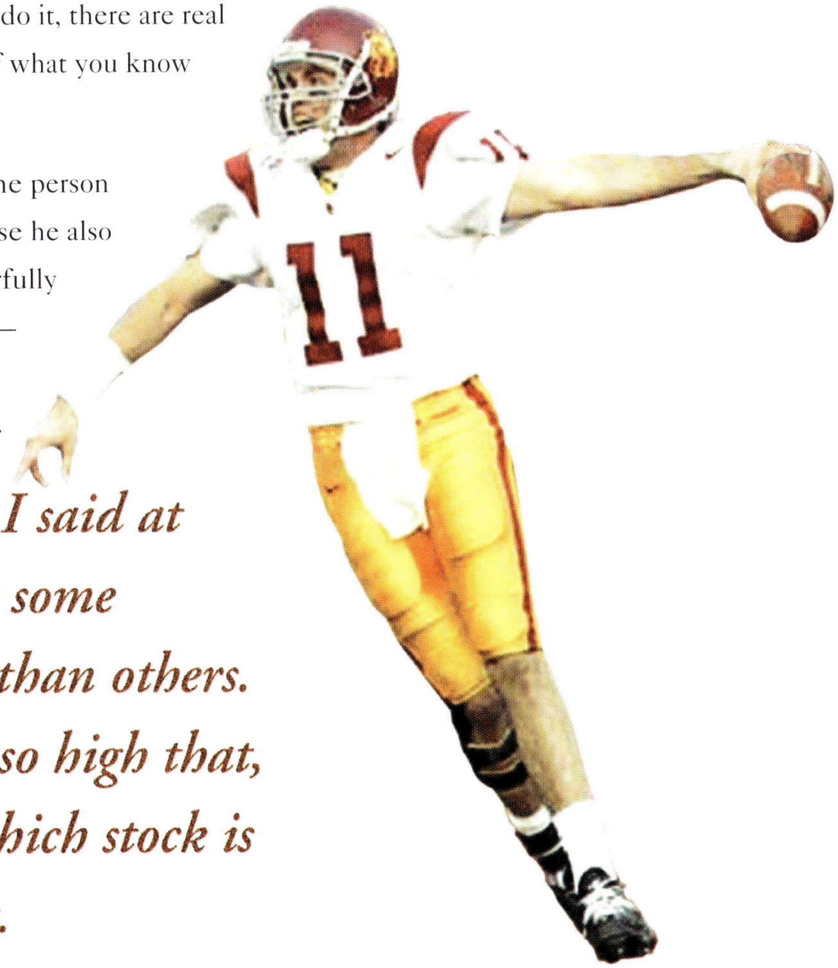

What makes investment hard, as I said at U.S.C., is that it's easy to see that some companies have better businesses than others. But the price of the stock goes up so high that, all of a sudden, the question of which stock is the best to buy gets quite difficult.

The University of Southern California, boasting recent back-to-back national football championships, was founded in 1880 and is the oldest private research university in the West. There are 16,500 undergraduate and 15,500 graduate and professional students attending the university.

Q: How do you incorporate psychology in your investment decisions? I think it would be more than just picking products that will appeal to everybody like Coke. After all, there are a lot of smart people out there who obviously think just the way that you showed us today. So are you looking for failure in the thinking of other investors when you go about picking successful companies?

What makes investment hard, as I said at U.S.C., is that it's easy to see that some companies have better businesses than others. But the price of the stock goes up so high that, all of a sudden, the question of which stock is the best to buy gets quite difficult.

We've never eliminated the difficulty of that problem. And ninety-eight percent of the time, our attitude toward the market is ... [that] we're agnostics. We don't know. Is GM valued properly vis-à-vis Ford? We don't know.

We're always looking for something where we think we have an insight which gives us a big statistical advantage. And sometimes it comes from psychology, but often it comes from something else. And we only find a few—maybe one or two a year. We have no system for having automatic good judgment on all investment decisions that can be made. Ours is a totally different system.

We just look for no-brainer decisions. As Buffett and I say over and over again, we don't leap seven-foot fences. Instead, we look for one-foot fences with big rewards on the other side. So we've succeeded by making the world easy for ourselves, not by solving hard problems.

Q: Based on statistical analysis and insight?

Well, certainly when we do make a decision, we think that we have an insight advantage. And it's true that some of the insight is statistical in nature. However, again, we find only a few of those.

We just look for no-brainer decisions. As Buffett and I say over and over again, we don't leap seven-foot fences.

It doesn't help us merely for favorable odds to exist. They have to be in a place where we can recognize them. So it takes a mispriced opportunity that we're smart enough to recognize. And that combination doesn't occur often.

But it doesn't have to. If you wait for the big opportunity and have the courage and vigor to grasp it firmly when it arrives, how many do you need? For example, take the top ten business investments Berkshire Hathaway's ever made. We would be very rich if we'd never done anything else—in two lifetimes.

So, once again, we don't have any system for giving you perfect investment judgment on all subjects at all times. That would be ridiculous. I'm just trying to give you a method you can use to sift reality to obtain an occasional opportunity for rational reaction.

If you take that method into something as competitive as common stock picking, you're competing with many brilliant people. So, even with our method, we only get a few opportunities. Fortunately, that happens to be enough.

Q: Have you been successful in creating an atmosphere where people below you can do the same things you're talking about doing yourself? For example, you talked about the tendency towards commitment and consistency....

Mostly about the terrible mistakes it causes you to make.

Q: How have you created an atmosphere comfortable [enough] for people to abandon that tendency and admit that they've made a mistake?

For example, someone here earlier this year from Intel talked about problems that occurred with their Pentium chip. One of the most difficult things for them to do was to realize they'd been going about it the wrong way and turn course. And it's very difficult to do that in a complex structure. How do you foster that?

Intel and its ilk create a coherent culture where teams solve difficult problems on the cutting edge of science. That's radically different from Berkshire Hathaway. Berkshire is a holding company. We've decentralized all the power except for natural headquarters-type capital allocation.

By and large, we've chosen people we admire enormously to have the power beneath us. It's easy for us to get along with them on average because we love and admire them. And they create the culture for whatever invention and reality recognition is going on in their businesses. And included in that reality recognition is the recognition that previous conclusions were incorrect.

But we're a totally different kind of company. It's not at all clear to me that Warren or I would be that good at doing what Andy Grove does. We don't have

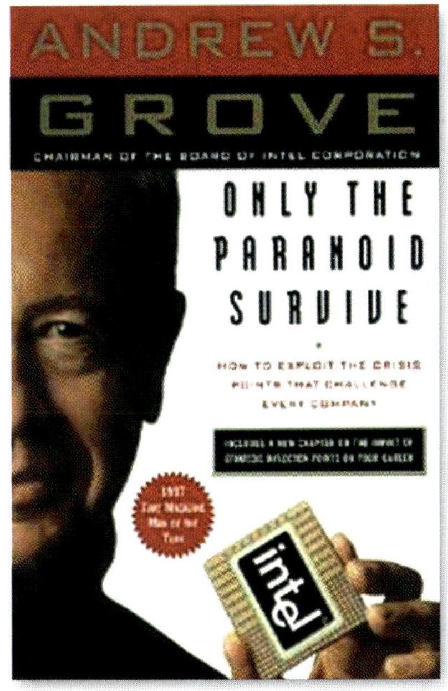

Andy Grove
(b. 1936)

Born András Grós in Budapest, Hungary, Grove earned a bachelor's degree in chemical engineering from the City College of New York and a Ph.D. from the University of California, Berkeley. He worked at Fairchild Semiconductor before becoming the fourth employee at the nascent Intel Corporation. He became Intel's president in 1979, its CEO in 1987, and its chairman and CEO in 1997. Author of several academic and mass-trade books, his 1996 work, *Only the Paranoid Survive*, was hugely popular. Grove continues to work at Intel as a senior advisor. This book is on Charlie's recommended book list.

special competence in that field. We are fairly good at relating to brilliant people we love. But we have defects. For example, some regard me as absent-minded and opinionated. I might be a mess at Intel.

However, both Warren and I are very good at changing our prior conclusions. We work at developing that facility because, without it, disaster often comes.

Q: Would you talk a little bit about your seeming predilection away from investing in high technology stocks—on your own part and the part of Berkshire Hathaway. One of the things I've found eye-opening and a little surprising is how the difficulties of running a low-tech business and those of running a high-tech business aren't all that different.

They're all hard. But why should it be easy to get rich? In a competitive world, shouldn't it be impossible for there to be an easy way for everybody to get rich? Of course, they're all hard.

And, yes—a low-tech business can be plenty hard. Just try to open a restaurant and make it succeed.

The reason we're not in high-tech businesses is that we have a special lack of aptitude in that area. And, yes—a low-tech business can be plenty hard. Just try to open a restaurant and make it succeed.

Q: You seem to be suggesting that there's special aptitude required in high-tech businesses—that they're harder. But aren't they equally difficult?

The advantage of low-tech stuff for us is that we think we understand it fairly well. The other stuff we don't. And we'd rather deal with what we understand.

Why should we want to play a competitive game in a field where we have no advantage—maybe a disadvantage—instead of in a field where we have a clear advantage?

Catching Up with George McGovern

Q: Someone mentioned to me that you tried to open up a bed-and-breakfast, and you ran into a lot of rules and regulations that made being a small businessman difficult.

A: I had a 140-room hotel in Stamford, Connecticut, for about three years, and it just didn't work. You know, the hotel business may be the most difficult place in the world to make a living unless you happen to own the Waldorf-Astoria. It was not a success.

I got sued a couple times by people who had accidents, one out in the parking lot of the hotel and one leaving the restaurant. I saw all the difficulties—record-keeping, keeping track of the tax applications, paying the help. It gave me a new appreciation for the problems of small businesses.

Saturday, 24 July 2004, Interview 2004 © by Bill Steigerwald and the *Pittsburgh Tribune-Review*

Each of you will have to figure out where your talents lie. And you'll have to use your advantages. But if you try to succeed in what you're worst at, you're going to have a very lousy career. I can almost guarantee it. To do otherwise, you'd have to buy a winning lottery ticket or get very lucky somewhere else.

Q: Warren Buffett has said that the investment Berkshire made in an airline was a good example of what not to do. What chain of thinking led to that wrong decision?

US Airways, like United Airlines and several other, smaller carriers, recently joined a long list of airlines that have sought bankruptcy protection. Other notables on the list (historically) include Continental, Eastern, and Pan Am.

We were not buying stock in USAir on the theory that the common shareholders were certain to prosper—because the history of the airline business in terms of taking care of shareholders has been terrible. It was a preferred stock with a mandatory redemption. In effect, we were loaning money to USAir, and we had this equity kicker.

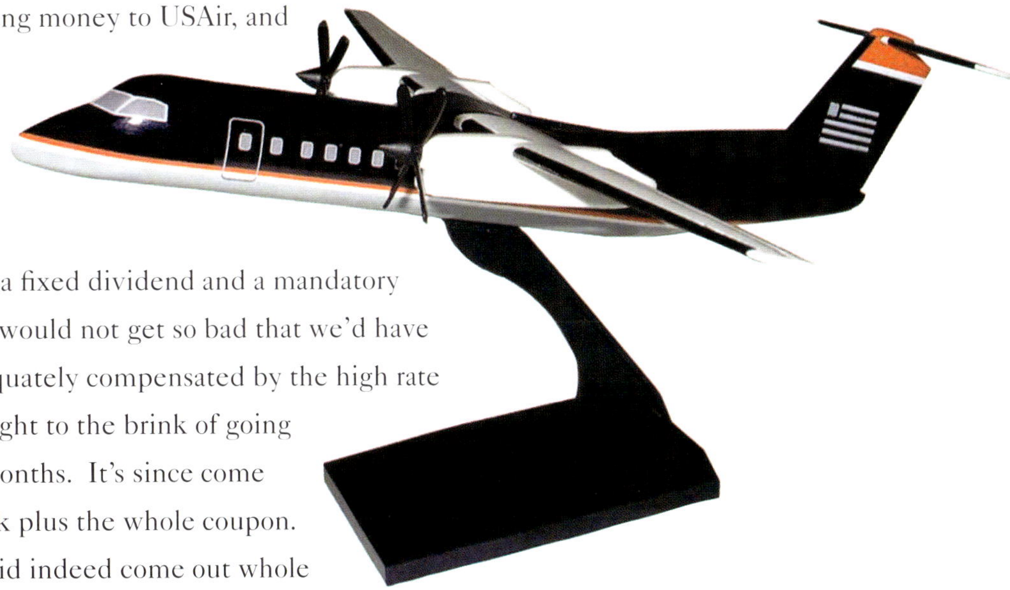

We weren't guessing whether it would be a great place for the shareholders. We were guessing whether it would remain prosperous enough to pay off a credit instrument—carrying a fixed dividend and a mandatory redemption. And we guessed that the business would not get so bad that we'd have a credit threat for which we were not being adequately compensated by the high rate we were getting. As it happened, USAir went right to the brink of going broke. It was hanging by a thread for several months. It's since come back. And we'll probably get all our money back plus the whole coupon. But it was a mistake. [Editor's note: Berkshire did indeed come out whole on its USAir investment.}

The history of the airline business in terms of taking care of shareholders has been terrible.

I don't want you to think we have any way of learning or behaving so you won't make a lot of mistakes. I'm just saying that you can learn to make fewer mistakes than other people—and how to fix your mistakes faster when you do make them.

The Card Players, Theodor Rombouts, Oil on canvas, Residenzgalerie, Salzburg

But there's no way that you can live an adequate life without [making] many mistakes.

In fact, one trick in life is to get so you can handle mistakes. Failure to handle psychological denial is a common way for people to go broke. You've made an enormous commitment to something. You've poured effort and money in. And the more you put in, the more that the whole consistency principle makes you think, "Now it has to work. If I put in just a little more, then it'll work."

Part of what you must learn is how to handle mistakes and new facts that change the odds. Life, in part, is like a poker game, wherein you have to learn to quit sometimes when holding a much-loved hand.

And deprival super-reaction syndrome also comes in: You're going to lose the whole thing if you don't put in a little more. People go broke that way—because they can't stop, rethink, and say, "I can afford to write this one off and live to fight again. I don't have to pursue this thing as an obsession—in a way that will break me."

Q: Could you talk about the thoughts that went into your decision to swap your Capital Cities stock for Disney rather than taking cash. In the media, it was reported that you mentioned thinking about taking the cash.

Disney's a perfectly marvelous company, but it's also very high-priced. Part of what it does is to make ordinary movies—which is not a business that attracts me at all. However, part of what Disney has is better than a great gold mine. My grandchildren—I mean, those videocassettes...

Disney is an amazing example of autocatalysis.... They had all those movies in the can. They owned the copyright. And just as Coke could prosper when refrigeration came, when the videocassette was invented, Disney didn't have to invent anything or do anything except take the thing out of the can and stick it on the cassette.

Disney is an amazing example of autocatalysis.... They had all those movies in the can. They owned the copyright. And just as Coke could prosper when refrigeration came, when the videocassette was invented, Disney didn't have to invent anything or do anything except take the thing out of the can and stick it on the cassette. And every parent and grandparent wanted his descendents to sit around and watch that stuff at home on videocassette. So Disney got this enormous tail wind from life. And it was billions of dollars worth of tail wind.

Obviously, that's a marvelous model if you can find it. You don't have to invent anything. All you have to do is to sit there while the world carries you forward....

The Value of a Spouse

At age 26, Walt Disney was already the head of a successful cartoon studio in Hollywood, California. But business was less than rosy for the young cartoonist, because his principal property, Oswald the Rabbit, had just been wrested from his control by his financial backers. "Mrs. Disney and I were coming back from New York on the train and I had to have something I could tell them," he recalled. "I've lost Oswald, but I had this mouse in the back of my head..." Walt's new creation was a little mouse in red velvet pants named "Mortimer." Walt's wife, Lillian, felt that was too pompous a name for such a cute character and suggested "Mickey" instead. The rest is Disney history.

Frank Wells
(1932–1994)

President of the Disney Company until his untimely death in 1994, Wells was greatly respected. For thirty years he carried a scrap of paper in his wallet that read, "Humility is the essence of life."

Disney's done a lot of new things right. Don't misunderstand me. But a lot of what happened to Disney was like what a friend of mine said about an ignorant fraternity brother of his who succeeded in life: "He was a duck sitting on a pond. And they raised the level of the pond."

Eisner and Wells were brilliant in how they ran Disney. But the huge tail wind from videocassette sales on all of the old stuff that was there when they came in, that was just an automatic break for the new management.

To be fair, they have been brilliant about creating new stuff—like *Pocahontas* and *The Lion King*—to catch the same tailwind. But by the time it's done, *The Lion King* alone is going to do plural billions. And, by the way, when I say "when it's done," I mean fifty years from now or something. But plural billions—from one movie?

Q: Could you talk about why you left the law?

I had a huge family. Nancy and I supported eight children…. And I didn't realize that the law was going to get as prosperous as it suddenly got. The big money came into law shortly after I left it. By 1962, I was mostly out. And I was totally out by 1965. So that was a long time ago.

Also, I preferred making the decisions and gambling my own money. I usually thought I knew better than the client anyway. So why should I have to do it his way? So partly, it was having an opinionated personality. And partly, it was a desire to get resources permitting independence.

Also, the bulk of my clients were terrific. But there were one or two I didn't enjoy. Plus, I like the independence of a capitalist. And I'd always had sort of a gambling personality. I like figuring things out and making bets. So I simply did what came naturally.

Q: Do you ever gamble Las Vegas–style?

I won't bet $100 against house odds between now and the grave. I don't do that. Why should I? I will gamble recreationally with my pals. And I'll occasionally play a much better bridge player, like Bob Hamman, who might be the best card player in the world. But I know I'm paying for the fun of playing with him. That's recreational.

As for gambling with simple mechanical house odds against me, why in the world would I ever want to do that—particularly given how I detest the manipulative culture of legalized gambling. So I don't like legalized gambling.

In 1931 the Nevada legislature approved a legalized gambling bill authored by Phil Tobin, a northern Nevada rancher. Tobin had never visited Las Vegas and said he had no interest in gambling. His legislation was designed "to raise needed taxes for public schools." The same rationale has been used to promote state lotteries.

And I'm not comfortable in Las Vegas, even though it does now include a higher percentage of wholesome family recreation. I don't like to be with many of the types who hang around card parlors and so forth.

On the other hand, I do like the manly art of wagering, so to speak. And I like light social gambling among friends. But I do not like the professional gambling milieu.

"Still the Best"

"The Intelligent Investor is still the best book on investing. It has the only three ideas you really need:

1) The Mr. Market analogy
2) A stock is a piece of a business
3) Margin of safety."

—Buffett

Important Books by Benjamin Graham

Security Analysis (1934)

The Interpretation of Financial Statements (1937)

World Commodities and World Currency (1944)

The Intelligent Investor (1949)

Benjamin Graham: The Memoirs of the Dean of Wall Street (1996, posthumous)

Q: Could you say something about how the mutual fund and money management business has changed since you got into it—and the growth of capital markets?

Actually, I didn't really get into it. I had a little private partnership for fourteen years—up until a little over twenty years ago. However, I never had enough money from other people to amount to a hill of beans—at least by current investment-management standards. So I've never really been part of the mutual fund business.

But the money management business has been one of the great growth businesses in the recent history of the United States. It's created many affluent professionals and multimillionaires. It's been a perfect gold mine for people who got in it early. The growth of pension funds, the value of American corporations, and the world's wealth have created a fabulous profession for many and carried lots of them up to affluence.

And we deal with them in a variety of ways. However, we haven't been part of it for many years. We've basically invested our own money for a long, long time.

Q: Do you expect this [bull] run to continue?

Well, I'd be amazed if the capitalized value of all American business weren't considerably higher twenty-five years from now. And if people continue to trade with one another and shuffle these pieces of paper around, then money management may continue to be a marvelous business for the managers. But except for what might be called our own money, we're really not in it.

Q: I was interested in the evolution of your investment strategy from when you first began—using the Ben Graham model—to the Berkshire Hathaway model. Would you recommend that model to a beginning investor—i.e., dumping most of it or all of it into one opportunity we think is a great one and leaving it there for decades? Or is that strategy really for a more mature investor?

Each person has to play the game given his own marginal utility considerations and in a way that takes into account his own psychology. If losses are going to make you miserable—and some losses are inevitable—you might be wise to utilize a very conservative pattern of investment and saving all your life. So you have to adapt your strategy to your own nature and your own talents. I don't think there's a one-size-fits-all investment strategy that I can give you.

Mine works for me. But, in part, that's because I'm good at taking losses. I can take 'em psychologically. And, besides, I have very few. The combination works fine.

Q: You and Buffett have said that Berkshire's stock is overvalued and you wouldn't recommend buying it.

We didn't say [we thought it was overvalued]. We just said that we wouldn't buy it or recommend that our friends buy it at the prices then prevailing. But that just related to Berkshire's intrinsic value as it was at that time.

Q: If I had the money, I would buy it—because you've been saying that your returns will go down for twenty years....

Well, I hope that your optimism is justified. But I do not change my opinion. After all, today, we're in uncharted territory. I sometimes tell my friends, "I'm doing the best I can. But I've never grown old before. I'm doing it for the first time. And I'm not sure that I'll do it right."

Charlie on Growing Old as Best He Can:

"Charlie, you look great, 20 years younger than your age."

Charlie: "That's part of my duty this evening, to listen to lots of factual inaccuracies. But thank you."

I sometimes tell my friends, "I'm doing the best I can. But I've never grown old before. I'm doing it for the first time. And I'm not sure that I'll do it right."

Warren and I have never been in this kind of territory—with high valuations and a huge amount of capital. We've never done it before. So we're learning.

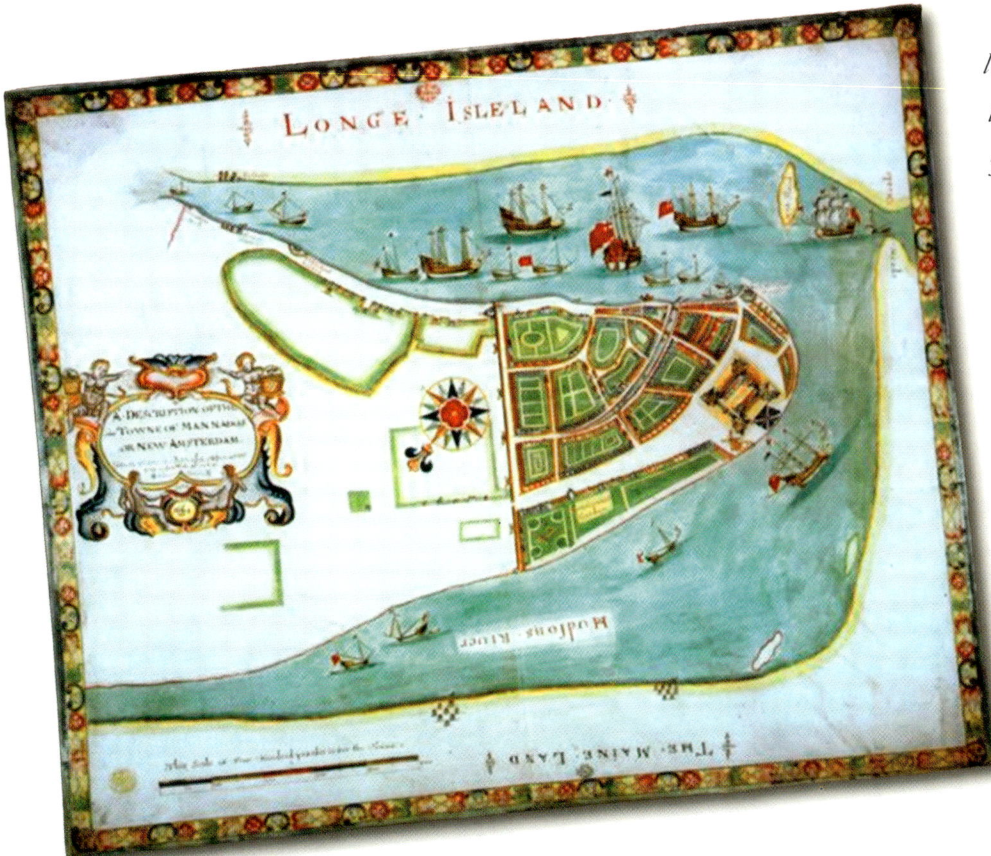

Q: Everything you and Buffett say seems logical. But it sounds like exactly the same language that Ben Graham was using thirty years ago when he was saying the stock market was overvalued—when it was at 900.

The wealth of the world will compound at no such rate.

Oh, I don't think that we share that with him. Graham, great though he was as a man, had a screw loose as he tried to predict outcomes for the stock market as a whole. In contrast, Warren and I are almost always agnostic about the market.

The Limits to Compounding

The $24 real estate investment by the Dutch to buy the island of Manhattan would today, by some estimates, be roughly equivalent to $3 trillion.

Over 378 years, that's about a seven percent annual compound rate of return.

On the other hand, we have said that common stocks generally have generated returns of ten to eleven percent after inflation for many years and that those returns can't continue for a very long period. And they can't. It's simply impossible. The wealth of the world will compound at no such rate. Whatever experience Stanford has had in its portfolio for the last fifteen years, its future experience is virtually certain to be worse. It may still be okay. But it's been a hog heaven period for investors over the last fifteen years. Bonanza effects of such scale can't last forever.

Q: Berkshire's annual report got a lot of press for being pessimistic and for expressing concern about the shrinking pool of opportunities as the company gets bigger and bigger. Where does that leave you ten years from now?

We've said over and over that our future rate of compounding our shareholders' wealth is going to go down compared to our past—and that our size will be an anchor dragging on performance. And we've said over and over again that this is not an opinion, but a promise.

However, let's suppose that we were able to compound our present book value at fifteen percent per annum from this point. That would not be so bad and would work out okay for our long-term shareholder. I'm just saying that we could afford to slow down some, as we surely will, and still do okay for the long-term shareholder.

By the way, I'm not promising that we will compound our present book value at fifteen percent per annum.

Q: You talked about how important it was not to have an extreme ideology. What responsibility, if any, do you think the business and legal communities have for helping inner-city areas, spreading the wealth and so on?

I'm all for fixing social problems. I'm all for being generous to the less fortunate.

I'm all for fixing social problems. I'm all for being generous to the less fortunate. And I'm all for doing things where, based on a slight preponderance of the evidence, you guess that it's likely to do more good than harm.

What I'm against is being very confident and feeling that you know, for sure, that your particular intervention will do more good than harm, given that you're dealing with highly complex systems wherein everything is interacting with everything else.

Q: So [what you're saying is to] just make sure that what you're doing [is doing more good]....

You can't make sure. That's my point....

On the other hand, I did recently reverse [the conclusions of] two sets of engineers. How did I have enough confidence in such a complicated field to do that? Well, you might think, "Oh, this guy is just an egomaniac who's made some money and thinks he knows everything."

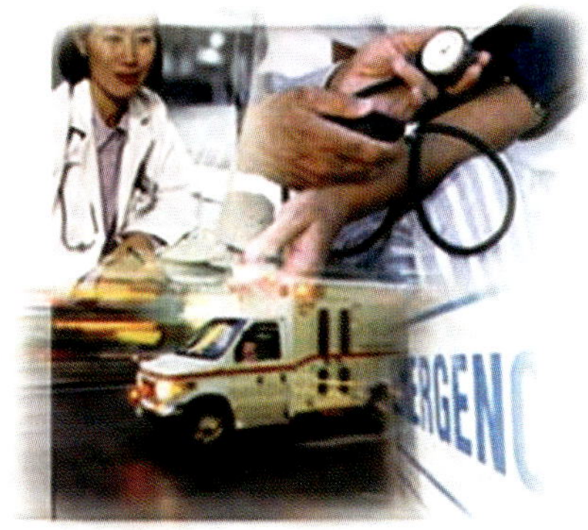

Good Samaritan

Good Samaritan Hospital of Los Angeles, founded in 1885, is a world-class academic medical center affiliated with the University of Southern California Keck School of Medicine. Performing about 4,200 surgeries and receiving 25,400 emergency room visits annually, it is organized as a not-for-profit corporation. Good Samaritan's longtime chairman of the board is Charles T. Munger.

Well, I may be an egomaniac, but I don't think I know everything. But I saw huge reasons in the circumstances for bias in each set of engineers as each recommended a course of action very advantageous to itself. And what each was saying was so consonant with a natural bias that it made me distrust it. Also, perhaps I knew enough engineering to know that [what they were saying] didn't make sense.

Finally, I found a third engineer who recommended a solution I approved. And, thereafter, the second engineer came to me and said, "Charlie, why didn't I think of that?"—which is to his credit. It was a much better solution, both safer and cheaper.

You must have the confidence to override people with more credentials than you whose cognition is impaired by incentive-caused bias or some similar psychological force that is obviously present. But there are also cases where you have to recognize that you have no wisdom to add—and that your best course is to trust some expert.

In effect, you've got to know what you know and what you don't know. What could possibly be more useful in life than that?

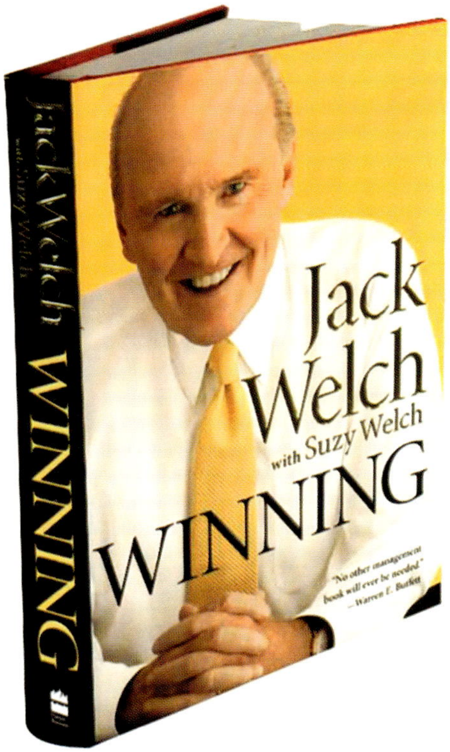

Jack Welch
(b. 1935)

Born John Francis Welch Jr. in Massachusetts, Welch earned a Ph.D. in chemical engineering before joining General Electric in 1960. He worked his way up the corporate ladder, becoming chairman and CEO in 1980. During his twenty years of leadership at GE, Welch increased the value of the company from $13 billion to several hundred billion dollars.

Q: You discussed Coke's mistake. Do you have any thoughts about where Apple went wrong?"

Let me give you a very good answer—one I'm copying from Jack Welch, the CEO of General Electric. He has a Ph.D. in engineering. He's a star businessman. He's a marvelous guy. And recently, in Warren's presence, someone asked him, "Jack, what did Apple do wrong?"

His answer? "I don't have any special competence that would enable me to answer that question." And I'll give you the very same answer. That's not a field in which I'm capable of giving you any special insight.

On the other hand, in copying Jack Welch, I am trying to teach you something. When you don't know and you don't have any special competence, don't be afraid to say so.

There's another type of person I compare to an example from biology: When a bee finds nectar, it comes back and does a little dance that tells the rest of the hive, as a matter of genetic programming, which direction to go and how far. So about forty or fifty years ago, some clever scientist stuck the nectar straight up. Well, the nectar's never straight up in the ordinary life of a bee. The nectar's out. So the bee finds the nectar and returns to the hive. But it doesn't have the genetic programming to do a dance that says straight up. So what does it do?

Well, if it were like Jack Welch, it would just sit there. But what it actually does is to dance this incoherent dance that gums things up. And a lot of people are like that bee. They attempt to answer a question like that. And that is a huge mistake. Nobody expects you to know everything about everything.

I try to get rid of people who always confidently answer questions about which they don't have any real knowledge. To me, they're like the bee dancing its incoherent dance. They're just screwing up the hive.

Q: As someone who's been in legal practice and business, how did you incorporate, or did you incorporate, these models into your legal practice? And how did it work? I suspect many of us have seen law firms that don't appear to adhere to these kinds of models.

Well, the models are there. But just as there are perverse incentives in academia, there are perverse incentives in law firms. In fact, in some respects, at the law firms, it's much worse.

Here's another model from law practice: When I was very young, my father practiced law. One of his best friends, Grant McFayden—Omaha's Pioneer Ford dealer—was a client. He was a perfectly marvelous man—a self-made Irishman

Apple Computer

With the 1976 release of the Apple 1 by Steven Jobs and Stephen Wozniak, Apple Computer was born. Through a series of improvements and innovations, Apple built a reputation for quality and the user-friendliest computers on the market. In the early 1990s, Apple began to lose its market share to Intel- and Windows-based computers. Despite what many observers maintained was superior technology and performance, Apple came close to irrelevance because of the marketing heft behind the Windows-based products. In the late 1990s, Apple's iMac and PowerBook products began an impressive resurgence. The recent introduction of the iPod personal audio device has greatly enhanced Apple's position in the market.

who'd run away uneducated from a farm as a youth because his father beat him. So he made his own way in the world. And he was a brilliant man of enormous charm and integrity—just a wonderful, wonderful man.

W. C. Fields as *The Bank Dick* (1940): a quintessential, unreasonable blowhard.

In contrast, my father had another client who was a blowhard, overreaching, unfair, pompous, difficult man. And I must have been fourteen years old or thereabouts when I asked, "Dad, why do you do so much work for Mr. X—this overreaching blowhard—instead of working more for wonderful men like Grant McFayden?"

My father said, "Grant McFayden treats his employees right, his customers right, and his problems right. And if he gets involved with a psychotic, he quickly walks over to where the psychotic is and works out an exit as fast as he can. Therefore, Grant McFayden doesn't have enough remunerative law business to keep you in Coca-Cola. But Mr. X is a walking minefield of wonderful legal business."

As you go through life, sell your services once in a while to an unreasonable blowhard if that's what you must do to feed your family. But run your own life like Grant McFayden. That was a great lesson.

This case demonstrates one of the troubles with practicing law. To a considerable extent, you're going to be dealing with grossly defective people. They create an enormous amount of the remunerative law business. And even when your own client is a paragon of virtue, you'll often be dealing with gross defectives on the other side or even on the bench. That's partly what drove me out of the profession.

The rest was my own greed, but my success in serving greed partly allowed me to make easier the process of being honorable and sensible. Like Ben Franklin observed, "It's hard for an empty sack to stand upright."

I'd argue that my father's model when I asked him about the two clients was totally correct didaction. He taught me the right lesson. The lesson? As you go through life, sell your services once in a while to an unreasonable blowhard if that's what you must do to feed your family. But run your own life like Grant McFayden. That was a great lesson.

And he taught it in a very clever way—because instead of just pounding it in, he told it to me in a way that required a slight mental reach. And I had to make the reach myself in order to get the idea that I should behave like Grant McFayden. And because I had to reach for it, he figured I'd hold it better. And, indeed, I've held it all the way through until today—through all of these decades. That's a very clever teaching method.

There, again, we're talking about elementary psychology. It's elementary literature. Good literature makes the reader reach a little for understanding. Then, it works better. You hold it better. It's the commitment and consistency tendency. If you've reached for it, the idea's pounded in better.

Good literature makes the reader reach a little for understanding. If you've reached for it, the idea's pounded in better.

As a lawyer or executive, you'll want to teach somebody what my father taught me or maybe you'll want to teach them something else. And you can use lessons like this. Isn't that a great way to teach a child? My father used indirection on purpose. And look at how powerfully it worked—like Captain Cook's wise use of psychology. I've been trying to imitate Grant McFayden ever since—for all my life. I may have had a few lapses. But at least I've been trying.

Good Literature

Irving Stone
(1903–1989)

An American writer known for his biographical novels of famous historical personalities and events, Irving Stone produced important works that included *Lust for Life*, based on the life of Vincent van Gogh (1934), *The Agony and the Ecstasy*, based on the life of Michelangelo (1961), and *Origin*, based on the life of Charles Darwin (1980). *Men to Match My Mountains* (1956) is an often spellbinding account about the bold pioneers who opened the Far West and California during the 1840s.

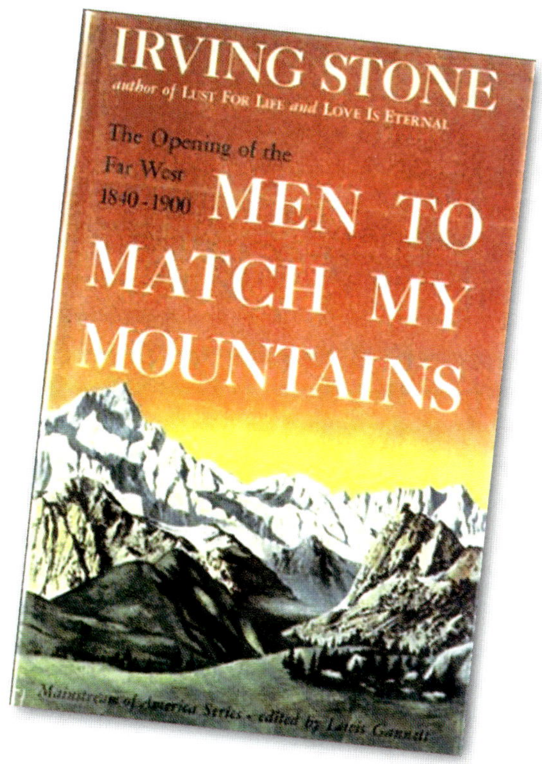

Henry Emerson
Editor and Publisher
Outstanding Investor Digest

Henry Emerson has spent eighteen years interacting with some of the world's greatest money managers—including both Warren Buffett and Charlie Munger. His indispensable newsletter is designed to "bring our subscribers the most valuable material that we can—the calendar be damned." Emerson's publication is a must-read for investors of every stripe.

Q: At the end of your article in OID, *you mentioned that only a select few investment managers actually add value. Since you're speaking to an audience of future lawyers, what would you encourage us to do in order to be able to add value in our profession?*

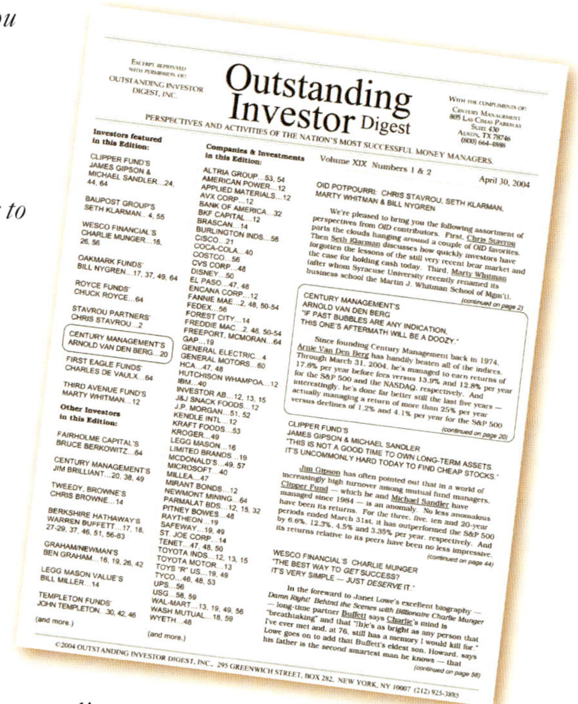

EXCERPT REPRINTED WITH PERMISSION OF: OUTSTANDING INVESTOR DIGEST, INC.

Outstanding Investor Digest

WITH THE COMPLIMENTS OF: CENTURY MANAGEMENT 805 LAS CIMAS PARKWAY SUITE 430 AUSTIN, TX 78746 (800) 664-4888

PERSPECTIVES AND ACTIVITIES OF THE NATION'S MOST SUCCESSFUL MONEY MANAGERS.

Volume XIX Numbers 1 & 2 April 30, 2004

Investors featured in this Edition:

CLIPPER FUND'S JAMES GIPSON & MICHAEL SANDLER...24, 44, 64

BAUPOST GROUP'S SETH KLARMAN...4, 55

WESCO FINANCIAL'S CHARLIE MUNGER...18, 26, 56

OAKMARK FUNDS' BILL NYGREN...17, 37, 49, 64

ROYCE FUNDS' CHUCK ROYCE...64

STAVROU PARTNERS' CHRIS STAVROU...2

CENTURY MANAGEMENT'S ARNOLD VAN DEN BERG...20

FIRST EAGLE FUNDS' CHARLES DE VAULX...64

THIRD AVENUE FUND'S MARTY WHITMAN...12

Other Investors in this Edition:

FAIRHOLME CAPITAL'S BRUCE BERKOWITZ...64

CENTURY MANAGEMENT'S JIM BRILLIANT...20, 38, 49

TWEEDY, BROWNE'S CHRIS BROWNE...14

BERKSHIRE HATHAWAY'S WARREN BUFFETT...17, 18, 27-29, 37, 46, 51, 56-63

GRAHAM/NEWMAN'S BEN GRAHAM...16, 19, 26, 42

LEGG MASON VALUE'S BILL MILLER...14

TEMPLETON FUNDS' JOHN TEMPLETON...30, 42, 46

(and more.)

Companies & Investments in this Edition:

ALTRIA GROUP...53, 54
AMERICAN POWER...12
APPLIED MATERIALS...12
AVX CORP...12
BANK OF AMERICA...32
BKF CAPITAL...12
BRASCAN...14
BURLINGTON INDS...58
CISCO...21
COCA-COLA...40
COSTCO...56
CVS CORP...48
DISNEY...50
EL PASO...47, 48
ENCANA CORP...12
FANNIE MAE...2, 48, 50-54
FEDEX...56
FOREST CITY...14
FREDDIE MAC...2, 48, 50-54
FREEPORT, MCMORAN...64
GAP...19
GENERAL ELECTRIC...4
GENERAL MOTORS...60
HCA...47, 48
HUTCHISON WHAMPOA...12
IBM...40
INVESTOR AB...12, 13, 15
J&J SNACK FOODS...12
J.P. MORGAN...51, 52
KENDLE INTL...12
KRAFT FOODS...53
KROGER...49
LEGG MASON...16
LIMITED BRANDS...19
MCDONALD'S...49, 57
MICROSOFT...40
MILLEA...47
MIRANT BONDS...12
NEWMONT MINING...64
PARMALAT BDS...12, 15, 32
PITNEY BOWES...48
RAYTHEON...19
SAFEWAY...19, 49
ST. JOE CORP...14
TENET...47, 48, 50
TOYOTA INDS...12, 13, 15
TOYOTA MOTOR...13
TOYS "R" US...19, 49
TYCO...46, 48, 53
UPS...56
USG...58, 59
WAL-MART...13, 19, 49, 56
WASH MUTUAL...18, 59
WYETH...48

(and more.)

OID POTPOURRI: CHRIS STAVROU, SETH KLARMAN, MARTY WHITMAN & BILL NYGREN

We're pleased to bring you the following assortment of perspectives from *OID* contributors. First, Chris Stavrou parts the clouds hanging around a couple of *OID* favorites. Then Seth Klarman discusses how quickly investors have forgotten the lessons of the still very recent bear market and the case for holding cash today. Third, Marty Whitman (after whom Syracuse University recently renamed its business school the Martin J. Whitman School of Mgm't).

(continued on page 2)

CENTURY MANAGEMENT'S ARNOLD VAN DEN BERG "IF PAST BUBBLES ARE ANY INDICATION, THIS ONE'S AFTERMATH WILL BE A DOOZY."

Since founding Century Management back in 1974, Arnie Van Den Berg has handily beaten all of the indices. Through March 31, 2004, he's managed to earn returns of 17.6% per year before fees versus 13.9% and 12.8% per year for the S&P 500 and the NASDAQ, respectively. And interestingly, he's done far better still the last five years — actually managing a return of more than 25% per year versus declines of 1.2% and 4.1% per year for the S&P 500

(continued on page 20)

CLIPPER FUND'S JAMES GIPSON & MICHAEL SANDLER "THIS IS NOT A GOOD TIME TO OWN LONG-TERM ASSETS. IT'S UNCOMMONLY HARD TODAY TO FIND CHEAP STOCKS."

Jim Gipson has often pointed out that in a world of increasingly high turnover among mutual fund managers, Clipper Fund — which he and Michael Sandler have managed since 1984 — is an anomaly. No less anomalous have been its returns. For the three, five, ten and 20-year periods ended March 31st, it has outperformed the S&P 500 by 6.6%, 12.3%, 4.5% and 3.35% per year, respectively. And its returns relative to its peers have been no less impressive.

(continued on page 44)

WESCO FINANCIAL'S CHARLIE MUNGER "THE BEST WAY TO *GET* SUCCESS? IT'S VERY SIMPLE — JUST *DESERVE* IT."

In the foreward to Janet Lowe's excellent biography — *Damn Right! Behind the Scenes with Billionaire Charlie Munger* — long-time partner Buffett says Charlie's mind is "breathtaking" and that "[h]e's as bright as any person that I've ever met and, at 76, still has a memory I would kill for." Lowe goes on to add that Buffett's eldest son, Howard, says his father is the second smartest man he knows — that

(continued on page 56)

To the extent you become a person who thinks correctly, you can add great value. To the extent you've learned it so well that you have enough confidence to intervene where it takes a little courage, you can add great value. And to the extent that you can prevent or stop some asininity that would otherwise destroy your firm, your client, or something that you care about, you can add great value.

And there are constructive tricks you can use. For example, one reason why my old classmate, Joe Flom of Skadden Arps, has been such a successful lawyer is that he's very good at dreaming up little, vivid examples that serve to pound the point home in a way that really works. It's enormously helpful when you're serving clients or otherwise trying to persuade someone in a good cause to come up with a little humorous example.

The ability to do that is a knack. So you could argue that the Joe Floms of the world are almost born with a gift. But he's honed the gift. And to one degree or another, all of you were born with the gift. And you can hone it, too.

Occasionally, you get into borderline stuff. For instance, suppose you've got a client who really wants to commit tax fraud. If he doesn't push the tax law way beyond the line, he can't stand it. He can't shave in the morning if he thinks there's been any cheating he could get by with that he hasn't done. And there are people like that. They just feel they aren't living aggressively enough.

You can approach that situation in either of two ways: (A) You can say, "I just won't work for him," and duck it. Or, (B) you can say, "Well, the circumstances of my life require that I work for him. And what I'm doing for him doesn't involve my cheating. Therefore, I'll do it."

And if you see he wants to do something really stupid, it probably won't work to tell him, "What you're doing is bad. I have better morals than you."

That offends him. You're young. He's old. Therefore, instead of being persuaded, he's more likely to react with, "Who in the hell are you to establish the moral code of the whole world?"

But, instead, you can say to him, "You can't do that without three other people beneath you knowing about it. Therefore, you're making yourself subject to blackmail. You're risking your reputation. You're risking your family, your money, etc."

That is likely to work. And you're telling him something that's true. Do you want to spend a lot of time working for people where you have to use methods like that to get them to behave well? I think the answer is no. But if you're hooked with it, appealing to his interest is likely to work better as a matter of human persuasion than appealing to anything else. That, again, is a powerful psychological principle with deep biological roots.

I saw that psychological principle totally blown at Salomon. Salomon's general counsel knew that the CEO, Gutfreund, should have promptly told the federal authorities all about Salomon's trading improprieties in which Gutfreund didn't participate and which he hadn't caused. And the general counsel urged Gutfreund to do it. He told Gutfreund, in effect, "You're probably not legally required to do that, but it's the right thing to do. You really should."

But it didn't work. The task was easy to put off—because it was unpleasant. So that's what Gutfreund did—he put it off.

And the general counsel had very little constituency within Salomon except for the CEO. If the CEO went down, the general counsel was going down with him. Therefore, his whole career was on the line. So to save his career, he needed to talk

John Gutfreund at Salomon Brothers

John Gutfreund, chairman and CEO of Salomon Brothers, paid a high price for inaction when he was put on notice of company misdeeds. In 1991, a Salomon trader made an illegal $3.2 billion bid for U.S. treasury securities. Although the transaction was reported to top management only days later, Gutfreund did not take the warning seriously and failed to report it for more than three months. Gutfreund knew as soon as the matter came out in the press that his delay in reporting had torpedoed his thirty-eight-year career with Salomon. He called in one of Salomon's outside directors, Warren Buffett, to save the company and restore its reputation. Buffett handled the complicated project masterfully, and the firm survived and prospered; it was later sold for $9 billion to Travelers.

the dilatory CEO into doing the right thing.

It would've been child's play to get that job done right. All the general counsel had to do was to tell his boss, "John, this situation could ruin your life. You could lose your wealth. You could lose your reputation." And it would have worked. CEOs don't like the idea of being ruined, disgraced, and fired.

March 3, 2004, New York, New York: Former WorldCom CEO Bernard Ebbers in handcuffs on his way to court for his arraignment after surrendering at FBI Headquarters in 26 Federal Plaza. Ebbers was charged with nine counts of conspiracy to commit securities fraud and making false statements to the SEC in connection with the collapse of WorldCom. He was found guilty in March of 2005 and, as of this writing, is headed to prison, perhaps for life.

Photo by Allan Tannenbaum / Polaris

CEOs don't like the idea of being ruined, disgraced, and fired.

And the ex–general counsel of Salomon is brilliant and generous—and he had the right idea. However, he lost his job because he didn't apply a little elementary psychology. He failed to recognize that what works best in most cases is to appeal to a man's interest.

But you don't have to get similarly lousy results when you face similar situations. Just remember what happened to Gutfreund and his general counsel. The right lessons are easily learned if you'll work at it. And if you do learn them, you can be especially useful at crucial moments when others fail. And to the extent that you do become wise, diligent, objective, and, especially able to persuade in a good cause, then you're adding value.

Q: Would you discuss how the threat of litigation—shareholder lawsuits and so forth—and legal complexity in general have affected decision-making in big business?

Well, every big business screams about its legal costs, screams about the amount of regulation, screams about the complexity of its life, screams about the plaintiffs' bar—particularly the class action plaintiffs' bar. So there's an absolute catechism on that where you could just copy the screams from one corporation to another and you'd hardly have to change a word.

But what causes the screams has, so far, been a godsend for the law firms. The big law firms have had a long updraft. And they now tend to kind of cluck like an undertaker in a plague. An undertaker, of course, would look very unseemly if he were jumping up and down and playing his fiddle during the plague. So law firm partners say, "Oh, isn't it sad—all this complexity, all this litigation, all this unfairness."

An undertaker, of course, would look very unseemly if he were jumping up and down and playing his fiddle during the plague.

The popular expression about fiddling during a disaster—commonly applied to the Roman Emperor Nero—has more to do with wasting time in frivolous pursuits than it does with playing a violin. In fact, the violin, or fiddle in the common vernacular, was not invented until many centuries after The Great Fire of Rome.

But, really, they're somewhat schizophrenic on the subject because it's been very good for [them]. Some recent California initiatives created some interesting conduct. Part of the defense bar lobbied quietly against certain propositions and, effectively, against their clients because they didn't want their clients to catch 'em in the process. And the reason that they did so was because it became harder for plaintiffs to bring cases.

If you make a living fighting overreaching and it keeps your children in school and somebody proposes a system that eliminates it—well, that's an adult experience and an adult choice that you have to make.

Officer Daniel Rodriguez, the so-called "singing cop," singing at the 2002 Winter Olympics [AP photo]. Officer Rodriguez was a great comfort to New Yorkers and America at large in the aftermath of the 9-11 tragedy.

So big corporations adapt. They have more litigation. They have to have a bigger legal department. They scream about what they don't like. But they adapt.

"As a matter of ideology, we're very pro-police."

Q: But hasn't that legal complexity consumed a lot more of companies' resources over the last few decades?

The answer is yes. There's hardly a corporation in America that isn't spending more on lawsuits and on compliance with various regulations than it was twenty years ago. And, yes, some of the new regulation is stupid and foolish. And some was damn well necessary. And it will ever be thus, albeit with some ebb and flow.

Q: But have you seen or experienced any change in decision making at corporations in their being less likely to take on riskier investments for fear of failure or liability?

The only place I saw—with another friend, not Warren [Buffett]—[was where] I was part owner of the biggest shareholder in a company that invented a better policeman's helmet. It was made of Kevlar or something of that sort. And they brought it to us and wanted us to [manufacture] it.

As a matter of ideology, we're very pro-police. I believe civilization needs a police force—although I don't believe in policemen creating too many widows and orphans unnecessarily either. But we like the idea of a better policeman's helmet.

However, we took one look at it and said to the people who invented it, "We're a rich corporation. We can't afford to make a better policeman's helmet. That's just how the civilization works. All risks considered, it can't work for us. But we want the civilization to have these."

"So we don't maximize what we sell it for it. Get somebody else to make it. Transfer the technology or whatever to somebody who can do it. But we're not going to."

Thus, we didn't try to disadvantage policemen [by keeping them from] getting new helmets, but we decided not to manufacture helmets ourselves.

There are businesses—given the way the civilization has developed—where being the only deep pocket around is bad business. In high school football, for example, a paraplegic or quadriplegic will inevitably be created occasionally. And who with deep pockets can the injured person best sue other than the helmet manufacturer? Then everyone feels sorry, the injuries are horrible, and the case is dangerous for the manufacturer....

I think big, rich corporations are seldom wise to make football helmets in the kind of a civilization we're in. And maybe it should be harder to successfully sue helmet makers.

Keeping it Simple

"The sign above the players' entrance to the field at Notre Dame reads 'Play Like a Champion Today.' I sometimes joke that the sign at Nebraska reads 'Remember Your Helmet.' Charlie and I are 'Remember Your Helmet' kind of guys. We like to keep it simple."

—Buffett

I think big, rich corporations are seldom wise to make football helmets in the kind of a civilization we're in.

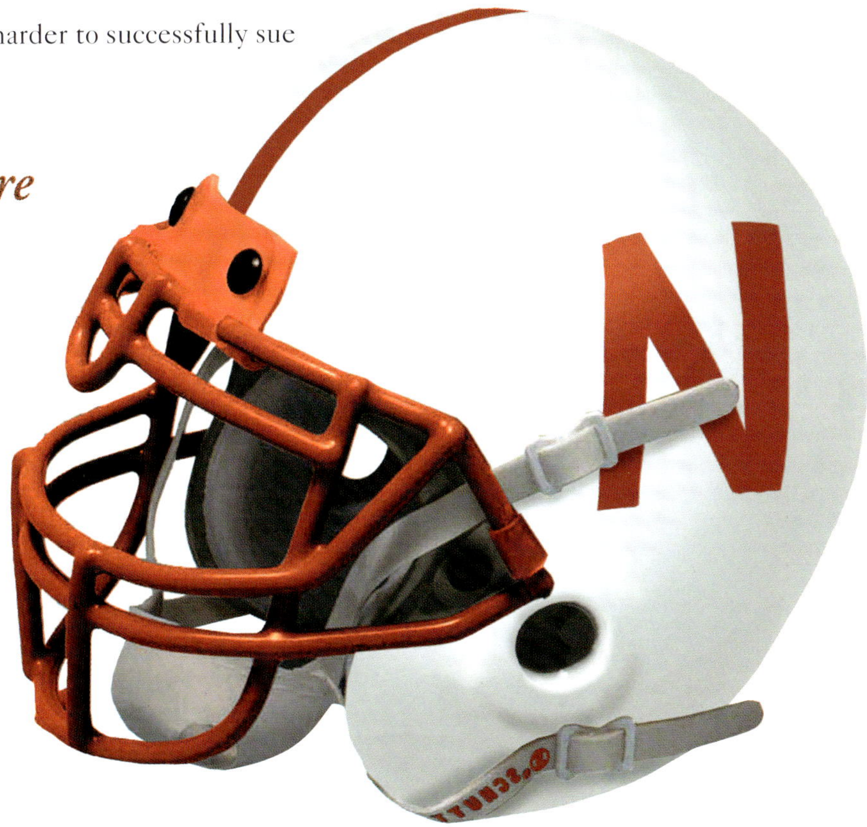

I know two different doctors—each of whom had a sound marriage. And when the malpractice premiums got high enough, they divorced their wives and transferred most of their property to their wives. And they continued to practice—only without malpractice insurance.

They were angry at the civilization. They needed to adapt. And they trusted their wives. So that was that. And they've not carried any malpractice insurance since.

People adapt to a changing litigation climate. They have various ways of doing it. That's how it's always been and how it's always going to be.

I like the Navy system.... If a captain... turns his ship over to a competent first mate in tough conditions and he takes the ship aground...the captain's naval career is over.

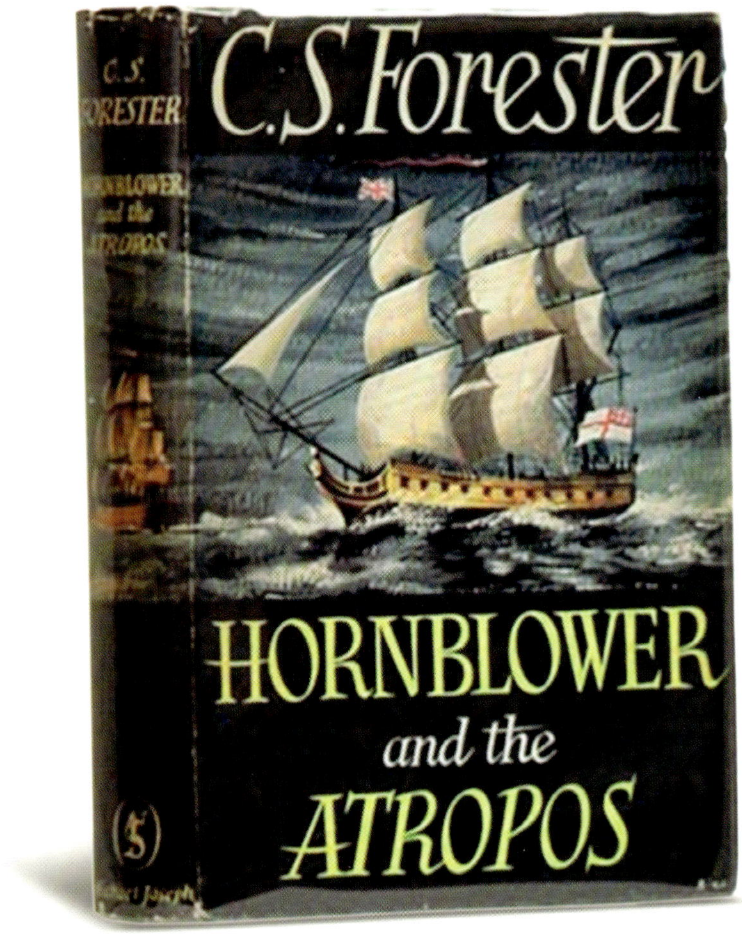

British Blockade of the French Coast
(1803–1814)

Winter in the Bay of Biscay brings ferocious gales, vicious tides, mountainous seas, and bitter discomfort for ships' crews. As chronicled by C. S. Forester in his *Hornblower* series, the consequences for any ship's captain who might allow his ship to go aground while on blockade duty were severe. Regardless of the circumstances, the officer faced almost certain court-martial and the severest of punishments, even including death. Not surprisingly, only one ship of the line was lost in all those years, and she ran on an uncharted rock.

What I personally hate most are systems that make fraud easy. Probably way more than half of all the chiropractic income in California comes from pure fraud. For example, I have a friend who had a little fender bender—an auto accident—in a tough neighborhood. And he got two chiropractors' cards and one lawyer's card before he'd even left the intersection. They're in the business of manufacturing claims that necks hurt.

In California, I believe the Rand statistics showed that we have twice as many personal injuries per accident as in many other states. And we aren't getting twice as much real injury per accident. So the other half of that is fraud. People just get so that they think everybody does it, and it's all right to do. I think it's terrible to let that stuff creep in.

If I were running the civilization, compensation for stress in workers' comp would be zero—not because there's no work-caused stress, but because I think the net social damage of allowing stress to be compensated at all is worse than what would happen if a few people that had real work-caused stress injuries went uncompensated.

I like the Navy system. If you're a captain in the Navy and you've been up for twenty-four hours straight and have to go to sleep and you turn the ship over to a competent first mate in tough conditions and he takes the ship aground—clearly through no fault of yours—they don't court-martial you, but your naval career is over.

You can say, "That's too tough. That's not law school. That's not due process." Well, the Navy model is better in its context than would be the law school model. The Navy model really forces people to pay attention when conditions are tough—because they know that there's no excuse.

Napoleon Bonaparte, Emperor of France, acquired control of most of western and central Europe by conquest or alliance until his defeat at the Battle of the Nations near Leipzig in 1813. He later staged a comeback known as the Hundred Days, before being defeated at the Battle of Waterloo in 1815. This painting, *Bonaparte Crossing the Alps at Grand-Saint-Bernard*, by Jacques-Louis David is in the collection of the Chateaux de Malmaison et Bois-Preau, Rueil-Malmaison, France.

Napoleon said he liked luckier generals—he wasn't into supporting losers. Well, the Navy likes luckier captains.

It doesn't matter why your ship goes aground, your career is over. Nobody's interested in your fault. It's just a rule that we happen to have—for the good of all, all effects considered.

I like some rules like that. I think that the civilization works better with some of these no-fault rules. But that stuff tends to be anathema around law schools. "It's not due process. You're not really searching for justice."

Well, I am searching for justice when I argue for the Navy rule—for the justice of fewer ships going aground. Considering the net benefit, I don't care if one captain has some unfairness in his life. After all, it's not like he's being court-martialed. He just has to look for a new line of work. And he keeps vested pension rights and so on. So it's not like it's the end of the world.

Sheep, blissfully uncomplicated and certainly with all the answers they will ever need in life, block a country road in the Yorkshire Dales in England.

So I like things like that. However, I'm in a minority.

Q: I'd like to hear you talk a little bit more about judgment. In your talk, you said we should read the psychology textbooks and take the fifteen or sixteen principles that are best of the ones that make sense….

The ones that are obviously important and obviously right. That's correct…. And then you stick in the ones that are obviously important and not in the books—and you've got a system.

Q: Right. My problem seems to be the prior step, which is determining which ones are obviously right. And that seems to me to be the more essential question to ask.

Well, if you're like me, it's kind of fun for it to be a little complicated. If you want it totally easy and laid out, maybe you should join some cult that claims to provide all the answers.

No, no. You overestimate the difficulty. Do you have difficulty understanding that people are heavily influenced by what other people think and what other people do—and that some of that happens on a subconscious level?

Q: No, I don't. I understand that.

Well, you can go right through the principles. And, one after another, they're like that. It's not that hard….

Do you have any difficulty with the idea that operant conditioning works—that people will repeat what worked for them the last time?

Q: It just seems to me like there's a lot of other things out there, as well, that also make a lot of sense. The system would quickly get too complicated, I imagine—as a result of too much cross-talk.

Well, if you're like me, it's kind of fun for it to be a little complicated. If you want it totally easy and totally laid out, maybe you should join some cult that claims to provide all the answers. I don't think that's a good way to go. I think you'll just have to endure the world—as complicated as it is. Einstein has a marvelous statement on that: "Everything should be made as simple as possible, but no more simple."

I'm afraid that's the way it is. If there are twenty factors and they interact some, you'll just have to learn to handle it—because that's the way the world is. But you won't find it that hard if you go at it Darwin-like, step by step with curious persistence. You'll be amazed at how good you can get.

Q: You've given us about three of the models that you use. I wondered where you found the other ones. And, second, do you have an easier way for us to find them than going through a psychology textbook? I'm not averse to doing that, but it takes longer.

There are a relatively small number of disciplines and a relatively small number of truly big ideas. And it's a lot of fun to figure it out. Plus, if you figure it out and do the outlining yourself, the ideas will stick better than if you memorize 'em using somebody else's cram list.

Even better, the fun never stops. I was miseducated horribly. And I hadn't bothered to pick up what's called modern Darwinism. I do a lot of miscellaneous reading, too. But I just missed it. And in the last year, I suddenly realized I was a total damned fool and hadn't picked it up properly. So I went back. And with the aid of Dawkins—Oxford's great biologist—and others, I picked it up.

Modern Darwinism or Modern Darwinian Synthesis

The terms, "modern Darwinism" and "modern Darwinian synthesis" describe work of the late 1930s and 1940s which blended the discoveries of geneticists and natural historians to determine how changes in genes could account for evolution of bio-diversity.

"Well, it was an absolute circus for me in my seventies to get the modern Darwinian synthesis in my head. It's so awesomely beautiful and so awesomely right [that the organism acts, and has evolved, to further the interests of its genes]. And it's so simple once you get it."

Were Charlie to teach a Remedial Worldly Wisdom course for law students, it would no doubt include his "Fundamental four-discipline combination of math, physics, chemistry, and engineering," (see page 313) as well as accounting, history, psychology, philosophy, statistics, biology, and economics. It might, in fact, last somewhat longer than "three weeks or a month."

Well, it was an absolute circus for me in my seventies to get the modern Darwinian synthesis in my head. It's so awesomely beautiful and so awesomely right. And it's so simple once you get it. So one beauty of my approach is that the fun never stops. I suppose that it does stop eventually when you're drooling in the convalescent home at the end. But, at least, it lasts a long time.

If I were czar of a law school—although, of course, no law school will permit a czar (they don't even want the dean to have much power)—I'd create a course that I'd call "Remedial Worldly Wisdom" that would, among other useful things, include a fair amount of properly taught psychology. And it might last three weeks or a month....

I think you could create a course that was so interesting—with pithy examples and powerful examples and powerful principles—that it would be a total circus. And I think that it would make the whole law school experience work better.

People raise their eyebrows at that idea. "People don't do that kind of thing." They may not like the derision that's implicit in the title: "Remedial Worldly Wisdom." But the title would be my way of announcing, "Everybody ought to know this." And, if you call it remedial, isn't that what you're saying? "This is really basic and everybody has to know it."

Such a course would be a perfect circus. The examples are so legion. I don't see why people don't do it. They may not do it mostly because they don't want to. But also, maybe they don't know how. And maybe they don't know what it is.

But the whole law school experience would be much more fun if the really basic ideas were integrated and pounded in with good examples for a month or so before you got into conventional law school material. I think the whole system of education would work better. But nobody has any interest in doing it.

And when law schools do reach out beyond traditional material, they often do it in what looks to me like a pretty dumb way. If you think psychology is badly taught in America, you should look at corporate finance. Modern portfolio theory? It's demented! It's truly amazing.

I don't know how these things happen. Hard science and engineering tend to be pretty reliably done. But the minute you get outside of those areas, a certain amount of inanity seems to creep into academia—even [in] academia involving people with very high I.Q.'s.

But, boy, what a school would be like that pounded a lot of the silliness out. But the right way to pound it out is not to have some seventy-plus-year-old capitalist come in and tell seniors, "Here's a little remedial worldly wisdom." This is not the way to do it.

Many of the legal doctrines are tied to other doctrines. They're joined at the hip. And, yet, they teach you those legal doctrines without pointing out how they're tied to the other important doctrines. That's insanity—absolute insanity.

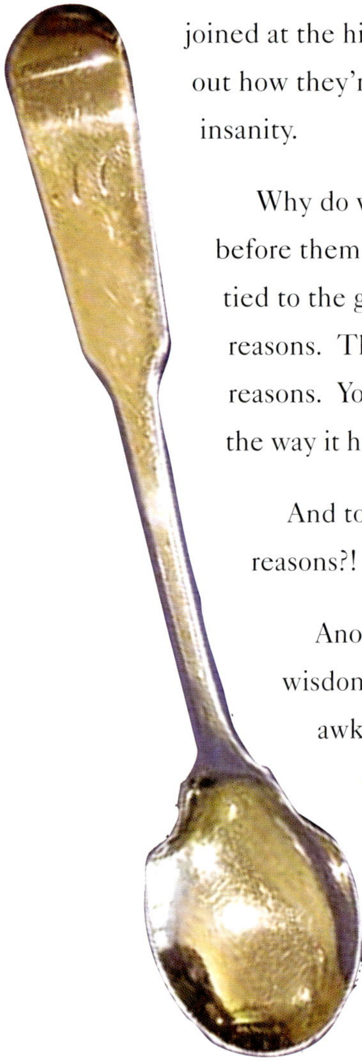

On the other hand, a month at the start of law school that really pounded in the basic doctrines.... Many of the legal doctrines are tied to other doctrines. They're joined at the hip. And, yet, they teach you those legal doctrines without pointing out how they're tied to the other important doctrines?! That's insanity—absolute insanity.

Why do we have a rule that judges shouldn't talk about legal issues that aren't before them? In my day, they taught us the rule, but not in a way giving reasons tied to the guts of undergraduate courses. It's crazy that people don't have those reasons. The human mind is not constructed so that it works well without having reasons. You've got to hang reality on a theoretical structure with reasons. That's the way it hangs together in usable form so that you're an effective thinker.

And to teach doctrines—either with no reasons or with poorly explained reasons?! That's wrong!

Another reason why I like the idea of having a course on remedial worldly wisdom is that it would force more sense on the professors. It would be awkward for them to teach something that was contravened by lessons that were obviously correct and emphasized in a course named "Remedial Worldly Wisdom." Professors doing so would really have to justify themselves.

Is that a totally crazy idea? It may be crazy to expect it to be done. However, if somebody had done it, would you have found it useful?

I'm always asked this question: "Spoon-feed me what you know." And, of course, what they're often saying is, "Teach me now to get rich with soft white hands faster. And not only let me get rich faster, but teach me faster, too."

Q: I think it would be a wonderful thing to have. Unfortunately, when it's created, we won't be here anymore. You're proposing that this would be good to teach people in a course form so it would be accessible to them. Is there any way that it could be more accessible to us—other than having to...

I get requests for pointers to easy learning all the time. And I'm trying to provide a little easy learning today. But one talk like this is not the right way to do it. The right way to do it would be in a book.

I hope what I'm saying will help you be more effective and better human beings. And if you don't get rich, that won't bother me. But I'm always asked this question: "Spoon-feed me what you know." And, of course, what they're often saying is, "Teach me now to get rich with soft white hands faster. And not only let me get rich faster, but teach me faster, too."

I don't have much interest in writing a book myself. Plus it would be a lot of work for somebody like me to try and do it in my seventies. And I have plenty else to do in life. So I'm not going to do it. But it's a screaming opportunity for somebody. And I'd provide funds to support the writing of an appropriate book if I found someone with the wisdom and the will to do the job right.

Let me turn to some of the probable reasons for present bad education. Part of the trouble is caused by the balkanization of academia. For instance, psychology is most powerful when combined with doctrines from other academic departments. But if your psychology professor doesn't know the other doctrines, then he isn't capable of doing the necessary integration.

And how would anyone get to be a psychology professor in the first place if he were good with nonpsychology doctrines and constantly worked nonpsychology doctrines into his material? Such a would-be professor would usually offend his peers and superiors.

There have been some fabulous psychology professors in the history of the world. Cialdini of Arizona State was very useful to me, as was B. F. Skinner—for his experimental results, if divorced from his monomania and utopianism. But averaged

B. F. Skinner
(1904–1990)

Born Burrhus Frederic Skinner in Pennsylvania to an attorney father and a strong and intelligent mother, B. F. Skinner enjoyed school and did well enough to get to college. Following graduation, he wrote newspaper articles on labor problems and lived in Greenwich Village. Tiring of a bohemian lifestyle, he decided to return to Harvard, where he earned a Ph.D. in psychology. Skinner's great contributions to psychology are his experiments in operant conditioning and behaviorism. Operant conditioning can be summarized as follows: "A behavior is followed by a consequence, and the nature of the consequence modifies the organism's tendency to repeat the behavior in the future."

out, I don't believe that psychology professors in America are people whose alternative career paths were in the toughest part of physics. And that may be one of the reasons why they don't get it quite right.

The schools of education, even at eminent universities, are pervaded by psychology. And they're almost an intellectual disgrace. It's not unheard of for academic departments—even at great institutions—to be quite deficient in important ways. And including a lot of material labeled as psychological is no cure-all.

And given academic inertia, all academic deficiencies are very hard to fix. Do you know how they tried to fix psychology at the University of Chicago? Having tenured professors who were terrible, the president there actually abolished the entire psychology department.

And Chicago, in due course, will probably bring back a new and different psychology department. Indeed, by now, it probably has. Perhaps conditions are now better. And I must admit that I admire a college president who will do something like that.

I do not wish to imply in my criticism that the imperfections of academic psychology teaching are all attributable to some kind of human fault common only to such departments. Instead, the causes of many of the imperfections lie deep in the nature of things—in irritating peculiarities that can't be removed from psychology.

Let me demonstrate by a "thought experiment" involving a couple of questions: Are there not many fields that need a synthesizing super-mind like that of James Clerk Maxwell, but are destined never to attract one? And is academic psychology, by its nature, one of the most unfortunate of all the would-be attractors of super-minds? I think the answers are yes and yes.

Yerkes Observatory
University of Chicago

The University of Chicago was founded in 1890 by the American Baptist Education Society and John D. Rockefeller. The University, which Rockefeller once described as, "the best investment I ever made," now has an enrollment of over 4,000 undergraduates and 9,000 graduate, professional and other students. It boasts more than seventy Nobel Prize winners among its faculty members, students and researchers.

One can see this by considering the case of any of the few members of each generation who can, as fast as fingers can move, accurately work through the problem sets in thermodynamics, electromagnetism, and physical chemistry. Such a person will be begged by some of the most eminent people alive to enter the upper reaches of hard science.

Will such a super-gifted person instead choose academic psychology wherein lie very awkward realities: (A) that the tendencies demonstrated by social psychology paradoxically grow weaker as more people learn them, and, (B) that clinical (patient-treating) psychology has to deal with the awkward reality that happiness, physiologically measured, is often improved by believing things that are not true? The answer, I think, is plainly no. The super-mind will be repelled by academic psychology much as Nobel laureate physicist Max Planck was repelled by economics, wherein he saw problems that wouldn't yield to his methods.

Q: We talk a lot about trade-offs between the quality of our life and our professional commitments. Is there time for a professional life, learning about these models, and doing whatever else interests you? Do you find time to do fun things besides learning?

I've always taken a fair amount of time to do what I really wanted to do—some of which was merely to fish or play bridge or play golf.

Each of us must figure out his or her own lifestyle. You may want to work seventy hours a week for ten years to make partner at Cravath and thereby obtain the obligation to do more of the same. Or you may say, "I'm not willing to pay that price." Either way, it's a totally personal decision that you have to make by your own lights.

But, whatever you decide, I think it's a huge mistake not to absorb elementary worldly wisdom if you're capable of doing it because it makes you better able to serve others, it makes you better able to serve yourself, and it makes life more fun. So if you have an aptitude for doing it, I think you'd be crazy not to. Your life will be enriched—not only financially, but in a host of other ways—if you do.

Max Planck
(1858–1947)

Max Planck, a German physicist—shown here with Albert Einstein—is known for his work on thermodynamics and radiation. His wisdom includes:

"Science cannot solve the ultimate mystery of nature. And that is because, in the last analysis, we ourselves are a part of the mystery that we are trying to solve."

"Scientific discovery and scientific knowledge have been achieved only by those who have gone in pursuit of it without any practical purpose whatsoever in view."

"A new scientific truth does not triumph by convincing its opponents and making them see the light, but rather because its opponents eventually die, and a new generation grows up that is familiar with it."

"It is not the possession of truth, but the success which attends the seeking after it, that enriches the seeker and brings happiness to him."

Now this has been a very peculiar talk for some businessman to come in and give at a law school—some guy who's never taken a course in psychology telling you that all of the psychology textbooks are wrong. This is very eccentric. But all I can tell you is that I'm sincere.

An Obligation to Teach

"Both Warren and I, in the makeup of our personalities and in our ethical systems, believe being an effective teacher is a high calling. My occasional speeches and my allowing this book to go forward and Warren's writing of those annual reports and his occasional speeches and his contact with business school students—it's all part of a teaching obligation. Properly done, if teaching isn't the highest calling of man, it is near it.

"We think it is such a high calling that we subject people to it all the time who don't have the slightest intention of ever learning anything from it. Very few people have taught with more rejection than we have and yet maintained as much enthusiasm."

—Munger

There's a lot of simple stuff that many of you are quite capable of learning. And your lives will work way better, too, if you do. Plus, learning it is a lot of fun. So I urge you to learn it.

Q: Are you, in effect, fulfilling your responsibility to share the wisdom that you've acquired over the years?

Sure. Look at Berkshire Hathaway. I call it the ultimate didactic enterprise. Warren's never going to spend any money. He's going to give it all back to society. He's just building a platform so people will listen to his notions. Needless to say, they're very good notions. And the platform's not so bad either. But you could argue that Warren and I are academics in our own way.

Q: Most of what you've said is very compelling. And your quest for knowledge and, therefore, command of the human condition and money are all laudable goals.

I'm not sure the quest for money is so laudable.

Q: Well, then—understandable.

That I'll take. I don't sneer, incidentally, at making sales calls or proofreading bond indentures. If you need the money, it's fun earning it. And if you have to try a bunch of cases in the course of your career, you'll learn something doing that. You ought to do something to earn money. Many activities are dignified by the fact that you earn money.

Q: I understand your skepticism about overly ideological people. But is there an ideological component to what you do? Is there something that you're irrationally passionate about?

Yeah, I'm passionate about wisdom. I'm passionate about accuracy and some kinds of curiosity. Perhaps I have some streak of generosity in my nature and a desire to serve values that transcend my brief life. But maybe I'm just here to show off. Who knows?

I believe in the discipline of mastering the best that other people have ever figured out. I don't believe in just sitting down and trying to dream it all up yourself. Nobody's that smart....

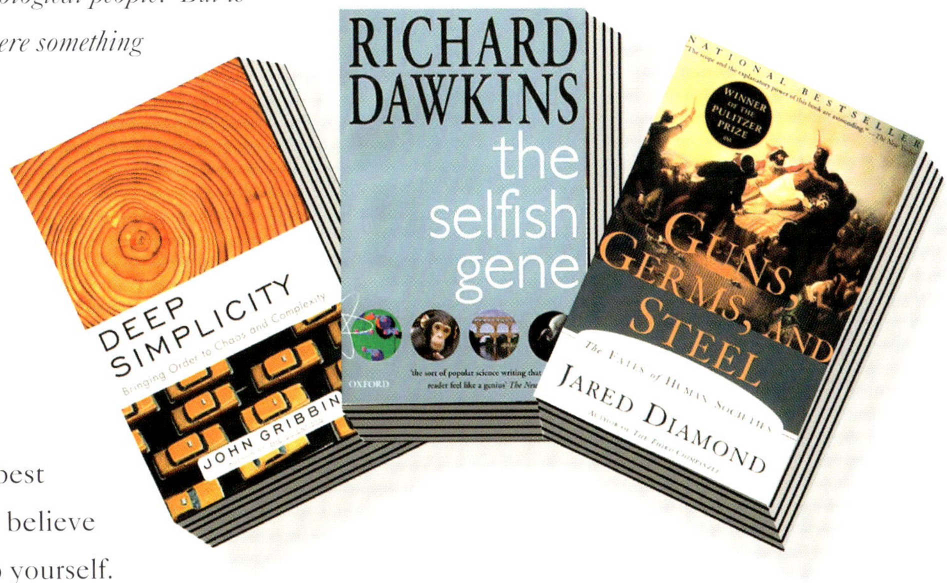

"The best that is known and taught in the world—nothing less can satisfy a teacher worthy of the name."

—Sir William Osler

Talk Three Revisited

When I gave Talk Three in 1996, I argued that intense political animosity should be avoided because it causes much mental malfunction, even in brilliant brains. Since then, political animosity has increased greatly, both on the left and right, with sad effects on the ability of people to recognize reality, exactly as I would have expected.

Naturally, I don't like this result. The grain of my emotional nature is to respond as Archimedes might respond if he complained now to God: "How could you put in those dark ages after I published my formulas?" Or as Mark Twain once complained: "These are sad days in literature. Homer is dead. Shakespeare is dead. And I myself am not feeling at all well."

Fortunately, I am still able to refrain from complaint in the mode of Mark Twain. After all, I never had more than a shred of an illusion that any views of mine would much change the world. Instead, I always knew that aiming low was the best path for me, and so I merely sought (1) to learn from my betters a few practical mental tricks that would help me avoid some of the worst miscognitions common in my age cohort, and (2) to pass on my mental tricks only to a few people who could easily learn from me because they already almost knew what I was telling them. Having pretty well accomplished these very limited objectives, I see little reason to complain now about the un-wisdom of the world. Instead, what works best for me in coping with all disappointment is what I call the Jewish method: humor.

As I revisit Talk Three in March of 2006, I still like its emphasis on the desirability of making human systems as cheating-proof as is practicable, even if this leaves some human misery unfixed. After all, the people who create rewarded cheating on a massive scale leave a trail of super-ruin in their wake, since the bad conduct speads by example and is so very hard to reverse.

And I fondly recall Talk Three's emphasis on both the life-handling lessons I learned from my father's friend, Grant McFayden, and one teaching method I learned from my father. I owe a lot to these long-dead predecessors, and if you like *Poor Charlie's Almanack*, so do you.

"The man who doesn't read good books has no advantage over the man who can't read them."

—Mark Twain

In this talk, Charlie explains how he makes decisions and solves problems by taking us step-by-step through a diverse set of "mental models." He presents a case study that asks rhetorically how the listener would go about producing a $2 trillion business from scratch, using as his example Coca-Cola. Naturally, he has his own solution, apt to strike you as both brilliant and perceptive.

Charlie's case study leads him to a discussion of academia's failures and its record of having produced generations of sloppy decision-makers. For this problem, he has other solutions.

This talk was delivered in 1996 to a group that has a policy of not publicizing its programs.

Editor's warning as suggested by Charlie: Most people don't understand this talk. Charlie says it was an extreme communication failure when made, and people have since found it difficult to understand even when read slowly, twice. To Charlie, these outcomes have "profound educational implications."

Practical Thought About Practical Thought?

An Informal Talk, July 20, 1996

"Without numerical fluency, in the part of life most of us inhabit, you are like a one-legged man in an ass-kicking contest."

The title of my talk is "Practical Thought About Practical Thought?"—with a question mark at the end. In a long career, I have assimilated various ultrasimple general notions that I find helpful in solving problems. Five of these helpful notions I will now describe. After that, I will present to you a problem of extreme scale. Indeed, the problem will involve turning start-up capital of $2 million into $2 trillion, a sum large enough to represent a practical achievement. Then, I will try to solve the problem, assisted by my helpful general notions. Following that, I will suggest that there are important educational implications in my demonstration. I will so finish because my objective is educational, my game today being a search for better methods of thought.

The first helpful notion is that it is usually best to simplify problems by deciding big "no-brainer" questions first.

Galileo Galilei
(1564–1642)

Galileo Galilei, born near Pisa, Italy, had early thoughts of joining a monastic order. Ultimately, though, his interests and education turned to mathematics and medicine, and he is credited with fundamental findings in pendulums, gravity, trajectories, and many other topics. He constructed the first astronomical telescope and used it to discover Jupiter's satellites and the Milky Way. In 1633, he was brought before the Inquisition in Rome, placed under house arrest for the remainder of his life, and made to renounce his beliefs in solar-centric Copernican theory. Despite the trying circumstances, he continued work on his *Discourses* and mathematical demonstrations concerning the two new sciences and completed it in 1638. Smuggled out of Italy and published in Holland, the *Discourses* delineates most of Galileo's contributions to physics.

The second helpful notion mimics Galileo's conclusion that scientific reality is often revealed only by math as if math was the language of God. Galileo's attitude also works well in messy, practical life. Without numerical fluency, in the part of life most of us inhabit, you are like a one-legged man in an ass-kicking contest.

The third helpful notion is that it is not enough to think problems through forward. You must also think in reverse, much like the rustic who wanted to know where he was going to die so that he'd never go there. Indeed, many problems can't be solved forward. And that is why the great algebraist Carl Jacobi so often said, "Invert, always invert." And why the Pythagoreans thought in reverse to prove that the square root of two was an irrational number.

It is not usually the conscious malfeasance of your narrow professional adviser that does you in. Instead, your troubles come from his subconscious bias.

The fourth helpful notion is that the best and most practical wisdom is elementary academic wisdom. But there is one extremely important qualification: You must think in a multidisciplinary manner. You must routinely use all the easy-to-learn concepts from the freshman course in every basic subject. Where elementary ideas will serve, your problem solving must not be limited, as academia and many business bureaucracies are limited, by extreme balkanization into disciplines and subdisciplines, with strong taboos against any venture outside assigned territory. Instead, you must do your multidisciplinary thinking in accord with Ben Franklin's prescription in *Poor Richard*: "If you want it done, go. If not, send."

If, in your thinking, you rely entirely on others, often through purchase of professional advice, whenever outside a small territory of your own, you will suffer much calamity. And it is not just difficulties in complex coordination that will do you in. You will also suffer from the reality evoked by the Shavian character who said, "In the last analysis, every profession is a conspiracy against the laity." Indeed, a Shavian character, for once, understated the horrors of something Shaw didn't like. It is not usually the conscious malfeasance of your narrow professional adviser that does you in. Instead, your troubles come from his subconscious bias. His cognition will often be impaired, for your purposes, by financial incentives different from yours. And he will also suffer from the psychological defect caught by the proverb: "To a man with a hammer, every problem looks like a nail."

The fifth helpful notion is that really big effects, lollapalooza effects, will often come only from large combinations of factors. For instance, tuberculosis was tamed, at least for a long time, only by routine, combined use in each case of three different drugs. And other lollapalooza effects, like the flight of an airplane, follow a similar pattern.

It is now time to present my practical problem. And here is the problem:

It is 1884 in Atlanta. You are brought, along with twenty others like you, before a rich and eccentric Atlanta citizen named Glotz. Both you and Glotz share two characteristics: First, you routinely use in problem solving the five helpful notions, and, second, you know all the elementary ideas in all the basic college courses, as taught in 1996. However, all discoverers and all examples demonstrating these elementary ideas come from dates before 1884. Neither you nor Glotz knows anything about anything that has happened after 1884.

Pythagoras and Irrational Numbers

Pythagoras (582–496 BC), an Ionian (Greek) mathematician and philosopher known as "the father of numbers," is often credited with the discovery of irrational numbers. More likely though, the credit belongs to one or more of his followers, the Pythagoreans, who produced a proof of the irrationality of the square root of two. But Pythagoras, believing that numbers were absolute, rejected irrational numbers and is said to have sentenced their leading proponent to death by drowning for his heresy.

Generally, an irrational number is any real number that cannot be written as a fraction "a/b," with "a" and "b" integers, and "b" not zero. For a number to be irrational, its expansion in any given base (decimal, binary, etc.) never ends and never enters a periodic pattern.

Pythagoras at *The School of Athens* (detail) 1509 Fresco, Vatican, Raffello Sanzio

Glotz offers to invest two million 1884 dollars, yet take only half the equity, for a Glotz Charitable Foundation, in a new corporation organized to go into the non-alcoholic beverage business and remain in that business only, forever. Glotz wants to use a name that has somehow charmed him: Coca-Cola.

The other half of the new corporation's equity will go to the man who most plausibly demonstrates that his business plan will cause Glotz's foundation to be worth a trillion dollars 150 years later, in the money of that later time, 2034, despite paying out a large part of its earnings each year as a dividend. This will make the whole new corporation worth $2 trillion, even after paying out many billions of dollars in dividends.

You have fifteen minutes to make your pitch. What do you say to Glotz?

Here is my solution, my pitch to Glotz, using only the helpful notions and what every bright college sophomore should know.

Well, Glotz, the big "no-brainer" decisions that, to simplify our problem, should be made first are as follows: First, we are never going to create something worth $2 trillion by selling some generic beverage. Therefore, we must make your name, "Coca-Cola," into a strong, legally protected trademark. Second, we can get to $2 trillion only by starting in Atlanta, then succeeding in the rest of the United States, then rapidly succeeding with our new beverage all over the world. This will require developing a product having universal appeal because it harnesses powerful elemental forces. And the right place to find such powerful elemental forces is in the subject matter of elementary academic courses.

We will next use numerical fluency to ascertain what our target implies. We can guess reasonably that by 2034 there will be about eight billion beverage consumers in the world. On average, each of these consumers will be much more prosperous in real terms than the average consumer of 1884. Each consumer is composed mostly of water and must ingest about sixty-four ounces of water per day. This is eight, eight-

Roman Drachma

The drachma was originally a unit of currency in Classical Greece. The word derives from the verb "to grasp." The drachma was also used in Ancient Rome in the third century BC and later. Most historians say one Roman drachma was equivalent to a day's wages for a laborer.

Currency Depreciation

A nation's currency depreciates with respect to another when its value falls in terms of the other.

ounce servings. Thus, if our new beverage, and other imitative beverages in our new market, can flavor and otherwise improve only twenty-five percent of ingested water worldwide, and we can occupy half of the new world market, we can sell 2.92 trillion eight-ounce servings in 2034. And if we can then net four cents per serving, we will earn $117 billion. This will be enough, if our business is still growing at a good rate, to make it easily worth $2 trillion.

A big question, of course, is whether four cents per serving is a reasonable

In essence, we are going into the business of creating and maintaining conditioned reflexes.

profit target for 2034. And the answer is yes if we can create a beverage with strong universal appeal. One hundred fifty years is a long time. The dollar, like the Roman drachma, will almost surely suffer monetary depreciation. Concurrently, real purchasing power of the average beverage consumer in the world will go way up. His proclivity to inexpensively improve his experience while ingesting water will go up considerably faster. Meanwhile, as technology improves, the cost of our simple product, in units of constant purchasing power, will go down. All four factors will work together in favor of our four-cents-per-serving profit target. Worldwide beverage-purchasing power in dollars will probably multiply by a factor of at least forty over 150 years. Thinking in reverse, this makes our profit-per-serving target,

"If you get to thinking you're a person of some influence, try ordering somebody else's dog around."

—Will Rogers

Ivan Pavlov
(1849–1936)

Ivan Pavlov was born in central Russia and attended seminary until age twenty-one, when he abandoned theology in favor of chemistry and physiology. Earning his M.D. in 1883, he excelled in physiology and surgical techniques. Later, he studied the secretory activity of digestion and ultimately formulated the laws of conditioned reflexes.

Pavlov's most famous experiment showed that dogs tend to salivate before food is actually delivered to their mouths. This result led him to a long series of experiments in which he manipulated the stimuli occurring before the presentation of food. He thereby established the basic laws for the establishment and extinction of what he called "conditional reflexes," later mistranslated from the original Russian as "conditioned reflexes." He was awarded the Nobel Prize in 1904 for his work on digestive secretions.

under 1884 conditions, a mere one fortieth of four cents or one tenth of a cent per serving. This is an easy-to-exceed target as we start out if our new product has universal appeal.

That decided, we must next solve the problem of invention to create universal appeal. There are two intertwined challenges of large scale: First, over 150 years, we must cause a new-beverage market to assimilate about one-fourth of the world's water ingestion. Second, we must so operate that half

> ***"I want a can of Coke within arm's reach of every American serviceman—something to remind him of home."***
>
> *—Dwight D. Eisenhower, Supreme Allied Commander, World War II*

the new market is ours while all our competitors combined are left to share the remaining half. These results are lollapalooza results. Accordingly, we must attack our problem by causing every favorable factor we can think of to work for us. Plainly, only a powerful combination of many factors is likely to cause the lollapalooza consequences we desire. Fortunately, the solution to these intertwined problems turns out to be fairly easy if one has stayed awake in all the freshman courses.

Let us start by exploring the consequences of our

simplifying "no-brainer" decision that we must rely on a strong trademark. This conclusion automatically leads to an understanding of the essence of our business in proper elementary academic terms. We can see from the introductory course in psychology that, in essence, we are going into the business of creating and maintaining conditioned reflexes. The "Coca-Cola" trade name and trade dress will act as the stimuli, and the purchase and ingestion of our beverage will be the desired responses.

The "Coca-Cola" trade name and trade dress will act as the stimuli, and the purchase and ingestion of our beverage will be the desired responses.

And how does one create and maintain conditioned reflexes? Well, the psychology text gives two answers: (1) by operant conditioning and (2) by classical conditioning, often called Pavlovian conditioning to honor the great Russian scientist. And, since we want a lollapalooza result, we must use both conditioning techniques—and all we can invent to enhance effects from each technique.

The operant conditioning part of our problem is easy to solve. We need only (1) maximize rewards of our beverage's ingestion and (2) minimize possibilities that desired reflexes, once created by us, will be extinguished through operant conditioning by proprietors of competing products.

For operant conditioning rewards, there are only a few categories we will find practical:

(1) Food value in calories or other inputs;

(2) Flavor, texture, and aroma acting as stimuli to consumption under neural preprogramming of man through Darwinian natural selection;

(3) Stimulus, as by sugar or caffeine;

(4) Cooling effect when man is too hot or warming effect when man is too cool.

Wanting a lollapalooza result, we will naturally include rewards in all the categories.

To start out, it is easy to decide to design our beverage for consumption cold. There is much less opportunity, without ingesting beverage, to counteract excessive heat, compared with excessive cold. Moreover, with excessive heat, much liquid must be consumed, and the reverse is not true. It is also easy to decide to include both sugar and caffeine. After all, tea, coffee, and lemonade are already

A competing product, if it is never tried, can't act as a reward creating a conflicting habit. Every spouse knows that.

widely consumed. And, it is also clear that we must be fanatic about determining, through trial and error, flavor and other characteristics that will maximize human pleasure while taking in the sugared water and caffeine we will provide. And, to counteract possibilities that desired operant-conditioned reflexes, once created by us, will be extinguished by operant-conditioning-employing competing products, there is also an obvious answer: We will make it a permanent obsession in our company that our beverage, as fast as practicable, will at all times be available everywhere throughout the world. After all, a competing product, if it is never tried, can't act as a reward creating a conflicting habit. Every spouse knows that.

We must next consider the Pavlovian conditioning we must also use. In Pavlovian conditioning, powerful effects come from mere association. The neural system of Pavlov's dog causes it to salivate at the bell it can't eat. And the brain of man yearns for the type of beverage held by the pretty woman he can't have. And so, Glotz, we must use every sort of decent, honorable Pavlovian conditioning we can think of. For as long as we are in business, our beverage and its promotion must be associated in consumer minds with all other things consumers like or admire.

The brain of man yearns for the type of beverage held by the pretty woman he can't have.

Such extensive Pavlovian conditioning will cost a lot of money, particularly for advertising. We will spend big money as far ahead as we can imagine. But the money will be effectively spent. As we expand fast in our new-beverage market, our competitors will face gross disadvantages of scale in buying advertising to create the Pavlovian conditioning they need. And this outcome, along with other volume-creates-power effects, should help us gain and hold at least fifty percent of the new market everywhere. Indeed, provided buyers are scattered, our higher volumes will give us very extreme cost advantages in distribution.

Moreover, Pavlovian effects from mere association will help us choose the flavor, texture, and color of our new beverage. Considering Pavlovian effects, we will have wisely chosen the exotic and expensive-sounding name "Coca-Cola," instead of a pedestrian name like "Glotz's Sugared, Caffeinated Water." For similar Pavlovian reasons, it will be wise to have our beverage look pretty much like wine instead of sugared water. And so, we will artificially color our beverage if it comes out clear. And we will carbonate our water, making our product seem like champagne, or some other expensive beverage, while also making its flavor better and imitation harder to arrange for competing products. And, because we are going to attach so many expensive psychological effects to our flavor, that flavor should be different from any other standard flavor so that we maximize difficulties for competitors and give no accidental same-flavor benefit to any existing product.

What else, from the psychology textbook, can help our new business? Well, there is that powerful "monkey-see, monkey-do" aspect of human nature that psychologists often call "social proof." Social proof, imitative consumption triggered by mere sight of consumption, will not only help induce trial of our beverage. It will also bolster perceived rewards from consumption. We will always take this powerful social-proof factor into account as we design advertising and sales promotion and as we forego present profit to enhance present and future consumption. More than with most other products, increased selling power will come from each increase in sales.

Autocatalytic Reaction

An autocatalytic reaction (also called autocatalysis) occurs when a single chemical reaction product is itself the catalyst for that reaction. For example, tin pest is an autocatalytic reaction of the element tin; at low temperatures, it causes deterioration of tin objects. Atmospheric ozone depletion is another example of an autocatalytic reaction.

We can now see, Glotz, that by combining (1) much Pavlovian conditioning, (2) powerful social-proof effects, and (3) a wonderful-tasting, energy-giving, stimulating, and desirably cold beverage that causes much operant conditioning, we are going to get sales that speed up for a long time by reason of the huge mixture of factors we have chosen. Therefore, we are going to start something like an autocatalytic reaction in chemistry, precisely the sort of multifactor-triggered lollapalooza effect we need.

The logistics and the distribution strategy of our business will be simple. There are only two practical ways to sell our beverage: (1) as syrup to fountains and restaurants and (2) as a complete carbonated-water product in containers. Wanting lollapalooza results, we will naturally do it both ways. And, wanting huge Pavlovian and social-proof effects, we will always spend on advertising and sales promotion, per serving, over forty percent of the fountain price for syrup needed to make the serving.

A few syrup-making plants can serve the world. However, to avoid needless shipping of mere space and water, we will need many bottling plants scattered over the world. We will maximize profits if (like early General Electric with light bulbs) we always set the first-sale price, either (1) for fountain syrup or (2) for any container of our complete product. The best way to arrange this desirable profit-maximizing control is to make any independent bottler we need a subcontractor, not a vendee of syrup, and certainly not a vendee of syrup under a perpetual franchise specifying a syrup price frozen forever at its starting level.

Being unable to get a patent or copyright on our superimportant flavor, we will work obsessively to keep our formula secret. We will make a big hoopla over our secrecy, which will enhance Pavlovian effects. Eventually, food-chemical engineering will advance so that our flavor can be copied with near exactitude. But, by that time, we will be so far ahead, with such strong trademarks and complete, "always available" worldwide distribution, that good flavor copying won't bar us from our objective. Moreover, the advances in food chemistry that help competitors will almost surely be accompanied by technological advances that will help us, including refrigeration, better transportation, and, for dieters, ability to insert a sugar taste without inserting sugar's calories. Also, there will be related beverage opportunities we will seize.

This brings us to a final reality check for our business plan. We will, once more, think in reverse like Jacobi. What must we avoid because we don't want it? Four answers seem clear:

The Ten Commandments

The commandments were a list of religious and moral imperatives that featured prominently in Judaism and Christianity. According to the Bible, the commandments represent the solemn utterances of God directly revealed to Moses and then by Moses to the people of Israel. The Bible indicates Moses wrote God's name with the Ten Commandments upon two tablets of stone. The commandments are:

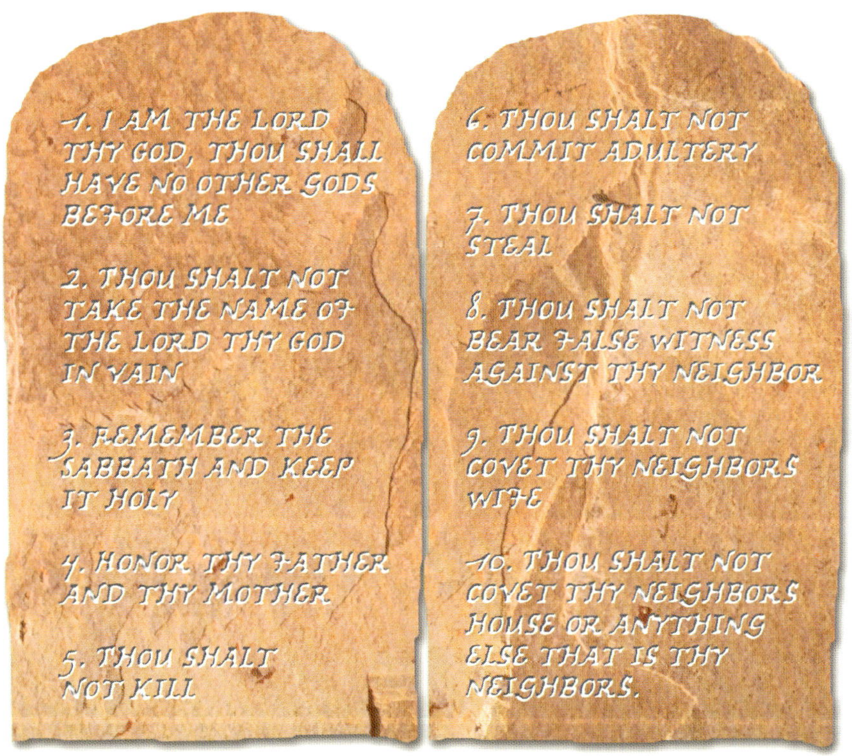

First, we must avoid the protective, cloying, stop-consumption effects of aftertaste that are a standard part of physiology, developed through Darwinian evolution to enhance the replication of man's genes by forcing a generally helpful moderation on the gene carrier. To serve our ends, on hot days, a consumer must be able to drink container after container of our product with almost no impediment from aftertaste. We will find a wonderful no-aftertaste flavor by trial and error and will thereby solve this problem.

Second, we must avoid ever losing even half of our powerful trademarked name. It will cost us mightily, for instance, if our sloppiness should ever allow sale of any other kind of "cola," for instance, a "peppy cola." If there is ever a "peppy cola," we will be the proprietor of the brand.

Third, with so much success coming, we must avoid bad effects from envy, which is given a prominent place in the Ten Commandments because envy is so much a part of human nature. The best way to avoid envy, recognized by Aristotle, is to plainly deserve the success we get. We will be fanatic about product quality, quality of product presentation, and reasonableness of prices, considering the harmless pleasure we will provide.

Fourth, after our trademarked flavor dominates our new market, we must avoid making any huge and sudden change in our flavor. Even if a new flavor performs better in blind taste tests, changing to that new flavor would be a foolish thing to do. This follows because, under such conditions, our old flavor will be so entrenched in consumer preference by psychological effects that a big flavor change would do us little good. And it would do immense harm by triggering in consumers the standard deprival super-reaction syndrome that makes "take-aways" so hard to get in any type of negotiation and helps make most gamblers so irrational. Moreover, such a large flavor change would allow a competitor, by copying our old flavor, to take advantage of both (1) the hostile consumer super-reaction to deprival and (2) the huge love of our original flavor created by our previous work.

Well, that is my solution to my own problem of turning \$2 million into \$2 trillion even after paying out billions of dollars in dividends. I think it would have won with Glotz in 1884 and should convince you more than you expected at the outset. After all, the correct strategies are clear after being related to elementary academic ideas brought into play by the helpful notions.

How consistent is my solution with the history of the real Coca-Cola Company? Well, as late as 1896, twelve years after the fictional Glotz was to start vigorously with two million 1884 dollars, the real Coca-Cola Company had a net worth under \$150,000 and earnings of about zero. And thereafter, the real Coca-Cola Company did lose half its trademark and did grant perpetual bottling franchises at fixed syrup prices. And some of the bottlers were not very effective and couldn't easily be changed. And the real Coca-Cola Company, with this system, did lose much pricing control that would have improved results, had it been retained. Yet, even so, the real Coca-Cola Company followed so much of the plan given to Glotz that it is now worth

Aristotle
(384–322 BC)

Aristotle, born at Stagyra, a Greek colony, was son to a court physician for the king of Macedonia. Joining the Academy in Athens, Aristotle studied under Plato for twenty years. Diverging from Plato's teaching, Aristotle ultimately established his own school, the Lyceum. Following Alexander's death and the overthrow of his government, Aristotle faced charges of impiety and was forced to flee. He died exiled from Athens.

Aristotle's works include treatises on physics, metaphysics, rhetoric, and ethics. He is also known for his observations about nature and the physical world, which formed the basis for the modern study of biology.

Michael Faraday
(1791–1867)

Child of a blacksmith in England, Michael Faraday was apprenticed at age fourteen to a bookbinder and bookseller. He became a voracious reader and his bookbinding duties also led him to the study of chemistry, at which he excelled. He discovered benzene and was the first to describe the compounds of chlorine and carbon. He also experimented with magnetism and electricity, leading him to produce continuous rotation using electric current—a necessary precursor to the electric motor. Faraday is also credited with the discovery of electromagnetic induction, principles of electrolysis, and a method to measure electrical charges, the voltameter.

about $125 billion and will have to increase its value at only eight percent per year until 2034 to reach a value of $2 trillion. And it can hit an annual physical volume target of 2.92 trillion servings if servings grow until 2034 at only six percent per year, a result consistent with much past experience and leaving plenty of plain-water ingestion for Coca-Cola to replace after 2034. So, I would guess that the fictional Glotz, starting earlier and stronger and avoiding the worst errors, would have easily hit his $2 trillion target. And he would have done it well before 2034.

This brings me, at last, to the main purpose of my talk. Large educational implications exist, if my answer to Glotz's problem is roughly right and you make one more assumption I believe true—that most Ph.D. educators, even psychology professors and business school deans, would not have given the same simple answer I did. And, if I am right in these two ways, this would indicate that our civilization now keeps in place a great many educators who can't satisfactorily explain Coca-Cola, even in retrospect, and even after watching it closely all their lives. This is not a satisfactory state of affairs.

Academic psychology, while it is admirable and useful as a list of ingenious and important experiments, lacks intradisciplinary synthesis.

Moreover—and this result is even more extreme—the brilliant and effective executives who, surrounded by business school and law school graduates, have run the Coca-Cola Company with glorious success in recent years also did not understand elementary psychology well enough to predict and avoid the "New Coke" fiasco, which dangerously threatened their company. That people so talented, surrounded by professional advisers from the best universities, should thus demonstrate a huge gap in their education is also not a satisfactory state of affairs.

Such extreme ignorance, in both the high reaches of academia and the high reaches of business is a lollapalooza effect of a negative sort, demonstrating grave defects in academia. Because the bad effect is a lollapalooza, we should expect to find intertwined, multiple academic causes. I suspect at least two such causes.

First, academic psychology, while it is admirable and useful as a list of ingenious and important experiments, lacks intradisciplinary synthesis. In particular, not enough attention is given to lollapalooza effects coming from combinations of psychological tendencies. This creates a situation reminding one of a rustic teacher who tries to simplify school work by rounding pi to an even three. And it violates Einstein's injunction that "everything should be made as simple as possible—but no more simple." In general, psychology is laid out and misunderstood as electromagnetism would now be misunderstood if physics had produced many brilliant experimenters like Michael Faraday and no grand synthesizer like James Clerk Maxwell.

Academic psychology departments are immensely more important and useful than other academic departments think. And, at the same time, the psychology departments are immensely worse than most of their inhabitants think. It is, of course, normal for self-appraisal to be more positive than external appraisal. Indeed, a problem of this sort may have given you your speaker today.

And, second, there is a truly horrible lack of synthesis blending psychology and other academic subjects. But only an interdisciplinary approach will correctly deal with reality—in academia as with the Coca-Cola Company.

In short, academic psychology departments are immensely more important and useful than other academic departments think. And, at the same time, the

James Clerk Maxwell
(1831–1879)

James Clerk Maxwell, born in Edinburgh, Scotland, demonstrated a very early interest in optics; a favorite childhood pastime of his was using a mirror to reflect the sun's rays. His unusual mode of dress earned him the nickname "Dafty" at Edinburgh Academy. Nonetheless, he was a brilliant student excelling in mathematics. He attended Cambridge University and joined its staff of lecturers following graduation. His interest in optics led him to study colors and astronomy. He also made significant contributions in the field of electromagnetism, including the first proposal that light is a form of electromagnetic radiation.

Sir Isaac Newton
(1642–1727)

Sir Isaac Newton, most famous for his conception of the law of universal gravitation, is also the source of these wise and pithy observations:

"Tact is the art of making a point without making an enemy."

"If I have ever made any valuable discoveries, it has been due more to patient attention, than to any other talent."

"No great discovery was ever made without a bold guess."

"We build too many walls and not enough bridges."

"If I am anything, which I highly doubt, I have made myself so by hard work."

"I keep the subject of my inquiry constantly before me, and wait till the first dawning opens gradually, by little and little, into a full and clear light."

"If I have done the public any service, it is due to my patient thought."

"If I have seen farther than others, it is because I was standing on the shoulders of giants."

psychology departments are immensely worse than most of their inhabitants think. It is, of course, normal for self-appraisal to be more positive than external appraisal. Indeed, a problem of this sort may have given you your speaker today. But the size of this psychology-department gap is preposterously large. In fact, the gap is so enormous that one very eminent university (Chicago) simply abolished its psychology department, perhaps with an undisclosed hope of later creating a better version.

In such a state of affairs, many years ago and with much that was plainly wrong already present, the "New Coke" fiasco occurred. Therein, Coke's executives came to the brink of destroying the most valuable trademark in the world. The academically correct reaction to this immense and well-publicized fiasco would have been the sort of reaction Boeing would display if three of its new airplanes crashed in a single week. After all, product integrity is involved in each case, and the plain educational failure was immense.

But almost no such responsible, Boeing-like reaction has come from academia. Instead, academia, by and large, continues in its balkanized way to tolerate psychology professors who misteach psychology, nonpsychology professors who fail to consider psychological effects obviously crucial in their subject matter, and professional schools that carefully preserve psychological ignorance coming in with each entering class and are proud of their inadequacies.

Even though this regrettable blindness and lassitude is now the normal academic result, are there exceptions providing hope that disgraceful shortcomings of the education establishment will eventually be corrected? Here, my answer is a very optimistic yes.

For instance, consider the recent behavior of the economics department of the University of Chicago. Over the last decade, this department has enjoyed a near monopoly of the Nobel prizes in economics, largely by getting good predictions out of "free market" models postulating man's rationality. And what is the reaction of this department after winning so steadily with its rational-man approach?

Well, it has just invited into a precious slot amid its company of greats a wise and witty Cornell economist, Richard Thaler. And it has done this because Thaler pokes fun at much that is holy at the University of Chicago. Indeed, Thaler believes, with me, that people are often massively irrational in ways predicted by psychology that must be taken into account in microeconomics.

In so behaving, the University of Chicago is imitating Darwin, who spent much of his long life thinking in reverse as he tried to disprove his own hardest-won and best-loved ideas. And so long as there are parts of academia that keep alive its best values by thinking in reverse like Darwin, we can confidently expect that silly educational practices will eventually be replaced by better ones, exactly as Carl Jacobi might have predicted.

Thaler pokes fun at much that is holy at the University of Chicago. Indeed, Thaler believes, with me, that people are often massively irrational in ways predicted by psychology that must be taken into account in microeconomics.

Richard Thaler
(b. 1945)

Richard Thaler, born in New Jersey, earned his Ph.D. at the University of Rochester. Serving professorships at Cornell and MIT in behavioral economics and decision research, he joined the faculty at University of Chicago in 1995. In addition to his work on behavioral economics and finance, he focuses on the psychology of decision making.

This will happen because the Darwinian approach, with its habitual objectivity taken on as a sort of hair shirt, is a mighty approach, indeed. No less a figure than Einstein said that one of the four causes of his achievement was self-criticism, ranking right up there alongside curiosity, concentration, and perseverance.

And, to further appreciate the power of self-criticism, consider where lies the grave of that very "ungifted" undergraduate, Charles Darwin. It is in Westminster Abbey, right next to the headstone of Isaac Newton, perhaps the most gifted student who ever lived, honored on that headstone in eight Latin words constituting the most eloquent praise in all graveyard print: "Hic depositum est, quod mortale fuit Isaaci Newtoni"—"Here lies that which was mortal of Isaac Newton."

A civilization that so places a dead Darwin will eventually develop and integrate psychology in a proper and practical fashion that greatly increases skills of all sorts. But all of us who have dollops of power and see the light should help the process along. There is a lot at stake. If, in many high places, a universal product as successful as Coca-Cola is not properly understood and explained, it can't bode well for our competency in dealing with much else that is important.

Ad that was a favorite of mine: "The company that needs a new machine tool, and hasn't bought it, is already paying for it."

Of course, those of you with fifty percent of net worth in Coca-Cola stock, occurring because you tried to so invest ten percent after thinking like I did in making my pitch to Glotz, can ignore my message about psychology as too elementary for useful transmission to you. But I am not so sure that this reaction is wise for the rest of you. The situation reminds me of the old-time Warner & Swasey ad that was a favorite of mine: "The company that needs a new machine tool, and hasn't bought it, is already paying for it."

Coca-Cola

Henry Kissinger was among many prominent individuals present when Charlie gave his talk "Practical Thought About Practical Thought?"

CHARLES T. MUNGER

Dear Henry,

July 23, 1996

As one self indulgent man addressing another, I am delighted to enclose the "Dine Out & Lose Weight" book that took 20 pounds off me. I went to its ridiculous system when I saw an even more indulgent friend (a wine and cheese importer) lose 50 pounds on the same diet.

I also enclose something that won't help you --- a more complete version of the talk I gave on July 20. This is sent from a former consultant to one still practicing and from a closet academic to a real one.

You were in great form last weekend, and it was a great pleasure to be with you.

Sincerely,

Charlie

CTM/do

Dr. Henry A. Kissinger
1800 K Street, N.W.
Suite 400
Washington, D.C. 20006

P.O. BOX 55007 • LOS ANGELES, CALIFORNIA 90055-2007 • (213) 624-7715

"Nothing to Add" Number Four

Charles T. Munger's office computer;
never turned on, gathering dust.

Question: "Do you use a computer?"

Answer: "I don't. I do have one in my office, but I've never turned it on. In fact, I wouldn't even know how to plug it in.

In my life there are not many questions I can't properly deal with using my $40 adding machine and dog-eared compound interest table."

Talk Four Revisited

In this talk I attempted to demonstrate large, correctable and important cognitive failure in U.S. academia and business. After all, I argued:

> (1) If academia and business functioned with best practicable results, most denizens would be able to explain the success of the Coca-Cola Company through parsimonious use of basic concepts and problem-solving techniques; yet
>
> (2) As the "new Coke" fiasco and its aftermath indicated, neither academia nor business had a respectable grasp of the simple realities causing the success of Coca-Cola.

As matters worked out, my 1996 talk failed to get through to almost all people hearing it. Then later, between 1996 and 2006, even when the talk's written version was slowly read twice by very intelligent people who admired me, its message likewise failed. In almost all cases the message did not get through in any constructive way. On the other hand, no one said to me that the talk was wrong. Instead, people were puzzled briefly, then moved on.

Thus my failure as a communicator was even more extreme than the cognitive failure I was trying to explain. Why?

The best explanation, I now think, is that I displayed gross folly as an amateur teacher. I attempted too much. I have always avoided all people who want to converse at length about the "meaning of meaning." Yet I chose as my title, "Practical Thought about Practical Thought?" This was a start into tough territory. Then I worked out a long, complex interplay of five generalized, powerful problem-solving tricks with basic ideas from a great many disciplines. I particularly included psychology, about which I wanted to demonstrate that there is much lamentable ignorance, even among highly educated people, some of some of whom teach psychology. My demonstration, naturally, relied on correct psychology as part of my would-be demonstration. This was logically sound. But, if psychological ignorance is widespread, why would most of my hearers recognize that my version of psychology was correct? Thus, for most hearers, I did the rough equivalent of trying to explain some hard-to-comprehend ideas by simply defining those ideas as equivalent to themselves.

And this was not the outer limit of my teaching folly. After I knew that the written version of my talk was hard to understand, I consented to an order of talks in the first edition of *Poor Charlie's Almanack* wherein my psychology talk was Talk Ten, inserted many pages after Talk Four. Instead, I should have recognized that the order of the two talks should be reversed, considering that Talk Four assumed that hearers had already mastered basic psychology, the subject of Talk Ten. Then, finally, in the Second Edition of the *Almanack*, I have preferred to maintain the original, unhelpful order of the two talks. I did this because I like closing the book with my most recent organization of psychology into a sort of check-list that has long been helpful to me.

Readers of the Second Edition, if they wish, can correct somewhat for the teaching defects that I have stubbornly retained. That is, they can re-read Talk Four after mastering Talk Ten. If they are willing to endure this ordeal, I predict that at least some of them will find the result worth the effort.

"Teachers open the door, but you must enter by yourself."

—Chinese proverb

Having ranted in the previous speech about all that is wrong in academia, Charlie holds forth here on the solutions. Delivered in 1998 at the fiftieth reunion of his Harvard Law School class, this talk focuses on a hugely complicated issue—the narrowness of elite education—and segments it into elements whose solutions, when taken together, form a satisfactory answer to the problem. Through a series of rhetorical questions, Charlie posits that professionals such as attorneys, to their own detriment, lack multidisciplinary skills. From his own extensive multidisciplinary studies, he recognizes that there are "subconscious mental tendencies" that keep people from broadening their own horizons sufficiently. Nonetheless, he brings unique and memorable solutions to the problem.

This talk—a favorite of your editor—clearly demonstrates Charlie's "uncommon, common sense." He says, "When it really matters, as with pilots and surgeons, educational systems employ highly-effective structures. Yet, they don't employ these same, well-understood structures in other areas of learning that are also important. If superior structures are known and available, why don't educators more broadly utilize them? What could be more simple?"

The Need for More Multidisciplinary Skills from Professionals: Educational Implications

Fiftieth Reunion of Harvard Law School Class of 1948, April 24, 1998

Today I am going to engage in a game reminding us of our old professors: Socratic solitaire. I will ask and briefly answer five questions:

1) Do broadscale professionals need more multidisciplinary skill?

2) Was our education sufficiently multidisciplinary?

3) In elite broadscale soft science, what is the essential nature of practicable best-form multidisciplinary education?

4) In the last fifty years, how far has elite academia progressed toward attainable best-form multidisciplinarity?

5) What educational practices would make progress faster?

William Tyndale
(1495–1536)

William Tyndale, born in Gloucestershire, England, earned a degree from Oxford and became a priest. He found England hostile to his beliefs and spent time in Germany and Belgium, where he expanded his beliefs and spread the teachings of Martin Luther. His books having been burned, and his having become a continuing target of hostility, he nonetheless continued to publish Bible translations and other tracts. After months of imprisonment, he was condemned for heresy, strangled to death, and publicly cremated. Later, Tyndale's translation formed the basis of the first royally approved English-language Bible and had great impact on the development of the English language.

We start with the question: Do broadscale professionals need more multidisciplinary skill?

To answer the first question, we must first decide whether more multidisciplinarity will improve professional cognition. And, to decide what will cure bad cognition, it will help to know what causes it. One of Bernard Shaw's characters explained professional defects as follows: "In the last analysis, every profession is a conspiracy against the laity." There is a lot of truth in Shaw's diagnosis, as was early demonstrated when in the sixteenth century, the dominant profession, the clergy, burned William Tyndale at the stake for translating the Bible into English.

But Shaw plainly understates the problem in implying that a conscious, self-interested malevolence is the main culprit. More important, there are frequent, terrible effects in professionals from intertwined subconscious mental tendencies, two of which are exceptionally prone to cause trouble:

1) Incentive-caused bias, a natural cognitive drift toward the conclusion that what is good for the professional is good for the client and the wider civilization; and

2) Man-with-a-hammer tendency, with the name taken from the proverb: "To a man with only a hammer, every problem tends to look pretty much like a nail."

One partial cure for man-with-a-hammer tendency is obvious: If a man has a vast set of skills over multiple disciplines, he, by definition, carries multiple tools and, therefore, will limit bad cognitive effects from man-with-a-hammer tendency. Moreover, when he is multidisciplinary enough to absorb from practical psychology the idea that all his life he must fight bad effects from both the tendencies I mentioned, both within himself and from others, he has taken a constructive step on the road to worldly wisdom.

If "A" is narrow professional doctrine and

"B" consists of the big, extra-useful concepts from other disciplines, then, clearly, the professional possessing "A" plus "B" will usually be better off than the poor possessor of "A" alone. How could it be otherwise? And thus, the only rational excuse for not acquiring more "B" is that it is not practical to do so, given the man's need for "A" and the other urgent demands in his life. I will later try to demonstrate that this excuse for unidisciplinarity, at least for our most gifted people, is usually unsound.

Broadscale problems, by definition, cross many academic disciplines.

My second question is so easy to answer that I won't give it much time. Our education was far too unidisciplinary. Broadscale problems, by definition, cross many academic disciplines. Accordingly, using a unidisciplinary attack on such problems is like playing a bridge hand by counting trumps while ignoring all else. This is "bonkers," sort of like the Mad Hatter's Tea Party. But, nonetheless, too much that is similar remains present in professional practice and, even worse, has long been encouraged in isolated departments of soft science, defined as everything less fundamental than biology.

Even in our youth, some of the best professors were horrified by bad effects from balkanization of academia into insular, turf-protecting enclaves wherein notions were maintained by leaps of faith plus exclusion of nonbelievers. Alfred North Whitehead, for one, long ago sounded an alarm in strong language when he spoke of "the fatal unconnectedness of academic disciplines." And, since then, elite educational institutions, agreeing more and more with Whitehead, have steadily fought unconnectedness by bringing in more multidisciplinarity, causing some awesome plaudits to be won in our time by great unconnectedness fighters at borders of academic disciplines, for instance, Harvard's E. O. Wilson and Caltech's Linus Pauling.

Modern academia now gives more multidisciplinarity than we received and is plainly right to do so.

Alfred North Whitehead
(1861–1947)

"Fools act on imagination without knowledge; pedants act on knowledge without imagination."

"True courage is not the brutal force of vulgar heroes, but the firm resolve of virtue and reason."

"Not ignorance, but ignorance of ignorance is the death of knowledge."

"The 'silly' question is the first intimation of some totally new development."

"Civilizations can only be understood by those who are civilized."

"No one who achieves success does so without acknowledging the help of others. The wise and confident acknowledge this help with gratitude."

"Almost all new ideas have a certain aspect of foolishness when they are first produced."

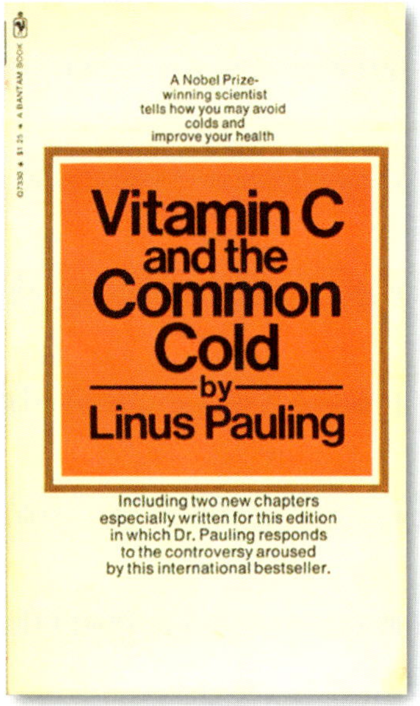

Linus Pauling
(1901–1994)

Encouraged by his parents to pursue his scientific interests, Linus Pauling was a gifted student in Portland, Oregon, and won scholarships to Oregon State University. He went on to earn a Ph.D. in chemistry at the California Institute of Technology, where he taught and carried out his research for the bulk of his career. Pauling made many contributions to his field, including applying quantum physics and wave theory to chemistry. He also made advances in antibody production and the atomic structure of proteins. Charlie believes he may have been the greatest chemist of the twentieth century.

He won Nobel Prizes for chemistry (1954) and peace (1962).

Late in life, Pauling wrote about the role of nutrition in fighting disease and recommended the use of vitamin C to ward off the common cold.

The natural third question then becomes: What is now the goal? What is the essential nature of best-form multidisciplinarity in elite education? This question, too, is easy to answer. All we have to do is examine our most successful narrow-scale education, identify essential elements, and scale up those elements to reach the sensible solution.

Yes, I am suggesting today that mighty Harvard would do better if it thought more about pilot training.

To find the best educational narrow-scale model, we have to look not at unthreatened schools of education and the like, too much driven by our two counterproductive psychological tendencies and other bad influences, but, instead, look where incentives for effective education are strongest and results are most closely measured. This leads us to a logical place: the hugely successful education now mandatory for pilots. (Yes, I am suggesting today that mighty Harvard would do better if it thought more about pilot training.) In piloting, as in other professions, one great hazard is bad effect from man-with-a-hammer tendency. We don't want a pilot, ever, to respond to a hazard as if it was hazard "X" just because his mind contains only a hazard "X" model. And so, for that and other reasons, we train a pilot in a strict six-element system:

1) His formal education is wide enough to cover practically everything useful in piloting.

2) His knowledge of practically everything needed by pilots is not taught just well enough to enable him to pass one test or two; instead, all his knowledge is raised to practice-based fluency, even in handling two or three intertwined hazards at once.

3) Like any good algebraist, he is made to think sometimes in a forward fashion and sometimes in reverse; and so he learns when to concentrate mostly on

what he wants to happen and also when to concentrate mostly on avoiding what he does not want to happen.

4) His training time is allocated among subjects so as to minimize damage from his later malfunctions; and so what is most important in his performance gets the most training coverage and is raised to the highest fluency levels.

5) "Checklist" routines are always mandatory for him.

6) Even after original training, he is forced into a special knowledge-maintenance routine: regular use of the aircraft simulator to prevent atrophy through long disuse of skills needed to cope with rare and important problems.

We need for best results to have multidisciplinary coverage of immense amplitude, with all needed skills raised to an ever-maintained practice-based fluency...

The need for this clearly correct six-element system, with its large demands in a narrow-scale field where stakes are high, is rooted in the deep structure of the human mind. Therefore, we must expect that the education we need for broadscale problem solving will keep all these elements but with awesomely expanded coverage for each element. How could it be otherwise?

Thus it follows, as the night the day, that in our most elite broadscale education wherein we are trying to make silk purses out of silk, we need for best results to have multidisciplinary coverage of immense amplitude, with all needed skills raised to an ever-maintained practice-based fluency, including considerable power of synthesis at boundaries between disciplines, with the highest fluency levels being achieved where they are most needed, with forward and reverse thinking techniques being employed in a manner reminding one of inversion in algebra, and with "checklist" routines being a permanent part of the knowledge system. There can be no

Al Ueltschi

FlightSafety International
Founded by Al Ueltschi

A Berkshire Hathaway company, FlightSafety has a unique corporate culture driven by founder Al Ueltschi. The culture is encapsulated in his "Six Pillars of Character" statement given to each employee and rigorously adhered to throughout the company. The "Pillars" are trustworthiness, fairness, respect, caring, responsibility, and citizenship.

One of the company's credos, no doubt inspired by the founder: "The best safety device in any aircraft is a well-trained pilot."

Pierre-Simon Laplace
(1749–1827)

Pierre-Simon Laplace, a French mathematician, astronomer, and philosopher, discovered many key ideas relating to inductive reasoning and probability, celestial movement, and causal determinism.

other way, no easier way, to broadscale worldly wisdom. Thus the task, when first identified in its immense breadth, seems daunting, verging on impossible.

But the task, considered in full context, is far from impossible when we consider three factors:

First, the concept of "all needed skills" lets us recognize that we don't have to raise everyone's skill in celestial mechanics to that of Laplace and also ask everyone to achieve a similar skill level in all other knowledge. Instead, it turns out that the truly big ideas in each discipline, learned only in essence, carry most of the freight. And they are not so numerous, nor are their interactions so complex, that a large and multidisciplinary understanding is impossible for many, given large amounts of talent and time.

Second, in elite education, we have available the large amounts of talent and time that we need. After all, we are educating the top one percent in aptitude, using teachers who, on average, have more aptitude than the students. And we have roughly thirteen long years in which to turn our most promising twelve-year-olds into starting professionals.

Third, thinking by inversion and through use of "checklists" is easily learned—in broadscale life as in piloting.

Moreover, we can believe in the attainability of broad multidisciplinary skill for the same reason the fellow from Arkansas gave for his belief in baptism: "I've seen it done." We all know of individuals, modern Ben Franklins, who have (1) achieved a massive multidisciplinary synthesis with less time in formal education than is now available to our numerous brilliant young and (2) thus become better performers in their own disciplines, not worse, despite diversion of learning time to matter outside the normal coverage of their own disciplines.

Given the time and talent available and examples of successful masters of multiple disciplines, what is shown by our present failure to minimize bad effects from man-with-a-hammer tendency is only that you can't win big in multidisciplinarity in soft-science academia if you are so satisfied with the status quo, or so frightened by the difficulties of change, that you don't try hard enough to win big.

Which brings us to our fourth question: Judged with reference to an optimized feasible multidisciplinary goal, how much has elite soft-science education been corrected after we left?

The answer is that many things have been tried as corrections in the direction of better multidisciplinarity. And, after allowing for some counterproductive results, there has been some considerable improvement, net. But much desirable correction is still undone and lies far ahead.

For instance, soft-science academia has increasingly found it helpful when professors from different disciplines collaborate or when a professor has been credentialed in more than one discipline. But a different sort of correction has usually worked best, namely augmentation, or "take what you wish" practice that encourages any discipline to simply assimilate whatever it chooses from other disciplines. Perhaps it has worked best because it bypassed academic squabbles rooted in the tradition and territoriality that had caused the unidisciplinary folly for which correction was now sought.

In his great work, *A Philosophical Essay on Probabilities,* Laplace sets out one of his signature ideas:

"We may regard the present state of the universe as the effect of its past and the cause of its future. An intellect which at a certain moment would know all forces that set nature in motion, and all positions of all items of which nature is composed, if this intellect were also vast enough to submit these data to analysis, it would embrace in a single formula the movements of the greatest bodies of the universe and those of the tiniest atom; for such an intellect nothing would be uncertain and the future just like the past would be present before its eyes."

Economics, in turn, took in from a biologist the "tragedy of the commons" model, thus correctly finding a wicked "invisible foot" in coexistence with Adam Smith's angelic "invisible hand."

Roger Fisher
(b. 1922)

Roger Fisher earned a law degree from Harvard in 1948 and stayed on as a faculty member in the Law School. He became director of the Harvard Negotiation Project in 1980. An expert in negotiation and conflict resolution, he coauthored (with Bill Ury) *Getting to YES*, a classic text in win-win negotiation techniques.

In any event, through increased use of "take what you wish," many soft-science disciplines reduced folly from man-with-a-hammer tendency. For instance, led by our classmate Roger Fisher, the law schools brought in negotiation, drawing on other disciplines. Over three million copies of Roger's wise and ethical negotiation book have now been sold, and his life's achievement may well be the best, ever, from our whole class. The law schools also brought in a lot of sound and useful economics, even some good game theory to enlighten antitrust law by better explaining how competition really works.

Economics, in turn, took in from a biologist the "tragedy of the commons" model, thus correctly finding a wicked "invisible foot" in coexistence with Adam Smith's angelic "invisible hand." These days, there is even some "behavioral economics," wisely seeking aid from psychology.

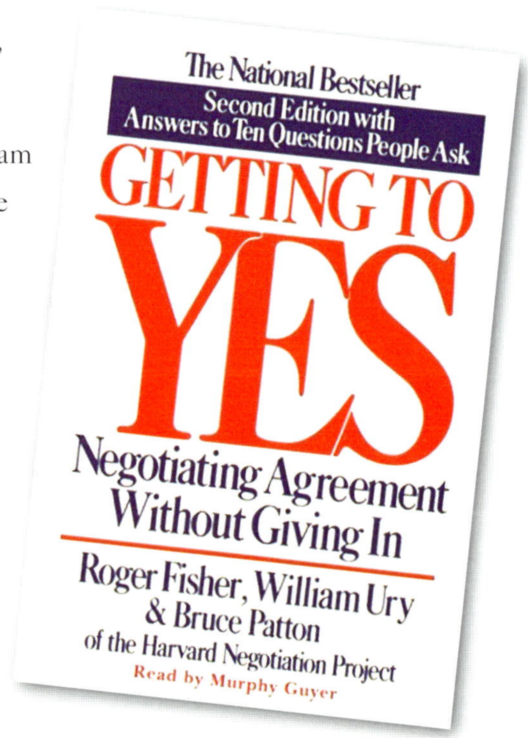

However, an extremely permissive practice like "take what you wish" was not destined to have one-hundred-percent-admirable results in soft science. Indeed, in some of its worst outcomes, it helped changes like (1) assimilation of Freudianism in some literature departments; (2) importation into many places of extremist political ideologies of the left or right that had, for their possessors, made regain of objectivity almost as unlikely as regain of virginity; and (3) importation into many law and business schools of hard-form, efficient-market theory by misguided would-be experts in corporate finance, one of whom kept explaining Berkshire Hathaway's investing success by adding standard deviations of luck until, at six standard deviations, he encountered enough derision to force a change in explanation.

Moreover, even when it avoided such lunacies, "take what you wish" had some serious defects. For instance, takings from more fundamental disciplines were often done without attribution, sometimes under new names, with little attention given to rank in a fundamentalness order for absorbed concepts. Such practices (1) act like a lousy filing system that must impair successful use and synthesis of absorbed knowledge and (2) do not maximize in soft science the equivalent of Linus Pauling's systematic mining of physics to improve chemistry. There must be a better way.

This brings us, finally, to our last question: In elite soft science, what practices would hasten our progress toward optimized disciplinarity? Here again, there are some easy answers:

First, many more courses should be mandatory, not optional. And this, in turn, requires that the people who decide what is mandatory must possess large, multidisciplinary knowledge maintained in fluency. This conclusion is as obvious in the training of the would-be broadscale problem solver as it is in the training of the would-be pilot. For instance, both psychology mastery and accounting mastery should be required as outcomes in legal education. Yet, in many elite places, even today, there are no such requirements. Often, such is the narrowness of mind of the program designers that they neither see what is needed and missing nor are able to fix deficiencies.

Taking What You Wish a la Kipling

When 'Omer smote 'is bloomin' lyre,
He'd 'eard men sing by land an' sea;
An' what he thought 'e might require,
'E went an' took—the same as me!

The market-girls an' fishermen,
The shepherds an' the sailors, too,
They 'eard old songs turn up again,
But kep' it quiet—same as you!

They knew 'e stole; 'e knew they knowed.
They didn't tell, nor make a fuss,
But winked at 'Omer down the road,
An' 'e winked back—the same as us!

Second, there should be much more problem-solving practice that crosses several disciplines, including practice that mimics the function of the aircraft simulator in preventing loss of skills through disuse. Let me give an example, roughly remembered, of this sort of teaching by a very wise but untypical Harvard Business School professor many decades ago.

This professor gave a test involving two unworldly old ladies who had just inherited a New England shoe factory making branded shoes and beset with serious business problems described in great detail. The professor then gave the students ample time to answer with written advice to the old ladies. In response to the answers, the professor next gave every student an undesirable grade except for one student who was graded at the top by a wide margin. What was the winning answer? It was very short and roughly as follows: "This business field and this particular business, in its particular location, present crucial problems that are so difficult that unworldly old ladies can not wisely try to solve them through hired help. Given the difficulties and unavoidable agency costs, the old ladies should promptly sell the shoe factory, probably to the competitor who would enjoy the greatest marginal-utility advantage." Thus, the winning answer relied not on what the students had most recently been taught in business school but, instead, on more fundamental concepts, like agency costs and marginal utility, lifted from undergraduate psychology and economics.

Two unworldly old ladies retired to lawn bowling.

Ah, my fellow members of the Harvard Law Class of 1948: If only we had been much more often tested like that, just think of what more we might have accomplished!

Incidentally, many elite private schools now wisely use such multidisciplinary methods in seventh grade science while, at the same time, many graduate schools have not yet seen the same light. This is one more sad example of Whitehead's "fatal unconnectedness" in education.

Third, most soft-science professional schools should increase use of the best business periodicals, like the *Wall Street Journal*, *Forbes*, *Fortune*, etc. Such periodicals are now quite good and perform the function of the aircraft simulator if used to prompt practice in relating events to multidisciplinary causes, often intertwined. And sometimes the periodicals even introduce new models for causes instead of merely refreshing old knowledge. Also, it is not just slightly sound to have the student practice in school what he must practice lifelong after formal education is over if he is going to maximize his good judgment. I know no person in business, respected for verified good judgment, whose wisdom-maintenance system does not include use of such periodicals. Why should academia be different?

Such periodicals are now quite good and perform the function of the aircraft simulator if used to prompt practice in relating events to multidisciplinary causes, often intertwined.

Another Voice on the Value of Reading

"I read everything: annual reports, 10K's, 10Q's, biographies, histories, five newspapers a day. On airplanes, I read the instructions on the backs of the seats. Reading is key. Reading has made me rich over time."

—Buffett

Fourth, in filling scarce academic vacancies, professors of superstrong, passionate, political ideology, whether on the left or right, should usually be avoided. So also for students. Best-form multidisciplinarity requires an objectivity such passionate people have lost, and a difficult synthesis is not likely to be achieved by minds in ideological fetters. In our day, some Harvard Law professors could and did point to a wonderful example of just such ideology-based folly. This, of course, was the law school at Yale, which was then viewed by many at Harvard as trying to improve legal education by importing a particular political ideology as a dominant factor.

Fifth, soft science should more intensely imitate the fundamental organizing ethos of hard science (defined as the "fundamental four-discipline combination" of math, physics, chemistry, and engineering). This ethos deserves more imitation.

Richard P. Feynman
(1918–1988)

Richard Feynman was born in Far Rockaway, New York. He earned an undergraduate degree in physics from the Massachusetts Institute of Technology and went on to Princeton for a Ph.D. He worked on the Manhattan Project and was instrumental in the development of the atomic bomb. He held faculty posts at Cornell University until 1951 and then settled at Caltech. Feynman's major contribution to physics was in quantum electrodynamics, the study of the interactions of electromagnetic radiation with atoms and more fundamental particles. He shared the Nobel Prize in physics in 1965.

Late in life, Feynman was named to the commission that investigated the Challenger Space Shuttle accident. He demonstrated the effect of cold temperatures on rubber O-rings and showed how the resulting shrinkage allowed hot gases to escape, causing the explosion.

After all, hard science has, by a wide margin, the best record for both (1) avoiding unidisciplinary folly and (2) making user-friendly a big patch of multidisciplinary domain, with frequent, good results like those of physicist Richard Feynman when he so quickly found in cold O-rings the cause of our greatest space shuttle disaster. And previous extensions of the ethos into softer fare have worked well. For instance, biology, starting 150 years ago with a descriptive mess not much related to deep theory, has gradually absorbed the fundamental organizing ethos with marvelous results as new generations have come to use better thinking methods, containing models that answer the question: why? And there is no clear reason why the ethos of hard science can't also help in disciplines far less fundamental than biology. Here, as I interpret it, is this fundamental organizing ethos I am talking about:

1) You must both rank and use disciplines in order of fundamentalness.

2) You must, like it or not, master to tested fluency and routinely use the truly essential parts of all four constituents of the fundamental four-discipline combination, with particularly intense attention given to disciplines more fundamental than your own.

3) You may never practice either cross-disciplinary absorption without attribution or departure from a "principle of economy" that forbids explaining in any

other way anything readily explainable from more fundamental material in your own or any other discipline.

4) But when the step (3) approach doesn't produce much new and useful insight, you should hypothesize and test to establishment new principles, ordinarily by using methods similar to those that created successful old principles. But you may not use any new principle inconsistent with an old one unless you can now prove that the old principle is not true.

There is an old two-part rule that often works wonders in business, science, and elsewhere: (1) Take a simple, basic idea and (2) take it very seriously.

You will note that, compared with much current practice in soft science, the fundamental organizing ethos of hard science is more severe. This reminds one of pilot training, and this outcome is not a coincidence. Reality is talking to anyone who will listen. Like pilot training, the ethos of hard science does not say "take what you wish" but "learn it all to fluency, like it or not." And rational organization of multidisciplinary knowledge is forced by making mandatory (1) full attribution for cross-disciplinary takings and (2) mandatory preference for the most fundamental explanation.

This simple idea may appear too obvious to be useful, but there is an old two-part rule that often works wonders in business, science, and elsewhere: (1) Take a simple, basic idea and (2) take it very seriously. And, as some evidence for the value of taking very seriously the fundamental organizing ethos, I offer the example of my own life.

To this day, I have never taken any course, anywhere, in chemistry, economics, psychology, or business.

"Any book, which is at all important, should be reread immediately."

—Schopenhauer

I came to Harvard Law School very poorly educated, with desultory work habits and no college degree. I was admitted over the objection of Warren Abner Seavey through the intervention of family friend Roscoe Pound. I had taken one silly course in biology in high school, briefly learning, mostly by rote, an obviously incomplete theory of evolution, portions of the anatomy of the paramecium and frog, plus a ridiculous concept of "protoplasm" that has since disappeared. To this day, I have never taken any course, anywhere, in chemistry, economics, psychology, or business. But I early took elementary physics and math and paid enough attention to somehow assimilate the fundamental organizing ethos of hard science, which I thereafter pushed further and further into softer and softer fare as my organizing guide and filing system in a search for whatever multidisciplinary worldly wisdom it would be easy to get.

Thus, my life became a sort of accidental educational experiment with respect to feasibility and utility of a very gross academic extension of the fundamental organizing ethos by a man who also learned well what his own discipline had to teach.

What I found, in my extended attempts to complete by informal means my stunted education, was that, plugging along with only ordinary will but with the fundamental organizing ethos as my guide, my ability to serve everything I loved was enhanced far beyond my deserts. Large gains came in places that seemed unlikely as I started out, sometimes making me like the only one without a blindfold in a high-stake game of "pin the tail on the donkey." For instance, I was productively led into psychology, where I had no plans to go, creating large advantages that deserve a story on another day.

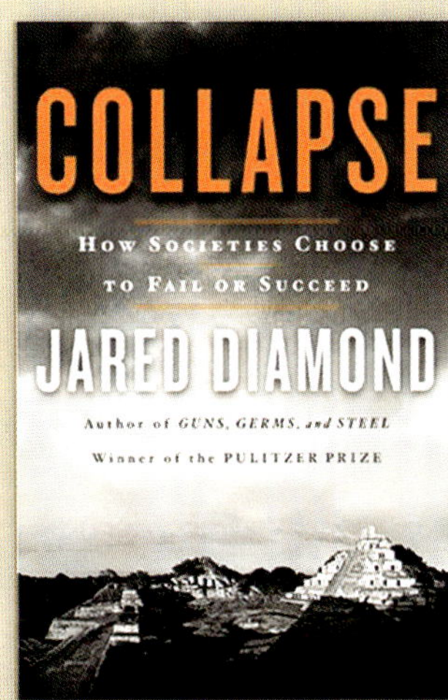

A Notable Exception: One Professor who is Multidisciplinary

Jared Diamond was awarded the 1999 National Medal of Science by President Clinton for his breakthrough discoveries in evolutionary biology and for landmark research in applying Darwinian theory to such diverse fields as physiology and ecology. A physiologist by training and currently a professor of geography at UCLA, Diamond brilliantly synthesizes the great models of many different academic disciplines. To the left is the latest work of this Pulitzer Prize-winning author.

Today, I have no more story. I have finished my talk by answering my own questions as best I could in a brief time. What is most interesting to me in my answers is that, while everything I have said is nonoriginal and has long been obvious to the point of banality to many sound and well-educated minds, all the evils I decry remain grossly overpresent in the best of our soft-science educational domains wherein virtually every professor has a too unidisciplinary habit of mind, even while a better model exists just across the aisle in his own university. To me, this ridiculous outcome implies that the soft-science departments tolerate perverse incentives. Wrong incentives are a major cause because, as Dr. Johnson so wisely observed, truth is hard to assimilate in any mind when opposed by interest. And, if institutional incentives cause the problem, then a remedy is feasible—because incentives can be changed.

"I've always been interested in a lot of things, and a lot of things at the same time, and I always tried to explain them to myself. I ask a lot of questions."

—Jared Diamond

It is neither inevitable nor advantageous for soft-science educational domains to tolerate as much unidisciplinary wrongheadedness as they now do.

I have tried to demonstrate today, and indeed by the example of my life, that it is neither inevitable nor advantageous for soft-science educational domains to tolerate as much unidisciplinary wrongheadedness as they now do. If I could somewhat fix

there is an ethos, also from Dr. Johnson, that is applicable. Please remember the word Dr. Johnson used to describe maintenance of academic ignorance that is removable through diligence. To Dr. Johnson, such conduct was "treachery."

As Dr. Johnson so wisely observed, truth is hard to assimilate in any mind when opposed by interest. And, if institutional incentives cause the problem, then a remedy is feasible—because incentives can be changed.

Portrait of Samuel Johnson by Gilbert Stuart, undated, Houghton Library, Harvard University

And if duty will not move improvement, advantage is also available. There will be immense worldly rewards, for law schools and other academic domains as for Charlie Munger, in a more multidisciplinary approach to many problems, common or uncommon. And more fun as well as more accomplishment. The happier mental realm I recommend is one from which no one willingly returns. A return would be like cutting off one's hands.

Talk Five Revisited

As I review Talk Five in 2006, I would not change a word. And I continue to believe that my ideas are important. In my attitude I may be displaying too much similarity to my long-dead relative, Reverend Theodore Munger, former chaplain of Yale.

Theodore published a collection of his sermons, laying out proper conduct with a strong, *ex cathedra* tone. Then, late in life, he published a final edition, reporting in his foreword that he had made no changes at all and was now producing the new edition only because the extreme popularity of his sermons had caused excessive wear in the original printing plates.

"Read over your compositions, and when you meet a passage which you think is particularly fine, strike it out."

—Samuel Johnson

Charlie's Checklists

> *"How can smart people so often be wrong? They don't do what I'm telling you to do: use a checklist to be sure you get all the main models and use them together in a multimodular way."*
>
> *—Munger*

"Charlie draws his confidence from the unusually rigorous process he follows to research, analyze, evaluate and decide. He knows he may not always be right, but that the odds are in his favor because his process is so disciplined and realistic. For this reason, he is never reluctant to make a decision and to act decisively upon it."

—Dick Esbenshade, friend and business associate since 1956

In Talk Five, Charlie lays out the case for checklists, both formal and informal, as indispensable tools for decision making and problem solving. Throughout the *Almanack*, he recommends four basic types of checklists that necessarily overlap and reinforce each other:

The Two-Track Analysis (Pages 63, 64):

- What are the factors that really govern the interests involved, rationally considered? (for example, macro and micro-level economic factors).
- What are the subconscious influences, where the brain at a subconscious level is automatically forming conclusions? (influences from instincts, emotions, cravings, and so on).

Investing and Decision Making Checklist (Pages 73-76):

- Charlie's informal, but extensive, list of factors worthy of consideration.

Ultra-Simple, General Problem-Solving Notions (Pages 279-281):

- Decide the big "no-brainer" questions first.
- Apply numerical fluency.
- Invert (think the problem through in reverse).
- Apply elementary multidisciplinary wisdom, never relying entirely upon others.
- Watch for combinations of factors—the Lollapalooza effect.

Psychology-Based Tendencies (Pages 420-478):

- His famous Twenty-Five Standard Causes of Human Misjudgment.

CALIFORNIA INSTITUTE OF TECHNOLOGY

Pasadena, California 91125

Mail Code 104-31
Telephone 626/395-6365
e-mail: dg@cco.caltech.edu
Fax 626/796-7820

David L. Goodstein
Vice Provost
Professor of Physics and Applied Physics
Frank J. Gilloon Distinguished Teaching and Service Professor

October 29, 1998

Mr. Charles T. Munger
Vice Chairman of the Board
Berkshire Hathaway Inc.
P.O. Box 55007
Los Angeles, CA 90055

Dear Charlie:

Thank you for your hilarious speech to the Financial Officers.

During the 20 years I knew him personally, Feynman, it is true, never fooled himself. Of course, by the time I met him he was already world-famous (at least among physicists) and maybe more worried about protecting his reputation than driven to come up with new results. Or, more likely he *was* driven to come up with new ideas, but was just an extraordinary person. In any case, I can assure you on the basis of first-hand knowledge that we physicists, unlike Feynman, but like financial officers, fool ourselves all the time.

It's always a pleasure to hear from you.

Best regards,

David

David L. Goodstein

DLG/jp

Although this letter from Caltech's David Goodstein was sent in response to the talk that follows, "Investment Practices of Leading Charitable Foundations," it is presented here because of the reference in this talk to Richard Feynman, whom Charlie extols for his multidisciplinary approach to problem solving.

This speech, delivered in October 1998 to the Foundation Financial Officers Group in Santa Monica, helps account for Charlie's line: "It's sad, but true: Not everybody loves me." In the talk, he attacks the accepted and practiced orthodoxy of his audience with sharp humor, though always without malice. Charlie has a deep and abiding belief in philanthropy, as is demonstrated by his own generous giving, and he seeks here to save the philanthropic community from itself.

Charlie believes foundations should serve as societal exemplars, which means they must discourage wasteful, non-productive practices. He posits a choice for his audience: the model of genius statesman Ben Franklin or that of disgraced fund manager Bernie Cornfeld. Referring back to his days as a limited partnership manager, Charlie employs, as is typical, self-deprecation and self-reflection: "Early Charlie Munger is a horrible career model for the young." If Charlie can emerge from that state successfully, he seems to be saying, so can the wayward foundation managers in his audience.

Investment Practices of Leading Charitable Foundations

Speech to the Foundation Financial Officers Group at Miramar Sheraton Hotel, Santa Monica, California, October 14, 1998, sponsored by the Conrad Hilton Foundation, the Amateur Athletic Foundation, the J. Paul Getty Trust, and Rio Hondo Memorial Foundation.

John C. Argue
(1932–2002)

John Argue divided his time between business and philanthropy. Long a senior partner of Los Angeles law firm Argue Pearson Harbison & Myers, he was one of the key reasons that Los Angeles got the 1984 Olympic Games. He also served on the University of Southern California Board of Trustees, becoming its chairman in 2000.

I am speaking here today because my friend, John Argue, asked me. And John well knew that I, who, unlike many other speakers on your agenda, having nothing to sell any of you, would be irreverent about much current investment practice in large institutions, including charitable foundations. Therefore any hostility my talk will cause should be directed at John Argue, who comes from the legal profession and may even enjoy it.

It was long the norm at large charitable foundations to invest mostly in unleveraged, marketable, domestic securities, mostly equities. The equities were selected by one or a very few investment counseling organizations. But, in recent years, there has been a drift toward more complexity. Some foundations, following the lead of institutions like Yale, have tried to become much better versions of Bernie Cornfeld's "fund of funds." This is an amazing development. Few would have predicted that long after Cornfeld's fall into disgrace, major universities would be leading foundations into Cornfeld's system.

Now, in some foundations, there are not few but many investment counselors, chosen by an additional layer of consultants who are hired to decide which investment counselors are best, help in allocating funds to various categories, make sure that foreign securities are not neglected in favor of domestic securities, check validity of claimed investment records, ensure that claimed investment styles are scrupulously followed, and help augment an already large diversification in a way that conforms to the latest notions of corporate finance professors about volatility and "beta."

Bernie Cornfeld, born in Turkey, came to America and became a mutual fund salesman in the 1950s. In the 1960s, he started selling his own family of mutual funds, Investors Overseas Services (IOS), incorporated in Switzerland. He hired thousands of salespeople, who sold the funds door-to-door all over Europe, especially in Germany. IOS raised $2.5 billion while Cornfeld engaged in lavish personal consumption.

Few would have predicted that, long after Cornfeld's fall into disgrace, major universities would be leading foundations into Cornfeld's system.

But even with this amazingly active, would-be-polymathic, new layer of consultant-choosing consultants, the individual investment counselors, in picking common stocks, still rely to a considerable extent on a third layer of consultants. The third layer consists of the security analysts employed by investment banks.

These security analysts receive enormous salaries, sometimes set in seven figures after bidding wars. The hiring investment banks recoup these salaries from two sources: (1) commissions and trading spreads borne by security buyers (some of which are rebated as "soft dollars" to money managers) plus (2) investment banking charges paid by corporations that appreciate the enthusiastic way their securities are being recommended by the security analysts.

In 1976, Carl Braun, an engineering entrepreneur greatly admired by Charlie (see page 170), self-published for his employees a small volume entitled *Objective Accounting*. Among his many insightful observations was, "The accountant takes the easy thing that comes before him, while failing to reach out for the things that count."

This full cost doesn't show up in conventional accounting. But that is because accounting has limitations and not because the full cost isn't present.

There is one thing sure about all this complexity, including its touches of behavior lacking the full punctilio of honor. Even when nothing but unleveraged stock picking is involved, the total cost of all the investment management, plus the frictional costs of fairly often getting in and out of many large investment positions, can easily reach three percent of foundation net worth per annum if foundations, urged on by consultants, add new activity, year after year. This full cost doesn't show up in conventional accounting. But that is because accounting has limitations and not because the full cost isn't present.

Next, we come to time for a little arithmetic: It is one thing each year to pay the croupiers three percent of starting wealth when the average foundation is enjoying a real return, say, of seventeen percent before the croupiers' take. But it is not written in the stars that foundations will always gain seventeen percent gross, a common result in recent years. And if the average annual gross real return from indexed investment in equities

goes back, say, to five percent over some long future period, and the croupiers' take turns out to remain the waste it has always been, even for the average intelligent player, then the average intelligent foundation will be in a prolonged, uncomfortable, shrinking mode. After all, five percent minus three percent minus five percent in donations leaves an annual shrinkage of three percent.

All the equity investors, in total, will surely bear a performance disadvantage per annum equal to the total croupiers' costs they have jointly elected to bear. This is an inescapable fact of life. And it is also inescapable that exactly half of the investors will get a result below the median result after the croupiers' take, which median result may well be somewhere between unexciting and lousy.

The croupiers' take turns out to remain the waste it has always been, even for the average intelligent player.

Human nature being what it is, most people assume away worries like those I raise. After all, centuries before Christ, Demosthenes noted, "What a man wishes, he will believe." And in self-appraisals of prospects and talents, it is the norm, as Demosthenes predicted, for people to be ridiculously over-optimistic. For instance, a careful survey in Sweden showed that ninety percent of automobile drivers considered themselves above average. And people who are successfully selling something, as investment counselors do, make Swedish drivers sound like depressives. Virtually every investment expert's public assessment is that he is above average, no matter what is the evidence to the contrary.

But, you may think, my foundation, at least, will be above average. It is well endowed, hires the best, and considers all investment issues at length and with objective professionalism. And to this I respond that an excess of what seems like professionalism will often hurt you horribly—precisely because the careful procedures themselves often lead to overconfidence in their outcome.

A careful survey in Sweden showed that ninety percent of automobile drivers considered themselves above average. And people who are successfully selling something, as investment counselors do, make Swedish drivers sound like depressives.

General Motors recently made just such a mistake, and it was a lollapalooza. Using fancy consumer surveys, its excess of professionalism, it concluded not to put a fourth door in a truck designed to serve also as the equivalent of a comfortable five-passenger car. Its competitors, more basic, had actually seen five people enter and exit cars. Moreover, they had noticed that people were used to four doors in a comfortable five-passenger car and that biological creatures ordinarily prefer effort minimization in routine activities and don't like removals of long-enjoyed benefits. There are only two words that come instantly to mind in reviewing General Motors' horrible decision, which has blown many hundreds of millions of dollars. And one of those words is "oops."

Biological creatures ordinarily prefer effort minimization in routine activities and don't like removals of long-enjoyed benefits.

Similarly, the hedge fund known as "Long-Term Capital Management" recently collapsed through overconfidence in its highly leveraged methods, despite I.Q.'s of its principals that must have averaged 160. Smart, hardworking people aren't exempted from professional disasters from overconfidence. Often, they just go aground in the more difficult voyages they choose, relying on their self-appraisals that they have superior talents and methods.

It is, of course, irritating that extra care in thinking is not all good but also introduces extra error. But most good things have undesired "side effects," and thinking is no exception. The best defense is that of the best physicists, who systematically criticize themselves to an extreme degree, using a mindset described by Nobel laureate Richard Feynman as follows: "The first principle is that you must not fool yourself, and you're the easiest person to fool."

But suppose that an abnormally realistic foundation, thinking like Feynman, fears a poor future investment outcome because it is unwilling to assume that its unleveraged equities will outperform equity indexes, minus all investment costs, merely because the foundation has adopted the approach of becoming a "fund of funds," with much investment turnover and layers of consultants that consider themselves above average. What are this fearful foundation's options as it seeks improved prospects?

There are at least three modern choices:

1. The foundation can both dispense with its consultants and reduce its investment turnover as it changes to indexed investment in equities.

2. The foundation can follow the example of Berkshire Hathaway, and thus get total annual croupier costs below one-tenth of one percent of principal per annum, by investing with virtually total passivity in a very few much-admired domestic corporations. And there is no reason why some outside advice can't be used in this process. All the fee payer has to do is suitably control the high talent in investment counseling organizations so that the servant becomes the useful tool of its master, instead of serving itself under the perverse incentives of a sort of Mad Hatter's Tea Party.

3. The foundation can supplement unleveraged investment in marketable equities with investment in limited partnerships that do some combination of the following: unleveraged investment in high-tech corporations in their infancy; leveraged investments in corporate buy-outs; leveraged relative value trades in equities; and leveraged convergence trades and other exotic trades in all kinds of securities and derivatives.

Long-Term Capital Management

Long-Term Capital Management, a hedge fund company founded in 1994 by a well-respected Wall Street bond trader and two Nobel Prize winners in economics, developed complex mathematical models to take advantage of arbitrage deals. Using high levels of debt—about $125 billion by 1998—the fund was poorly positioned for two consecutive months of negative returns combined with Salomon Brothers' exit from the arbitrage business combined with foreign financial panics. Within a few months, the fund lost almost $2 billion in capital. It became necessary for the Federal Reserve Bank to organize a bailout of the fund to avoid a chain reaction of liquidity requests throughout the economy. The debacle reminded the financial community of the potential seriousness of liquidity risk. The seminal book on the subject, *When Genius Failed,* was translated into many languages.

For the obvious reasons given by purveyors of indexed equities, I think choice (1), indexing, is a wiser choice for the average foundation than what it is now doing in unleveraged equity investment. And particularly so, as its present total croupier costs exceed one percent of principal per annum. Indexing can't work well forever if almost everybody turns to it. But it will work all right for a long time.

Choice (3), investment in fancy limited partnerships, is largely beyond the scope of this talk. I will only say that the Munger Foundation does not so invest and briefly mention two considerations bearing on LBO funds.

The first consideration bearing on LBO funds is that buying one hundred percent of corporations with much financial leverage and two layers of promotional carry (one for the management and one for the general partners in the LBO fund) is no sure thing to outperform equity indexes in the future if equity indexes perform poorly in the future. In substance, an LBO fund is a better way of buying equivalents of marketable equities on margin, and the debt could prove disastrous if future marketable equity performance is bad. And particularly so, if the bad performance comes from generally bad business conditions.

There are now very many LBO funds, both large and small, mostly awash in money and with general partners highly incentivized to buy something.

The second consideration is increasing competition for LBO candidates. For instance, if the LBO candidates are good service corporations, General Electric can now buy more than $10 billion worth per year in GE's credit corporation, with one hundred percent debt financing at an interest rate only slightly higher than the U.S. government is paying. This sort of thing is not ordinary competition, but supercompetition. And there are now very many LBO funds, both large and small, mostly awash in money and with general partners highly incentivized to buy something. In addition, there is increased buying competition from corporations other than GE using some combination of debt and equity.

In short, in the LBO field, there is a buried covariance with marketable equities—toward disaster in generally bad business conditions—and competition is now extreme.

Given time limitations, I can say no more about limited partnerships, one of which I once ran. This leaves for extensive discussion only foundation choice (2), more imitation of the investment practices of Berkshire Hathaway in maintaining marketable equity portfolios with virtually zero turnover and with only a very few stocks chosen. This brings us to the question of how much investment diversification is desirable at foundations.

I have more than skepticism regarding the orthodox view that huge diversification is a must for those wise enough so that indexation is not the logical mode for equity investment. I think the orthodox view is grossly mistaken.

In the United States, a person or institution with almost all wealth invested long-term, in just three fine domestic corporations, is securely rich. And why should such an owner care if, at any time, most other investors are faring somewhat better or worse? And particularly so when he rationally believes, like Berkshire, that his long-term results will be superior by reason of his lower costs, required emphasis on long-term effects, and concentration in his most preferred choices.

Robert W. Woodruff
(1889–1985)

Robert Woodruff was born in Georgia to a father who was president of a major trust company. Woodruff had an unremarkable school career, but once in the workforce, he succeeded quickly. Although he started in car sales, by age thirty-three he had taken over the Coca-Cola Company. He turned a fairly small soft-drink manufacturer and bottler into a corporate giant known worldwide. Over the remainder of his life, Woodruff was unusually philanthropic and established a large foundation that now bears his name.

Woodruff's personal creed gives one a good sense of how he accomplished so much in his long life:

"There is no limit to what a man can do or where he can go if he doesn't mind who gets the credit."

Peter F. Drucker
(1909 - 2005)

Peter Drucker, born in Austria, was educated there and in England. He earned a Ph.D. in public and international law while working as a newspaper reporter in Germany. Later, he worked as an economist in a London bank and came to the United States in 1937. His academic career has included professorships at Bennington College, New York University, and, starting in 1971, Claremont Graduate University, where the graduate management school is named after him. For decades, he consulted for businesses and nonprofit organizations.

Author of some thirty books on management, philosophy, and other topics, Drucker is considered a seminal thinker, writer, and lecturer on the contemporary organization. In 2002, he received the Presidential Medal of Freedom.

I go even further. I think it can be a rational choice, in some situations, for a family or a foundation to remain ninety percent concentrated in one equity. Indeed, I hope the Mungers follow roughly this course. And I note that the Woodruff foundations have, so far, proven extremely wise to retain an approximately ninety percent concentration in the founder's Coca-Cola stock. It would be interesting to calculate just how all American foundations would have fared if they had never sold a share of founder's stock. Very many, I think, would now be much better off. But, you may say, the diversifiers simply took out insurance against a catastrophe that didn't occur. And I reply: There are worse things than some foundation's losing relative clout in the world, and rich institutions, like rich individuals, should do a lot of self-insurance if they want to maximize long-term results.

Some important factor doesn't lose share of force just because some "expert" can better measure other types of force.

Furthermore, all the good in the world is not done by foundation donations. Much more good is done through the ordinary business operations of the corporations in which the foundations invest. And some corporations do much more good than others do in a way that gives investors therein better-than-average long-term prospects. And I don't consider it foolish, stupid, evil, or illegal for a foundation to greatly concentrate investment in what it admires or even loves. Indeed, Ben Franklin required just such an investment practice for the charitable endowment created by his will.

One other aspect of Berkshire's equity investment practice deserves comparative mention. So far, there has been almost no direct foreign investment at Berkshire and much foreign investment at foundations.

Regarding this divergent history, I wish to say that I agree with Peter Drucker that the culture and legal systems of the United States are especially favorable

The "Gillette Young Guns"—from left to right: Kurt Busch, Jimmie Johnson, Kevin Harvick, Matt Kenseth, Ryan Newman, and Dale Earnhardt Jr.—dominated their inaugural 2004 season, winning over fifty percent of the thirty-six NASCAR Cup races. Popularity is increasing worldwide for NASCAR Stock Car Racing.

to shareholder interests compared to other interests and compared to most other countries. Indeed, there are many other countries where any good going to public shareholders has a very low priority and almost every other constituency stands higher in line. This factor, I think, is underweighed at many investment institutions, probably because it does not easily lead to quantitative thinking using modern financial technique. But some important factor doesn't lose share of force just because some "expert" can better measure other types of force. Generally, I tend to prefer over direct foreign investment Berkshire's practice of participating in foreign economies through the likes of Coca-Cola and Gillette.

I tend to prefer over direct foreign investment Berkshire's practice of participating in foreign economies through the likes of Coca-Cola and Gillette.

To conclude, I will make one controversial prediction and one controversial argument.

The controversial prediction is that, if some of you make your investment style more like Berkshire Hathaway's, in a long-term retrospect, you will be unlikely to have cause for regret, even if you can't get Warren Buffett to work for nothing. Instead, Berkshire will have cause for regret as it faces more intelligent investment competition. But Berkshire won't actually regret any disadvantage from your enlightenment. We only want what success we can get despite encouraging others to share our general views about reality.

My controversial argument is an additional consideration weighing against the complex, high-cost investment modalities becoming ever more popular at foundations. Even if, contrary to my suspicions, such modalities should turn out to work pretty well, most of the money-making activity would contain profoundly antisocial effects. This would be so because the activity would exacerbate the current, harmful trend in which ever more of the nation's ethical young brainpower is attracted into lucrative money management and its attendant modern frictions, as distinguished from work providing much more value to others. Money management does not create the right examples. Early Charlie Munger is a horrible career model for the young because not enough was delivered to civilization in return for what was wrested from capitalism. And other similar career models are even worse.

Money management does not create the right examples. Early Charlie Munger is a horrible career model for the young because not enough was delivered to civilization in return for what was wrested from capitalism.

Rather than encourage such models, a more constructive choice at foundations is long-term investment concentration in a few domestic corporations that are wisely admired.

Why not thus imitate Ben Franklin? After all, old Ben was very effective in doing public good. And he was a pretty good investor, too. Better his model, I think, than Bernie Cornfeld's. The choice is plainly yours to make.

FRANKLIN
CORNFELD

Talk Six Revisited

A lot of water has passed under the bridge since this talk was made in 1998. And what has happened by 2006 is that we now see much more of the conduct I criticized.

In particular, frictional costs for stockmarket investors have increased markedly, and there has been an increase in the share of young brainpower becoming, with respect to investments, what the tout is with respect to horseracing tracks.

Indeed, I recently heard Warren Buffett say that if present investment trends spread to racetracks, most bettors will try to improve results by always bringing along a well-paid personal tout.

However, at the same time that lovers of frictional costs have been spending more on what they love, there has also been an increase in holdings of stocks that track market indexes in a manner imposing negligible costs. This cost-averse, index-mimicking group does not grow fast enough to prevent an increase in total frictional costs, but more stockholding is slowly being converted to the passive, indexed mode.

Handicapping Is Investing, Investing Is Handicapping

Charlie likes to cite similarities between the pari-mutuel betting system used at horse races and the stock market (see pages 196 and 197). Further, he compares the best investing opportunities to mispriced bets on horses, saying, "What we're really looking for are 50-50 odds which pay three to one" (see page 64).

Equally attuned to race track analogies is Warren Buffett. Intrigued as a boy by the voluminous data involving variables such as weights, speed ratings, pace, past performance, and breeding, Buffett developed a keen interest in horse racing. Along with a friend, he formed a partnership to produce a tipsheet, *Stable Boy Selections,* which was then sold at Omaha's Ak-Sar-Ben racetrack ("Nebraska" spelled backwards).

Buffett's early days as a horse handicapper may continue to benefit him today as an investor. In both arenas, voluminous data, variables and unknowns exist, together with different schools of thought as to how such factors should best be evaluated. Not surprisingly, Buffett applies a similar methodology to both pursuits.

Witness this excerpt from Innisfree Farms *Rice's Derby Journal, 14th Edition, 1993:*

Back on the subject of handicapping, there are two schools to which most practitioners belong: speed or trip. Much like the momentum investor in the stock market, the speed handicapper likes to bet horses that win races in fast times (don't we all?). The trip handicapper is more concerned with the nuances of the "trip" the horse had. Did the track favor closers that day? Was the horse hindered? Was there a lot of speed in the race, no speed? The legendary stock market investor, Warren Buffett, began his adult life publishing a race track tip sheet. He once defined his investing style by calling himself a trip handicapper. Few of his followers likely comprehended his remark; racetrackers certainly did.

Adding to the credibility of the above view by *Rice's Derby Journal,* is the fact that its predicted winner of the 1993 Kentucky Derby, Sea Hero, indeed won, paying a hefty $27.80 for those astute enough to place a $2 win bet.

ARGUE PEARSON HARBISON & MYERS, LLP
ATTORNEYS AT LAW

DON M. PEARSON*
STEPHEN F. HARBISON
WILLIAM A. JONES
ANTHONY M. VIENNA
THOMAS R. SCHALOW
*A LAW CORPORATION

801 SOUTH FLOWER STREET
LOS ANGELES, CALIFORNIA 90017-4699
(213) 622-3100
FAX
(213) 622-7575
JOHN C. ARGUE
OF COUNSEL
LOUIS W. MYERS
(1945-1993)
OUR FILE NUMBER

July 31, 1998

Charles T. Munger, Esq.
HCR 00 Box 94
Cass Lake, MN 56633

Dear Charlie:

This is further in connection with our brief meeting at breakfast this week. I was asked to request that you speak at the Foundation Financial Officers Group meeting at lunch on Wednesday, October 14th. That group will be meeting in Los Angeles at that time. It consists of the chief investment and chief financial officers of most of the major private foundations in the United States, and collectively represents about $130 billion in invested assets. In addition, some representatives of prominent European foundations will be present.

The purpose of the group is to share investment knowledge and experiences, and to develop a strong network whereby they help one another separate the wheat from the chaff in the myriad of investment decisions that must be made.

The meeting is being held at the Miramar Sheraton Hotel in Santa Monica, and is being organized by the Amateur Athletic Foundation, the Conrad Hilton Foundation, the J. Paul Getty Trust, and the Rio Hondo Foundation. The theme of the conference is to focus on the current lofty level of the U.S. large cap market, and to explore possible alternatives to this market.

You have a great deal of flexibility with respect to your topic. I think they are willing to be challenged with strong opinions formed by your wealth of investment experience. Speaking on the same program as you will be Barry Munitz, the new head of the Getty.

I respectfully urge that you do this. You have a great deal to offer these investment and financial officers, and they can use your advice. You will also be in very good company with respect to the other speakers and the sponsoring organizations. Many thanks.

Sincerely,

John C. Argue

John C. Argue

Above is the letter from John C. Argue inviting Charlie to speak to the Foundation Financial Officers Group.

In his letter below, John Bogle of Vanguard asks for a copy of the talk.

THE Vanguard GROUP.

John C. Bogle
Senior Chairman

December 9, 1998

Mr. Charles T. Munger
Munger, Tolles & Olson LLP
355 South Grand Avenue
Thirty-Fifth Floor
Los Angeles, CA 90071-1560

Dear Mr. Munger:

I was delighted to read Barton Biggs' complimentary report on your speech of October 14. I'm almost embarrassed to put myself in your awesome company, but I share virtually all of your ideas. In any event, I would be most appreciative if you could send me a copy of the speech itself.

I've known Warren Buffett over the years, and in recent years also Bob Denham, a fellow Director of the Independence Standards Board. I've been very impressed by the talents he brings to that group. Perhaps one day I'll have an opportunity to meet you too. I hope so.

Best regards.

Sincerely,

Jack Bogle

JCB/eas

Post Office Box 2600, Valley Forge, Pennsylvania 19482-2600
610-669-1000 • www.vanguard.com

"Nothing to Add" Number Five

We continue with this question on the subject of performing arts:

Question: "Do you play the piano?"

Answer: "I don't know. I've never tried."

This speech was delivered in November 2000 to the Philanthropy Roundtable in Pasadena. Startling Charlie's family and friends, Jody Curtis, of *Foundation News & Commentary*, characterized Charlie as "a friendly old uncle, one with a jolly sense of humor at that."

Charlie's goal, as was the case in the previous speech, was to save foundations from their own mistakes by getting them to invest effectively, with minimum waste. Charlie warns foundations that they often act unwisely because of "a failure to understand their own investment operations, related to the larger system" of which they're a part. Never one to pull punches, he boldly and bluntly challenges his listeners to cure the ignorance that is jeopardizing their foundations and those who depend on them. Charlie coins the term "febezzlement"—the functional equivalent of embezzlement—to explain how wealth is stripped away by layers of unnecessary investment managers and consultants.

Talk Seven

Breakfast Meeting of the Philanthropy Roundtable

November 10, 2000

I am here today to talk about so-called "wealth effects" from rising prices for U.S. common stocks.

I should concede, at the outset, that "wealth effects" are part of the academic discipline of economics and that I have never taken a single course in economics, nor tried to make a single dollar, ever, from foreseeing macroeconomic changes.

Nonetheless, I have concluded that most Ph.D. economists underappraise the power of the common-stock-based "wealth effect," under current extreme conditions.

Everyone now agrees on two things. First, spending proclivity is influenced in an upward direction when stock prices go up and in a downward direction when stock prices go down. And, second, the proclivity to spend is terribly important in macroeconomics. However, the professionals disagree about size and timing of "wealth effects," and how they interact with other effects, including the obvious

The Philanthropy Roundtable

The Philanthropy Roundtable

Founded in the 1970s in Washington, D.C., the Philanthropy Roundtable is an informal network of grantmakers seeking to promote private, voluntary approaches to individual and community betterment. Currently, there are more than 600 Roundtable Associates.

complication that increased spending tends to drive up stock prices while stock prices are concurrently driving up spending. Also, of course, rising stock prices increase corporate earnings even when spending is static, for instance, by reducing pension cost accruals after which stock prices tend to rise more. Thus, "wealth effects" involve mathematical puzzles that are not nearly so well worked out as physics theories and never can be.

I have never taken a single course in economics, nor tried to make a single dollar, ever, from foreseeing macroeconomic changes.

The "wealth effect" from rising U.S. stock prices is particularly interesting right now for two reasons. First, there has never been an advance so extreme in the price of widespread stock holdings and, with stock prices going up so much faster than GNP, the related "wealth effect" must now be bigger than was common before. And second, what has happened in Japan over roughly the last ten years has shaken up academic economics, as it obviously should, creating strong worries about recession from "wealth effects" in reverse.

In Japan, with much financial corruption, there was an extreme rise in stock and real estate prices for a very long time, accompanied by extreme real economic growth, compared to the United States. Then, asset values crashed, and the Japanese economy stalled out at a very suboptimal level. After this, Japan, a modern economy that had learned all the would-be-corrective Keynesian and monetary tricks, pushed these tricks hard and long. Japan, for many years, not only ran an immense government deficit but also reduced interest rates to a place within hailing distance of zero and kept them there. Nonetheless, the Japanese economy, year after year, stays stalled, as Japanese proclivity to spend stubbornly resists all the tricks of the economists. And Japanese stock prices stay down. This Japanese experience is a disturbing example for everyone and, if something like it happened here, would leave shrunken charitable foundations feeling clobbered by fate. Let us hope, as is probably the case, that the sad situation in Japan is caused in some large part by social psychological effects and corruption peculiar to Japan. In such case, our country may be at least half as safe as is widely assumed.

In 1974, Erno Rubik, a lecturer in the Department of Interior Design at the Academy of Applied Arts and Crafts in Budapest, patented the now well-known "Rubik's Cube." Rubik set out to create a three dimensional object that would both be aesthetically pleasing and present a greater mental challenge than any puzzle in existence.

"Wealth effects" involve mathematical puzzles that are not nearly so well worked out as physics theories and never can be.

Well, grant that spending proclivity, as influenced by stock prices, is now an important subject and that the long Japanese recession is disturbing. How big are the economic influences of U.S. stock prices? A median conclusion of the economics professionals, based mostly on data collected by the Federal Reserve System, would probably be that the "wealth effect" on spending from stock prices is not all that big. After all, even now, real household net worth, excluding pensions, is probably up by less than one hundred percent over the last ten years and remains a pretty modest figure per household, while market value of common stock is probably not yet one-third of aggregate household net worth, excluding pensions. Moreover, such household wealth in common stocks is almost incredibly concentrated, and the super-rich don't consume in proportion to their wealth. Leaving out pensions, the top one percent of households probably hold about fifty percent of common stock value, and the bottom eighty percent probably hold about four percent.

Based on such data plus unexciting past correlation between stock prices and spending, it is easy for a professional economist to conclude, say, that even if the average household spends incrementally at a rate of three percent of asset values in stock, consumer spending would have risen less than one-half percent per year over the last ten years as a consequence of the huge, unprecedented, long-lasting, consistent boom in stock prices.

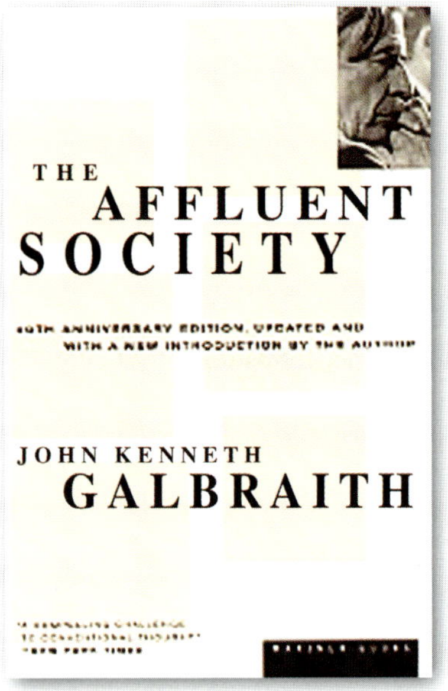

John Kenneth Galbraith
(b. 1908)

John Kenneth Galbraith, born in Ontario, Canada, graduated from Ontario Agricultural College and went on for a Ph. D. from the University of California, Berkeley. In 1949, he joined the economics faculty at Harvard University. A friend of President John F. Kennedy, Galbraith served as U.S. ambassador to India from 1961 to 1963.

As an economist, Galbraith holds progressive values and writes accessible books that often describe how economic theory does not always mesh with real life. Among his best known works are *American Capitalism: The Concept of Countervailing Power* (1952), *The Affluent Society* (1958), and *The New Industrial State* (1967).

I believe that such economic thinking widely misses underlying reality right now. To me, such thinking looks at the wrong numbers and asks the wrong questions. Let me, the ultimate amateur, boldly try to do a little better, or at least a little differently.

For one thing, I have been told, probably correctly, that Federal Reserve data collection, due to practical obstacles, doesn't properly take into account pension effects, including effects from 401(k) and similar plans. Assume some sixty-three-year-old dentist has $1 million in GE stock in a private pension plan. The stock goes up in value to $2 million, and the dentist, feeling flush, trades in his very old Chevrolet and leases a new Cadillac at the giveaway rate now common. To me, this is an obvious large "wealth effect" in the dentist's spending. To many economists, using Federal Reserve data, I suspect the occasion looks like profligate dissaving by the dentist. To me, the dentist, and many others like him, seems to be spending a lot more because of a very strong pension-related "wealth effect." Accordingly, I believe that present-day "wealth effect" from pension plans is far from trivial and much larger than it was in the past.

For another thing, the traditional thinking of economists often does not take into account implications from the idea of "bezzle." Let me repeat: "bezzle," B-E-Z-Z-L-E.

The word "bezzle" is a contraction of the word "embezzle," and it was coined by Harvard Economics Professor John Kenneth Galbraith to stand for the increase in any period of undisclosed embezzlement. Galbraith coined the "bezzle" word because he saw that undisclosed embezzlement, per dollar, has a very powerful stimulating effect on spending. After all, the embezzler spends more because he has more income, and his employer spends as before because he doesn't know any of his assets are gone.

"Worldly wisdom teaches that it is better for reputation to fail conventionally than to succeed unconventionally."

—John Maynard Keynes

But Galbraith did not push his insight on. He was content to stop with being a stimulating gadfly. So, I will now try to push Galbraith's "bezzle" concept on to the next logical level. As Keynes showed, in a native economy relying on earned income, when the seamstress sells a coat to the shoemaker for twenty dollars, the shoemaker has twenty dollars less to spend, and the seamstress has twenty dollars more to spend. There is no lollapalooza effect on aggregate spending. But when the government prints another twenty-dollar bill and uses it to buy a pair of shoes, the shoemaker has another twenty dollars, and no one feels poorer. And when the shoemaker next buys a coat, the process goes on and on, not to an infinite increase, but with what is now called the Keynesian multiplier effect, a sort of lollapalooza effect on spending. Similarly, an undisclosed embezzlement has stronger stimulative effects per dollar on spending than a same-sized honest exchange of goods. Galbraith, being Scottish, liked the bleakness of life demonstrated by his insight. After all, the Scottish enthusiastically accepted the idea of pre-ordained, unfixable infant damnation. But the rest of us don't like Galbraith's insight. Nevertheless, we have to recognize that Galbraith was roughly right.

Undisclosed embezzlement, per dollar, has a very powerful stimulating effect on spending. After all, the embezzler spends more because he has more income, and his employer spends as before because he doesn't know any of his assets are gone.

No doubt Galbraith saw the Keynesian-multiplier-type economic effects promised by increases in "bezzle." But he stopped there. After all, "bezzle" could not grow very big because discovery of massive theft was nearly inevitable and sure to have reverse effects in due course. Thus, increase in private "bezzle" could not drive economies up and up, and on and on, at least for a considerable time, like government spending.

Deterred by the apparent smallness of economic effects from his insight, Galbraith did not ask the next logical question: Are there important functional equivalents of "bezzle" that are large and not promptly self-destructive? My answer to this question is yes. I will next describe only one. I will join Galbraith in coining new words: first, "febezzle," to stand for the functional equivalent of "bezzle"; second, "febezzlement," to describe the process of creating "febezzle"; and third, "febezzlers," to describe persons engaged in "febezzlement." Then, I will identify an important source of "febezzle" right in this room. You people, I think, have created a lot of "febezzle" through your foolish investment management practices in dealing with your large holdings of common stock.

If a foundation, or other investor, wastes three percent of assets per year in unnecessary, nonproductive investment costs in managing a strongly rising stock portfolio, it still feels richer, despite the waste, while the people getting the wasted three percent, "febezzlers" though they are, think they are virtuously earning income. The situation is functioning like undisclosed embezzlement without being self-limited. Indeed, the process can expand for a long while by feeding on itself. And, all the while, what looks like spending from earned income of the receivers of the wasted three percent is, in substance, spending from a disguised "wealth effect" from rising stock prices.

It is paradoxical and disturbing to us that economists have long praised foolish spending as a necessary ingredient of a successful economy.

This room contains many people pretty well stricken by expired years—in my generation or the one following. We tend to believe in thrift and avoiding waste as good things, a process that has worked well for us. It is paradoxical and disturbing to us that economists have long praised foolish spending as a necessary ingredient of

a successful economy. Let us call foolish expenditures "foolexures." And now you holders of old values are hearing one of your own add to the case for "foolexures" the case for "febezzlements"—the functional equivalent of embezzlements. This may not seem like a nice way to start a new day. Please be assured that I don't like "febezzlements." It is just that I think "febezzlements" are widespread and have powerful economic effects. And I also think that one should recognize reality even when one doesn't like it, indeed, especially when one doesn't like it. Also, I think one should cheerfully endure paradox that one can't remove by good thinking. Even in pure mathematics, they can't remove all paradox, and the rest of us should also recognize we are going to have to endure a lot of paradox, like it or not.

I also think that one should recognize reality even when one doesn't like it, indeed, especially when one doesn't like it.

Let me also take this occasion to state that my previous notion of three percent of assets per annum in waste in much institutional investment management related to stocks is quite likely too low in a great many cases. A friend, after my talk to foundation financial officers, sent me a summary of a study about mutual fund investors. The study concluded that the typical mutual fund investor gained at

7.25 percent per year in a fifteen-year period when the average stock fund gained at 12.8 percent per year (presumably after expenses). Thus, the real performance lag for investors was over five percent of assets per year in addition to whatever percentage per year the mutual funds, after expenses, lagged behind stock market averages. If this mutual fund study is roughly right, it raises huge questions about foundation wisdom in changing investment managers all the time as mutual fund investors do. If the extra lag reported in the mutual fund study exists, it is probably caused in considerable measure by folly in constant removal of assets from lagging portfolio managers being forced to liquidate stockholdings, followed by placement of removed assets with new investment managers that have high-pressure, asset-gaining hoses in their mouths and clients whose investment results will not be improved by the super-rapid injection of new funds. I am always having trouble like that caused by this new mutual fund study. I describe something realistically that looks so awful that my description is disregarded as extreme satire instead of reality. Next, new reality tops the horror of my disbelieved description by some large amount. No wonder Munger notions of reality are not widely welcome. This may be my last talk to charitable foundations.

This may be my last talk to charitable foundations.

Now, toss in with "febezzlement" in investment management about $750 billion in floating, ever-growing, ever-renewing wealth from employee stock options and you get lot more common-stock-related "wealth effect" driving consumption, with some of the "wealth effect" from employee stock options being, in substance, "febezzle" effect, facilitated by the corrupt accounting practice now required by standard practice.

Girl with a Pearl Earring
Vermeer Van Delft
c. 1665
Oil on canvas, 46.5 x 40 cm
Mauritshuis, The Hague

Next, consider that each one-hundred-point advance in the S&P adds about $1 trillion in stock market value, and throw in some sort of Keynesian-type multiplier effect related to all "febezzlement." The related macroeconomic "wealth effects," I believe, become much larger than is conventionally supposed.

And aggregate "wealth effect" from stock prices can get very large indeed. It is an unfortunate fact that great and foolish excess can come into prices of common stocks in the aggregate. They are valued partly like bonds, based on roughly rational projections of use value in producing future cash. But they are also valued partly like Rembrandt paintings, purchased mostly because their prices have gone up, so far. This situation, combined with big "wealth effects," at first up and later down, can conceivably produce much mischief. Let us try to investigate this by a "thought experiment." One of the big British pension funds once bought a lot of ancient art, planning to sell it ten years later, which it did, at a modest profit. Suppose all pension funds purchased ancient art, and only ancient art, with all their assets. Wouldn't we eventually have a terrible mess on our hands, with great and undesirable macroeconomic consequences? And wouldn't the mess be bad if only half of all pension funds were invested in ancient art? And if half of all stock value became a consequence of mania, isn't the situation much like the case wherein half of pension assets are ancient art?

One of the big British pension funds once bought a lot of ancient art, planning to sell it ten years later, which it did, at a modest profit.

My foregoing acceptance of the possibility that stock value in aggregate can become irrationally high is contrary to the hard-form "efficient market" theory that many of you once learned as gospel from your mistaken professors of yore. Your mistaken professors were too much influenced by "rational man" models of human behavior from economics and too little by "foolish man" models from psychology and real-world experience. "Crowd folly," the tendency of humans, under some circumstances, to resemble lemmings, explains much foolish thinking of brilliant men and much foolish behavior—like investment management practices of many foundations represented here today. It is sad that today each institutional investor apparently fears most of all that its investment practices will be different from practices of the rest of the crowd.

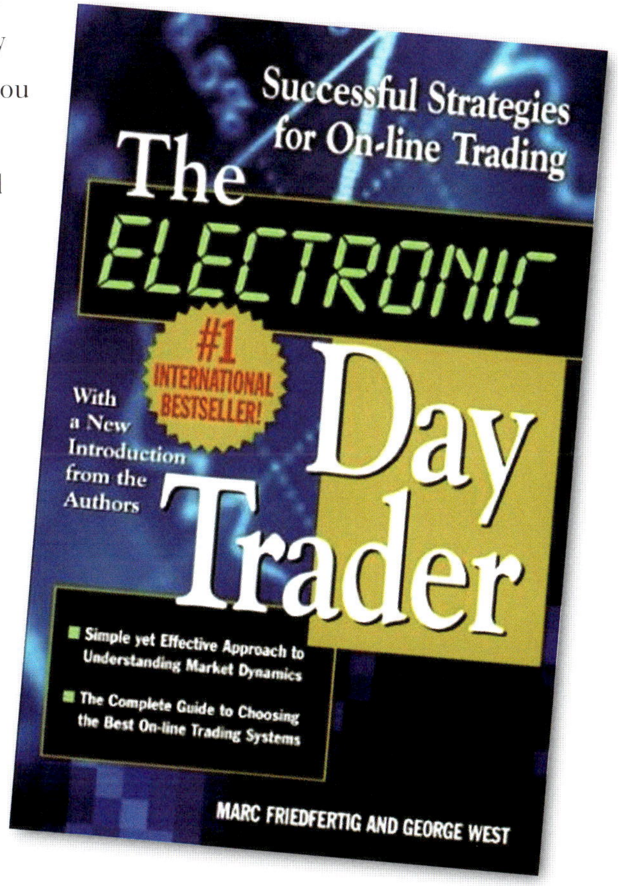

Some might view day-trading in the 1990s as a classic illustration of "crowd folly."

Well, this is enough uncredentialed musing for one breakfast meeting. If I am at all right, our present prosperity has had a stronger boost from common-stock-price-related "wealth effects," some of them disgusting, than has been the case in many former booms. If so, what was greater on the upside in the recent boom could also be greater on the downside at some time of future stock price decline. Incidentally, the economists may well conclude, eventually, that, when stock market advances and declines are regarded as long-lasting, there is more downside force on optional consumption per dollar of stock market decline than there is upside force per dollar of stock market rise. I suspect that economists would believe this already if they were more willing to take assistance from the best ideas outside their own discipline, or even to look harder at Japan.

Remembering Japan, I also want to raise the possibility that there are, in the very long term, "virtue effects" in economics—for instance, that widespread corrupt accounting will eventually create bad long-term consequences as a sort of obverse

James Boswell and Samuel Johnson

A Scottish lawyer and essayist, James Boswell (1740–1795) became reknowned for his two-volume biography, *The Life of Samuel Johnson, LLD,* published in 1791, seven years after the death of his famous subject. Boswell and Johnson met in 1763 in Davies' London bookshop and became fast friends.

effect from the virtue-based boost double-entry bookkeeping gave to the heyday of Venice. I suggest that when the financial scene starts reminding you of Sodom and Gomorrah, you should fear practical consequences even if you like to participate in what is going on.

Finally, I believe that implications for charitable foundations of my conclusions today, combined with conclusions in my former talk to foundation financial officers, go way beyond implications for investment techniques. If I am right, almost all U.S. foundations are unwise through failure to understand their own investment operations, related to the larger system. If so, this is not good. A rough rule in life is that an organization foolish in one way in dealing with a complex system is all too likely to be foolish in another. So the wisdom of foundation donations may need as much improvement as investment practices of foundations. And here we have two more old rules to guide us. One rule is ethical, and the other is prudential.

The ethical rule is from Samuel Johnson, who believed that maintenance of easily removable ignorance by a responsible office-holder was treacherous malfeasance in meeting moral obligation.

The ethical rule is from Samuel Johnson, who believed that maintenance of easily removable ignorance by a responsible officeholder was treacherous malfeasance in meeting moral obligation. The prudential rule is that underlying the old Warner & Swasey advertisement for machine tools: "The man who needs a new machine tool and hasn't bought it is already paying for it." The Warner & Swasey rule also applies, I believe, to thinking tools. If you don't have the right thinking tools, you, and the people you seek to help, are already suffering from your easily removable ignorance.

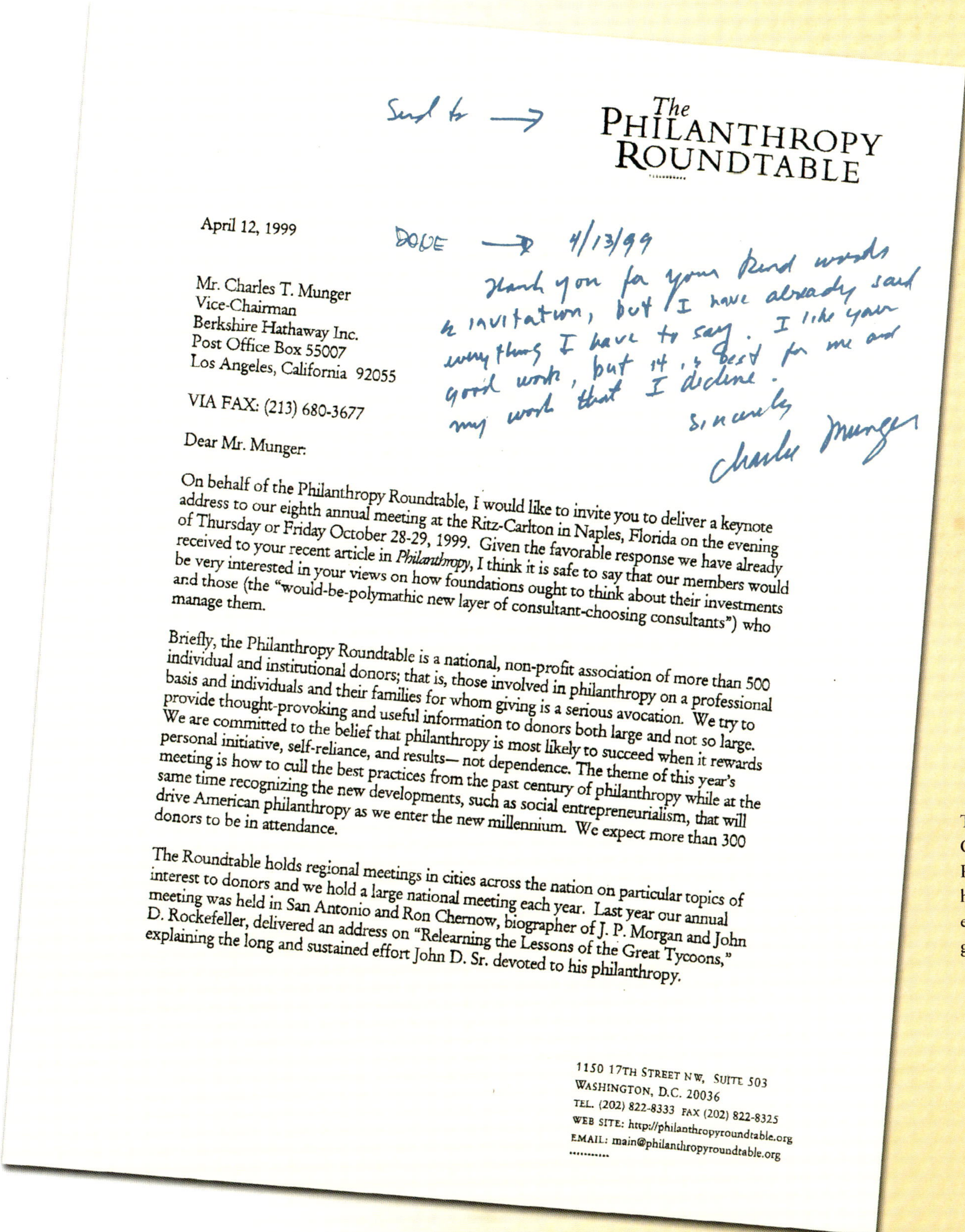

Send to →

The PHILANTHROPY ROUNDTABLE

April 12, 1999

DONE → 4/13/99

Mr. Charles T. Munger
Vice-Chairman
Berkshire Hathaway Inc.
Post Office Box 55007
Los Angeles, California 92055

VIA FAX: (213) 680-3677

Thank you for your kind words
& invitation, but I have already said
everything I have to say. I like your
good work, but it is best for me and
my work that I decline.
Sincerely
Charlie Munger

Dear Mr. Munger:

On behalf of the Philanthropy Roundtable, I would like to invite you to deliver a keynote address to our eighth annual meeting at the Ritz-Carlton in Naples, Florida on the evening of Thursday or Friday October 28-29, 1999. Given the favorable response we have already received to your recent article in *Philanthropy*, I think it is safe to say that our members would be very interested in your views on how foundations ought to think about their investments and those (the "would-be-polymathic new layer of consultant-choosing consultants") who manage them.

Briefly, the Philanthropy Roundtable is a national, non-profit association of more than 500 individual and institutional donors; that is, those involved in philanthropy on a professional basis and individuals and their families for whom giving is a serious avocation. We try to provide thought-provoking and useful information to donors both large and not so large. We are committed to the belief that philanthropy is most likely to succeed when it rewards personal initiative, self-reliance, and results— not dependence. The theme of this year's meeting is how to cull the best practices from the past century of philanthropy while at the same time recognizing the new developments, such as social entrepreneurialism, that will drive American philanthropy as we enter the new millennium. We expect more than 300 donors to be in attendance.

The Roundtable holds regional meetings in cities across the nation on particular topics of interest to donors and we hold a large national meeting each year. Last year our annual meeting was held in San Antonio and Ron Chernow, biographer of J. P. Morgan and John D. Rockefeller, delivered an address on "Relearning the Lessons of the Great Tycoons," explaining the long and sustained effort John D. Sr. devoted to his philanthropy.

1150 17TH STREET NW, SUITE 503
WASHINGTON, D.C. 20036
TEL. (202) 822-8333 FAX (202) 822-8325
WEB SITE: http://philanthropyroundtable.org
EMAIL: main@philanthropyroundtable.org

This is the initial letter inviting Charlie to address the Philanthropy Roundtable, with Charlie's handwritten declination. Charlie eventually relented and agreed to give the talk the next year.

Talk Seven Revisited

This talk in November 2000 turned out to be pretty timely, because stockmarket unpleasantness thereafter greatly increased, particularly for high-tech stocks.

But, as nearly as I can tell, there has been absolutely no theoretical reaction from anyone who heard or read the talk. I still believe everything I said about significant macroeconomic effects from "febezzlement" through excessive investment costs. But no one trained in economics has ever tried to engage with me on this subject.

Undeterred by this apathy, I am now going to push my reasoning one notch further by laying out a "thought experiment" extrapolating the combined reasoning of Talks Six and Seven to an assumed higher level of investment costs.

Assume that 2006 stock prices rise by 200% while corporate earnings do not rise, at which point all the sensibly distributable earnings of all U.S. corporations combined amount to less than the total of all stockholder investment costs, because such costs rise proportionally with stock prices. Now, so long as this situation continues, no money at all, net of investment costs, is going out of all corporations to all corporate owners combined. Instead, frictional cost imposers get more than all sensibly distributable corporate earnings. And at the end of any year, the corporate owners in aggregate can get money by reason of their stockholding only by making stock sales to providers of "new money" who, considering high continuing investment costs for themselves and others, must expect that stock prices will keep rising indefinitely while all stock owners, combined, are getting nothing, net, except by selling stock to more "new money."

To many imposers of frictional investment costs, this peculiar state of affairs would seem ideal, with more than 100% of sensibly distributable corporate earnings going to precisely the right sort of people, instead of being wasted on the shareholders. And some economists would regard the result as good because it came about in a market. But to me it would resemble a weird and disturbing combination of (1) a gambling casino imposing an unreasonably greedy take for the house, plus (2) a form of Ponzi-like scheme, similar to the market for expensive art, in which participation would be unsuitable for pension funds, etc., plus (3) a bubble of speculation that would eventually burst, probably with unfortunate macroeconomic consequences. And what the situation would not look like is a state of affairs likely to function well in guiding the capital development of the surrounding civilization.

Such a state of affairs, or even a lesser version, would, I think, reduce the reputation of our country, and deservedly so.

"Regard your good name as the richest jewel you can possibly be possessed of - for credit is like fire; when once you have kindled it you may easily preserve it, but if you once extinguish it, you will find it an arduous task to rekindle it again. The way to gain a good reputation is to endeavor to be what you desire to appear."

— Socrates (469 BC - 399 BC)

This parable and morality play gives Charlie a chance to vent his anger at the accounting profession's role in corporate malfeasance. Handwritten by Charlie when he was vacationing in the summer of 2000, the speech is an eerie prediction of the scandals that surfaced well before his predicted date of 2003 and that continue today to be an important issue.

The early Quant Tech appears to be loosely based on C. F. Braun Engineering, a firm whose brilliant founder, Carl F. Braun, and business practices Charlie greatly admired. (The firm was ultimately sold to the Kuwaiti government; so the later Quant Tech is not modeled in any way on C. F. Braun Engineering).

Charlie chronicles how leadership change in a very successful company can consign the firm to mediocrity—or worse, to disrepute and failure. When new management adopts modern financial engineering techniques, especially the use of stock options that aren't expensed, all is lost.

Shakespeare's King Henry VI said, "First thing we do, let's kill all the lawyers." Charlie, an attorney, might reject that idea, but accountants? Well…

Talk Eight

The Great Financial Scandal of 2003

An Account by Charles T. Munger, Summer 2000

The great financial scandal erupted in 2003 with the sudden, deserved disgrace of Quant Technical Corporation, always called "Quant Tech." By this time, Quant Tech was the country's largest pure engineering firm, having become so as a consequence of the contributions of its legendary founder, engineer Albert Berzog Quant.

After 2003, people came to see the Quant Tech story as a sort of morality play, divided into two acts. Act One, the era of the great founding engineer, was seen as a golden age of sound values. Act Two, the era of the founder's immediate successors, was seen as the age of false values with Quant Tech becoming, in the end, a sort of latter-day Sodom or Gomorrah.

In fact, as this account will make clear, the change from good to evil did not occur all at once when Quant Tech's founder died in 1982. Much good continued after 1982, and serious evil had existed for many years prior to 1982 in the financial culture in which Quant Tech had to operate.

Quant Tech is a fictitious engineering company that, in our story, experiences many of the common maladies of real companies—especially the fatal flaw of not accounting properly for the real costs of employee stock options.

On November 7, 1940, the first Tacoma Narrows suspension bridge in the Puget Sound of Washington State collapsed due to substandard engineering, which did not properly take into account the effects of high winds common in the area. The bridge had only been open to traffic a few months.

The Quant Tech story is best understood as a classic sort of tragedy in which a single flaw is inexorably punished by remorseless Fate. The flaw was the country's amazingly peculiar accounting treatment for employee stock options. The victims were Quant Tech and its country. The history of the Great Financial Scandal, as it actually happened, could have been written by Sophocles.

As his life ended in 1982, Albert Berzog Quant delivered to his successors and his Maker a wonderfully prosperous and useful company. The sole business of Quant Tech was designing, for fees, all over the world, a novel type of superclean and superefficient small power plant that improved electricity generation.

He no more wanted bad accounting in his business than he wanted bad engineering.

By 1982, Quant Tech had a dominant market share in its business and was earning $100 million on revenues of $1 billion. Its costs were virtually all costs to compensate technical employees engaged in design work. Direct employee compensation cost amounted to seventy percent of revenues. Of this seventy percent, thirty percent was base salaries and forty percent was incentive bonuses being paid out under an elaborate system designed by the founder. All compensation was paid in cash. There were no stock options because the old man had considered the accounting treatment required for stock options to be "weak, corrupt, and contemptible," and he no more wanted bad accounting in his business than he wanted bad engineering. Moreover, the old man believed in tailoring his huge incentive bonuses to precise performance standards established for individuals or small groups, instead of allowing what he considered undesirable compensation outcomes, both high and low, such as he believed occurred under other companies' stock option plans.

Yet, even under the old man's system, most of Quant Tech's devoted longtime employees were becoming rich, or sure to get rich. This was happening because the employees were buying Quant Tech stock in the market, just like nonemployee shareholders. The old man had always figured that people smart enough, and self-disciplined enough, to design power plants could reasonably be expected to take care of their own financial affairs in this way. He would sometimes advise an employee to buy Quant Tech stock, but more paternalistic than that he would not become.

By the time the founder died in 1982, Quant Tech was debt free and, except as a reputation-enhancer, really didn't need any shareholders' equity to run its business, no matter how fast revenues grew. However, the old man believed with Ben Franklin that "it is hard for an empty sack to stand upright," and he wanted Quant Tech to stand upright. Moreover, he loved his business and his coworkers and always wanted to have on hand large amounts of cash equivalents so as to be able to maximize work-out or work-up chances if an unexpected adversity or opportunity came along. And so, in 1982, Quant Tech had on hand $500 million in cash equivalents, amounting to fifty percent of revenues.

Possessing a strong balance sheet and a productive culture and also holding a critical mass of expertise in a rapidly changing and rapidly growing business, Quant Tech, using the old man's methods, by 1982 was destined for twenty years ahead to maintain profits at ten percent of revenues while revenues increased at twenty percent per year. After these twenty years, commencing in 2003, Quant Tech's profit margin would hold for a very long time at ten percent while revenue growth would slow down to four percent per year. But no one at Quant Tech knew precisely when its inevitable period of slow revenue growth would begin.

The old man's dividend policy for Quant Tech was simplicity itself: He never paid a dividend. Instead, all earnings simply piled up in cash equivalents.

Every truly sophisticated investor in common stocks could see that the stock of cash-rich Quant Tech provided a splendid investment opportunity in 1982 when it sold at a mere fifteen times earnings and, despite its brilliant prospects, had a market capitalization of only $1.5 billion. This low market capitalization, despite brilliant

Sophocles
(496–406 BC)

Sophocles, an ancient Greek playwright, dramatist, priest, and politician of Athens, is best known as one of the three great Greek tragedians (the others being Aeschylus and Euripides, with whom he often competed in dramatic contests). Sophocles wrote over one hundred plays; many scholars, including Aristotle, considered him to be the greatest playwright in ancient Greek theater. The most famous of his surviving works are the tragedies of *Oedipus Rex* and *Antigone.*

prospects, existed in 1982 because other wonderful common stocks were also then selling at fifteen times earnings, or less, as a natural consequence of high interest rates then prevailing plus disappointing investment returns that had occurred over many previous years for holders of typical diversified portfolios of common stocks.

One result of Quant Tech's low market capitalization in 1982 was that it made Quant Tech's directors uneasy and dissatisfied right after the old man's death. A wiser board would then have bought in Quant Tech's stock very aggressively, using up all cash on hand and also borrowing funds to use in the same way. However, such a decision was not in accord with conventional corporate wisdom in 1982. And so the directors made a conventional decision. They recruited a new CEO and CFO from outside Quant Tech, in particular from a company that then had a conventional stock option plan for employees and also possessed a market capitalization at twenty times reported earnings, even though its balance sheet was weaker than Quant Tech's and its earnings were growing more slowly than earnings at Quant Tech. Incident to the recruitment of the new executives, it was made plain that Quant Tech's directors wanted a higher market capitalization as soon as feasible.

The newly installed Quant Tech officers quickly realized that the company could not wisely either drive its revenues up at an annual rate higher than the rate in place or increase Quant Tech profit margin. The founder had plainly achieved an optimum in each case. Nor did the new officers dare tinker with an engineering culture that was working so well. Therefore, the new officers were attracted to employing what they called "modern financial engineering," which required prompt use of any and all arguably lawful methods for driving up reported earnings, with big, simple changes to be made first.

By a strange irony of fate, the accounting convention for stock options that had so displeased Quant Tech's founder now made the new officers' job very easy and would ultimately ruin Quant Tech's reputation. There was now an accounting convention in the United States that, provided employees were first given options, required that when easily marketable stock was issued to employees at a below-market price, the bargain element for the employees, although roughly equivalent to cash, could not count as compensation expense in determining a company's reported profits. This amazingly peculiar accounting convention had been selected by the accounting profession, over the objection of some of its wisest and most ethical members, because corporate managers, by and large, preferred that their gains from exercising options covering their employers' stock not be counted as expense in determining their employers' earnings. The accounting profession, in making its amazingly peculiar decision, had simply followed the injunction so often followed by persons quite different from prosperous, entrenched accountants. The injunction was that normally followed by insecure and powerless people: "Whose bread I eat, his song I sing." Fortunately, the income tax authorities did not have the same amazingly peculiar accounting idea as the accounting profession. Elementary common sense prevailed, and the bargain element in stock option exercises was treated as an obvious compensation expense, deductible in determining income for tax purposes.

Upton Sinclair
(1878–1968)

"It is difficult to get a man to understand something when his salary depends on his not understanding it."

The injunction was that normally followed by insecure and powerless people: "Whose bread I eat, his song I sing."

Quant Tech's new officers, financially shrewd as they were, could see at a glance that, given the amazingly peculiar accounting convention and the sound income tax rules in place, Quant Tech had a breathtakingly large opportunity to increase its reported profits by taking very simple action. The fact that so large a share of Quant Tech's annual expense was incentive bonus expense provided a "modern financial engineering" opportunity second to none.

For instance, it was mere child's play for the executives to realize that if in 1982 Quant Tech had substituted employee stock option exercise profits for all its incentive bonus expense of $400 million while using bonus money saved plus option prices paid to buy back all shares issued in option exercises and keeping all else the same, the result would have been to drive Quant Tech 1982 reported earnings up by 400 percent to $500 million from $100 million while shares outstanding remained exactly the same! And so it seemed that the obviously correct ploy for the officers was to start substituting employee stock option exercise profits for incentive bonuses. Why should a group of numerate engineers care whether their bonuses were in cash or virtually perfect equivalents of cash? Arranging such substitutions, on any schedule desired, seemed like no difficult chore.

However, it was also mere child's play for the new officers to realize that a certain amount of caution and restraint would be desirable in pushing their new ploy. Obviously, if they pushed their new ploy too hard in any single year, there might be rebellion from Quant Tech's accountants or undesirable hostility from other sources. This, in turn, would risk killing a goose with a vast ability to deliver golden eggs, at least to the officers. After all, it was quite clear that their ploy would be increasing reported earnings only by adding to real earnings an element of phony earnings—phony in the sense that Quant Tech would enjoy no true favorable economic effect (except temporary fraud-type effect similar to that from overcounting closing inventory) from that part of reported earnings increases attributable to use of the ploy. The new CEO privately called the desirable, cautious approach "wisely restrained falsehood."

"The Right Way to Behave is to Never Let Improper Accounting Start"

In 1991, the Financial Accounting Standards Board proposed that part of the real cost of employee stock options be recognized as an expense. Because of stiff opposition from both the business community and Congress, the proposal was greatly diluted, requiring only some disclosure in footnotes. Today, however, generally accepted accounting principles in the U.S. require some part of the real cost of employee stock options to be recorded as an expense in the income statement. Charlie remains skeptical: "By the time stock options are exercised, the total cost charged is usually far less than total cost incurred. Moreover, the part of cost that is charged to earnings is often manipulated downward by dubious techniques. This kind of thing has always been hard to stamp out. The right way to behave is to never let improper accounting start."

Plainly, the new officers saw, it would be prudent to shift bonus payments to employee stock option exercise profits in only a moderate amount per year over many years ahead. They privately called the prudent plan they adopted their "dollop by dollop system," which they believed had four obvious advantages:

The outside accountants...would probably find it unendurably embarrassing not to bless new financial statements containing only the same phony proportion of reported earnings increase.

"Those principles upon which his business was built and with which it is synonymous must be preserved. His name must never be associated with any program or action that is not the highest and the best. I am sure he would rather the doors be closed than it should continue to exist on principles other than those he established. To you he has left a great name. Your opportunity is tremendous, your responsibility is great."

—The Rev. Dr. Duncan E. Littlefair, closing words, eulogy for Arthur Andersen (above), January 13, 1947

First, a moderate dollop of phony earnings in any single year would be less likely to be noticed than a large dollop.

Second, the large long-term effect from accumulating many moderate dollops of phony earnings over the years would also tend to be obscured in the "dollop by dollop system." As the CFO pithily and privately said, "If we mix only a moderate minority share of turds with the raisins each year, probably no one will recognize what will ultimately become a very large collection of turds."

Third, the outside accountants, once they had blessed a few financial statements containing earnings increases, only a minority share of which were phony, would probably find it unendurably embarrassing not to bless new financial statements containing only the same phony proportion of reported earnings increase.

Fourth, the "dollop by dollop system" would tend to prevent disgrace, or something more seriously harmful, for Quant Tech's officers. With virtually all corporations except Quant Tech having ever-more-liberal stock option plans, the officers could always explain that a moderate dollop of shift toward compensation in option-exercise form was needed to help attract or retain employees. Indeed, given

Carlo "Charles" Ponzi
(1882–1949)

The Ponzi Scheme

One of the most famous examples of modern financial engineering was the Ponzi scheme, which started in Boston in 1919. Claiming an ability to exploit an unforeseen arbitrage in international postal coupons, Carlo "Charles" Ponzi attracted thousands of investors by promising fifty percent interest in ninety days. To build credibility, he used funds from recent investors to provide returns to earlier participants—a standard pyramid-scheme tactic. Soon, Ponzi had taken in millions. In 1920, the *Boston Post* ran a story questioning Ponzi's practices, which provoked an independent audit. The audit revealed the fraud, and investors demanded their money back. In the end, the average participant had only thirty-seven percent of invested funds returned, and Ponzi spent several years in prison. Unrepentant, Ponzi turned up again in the late 1920s selling worthless land in Florida.

corporate culture and stock market enthusiasm likely to exist as a consequence of the strange accounting convention for stock options, this claim would often be true.

With these four advantages, the "dollop by dollop system" seemed so clearly desirable that it only remained for Quant Tech's officers to decide how big to make their annual dollops of phony earnings. This decision, too, turned out to be easy. The officers first decided upon three reasonable conditions they wanted satisfied:

First, they wanted to be able to continue their "dollop by dollop system" without major discontinuities for twenty years.

Second, they wanted Quant Tech's reported earnings to go up by roughly the same percentage each year throughout the whole twenty years because they believed that financial analysts, representing institutional investors, would value Quant Tech's stock higher if reported annual earnings growth never significantly varied.

Third, to protect credibility for reported earnings, they never wanted to strain credulity of investors by reporting, even in their twentieth year, that Quant Tech was earning more than forty percent of revenues from designing power plants.

With these requirements, the math was easy, given the officers' assumption that Quant Tech's non-phony earnings and revenues were both going to grow at twenty percent per year for twenty years. The officers quickly decided to use their "dollop by dollop system" to make Quant Tech's reported earnings increase by twenty-eight percent per year instead of the twenty percent that would have been reported by the founder.

And so, the great scheme of "modern financial engineering" went forward toward tragedy at Quant Tech.

And so, the great scheme of "modern financial engineering" went forward toward tragedy at Quant Tech. And few disreputable schemes of man have ever worked better in achieving what was attempted. Quant Tech's reported earnings, certified by its accountants, increased regularly at twenty-eight percent per year. No one criticized Quant Tech's financial reporting except a few people widely regarded as impractical, overly theoretical, misanthropic cranks. It turned out that the founder's policy of never paying dividends, which was continued, greatly helped in preserving credibility for Quant Tech's reports that its earnings were rising steadily at twenty-eight percent per year. With cash equivalents on hand so remarkably high, the Pavlovian mere-association effects that so often impair reality recognition served well to prevent detection of the phony element in reported earnings.

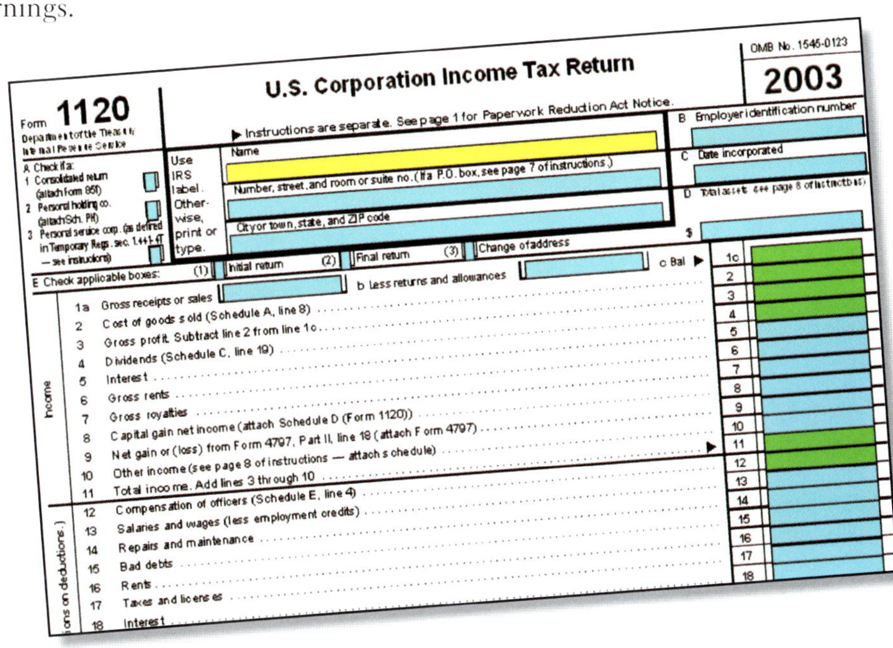
Form 1120
U.S. Corporation Income Tax Return
OMB No. 1545-0123
2003
Department of the Treasury
Internal Revenue Service
Instructions are separate. See page 1 for Paperwork Reduction Act Notice.
A Check if a:
1 Consolidated return (attach Form 851)
2 Personal holding co. (attach Sch. PH)
3 Personal service corp. (as defined in Temporary Regs. sec. 1.441-4T — see instructions)
Use IRS label. Otherwise, print or type.
Name
Number, street, and room or suite no. (If a P.O. box, see page 7 of instructions.)
City or town, state, and ZIP code
B Employer identification number
C Date incorporated
D Total assets (see page 8 of instructions)
$
E Check applicable boxes: (1) Initial return (2) Final return (3) Change of address

Income
1a Gross receipts or sales | b Less returns and allowances | c Bal ▶ 1c
2 Cost of goods sold (Schedule A, line 8) 2
3 Gross profit. Subtract line 2 from line 1c 3
4 Dividends (Schedule C, line 19) 4
5 Interest 5
6 Gross rents 6
7 Gross royalties 7
8 Capital gain net income (attach Schedule D (Form 1120)) 8
9 Net gain or (loss) from Form 4797, Part II, line 18 (attach Form 4797) 9
10 Other income (see page 8 of instructions — attach schedule) 10
11 Total income. Add lines 3 through 10 ▶ 11

Deductions (See instructions for limitations on deductions.)
12 Compensation of officers (Schedule E, line 4) 12
13 Salaries and wages (less employment credits) 13
14 Repairs and maintenance 14
15 Bad debts 15
16 Rents 16
17 Taxes and licenses 17
18 Interest 18

It was, therefore, natural, after the "dollop by dollop system" had been in place for a few years, for Quant Tech's officers to yearn to have Quant Tech's reported earnings per share keep going up at twenty-eight percent per year while cash equivalents grew much faster than they were then growing. This turned out to be a snap. By this time, Quant Tech's stock was selling at a huge multiple of reported earnings, and the officers simply started causing some incremental stock-option exercises that were not matched either by reductions in cash bonuses paid or by repurchases of Quant Tech's stock. This change, the officers easily recognized, was a very helpful revision of their original plan. Not only was detection of the phony element in reported earnings made much more difficult as cash accumulation greatly accelerated, but also a significant amount of Ponzi-scheme or chain-letter effect was being introduced into Quant Tech, with real benefits for present shareholders, including the officers.

At this time, the officers also fixed another flaw in their original plan. They saw that as Quant Tech's reported earnings, containing an increasing phony element, kept rising at twenty-eight percent, Quant Tech's income taxes as a percentage of reported pre-tax earnings kept going lower and lower. This plainly increased chances for causing undesired questions and criticism. This problem was soon

Trust, But Verify

A useful technique in assessing the veracity of reported earnings is to compare the purported good news in the annual report with the stark reality of income taxes *actually* being paid. Since managers are seldom as eager to juice reported results to the IRS as they are to shareholders, the "cash income taxes paid" footnote in a corporation's 10K is often a more accurate and truthful indicator of the company's real earnings.

eliminated. Many power plants in foreign nations were built and owned by governments, and it proved easy to get some foreign governments to raise Quant Tech's design fees, provided that in each case slightly more than the fee increase was paid back in additional income taxes to the foreign government concerned.

Finally, for 2002, Quant Tech reported $16 billion in earnings on $47 billion of revenues that now included a lot more revenue from interest on cash equivalents than would have been present without net issuances of new stock over the years. Cash equivalents on hand now amounted to an astounding $85 billion, and somehow it didn't seem impossible to most investors that a company virtually drowning in so much cash could be earning the $16 billion it was reporting. The market capitalization of Quant Tech at its peak early in 2003 became $1.4 trillion, about ninety times earnings reported for 2002.

All man's desired geometric progressions, if a high rate of growth is chosen, at last come to grief on a finite earth.

However, all man's desired geometric progressions, if a high rate of growth is chosen, at last come to grief on a finite earth. And the social system for man on earth is fair enough, eventually, that almost all massive cheating ends in disgrace. And in 2003, Quant Tech failed in both ways.

By 2003, Quant Tech's real earning power was growing at only four percent per year after sales growth had slowed to four percent. There was now no way for Quant Tech to escape causing a big disappointment for its shareholders, now largely consisting of institutional investors. This disappointment triggered a shocking decline in the price of Quant Tech stock, which went down suddenly by fifty percent. This price decline, in turn, triggered a careful examination of Quant Tech's financial reporting practices, which, at long last, convinced nearly everyone that a very large majority of Quant Tech's reported earnings had long been phony earnings and that massive and deliberate misreporting had gone on for a great many years.

Geometric Progressions:
Highly Counter-Intuitive

Seeking to teach his young charge a lesson in the power of compounding, a teacher made an intriguing offer:

"I will give you one of the following, but you cannot change your mind later, so think carefully before you decide. I will give you $1,000 per day for thirty days that you can begin spending immediately. Alternatively, I will give you a penny on day one, double it on day two, double the resulting sum again on day three, and continue doubling your holdings every day for thirty days, but you may not spend a single cent until the thirtieth day has passed."

The young charge, enticed by the prospect of spending $1,000 per day for a month compared to what he believed would be just a few pennies jingling around in his pocket a month from now, chose the $1,000 per day for a month. Did he choose wisely?

Under the first choice, the young charge would receive a total of $30,000. Under the second choice, the power of compounding would run the total to $5,368,709.12.

This triggered even more price decline for Quant Tech stock until in mid-2003 the market capitalization of Quant Tech was only $140 billion, down ninety percent from its peak only six months earlier.

A quick ninety percent decline in the price of the stock of such an important company that was previously so widely owned and admired caused immense human suffering, considering the $1.3 trillion in market value that had disappeared. And naturally, with Quant Tech's deserved disgrace, the public and political reaction included intense hatred and revulsion directed at Quant Tech even though its admirable engineers were still designing the nation's best power plants.

Moreover, the hatred and revulsion did not stop with Quant Tech. It soon spread to other corporations, some of which plainly had undesirable financial cultures different from Quant Tech's only in degree. The public and political hatred, like the behavior that had caused it, soon went to gross excess and fed upon itself. Financial misery spread far beyond investors into a serious recession like that of Japan in the 1990s following the long period of false Japanese accounting.

There was huge public antipathy to professions following the Great Scandal. The accounting profession, of course, got the most blame. The rule-making body for accountants had long borne the acronym "F.A.S.B." And now, nearly everyone said this stood for "Financial Accounts Still Bogus."

Economics professors, likewise, drew much criticism for failing to blow the whistle on false accounting and for not sufficiently warning about eventual bad macroeconomic effects of widespread false accounting. So great was the disappointment with conventional economists that Harvard's John Kenneth Galbraith received the Nobel Prize in economics. After all, he had once predicted that massive, undetected corporate embezzlement would have a wonderfully

John Kenneth Galbraith
(b. 1908)

Famed economist John Kenneth Galbraith offers his wisdom:

"We all agree that pessimism is a mark of superior intellect."

"There is certainly no absolute standard of beauty. That precisely is what makes its pursuit so interesting."

"Meetings are indispensable when you don't want to do anything."

"The only function of economic forecasting is to make astrology look respectable."

"The modern conservative is engaged in one of man's oldest exercises in moral philosophy; that is, the search for a superior moral justification for selfishness."

"More die in the United States of too much food than of too little."

"Faced with the choice between changing one's mind and proving there is no need to do so, almost everyone gets busy on the proof."

"People who are in a fortunate position always attribute virtue to what makes them so happy."

"Do you understand 'it is a far, far better thing to have a firm anchor in nonsense than to put out on the troubled seas of thought.'"

"People of privilege will always risk their complete destruction rather than surrender any material part of their advantage."

"In any great organization it is far, far safer to be wrong with the majority than to be right alone."

"How do you fall dramatically off a pancake?"

stimulating effect on the economy. And people could now see that something very close to what Galbraith had predicted had actually happened in the years preceding 2003 and had thereafter helped create a big, reactive recession.

With Congress and the S.E.C. so heavily peopled by lawyers, and with lawyers having been so heavily involved in drafting financial disclosure documents now seen as bogus, there was a new "lawyer" joke every week. One such was: "The butcher says, 'The reputation of lawyers has fallen dramatically,' and the checkout clerk replies, 'How do you fall dramatically off a pancake?'"

But the hostility to established professions did not stop with accountants, economists, and lawyers. There were many adverse "rub-off" effects on reputations of professionals that had always performed well, like engineers, who did not understand the financial fraud that their country had made a conventional requirement.

In the end, much that was good about the country, and needed for its future felicity, was widely and unwisely hated.

At this point, action came from a Higher Realm. God himself, who reviews all, changed His decision schedule to bring to the fore the sad case of the Great Financial Scandal of 2003. He called in his chief detective and said, "Smith, bring in for harsh but fair judgment the most depraved of those responsible for this horrible outcome."

But when Smith brought in a group of security analysts who had long and uncritically touted the stock of Quant Tech, the Great Judge was displeased. "Smith," he said, "I can't come down hardest on low-level cognitive error, much of it subconsciously caused by the standard incentive systems of the world."

Next, Smith brought in a group of S.E.C. commissioners and powerful politicians. "No, no," said the Great Judge, "These people operate in a virtual maelstrom of regrettable forces and can't reasonably be expected to meet the behavioral standard you seek to impose."

Now the chief detective thought he had gotten the point. He next brought in the corporate officers who had practiced their version of "modern financial engineering" at Quant Tech. "You are getting close," said the Great Judge, "but I told you to bring in the most depraved. These officers will, of course, get strong punishment for their massive fraud and disgusting stewardship of the great engineer's legacy. But I want you to bring in the miscreants who will soon be in the lowest circle in Hell, the ones who so easily could have prevented all this calamity."

William Blake created this image, *God Judging Adam* (1795), in a variety of media—as a drawing, etching, prints and watercolor. One prominent version of the image is the color-printed relief etching finished in pen and ink and watercolor at the Metropolitan Museum of Art in New York.

At last, the chief detective truly understood. He remembered that the lowest circle of Hell was reserved for traitors. And so he now brought in from Purgatory a group of elderly persons who, in their days on earth, had been prominent partners in major accounting firms. "Here are your traitors," said the chief detective. "They adopted the false accounting convention for employee stock options. They occupied high positions in one of the noblest professions, which, like yours, help make

society work right by laying down the right rules. They were very smart and securely placed, and it is inexcusable that they deliberately caused all this lying and cheating that was so obviously predictable. They well knew what they were doing was disastrously wrong, yet they did it anyway. Owing to press of business in Your Judicial System, you made a mistake at first in punishing them so lightly. But now you can send them into the lowest circle in Hell."

Startled by the vehemence and presumption, the Great Judge paused. Then He quietly said, "Well done, my good and faithful servant."

This account is not an implied prediction about 2003. It is a work of fiction. Except in the case of Professor Galbraith, any resemblance to real persons or companies is accidental. It was written in an attempt to focus possibly useful attention on certain modern behaviors and belief systems.

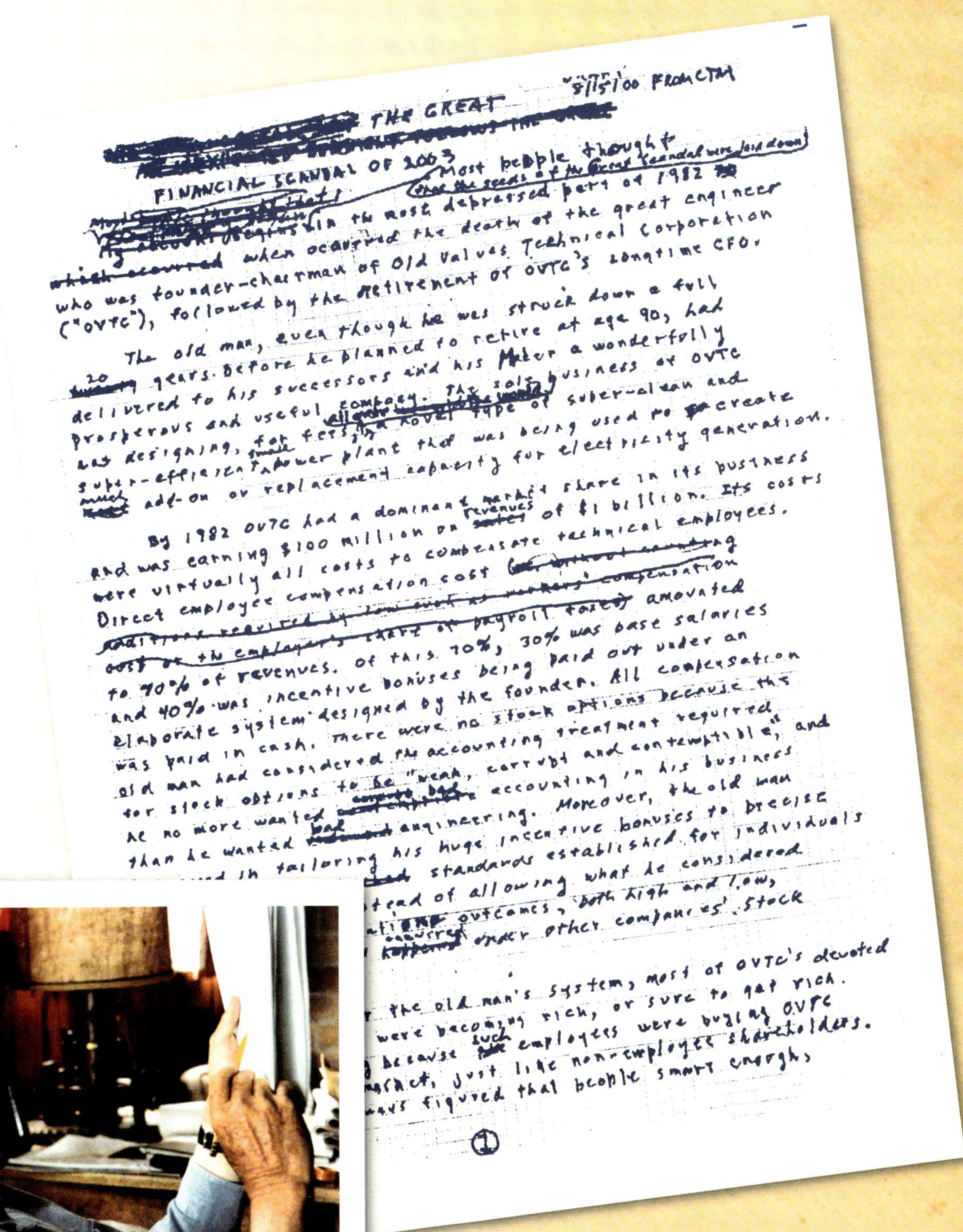

8/15/00 FROM CTM

THE GREAT FINANCIAL SCANDAL OF 2003

Most people thought that the seeds of the Great Scandal were laid down in the most depressed part of 1982 when occurred the death of the great engineer who was founder-chairman of Old Values Technical Corporation ("OVTC"), followed by the retirement of OVTC's longtime CFO.

The old man, even though he was struck down a full 20 years before he planned to retire at age 90, had delivered to his successors and his heir a wonderfully prosperous and useful company. The sole business of OVTC was designing, for fees, a novel type of super-clean and super-efficient small power plant that was being used to create much add-on or replacement capacity for electricity generation.

By 1982 OVTC had a dominant market share in its business and was earning $100 million on revenues of $1 billion. Its costs were virtually all costs to compensate technical employees. Direct employee compensation cost amounted to 70% of revenues. Of this 70%, 30% was base salaries and 40% was incentive bonuses being paid out under an elaborate system designed by the founder. All compensation was paid in cash. There were no stock options because the old man had considered the accounting treatment required for stock options to be "weak, corrupt and contemptible," and he no more wanted bad accounting in his business than he wanted bad engineering. Moreover, the old man [illegible] precise [illegible] in tailoring his huge incentive bonuses to individuals [illegible] standards established for [illegible] he considered [illegible] instead of allowing what [illegible] outcomes, both high and low, [illegible] occurred under other companies' stock [illegible]

[illegible] the old man's system, most of OVTC's devoted [illegible] were becoming rich, or sure to get rich. [illegible] because such employees were buying OVTC [illegible] market, just like non-employee shareholders. [illegible] figured that people smart enough [illegible]

1

The first manuscript page of "The Great Financial Scandal of 2003," which Charlie wrote while on vacation in Minnesota in 2000.

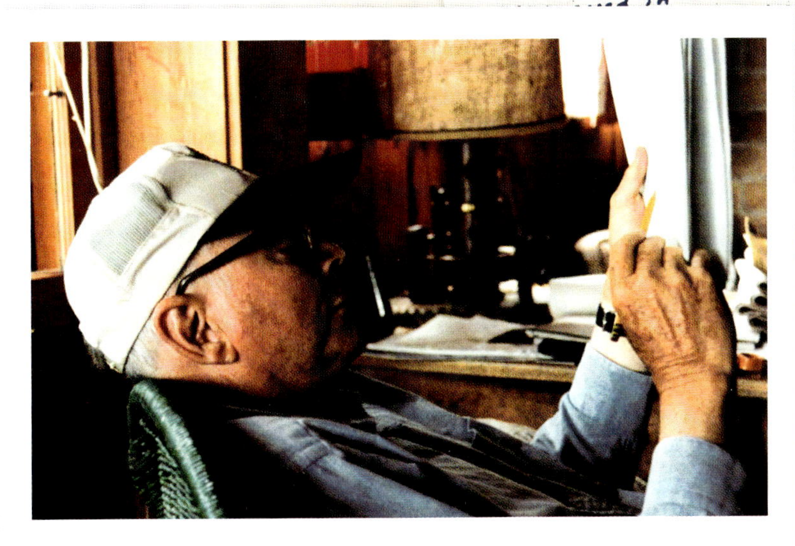

Talk Eight Revisited

I had a lot of fun composing this account in the summer of 2000. But I was serious as I tried to show how standard accounting treatment for stock options was functionally equivalent to simpler types of promotional fraud.

To me, a profession and a nation that allow unsound accounting for management cost are leaning in the same moral direction as the group that leaves most of the steel out of the concrete in erecting high-rise apartment buildings. Moreover, the unsound accounting is more virulent than the murderous construction practice. After all, the defective constructors have a harder time rationalizing their deplorable behavior. And, therefore, the bad accounting will more easily spread than the defective construction. Which is exactly what happened, as defective accounting for stock options became ubiquitous.

Close-up view of Taiwan 7.6 magnitude Chi-Chi earthquake damage. Much of the damage resulted from inadequate steel reinforcement in concrete structures.

There has been some good news since Talk Eight was delivered. The accounting profession now requires that some provision for stock option cost be charged against earnings. However, by the time stock options are exercised, the total cost charged is usually far less than total cost incurred. Moreover the part of cost that is charged to earnings is often manipulated downward by dubious techniques.

What this accounting saga constitutes is one more sad example of evil rewarded dying hard, as a great many people conclude that something can't be evil if they are profiting from it.

"Pleasure is the greatest incentive to evil."

—Plato

The editor of this book spent twelve consecutive hours with Charlie on the day he delivered this speech at the University of California at Santa Barbara. Our schedule that day: a two-hour drive each way from Los Angeles, lunch, pre-talk meetings, the talk itself, a post-talk reception, and finally dinner at the home of Jeff Henley, chief financial officer (and now chairman) of Oracle Corp. Despite then being within a few months of his eightieth birthday, Charlie performed like a tireless virtuoso. His sharpness, stamina, and good humor during that long day were astounding and inspiring.

What Charlie laid forth on that occasion might be considered the Grand Unified Theory of the Munger approach. The talk incorporates the many ideas that Charlie discussed in his previous talks and presents them, checklist-style, as a coherent philosophy.

Charlie's audience, the economics department of this major university, was the perfect group on which to unleash this lament—and remediation proposals besides—about the lack of multidisciplinarianism in the soft sciences.

Academic Economics: Strengths and Faults after Considering Interdisciplinary Needs

Herb Kay Undergraduate Lecture University of California, Santa Barbara Economics Department, October 3, 2003

I have outlined some remarks in a rough way, and after I'm finished talking from that outline, I'll take questions as long as anybody can endure listening, until they drag me away to wherever else I'm supposed to go. As you might guess, I agreed to do this because the subject of getting the soft sciences so they talk better to each other has been one that has interested me for decades. And, of course, economics is, in many respects, the queen of the soft sciences. It's expected to be better than the rest. It's my view that economics is better at the multidisciplinary stuff than the rest of the soft science. And it's also my view that it's still lousy, and I'd like to discuss this failure in this talk.

A Second Black Belt

Twenty years after he first introduced the Black Belt in Chutzpah, Charlie appropriately awards himself a second one in this talk at UC Santa Barbara.

As I talk about strengths and weaknesses in academic economics, one interesting fact you are entitled to know is that I never took a course in economics. And with this striking lack of credentials, you may wonder why I have the chutzpah to be up here giving this talk. The answer is I have a black belt in chutzpah. I was born with it. Some people, like some of the women I know, have a black belt in spending. They were born with that. But what they gave me was a black belt in chutzpah.

But, I come from two peculiar strands of experience that may have given me some useful economic insights. One is Berkshire Hathaway, and the other is my personal educational history. Berkshire, of course, has finally gotten interesting. When Warren took over Berkshire, the market capitalization was about $10 million. And forty-something years later, there are not many more shares outstanding now than there were then, and the market capitalization is about a $100 billion, ten thousand for one. And since that has happened, year after year, in kind of a grind-ahead fashion with very few failures, it eventually drew some attention, indicating that maybe Warren and I knew something useful in microeconomics.

"If you would persuade, appeal to interest and not to reason."

For a long time there was a Nobel Prize–winning economist who explained Berkshire Hathaway's success as follows:

First, he said Berkshire beat the market in common stock investing through one sigma of luck because nobody could beat the market except by luck. This hard-form version of efficient market theory was taught in most schools of economics at the time. People were taught that nobody could beat the market. Next, the professor went to two sigmas, and three sigmas, and four sigmas, and when he finally got to six sigmas of luck, people were laughing so hard he stopped doing it.

Then, he reversed the explanation 180 degrees. He said, "No, it was still six sigmas, but it was six sigmas of skill." Well, this very sad history demonstrates the truth of Benjamin Franklin's observation in *Poor Richard's Almanack*, "If you would persuade, appeal to interest and not to reason." The man changed his silly view when his incentives made him change it and not before.

I watched the same thing happen at the Jules Stein Eye Institute at UCLA. I asked, at one point, "Why are you treating cataracts only with a totally obsolete cataract operation?" And the man said to me, "Charlie, it's such a wonderful operation to teach." When he stopped using that operation, it was because almost all the patients had voted with their feet. Again, appeal to interest and not to reason if you want to change conclusions.

Well, Berkshire's whole record has been achieved without paying one ounce of attention to the efficient market theory in its hard form. And not one ounce of attention to the descendants of that idea, which came out of academic economics and went into corporate finance and morphed into such obscenities as the capital asset pricing model, which we also paid no attention to. I think you'd have to believe in the tooth fairy to believe that you could easily outperform the market by seven percentage points per annum just by investing in high-volatility stocks.

Yet, believe it or not, like the Jules Stein doctor, people once believed this stuff. And the belief was rewarded. And it spread. And many people still believe it. But Berkshire never paid any attention to it. And now, I think the world is coming our way, and the idea of perfection in all market outcomes is going the way of the dodo.

It was always clear to me that the stock market couldn't be perfectly efficient, because, as a teenager, I'd been to the racetrack in Omaha where they had the pari-mutuel system. And it was quite obvious to me that if the house take, the croupier's take, was seventeen percent, some people consistently lost a lot less then seventeen percent of all their bets, and other people consistently lost more than seventeen percent of all their bets. So the pari-mutuel system in Omaha had no perfect

The Jules Stein Eye Institute

The Jules Stein Eye Institute, established in 1966 by Dr. and Mrs. Jules Stein, is a center for the vision sciences, dedicated to the preservation of vision and the prevention of blindness.

The Institute carries out patient care, research, and education in the vision sciences. It is affiliated with UCLA.

efficiency. And so I didn't accept the argument that the stock market was always perfectly efficient in creating rational prices.

Indeed, there have been some documented cases since of people getting so good at understanding horses and odds that they actually are able to beat the house in off-track betting. There aren't many people who can do that, but there are a few people in America who can.

Next, my personal education history is interesting because its deficiencies and my peculiarities eventually created advantages. For some odd reason, I had an early and extreme multidisciplinary cast of mind. I couldn't stand reaching for a small idea in my own discipline when there was a big idea right over the fence in somebody else's discipline. So I just grabbed in all directions for the big ideas that would really work. Nobody taught me to do that; I was just born with that yen. I also was born with a huge craving for synthesis. And when it didn't come easily, which was often, I would rag the problem, and then when I failed, I would put it aside, and I'd come back to it and rag it again. It took me twenty years to figure out how and why cult conversion methods worked. But the psychology departments haven't figured it out yet, so I'm ahead of them.

Originally part of the U.S. Army, the U.S. Army Air Corps was established by an act of Congress in 1926. The role of the Corps grew as aviators, like Jimmy Doolittle and others, demonstrated the value of air power. Today, the Corps is known as the U.S. Air Force.

But anyway, I have this tendency to want to rag the problems. Because WWII caught me, I drifted into some physics, and the Air Corps sent me to Caltech, where I did a little more physics as part of being made into a meteorologist. And there, at a very young age, I absorbed what I call the fundamental full attribution ethos of hard science. And that was enormously useful to me. Let me explain that ethos.

Under this ethos, you've got to know all the big ideas in all the disciplines more fundamental than your own. You can never make any explanation that can be made in a more fundamental way in any other way than the most fundamental way. And you always take with full attribution to the most fundamental ideas that

you are required to use. When you're using physics, you say you're using physics. When you're using biology, you say you're using biology. And so on and so on. I could early see that that ethos would act as a fine organizing system for my thought. And I strongly suspected that it would work really well in the soft sciences as well as the hard sciences, so I just grabbed it and used it all through my life in soft science as well as hard science. That was a very lucky idea for me.

Let me explain how extreme that ethos is in hard science. There is a constant, one of the fundamental constants in physics, known as Boltzmann's constant. You probably all know it very well. And the interesting thing about Boltzmann's constant is that Boltzmann didn't discover it. So why is Boltzmann's constant now named for Boltzmann? Well, the answer is that Boltzmann derived that constant from basic physics in a more fundamental way than the poor forgotten fellow who found the constant in the first place in some less fundamental way. The ethos of hard science is so strong in favor of reductionism to the more fundamental body of knowledge that you can wash the discoverer right out of history when somebody else handles his discovery in a more fundamental way. I think that is correct. I think Boltzmann's constant should be named for Boltzmann.

At any rate, in my history and Berkshire's history, Berkshire went on and on into considerable economic success while ignoring the hard-form efficient markets doctrine once very popular in academic economics and ignoring the descendants of that doctrine in corporate finance where the results became even sillier than they were in economics. This naturally encouraged me.

Boltzmann's Constant

Boltzmann's constant derives its name from Austrian physicist Ludwig Boltzmann (1844–1906); it defines the relation between absolute temperature and the kinetic energy contained in each molecule of an ideal gas. In general, the energy in a gas molecule is directly proportional to the absolute temperature. As the temperature increases, the kinetic energy per molecule increases. As a gas is heated, its molecules move more rapidly. This movement produces increased pressure if the gas is confined in a space of constant volume, or increased volume if the pressure remains constant.

1.381E -23

Finally, with my peculiar history, I'm also bold enough to be here today because, at least when I was young, I wasn't a total klutz. For one year at the Harvard Law School, I was ranked second in a very large group, and I always figured that, while there were always a lot of people much smarter than I was, I didn't have to hang back totally in the thinking game.

N. Gregory Mankiw
(b. 1958)

N. Gregory Mankiw studied economics at Princeton University, earned a Ph. D. from MIT, and is on the faculty at Harvard University. In 2003, he was appointed chairman of the Council of Economic Advisers.

Let me begin by discussing the obvious strengths of academic economics. The first obvious strength, and this is true of a lot of places that get repute, is that it was in the right place at the right time. Two hundred years ago, aided by the growth of technology and the growth of other developments in the civilization, the real output per capita of the civilized world started going up at about two percent per annum, compounded. And before that, for the previous thousands of years, it had gone up at a rate that hovered just a hair's-breadth above zero. And, of course, economics grew up amid this huge success. Partly it helped the success, and partly it explained it. So, naturally, academic economics grew. And, lately, with the collapse of all the communist economies, as the free market economies or partially free market economies flourished, that added to the reputation of economics. Economics has been a very favorable place to be if you're in academia.

Economics was always more multidisciplinary than the rest of soft science. It just reached out and grabbed things as it needed to. And that tendency to just grab whatever you need from the rest of knowledge if you're an economist has reached a fairly high point in N. Gregory Mankiw's new textbook. I checked out that textbook. I must have been one of the few businessmen in America that bought it immediately when it came out because it had gotten such a big advance. I wanted to figure out what the guy was doing where he could get an advance that great. So this is how I happened to riffle through Mankiw's freshman textbook. And there I found laid out as principles of economics: Opportunity cost is a superpower, to be used by all people who have any hope of getting the right answer. Also, incentives are superpowers.

And lastly, the tragedy of the commons model, popularized by my longtime friend, UCSB's Garrett Hardin. Hardin caused the delightful introduction into economics—alongside Smith's beneficent invisible hand—of Hardin's wicked evildoing invisible foot. Well, I thought that the Hardin model made economics more complete, and I knew when Hardin introduced me to his model, the tragedy of the commons, that it would be in the economics textbooks eventually. And, lo and behold, it finally made it about twenty years later. And it's right for Mankiw to reach out into other disciplines and grab Hardin's model and anything else that works well.

Another thing that helped economics is that, from the beginning, it attracted the best brains in soft science. Its denizens also interacted more with the practical world than was at all common in soft science and the rest of academia, and that resulted in very creditable outcomes like the three cabinet appointments of economics Ph.D. George Shultz and the cabinet appointment of Larry Summers. So this has been a very favored part of academia.

Also, economics early on attracted some of the best writers of language in the history of the Earth. You start out with Adam Smith. Adam Smith was so good a thinker and so good a writer that, in his own time, Emmanuel Kant, then the greatest intellectual in Germany, simply announced that there was nobody in Germany to equal Adam Smith. Well, Voltaire, being an even pithier speaker than Kant, which wouldn't be that hard, immediately said, "Oh well, France doesn't have anybody who can even be compared to Adam Smith." So economics started with some very great men and great writers.

Garrett Hardin
(1915–2003)

Garrett Hardin, born in Dallas, spent his childhood in the Midwest. He earned an undergraduate degree from the University of Chicago and a Ph.D. in biology from Stanford University. In 1946, he joined the faculty at UC Santa Barbara.

His essay, "The Tragedy of the Commons," became a staple of ecological thought. His philosophical and political positions influenced debates on abortion, immigration, foreign aid, and other issues for decades.

Alfred North Whitehead
(1861–1947)

Alfred North Whitehead, a British philosopher and mathematician, worked in logic, mathematics, philosophy of science, and metaphysics. Whitehead is known for developing process philosophy, a view holding that fundamental elements of the universe are occasions of experience. In this view, concrete objects are actually successions of these occasions of experience. By grouping occasions of experience, something as complex as a human being can be defined. Whitehead's views evolved into process theology, a way of understanding God. His best-known mathematics work is *Principia Mathematica*, cowritten with Bertrand Russell.

And then, there have been later great writers like John Maynard Keynes, whom I quote all the time and who has added a great amount of illumination to my life. And finally, even in the present era, if you take Paul Krugman and read his essays, you will be impressed by his fluency. I can't stand his politics; I'm on the other side. But I love this man's essays. I think Paul Krugman is one of the best essayists alive. And so, economics has constantly attracted these fabulous writers. And they are so good that they have this enormous influence far outside their economic discipline, and that's very uncommon in other academic departments.

Okay, now it's time to extend criticism instead of praise. We've recognized that economics is better than other soft science academic departments in many ways. And one of the glories of civilization. Now it's only fair that we outline a few things that are wrong with academic economics.

What's Wrong with Economics?

1) Fatal Unconnectedness, Leading to Man-with-a-Hammer Syndrome, Often Causing Overweighing What Can Be Counted

I think I've got eight, no nine objections, some being logical subdivisions of a big general objection. The big general objection to economics was the one early described by Alfred North Whitehead when he spoke of the fatal unconnectedness of academic disciplines, wherein each professor didn't even know the models of the other disciplines, much less try to synthesize those disciplines with his own.

I think there's a modern name for this approach that Whitehead didn't like, and that name is "bonkers." This is a perfectly crazy way to behave. Yet economics, like much else in academia, is too insular.

The nature of this failure is that it creates what I always call man-with-a-hammer syndrome. And that's taken from the folk saying: To the man with only a hammer, every problem looks pretty much like a nail. And that works marvelously to gum up all professions and all departments of academia and, indeed, most practical life. The only antidote for being an absolute klutz due to the presence of a man-with-a-hammer syndrome is to have a full kit of tools. You don't have just a hammer.

You've got all the tools. And you've got to have one more trick. You've got to use those tools checklist-style because you'll miss a lot if you just hope that the right tool is going to pop up unaided whenever you need it. But if you've got a full list of tools and go through them in your mind, checklist-style, you will find a lot of answers that you won't find any other way. So limiting this big general objection that so disturbed Alfred North Whitehead is very important, and there are mental tricks that help do the job.

"I had an early and extreme multidisciplinary cast of mind. I couldn't stand reaching for a small idea in my own discipline when there was a big idea right over the fence in somebody else's discipline. So I just grabbed in all directions for the big ideas that would really work."

—Munger

I think there's a modern name for this approach that Whitehead didn't like, and that name is "bonkers."

A special version of this man-with-a-hammer syndrome is terrible, not only in economics but practically everywhere else, including business. It's really terrible in business. You've got a complex system, and it spews out a lot of wonderful numbers that enable you to measure some factors. But there are other factors that are terribly important, [yet] there's no precise numbering you can put to these factors. You know they're important, but you don't have the numbers. Well, practically everybody (1) overweighs the stuff that can be numbered because it yields to the statistical techniques they're taught in academia and (2) doesn't mix in the hard-to-measure stuff that may be more important. That is a mistake I've tried all my life to avoid, and I have no regrets for having done that.

The late, great Thomas Hunt Morgan, who was one of greatest biologists who ever lived, when he got to Caltech, had a very interesting, extreme way of avoiding some mistakes from overcounting what could be measured and undercounting

Far less efficient than Munger's preferred approach of simply "reaching down and picking up big nuggets of gold," placer mining (pronounced "plass-er") is an open-pit or open-cast form of mining in which miniscule amounts of valuable minerals are extracted from great volumes of earth using water pressure or surface excavating equipment. The name derives from the Spanish word, "placer," meaning "sand bank" and refers to precious metal deposits (particularly gold and gem stones) found in alluvial deposits.

what couldn't. At that time, there were no computers, and the computer substitute then available to science and engineering was the Friden calculator, and Caltech was full of Friden calculators. And Thomas Hunt Morgan banned the Friden calculator from the biology department. And when they said, "What the hell are you doing, Dr. Morgan?" he said, "Well, I am like a guy who is prospecting for gold along the banks of the Sacramento River in 1849. With a little intelligence, I can reach down and pick up big nuggets of gold. And as long as I can do that, I'm not going to let any people in my department waste scarce resources in placer mining." And that's the way Thomas Hunt Morgan got through life.

I've adopted the same technique, and here I am in my eightieth year. I haven't had to do any placer mining yet. And it begins to look like I'm going to get all the way through, as I'd always hoped, without doing any of that damned placer mining. Of course, if I were a physician, particularly an academic physician, I'd have to do the statistics, do the placer mining. But it's amazing what you can do in life without the placer mining if you've got a few good mental tricks and just keep ragging the problems the way Thomas Hunt Morgan did.

2) Failure to Follow the Fundamental Full-Attribution Ethos of Hard Science

What's wrong with the way Mankiw does economics is that he grabs from other disciplines without attribution. He doesn't label the grabbed items as physics or biology or psychology or game theory or whatever they really are, fully attributing the concept to the basic knowledge from which it came. If you don't do that, it's like running a business with a sloppy filing system. It reduces your power to be as good as you can be. Now, Mankiw is so smart he does pretty well even when his technique is imperfect. He got the largest advance any textbook writer ever got.

But, nonetheless, he'd be better if he had absorbed a hard-science ethos, which has been helpful to me.

It's like running a business with a sloppy filing system. It reduces your power to be as good as you can be.

Joseph Rudyard Kipling
(1865–1936)

Rudyard Kipling, born in Bombay, India, to a father who taught at a local art school, attended boarding school in England. He returned to India and traveled around the subcontinent as a correspondent. He also wrote fiction and poetry, publishing *The Jungle Book* in 1894, *Captains Courageous* in 1897, and *Gunga Din* in 1892. He won the Nobel Prize for literature in 1907.

I have names for Mankiw's approach, grabbing whatever you need without attribution. Sometimes I call it "take what you wish," and sometimes I call it "Kiplingism." And when I call it Kiplingism, I'm reminding you of Kipling's stanza of poetry, which went something like this: "When Homer smote his blooming lyre, he'd heard men sing by land and sea, and what he thought he might require, he went and took, the same as me." Well, that's the way Mankiw does it. He just grabs. This is much better than not grabbing. But it is much worse than grabbing with full attribution and full discipline, using all knowledge plus extreme reductionism where feasible.

3) Physics Envy

The third weakness that I find in economics is what I call physics envy. And, of course, that term has been borrowed from penis envy as described by one of the world's great idiots, Sigmund Freud. But he was very popular in his time, and the concept got a wide vogue.

One of the worst examples of what physics envy did to economics was cause adoption of hard-form efficient market theory. And then, when you logically derived consequences from this wrong theory, you would get conclusions such as it can never be correct for any corporation to buy its own stock. Because the stock price, by definition, is totally efficient, there could never be any advantage. QED. And they taught this theory to some partner at McKinsey when he was at some school of business that had adopted this crazy line of reasoning

from economics, and the partner became a paid consultant for the *Washington Post*. And *Washington Post* stock was selling at a fifth of what an orangutan could figure was the plain value per share by just counting up the values and dividing. But he so believed what he'd been taught in graduate school that he told the *Washington Post* it shouldn't buy its own stock. Well, fortunately, they put Warren Buffett on the board, and he convinced them to buy back more than half of the outstanding stock, which enriched the remaining shareholders by much more than a billion dollars. So, there was at least one instance of a place that quickly killed a wrong academic theory.

LSU Wins Sugar Bowl; Packers, Colts Advance in Playoffs

The Washington Post

Dean Absorbs Most Attacks From Rivals

Afghan Delegates Approve Charter

The Washington Post

Over the years, *The Washington Post* has featured many important contributors, including political cartoonist Herbert Block (Herblock), and reporters Bob Woodward and Carl Bernstein, who are credited with breaking the story of the Watergate scandals of the Richard M. Nixon administration in the early 1970s.

And* Washington Post *stock was selling at a fifth of what an orangutan could figure was the plain value per share by just counting up the values and dividing.

It's my view that economics could avoid a lot of this trouble that comes from physics envy. I want economics to pick up the basic ethos of hard science, the full attribution habit, but not the craving for an unattainable precision that comes from physics envy. The sort of precise, reliable formula that includes Boltzmann's constant is not going to happen, by and large, in economics. Economics involves too complex a system. And the craving for that physics-style precision does little but get you in terrible trouble, like the poor fool from McKinsey.

I think that economists would be way better off if they paid more attention to Einstein and Sharon Stone. Well, Einstein is easy because Einstein is famous

for saying, "Everything should be made as simple as possible, but no more simple." Now, the saying is a tautology, but it's very useful, and some economist—it may have been Herb Stein—had a similar tautological saying that I dearly love: "If a thing can't go on forever, it will eventually stop."

Sharon Stone contributed to the subject because someone once asked her if she was bothered by penis envy. And she said, "Absolutely not. I have more trouble than I can handle with what I've got."

Albert Einstein
(1879–1955)

Albert Einstein earned a teaching diploma from a Swiss university and, while working in the Swiss patent office in 1904, wrote his doctoral dissertation on a method to determine molecular dimensions. That same year and the next, he wrote several articles that form the foundation of modern physics. Topics included Brownian motion, the photoelectric effect, and special relativity. He went on to make major contributions to the development of quantum mechanics, statistical mechanics, and cosmology. He won the Nobel Prize for physics in 1921.

When I talk about this false precision, this great hope for reliable, precise formulas, I am reminded of Arthur Laffer, who's in my political party, and who takes a mistaken approach, sometimes, when it comes to doing economics. His trouble is his craving for false precision, which is not an adult way of dealing with his subject matter.

Einstein is easy because Einstein is famous for saying, "Everything should be made as simple as possible, but no more simple."

The situation of people like Laffer reminds me of a rustic legislator—and this really happened in America. I don't invent these stories. Reality is always more ridiculous than what I'm going to tell you. At any rate, this rustic legislator proposed a new law in his state. He wanted to pass a law rounding pi to an even 3.2 so it would be easier for the school children to make the computations. Well, you can say that this is too ridiculous, and it can't be fair to liken economics professors like Laffer to a rustic legislator like this. I say I'm undercriticizing the professors. At least when this rustic legislator rounded pi to an even number, the error was relatively small. But once you try to put a lot of false precision into a complex system like economics, the errors can compound to the point where they're worse than those of the McKinsey partner when he was incompetently advising the *Washington Post*. So, economics should emulate physics' basic ethos, but its search for precision in physics-like formulas is almost always wrong in economics.

Nebraska Furniture Mart

Founded in 1937 by Russian immigrant Rose Blumkin, the Nebraska Furniture Mart began in a basement in Omaha. Responding to her simple principle of "Sell cheap and tell the truth," customers supported the shop and fueled exponential growth. In 1983, Berkshire Hathaway purchased ninety percent of the business. By 1994, the Omaha store had grown to several hundred thousand square feet on a seventy-seven-acre campus. In 2003, the store added a 700,000-square-foot operation in Kansas City; it is perhaps the largest free-standing home furnishings store in the country.

4) Too Much Emphasis on Macroeconomics

My fourth criticism is that there's too much emphasis on macroeconomics and not enough on microeconomics. I think this is wrong. It's like trying to master medicine without knowing anatomy and chemistry. Also, the discipline of microeconomics is a lot of fun. It helps you correctly understand macroeconomics, and it's a perfect circus to do. In contrast, I don't think macroeconomics people have all that much fun. For one thing, they are often wrong because of extreme complexity in the system they wish to understand.

Let me demonstrate the power of microeconomics by solving two microeconomic problems. One simple and one a little harder. The first problem is this: Berkshire Hathaway just opened a furniture and appliance store in Kansas City, Kansas. At the time Berkshire opened it, the largest selling furniture and appliance store in the world was another Berkshire Hathaway store, selling $350 million worth of goods per year. The new store in a strange city opened up selling at the rate of more than $500 million a year. From the day it opened, the 3,200 spaces in the parking lot were full. The women had to wait outside the ladies restroom because the architects didn't understand biology. It's hugely successful.

Well, I've given you the problem. Now, tell me what explains the runaway success of this new furniture and appliance store that is outselling everything else in the world? Well, let me do it for you. Is this a low-priced store or a high-priced store? It's not going to have a runaway success in a strange city as a high-priced store. That would take time. Number two, if it's moving $500 million worth of furniture through it, it's one hell of a big store, furniture being as bulky as it is. And what does a big store do? It provides a big selection. So what could this possibly be except a low-priced store with a big selection?

But, you may wonder, why wasn't it done before, preventing its being done first now? Again, the answer just pops into your head: It costs a fortune to open a store this big. So, nobody's done it before. So, you quickly know the answer. With a few basic concepts, these microeconomic problems that seem hard can be solved much as you put a hot knife through butter. I like such easy ways of thought that are very remunerative. And I suggest that you people should also learn to do microeconomics better.

Now I'll give you a harder problem. There's a tire store chain in the Northwest that has slowly succeeded over fifty years, the Les Schwab tire store chain. It just ground ahead. It started competing with the stores that were owned by the big tire companies that made all the tires, the Goodyears and so forth. And, of course, the manufacturers favored their own stores. Their "tied stores" had a big cost advantage. Later, Les Schwab rose in competition with the huge price discounters like Costco and Sam's Club and before that Sears, Roebuck and so forth. And yet, here is Schwab now, with hundreds of millions of dollars in sales. And here's Les Schwab in his eighties, with no education, having done the whole thing. How did he do it? I don't see a whole lot of people looking like a light bulb has come on. Well, let's think about it with some microeconomic fluency.

Is there some wave that Schwab could have caught? The minute you ask the question, the answer pops in. The Japanese had a zero position in tires, and they got big. So this guy must have ridden that wave some in the early times. Then, the slow following success has to have some other causes. And what probably

Les Schwab
(b. 1917)

Leslie Schwab was born in Bend, Oregon. After service in the Air Cadet Corps during World War II, he returned to Oregon and bought OK Rubber Welders, a small tire shop that he turned from a $32,000-a-year business into one generating $150,000 annually. In the 1950s, Schwab began expanding his business throughout the Pacific Northwest. Through innovations such as profit sharing, "supermarket" product selection, and independence from the tire manufacturing companies, the company now operates over three hundred stores with sales exceeding $1 billion annually. Schwab is still involved in company decision-making.

He must have a very clever incentive structure driving his people. And a clever personnel selection system, etc. And he must be pretty good at advertising. Which he is. He's an artist.

happened here, obviously, is this guy did one hell of a lot of things right. And among the things that he must have done right is he must have harnessed what Mankiw calls the superpower of incentives. He must have a very clever incentive structure driving his people. And a clever personnel selection system, etc. And he must be pretty good at advertising. Which he is. He's an artist. So, he had to get a wave in Japanese tire invasion, the Japanese being as successful as they were. And then a talented fanatic had to get a hell of a lot of things right and keep them right with clever systems. Again, not that hard of an answer. But what else would be a likely cause of the peculiar success?

We hire business school graduates, and they're no better at these problems than you were. Maybe that's the reason we hire so few of them.

We hire business school graduates, and they're no better at these problems than you were. Maybe that's the reason we hire so few of them.

Well, how did I solve those problems? Obviously, I was using a simple search engine in my mind to go through checklist-style, and I was using some rough algorithms that work pretty well in a great many complex systems, and those algorithms run something like this: Extreme success is likely to be caused by some combination of the following factors:

A) Extreme maximization or minimization of one or two variables. Example, Costco or our furniture and appliance store.

B) Adding success factors so that a bigger combination drives success, often in nonlinear fashion, as one is reminded by the concept of breakpoint and the concept of critical mass in physics. Often results are not linear. You get a little bit more mass, and you get a lollapalooza result. And, of course, I've been searching for lollapalooza results all my life, so I'm very interested in models that explain their occurrence.

C) An extreme of good performance over many factors. Example, Toyota or Les Schwab.

D) Catching and riding some sort of big wave. Example, Oracle. By the way, I cited Oracle before I knew that the Oracle CFO (Jeff Henley) was a big part of the proceedings here today.

Generally I recommend and use in problem solving cut-to-the quick algorithms, and I find you have to use them both forward and backward. Let me give you an example. I irritate my family by giving them little puzzles, and one of the puzzles that I gave my family not very long ago was when I said, "There's an activity in America, with one-on-one contests and a national championship. The same person won the championship on two occasions about sixty-five years apart." "Now," I said, "name the activity." Again, I don't see a lot of light bulbs going on. And in my family, not a lot of light bulbs were flashing. But I have a physicist son who has been trained more in the type of thinking I like. And he immediately got the right answer, and here's the way he reasoned:

It can't be anything requiring a lot of hand-eye coordination. Nobody eighty-five years of age is going to win a national billiards tournament, much less a national tennis tournament. It just can't be. Then, he figured it couldn't be chess, which this physicist plays very well, because it's too hard. The complexity of the

Checkers

A board game very similar to checkers dating to 3000 BC was discovered in the ruins of the ancient city of Ur (located in today's Iraq). Checkers as we know it today was first played in Egypt around 1400 BC.

system and the stamina required are too great. But that led into checkers. And he thought, "Ah ha! There's a game where vast experience might guide you to be the best even though you're eighty-five years of age."

And sure enough, that was the right answer.

Anyway, I recommend that sort of mental puzzle solving to all of you, flipping one's thinking both backward and forward. And I recommend that academic economics get better at very small-scale microeconomics as demonstrated here.

5) Too Little Synthesis in Economics

My fifth criticism is there is too little synthesis in economics, not only with matter outside traditional economics, but also within economics. I have posed before two different business school classes the following problem. I say, "You have studied supply and demand curves. You have learned that when you raise the price, ordinarily, the volume you can sell goes down, and when you reduce the price, the volume you can sell goes up. Is that right? That's what you've learned?" They all nod yes. And I say, "Now tell me several instances when, if you want the physical volume to go up, the correct answer is to increase the price." And there's this long and ghastly pause. And finally, in each of the two business schools in which I've tried this,

Luxury goods: Raising the price can improve the product's utility as a "show-off" item, sometimes increasing sales. Purchasers may also assume that a higher price equates to a better product.

“Nothing to Add” Number Six

ROLEX

Question: “I have posed at two different business schools the following problem. I say, “You have studied supply and demand curves. You have learned that when you raise the price, ordinarily the volume you can sell goes down, and when you reduce the price, the volume you can sell goes up. Is that right? That’s what you’ve learned?” They all nod yes. And I say, “Now tell me several instances when, if you want the physical volume to go up, the correct answer is to increase the price?” And there’s this long and ghastly pause. And finally, in each of the two business schools in which I’ve tried this, maybe one person in fifty could name one instance. But only one in fifty can come up with this sole instance in a modern business school—one of the business schools being Stanford, which is hard to get into. And nobody has yet come up with the main answer that I like. ”

Answer: “There are four categories of answers to this problem. A few people get the first category but rarely any of the others.

1. Luxury goods: Raising the price can improve the product’s ability as a ‘show-off’ item, i.e., by raising the price the utility of the goods is improved to someone engaging in conspicuous consumption. Further, people will frequently assume that the high price equates to a better product, and this can sometimes lead to increased sales.

2. Non-luxury goods: same as second factor cited above, i.e., the higher price conveys information assumed to be correct by the consumer, that the higher price connotes higher value. This can especially apply to industrial goods where high reliability is an important factor.

3. Raise the price and use the extra revenue in legal ways to make the product work better or to make the sales system work better.

4. Raise the price and use the extra revenue in illegal or unethical ways to drive sales by the functional equivalent of bribing purchasing agents or in other ways detrimental to the end consumer, i.e., mutual fund commission practices. [This is the answer I like the most, but never get.]”

"Nothing to Add" Number Seven

Carlo "Charles" Ponzi
(1882–1949)

Here is a question that arose concerning the content of Talk Nine:

Question: "You once said you left 'Mystery Defect Number Ten' out of your UCSB talk. What was it?"

Answer: "Oh, yes. I should have included it, but I didn't, and I think we should just leave it as it was delivered. The tenth defect is what I call 'Not Enough Attention to the Effects of Embedded Ponzi Schemes at the Microeconomic Level.' This is easily demonstrated by the unfunded pension plans at the major law firms where a clear and enormous potential future impact goes unnoticed—and blissfully ignored."

maybe one person in fifty could name one instance. They come up with the idea that, under certain circumstances a higher price acts as a rough indicator of quality and thereby increases sales volumes.

"Now tell me several instances when, if you want the physical volume to go up, the correct answer is to increase the price?"

This happened in the case of my friend, Bill Ballhaus. When he was head of Beckman Instruments, it produced some complicated product where, if it failed, it caused enormous damage to the purchaser. It wasn't a pump at the bottom of an oil well, but that's a good mental example. And he realized that the reason this thing was selling so poorly, even though it was better than anybody else's product, was because it was priced lower. It made people think it was a low-quality gizmo. So he raised the price by twenty percent or so, and the volume went way up.

But only one in fifty can come up with this sole instance in a modern business school—one of the business schools being Stanford, which is hard to get into. And nobody has yet come up with the main answer that I like. (See the "I Have Nothing to Add" feature on page 393 for Charlie's full answers to this question.) Suppose you raise that price and use the extra money to bribe the other guy's purchasing agent? Is that going to work? And are there functional equivalents in economics—microeconomics—of raising the price and using the extra sales proceeds to drive sales higher? And, of course, there are a zillion, once you've made that mental jump. It's so simple.

One of the most extreme examples is in the investment management field. Suppose you're the manager of a mutual fund, and you want to sell more. People commonly come to the following answer: You raise the commissions, which, of course, reduces the number of units of real investments delivered to the ultimate buyer, so you're increasing the price per unit of real investment that you're selling the ultimate customer. And you're using that extra commission to bribe the customer's purchasing agent. You're bribing the broker to betray his client and put the client's money into the high-commission product. This has worked to produce at least a trillion dollars of mutual fund sales.

The second interesting problem with synthesis involves two of the most famous examples in economics. Number one is Ricardo's principle of comparative advantage in trade, and the other is Adam Smith's pin factory.

David Ricardo
(1772–1823)

David Ricardo, born in London, began working with his father at the London Stock Exchange at age fourteen. His wealth allowed him to retire young, and he secured a seat in Parliament. He became interested in economics after reading Adam Smith's *The Wealth of Nations* and made many significant contributions to the field. Ricardo is often credited with the theory of comparative advantage, which explains why it can be beneficial for two countries to trade, even though one of them may be able to produce every kind of item more cheaply than the other. The concept was first described by Robert Torrens in 1815 in an essay on the wheat trade, but Ricardo explained it more clearly in his 1817 book *The Principles of Political Economy and Taxation.*

This tactic is not an attractive part of human nature, and I want to tell you that I pretty completely avoided it in my life. I don't think it's necessary to spend your life selling what you would never buy. Even though it's legal, I don't think it's a good idea. But you shouldn't accept all my notions because you'll risk becoming unemployable. You shouldn't take my notions unless you're willing to risk being unemployable by all but a few.

I think my experience with my simple question is an example of how little synthesis people get, even in advanced academic settings, considering economic questions. Obvious questions, with such obvious answers. Yet, people take four courses in economics, go to business school, have all these I.Q. points, and write all these essays, but they can't synthesize worth a damn. This failure is not because the professors know all this stuff and they're deliberately withholding it from the students. This failure happens because the professors aren't all that good at this kind of synthesis. They were trained in a different way. I can't remember if it was Keynes or Galbraith who said that economics professors are most economical with ideas. They make a few they learned in graduate school last a lifetime.

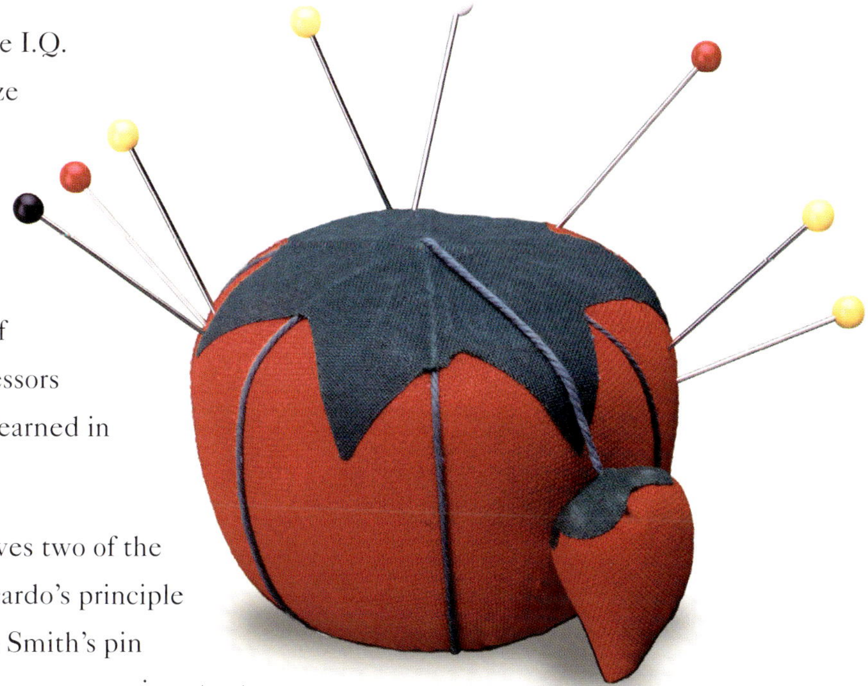

The second interesting problem with synthesis involves two of the most famous examples in economics. Number one is Ricardo's principle of comparative advantage in trade, and the other is Adam Smith's pin factory. And both of these, of course, work to vastly increase economic output per person, and they're similar in that each somehow directs functions into the hands of people who are very good at doing the functions. Yet, they're radically different examples in that one of them is the ultimate example of central planning—the pin factory—where the whole system was planned by somebody, while the other example, Ricardo's, happens automatically as a natural consequence of trade.

And, of course, once you get into the joys of synthesis, you immediately think, "Do these things interact?" Of course they interact. Beautifully. And that's one of the causes of the power of a modern economic system. I saw an example of that kind of interaction years ago. Berkshire had this former savings and loan company, and it had made this loan on a hotel right opposite the Hollywood Park Racetrack. In due time, the neighborhood changed, and it was full of gangs, pimps, and dope dealers. They tore copper pipe out of the wall for dope fixes, and there were people hanging around the hotel with guns, and nobody would come. We foreclosed on it two or three times, and the loan value went down to nothing. We seemed to have an insolvable economic problem—a microeconomic problem.

Now, we could have gone to McKinsey, or maybe a bunch of professors from Harvard, and we would have gotten a report about ten inches thick about the ways

Adam Smith's Pin Factory

Adam Smith recorded in *An Inquiry into the Nature and Causes of the Wealth of Nations* (1776) his observations at a pin factory. He found that only ten workers were able to produce 48,000 pins per day because of divided and specialized labor. If each worker handled all the steps required to make a pin, he could only make twenty per day, for a total factory output of two hundred pins daily. Smith recognized and extolled the great productivity gains and economic progress represented by the pin factory and its embrace of specialized labor.

we could approach this failing hotel in this terrible neighborhood. But instead, we put a sign on the property that said: "For sale or rent." And in came, in response to that sign, a man who said, "I'll spend $200,000 fixing up your hotel and buy it at a high price on credit, if you can get zoning so I can turn the parking lot into a putting green." "You've got to have a parking lot in a hotel," we said. "What do you have in mind?" He said, "No, my business is flying seniors in from Florida, putting them near the airport, and then letting them go out to Disneyland and various places by bus and coming back. And I don't care how bad the neighborhood is going to be because my people are self-contained behind walls. All they have to do is get on the bus in the morning and come home in the evening, and they don't need a parking lot; they need a putting green." So we made the deal with the guy. The whole thing worked beautifully, and the loan got paid off, and it all worked out.

Ronald Coase
(b. 1910)

Ronald Coase, born in a suburb of London, graduated from secondary school at age twelve and enrolled in the University of London only two years later. He earned degrees in law and economics and began research into transaction costs. He came to the United States in 1951 for an academic career that started at the University of Buffalo. He settled into the University of Chicago in 1964 and remains there as professor emeritus. His work, "The Nature of the Firm" (1937), was cited as a major consideration in his receipt of the Nobel Prize in economics in 1991.

The odd system that this guy had designed to amuse seniors was pure pin factory, and finding the guy with this system was pure Ricardo.

Obviously, that's an interaction of Ricardo and the pin factory examples. The odd system that this guy had designed to amuse seniors was pure pin factory, and finding the guy with this system was pure Ricardo. So these things are interacting.

Well, I've taken you part way through the synthesis. It gets harder when you want to figure out how much activity should be within private firms, and how much should be within the government, and what are the factors that determine which functions are where, and why do the failures occur, and so on and so on.

It's my opinion that anybody with a high I.Q. who graduated in economics ought to be able to sit down and write a ten-page synthesis of all these ideas that's quite persuasive. And I would bet a lot of money that I could give this test in practically every economics department in the country and get a perfectly lousy bunch of synthesis. They'd give me Ronald Coase. They'd talk about transaction costs. They'd click off a little something that their professors gave them and spit it back. But in terms of really understanding how it all fits together, I would confidently predict that most people couldn't do it very well.

Why did Max Planck, one of the smartest people who ever lived, give up economics? The answer is, he said, "It's too hard. The best solution you can get is messy and uncertain."

Max Planck
(1858–1947)

Born in Germany in 1858 to a law professor father, Max Planck earned his doctorate at age twenty-one. His earliest work on thermodynamics evolved into an interest in radiation. From these studies, he was led to work on the distribution of energy in the spectrum of radiation. Planck's work on energy emissions was essential to the field of physics and came to be known as the "quantum theory." He was awarded the Nobel Prize for physics in 1918.

By the way, if any of you want to try and do this, go ahead. I think you'll find it hard. In this connection, one of the interesting things that I want to mention is that Max Planck, the great Nobel laureate who found Planck's constant, tried once to do economics. He gave it up. Now why did Max Planck, one of the smartest people who ever lived, give up economics? The answer is, he said, "It's too hard. The best solution you can get is messy and uncertain." It didn't satisfy Planck's craving for order, and so he gave it up. And if Max Planck early on realized he was never going to get perfect order, I will confidently predict that all of the rest of you are going to have exactly the same result.

By the way, there's a famous story about Max Planck that is apocryphal: After he won his prize, he was invited to lecture everywhere, and he had this chauffeur who drove him around to give public lectures all through Germany. And the chauffeur memorized the lecture, and so one day he said, "Gee, Professor Planck, why don't

you let me try it by switching places?" And so he got up and gave the lecture. At the end of it, some physicist stood up and posed a question of extreme difficulty. But the chauffeur was up to it. "Well," he said, "I'm surprised that a citizen of an advanced city like Munich is asking so elementary a question, so I'm going to ask my chauffeur to respond."

6) Extreme and Counterproductive Psychological Ignorance

All right, I'm down to the sixth main defect, and this is a subdivision of the lack of adequate multidisciplinarity: extreme and counterproductive psychological ignorance in economics. Here, I want to give you a very simple problem. I specialize in simple problems.

You own a small casino in Las Vegas. It has fifty standard slot machines. Identical in appearance, they're identical in the function. They have exactly the same payout ratios. The things that cause the payouts are exactly the same. They occur in the same percentages. But there's one machine in this group of slot machines that, no matter where you put it among the fifty, in fairly short order, when you go to the machines at the end of the day, there will be twenty-five percent more winnings from this one machine than from any other machine. Now surely, I'm not going to have a failure here. What is different about that heavy-winning machine? Can anybody do it?

In one of his most famous roles, Morgan Freeman played Hoke Colburn, the chauffeur, in the 1989 film *Driving Miss Daisy*. Freeman had great roles in many other films, notably *The Shawshank Redemption*. He won a well-deserved Academy Award in 2005 for his work in *Million Dollar Baby*.

In the real world, it is critical to distinguish when you are "Max Planck" and when you are the "chauffeur." If you cannot legitimately respond to the *next* question, you are most likely outside your "Circle of Competence."

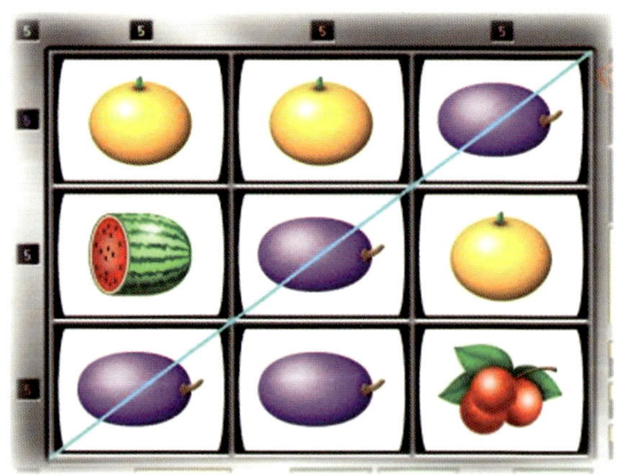

Male: More people play it.

Munger: No, no, I want to know why more people play it. What's different about that machine is people have used modern electronics to give a higher ratio of *near misses*. That machine is going bar, bar, lemon, bar, bar, grapefruit, way more often than normal machines, and that will cause heavier play. How do you get an answer like that? Easy. Obviously, there's a psychological cause: That machine is doing something to trigger some basic psychological response.

If you know the psychological factors, if you've got them on a checklist in your head, you just run down the factors, and, boom! you get to one that must explain this occurrence. There isn't any other way to do it effectively. These answers are not going to come to people who don't learn these problem-solving methods. If you want to go through life like a one-legged man in an ass-kicking contest, why, be my guest. But if you want to succeed like a strong man with two legs, you have to pick up these methods, including doing micro- and macro-economics while knowing psychology.

In this vein, I next want to mention a strange Latin American case of a dysfunctional economy that got fixed. In this little subdivision of Latin America, a culture had arisen wherein everybody stole everything. They embezzled from the company; they stole everything that was loose in the community. And, of course, the economy came practically to a halt. And this thing got fixed. Now, where did I read about this case? I'll give you a hint. It wasn't in the annals of economics. I found this case in the annals of psychology. Clever people went down and used a bunch of psychological tricks. And they fixed it.

Somewhere in a little subdivision of Latin America: An interesting case history of fixing a dysfunctional economy, drawn from the annals of Psychology (see page 501).

Well, I think there's no excuse if you're an economist, when there are wonderful cases like that of the dysfunctional economy becoming fixed, and these simple tricks that solve so many problems, and you don't know how to do the fixes and understand the problems. Why be so

Mars, Surrounded by the Liberal Arts, Vanquishing Ignorance Antoon Claessens, 1605, oil on canvas
Groeninge Museum, Bruges

ignorant about psychology that you don't even know psychology's tricks that will fix your own dysfunctional economic systems?

Here, I want to give you an extreme injunction. This is even tougher than the fundamental organizing ethos of hard science. This has been attributed to Samuel Johnson. He said, in substance, that if an academic maintains in place an ignorance that can be easily removed with a little work, the conduct of the academic amounts to treachery. That was his word, "treachery." You can see why I love this stuff. He says you have a duty if you're an academic to be as little of a klutz as you can possibly be, and, therefore, you have got to keep grinding out of your system as much removable ignorance as you can remove.

7) Too Little Attention to Second- and Higher-Order Effects

On to the next one, the seventh defect: too little attention in economics to second-order and even higher-order effects. This defect is quite understandable because the consequences have consequences, and the consequences of the consequences have consequences, and so on. It gets very complicated. When I was a meteorologist, I found this stuff very irritating. And economics makes meteorology look like a tea party.

Extreme economic ignorance was displayed when various experts, including Ph. D. economists, forecast the cost of the original Medicare law. They did simple extrapolations of past costs.

Well, the cost forecast was off by a factor of more than one thousand percent. The cost they projected was less than ten percent of the cost that happened. Once they put in place various new incentives, the behavior changed in response to the incentives, and the numbers became quite different from their projection. And medicine invented new and expensive remedies, as it was sure to do. How could a great group of experts make such a silly forecast? Answer: They oversimplified to get easy figures, like the rube rounding pi to 3.2! They chose not to consider effects of effects on effects, and so on.

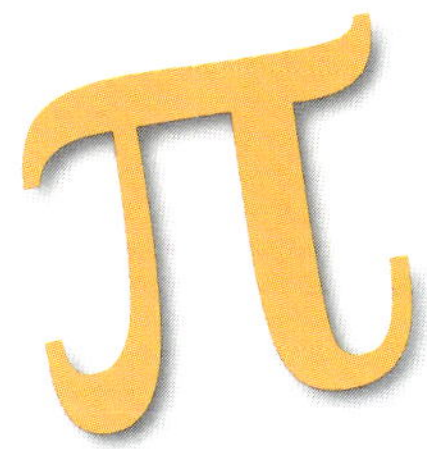

The Discovery of Pi

"Pi" (usually represented by the Greek letter) is the ratio of the circumference (the distance around) to the diameter (the distance across) of any circle. The Greeks revealed that Pi is an irrational number, which cannot be represented by a fraction. Pi is a unique constant of nature used today in such diverse fields as architecture and quantum mechanics.

One good thing about this common form of misthinking from the viewpoint of academia is that business people are even more foolish about microeconomics. The business version of the Medicare-type insanity is when you own a textile plant and a guy comes in and says, "Oh, isn't this wonderful? They invented a new loom. It'll pay for itself in three years at current prices because it adds so much efficiency to the production of textiles." And you keep buying these looms, and their equivalent, for twenty years, and you keep making four percent on capital; you never go anywhere. And the answer is, it wasn't that technology didn't work, it's that the laws of economics caused the benefit from the new looms to go to the people that bought the textiles, not the guy that owned the textile plant. How could anybody not know that if he'd taken freshman economics or been through business school? I think the schools are doing a lousy job. Otherwise, such insanities wouldn't happen so often.

Usually, I don't use formal projections. I don't let people do them for me because I don't like throwing up on the desk, but I see them made in a very foolish way all the time, and many people believe in them, no matter how foolish they are. It's an effective sales technique in America to put a foolish projection on a desk.

And if you're an investment banker, it's an art form. I don't read their projections either. Once Warren and I bought a company, and the seller had a big study done by an investment banker. It was about this thick. We just turned it over as if it were a diseased carcass. He said, "We paid $2 million for that." I said, "We don't use them. Never look at them."

Anyway, as the Medicare example showed, all human systems are gamed, for reasons rooted deeply in psychology, and great skill is displayed in the gaming because game theory has so much potential. That's what's wrong with the workers' comp system in California. Gaming has been raised to an art form. In the course of gaming the system, people learn to be crooked. Is this good for civilization? Is it good for economic performance? Hell, no. The people who design easily gameable systems belong in the lowest circle of hell.

They just don't think about what terrible things they're doing to the civilization because they don't take into account the second-order effects and the third-order effects in lying and cheating.

By way of analogy, the game of chess, particularly the three-dimensional version played here by Mr. Spock, is a perfect illustration of second-order and higher levels of effect. The movement of any individual piece on the board affects, sometimes dramatically, the overall composition of the game.

I've got a friend whose family controls about eight percent of the truck trailer market. He just closed his last factory in California, and he had one in Texas that was even worse. The workers' comp cost in his Texas plant got to be double-digit percentages of payroll. Well, there's no such profit in making truck trailers. He closed his plant and moved it to Ogden, Utah, where a bunch of believing Mormons are raising big families and don't game the workers' comp system. The workers' comp expense is two percent of payroll.

Are the Latinos who were peopling his plant in Texas intrinsically dishonest or bad compared to the Mormons? No. It's just the incentive structure that so rewards all this fraud is put in place by these ignorant legislatures, many members of which have been to law school, and they just don't think about what terrible things they're doing to the civilization because they don't take into account the second-order effects and the third-order effects in lying and cheating. So, this happens everywhere, and when economics is full of it, it is just like the rest of life.

There was a wonderful example of gaming a human system in the career of Victor Niederhoffer in the Economics Department of Harvard. Victor Niederhoffer was the son of a police lieutenant, and he needed to get A's at Harvard. But he didn't want to do any serious work at Harvard because what he really liked doing was, one, playing world-class checkers; two, gambling in high-stakes card games, at which he was very good, all hours of the day and night; three, being the squash champion of the United States, which he was for years; and, four, being about as good a tennis player as a part-time tennis player could be.

Victor Niederhoffer
(b. 1943)

Victor Niederhoffer studied statistics and economics, earning an undergraduate degree at Harvard and a Ph. D. at the University of Chicago. He taught at the University of California, Berkeley, for five years and simultaneously ran Niederhoffer, Cross and Zeckhauser, Inc., involved in selling private firms to public companies. In the late 1970s, Niederhoffer started trading futures and options; he founded a trading firm, Niederhoffer Investments, in 1980 to provide financial management for institutional clients. He is also a past multiyear national squash champion.

This did not leave much time for getting A's at Harvard, so he went into the Economics Department. You'd think he would have chosen French poetry. But remember, this was a guy who could play championship checkers. He thought he was up to outsmarting the Harvard Economics Department. And he was. He noticed that the graduate students did most of the boring work that would otherwise go to the professors, and he noticed that because it was so hard to get to be a graduate student at Harvard, they were all very brilliant and organized and hardworking, as well as much needed by grateful professors.

And, therefore, by custom, and as would be predicted from the psychological force called "reciprocity tendency," in a really advanced graduate course, the professors always gave an A. So Victor Niederhoffer signed up for nothing but the most advanced graduate courses in the Harvard Economics Department, and, of course, he got A, after A, after A, after A, and was hardly ever near a class. And, for a while, some people at Harvard may have thought it had a new prodigy on its hands. That's a ridiculous story, but the scheme will work still. And Niederhoffer is famous: They call his style "Niederhoffering the curriculum."

This shows how all human systems are gamed. Another example of not thinking through the consequences of the consequences is the standard reaction in economics

Comparative Advantage

The often overlooked benefits of comparative advantage through free trade were famously revealed by David Ricardo in his 1817 book The Principles of Political Economy and Taxation:

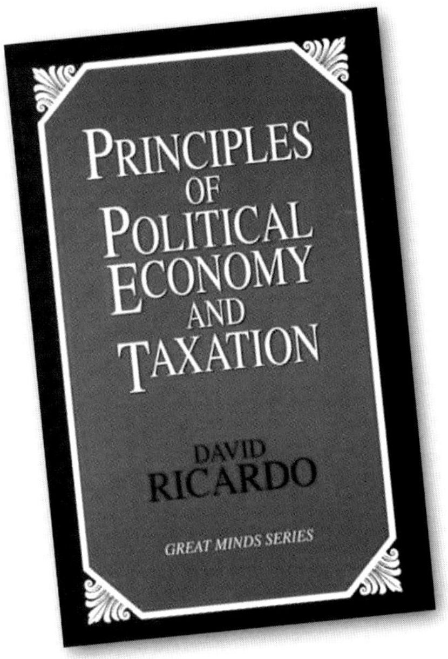

"In Portugal it is possible to produce both wine and cloth with less work than it takes in England. However, the relative costs of producing those two goods are different in the two countries. In England it is very hard to produce wine, but only moderately difficult to produce cloth. In Portugal both are easy to produce. Therefore, while it is cheaper to produce cloth in Portugal than England, it is cheaper still for Portugal to produce excess wine, and trade it for English cloth. Conversely, England benefits from this trade because its cost for producing cloth has not changed but it can now get wine at closer to the cost of cloth".

Frequently overlooked is that Ricardo's comparative advantage in "delegating" tasks among nations is equally applicable for managers delegating work. Even if a manager can perform the full range of tasks better himself, it is still mutually advantageous to divide them up.

to Ricardo's law of comparative advantage giving benefit on both sides of trade. Ricardo came up with a wonderful, non-obvious explanation that was so powerful that people were charmed with it, and they still are because it's a very useful idea. Everybody in economics understands that comparative advantage is a big deal when one considers first-order advantages in trade from the Ricardo effect. But suppose you've got a very talented ethnic group, like the Chinese, and they're very poor and backward, and you're an advanced nation, and you create free trade with China, and it goes on for a long time.

Now let's follow second- and third-order consequences. You are more prosperous than you would have been if you hadn't traded with China in terms of average well-being in the United States, right? Ricardo proved it. But which nation is going to be growing faster in economic terms? It's obviously China. They're absorbing all the modern technology of the world through this great facilitator in free trade, and, like the Asian Tigers have proved, they will get ahead fast. Look at Hong Kong. Look at Taiwan. Look at early Japan. So, you start in a place where you've got a weak nation of backward peasants, a billion and a quarter of them, and, in the end, they're going to be a much bigger, stronger nation than you are, maybe even having more and better atomic bombs. Well, Ricardo did not prove that that's a wonderful outcome for the former leading nation. He didn't try to determine second-order and higher-order effects.

If you try and talk like this to economics professors, and I've done this three times, they shrink in horror and offense because they don't like this kind of talk. It really gums up this nice discipline of theirs, which is so much simpler when you ignore second- and third-order consequences.

The best answer I ever got on that subject—in three tries—was from George Shultz. He said, "Charlie, the way I figure it is if we stop trading with China, the other advanced nations will do it anyway, and we wouldn't stop the ascent of China compared to us, and we'd lose the Ricardo-diagnosed advantages of trade." Which is obviously correct. And I said, "Well, George, you've just invented a new form of the tragedy of the commons. You're locked in this system, and you can't fix it. You're going to go to a tragic hell in a handbasket, if going to hell involves being once the great leader of the world and finally going to the shallows in terms of leadership." And he said, "Charlie, I do not want to think about this." I think he's wise. He's even older than I am, and maybe I should learn from him.

8) Not Enough Attention to the Concept of Febezzlement

Okay, I'm now down to my eighth objection: too little attention within economics to the simplest and most fundamental principle of algebra. Now, this sounds outrageous, that economics doesn't do algebra, right? Well, I want to try an example—I may be wrong on this. I'm old and I'm iconoclastic—but I throw it out anyway. I say that economics doesn't pay enough attention to the concept of febezzlement. And that I derive from Galbraith's idea. Galbraith's idea was that, if you have an undisclosed embezzlement, it has a wonderful Keynesian stimulating effect on the economy because the guy who's been embezzled thinks he is as rich as he always was and spends accordingly, and the guy that has stolen the money gets all this new purchasing power. I think that's correct analysis on Galbraith's part. The trouble with his notion is that he's described a minor phenomenon. Because when the embezzlement is discovered, as it almost surely will be, the effect will quickly reverse. So the effect quickly cancels out.

But suppose you paid a lot of attention to algebra, which I guess Galbraith didn't, and you think, "Well, the fundamental principle of algebra is, 'If A is equal to B and B is equal to C, then A is equal to C.'" You've then got a fundamental principle that demands that you look for functional equivalents, all you can find. So suppose you ask the question, "Is there such a thing in economics as a febezzlement?" By the way, Galbraith invented the word "bezzle" to describe the amount of undisclosed embezzlement, so I invented the word "febezzlement": the functional equivalent of embezzlement.

This happened after I asked the question, "Is there a functional equivalent of embezzlement?" I came up with a lot of wonderful, affirmative answers. Some were in investment management. After all, I'm near investment management. I considered the billions of dollars totally wasted in the course of investing common

George P. Shultz
(b. 1920)

George Shultz, born in New York City, earned an undergraduate degree in economics from Princeton University and a Ph.D. in industrial economics at MIT. Following several years on the MIT faculty, he moved on to the University of Chicago. He served as President Richard M. Nixon's secretary of the treasury for two years until Nixon was forced to resign. President Ronald Reagan appointed him secretary of state in 1982; Shultz served both of Reagan's terms. He is a member of the Hoover Institution and on the board of directors for the Bechtel Corporation, Gilead Sciences, and Charles Schwab & Company. During Arnold Schwarzenegger's successful bid to replace California governor Gray Davis in 2003, Shultz was named an advisor to Schwarzenegger's campaign.

Economist John Kenneth Galbraith was awarded the nation's highest civilian honor, the Presidential Medal of Freedom, at an August 9, 2000 ceremony at the White House.

stock portfolios for American owners. As long as the market keeps going up, the guy who's wasting all this money doesn't feel it because he's looking at these steadily rising values. And to the guy who is getting the money for investment advice, the money looks like well-earned income when he's really selling detriment for money, surely the functional equivalent of undisclosed embezzlement. You can see why I don't get invited to many lectures.

So I say, if you look in the economy for febezzlement, the functional equivalent of embezzlement, you'll find some enormously powerful factors. They create some "wealth effect" that is on steroids compared to the old "wealth effect." But practically nobody thinks as I do, and I quitclaim my idea to any hungry graduate student who has independent means, which he will need before his thesis topic is approved.

9) Not Enough Attention to Virtue and Vice Effects

Okay, my ninth objection: not enough attention to virtue and vice effects in economics. It has been plain to me since early life that there are enormous virtue effects in economics and also enormous vice effects. But economists get very uncomfortable when you talk about virtue and vice. It doesn't lend itself to a lot of columns of numbers. But, I would argue that there are big virtue effects in economics. I would say that the spreading of double-entry bookkeeping by the monk, Fra Luca de Pacioli, was a big virtue effect in economics. It made business more controllable, and it made it more honest. Then, the cash register. The cash register did more for human morality than the Congregational Church. It was a really powerful phenomenon to make an economic system work better, just as, in reverse, a system that can be easily defrauded ruins a civilization. A system that's very hard to defraud, like a cash register–based system, helps the economic performance of a civilization by reducing vice, but very few people within economics talk about it in those terms.

I'll go further: I say economic systems work better when there's an extreme reliability ethos. And the traditional way to get a reliability ethos, at least in past generations in America, was through religion. The religions instilled guilt. We have a charming Irish Catholic priest in our neighborhood, and he loves to say, "Those old Jews may have invented guilt, but we perfected it." And this guilt, derived from religion, has been a huge driver of a reliability ethos, which has been very helpful to economic outcomes for man.

"Few things are harder to put up with than the annoyance of a good example."

—Mark Twain

But economists get very uncomfortable when you talk about virtue and vice. It doesn't lend itself to a lot of columns of numbers.

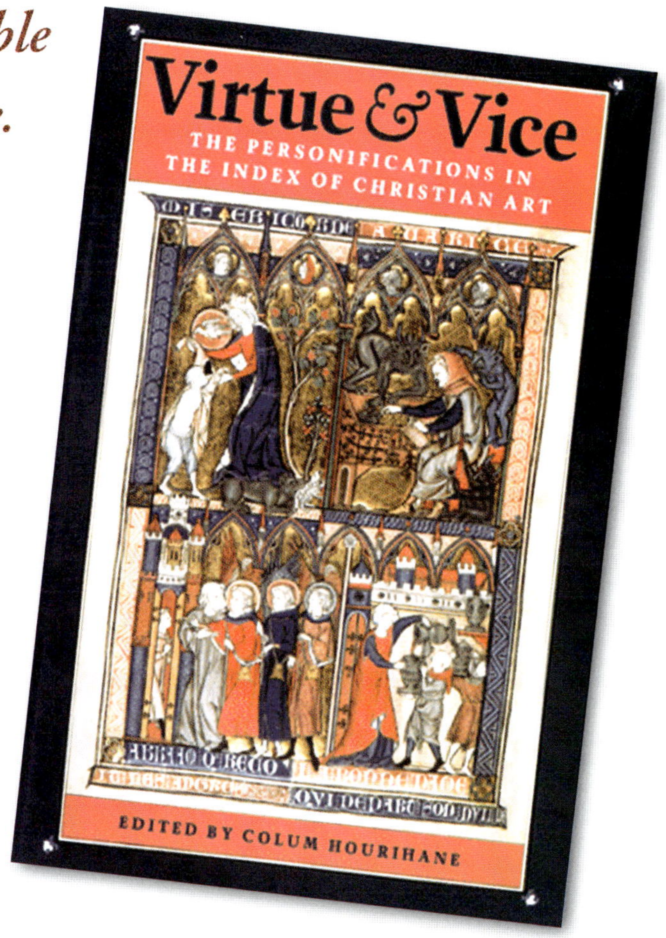

Many bad effects from vice are clear. You've got the crazy booms and crooked promotions—all you have to do is read the paper over the last six months. There's enough vice to make us all choke. And, by the way, everybody's angry about unfair compensation at the top of American corporations, and people should be. We now face various crazy governance nostrums invented by lawyers and professors that won't give us a fix for unfair compensation, yet a good partial solution is obvious: If directors were significant shareholders who got a pay of zero, you'd be amazed what would happen to unfair compensation of corporate executives as we dampened effects from reciprocity tendency.

Luca de Pacioli
(1445–1517)

Luca de Pacioli, in 1494, published his seminal work, *The Collected Knowledge of Arithmetic, Geometry, Proportion, and Proportionality.* In one section of the book, Pacioli described a novel concept, double-entry accounting. This invention revolutionized business practice and made Pacioli a celebrity. His was one of the first books to be printed on the Gutenberg press.

A roughly similar equivalent of this no-pay system has been tried in a strange place. In England, lay magistrates staff the lower criminal courts, which can send you to prison for a year or fine you substantially. You've got three judges sitting up there, and they all get a pay of zero. Their expenses are reimbursed, but not too liberally. And they work about forty half-days a year, as volunteers. It's worked beautifully for about seven hundred years. Able and honest people compete to become magistrates, to perform the duty and get the significance, but no pay.

This is the system Benjamin Franklin, near the end of his life, wanted for the U.S. government. He didn't want the high executives of government to be paid, but to be like himself or the entirely unpaid, well-off ministers and rulers of the Mormon Church. And when I see what's happened in California, I'm not sure he wasn't right. At any rate, no one now drifts in Franklin's direction. For one thing, professors—and most of them need money—get appointed directors.

It is not always recognized that, to function best, morality should sometimes appear unfair, like most worldly outcomes. The craving for perfect fairness causes a lot of terrible problems in system function. Some systems should be made deliberately unfair to individuals because they'll be fairer on average for all of us. Thus, there can be virtue in apparent non-fairness. I frequently cite the example of having your career over, in the Navy, if your ship goes aground, even if it wasn't your fault. I say the lack of justice for the one guy that wasn't at fault is way more than made up by a greater justice for everybody when every captain of a ship always sweats blood to make sure the ship doesn't go aground. Tolerating a little unfairness to some to get a greater fairness for all is a model I recommend to all of you. But again, I wouldn't put it in your assigned college work if you want to be graded well, particularly in a modern law school wherein there is usually an over-love of fairness-seeking process.

There are, of course, enormous vice effects in economics. You have these bubbles with so much fraud and folly. The aftermath is frequently very unpleasant, and we've had some of that lately. One of the first big bubbles, of course, was the huge and horrible South Sea Bubble in England. And the aftermath was interesting. Many of you probably don't remember what happened after the South Sea Bubble, which caused an enormous financial contraction and a lot of pain. Except in certain rare cases, they banned publicly traded stock in England for decades. Parliament passed a law that said you can have a partnership with a few partners, but you can't have publicly-traded stock. And, by the way, England continued to grow without publicly-traded stock. The people who are in the business of prospering because there's a lot of stock being traded in casino-like frenzy wouldn't like this example if they studied it enough. It didn't ruin England to have a long period when they didn't have publicly-traded shares.

Just as in real estate. We had all the shopping centers and auto dealerships, and so on, we needed for years when we didn't have publicly-traded real estate shares. It's a myth that once you've got some capital market, economic considerations demand that it has to be as fast and efficient as a casino. It doesn't.

Another interesting problem is raised by vice effects involving envy. Envy wisely got a very strong condemnation in the laws of Moses. You remember how they laid it on with

The South Sea Bubble

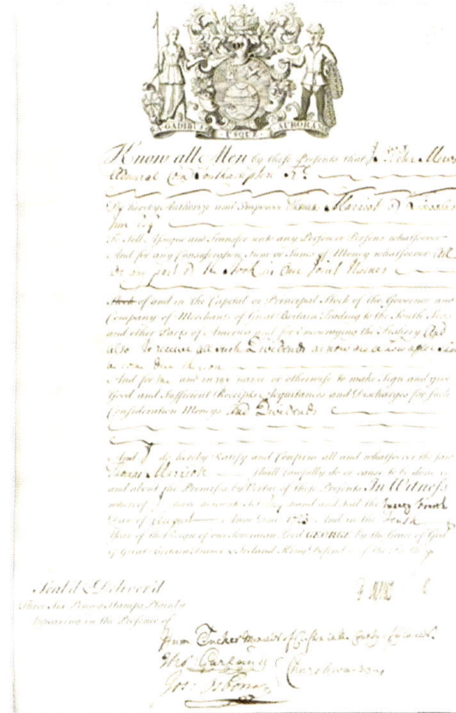

Know all Men by these Presents that

of and in the Capital or Principal Stock of the Governor and Company of Merchants of Great Britain Trading to the South Seas and other Parts of America and for Encouraging the Fishery

Sealed & Delivered

The South Sea Bubble

The South Sea Bubble was an economic frenzy in England that occurred when speculation in South Sea Company shares peaked during 1720. The share price rose from £128 in January to a high of £1,000 in August, and then fell back to £150 in September.

The company had been granted exclusive trading rights in Spanish South America. When results ultimately proved skimpy, the company engineered a public debt scheme that appeared to bolster profits. Company leaders and other shareholders also talked up future revenues, causing the speculative frenzy. Public outcry following disclosure of the fraud led to imposition of the Bubble Act of 1720, requiring publicly-traded companies to have a royal charter.

a trowel: You couldn't covet thy neighbor's ass, you couldn't covet thy neighbor's servant girl, you couldn't covet.... Those old Jews knew how envious people are and how much trouble it caused. They really laid it on hard, and they were right. But Mandeville—remember his fable of bees? He demonstrated convincingly—to me, anyway—that envy was a great driver of proclivity to spend. And so, here's this terrible vice, which is forbidden in the Ten Commandments, and here it's driving all these favorable results in economics. There's some paradox in economics that nobody's going to get out.

When I was young, everybody was excited by Gödel, who came up with proof that you couldn't have a mathematical system without a lot of irritating incompleteness in it. Well, since then, my betters tell me that they've come up with more irremovable defects in mathematics and have decided that you're never going to get mathematics without some paradox in it. No matter how hard you work, you're going to have to live with some paradox if you're a mathematician.

Well, if the mathematicians can't get the paradox out of their system when they're creating it themselves, the poor economists are never going to get rid of paradoxes, nor are any of the rest of us. It doesn't matter. Life is interesting with some paradox. When I run into a paradox, I think either I'm a total horse's ass to have gotten to this point, or I'm fruitfully near the edge of my discipline. It adds excitement to life to wonder which it is.

As I conclude, I want to tell one more story demonstrating how awful it is to get a wrong idea from a limited repertoire and just stick to it. And this is the story of Hyman Liebowitz, who came to America from the old country. In the new country, as in the old, he tried to make his way in the family trade, which was manufacturing nails. And he struggled, and he struggled, and, finally, his little nail business got to vast prosperity, and his wife said to him, "You are old, Hyman, it's time to go to Florida and turn the business over to our son."

So down he went to Florida, turning his business over to the son, but he got weekly financial reports. And he hadn't been in Florida very long before they turned sharply negative. In fact, they were terrible. So he got on an airplane, and he went

In his 1989 Pulitzer Prize–winning book, Douglas Hofstadter ties together the work of mathematician Gödel, graphic artist Escher, and composer Bach.

Kurt Gödel
(1906–1978)

Kurt Gödel, a logician, mathematician, and philosopher of mathematics from Austria-Hungary, wrote a dissertation for his Ph.D. at the University of Vienna that included his famous, but somewhat obscure, incompleteness theorems. The first theorem holds that one can use the mathematical system to construct a statement that can be neither proved nor disproved within that system. The second theorem, arrived at by proving the first, states that no consistent system can be used to prove its own consistency.

back to New Jersey where the factory was. As he left the airport on the way to the factory, he saw this enormous outdoor advertising sign lighted up. And there was Jesus, spread out on the cross. And under it was a big legend, "They Used Liebowitz's Nails." So he stormed into the factory and said, "You dumb son! What do you think you're doing? It took me fifty years to create this business!" "Papa," he said, "trust me. I will fix it."

So back he went to Florida, and while he was in Florida, he got more reports, and the results kept getting worse. So he got on the airplane again. Left the airport, drove by the sign, looked up at this big lighted sign, and now there's a vacant cross. And, lo and behold, Jesus is crumpled on the ground under the cross, and the sign said, "They Didn't Use Liebowitz's Nails."

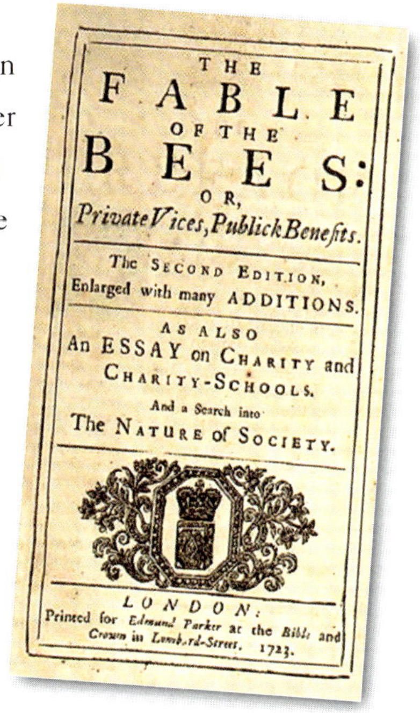
THE FABLE OF THE BEES: OR, *Private Vices, Publick Benefits.*

The SECOND EDITION, Enlarged with many ADDITIONS.

AS ALSO An ESSAY on CHARITY and CHARITY-SCHOOLS. And a Search into The NATURE of SOCIETY.

LONDON: Printed for *Edmund Parker* at the *Bible* and *Crown* in *Lombard-Street*. 1723.

Bernard de Mandeville
(1670–1733) and
"The Fable of the Bees"

Bernard de Mandeville, philosopher and satirist, published a poem, "The Fable of the Bees: or, Private Vices, Publick Benefits," in 1705 as a political satire. Mandeville's philosophy suggests that altruism harms the state and its intellectual progress and that self-interested human vice is the real engine of progress. Thus he arrives at the paradox that "private vices are public benefits."

Well, you can laugh at that. It is ridiculous, but it's no more ridiculous than the way a lot of people cling to failed ideas. Keynes said, "It's not bringing in the new ideas that's so hard. It's getting rid of the old ones." And Einstein said it better, attributing his mental success to "curiosity, concentration, perseverance, and self-criticism." By self-criticism, he meant becoming good at destroying your own best-loved and hardest-won ideas. If you can get really good at destroying your own wrong ideas, that is a great gift.

Well, it's time to repeat the big lesson in this little talk. What I've urged is the use of a bigger multidisciplinary bag of tricks, mastered to fluency, to help economics and everything else. And I also urged that people not be discouraged by irremovable complexity and paradox. It just adds more fun to the problems. My inspiration again is Keynes: Better roughly right than precisely wrong.

And so, I end by repeating what I said once before on a similar occasion. If you skillfully follow the multidisciplinary path, you will never wish to come back. It would be like cutting off your hands.

John Maynard Keynes, Baron Keynes and Lydia Lopokova (Lady Keynes) by William Roberts, exhibited 1932 (NPG 5587), oil on canvas. National Portrait Gallery, London

John Maynard Keynes
(1883–1946)

John Maynard Keynes, son of an economics lecturer at Cambridge University and a social reformist, seemed destined to become a great economist and political thinker. His book, *The General Theory of Employment, Interest, and Money*, published in 1936, advocated that government stimulate demand in times of high unemployment—for example, by spending on public works. The book serves as the foundation of modern macroeconomics.

Well, that's the end. I'll take questions as long as people can endure me.

Male: ...financial destruction from trading of derivative contracts. Buffett said that the genie's out of the bottle and the hangover may be proportionate to the binge. Would you speculate for us how that scenario can play out? [The question was garbled, but the person asked about derivatives, which Buffett has called "financial weapons of mass destruction."]

Munger: Well, of course, catastrophe predictions have always been quite difficult to make with success. But I confidently predict that there are big troubles to come. The system is almost insanely irresponsible. And what people think are fixes aren't really fixes. It's so complicated I can't do it justice here—but you can't believe the trillions of dollars involved. You can't believe the complexity. You can't believe how difficult it is to do the accounting. You can't believe how big the incentives are to have wishful thinking about values and wishful thinking about ability to clear.

Running off a derivative book is agony and takes time. And you saw what happened when they tried to run off the derivative books at Enron. Its certified net worth vanished. In the derivative books of America, there are a lot of reported profits that were never earned and assets that never existed.

And there are large febezzlement effects and some ordinary embezzlement effects that come from derivative activity. And the reversal of these is going to cause pain. How big the pain will be and how well it will be handled, I can't tell you. But you would be disgusted if you had a fair mind and spent a month really delving into a big derivative operation. You would think it was Lewis Carroll [author of *Alice's Adventures in Wonderland*]. You would think it was the Mad Hatter's Tea Party.

And the false precision of these people is just unbelievable. They make the worst economics professors look like gods. Moreover, there is depravity augmenting the folly. Read the book *F.I.A.S.C.O.*, by law professor and former derivatives trader Frank Partnoy, an insider account of depravity in derivative trading at one of the biggest and best-regarded Wall Street firms. The book will turn your stomach.

Rajneesh Mehta: We'll take one more question. There's a class outside that has to come in. So one more question.

Male: Could you describe Warren's reactions to the advice about the negative reaction that he got from musing about defects of California's Prop Thirteen? Was he shocked, surprised?

Munger: It's hard to shock Warren. He's past seventy, he's seen a lot. And his brain works quickly. He generally avoids certain subjects before elections; and that is what I am going to do here.

California's Proposition 13

In 1978, nearly two-thirds of California voters passed Proposition 13, which limits property taxes to one percent of a property's market value, and to two percent per year any increase in the property's valuation assessment unless the property is sold. Prior to Proposition 13, there were no real limits on increases either for the tax rate or property value assessments in the state of California. Prop 13 set the stage for a broader "taxpayer revolt" that contributed to Ronald Reagan's election as president in 1980.

In the 2003 California gubernatorial recall election in which Arnold Schwarzenegger was elected, Schwarzenegger advisor Warren Buffett suggested that Proposition 13, still very popular with many homeowners, be repealed or changed to help balance the state's budget. Politically, Buffett's suggestion proved to be highly charged. Below is Schwarzenegger's reaction.

"Warren, if you mention Prop Thirteen one more time, you owe me five hundred sit-ups."

Talk Nine Revisited

This waggish talk on economics, given in 2003, gave me pleasure as I put it together. But I hope it provided more than harmless fun. I even hope that some shred of my ideas eventually gets into academic economics, not because I want recognition, but because I think academic economics needs some improvement.

Since the talk was given, I came across a book, published by Alfred A. Knopf in 2005. It was written by a distinguished Harvard economics professor, Benjamin M. Friedman, and dealt with the interplay of economics and morals, much as I wished in my talk. The title of this book is "The Moral Consequences of Economic Growth." As readers will note from the title, Professor Friedman is particularly interested in the impact of economic growth on morals, whereas my interest is mostly in the reverse direction, the impact of morals on economic growth. This difference is not a big deal, because every educated person can see reciprocal effects, for good or ill, between the two factors, creating what is often called either a "virtuous circle" or "vicious circle." Professor Friedman supplies a marvelous quotation on this subject from Rabbi Elizar Ben Azariah: "Where there is no bread, there is no law; where there is no law, there is no bread."

A Matter of Trust

"Capitalism works best when there is trust in the system."

—Munger

Arguably the most important theme in this book is the need for *trust*: deserved reliance upon the character, values and integrity of those you live and work with. Charlie Munger and Warren Buffett are renowned for their steadfast commitment to unblemished integrity—believing, like Elbert Gary (Chairman of US Steel from 1901 to 1927) that, "Ethical practices aren't good because they pay; they pay because they are good."

Charlie recalls a meeting of the "Ben Graham Group" in San Diego many years ago. Ben Graham gave his brilliant followers a "cognitive assessment test," containing some extremely tricky questions. As Ben anticipated, the test takers did not fare well, allowing him to deliver a vital lesson regarding the fundamental importance of trust:

"Charlie and I were introduced in 1959 by the Davis family. We were two personalities who tended towards dominance. Yet, we've never had an argument since."

—Buffett

"No matter how smart you are, there are smart people out there who can fool you if they really want to. So, be sure you can trust the smart people you work with."

Raznick Realty Group

Aaron L. Raznick
CHAIRMAN / CEO

Raznick & Sons, Inc.
Raznick Community Builders
Raznick Family Ventures
DoubleHigh Financial

October 8, 2003

Mr. Charlie Munger
Wesco Financial Corporation
301 E. Colorado, Suite 300
Pasadena, CA 91101

Dear Mr. Munger,

Please let me introduce myself, I am Aaron Raznick, a Berkshire Hathaway stockholder, a 1944 Central High graduate, and the person who requested the UCSB Economics Department to ask you to speak. Unhappily and unfortunately, I was unable to attend your lecture due to snarls in traffic outside Oxnard and again outside Santa Barbara. By the time I arrived in Santa Barbara your lecture was long over and I was disgusted.

I had originally written to Mr. Buffet to ask him to speak at UCSB and he responded by telling that I should ask you instead, and that's when I made the suggestion to the Economics Department. My wife and I had endowed a Chair in Economics to UCSB and we have been actively involved with the university for almost 30 years. I was Chairman of the Board of Trustees for two terms and retired from the Board in 2001 after serving over 20 years.

My wife and I are disappointed that we did not have a chance to hear you and meet with you, but I hope we can do so soon. I have attended several of the stockholder meetings in Omaha but have skipped the last two years because of an accident that resulted in my using a walker that I hope will be past history in the next few months. I do plan to attend the stockholder meeting in 2004.

Best wishes,

Aaron L. Raznick

FAXED THIS LTR
11-26-03

11/20/03
What a nice letter. I have ordered a transcript of my talk at UCSB. I will ask my secretary to send you a copy of the talk when it arrives.
Charlie Munger

Real Estate Developers Since 1930
kdale Avenue Suite 200 Woodland Hills, CA 91364-2695 818 884-7770 FAX 818 884-6769
After Hours: (818) 715-1430 email: raznicksons@aol.com

ABC, Inc.

Thomas S. Murphy

June 10, 2004

Mr. Charles T. Munger
Vice Chairman of the Board
Berkshire Hathaway Inc.
P. O. Box 55007
Los Angeles, California 90055

Dear Charlie:

Belated thanks for sending me a copy of your lecture at the University of California in Santa Barbara.

First, I have to admit I haven't read it yet, but I was on the internet today and found a report on your talk by Whitney Tilson. One section gave three problems to solve. I am now so intrigued that I plan to read the entire transcript this weekend.

Thanks for sending it on, and I look forward to seeing you soon.

All the best,

Tom

Thomas S. Murphy

TSM:ekl

Letters from Tom Murphy of ABC, Inc., and Donald Keough expressing anticipation and enthusiasm for "Academic Economics: Strengths and Faults after Considering Interdisciplinary Needs."

Donald R. Keough

June 10, 2004

Mr. Charles T. Munger
Vice Chairman of the Board
Berkshire Hathaway Inc.
P.O. Box 55007
Los Angeles, CA 90055

Dear Charlie:

Even at my advanced age, I can still learn.

Having the opportunity to read and study your October 3 lecture at the University of California, I became a student again!

You followed Einstein's principle – you made it as simple as possible but I still had to study it.

Thanks, Charlie.

All the best.

Sincerely,

/jl

In the run-up to publishing this book, Charlie remarked that one of the most important talks in our list, "The Psychology of Human Misjudgment," could use "a little revising" to bring it in line with his most current views on the subject. Little did we know, Charlie's "little" revision would amount to a full-scale rewrite, with loads of new material, and a "stop-the-press" completion schedule. The talk features Charlie's original concept of "behavioral finance," which has now burgeoned into its own academic field of study. As attendee Donald Hall recalls, "Charlie was espousing his well-reasoned views on behavioral finance before the term was even coined."

Charlie also addresses the importance of recognizing patterns to determine how humans behave, both rationally and irrationally. He shares with us his checklist of twenty-five standard causes of human misjudgment, which contains observations that are ingenious, counterintuitive, and important—values Charlie treasures in the work of other great thinkers throughout history. He also emphasizes the "lollapalooza" power of psychological misjudgments in combination.

Here then, written exclusively for *Poor Charlie's Almanack*, is Charlie's magnum opus on why we behave the way we do. We wish you success in the application of these ideas in your own personal and business endeavors.

Talk Ten

The Psychology of Human Misjudgment

Selections from three of Charlie's talks, combined into one talk never made, after revisions by Charlie in 2005 that included considerable new material.

The three talks were:

(1) The Bray Lecture at the Caltech Faculty Club, February 2, 1992;

(2) Talk under the Sponsorship of the Cambridge Center for Behavioral Studies at the Harvard Faculty Club, October 6, 1994; and

(3) Talk under the Sponsorship of the Cambridge Center for Behavioral Studies at the Boston Harbor Hotel, April 24, 1995.

The extensive revision by Charlie in 2005, made from memory unassisted by any research, occurred because Charlie thought he could do better at age eighty-one than he did more than ten years earlier when he (1) knew less and was more harried by a crowded life and (2) was speaking from rough notes instead of revising transcripts.

PREFACE

When I read transcripts of my psychology talks given about fifteen years ago, I realized that I could now create a more logical but much longer "talk," including most of what I had earlier said.

But I immediately saw four big disadvantages.

First, the longer "talk," because it was written out with more logical completeness, would be more boring and confusing to many people than any earlier talk. This would happen because I would use idiosyncratic definitions of psychological tendencies in a manner reminiscent of both psychology textbooks and Euclid. And who reads textbooks for fun or revisits Euclid?

Second, because my formal psychological knowledge came only from skimming three psychology textbooks about fifteen years ago, I know virtually nothing about any academic psychology later developed. Yet, in a longer talk containing guesses, I would be criticizing much academic psychology. This sort of intrusion into a professional territory by an amateur would be sure to be resented by professors who would rejoice in finding my errors and might be prompted to respond to my published criticism by providing theirs. Why should I care about new criticism? Well, who likes new hostility from articulate critics with an information advantage?

Third, a longer version of my ideas would surely draw some disapproval from people formerly disposed to like me. Not only would there be stylistic and substantive objections, but also there would be perceptions of arrogance in an old man who displayed much disregard for conventional wisdom while "popping-off" on a subject in which he had never taken a course. My old Harvard Law classmate, Ed Rothschild, always called such a popping-off "the shoe button complex," named for the condition of a family friend who spoke in oracular style on all subjects after becoming dominant in the shoe button business.

Fourth, I might make a fool of myself.

Despite these four very considerable objections, I decided to publish the much-expanded version. Thus, after many decades in which I have succeeded mostly by restricting action to jobs and methods in which I was unlikely to fail, I have now chosen a course of action in which (1) I have no significant personal benefit to gain, (2) I will surely give some pain to family members and friends, and (3) I may make myself ridiculous. Why am I doing this?

One reason may be that my nature makes me incline toward diagnosing and talking about errors in conventional wisdom. And despite years of being smoothed out by the hard knocks that were inevitable for one with my attitude, I don't believe life ever knocked all the boy's brashness out of the man.

A second reason for my decision is my approval of the attitude of Diogenes when he asked: "Of what use is a philosopher who never offends anybody?"

My third and final reason is the strongest. I have fallen in love with my way of laying out psychology because it has been so useful for me. And so, before I die, I want to imitate to some extent the bequest practices of three characters: the protagonist in John Bunyan's *Pilgrim's Progress*, Benjamin Franklin, and my first employer, Ernest Buffett. Bunyan's character, the knight wonderfully named "Old Valiant for Truth," makes the only practical bequest available to him when he says at the end of his life: "My sword I leave to him who can wear it." And like this man, I don't mind if I have misappraised my sword, provided I have tried to see it correctly, or that many will not wish to try it, or that some who try to wield it may find it serves them not. Ben Franklin, to my great benefit, left behind his autobiography, his *Almanacks*, and much else. And Ernest Buffett did the best he could in the same mode when he left behind "How to Run a Grocery Store and a Few Things I Have Learned about Fishing." Whether or not this last contribution to the genre was the best, I will not say. But I will report that I have now known four generations of Ernest Buffett's descendants and that the results have encouraged my imitation of the founder.

The Psychology of Human Misjudgment

I have long been very interested in standard thinking errors.

However, I was educated in an era wherein the contributions of non-patient-treating psychology to an understanding of misjudgment met little approval from members of the mainstream elite. Instead, interest in psychology was pretty well confined to a group of professors who talked and published mostly for themselves, with much natural detriment from isolation and groupthink.

And so, right after my time at Caltech and Harvard Law School, I possessed a vast ignorance of psychology. Those institutions failed to require knowledge of the subject. And, of course, they couldn't integrate psychology with their other subject matter when they didn't know psychology. Also, like the Nietzsche character who was proud of his lame leg, the institutions were proud of their willful avoidance of "fuzzy" psychology and "fuzzy" psychology professors.

I shared this ignorant mindset for a considerable time. And so did a lot of other people. What are we to think, for instance, of the Caltech course catalogue that for years listed just one psychology professor, self-described as a "Professor of Psychoanalytical Studies," who taught both "Abnormal Psychology" and "Psychoanalysis in Literature"?

Soon after leaving Harvard, I began a long struggle to get rid of the most dysfunctional part of my psychological ignorance. Today, I will describe my long struggle for elementary wisdom and a brief summary of my ending notions. After that, I will give examples, many quite vivid and interesting to me, of both psychology at work and antidotes to psychology-based dysfunction. Then, I will end by asking and answering some general questions raised by what I have said. This will be a long talk.

When I started law practice, I had respect for the power of genetic evolution and appreciation of man's many evolution-based resemblances to less cognitively-gifted animals and insects. I was aware that man was a "social animal," greatly and automatically influenced by behavior he observed in men around him. I also knew that man lived, like barnyard animals and monkeys, in limited-size dominance hierarchies, wherein he tended to respect authority and to like and cooperate with his own hierarchy members while displaying considerable distrust and dislike for competing men not in his own hierarchy.

But this generalized, evolution-based theory structure was inadequate to enable me to cope properly with the cognition I encountered. I was soon surrounded by much extreme irrationality, displayed in patterns and subpatterns. So surrounded, I could see that I was not going to cope as well as I wished with life unless I could acquire a better theory-structure on which to hang my observations and experiences. By then, my craving for more theory had a long history. Partly, I had always loved theory as an aid in puzzle solving and as a means of satisfying my monkey-like curiosity. And, partly, I had found that theory-structure was a superpower in helping one get what one wanted, as I had early discovered in school wherein I had excelled without labor, guided by theory, while many others, without mastery of theory, failed despite monstrous effort. Better theory, I thought, had always worked for me and, if now available, could make me acquire capital and independence faster and better assist everything I loved. And so I slowly developed my own system of psychology, more or less in the self-help style of Ben Franklin and with the determination displayed in the refrain of the nursery story: "'Then I'll do it myself,' said the little red hen."

I was greatly helped in my quest by two turns of mind. First, I had long looked for insight by inversion in the intense manner counseled by the great algebraist, Jacobi: "Invert, always invert." I sought good judgment mostly by collecting instances of bad judgment, then pondering ways to avoid such outcomes. Second, I became so avid a collector of instances of bad judgment that I paid no attention to boundaries between professional territories. After all, why should I search for some tiny, unimportant, hard-to-find new stupidity in my own field when some large, important, easy-to-find stupidity was just over the fence in the other fellow's professional territory? Besides, I could already see that real-world problems didn't neatly lie within territorial boundaries. They jumped right across. And I was dubious of any approach that, when two things were inextricably intertwined and interconnected, would try and think about one thing but not the other. I was afraid, if I tried any such restricted approach, that I would end up, in the immortal words of John L. Lewis, "with no brain at all, just a neck that had haired over."

Pure curiosity, somewhat later, made me wonder how and why destructive cults were often able, over a single long weekend, to turn many tolerably normal people into brainwashed zombies and thereafter keep them in that state indefinitely. I resolved that I would eventually find a good answer to this cult question if I could do so by general reading and much musing.

I also got curious about social insects. It fascinated me that both the fertile female honeybee and the fertile female harvester ant could multiply their quite different normal life expectancies by exactly twenty by engaging in one gangbang in the sky. The extreme success of the ants also fascinated me—how a few behavioral algorithms caused such extreme evolutionary success grounded in extremes of cooperation within the breeding colony and, almost always, extremes of lethal hostility toward ants outside the breeding colony, even ants of the same species.

Motivated as I was, by midlife I should probably have turned to psychology textbooks, but I didn't, displaying my share of the outcome predicted by the German folk saying: "We are too soon old and too late smart." However, as I later found out, I may have been lucky to avoid for so long the academic psychology that was then laid out in most textbooks. These would not then have guided me well with respect to cults and were often written as if the authors were collecting psychology experiments as a boy collects butterflies—with a passion for more butterflies and more contact with fellow collectors and little craving for synthesis in what is already possessed. When I finally got to the psychology texts, I was reminded of the observation of Jacob Viner, the great economist, that many an academic is like the truffle hound, an animal so trained and bred for one narrow purpose that it is no good at anything else. I was also appalled by hundreds of pages of extremely nonscientific musing about comparative weights of nature and nurture in human outcomes. And I found that introductory psychology texts, by and large, didn't deal appropriately with a fundamental issue: Psychological tendencies tend to be both numerous and inseparably intertwined, now and forever, as they interplay in life. Yet the complex parsing out of effects from intertwined tendencies was usually avoided by the writers of the elementary texts. Possibly the authors did not wish, through complexity, to repel entry of new devotees to their discipline. And, possibly, the cause of their inadequacy was the one given by Samuel Johnson in response to a woman who inquired as to what accounted for his dictionary's misdefinition of the word "pastern." "Pure ignorance," Johnson replied. And, finally, the text writers showed little interest in describing standard antidotes to standard psychology-driven folly, and they thus avoided most discussion of exactly what most interested me.

But academic psychology has some very important merits alongside its defects. I learned this eventually, in the course of general reading, from a book, *Influence*, aimed at a popular audience, by a distinguished psychology professor, Robert Cialdini, at Arizona State, a very big university. Cialdini had made himself into a super-tenured "Regents' Professor" at a very young age by devising, describing, and explaining a vast group of clever experiments in which man manipulated man to his detriment, with all of this made possible by man's intrinsic thinking flaws.

I immediately sent copies of Cialdini's book to all my children. I also gave Cialdini a share of Berkshire stock [Class A] to thank him for what he had done for me and the public. Incidentally, the sale by Cialdini of hundreds of thousands of copies of a book about social psychology was a huge feat, considering that Cialdini didn't claim that he was going to improve your sex life or make you any money.

Part of Cialdini's large book-buying audience came because, like me, it wanted to learn how to become less often tricked by salesmen and circumstances. However, as an outcome not sought by Cialdini, who is a profoundly ethical man, a huge number of his books were bought by salesmen who wanted to learn how to become more effective in misleading customers. Please remember this perverse outcome when my discussion comes to incentive-caused bias as a consequence of the superpower of incentives.

With the push given by Cialdini's book, I soon skimmed through three much used textbooks covering introductory psychology. I also pondered considerably while craving synthesis and taking into account all my previous training and experience. The result was Munger's partial summary of the non-patient-treating, non-nature vs. nurture-weighing parts of nondevelopmental psychology. This material was stolen from its various discoverers (most of whose names I did not even try to learn), often with new descriptions and titles selected to fit Munger's notion of what makes recall easy for Munger, then revised to make Munger's use easy as he seeks to avoid errors.

I will start my summary with a general observation that helps explain what follows. This observation is grounded in what we know about social insects. The limitations inherent in evolution's development of the nervous-system cells that control behavior are beautifully demonstrated by these insects, which often have a mere 100,000 or so cells in their entire nervous systems, compared to man's multiple billions of cells in his brain alone.

Each ant, like each human, is composed of a living physical structure plus behavioral algorithms in its nerve cells. In the ant's case, the behavioral algorithms are few in number and almost entirely genetic in origin. The ant learns a little behavior from experiences, but mostly it merely responds to ten or so stimuli with a few simple responses programmed into its nervous system by its genes.

Naturally, the simple ant behavior system has extreme limitations because of its limited nerve-system repertoire. For instance, one type of ant, when it smells a pheromone given off by a dead ant's body in the hive, immediately responds by cooperating with other ants in carrying the dead body out of the hive. And Harvard's great E.O. Wilson performed one of the best psychology experiments ever done when he painted dead-ant pheromone on a live ant. Quite naturally, the other ants dragged this useful live ant out of the hive even though it kicked and otherwise protested throughout the entire process. Such is the brain of the ant. It has a simple program of responses that generally work out all right, but which are imprudently used by rote in many cases.

Another type of ant demonstrates that the limited brain of ants can be misled by circumstances as well as by clever manipulation from other creatures. The brain of this ant contains a simple behavioral program that directs the ant, when walking, to follow the ant ahead. And when these ants stumble into walking in a big circle, they sometimes walk round and round until they perish.

It seems obvious, to me at least, that the human brain must often operate counterproductively just like the ant's, from unavoidable oversimplicity in its mental process, albeit usually in trying to solve problems more difficult than those faced by ants that don't have to design airplanes.

The perception system of man clearly demonstrates just such an unfortunate outcome. Man is easily fooled, either by the cleverly thought out manipulation of man, by circumstances occurring by accident, or by very effective manipulation practices that man has stumbled into during "practice evolution" and kept in place because they work so well. One such outcome is caused by a quantum effect in human perception. If stimulus is kept below a certain level, it does not get through. And, for this reason, a magician was able to make the Statue of Liberty disappear after a certain amount of magician lingo expressed in the dark. The audience was not aware that it was sitting on a platform that was rotating so slowly, below man's sensory threshold, that no one could feel the acceleration implicit in the considerable rotation. When a surrounding curtain was then opened in the place on the platform where the Statue had earlier appeared, it seemed to have disappeared.

And even when perception does get through to man's brain, it is often misweighted, because what is registered in perception is in shockingness of apparent contrast, not the standard scientific units that make possible science and good engineering.

A magician demonstrates this sort of contrast-based error in your nervous system when he removes your wristwatch without your feeling it. As he does this, he applies pressure of touch on your wrist that you would sense if it was the only pressure of touch you were experiencing. But he has concurrently applied other intense pressure of touch on your body, but not on your wrist, "swamping" the wrist pressure by creating a high-contrast touch pressure elsewhere. This high contrast takes the wrist pressure below perception.

Some psychology professors like to demonstrate the inadequacy of contrast-based perception by having students put one hand in a bucket of hot water and one hand in a bucket of cold water. They are then suddenly asked to remove both hands and place them in a single bucket of room-temperature water. Now, with both hands in the same water, one hand feels as if it has just been put in cold water and the other hand feels as if it has just been placed in hot water. When one thus sees perception so easily fooled by mere contrast, where a simple temperature gauge would make no error, and realizes that cognition mimics perception in being misled by mere contrast, he is well on the way toward understanding, not only how magicians fool one, but also how life will fool one. This can occur, through deliberate human manipulation or otherwise, if one doesn't take certain precautions against often-wrong effects from generally useful tendencies in his perception and cognition.

Man's—often wrong but generally useful—psychological tendencies are quite numerous and quite different. The natural consequence of this profusion of tendencies is the grand general principle of social psychology: cognition is ordinarily situation-dependent so that different situations often cause different conclusions, even when the same person is thinking in the same general subject area.

With this introductory instruction from ants, magicians, and the grand general principle of social psychology, I will next simply number and list psychology-based tendencies that, while generally useful, often mislead. Discussion of errors from each tendency will come later, together with description of some antidotes to errors, followed by some general discussion. Here are the tendencies:

One:	Reward and Punishment Superresponse Tendency
Two:	Liking/Loving Tendency
Three:	Disliking/Hating Tendency
Four:	Doubt-Avoidance Tendency
Five:	Inconsistency-Avoidance Tendency
Six:	Curiosity Tendency

Seven:	Kantian Fairness Tendency
Eight:	Envy/Jealousy Tendency
Nine:	Reciprocation Tendency
Ten:	Influence-from-Mere-Association Tendency
Eleven:	Simple, Pain-Avoiding Psychological Denial
Twelve:	Excessive Self-Regard Tendency
Thirteen:	Overoptimism Tendency
Fourteen:	Deprival-Superreaction Tendency
Fifteen:	Social-Proof Tendency
Sixteen:	Contrast-Misreaction Tendency
Seventeen:	Stress-Influence Tendency
Eighteen:	Availability-Misweighing Tendency
Nineteen:	Use-It-or-Lose-It Tendency
Twenty:	Drug-Misinfluence Tendency
Twenty-One:	Senescence-Misinfluence Tendency
Twenty-Two:	Authority-Misinfluence Tendency
Twenty-Three:	Twaddle Tendency
Twenty-Four:	Reason-Respecting Tendency
Twenty-Five:	Lollapalooza Tendency—The Tendency to Get Extreme Consequences from Confluences of Psychological Tendencies Acting in Favor of a Particular Outcome

One:
Reward and Punishment Superresponse Tendency

I place this tendency first in my discussion because almost everyone thinks he fully recognizes how important incentives and disincentives are in changing cognition and behavior. But this is not often so. For instance, I think I've been in the top five percent of my age cohort almost all my adult life in understanding the power of incentives, and yet I've always underestimated that power. Never a year passes but I get some surprise that pushes a little further my appreciation of incentive superpower.

One of my favorite cases about the power of incentives is the Federal Express case. The integrity of the Federal Express system requires that all packages be shifted rapidly among airplanes in one central airport each night. And the system has no integrity for the customers if the night work shift can't accomplish its assignment fast. And Federal Express had one hell of a time getting the night shift to do the right thing. They tried moral suasion. They tried everything in the world without luck. And, finally, somebody got the happy thought that it was foolish to pay the night shift by the hour when what the employer wanted was not maximized billable hours of employee service but fault-free, rapid performance of a particular task. Maybe, this person thought, if they paid the employees per shift and let all night shift employees go home when all the planes were loaded, the system would work better. And, lo and behold, that solution worked.

Early in the history of Xerox, Joe Wilson, who was then in the government, had a similar experience. He had to go back to Xerox because he couldn't understand why its new machine was selling so poorly in relation to its older and inferior machine. When he got back to Xerox, he found out that the commission arrangement with the salesmen gave a large and perverse incentive to push the inferior machine on customers, who deserved a better result.

And then there is the case of Mark Twain's cat that, after a bad experience with a hot stove, never again sat on a hot stove, or a cold stove either.

We should also heed the general lesson implicit in the injunction of Ben Franklin in *Poor Richard's Almanack*: "If you would persuade, appeal to interest and not to reason." This maxim is a wise guide to a great and simple precaution in life: Never, ever, think about something else when you should be thinking about the power of incentives. I once saw a very smart house counsel for a major investment bank lose his job, with no moral fault, because he ignored the lesson in this maxim of Franklin. This counsel failed to persuade his client because he told him his moral duty, as correctly conceived by the counsel, without also telling the client in vivid terms that he was very likely to be clobbered to smithereens if he didn't behave as his counsel recommended. As a result, both client and counsel lost their careers.

We should also remember how a foolish and willful ignorance of the superpower of rewards caused Soviet communists to get their final result as described by one employee: "They pretend to pay us and we pretend to work." Perhaps the most important rule in management is "Get the incentives right."

But there is some limit to a desirable emphasis on incentive superpower. One case of excess emphasis happened at Harvard, where B. F. Skinner, a psychology professor, finally made himself ridiculous. At one time, Skinner may have been the best-known psychology professor in the world. He partly deserved his peak reputation because his early experiments using rats and pigeons were ingenious, and his results were both counterintuitive and important. With incentives, he could cause more behavior change, culminating in conditioned reflexes in his rats and pigeons, than he could in any other way. He made obvious the extreme stupidity, in dealing with children or employees, of rewarding behavior one didn't want more of. Using food rewards, he even caused strong superstitions, predesigned by himself, in his pigeons. He demonstrated again and again a great recurring, generalized behavioral algorithm in nature: "Repeat behavior that works." He also demonstrated that prompt rewards worked much better than delayed rewards in changing and maintaining behavior. And, once his rats and pigeons had conditioned reflexes, caused by food rewards, he found what withdrawal pattern of rewards kept the reflexive behavior longest in place: random distribution. With this result, Skinner thought he had pretty well explained man's misgambling compulsion whereunder he often foolishly proceeds to ruin. But, as we shall later see when we discuss other psychological tendencies that contribute to misgambling compulsion, he was only partly right. Later, Skinner lost most of his personal reputation (a) by overclaiming for incentive superpower to the point of thinking he could create a human utopia with it and (b) by displaying hardly any recognition of the power of the rest of psychology. He thus behaved like one of Jacob Viner's truffle hounds as he tried to explain everything with incentive effects. Nonetheless, Skinner was right in his main idea: Incentives are superpowers. The outcome of his basic experiments will always remain in high repute in the annals of experimental science. And his method of monomaniacal reliance on rewards, for many decades after his death, did more good than anything else in improving autistic children.

When I was at Harvard Law School, the professors sometimes talked about an overfocused, Skinner-like professor at Yale Law School. They used to say: "Poor old Eddie Blanchard, he thinks declaratory judgments will cure cancer." Well, that's the way Skinner got with his very extreme emphasis on incentive superpower. I always call the "Johnny-one-note" turn of mind that eventually so diminished Skinner's reputation the man-with-a-hammer tendency, after the folk saying: "To a man with only a hammer every problem looks pretty much like a nail." Man-with-a-hammer tendency does not exempt smart people like Blanchard and Skinner. And it won't exempt you if you don't watch out. I will return to man-with-a-hammer tendency at various times in this talk because, fortunately, there are effective antidotes that reduce the ravages of what pretty much ruined the personal reputation of the brilliant Skinner.

One of the most important consequences of incentive superpower is what I call "incentive-caused bias." A man has an acculturated nature making him a pretty decent fellow, and yet, driven both consciously and subconsciously by incentives, he drifts into immoral behavior in order to get what he wants, a result he facilitates by rationalizing his bad behavior, like the salesmen at Xerox who harmed customers in order to maximize their sales commissions.

Here, my early education involved a surgeon who over the years sent bushel baskets full of normal gall bladders down to the pathology lab in the leading hospital in Lincoln, Nebraska, my grandfather's town. And, with that permissive quality control for which community hospitals are famous, many years after this surgeon should've been removed from the medical staff, he was. One of the doctors who participated in the removal was a family friend, and I asked him: "Did this surgeon think, 'Here's a way for me to exercise my talents'—this guy was very skilled technically—'and make a high living by doing a few maimings and murders every year in the course of routine fraud?'" And my friend answered: "Hell no, Charlie. He thought that the gall bladder was the source of all medical evil, and, if you really loved your patients, you couldn't get that organ out rapidly enough."

Now that's an extreme case, but in lesser strength, the cognitive drift of that surgeon is present in every profession and in every human being. And it causes perfectly terrible behavior. Consider the presentations of brokers selling commercial real estate and businesses. I've never seen one that I thought was even within hailing distance of objective truth. In my long life, I have never seen a management consultant's report that didn't end with the same advice: "This problem needs more management consulting services." Widespread incentive-caused bias requires that one should often distrust, or take with a grain of salt, the advice of one's professional advisor, even if he is an engineer. The general antidotes here are: (1) especially fear professional advice when it is especially good for the advisor; (2) learn and use the basic elements of your advisor's trade as you deal with your advisor; and (3) double check, disbelieve, or replace much of what you're told, to the degree that seems appropriate after objective thought.

The power of incentives to cause rationalized, terrible behavior is also demonstrated by Defense Department procurement history. After the Defense Department had much truly awful experience with misbehaving contractors motivated under contracts paying on a cost-plus-a-percentage-of-cost basis, the reaction of our republic was to make it a crime for a contracting officer in the Defense Department to sign such a contract, and not only a crime, but a felony.

And, by the way, although the government was right to create this new felony, much of the way the rest of the world is run, including the operation of many law firms and a lot of other firms, is still under what is, in essence, a cost-plus-a-percentage-of-cost reward system. And human nature, bedeviled by incentive-caused bias, causes a lot of ghastly abuse under these standard incentive patterns of the world. And many of the people who are behaving terribly you would be glad to have married into your family, compared to what you're otherwise likely to get.

Now there are huge implications from the fact that the human mind is put together this way. One implication is that people who create things like cash registers, which make dishonest behavior hard to accomplish, are some of the effective saints of our civilization because, as Skinner so well knew, bad behavior is intensely habit-forming when it is rewarded. And so the cash register was a great moral instrument when it was created. And, by the way, Patterson, the great evangelist of the cash register, knew that from his own experience. He had a little store, and his employees were stealing him blind, so that he never made any money. Then people sold him a couple of cash registers, and his store went to profit immediately. He promptly closed the store and went into the cash register business, creating what became the mighty National Cash Register Company, one of the glories of its time. "Repeat behavior that works" is a behavioral guide that really succeeded for Patterson, after he applied one added twist. And so did high moral cognition. An eccentric, inveterate do-gooder (except when destroying competitors, all of which he regarded as would-be patent thieves), Patterson, like Carnegie, pretty well gave away all his money to charity before he died, always pointing out that "shrouds have no pockets." So great was the contribution of Patterson's cash register to civilization, and so effectively did he improve the cash register and spread its use, that in the end, he probably deserved the epitaph chosen for the Roman poet Horace: "I did not completely die."

The strong tendency of employees to rationalize bad conduct in order to get rewards requires many antidotes in addition to the good cash control promoted by Patterson. Perhaps the most important of these antidotes is use of sound accounting theory and practice. This was seldom better demonstrated than at Westinghouse, which had a subsidiary that made loans having no connection to the rest of Westinghouse's businesses. The officers of Westinghouse, perhaps influenced by envy of General Electric, wanted to expand profits from loans to outsiders. Under Westinghouse's accounting practice, provisions for future credit losses on these loans depended largely on the past credit experience of its lending subsidiary, which mainly made loans unlikely to cause massive losses.

Now there are two special classes of loans that naturally cause much trouble for lenders. The first is ninety-five percent-of-value construction loans to any kind of real estate developer, and the second is any kind of construction loan on a hotel. So, naturally, if one was willing to loan approximately ninety-five percent of the real cost to a developer constructing a hotel, the loan would bear a much-higher-than-normal interest rate because the credit-loss danger would be much higher than normal. So, sound accounting for Westinghouse in making a big, new mass of ninety-five percent-of-value construction loans to hotel developers would have been to report almost no profit, or even a loss, on each loan until, years later, the loan became clearly worth par. But Westinghouse instead plunged into big-time construction lending on hotels, using accounting that made its lending officers look good because it showed extremely high starting income from loans that were very inferior to the loans from which the company had suffered small credit losses in the past. This terrible accounting was allowed by both international and outside accountants for Westinghouse as they displayed the conduct predicted by the refrain: "Whose bread I eat, his song I sing."

The result was billions of dollars of losses. Who was at fault? The guy from the refrigerator division, or some similar division, who as lending officer was suddenly in charge of loans to hotel developers? Or the accountants and other senior people who tolerated a nearly insane incentive structure, almost sure to trigger incentive-caused bias in a lending officer? My answer puts most blame on the accountants and other senior people who created the accounting system. These people became the equivalent of an armored car cash-carrying service that suddenly decided to dispense with vehicles and have unarmed midgets hand-carry its customers' cash through slums in open bushel baskets.

I wish I could tell you that this sort of thing no longer happens, but this is not so. After Westinghouse blew up, General Electric's Kidder Peabody subsidiary put a silly computer program in place that allowed a bond trader to show immense fictional profits. And after that, much accounting became even worse, perhaps reaching its nadir at Enron.

And so incentive-caused bias is a huge, important thing, with highly important antidotes, like the cash register and a sound accounting system. But when I came years ago to the psychology texts, I found that, while they were about one thousand pages long, there was little therein that dealt with incentive-caused bias and no mention of Patterson or sound accounting systems. Somehow incentive-caused bias and its antidotes pretty well escaped the standard survey courses in psychology, even though incentive-caused bias had long been displayed prominently in much of the world's great literature, and antidotes to it had long existed in standard business routines. In the end, I concluded that when something was obvious in life but not easily demonstrable in certain kinds of easy-to-do, repeatable academic experiments, the truffle hounds of psychology very often missed it.

In some cases, other disciplines showed more interest in psychological tendencies than did psychology, at least as explicated in psychology textbooks. For instance, economists, speaking from the employer's point of view, have long had a name for the natural results of incentive-caused bias: "agency cost." As the name implies, the economists have typically known that, just as grain is always lost to rats, employers always lose to employees who improperly think of themselves first. Employer-installed antidotes include tough internal audit systems and severe public punishment for identified miscreants, as well as misbehavior-preventing routines and such machines as cash registers. From the employee's point of view, incentive-caused bias quite naturally causes opposing abuse from the employer: the sweatshop, the unsafe work place, etc. And these bad results for employees have antidotes not only in pressure from unions but also in government action, such as wage and hour laws, work-place-safety rules, measures fostering unionization, and workers' compensation systems. Given the opposing psychology-induced strains that naturally occur in employment because of incentive-caused bias on both sides of the relationship, it is no wonder the Chinese are so much into Yin and Yang.

The inevitable ubiquity of incentive-caused bias has vast, generalized consequences. For instance, a sales force living only on commissions will be much harder to keep moral than one under less pressure from the compensation arrangement. On the other hand, a purely commissioned sales force may well be more efficient per dollar spent. Therefore, difficult decisions involving trade-offs are common in creating compensation arrangements in the sales function.

The extreme success of free-market capitalism as an economic system owes much to its prevention of many of bad effects from incentive-caused bias. Most capitalist owners in a vast web of free-market economic activity are selected for ability by surviving in a brutal competition with other owners and have a strong incentive to prevent all waste in operations within their ownership. After all, they live on the difference between their competitive prices and their overall costs and their businesses will perish if costs exceed sales. Replace such owners by salaried employees of the state and you will normally get a substantial reduction in overall efficiency as each employee who replaces an owner is subject to incentive-caused bias as he determines what service he will give in exchange for his salary and how much he will yield to peer pressure from many fellow employees who do not desire his creation of any strong performance model.

Another generalized consequence of incentive-caused bias is that man tends to "game" all human systems, often displaying great ingenuity in wrongly serving himself at the expense of others. Anti-gaming features, therefore, constitute a huge and necessary part of almost all system design. Also needed in system design is an admonition: Dread, and avoid as much you can, rewarding people for what can be easily faked. Yet our legislators and judges, usually including many lawyers educated in eminent universities, often ignore this injunction. And society consequently pays a huge price in the deterioration of behavior and efficiency, as well as the incurrence of unfair costs and wealth transfers. If education were improved, with psychological reality becoming better taught and assimilated, better system design might well come out of our legislatures and courts.

Of course, money is now the main reward that drives habits. A monkey can be trained to seek and work for an intrinsically worthless token, as if it were a banana, if the token is routinely exchangeable for a banana. So it is also with humans working for money—only more so, because human money is exchangeable for many desired things in addition to food, and one ordinarily gains status from either holding or spending it. Moreover, a rich person will often, through habit, work or connive energetically for more money long after he has almost no real need for more. Averaged out, money is a mainspring of modern civilization, having little precedent in the behavior of nonhuman animals. Money rewards are also intertwined with other forms of reward. For instance, some people use money to buy status and others use status to get money, while still others sort of do both things at the same time.

Although money is the main driver among rewards, it is not the only reward that works. People also change their behavior and cognition for sex, friendship, companionship, advancement in status, and other nonmonetary items.

"Granny's Rule" provides another example of reward superpower, so extreme in its effects that it must be mentioned here. You can successfully manipulate your own behavior with this rule, even if you are using as rewards items that you already possess! Indeed, consultant Ph. D. psychologists often urge business organizations to improve their reward systems by teaching executives to use "Granny's Rule" to govern their own daily behavior. Granny's Rule, to be specific, is the requirement that children eat their carrots before they get dessert. And the business version requires that executives force themselves daily to first do their unpleasant and necessary tasks before rewarding themselves by proceeding to their pleasant tasks. Given reward superpower, this practice is wise and sound. Moreover, the rule can also be used in the nonbusiness part of life. The emphasis on daily use of this practice is not accidental. The consultants well know, after the teaching of Skinner, that prompt rewards work best.

Punishments, of course, also strongly influence behavior and cognition, although not so flexibly and wonderfully as rewards. For instance, illegal price fixing was fairly common in America when it was customarily punished by modest fines. Then, after a few prominent business executives were removed from their eminent positions and sent to federal prisons, price-fixing behavior was greatly reduced.

Military and naval organizations have very often been extreme in using punishment to change behavior, probably because they needed to cause extreme behavior. Around the time of Caesar, there was a European tribe that, when the assembly horn blew, always killed the last warrior to reach his assigned place, and no one enjoyed fighting this tribe. And George Washington hanged farm-boy deserters forty feet high as an example to others who might contemplate desertion.

Two:
Liking/Loving Tendency

A newly hatched baby goose is programmed, through the economy of its genetic program, to "love" and follow the first creature that is nice to it, which is almost always its mother. But, if the mother goose is not present right after the hatching, and a man is there instead, the gosling will "love" and follow the man, who becomes a sort of substitute mother.

Somewhat similarly, a newly arrived human is "born to like and love" under the normal and abnormal triggering outcomes for its kind. Perhaps the strongest inborn tendency to love—ready to be triggered—is that of the human mother for its child. On the other hand, the similar "child-loving" behavior of a mouse can be eliminated by the deletion of a single gene, which suggests there is some sort of triggering gene in a mother mouse as well as in a gosling.

Each child, like a gosling, will almost surely come to like and love, not only as driven by its sexual nature, but also in social groups not limited to its genetic or adoptive "family." Current extremes of romantic love almost surely did not occur in man's remote past. Our early human ancestors were surely more like apes triggered into mating in a pretty mundane fashion.

And what will a man naturally come to like and love, apart from his parent, spouse and child? Well, he will like and love being liked and loved. And so many a courtship competition will be won by a person displaying exceptional devotion, and man will generally strive, lifelong, for the affection and approval of many people not related to him.

One very practical consequence of Liking/Loving Tendency is that it acts as a conditioning device that makes the liker or lover tend (1) to ignore faults of, and comply with wishes of, the object of his affection, (2) to favor people, products, and actions merely associated with the object of his affection (as we shall see when we get to "Influence-from-Mere-Association Tendency," and (3) to distort other facts to facilitate love.

The phenomenon of liking and loving causing admiration also works in reverse. Admiration also causes or intensifies liking or love. With this "feedback mode" in place, the consequences are often extreme, sometimes even causing deliberate self-destruction to help what is loved.

Liking or loving, intertwined with admiration in a feedback mode, often has vast practical consequences in areas far removed from sexual attachments. For instance, a man who is so constructed that he loves admirable persons and ideas with a special intensity has a huge advantage in life. This blessing came to both Buffett and myself in large measure, sometimes from the same persons and ideas. One common, beneficial example for us both was Warren's uncle, Fred Buffett, who cheerfully did the endless grocery-store work that Warren and I ended up admiring from a safe distance. Even now, after I have known so many other people, I doubt if it is possible to be a nicer man than Fred Buffett was, and he changed me for the better.

There are large social policy implications in the amazingly good consequences that ordinarily come from people likely to trigger extremes of love and admiration boosting each other in a feedback mode. For instance, it is obviously desirable to attract a lot of lovable, admirable people into the teaching profession.

Three:
Disliking/Hating Tendency

In a pattern obverse to Liking/Loving Tendency, the newly arrived human is also "born to dislike and hate" as triggered by normal and abnormal triggering forces in its life. It is the same with most apes and monkeys.

As a result, the long history of man contains almost continuous war. For instance, most American Indian tribes warred incessantly, and some tribes would occasionally bring captives home to women so that all could join in the fun of torturing captives to death. Even with the spread of religion, and the advent of advanced civilization, much modern war remains pretty savage. But we also get what we observe in present-day Switzerland and the United States, wherein the clever political arrangements of man "channel" the hatreds and dislikings of individuals and groups into nonlethal patterns including elections.

But the dislikings and hatreds never go away completely. Born into man, these driving tendencies remain strong. Thus, we get maxims like the one from England: "Politics is the art of marshalling hatreds." And we also get the extreme popularity of very negative political advertising in the United States.

At the family level, we often see one sibling hate his other siblings and litigate with them endlessly if he can afford it. Indeed, a wag named Buffett has repeatedly explained to me that "a major difference between rich and poor people is that the rich people can spend their lives suing their relatives." My father's law practice in Omaha was full of such intrafamily hatreds. And when I got to the Harvard Law School and its professors taught me "property law" with no mention of sibling rivalry in the family business, I appraised the School as a pretty unrealistic place that wore "blinders" like the milk-wagon horses of yore. My current guess is that sibling rivalry has not yet made it into property law as taught at Harvard.

Disliking/Hating Tendency also acts as a conditioning device that makes the disliker/hater tend to (1) ignore virtues in the object of dislike, (2) dislike people, products, and actions merely associated with the object of his dislike, and (3) distort other facts to facilitate hatred.

Distortion of that kind is often so extreme that miscognition is shockingly large. When the World Trade Center was destroyed, many Pakistanis immediately concluded that the Hindus did it, while many Muslims concluded that the Jews did it. Such factual distortions often make mediation between opponents locked in hatred either difficult or impossible. Mediations between Israelis and Palestinians are difficult because facts in one side's history overlap very little with facts from the other side's.

Four:
Doubt-Avoidance Tendency

The brain of man is programmed with a tendency to quickly remove doubt by reaching some decision.

It is easy to see how evolution would make animals, over the eons, drift toward such quick elimination of doubt. After all, the one thing that is surely counterproductive for a prey animal that is threatened by a predator is to take a long time in deciding what to do. And so man's Doubt-Avoidance Tendency is quite consistent with the history of his ancient, nonhuman ancestors.

So pronounced is the tendency in man to quickly remove doubt by reaching some decision that behavior to counter the tendency is required from judges and jurors. Here, delay before decision making is forced. And one is required to so comport himself, prior to conclusion time, so that he is wearing a "mask" of objectivity. And the "mask" works to help real objectivity along, as we shall see when we next consider man's Inconsistency-Avoidance Tendency.

Of course, once one has recognized that man has a strong Doubt-Avoidance Tendency, it is logical to believe that at least some leaps of religious faith are greatly boosted by this tendency. Even if one is satisfied that his own faith comes from revelation, one still must account for the inconsistent faiths of others. And man's Doubt-Avoidance Tendency is almost surely a big part of the answer.

What triggers Doubt-Avoidance Tendency? Well, an unthreatened man, thinking of nothing in particular, is not being prompted to remove doubt through rushing to some decision. As we shall see later when we get to Social-Proof Tendency and Stress-Influence Tendency, what usually triggers Doubt-Avoidance Tendency is some combination of (1) puzzlement and (2) stress. And both of these factors naturally occur in facing religious issues.

Thus, the natural state of most men is in some form of religion. And this is what we observe.

Five:
Inconsistency-Avoidance Tendency

The brain of man conserves programming space by being reluctant to change, which is a form of inconsistency avoidance. We see this in all human habits, constructive and destructive. Few people can list a lot of bad habits that they have eliminated, and some people cannot identify even one of these. Instead, practically everyone has a great many bad habits he has long maintained despite their being known as bad. Given this situation, it is not too much in many cases to appraise early-formed habits as destiny. When Marley's miserable ghost says, "I wear the chains I forged in life," he is talking about chains of habit that were too light to be felt before they became too strong to be broken.

The rare life that is wisely lived has in it many good habits maintained and many bad habits avoided or cured. And the great rule that helps here is again from Franklin's *Poor Richard's Almanack*: "An ounce of prevention is worth a pound of cure." What Franklin is here indicating, in part, is that Inconsistency-Avoidance Tendency makes it much easier to prevent a habit than to change it.

Also tending to be maintained in place by the anti-change tendency of the brain are one's previous conclusions, human loyalties, reputational identity, commitments, accepted role in a civilization, etc. It is not entirely clear why evolution would program into man's brain an anti-change mode alongside his tendency to quickly remove doubt. My guess is the anti-change mode was significantly caused by a combination of the following factors:

(1) It facilitated faster decisions when speed of decision was an important contribution to the survival of nonhuman ancestors that were prey.

(2) It facilitated the survival advantage that our ancestors gained by cooperating in groups, which would have been more difficult to do if everyone was always changing responses.

(3) It was the best form of solution that evolution could get to in the limited number of generations between the start of literacy and today's complex modern life.

It is easy to see that a quickly reached conclusion, triggered by Doubt-Avoidance Tendency, when combined with a tendency to resist any change in that conclusion, will naturally cause a lot of errors in cognition for modern man. And so it observably works out. We all deal much with others whom we correctly diagnose as imprisoned in poor conclusions that are maintained by mental habits they formed early and will carry to their graves.

So great is the bad-decision problem caused by Inconsistency-Avoidance Tendency that our courts have adopted important strategies against it. For instance, before making decisions, judges and juries are required to hear long and skillful presentations of evidence and argument from the side they will not naturally favor, given their ideas in place. And this helps prevent considerable bad thinking from "first conclusion bias." Similarly, other modern decision makers will often force groups to consider skillful counterarguments before making decisions.

And proper education is one long exercise in augmentation of high cognition so that our wisdom becomes strong enough to destroy wrong thinking maintained by resistance to change. As Lord Keynes pointed out about his exalted intellectual group at one of the greatest universities in the world, it was not the intrinsic difficulty of new ideas that prevented their acceptance. Instead, the new ideas were not accepted because they were inconsistent with old ideas in place. What Keynes was reporting is that the human mind works a lot like the human egg. When one sperm gets into a human egg, there's an automatic shut-off device that bars any other sperm from getting in. The human mind tends strongly toward the same sort of result.

And so, people tend to accumulate large mental holdings of fixed conclusions and attitudes that are not often reexamined or changed, even though there is plenty of good evidence that they are wrong.

Moreover, this doesn't just happen in social science departments, like the one that once thought Freud should serve as the only choice as a psychology teacher for Caltech. Holding to old errors even happens, although with less frequency and severity, in hard science departments. We have no less an authority for this than Max Planck, Nobel laureate, finder of "Planck's constant." Planck is famous not only for his science but also for saying that even in physics the radically new ideas are seldom really accepted by the old guard. Instead, said Planck, the progress is made by a new generation that comes along, less brain-blocked by its previous conclusions. Indeed, precisely this sort of brain-blocking happened to a degree in Einstein. At his peak, Einstein was a great destroyer of his own ideas, but an older Einstein never accepted the full implications of quantum mechanics.

One of the most successful users of an antidote to first conclusion bias was Charles Darwin. He trained himself, early, to intensively consider any evidence tending to disconfirm any hypothesis of his, more so if he thought his hypothesis was a particularly good one. The opposite of what Darwin did is now called confirmation bias, a term of opprobrium. Darwin's practice came from his acute recognition of man's natural cognitive faults arising from Inconsistency-Avoidance Tendency. He provides a great example of psychological insight correctly used to advance some of the finest mental work ever done.

Inconsistency-Avoidance Tendency has many good effects in civilization. For instance, rather than act inconsistently with public commitments, new or old public identities, etc., most people are more loyal in their roles in life as priests, physicians, citizens, soldiers, spouses, teachers, employees, etc.

One corollary of Inconsistency-Avoidance Tendency is that a person making big sacrifices in the course of assuming a new identity will intensify his devotion to the new identity. After all, it would be quite inconsistent behavior to make a large sacrifice for something that was no good. And thus civilization has invented many tough and solemn initiation ceremonies, often public in nature, that intensify new commitments made.

Tough initiation ceremonies can intensify bad contact as well as good. The loyalty of the new, "made-man" mafia member, or of the military officer making the required "blood oath" of loyalty to Hitler, was boosted through the triggering of Inconsistency-Avoidance Tendency.

Moreover, the tendency will often make man a "patsy" of manipulative "compliance-practitioners," who gain advantage from triggering his subconscious Inconsistency-Avoidance Tendency. Few people demonstrated this process better than Ben Franklin. As he was rising from obscurity in Philadelphia and wanted the approval of some important man, Franklin would often maneuver that man into doing Franklin some unimportant favor, like lending Franklin a book. Thereafter, the man would admire and trust Franklin more because a nonadmired and nontrusted Franklin would be inconsistent with the appraisal implicit in lending Franklin the book.

During the Korean War, this technique of Franklin's was the most important feature of the Chinese brainwashing system that was used on enemy prisoners. Small step by small step, the technique often worked better than torture in altering prisoner cognition in favor of Chinese captors.

The practice of Franklin, whereunder he got approval from someone by maneuvering him into treating Franklin favorably, works viciously well in reverse. When one is maneuvered into deliberately hurting some other person, one will tend to disapprove or even hate that person. This effect, from Inconsistency-Avoidance Tendency, accounts for the insight implicit in the saying: "A man never forgets where he has buried the hatchet." The effect accounts for much prisoner abuse by guards, increasing their dislike and hatred for prisoners that exists as a consequence of the guards' reciprocation of hostility from prisoners who are treated like animals. Given the psychology-based hostility natural in prisons between guards and prisoners, an intense, continuous effort should be made (1) to prevent prisoner abuse from starting and (2) to stop it instantly when it starts because it will grow by feeding on itself, like a cluster of infectious disease. More psychological acuity on this subject, aided by more insightful teaching, would probably improve the overall effectiveness of the U.S. Army.

So strong is Inconsistency-Avoidance Tendency that it will often prevail after one has merely pretended to have some identity, habit, or conclusion. Thus, for a while, many an actor sort of believes he is Hamlet, Prince of Denmark. And many a hypocrite is improved by his pretensions of virtue. And many a judge and juror, while pretending objectivity, is gaining objectivity. And many a trial lawyer or other advocate comes to believe what he formerly only pretended to believe.

While Inconsistency-Avoidance Tendency, with its "status quo bias," immensely harms sound education, it also causes much benefit. For instance, a near-ultimate inconsistency would be to teach something to others that one did not believe true. And so, in clinical medical education, the learner is forced to "see one, do one, and then teach one," with the teaching pounding the learning into the teacher. Of course, the power of teaching to influence the cognition of the teacher is not always a benefit to society. When such power flows into political and cult evangelism, there are often bad consequences.

For instance, modern education often does much damage when young students are taught dubious political notions and then enthusiastically push these notions on the rest of us. The pushing seldom convinces others. But as students pound into their mental habits what they are pushing out, the students are often permanently damaged. Educational institutions that create a climate where much of this goes on are, I think, irresponsible. It is important not to thus put one's brain in chains before one has come anywhere near his full potentiality as a rational person.

Six:
Curiosity Tendency

There is a lot of innate curiosity in mammals, but its nonhuman version is highest among apes and monkeys. Man's curiosity, in turn, is much stronger than that of his simian relatives. In advanced human civilization, culture greatly increases the effectiveness of curiosity in advancing knowledge. For instance, Athens (including its colony, Alexandria) developed much math and science out of pure curiosity while the Romans made almost no contribution to either math or science. They instead concentrated their attention on the "practical" engineering of mines, roads, aqueducts, etc. Curiosity, enhanced by the best of modern education (which is by definition a minority part in many places), much helps man to prevent or reduce bad consequences arising from other psychological tendencies. The curious are also provided with much fun and wisdom long after formal education has ended.

Seven:
Kantian Fairness Tendency

Kant was famous for his "categorical imperative," a sort of a "golden rule" that required humans to follow those behavior patterns that, if followed by all others, would make the surrounding human system work best for everybody. And it is not too much to say that modern acculturated man displays, and expects from others, a lot of fairness as thus defined by Kant.

In a small community having a one-way bridge or tunnel for autos, it is the norm in the United States to see a lot of reciprocal courtesy, despite the absence of signs or signals. And many freeway drivers, including myself, will often let other drivers come in front of them, in lane changes or the like, because that is the courtesy they desire when roles are reversed. Moreover, there is, in modern human culture, a lot of courteous lining up by strangers so that all are served on a "first-come-first-served" basis.

Also, strangers often voluntarily share equally in unexpected, unearned good and bad fortune. And, as an obverse consequence of such "fair-sharing" conduct, much reactive hostility occurs when fair-sharing is expected yet not provided.

It is interesting how the world's slavery was pretty well abolished during the last three centuries after being tolerated for a great many previous centuries during which it coexisted with the world's major religions. My guess is that Kantian Fairness Tendency was a major contributor to this result.

Eight:
Envy/Jealousy Tendency

A member of a species designed through evolutionary process to want often-scarce food is going to be driven strongly toward getting food when it first sees food. And this is going to occur often and tend to create some conflict when the food is seen in the possession of another member of the same species. This is probably the evolutionary origin of the envy/jealousy Tendency that lies so deep in human nature.

Sibling jealousy is clearly very strong and usually greater in children than adults. It is often stronger than jealousy directed at strangers. Kantian Fairness Tendency probably contributes to this result.

Envy/jealousy is extreme in myth, religion, and literature wherein, in account after account, it triggers hatred and injury. It was regarded as so pernicious by the Jews of the civilization that preceded Christ that it was forbidden, by phrase after phrase, in the laws of Moses. You were even warned by the Prophet not to covet your neighbor's donkey.

And envy/jealousy is also extreme in modern life. For instance, university communities often go bananas when some university employee in money management, or some professor in surgery, gets annual compensation in multiples of the standard professorial salary. And in modern investment banks, law firms, etc., the envy/jealousy effects are usually more extreme than they are in university faculties. Many big law firms, fearing disorder from envy/jealousy, have long treated all senior partners alike in compensation, no matter how different their contributions to firm welfare. As I have shared the observation of life with Warren Buffett over decades, I have heard him wisely say on several occasions: "It is not greed that drives the world, but envy."

And, because this is roughly right, one would expect a vast coverage of envy/jealousy in psychology textbooks. But no such vast coverage existed when I read my three textbooks. Indeed, the very words "envy" and "jealousy" were often absent from indexes.

Nondiscussion of envy/jealousy is not a phenomenon confined to psychology texts. When did any of you last engage in any large group discussion of some issue wherein adult envy/jealousy was identified as the cause of someone's argument? There seems to be a general taboo against any such claim. If so, what accounts for the taboo?

My guess is that people widely and generally sense that labeling some position as driven by envy/jealousy will be regarded as extremely insulting to the position taker, possibly more so when the diagnosis is correct than when it is wrong. And if calling a position "envy-driven" is perceived as the equivalent of describing its holder as a childish mental basket case, then it is quite understandable how a general taboo has arisen.

But should this general taboo extend to psychology texts when it creates such a large gap in the correct, psychological explanation of what is widespread and important? My answer is no.

Nine:
Reciprocation Tendency

The automatic tendency of humans to reciprocate both favors and disfavors has long been noticed as extreme, as it is in apes, monkeys, dogs, and many less cognitively gifted animals. The tendency clearly facilitates group cooperation for the benefit of members. In this respect, it mimics much genetic programming of the social insects.

We see the extreme power of the tendency to reciprocate disfavors in some wars, wherein it increases hatred to a level causing very brutal conduct. For long stretches in many wars, no prisoners were taken; the only acceptable enemy being a dead one. And sometimes that was not enough, as in the case of Genghis Khan, who was not satisfied with corpses. He insisted on their being hacked into pieces.

One interesting mental exercise is to compare Genghis Khan, who exercised extreme, lethal hostility toward other men, with ants that display extreme, lethal hostility toward members of their own species that are not part of their breeding colony. Genghis looks sweetly lovable when compared to the ants. The ants are more disposed to fight and fight with more extreme cruelty. Indeed, E. O. Wilson once waggishly suggested that if ants were suddenly to get atom bombs, all ants would be dead within eighteen hours. What both human and ant history suggest is (1) that nature has no general algorithm making intraspecies, turn-the-other-cheek behavior a booster of species survival, (2) that it is not clear that a country would have good prospects were it to abandon all reciprocate-disfavor tendency directed at outsiders, and (3) if turn-the-other-cheek behavior is a good idea for a country as it deals with outsiders, man's culture is going to have to do a lot of heavy lifting because his genes won't be of much help.

I next turn to man's reciprocated hostility that falls well short of war. Peacetime hostility can be pretty extreme, as in many modern cases of "road rage" or injury-producing temper tantrums on athletic fields.

The standard antidote to one's overactive hostility is to train oneself to defer reaction. As my smart friend Tom Murphy so frequently says, "You can always tell the man off tomorrow, if it is such a good idea."

Of course, the tendency to reciprocate favor for favor is also very intense, so much so that it occasionally reverses the course of reciprocated hostility. Weird pauses in fighting have sometimes occurred right in the middle of wars, triggered by some minor courtesy or favor on the part of one side, followed by favor reciprocation from the other side, and so on, until fighting stopped for a considerable period. This happened more than once in the trench warfare of World War I, over big stretches of the front and much to the dismay of the generals.

It is obvious that commercial trade, a fundamental cause of modern prosperity, is enormously facilitated by man's innate tendency to reciprocate favors. In trade, enlightened self-interest joining with Reciprocation Tendency results in constructive conduct. Daily interchange in marriage is also assisted by Reciprocation Tendency, without which marriage would lose much of its allure.

And Reciprocation Tendency, insomuch as it causes good results, does not join forces only with the superpower of incentives. It also joins Inconsistency-Avoidance Tendency in helping cause (1) the fulfillment of promises made as part of a bargain, including loyalty promises in marriage ceremonies, and (2) correct behavior expected from persons serving as priests, shoemakers, physicians, and all else.

Like other psychological tendencies, and also man's ability to turn somersaults, reciprocate-favor tendency operates to a very considerable degree at a subconscious level. This helps make the tendency a strong force that can sometimes be used by some men to mislead others, which happens all the time.

For instance, when an automobile salesman graciously steers you into a comfortable place to sit and gives you a cup of coffee, you are very likely being tricked, by this small courtesy alone, into parting with an extra five hundred dollars. This is far from the most extreme case of sales success that is rooted in a salesman dispensing minor favors. However, in this scenario of buying a car, you are going to be disadvantaged by parting with an extra five hundred dollars of your own money. This potential loss will protect you to some extent.

But suppose you are the purchasing agent of someone else—a rich employer, for instance. Now the minor favor you receive from the salesman is less opposed by the threat of extra cost to you because someone else is paying the extra cost. Under such circumstances, the salesman is often able to maximize his advantage, particularly when government is the purchaser.

Wise employers, therefore, try to oppose reciprocate-favor tendencies of employees engaged in purchasing. The simplest antidote works best: Don't let them accept any favors from vendors. Sam Walton agreed with this idea of absolute prohibition. He wouldn't let purchasing agents accept so much as a hot dog from a vendor. Given the subconscious level at which much Reciprocation Tendency operates, this policy of Walton's was profoundly correct. If I controlled the Defense Department, its policies would mimic Walton's.

In a famous psychology experiment, Cialdini brilliantly demonstrated the power of "compliance practitioners" to mislead people by triggering their subconscious Reciprocation Tendency.

Carrying out this experiment, Cialdini caused his "compliance practitioners" to wander around his campus and ask strangers to supervise a bunch of juvenile delinquents on a trip to a zoo. Because this happed on a campus, one person in six out of a large sample actually agreed to do this. After accumulating this one-in-six statistic, Cialdini changed his procedure. His practitioners next wandered around the campus asking strangers to devote a big chunk of time every week for two years to the supervision of juvenile delinquents. This ridiculous request got him a one hundred percent rejection rate. But the practitioner had a follow-up question: "Will you at least spend one afternoon taking juvenile delinquents to a zoo?" This raised Cialdini's former acceptance rate of 1/6 to 1/2—a tripling.

What Cialdini's "compliance practitioners" had done was make a small concession, which was reciprocated by a small concession from the other side. This subconscious reciprocation of a concession by Cialdini's experimental subjects actually caused a much increased percentage of them to end up irrationally agreeing to go to a zoo with juvenile delinquents. Now, a professor who can invent an experiment like that, which so powerfully demonstrates something so important, deserves much recognition in the wider world, which he indeed got to the credit of many universities that learned a great deal from Cialdini.

Why is Reciprocation Tendency so important? Well, consider the folly of having law students graduate, and go out in the world representing clients in negotiations, not knowing the nature of the subconscious processes of the mind as exhibited in Cialdini's experiment. Yet such folly was prevalent in the law schools of the world for decades, in fact, generations. The correct name for that is educational malpractice. The law schools didn't know, or care to teach, what Sam Walton so well knew.

The importance and power of reciprocate-favor tendency was also demonstrated in Cialdini's explanation of the foolish decision of the attorney general of the United States to authorize the Watergate burglary. There, an aggressive subordinate made some extreme proposal for advancing Republican interests through use of some combination of whores and a gigantic yacht. When this ridiculous request was rejected, the subordinate backed off, in gracious concession, to merely asking for consent to a burglary, and the attorney general went along. Cialdini believes that subconscious Reciprocation Tendency thus became one important cause of the resignation of a United States president in the Watergate debacle, and so do I. Reciprocation Tendency subtly causes many extreme and dangerous consequences, not just on rare occasions but pretty much all the time.

Man's belief in reciprocate-favor tendency, following eons of his practicing it, has done some queer and bad things in religions. The ritualized murder of the Phoenicians and the Aztecs, in which they sacrificed human victims to their gods, was a particularly egregious example. And we should not forget that as late as the Punic Wars, the civilized Romans, out of fear of defeat, returned in a few instances to the practice of human sacrifice. On the other hand, the reciprocity-based, religion-boosting idea of obtaining help from God in reciprocation for good human behavior has probably been vastly constructive.

Overall, both inside and outside religions, it seems clear to me that Reciprocation Tendency's constructive contributions to man far outweigh its destructive effects. In cases of psychological tendencies being used to counter or prevent bad results from one or more other psychological tendencies—for instance, in the case of interventions to end chemical dependency—you will usually find Reciprocation Tendency performing strongly on the constructive side.

And the very best part of human life probably lies in relationships of affection wherein parties are more interested in pleasing than being pleased—a not uncommon outcome in display of reciprocate-favor tendency.

Before we leave reciprocate-favor tendency, the final phenomenon we will consider is widespread human misery from feelings of guilt. To the extent the feeling of guilt has an evolutionary base, I believe the most plausible cause is the mental conflict triggered in one direction by reciprocate-favor tendency and in the opposite direction by reward superresponse tendency pushing one to enjoy one hundred percent of some good thing. Of course, human culture has often greatly boosted the genetic tendency to suffer from feelings of guilt. Most especially, religious culture has imposed hard-to-follow ethical and devotional demands on people. There is a charming Irish Catholic priest in my neighborhood who, with rough accuracy, often says, "The old Jews may have invented guilt, but we Catholics perfected it." And if you, like me and this priest, believe that, averaged out, feelings of guilt do more good than harm, you may join in my special gratitude for reciprocate-favor tendency, no matter how unpleasant you find feelings of guilt.

Ten:
Influence-from-Mere-Association Tendency

In the standard conditioned reflexes studied by Skinner and most common in the world, responsive behavior, creating a new habit, is directly triggered by rewards previously bestowed. For instance, a man buys a can of branded shoe polish, has a good experience with it when shining his shoes, and because of this "reward," buys the same shoe polish when he needs another can.

But there is another type of conditioned reflex wherein mere association triggers a response. For instance, consider the case of many men who have been trained by their previous experience in life to believe that when several similar items are presented for purchase, the one with the highest price will have the highest quality. Knowing this, some seller of an ordinary industrial product will often change his product's trade dress and raise its price significantly hoping that quality-seeking buyers will be tricked into becoming purchasers by mere association of his product and its high price. This industrial practice frequently is effective in driving up sales and even more so in driving up profits. For instance, it worked wonderfully with high-priced power tools for a long time. And it would work better yet with high-priced pumps at the bottom of oil wells. With luxury goods, the process works with a special boost because buyers who pay high prices often gain extra status from thus demonstrating both their good taste and their ability to pay.

Even association that appears to be trivial, if carefully planned, can have extreme and peculiar effects on purchasers of products. The target purchaser of shoe polish may like pretty girls. And so he chooses the polish with the pretty girl on the can or the one with the pretty girl in the last ad for shoe polish that he saw.

Advertisers know about the power of mere association. You won't see Coke advertised alongside some account of the death of a child. Instead, Coke ads picture life as happier than reality.

Similarly, it is not from mere chance that military bands play such impressive music. That kind of music, appearing in mere association with military service, helps to attract soldiers and keep them in the army. Most armies have learned to use mere association in this successful way.

However, the most damaging miscalculations from mere association do not ordinarily come from advertisers and music providers.

Some of the most important miscalculations come from what is accidentally associated with one's past success, or one's liking and loving, or one's disliking and hating, which includes a natural hatred for bad news.

To avoid being misled by the mere association of some fact with past success, use this memory clue. Think of Napoleon and Hitler when they invaded Russia after using their armies with much success elsewhere. And there are plenty of mundane examples of results like those of Napoleon and Hitler. For instance, a man foolishly gambles in a casino and yet wins. This unlikely correlation causes him to try the casino again, or again and again, to his horrid detriment. Or a man gets lucky in an odds-against venture headed by an untalented friend. So influenced, he tries again what worked before—with terrible results.

The proper antidotes to being made such a patsy by past success are (1) to carefully examine each past success, looking for accidental, non-causative factors associated with such success that will tend to mislead as one appraises odds implicit in a proposed new undertaking and (2) to look for dangerous aspects of the new undertaking that were not present when past success occurred.

The damage to the mind that can come from liking and loving was once demonstrated by obviously false testimony given by an otherwise very admirable woman, the wife of a party in a jury case. The famous opposing counsel wanted to minimize his attack on such an admirable woman yet destroy the credibility of her testimony. And so, in his closing argument, he came to her testimony last. He then shook his head sadly and said, "What are we to make of such testimony? The answer lies in the old rhyme:

> 'As the husband is,
> So the wife is.
> She is married to a clown,
> And the grossness of his nature
> Drags her down.'"

The jury disbelieved the woman's testimony. They easily recognized the strong misinfluence of love on her cognition. And we now often see even stronger misinfluence from love as tearful mothers, with heartfelt conviction, declare before TV cameras the innocence of their obviously guilty sons.

People disagree about how much blindness should accompany the association called love. In *Poor Richard's Almanack* Franklin counseled: "Keep your eyes wide open before marriage and half shut thereafter." Perhaps this "eyes-half-shut" solution is about right, but I favor a tougher prescription: "See it like it is and love anyway."

Hating and disliking also cause miscalculation triggered by mere association. In business, I commonly see people underappraise both the competency and morals of competitors they dislike. This is a dangerous practice, usually disguised because it occurs on a subconscious basis.

Another common bad effect from the mere association of a person and a hated outcome is displayed in "Persian Messenger Syndrome." Ancient Persians actually killed some messengers whose sole fault was that they brought home truthful bad news, say, of a battle lost. It was actually safer for the messenger to run away and hide, instead of doing his job as a wiser boss would have wanted it done.

And Persian Messenger Syndrome is alive and well in modern life, albeit in less lethal versions. It is actually dangerous in many careers to be a carrier of unwelcome news. Union negotiators and employer representatives often know this, and it leads to many tragedies in labor relations. Sometimes lawyers, knowing their clients will hate them if they recommend an unwelcome but wise settlement, will carry on to disaster. Even in places well known for high cognition, one will sometimes find Persian Messenger Syndrome. For instance, years ago, two major oil companies litigated in a Texas trial court over some ambiguity in an operating agreement covering one of the largest oil reservoirs in the Western hemisphere. My guess is that the cause of the trial was some general counsel's unwillingness to carry bad news to a strong-minded CEO.

CBS, in its late heyday, was famous for occurrence of Persian Messenger Syndrome because Chairman Paley was hostile to people who brought him bad news. The result was that Paley lived in a cocoon of unreality, from which he made one bad deal after another, even exchanging a large share of CBS for a company that had to be liquidated shortly thereafter.

The proper antidote to creating Persian Messenger Syndrome and its bad effects, like those at CBS, is to develop, through exercise of will, a habit of welcoming bad news. At Berkshire, there is a common injunction: "Always tell us the bad news promptly. It is only the good news that can wait." It also helps to be so wise and informed that people fear not telling you bad news because you are so likely to get it elsewhere.

Influence-from-Mere-Association Tendency often has a shocking effect that helps swamp the normal tendency to return favor for favor. Sometimes, when one receives a favor, his condition is unpleasant, due to poverty, sickness, subjugation, or something else. In addition, the favor may trigger an envy-driven dislike for the person who was in so favorable a state that he could easily be a favor giver. Under such circumstances, the favor receiver, prompted partly by mere association of the favor giver with past pain, will not only dislike the man who helped him but also try to injure him. This accounts for a famous response, sometimes dubiously attributed to Henry Ford: "Why does that man hate me so? I never did anything for him." I have a friend, whom I will now call "Glotz," who had an amusing experience in favor-giving. Glotz owned an apartment building that he had bought because he wanted, eventually, to use the land in different development. Pending this outcome, Glotz was very lenient in collecting below-market rents from tenants. When, at last, there was a public hearing on Glotz's proposal to tear down the building, one tenant who was far behind in his rent payments was particularly angry and hostile. He came to the public hearing and said, "This proposal is outrageous. Glotz doesn't need any more money. I know this because I was supported in college by Glotz fellowships."

A final serious clump of bad thinking caused by mere association lies in the common use of classification stereotypes. Because Pete knows that Joe is ninety years old and that most ninety-year-old persons don't think very well, Pete appraises old Joe as a thinking klutz even if old Joe still thinks very well. Or, because Jane is a white-haired woman, and Pete knows no old women good at higher math, Pete appraises Jane as no good at it even if Jane is a whiz. This sort of wrong thinking is both natural and common. Pete's antidote is not to believe that, on average, ninety-year-olds think as well as forty-year-olds or that there are as many females as males among Ph. D.'s in math. Instead, just as he must learn that trend does not always correctly predict destiny, he must learn that the average dimension in some group will not reliably guide him to the dimension of some specific item. Otherwise Pete will make many errors, like that of the fellow who drowned in a river that averaged out only eighteen inches deep.

Eleven:
Simple, Pain-Avoiding Psychological Denial

This phenomenon first hit me hard in World War II when the superathlete, superstudent son of a family friend flew off over the Atlantic Ocean and never came back. His mother, who was a very sane woman, then refused to believe he was dead. That's Simple, Pain-Avoiding Psychological Denial. The reality is too painful to bear, so one distorts the facts until they become bearable. We all do that to some extent, often causing terrible problems. The tendency's most extreme outcomes are usually mixed up with love, death, and chemical dependency.

Where denial is used to make dying easier, the conduct meets almost no criticism. Who would begrudge a fellow man such help at such a time? But some people hope to leave life hewing to the iron prescription, "It is not necessary to hope in order to persevere." And there is something admirable in anyone able to do this.

In chemical dependency, wherein morals usually break down horribly, addicted persons tend to believe that they remain in respectable condition, with respectable prospects. They thus display an extremely unrealistic denial of reality as they go deeper and deeper into deterioration. In my youth, Freudian remedies failed utterly in reversing chemical dependency, but nowadays Alcoholics Anonymous routinely achieves a fifty percent cure rate by causing several psychological tendencies to act together to counter addiction. However, the cure process is typically difficult and draining, and a fifty percent success rate implies a fifty percent failure rate. One should stay far away from any conduct at all likely to drift into chemical dependency. Even a small chance of suffering so great a damage should be avoided.

Twelve:
Excessive Self-Regard Tendency

We all commonly observe the excessive self-regard of man. He mostly misappraises himself on the high side, like the ninety percent of Swedish drivers that judge themselves to be above average. Such misappraisals also apply to a person's major "possessions." One spouse usually overappraises the other spouse. And a man's children are likewise appraised higher by him than they are likely to be in a more objective view. Even man's minor possessions tend to be overappraised. Once owned, they suddenly become worth more to him than he would pay if they were offered for sale to him and he didn't already own them. There is a name in psychology for this overappraise-your-own-possessions phenomenon: the "endowment effect." And all man's decisions are suddenly regarded by him as better than would have been the case just before he made them.

Man's excess of self-regard typically makes him strongly prefer people like himself. Psychology professors have had much fun demonstrating this effect in "lost-wallet" experiments. Their experiments all show that the finder of a lost wallet containing identity clues will be most likely to return the wallet when the owner most closely resembles the finder. Given this quality in psychological nature, cliquish groups of similar persons will always be a very influential part of human culture, even after we wisely try to dampen the worst effects.

Some of the worst consequences in modern life come when dysfunctional groups of cliquish persons, dominated by Excessive Self-Regard Tendency, select as new members of their organizations persons who are very much like themselves. Thus if the English department at an elite university becomes mentally dysfunctional or the sales department of a brokerage firm slips into routine fraud, the problem will have a natural tendency to get worse and to be quite resistant to change for the better. So also with a police department or prison-guard unit or political group gone sour and countless other places mired in evil and folly, such as the worst of our big-city teachers' unions that harm our children by preventing discharge of ineffective teachers. Therefore, some of the most useful members of our civilization are those who are willing to "clean house" when they find a mess under their ambit of control.

Well, naturally, all forms of excess of self-regard cause much error. How could it be otherwise?

Let us consider some foolish gambling decisions. In lotteries, the play is much lower when numbers are distributed randomly than it is when the player picks his own number. This is quite irrational. The odds are almost exactly the same and much against the player. Because state lotteries take advantage of man's irrational love of self-picked numbers, modern man buys more lottery tickets than he otherwise would have, with each purchase foolish.

Intensify man's love of his own conclusions by adding the possessory wallop from the "endowment effect," and you will find that a man who has already bought a pork-belly future on a commodity exchange now foolishly believes, even more strongly than before, in the merits of his speculative bet.

And foolish sports betting, by people who love sports and think they know a lot about relative merits of teams, is a lot more addictive than race track betting—partly because of man's automatic overappraisal of his own complicated conclusions.

Also extremely counterproductive is man's tendency to bet, time after time, in games of skill, like golf or poker, against people who are obviously much better players. Excessive Self-Regard Tendency diminishes the foolish bettor's accuracy in appraising his relative degree of talent.

More counterproductive yet are man's appraisals, typically excessive, of the quality of the future service he is to provide to his business. His overappraisal of these prospective contributions will frequently cause disaster.

Excesses of self-regard often cause bad hiring decisions because employers grossly overappraise the worth of their own conclusions that rely on impressions in face-to-face contact. The correct antidote to this sort of folly is to underweigh face-to-face impressions and overweigh the applicant's past record.

I once chose exactly this course of action while I served as chairman of an academic search committee. I convinced fellow committee members to stop all further interviews and simply appoint a person whose achievement record was much better than that of any other applicant. And when it was suggested to me that I wasn't giving "academic due process," I replied that I was the one being true to academic values because I was using academic research showing poor predictive value of impressions from face-to-face interviews.

Because man is likely to be overinfluenced by face-to-face impressions that by definition involve his active participation, a job candidate who is a marvelous "presenter" often causes great danger under modern executive-search practice. In my opinion, Hewlett-Packard faced just such a danger when it interviewed the articulate, dynamic Carly Fiorina in its search for a new CEO. And I believe (1) that Hewlett-Packard made a bad decision when it chose Ms. Fiorina and (2) that this bad decision would not have been made if Hewlett-Packard had taken the methodological precautions it would have taken if it knew more psychology.

There is a famous passage somewhere in Tolstoy that illuminates the power of Excessive Self-Regard Tendency. According to Tolstoy, the worst criminals don't appraise themselves as all that bad. They come to believe either (1) that they didn't commit their crimes or (2) that, considering the pressures and disadvantages of their lives, it is understandable and forgivable that they behaved as they did and became what they became.

The second half of the "Tolstoy effect", where the man makes excuses for his fixable poor performance, instead of providing the fix, is enormously important. Because a majority of mankind will try to get along by making way too many unreasonable excuses for fixable poor performance, it is very important to have personal and institutional antidotes limiting the ravages of such folly. On the personal level a man should try to face the two simple facts: (1) fixable but unfixed bad performance is bad character and tends to create more of itself, causing more damage to the excuse giver with each tolerated instance, and (2) in demanding places, like athletic teams and General Electric, you are almost sure to be discarded in due course if you keep giving excuses instead of behaving as you should. The main institutional antidotes to this part of the "Tolstoy effect" are (1) a fair, meritocratic, demanding culture plus personnel handling methods that build up morale and (2) severance of the worst offenders. Of course, when you can't sever, as in the case of your own child, you must try to fix the child as best you can. I once heard of a child-teaching method so effective that the child remembered the learning experience over fifty years later. The child later became Dean of the USC School of Music and then related to me what his father said when he saw his child taking candy from the stock of his employer with the excuse that he intended to replace it later. The father said, "Son, it would be better for you to simply take all you want and call yourself a thief every time you do it."

The best antidote to folly from an excess of self-regard is to force yourself to be more objective when you are thinking about yourself, your family and friends, your property, and the value of your past and future activity. This isn't easy to do well and won't work perfectly, but it will work much better than simply letting psychological nature take its normal course.

While an excess of self-regard is often counterproductive in its effects on cognition, it can cause some weird successes from overconfidence that happens to cause success. This factor accounts for the adage: "Never underestimate the man who overestimates himself."

Of course, some high self-appraisals are correct and serve better than false modesty. Moreover, self-regard in the form of a justified pride in a job well done, or a life well lived, is a large constructive force. Without such justified pride, many more airplanes would crash. "Pride" is another word generally left out of psychology textbooks, and this omission is not a good idea. It is also not a good idea to construe the bible's parable about the Pharisee and the Publican as condemning all pride.

Of all forms of useful pride, perhaps the most desirable is a justified pride in being trustworthy. Moreover, the trustworthy man, even after allowing for the inconveniences of his chosen course, ordinarily has a life that averages out better than he would have if he provided less reliability.

Thirteen:
Overoptimism Tendency

About three centuries before the birth of Christ, Demosthenes, the most famous Greek orator, said, "What a man wishes, that also will he believe."

Demosthenes, parsed out, was thus saying that man displays not only Simple, Pain-Avoiding Psychological Denial but also an excess of optimism even when he is already doing well.

The Greek orator was clearly right about an excess of optimism being the normal human condition, even when pain or the threat of pain is absent. Witness happy people buying lottery tickets or believing that credit-furnishing, delivery-making grocery stores were going to displace a great many superefficient cash-and-carry supermarkets.

One standard antidote to foolish optimism is trained, habitual use of the simple probability math of Fermat and Pascal, taught in my youth to high school sophomores. The mental rules of thumb that evolution gives you to deal with risk are not adequate. They resemble the dysfunctional golf grip you would have if you relied on a grip driven by evolution instead of golf lessons.

Fourteen:
Deprival-Superreaction Tendency

The quantity of man's pleasure from a ten-dollar gain does not exactly match the quantity of his displeasure from a ten-dollar loss. That is, the loss seems to hurt much more than the gain seems to help. Moreover, if a man almost gets something he greatly wants and has it jerked away from him at the last moment, he will react much as if he had long owned the reward and had it jerked away. I include the natural human reactions to both kinds of loss experience—the loss of the possessed reward and the loss of the almost-possessed reward—under one description, Deprival-Superreaction Tendency.

In displaying Deprival-Superreaction Tendency, man frequently incurs disadvantage by misframing his problems. He will often compare what is near instead of what really matters. For instance, a man with $10 million in his brokerage account will often be extremely irritated by the accidental loss of $100 out of the $300 in his wallet.

The Mungers once owned a tame and good-natured dog that displayed the canine version of Deprival-Superreaction Tendency. There was only one way to get bitten by this dog. And that was to try and take some food away from him after he already had it in his mouth. If you did that, this friendly dog would automatically bite. He couldn't help it. Nothing could be more stupid than for the dog to bite his master. But the dog couldn't help being foolish. He had an automatic Deprival-Superreaction Tendency in his nature.

Humans are much the same as this Munger dog. A man ordinarily reacts with irrational intensity to even a small loss, or threatened loss, of property, love, friendship, dominated territory, opportunity, status, or any other valued thing. As a natural result, bureaucratic infighting over the threatened loss of dominated territory often causes immense damage to an institution as a whole. This factor, among others, accounts for much of the wisdom of Jack Welch's long fight against bureaucratic ills at General Electric. Few business leaders have ever conducted wiser campaigns.

Deprival-Superreaction Tendency often protects ideological or religious views by triggering dislike and hatred directed toward vocal nonbelievers. This happens, in part, because the ideas of the nonbelievers, if they spread, will diminish the influence of views that are now supported by a comfortable environment including a strong belief-maintenance system. University liberal arts departments, law schools, and business organizations all display plenty of such ideology-based groupthink that rejects almost all conflicting inputs. When the vocal critic is a former believer, hostility is often boosted both by (1) a concept of betrayal that triggers additional Deprival-Superreaction Tendency because a colleague is lost and (2) fears that conflicting views will have extra persuasive power when they come from a former colleague. The foregoing considerations help account for the old idea of heresy, which for centuries justified much killing of heretics, frequently after torture and frequently accomplished by burning the victim alive.

It is almost everywhere the case that extremes of ideology are maintained with great intensity and with great antipathy to non-believers, causing extremes of cognitive dysfunction. This happens, I believe, because two psychological tendencies are usually acting concurrently toward this same sad result: (1) Inconsistency-Avoidance Tendency, plus (2) Deprival-Superreaction Tendency.

One antidote to intense, deliberate maintenance of groupthink is an extreme culture of courtesy, kept in place despite ideological differences, like the behavior of the justices now serving on the U.S. Supreme Court. Another antidote is to deliberately bring in able and articulate disbelievers of incumbent groupthink. Successful corrective measures to evil examples of groupthink maintenance have included actions like that of Derek Bok when, as president of Harvard, he started disapproving tenure appointments proposed by ideologues at Harvard Law School.

Even a one-degree loss from a 180-degree view will sometime create enough Deprival-Superreaction Tendency to turn a neighbor into an enemy, as I once observed when I bought a house from one of two neighbors locked into hatred by a tiny tree newly installed by one of them.

As the case of these two neighbors illustrated, the clamor of almost any group of neighbors displaying irrational, extreme deprival-superreaction over some trifle in a zoning hearing is not a pretty thing to watch. Such bad behavior drives some people from the zoning field. I once bought some golf clubs from an artisan who was formerly a lawyer. When I asked him what kind of law he had practiced, I expected to hear him say, "divorce law." But his answer was, "zoning law."

Deprival-Superreaction Tendency has ghastly effects in labor relations. Most of the deaths in the labor strife that occurred before World War I came when employers tried to reduce wages. Nowadays, we see fewer deaths and more occasions when whole companies disappear, as competition requires either takeaways from labor—which it will not consent to—or death of the business. Deprival-Superreaction Tendency causes much of this labor resistance, often in cases where it would be in labor's interest to make a different decision.

In contexts other than labor relations, takeaways are also difficult to get. Many tragedies, therefore, occur that would have been avoided had there been more rationality and less subconscious heed of the imperative from Deprival-Superreaction Tendency.

Deprival-Superreaction Tendency is also a huge contributor to ruin from compulsion to gamble. First, it causes the gambler to have a passion to get even once he has suffered loss, and the passion grows with the loss. Second, the most addictive forms of gambling provide a lot of near misses and each one triggers Deprival-Superreaction Tendency. Some slot machine creators are vicious in exploiting this weakness of man. Electronic machines enable these creators to produce a lot of meaningless bar-bar-lemon results that greatly increase play by fools who think they have very nearly won large rewards.

Deprival-Superreaction Tendency often does much damage to man in open-outcry auctions. The "social proof" that we will next consider tends to convince man that the last price from another bidder was reasonable, and then Deprival-Superreaction Tendency prompts him strongly to top the last bid. The best antidote to being thus triggered into paying foolish prices at open-outcry auctions is the simple Buffett practice: Don't go to such auctions.

Deprival-Superaction Tendency and Inconsistency-Avoidance Tendency often join to cause one form of business failure. In this form of ruin, a man gradually uses up all his good assets in a fruitless attempt to rescue a big venture going bad. One of the best antidotes to this folly is good poker skill learned young. The teaching value of poker demonstrates that not all effective teaching occurs on a standard academic path.

I myself, the would-be instructor here, many decades ago made a big mistake caused in part by subconscious operation of my Deprival-Superreaction Tendency. A friendly broker called and offered me 300 shares of ridiculously underpriced, very thinly traded Belridge Oil at $115 per share, which I purchased using cash I had on hand. The next day, he offered me 1,500 more shares at the same price, which I declined to buy partly because I could only have made the purchase had I sold something or borrowed the required $173,000. This was a very irrational decision. I was a well-to-do man with no debt; there was no risk of loss; and similar no-risk opportunities were not likely to come along. Within two years, Belridge Oil sold out to Shell at a price of about $3,700 per share, which made me about $5.4 million poorer than I would have been had I then been psychologically acute. As this tale demonstrates, psychological ignorance can be very expensive.

Some people may question my defining Deprival-Superreaction Tendency to include reaction to profit barely missed, as in the well-documented responses of slot machine players. However, I believe that I haven't defined the tendency as broadly as I should. My reason for suggesting an even broader definition is that many Berkshire Hathaway shareholders I know never sell or give away a single share after immense gains in market value have occurred. Some of this reaction is caused by rational calculation, and some is, no doubt, attributable to some combination of (1) reward superresponse, (2) "status quo bias" from Inconsistency-Avoidance Tendency, and (3) "the endowment effect" from Excessive Self-Regard Tendency. But I believe the single strongest irrational explanation is a form of Deprival-Superreaction Tendency. Many of these shareholders simply can't stand the idea of having their Berkshire Hathaway holdings smaller. Partly they dislike facing what they consider an impairment of identity, but mostly they fear missing out on future gains from stock sold or given away.

Fifteen:
Social-Proof Tendency

The otherwise complex behavior of man is much simplified when he automatically thinks and does what he observes to be thought and done around him. And such followership often works fine. For instance, what simpler way could there be to find out how to walk to a big football game in a strange city than by following the flow of the crowd. For some such reason, man's evolution left him with Social-Proof Tendency, an automatic tendency to think and act as he sees others around him thinking and acting.

Psychology professors love Social-Proof Tendency because in their experiments it causes ridiculous results. For instance, if a professor arranges for some stranger to enter an elevator wherein ten "compliance practitioners" are all silently standing so that they face the rear of the elevator, the stranger will often turn around and do the same. The psychology professors can also use Social-Proof Tendency to cause people to make large and ridiculous measurement errors.

And, of course, teenagers' parents usually learn more than they would like about teenagers' cognitive errors from Social-Proof Tendency. This phenomenon was recently involved in a break-through by Judith Rich Harris who demonstrated that superrespect by young people for their peers, rather than for parents or other adults, is ordained to some considerable extent by the genes of the young people. This makes it wise for parents to rely more on manipulating the quality of the peers than on exhortations to their own offspring. A person like Ms. Harris, who can provide an insight of this quality and utility, backed by new reasons, has not lived in vain.

And in the highest reaches of business, it is not all uncommon to find leaders who display followership akin to that of teenagers. If one oil company foolishly buys a mine, other oil companies often quickly join in buying mines. So also if the purchased company makes fertilizer. Both of these oil company buying fads actually bloomed, with bad results.

Of course, it is difficult to identify and correctly weigh all the possible ways to deploy the cash flow of an oil company. So oil company executives, like everyone else, have made many bad decisions that were quickly triggered by discomfort from doubt. Going along with social proof provided by the action of other oil companies ends this discomfort in a natural way.

When will Social-Proof Tendency be most easily triggered? Here the answer is clear from many experiments: Triggering most readily occurs in the presence of puzzlement or stress, and particularly when both exist.

Because stress intensifies Social-Proof Tendency, disreputable sales organizations, engaged, for instance, in such action as selling swampland to schoolteachers, manipulate targets into situations combining isolation and stress. The isolation strengthens the social proof provided by both the knaves and the people who buy first, and the stress, often increased by fatigue, augments the targets' susceptibility to the social proof. And, of course, the techniques of our worst "religious" cults imitate those of the knavish salesmen. One cult even used rattlesnakes to heighten the stress felt by conversion targets.

Because both bad and good behavior are made contagious by Social-Proof Tendency, it is highly important that human societies (1) stop any bad behavior before it spreads and (2) foster and display all good behavior.

My father once told me that just after commencing law practice in Omaha, he went with a large group from Nebraska to South Dakota to hunt pheasants. A South Dakota hunting license was, say, $2 for South Dakota residents and $5 for nonresidents. All the Nebraska residents, one by one, signed up for South Dakota licenses with phony South Dakota addresses until it was my father's turn. Then, according to him, he barely prevented himself from doing what the others were doing, which was some sort of criminal offense.

Not everyone so resists the social contagion of bad behavior. And, therefore, we often get "Serpico Syndrome," named to commemorate the state of a near-totally corrupt New York police division joined by Frank Serpico. He was then nearly murdered by gunfire because of his resistance to going along with the corruption in the division. Such corruption was being driven by social proof plus incentives, the combination that creates Serpico Syndrome. The Serpico story should be taught more than it now is because the didactic power of its horror is aimed at a very important evil, driven substantially by a very important force: social proof.

In social proof, it is not only action by others that misleads but also their inaction. In the presence of doubt, inaction by others becomes social proof that inaction is the right course. Thus, the inaction of a great many bystanders led to the death of Kitty Genovese in a famous incident much discussed in introductory psychology courses.

In the ambit of social proof, the outside directors on a corporate board usually display the near ultimate form of inaction. They fail to object to anything much short of an axe murder until some public embarrassment of the board finally causes their intervention. A typical board-of-directors' culture was once well described by my friend, Joe Rosenfield, as he said, "They asked me if I wanted to become a director of Northwest Bell, and it was the last thing they ever asked me."

In advertising and sales promotion, Social-Proof Tendency is about as strong a factor as one could imagine. "Monkey-see, monkey-do" is the old phrase that reminds one of how strongly John will often wish to do something, or have something, just because Joe does or has it. One interesting consequence is that an advertiser will pay a lot to have its soup can, instead of someone else's, in a movie scene involving soup consumption only in a peripheral way.

Social-Proof Tendency often interacts in a perverse way with Envy/Jealousy and Deprival-Superreaction Tendency. One such interaction amused my family for years as people recalled the time when my cousin Russ and I, at ages three and four, fought and howled over a single surplus shingle while surrounded by a virtual sea of surplus shingles.

But the adult versions of this occasion, boosted by psychological tendencies preserving ideologies, are not funny and can bring down whole civilizations. The Middle East now presents just such a threat. By now the resources spent by Jews, Arabs and all others over a small amount of disputed land if divided arbitrarily among land claimants, would have made every one better off, even before taking into account any benefit from reduced threat of war, possibly nuclear.

Outside domestic relations it is rare now to try to resolve disputes by techniques including discussion of impacts from psychological tendencies. Considering the implications of childishness that would be raised by such inclusion, and the defects of psychology as now taught, this result may be sound. But, given the nuclear stakes now involved and the many failures in important negotiations lasting decades, I often wonder if some day, in some way, more use of psychological insight will eventually improve outcomes. If so, correct teaching of psychology matters a lot. And, if old psychology professors are even less likely than old physics professors to learn new ways, which seems nearly certain, then we may, as Max Planck predicted, need a new generation of psychology professors who have grown up to think in a different way.

If only one lesson is to be chosen from a package of lessons involving Social-Proof Tendency, and used in self improvement, my favorite would be: Learn how to ignore the examples from others when they are wrong, because few skills are more worth having.

Sixteen:
Contrast-Misreaction Tendency

Because the nervous system of man does not naturally measure in absolute scientific units, it must instead rely on something simpler. The eyes have a solution that limits their programming needs: the contrast in what is seen is registered. And as in sight, so does it go, largely, in the other senses. Moreover, as perception goes, so goes cognition. The result is man's Contrast-Misreaction Tendency.

Few psychological tendencies do more damage to correct thinking. Small-scale damages involve instances such as man's buying an overpriced $1,000 leather dashboard merely because the price is so low compared to his concurrent purchase of a $65,000 car. Large- scale damages often ruin lives, as when a wonderful woman having terrible parents marries a man who would be judged satisfactory only in comparison to her parents. Or as when a man takes wife number two who would be appraised as all right only in comparison to wife number one.

A particularly reprehensible form of sales practice occurs in the offices of some real estate brokers. A buyer from out of the city, perhaps needing to shift his family there, visits the office with little time available. The salesman deliberately shows the customer three awful houses at ridiculously high prices. Then he shows him a merely bad house at a price only moderately too high. And, boom, the broker often makes an easy sale.

Contrast-Misreaction Tendency is routinely used to cause disadvantage for customers buying merchandise and services. To make an ordinary price seem low, the vendor will very frequently create a highly artificial price that is much higher than the price always sought, then advertise his standard price as a big reduction from his phony price. Even when people know that this sort of customer manipulation is being attempted, it will often work to trigger buying. This phenomenon accounts in part for much advertising in newspapers. It also demonstrates that being aware of psychological ploys is not a perfect defense.

When a man's steps are consecutively taken toward disaster, with each step being very small, the brain's Contrast-Misreaction Tendency will often let the man go too far toward disaster to be able to avoid it. This happens because each step presents so small a contrast from his present position.

A bridge-playing pal of mine once told me that a frog tossed into very hot water would jump out, but that the same frog would end up dying if placed in room-temperature water that was later heated at a very slow rate. My few shreds of physiological knowledge make me doubt this account. But no matter because many businesses die in just the manner claimed by my friend for the frog. Cognition, misled by tiny changes involving low contrast, will often miss a trend that is destiny.

One of Ben Franklin's best-remembered and most useful aphorisms is "A small leak will sink a great ship." The utility of the aphorism is large precisely because the brain so often misses the functional equivalent of a small leak in a great ship.

Seventeen:
Stress-Influence Tendency

Everyone recognizes that sudden stress, for instance from a threat, will cause a rush of adrenaline in the human body, prompting faster and more extreme reaction. And everyone who has taken Psych 101 knows that stress makes Social-Proof Tendency more powerful.

In a phenomenon less well recognized but still widely known, light stress can slightly improve performance—say, in examinations—whereas heavy stress causes dysfunction.

But few people know more about really heavy stress than that it can cause depression. For instance, most people know that an "acute stress depression" makes thinking dysfunctional because it causes an extreme of pessimism, often extended in length and usually accompanied by activity-stopping fatigue. Fortunately, as most people also know, such a depression is one of mankind's more reversible ailments. Even before modern drugs were available, many people afflicted by depression, such as Winston Churchill and Samuel Johnson, gained great achievement in life.

Most people know very little about nondepressive mental breakdowns influenced by heavy stress. But there is at least one exception, involving the work of Pavlov when he was in his seventies and eighties. Pavlov had won a Nobel Prize early in life by using dogs to work out the physiology of digestion. Then he became world-famous by working out mere-association responses in dogs, initially salivating dogs—so much so that changes in behavior triggered by mere-association, like those caused by much modern advertisement, are today often said to come from "Pavlovian" conditioning.

What happened to cause Pavlov's last work was especially interesting. During the great Leningrad Flood of the 1920s, Pavlov had many dogs in cages.

Their habits had been transformed, by a combination of his "Pavlovian conditioning" plus standard reward responses, into distinct and different patterns. As the waters of the flood came up and receded, many dogs reached a point where they had almost no airspace between their noses and the tops of their cages. This subjected them to maximum stress. Immediately thereafter, Pavlov noticed that many of the dogs were no longer behaving as they had. The dog that formerly had liked his trainer now disliked him, for example. This result reminds one of modern cognition reversals in which a person's love of his parents suddenly becomes hate, as new love has been shifted suddenly to a cult. The unanticipated, extreme changes in Pavlov's dogs would have driven any good experimental scientist into a near-frenzy of curiosity. That was indeed Pavlov's reaction. But not many scientists would have done what Pavlov next did.

And that was to spend the rest of his long life giving stress-induced nervous breakdowns to dogs, after which he would try to reverse the breakdowns, all the while keeping careful experimental records. He found (1) that he could classify dogs so as to predict how easily a particular dog would breakdown; (2) that the dogs hardest to break down were also the hardest to return to their pre-breakdown state; (3) that any dog could be broken down; and (4) that he couldn't reverse a breakdown except by reimposing stress.

Now, practically everyone is revolted by such experimental treatment of man's friend, the dog. Moreover, Pavlov was Russian and did his last work under the Communists. And maybe those facts account for the present extreme, widespread ignorance of Pavlov's last work. The two Freudian psychiatrists with whom I tried many years ago to discuss this work had never heard of it. And the dean of a major medical school actually asked me, several years ago, if any of Pavlov's experiments were "repeatable" in experiments of other researchers. Obviously, Pavlov is now a sort of forgotten hero in medical science.

I first found a description of Pavlov's last work in a popular paperback, written by some Rockefeller-financed psychiatrist, when I was trying to figure out (1) how cults worked their horrible mischief and (2) what should the law say about what parents could do to "deprogram" children who had become brainwashed zombies. Naturally, mainstream law objected to the zombies being physically captured by their parents and next subjected to stress that would help to deprogram the effects of the stress they had endured in cult conversions.

I never wanted to get into the legal controversy that existed about this subject. But I did conclude that the controversy couldn't be handled with maximized rationality without considering whether, as Pavlov's last work suggests, the heavy-handed imposition of stress might be the only reversal method that would work to remedy one of the worst evils imaginable: a stolen mind. I have included this discussion of Pavlov (1) partly out of general antagonism toward taboos, (2) partly to make my talk reasonably complete as it considers stress and (3) partly because I hope some listener may continue my inquiry with more success.

Eighteen:
Availability-Misweighing Tendency

This mental tendency echoes the words of the song: "When I'm not near the girl I love, I love the girl I'm near." Man's imperfect, limited-capacity brain easily drifts into working with what's easily available to it. And the brain can't use what it can't remember or what it is blocked from recognizing because it is heavily influenced by one or more psychological tendencies bearing strongly on it, as the fellow is influenced by the nearby girl in the song. And so the mind overweighs what is easily available and thus displays Availability-Misweighing Tendency.

The main antidote to miscues from Availability-Misweighing Tendency often involve procedures, including use of checklists, which are almost always helpful.

Another antidote is to behave somewhat like Darwin did when he emphasized disconfirming evidence. What should be done is to especially emphasize factors that don't produce reams of easily available numbers, instead of drifting mostly or entirely into considering factors that do produce such numbers. Still another antidote is to find and hire some skeptical, articulate people with far-reaching minds to act as advocates for notions that are opposite to the incumbent notions.

One consequence of this tendency is that extra-vivid evidence, being so memorable and thus more available in cognition, should often consciously be underweighed while less vivid evidence should be overweighed.

Still, the special strength of extra-vivid images in influencing the mind can be constructively used (1) in persuading someone else to reach a correct conclusion or (2) as a device for improving one's own memory by attaching vivid images, one after the other, to many items one doesn't want to forget. Indeed, such use of vivid images as memory boosters is what enabled the great orators of classical Greece and Rome to give such long, organized speeches without using notes.

The great algorithm to remember in dealing with this tendency is simple: An idea or a fact is not worth more merely because it is easily available to you.

Nineteen:
Use-It-or-Lose-It Tendency

All skills attenuate with disuse. I was a whiz at calculus until age twenty, after which the skill was soon obliterated by total nonuse. The right antidote to such a loss is to make use of the functional equivalent of the aircraft simulator employed in pilot training. This allows a pilot to continuously practice all of the rarely used skills that he can't afford to lose.

Throughout his life, a wise man engages in practice of all his useful, rarely used skills, many of them outside his discipline, as a sort of duty to his better self. If he reduces the number of skills he practices and, therefore, the number of skills he retains, he will naturally drift into error from man with a hammer tendency. His learning capacity will also shrink as he creates gaps in the latticework of theory he needs as a framework for understanding new experience. It is also essential for a thinking man to assemble his skills into a checklist that he routinely uses. Any other mode of operation will cause him to miss much that is important.

Skills of a very high order can be maintained only with daily practice. The pianist Paderewski once said that if he failed to practice for a single day, he could notice his performance deterioration and that, after a week's gap in practice, the audience could notice it as well.

The hard rule of Use-It-or-Lose-It Tendency tempers its harshness for the diligent. If a skill is raised to fluency, instead of merely being crammed in briefly to enable one to pass some test, then the skill (1) will be lost more slowly and (2) will come back faster when refreshed with new learning. These are not minor advantages, and a wise man engaged in learning some important skill will not stop until he is really fluent in it.

Twenty:
Drug-Misinfluence Tendency

This tendency's destructive power is so widely known to be intense, with frequent tragic consequences for cognition and the outcome of life, that it needs no discussion here to supplement that previously given under "Simple, Pain-Avoiding Psychological Denial."

Twenty-One:
Senescence-Misinfluence Tendency

With advanced age, there comes a natural cognitive decay, differing among individuals in the earliness of its arrival and the speed of its progression. Practically no one is good at learning complex new skills when very old. But some people remain pretty good in maintaining intensely practiced old skills until late in life, as one can notice in many a bridge tournament.

Old people like me get pretty skilled, without working at it, at disguising age-related deterioration because social convention, like clothing, hides much decline.

Continuous thinking and learning, done with joy, can somewhat help delay what is inevitable.

Twenty-Two:
Authority-Misinfluence Tendency

Living in dominance hierarchies as he does, like all his ancestors before him, man was born mostly to follow leaders, with only a few people doing the leading. And so, human society is formally organized into dominance hierarchies, with their culture augmenting the natural follow-the-leader tendency of man.

But automatic as most human reactions are, with the tendency to follow leaders being no exception, man is often destined to suffer greatly when the leader is wrong or when his leader's ideas don't get through properly in the bustle of life and are misunderstood. And so, we find much miscognition from man's Authority-Misinfluence Tendency.

Some of the misinfluences are amusing, as in a case described by Cialdini. A physician left a written order for a nurse treating an earache, as follows: "Two drops, twice a day, 'r. ear.'" The nurse then directed the patient to turn over and put the eardrops in his anus.

Other versions of confused instructions from authority figures are tragic. In World War II, a new pilot for a general, who sat beside him in the copilot's seat, was so anxious to please his boss that he misinterpreted some minor shift in the general's position as a direction to do some foolish thing. The pilot crashed the plane and became a paraplegic.

Well, naturally, cases like this one get the attention of careful thinkers like Boss Buffett, who always acts like an overquiet mouse around his pilots.

Such cases are also given attention in the simulator training of copilots who have to learn to ignore certain really foolish orders from boss pilots because boss pilots will sometimes err disastrously. Even after going through such a training regime, however, copilots in simulator exercises will too often allow the simulated plane to crash because of some extreme and perfectly obvious simulated error of the chief pilot.

After Corporal Hitler had risen to dominate Germany, leading a bunch of believing Lutherans and Catholics into orgies of genocide and other mass destruction, one clever psychology professor, Stanley Milgram, decided to do an experiment to determine exactly how far authority figures could lead ordinary people into gross misbehavior. In this experiment, a man posing as an authority figure, namely a professor governing a respectable experiment, was able to trick a great many ordinary people into giving what they had every reason to believe were massive electric shocks that inflicted heavy torture on innocent fellow citizens. This experiment did demonstrate a terrible result contributed to by Authority-Misinfluence Tendency, but it also demonstrated extreme ignorance in the psychology professoriate right after World War II.

Almost any intelligent person with my checklist of psychological tendencies in his hand would, by simply going down the checklist, have seen that Milgram's experiment involved about six powerful psychological tendencies acting in confluence to bring about his extreme experimental result. For instance, the person pushing Milgram' s shock lever was given much social proof from presence of inactive bystanders whose silence communicated that his behavior was okay. Yet it took over a thousand psychological papers, published before I got to Milgram, for the professoriate to get his experiment only about ninety percent as well understood as it would have immediately been by any intelligent person who used (1) any sensible organization of psychology along the lines of this talk, plus (2) a checklist procedure. This outcome displaying the dysfunctional thinking of long-dead professors deserves a better explanation. I will later deal with the subject in a very hesitant fashion.

We can be pleased that the psychology professoriate of a former era wasn't quite as dysfunctional as the angler in my next-to-last illustration of Authority-Misinfluence Tendency.

When I once fished in the Rio Colorado in Costa Rica, my guide, in a state of shock, told me a story about an angler who'd earlier come to the river without ever having fished for tarpon. A fishing guide like the one I had runs the boat and gives fishing advice, establishing himself in this context as the ultimate authority figure. In the case of this guide, his native language was Spanish, while the angler's native language was English. The angler got a big tarpon on and began submitting to many directions from this authority figure called a guide: tip up, tip down, reel in, etc. Finally, when it was necessary to put more pressure on the fish by causing more bending of the angler's rod, the guide said in English: "Give him the rod, give him the rod." Well, the angler threw his expensive rod at the fish, and when last seen, it was going down the Rio Colorado toward the ocean. This example shows how powerful is the tendency to go along with an authority figure and how it can turn one's brain into mush.

My final example comes from business. A psychology Ph. D. once became a CEO of a major company and went wild, creating an expensive new headquarters, with a great wine cellar, at an isolated site. At some point, his underlings remonstrated that money was running short. "Take the money out of the depreciation reserves," said the CEO. Not too easy because a depreciation reserve is a liability account.

So strong is undue respect for authority that this CEO, and many even worse examples, have actually been allowed to remain in control of important business institutions for long periods after it was clear they should be removed. The obvious implication: Be careful whom you appoint to power because a dominant authority figure will often be hard to remove, aided as he will be by Authority-Misinfluence Tendency.

Twenty-Three:
Twaddle Tendency

Man, as a social animal who has the gift of language, is born to prattle and to pour out twaddle that does much damage when serious work is being attempted. Some people produce copious amounts of twaddle and others very little.

A trouble from the honeybee version of twaddle was once demonstrated in an interesting experiment. A honeybee normally goes out and finds nectar and then comes back and does a dance that communicates to the other bees where the nectar is. The other bees then go out and get it. Well some scientist—clever, like B. F. Skinner—decided to see how well a honeybee would do with a handicap. He put the nectar straight up. Way up. Well, in a natural setting, there is no nectar a long way straight up, and the poor honeybee doesn't have a genetic program that is adequate to handle what she now has to communicate. You might guess that this honeybee would come back to the hive and slink into a corner, but she doesn't. She comes into the hive and does an incoherent dance. Well, all my life I've been dealing with the human equivalent of that honeybee. And it's a very important part of wise administration to keep prattling people, pouring out twaddle, far away from the serious work. A rightly famous Caltech engineering professor, exhibiting more insight than tact, once expressed his version of this idea as follows: "The principal job of an academic administration is to keep the people who don't matter from interfering with the work of the people that do." I include this quotation partly because I long suffered from backlash caused by my version of this professor's conversational manner. After much effort, I was able to improve only slightly, so one of my reasons for supplying the quotation is my hope that, at least in comparison, I will appear tactful.

Twenty-Four:
Reason-Respecting Tendency

There is in man, particularly one in an advanced culture, a natural love of accurate cognition and a joy in its exercise. This accounts for the widespread popularity of crossword puzzles, other puzzles, and bridge and chess columns, as well as all games requiring mental skill.

This tendency has an obvious implication. It makes man especially prone to learn well when a would-be teacher gives correct reasons for what is taught, instead of simply laying out the desired belief ex cathedra with no reasons given. Few practices, therefore, are wiser than not only thinking through reasons before giving orders but also communicating these reasons to the recipient of the order.

No one knew this better than Carl Braun, who designed oil refineries with spectacular skill and integrity. He had a very simple rule, one of many in his large, Teutonic company: You had to tell Who was to do What, Where, When, and Why. And if you wrote a communication leaving out your explanation of why the addressee was to do what was ordered, Braun was likely to fire you because Braun well knew that ideas got through best when reasons for the ideas were meticulously laid out.

In general, learning is most easily assimilated and used when, life long, people consistently hang their experience, actual and vicarious, on a latticework of theory answering the question: Why? Indeed, the question "Why?" is a sort of Rosetta stone opening up the major potentiality of mental life.

Unfortunately, Reason-Respecting Tendency is so strong that even a person's giving of meaningless or incorrect reasons will increase compliance with his orders and requests. This has been demonstrated in psychology experiments wherein "compliance practitioners" successfully jump to the head of the lines in front of copying machines by explaining their reason: "I have to make some copies." This sort of unfortunate byproduct of Reason-Respecting Tendency is a conditioned reflex, based on a widespread appreciation of the importance of reasons. And, naturally, the practice of laying out various claptrap reasons is much used by commercial and cult "compliance practitioners" to help them get what they don't deserve.

Twenty-Five:

Lollapalooza Tendency—The Tendency to Get Extreme Consequences from Confluences of Psychological Tendencies Acting in Favor of a Particular Outcome

This tendency was not in any of the psychology texts I once examined, at least in any coherent fashion, yet it dominates life. It accounts for the extreme result in the Milgram experiment and the extreme success of some cults that have stumbled through practice evolution into bringing pressure from many psychological tendencies to bear at the same time on conversion targets. The targets vary in susceptibility, like the dogs Pavlov worked with in his old age, but some of the minds that are targeted simply snap into zombiedom under cult pressure. Indeed, that is one cult's name for the conversion phenomenon: snapping.

What are we to make of the extreme ignorance of the psychology textbook writers of yesteryear? How could anyone who had taken a freshman course in physics or chemistry not be driven to consider, above all, how psychological tendencies combine and with what effects? Why would anyone think his study of psychology was adequate without his having endured the complexity involved in dealing with intertwined psychological tendencies? What could be more ironic than professors using oversimplified notions while studying bad cognitive effects grounded in the mind's tendency to use oversimplified algorithms?

I will make a few tentative suggestions. Maybe many of the long-dead professors wanted to create a whole science from one narrow type of repeatable psychology experiment that was conductible in a university setting and that aimed at one psychological tendency at a time. If so, these early psychology professors made a massive error in so restricting their approach to their subject. It would be like physics ignoring (1) astrophysics because it couldn't happen in a physics lab, plus (2) all compound effects. What psychological tendencies could account for early psychology professors adopting an over-restricted approach to their own subject matter? One candidate would be Availability-Misweighing Tendency grounded in a preference for easy-to-control data. And then the restrictions would eventually create an extreme case of man with a hammer tendency. Another candidate might be envy/jealousy Tendency through which early psychology professors displayed some weird form of envy of a physics that was misunderstood. And this possibility tends to demonstrate that leaving envy/jealousy out of academic psychology was never a good idea.

I now quitclaim all these historical mysteries to my betters.

Well, that ends my brief description of psychological tendencies.

Questions and Answers:

Now, as promised, I will ask and answer a few general questions.

My first is a compound question: Isn't this list of psychological tendencies tautological to some extent compared to the system of Euclid? That is, aren't there overlaps in the tendencies? And couldn't the system be laid out just as plausibly in a somewhat different way? The answers are yes, yes, and yes, but this matters only moderately. Further refinement of these tendencies, while desirable, has a limited practical potential because a significant amount of messiness is unfixable in a soft science like psychology.

My second question is: Can you supply a real-world model, instead of a Milgram-type controlled psychology experiment, that uses your system to illustrate multiple psychological tendencies interacting in a plausibly diagnosable way? The answer is yes. One of my favorite cases involves the McDonnell Douglas airliner evacuation test. Before a new airliner can be sold, the government requires that it pass an evacuation test, during which a full load of passengers must get out in some short period of time. The government directs that the test be realistic. So you can't pass by evacuating only twenty-year-old athletes. So McDonnell Douglas scheduled such a test in a darkened hangar using a lot of old people as evacuees. The passenger cabin was, say, twenty feet above the concrete floor of the hangar and was to be evacuated through moderately flimsy rubber chutes. The first test was made in the morning. There were about twenty very serious injuries, and the evacuation took so long it flunked the time test. So what did McDonnell Douglas next do? It repeated the test in the afternoon, and this time there was another failure, with about twenty more serious injuries, including one case of permanent paralysis.

What psychological tendencies contributed to this terrible result? Well, using my tendency list as a checklist, I come up with the following explanation. Reward-Superresponse Tendency drove McDonnell Douglas to act fast. It couldn't sell its airliner until it passed the test. Also pushing the company was Doubt-Avoidance Tendency with its natural drive to arrive at a decision and run with it. Then the government's direction that the test be realistic drove Authority-Misinfluence Tendency into the mischief of causing McDonnell Douglas to overreact by using what was obviously too dangerous a test method. By now the course of action had been decided, so Inconsistency-Avoidance Tendency helped preserve the near-idiotic plan. When all the old people got to the dark hangar, with its high airline cabin and concrete floor, the situation must have made McDonnell Douglas employees very queasy, but they saw other employees and supervisors not objecting. Social-Proof Tendency, therefore, swamped the queasiness. And this allowed continued action as planned, a continuation that was aided by more Authority-Misinfluence Tendency. Then came the disaster of the morning test with its failure, plus serious injuries. McDonnell Douglas ignored the strong disconfirming evidence from the failure of the first test because confirmation bias, aided by the triggering of strong Deprival-Superreaction Tendency, favored maintaining the original plan. McDonnell Douglas' Deprival-Superreaction Tendency was now like that which causes a gambler, bent on getting even after a huge loss, to make his final big bet. After all, McDonnell Douglas was going to lose a lot if it didn't pass its test as scheduled. More psychology-based explanation can probably be made, but the foregoing discussion is complete enough to demonstrate the utility of my system when used in a checklist mode.

My third question is also compound: In the practical world, what good is the thought system laid out in this list of tendencies? Isn't practical benefit prevented because these psychological tendencies are so thoroughly programmed into the human mind by broad evolution [the combination of genetic and cultural evolution] that we can't get rid of them? Well, the answer is that the tendencies are probably much more good than bad. Otherwise, they wouldn't be there, working pretty well for man, given his condition and his limited brain capacity. So the tendencies can't be simply washed out automatically, and shouldn't be. Nevertheless, the psychological thought system described, when properly understood and used, enables the spread of wisdom and good conduct and facilitates the avoidance of disaster. Tendency is not always destiny, and knowing the tendencies and their antidotes can often help prevent trouble that would otherwise occur. Here is a short list of examples reminding us of the great utility of elementary psychological knowledge:

One: Carl Braun's communication practices.

Two: The use of simulators in pilot training.

Three: The system of Alcoholics Anonymous.

Four: Clinical training methods in medical schools.

Five: The rules of the U.S. Constitutional Convention: totally secret meetings, no recorded vote by name until the final vote, votes reversible at any time before the end of the convention, then just one vote on the whole Constitution. These are very clever psychology-respecting rules. If the founders had used a different procedure, many people would have been pushed by various psychological tendencies into inconsistent, hardened positions. The elite founders got our Constitution through by a whisker only because they were psychologically acute.

Six: The use of Granny's incentive-driven rule to manipulate oneself toward better performance of one's duties.

Seven: The Harvard Business School's emphasis on decision trees. When I was young and foolish I used to laugh at the Harvard Business School. I said, "They're teaching twenty-eight-year-old people that high school algebra works in real life?" But later, I wised up and realized that it was very important that they do that to counter some bad effects from psychological tendencies. Better late than never.

Eight: The use of autopsy equivalents at Johnson & Johnson. At most corporations, if you make an acquisition and it turns out to be a disaster, all the people, paperwork, and presentations that caused the foolish acquisition are quickly forgotten. Nobody wants to be associated with the poor outcome by mentioning it. But at Johnson & Johnson, the rules make everybody revisit old acquisitions, comparing predictions with outcomes. That is a very smart thing to do.

Nine: The great example of Charles Darwin as he avoided confirmation bias, which has morphed into the extreme anti-confirmation-bias method of the "double blind" studies wisely required in drug research by the F.D.A.

Ten: The Warren Buffett rule for open-outcry auctions: Don't go.

My fourth question is: What special knowledge problems lie buried in the thought system demonstrated by your list?

Well, one answer is paradox. In social psychology, the more people learn about the system the less it is true, and this is what gives the system its great value as a preventer of bad outcomes and a driver of good outcomes. This result is paradoxical, and doesn't remind one of elementary physics, but so what. One can't get all the paradox out of pure math, so why should psychology be shocked by some paradox?

There is also some paradox in cognition change that works even when the manipulated person knows he is being manipulated. This creates a sort of paradox in a paradox, but, again, so what. I once much enjoyed an occasion of this sort. I drew this beautiful woman as my dinner partner many years ago. I'd never seen her before. She was married to a prominent Los Angeles man. She sat down next to me, turned her beautiful face up, and said, "Charlie, what one word accounts for your remarkable success in life?" I knew I was being manipulated by a practiced routine, and I just loved it. I never see this woman without a little lift in my spirits. And, by the way, I told her I was rational. You'll have to judge yourself whether that's true. I may be demonstrating some psychological tendency I hadn't planned on demonstrating.

My fifth question is: Don't we need more reconciliation of psychology and economics? My answer is yes, and I suspect that some slight progress is being made. I have heard of one such example. Colin Camerer of Caltech, who works in "experimental economics," devised an interesting experiment in which he caused high I.Q. students, playing for real money, to pay price A+B for a "security" they knew would turn into A dollars at the end of the day. This foolish action occurred because the students were allowed to trade with each other in a liquid market for the security. And some students then paid price A+B because they hoped to unload on other students at a higher price before the day was over. What I will now confidently predict is that, despite Camerer's experimental outcome, most economics and corporate finance professors who still believe in the "hard-form efficient market hypothesis" will retain their original belief. If so, this will be one more indication of how irrational smart people can be when influenced by psychological tendencies.

My sixth question is: Don't moral and prudential problems come with knowledge of these psychological tendencies? The answer is yes. For instance, psychological knowledge improves persuasive power and, like other power, it can be used for good or ill. Captain Cook once played a psychology-based trick on his seamen to cause them to eat sauerkraut and avoid scurvy. In my opinion, this action was both ethical and wise under the circumstances, despite the deliberate manipulation involved. But ordinarily, when you try to use your knowledge of psychological tendencies in the artful manipulation of someone whose trust you need, you will be making both a moral and prudential error.

The moral error is obvious. The prudential error comes because many intelligent people, targeted for conscious manipulation, are likely to figure out what you are trying to do and resent your action.

My final question is: Aren't there factual and reasoning errors in this talk? The answer is yes, almost surely yes. The final revision was made from memory over about fifty hours by a man eighty-one years old, who never took a course in psychology and has read none of it, except one book on developmental psychology, for nearly fifteen years. Even so, I think the totality of my talk will stand up very well, and I hope all my descendants and friends will carefully consider what I have said. I even hope that more psychology professors will join me in: (1) making heavy use of inversion; (2) driving for a complete description of the psychological system so that it works better as a checklist; and (3) especially emphasizing effects from combinations of psychological tendencies.

Well that ends my talk. If in considering what I have said you had ten percent the fun I had saying it, you were lucky recipients.

"Peter, you and Warren sucked me into rewriting this thing, and it's taken over my life." (February 2005)

Talk Ten Revisited

In this Talk Ten, made in 2000, I gave favorable mention to Judith Rich Harris' strong-selling book *The Nurture Assumption*. You will recall that this work demonstrated that peer pressure on the young is far more important, and parental nurture is much less important, than had been commonly recognized. The success of the book, with its vast practical implications, has an interesting story behind it: Long before the book was published, Ms. Harris, now 67, was kicked out of Harvard's Ph. D. program in psychology because Harvard believed that she lacked qualities ideal in psychological research. Then, later, out of illness and obscurity, as she was pretty much housebound throughout adult life by unfixable autoimmune disease, she published an academic paper on which her subsequent book was based. And for that paper she won a prestigious medal, named after the man who signed her dismissal notice from Harvard, awarded annually by the American Psychological Association for distinction in published writing.

When I learned from her impressive book that this ironic result had occurred, I wrote to Harvard, my alma mater, urging it to award Ms. Harris, whom I did not know, an honorary Ph. D., or, better yet, a real Ph. D. I cited the example of Oxford. That great university once allowed its best student, Samuel Johnson, to leave without a degree because he was too poor to continue paying tuition. But Oxford later made gracious amends. It gave Johnson a doctorate after he conquered sickness and became famous in a tough climb once described in his own words: "Slow rises worth, by poverty oppressed." I failed utterly in my effort to convince Harvard to imitate Oxford in this way. But Harvard did later recruit from MIT one of the most famous living psychology professors, Steven Pinker, and Pinker is a big admirer of Ms. Harris. From this step, we can see one reason why its liberal arts division is more highly regarded than most others. The division's extreme depth often allows partial correction of bonehead errors that would flourish unopposed elsewhere.

Judith Rich Harris
(b. 1938)

Judith Rich Harris is an independent investigator and author. Her significant professional accomplishments include a mathematical model of visual speech, textbooks in developmental psychology, and many influential professional articles. She is best known for *The Nurture Assumption* (1998) and *No Two Alike* (2006). Ms. Harris lives with her husband in New Jersey.

In 2006, Ms. Harris, struggling further through her unfixable illness, has published another book, *No Two Alike.* The title is apt because one central question the author assaults is why identical twins turn out to be so different in important aspects of personality. Her dogged curiosity and rigor in dealing with this question remind me of both Darwin and Sherlock Holmes. And her solution is very plausible as she collects and explains data from professional literature, including an interesting case wherein one of two identical twins became a success in business and family life while the other twin went to Skid Row. I won't here disclose Ms. Harris' desirably generalized answer to her central question, because it would be better for *Almanack* readers to first guess the answer, then read her book. If Ms. Harris is roughly right, which seems very likely to me, she has twice, from a very handicapped position, produced academic insights of great practical importance in child rearing, education and much else.

How could this rare and desirable result happen? Well, by Ms. Harris' own account, she was "impertinent and skeptical, even as a child," and these qualities, plus patient, determined skill, have obviously served her truth-seeking well, all the way through to age 67. No doubt, she was also assisted by her enthusiasm in destroying her own ideas, as she now demonstrates by apologizing for her former work as a textbook writer who repeated wrong notions, now outgrown.

In Talk Ten I displayed some impertinency of my own by delivering an extreme-sounding message. It claims nothing less than (1) that academic psychology is hugely important; (2) that, even so, it is usually ill thought out and ill presented by its Ph. D. denizens; and (3) that my way of presenting psychology often has a large superiority in practical utility, compared to most textbooks. Naturally, I believe these extreme claims are correct. After all, I assembled the material contained in Talk Ten to help me succeed in practical thinking and not to gain advantage by making public any would-be-clever notions.

If I am even partly right, the world will eventually see more psychology in roughly the form of Talk Ten. If so, I confidently predict that the change in practice will improve general competency.

"And with that, I have nothing more to add."

Charles T. Munger

March 7, 2006

Charlie Munger's Recommended Books

"In my whole life, I have known no wise people (over a broad subject matter area) who didn't read all the time—none, zero. You'd be amazed at how much Warren reads—and at how much I read. My children laugh at me. They think I'm a book with a couple of legs sticking out."

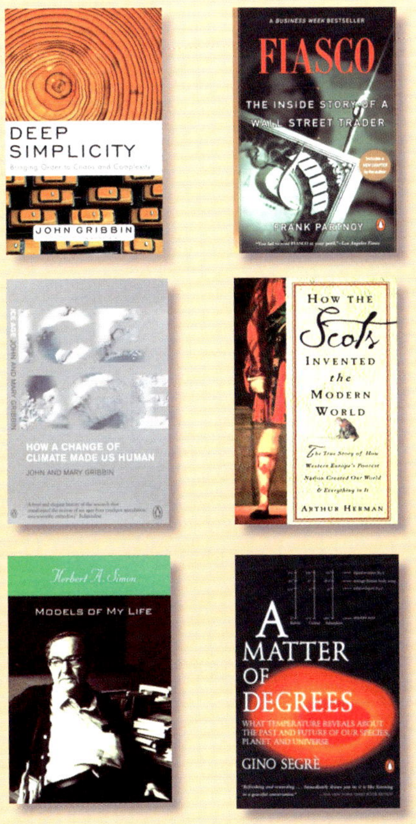

- *Deep Simplicity: Bringing Order to Chaos and Complexity*
  John Gribbin, Random House (2005)
- *F.I.A.S.C.O.: The Inside Story of a Wall Street Trader*
  Frank Partnoy, Penguin Books (1999)
- *Ice Age*
  John & Mary Gribbin, Barnes & Noble (2002)
- *How the Scots Invented the Modern World: The True Story of How Western Europe's Poorest Nation Created Our World & Everything in It*
  Arthur Herman, Three Rivers Press (2002)
- *Models of My Life*
  Herbert A. Simon, The MIT Press (1996)
- *A Matter of Degrees: What Temperature Reveals About the Past and Future of Our Species, Planet, and Universe*
  Gino Segre, Viking Books (2002)

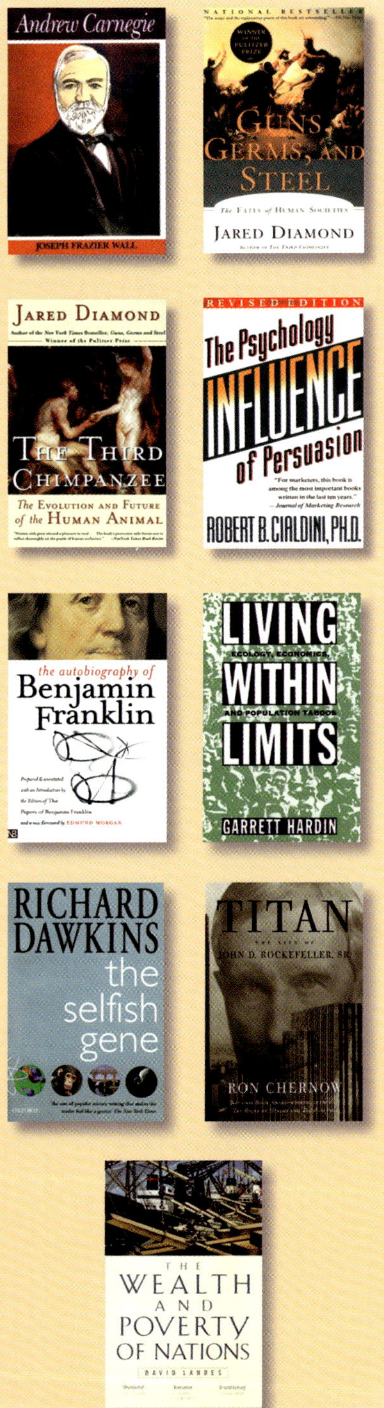

- *Andrew Carnegie*
  Joseph Frazier Wall,
  Oxford University Press
  (1970)
- ***Guns, Germs, and Steel: The Fates of Human Societies***
  Jared M. Diamond, W. W. Norton & Company
  (1999)
- ***The Third Chimpanzee: The Evolution and Future of the Human Animal***
  Jared M. Diamond, Perennial (1992)
- ***Influence: The Psychology of Persuasion***
  Robert B. Cialdini, Perennial Currents (1998)
- ***The Autobiography of Benjamin Franklin***
  Benjamin Franklin, Yale Nota Bene (2003)
- ***Living Within Limits: Ecology, Economics, and Population Taboos***
  Garrett Hardin, Oxford University Press (1995)
- ***The Selfish Gene***
  Richard Dawkins, Oxford University Press (1990)
- ***Titan: The Life of John D. Rockefeller, Sr.***
  Ron Chernow, Vintage (2004)
- ***The Wealth and Poverty of Nations: Why Some Are So Rich and Some So Poor***
  David S. Landes, W. W. Norton & Company (1998)

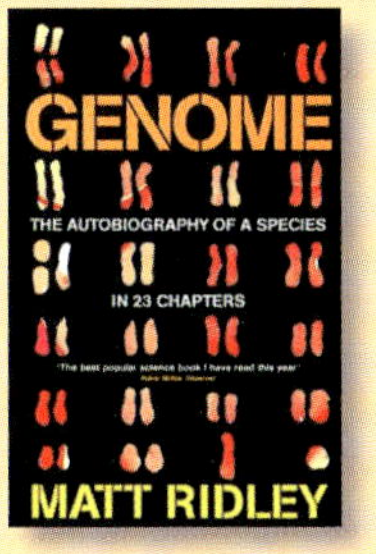

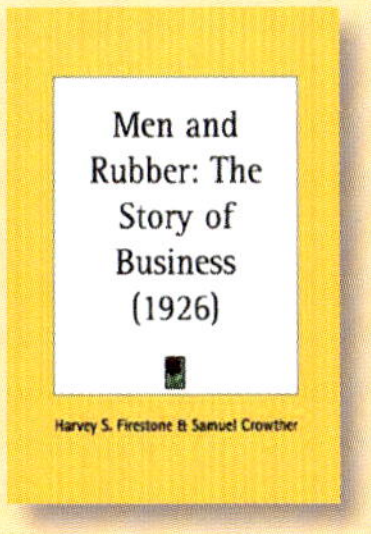

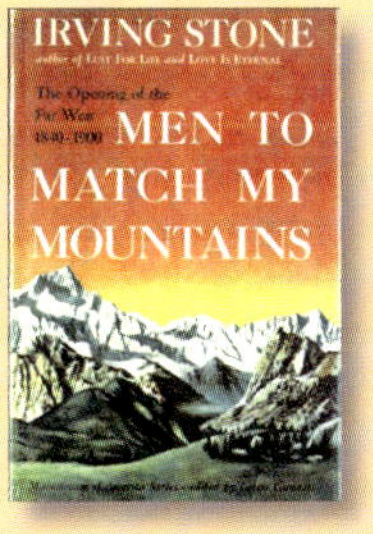

- *The Warren Buffett Portfolio:*
  Mastering the Power of the Focus Investment Strategy
  Robert G. Hagstrom, Wiley (2000)
- *Genome:*
  The Autobiography of a Species in 23 Chapters
  Matt Ridley, HarperCollins Publishers (2000)
- *Getting to Yes:*
  Negotiating Agreement Without Giving In
  Roger Fisher, William Ury, and Bruce Patton, Penguin Books (1991)
- *Three Scientists and Their Gods:*
  Looking for Meaning in an Age of Information
  Robert Wright, HarperCollins Publishers (1989)
- *Only the Paranoid Survive*
  Andy Grove, Currency (1996)

And a few from your editor...

- *Les Schwab:*
  Pride in Performance
  Les Schwab, Pacific Northwest Books (1986)
- *Men and Rubber:*
  The Story of Business
  Harvey S. Firestone, Kessinger Publishing (2003)
- *Men to Match My Mountains:*
  The Opening of the Far West, 1840–1900
  Irving Stone, Book Sales (2001)

Articles, Editorials, and Opinion Pieces

Los Angeles Times Sun., Oct. 1, 1978 Part VI 3

If Standard Oil Is Trying to Be Greedy, It's Doing a Poor Job of It

BY CHARLES T. MUNGER

A Tribute to the Good Gray Engineers

I am increasingly baffled by the current wave of criticism of the Standard Oil Company of California (and other "Big Oil" companies). Faultfinders accuse them of greed, of antisocial conduct, and of huge profits.

I keep track of the fortunes of Standard Oil because some years ago my mother gave my wife $300 as a wedding gift. My wife invested the money in Standard's common stock. As a result, I have become a regular reader of Standard's annual reports, although my reading has never prompted me to purchase more Standard shares. There is a reason for my reticence.

If Standard Oil is trying to be a greedy oligopolist, it is certainly doing a poor job of it. Since the end of 1965, the market price per present share has increased about 22%. Meanwhile, inflation has increased consumer prices by about 102%. Dividends have increased, to be sure, from $1.03 per share in 1965 to an expected $2.55 per share in 1978. But although this dividend increase has exceeded the inflation rate by about one percentage point per year, it is considerably less than the average wage increase during the same period.

Charles T. Munger, a Los Angeles attorney, is the chairman of the board of Blue Chip Stamps.

A Standard Oil shareholder who purchased at the end of 1965, and paid income taxes of 40% on dividends received since then has actually lost purchasing power. The combined effect of inflation and income taxes on the overall investment return (considering both capital value and income) has produced a negative real return. There has been an average overall 2% loss per year in the purchasing power of the 1965 dollars committed.

That in itself is discouraging, but what kept me from adding to my wife's small stake over the years was Standard's poor earnings from the only assets I considered to be safely located—those in the United States.

In the five years between 1968 and 1972, before the foreign countries of the OPEC oil cartel increased the price of oil by more than 400%, Standard's annual return on net assets located in the United States was very low. Even in 1973 its $184 million in reported U.S. earnings amounted to a return of only about 6% per year on net U.S. assets. The substandard return from U.S. assets was compensated by far-above-average earnings abroad. By 1973, Standard, controlling oceans of cheap oil in Saudi Arabia and elsewhere, was earning $529 million, or well over 30% per year, on the $1.6 billion invested in the eastern hemisphere. The combination of very high foreign earnings and very low U.S. earnings made the average return on worldwide net assets approximately 10% per year between 1968 and 1972—a substandard overall return for a healthy corporation.

But this situation changed in Standard's favor after 1972 when OPEC, the oil cartel, made dramatic price increases. As a result, owners of oil located in the United States made higher profits. At the same time, Standard was forced to sell major parts of its foreign assets at low prices to host governments. In 1977, Standard earned about 10% on its net U.S. assets, while foreign earnings, although they had declined greatly in relative significance, still produced a high return of about 19% on net foreign assets. Average return on worldwide net assets was about 14%, compared to only 10% in the 1968-72 period.

Should I as a consumer be annoyed because Standard Oil's profits are now a little higher? Or because it now earns 10% on net U.S. assets instead of the lower return it used to earn?

I think not. Too often, because its subnormal U.S. earnings have been masked by its high profits from the production and sale of huge amounts of cheap Arabian oil, Standard has been criticized as a profiteer. Once the company did earn extraordinary—but now decreasing—returns from foreign investment. Risky pioneering oil exploration projects undertaken by Standard Oil eventually led to the discovery of large amounts of oil in the Middle East. Since this oil is cheap to produce, Standard realized large earnings, mostly from foreigners.

My whole acquaintance with Standard Oil, though casual, irregular and remote, has left me with a favorable impression of the company—at least compared to other large institutions I have dealt with. Standard's products have never given me any trouble. As a customer at its wholly owned gas stations, when I have negotiated transactions I have been dealt with promptly and fairly. In my 30 years in California, Standard has not irritated me by causing major scandals. When I dealt with Standard a few times as a young lawyer representing other interests, I found it ponderous and bureaucratic (as it probably had to be to maintain internal control and avoid scandals at its size) but the soul of honor and essentially rational on all points.

Over the decades I have observed Standard's personnel policies. I found it to be a paternalistic meritocracy—promoting its workers based on ability, and separating them only occasionally and then with financial compassion.

My wife regularly receives proxy statements from Standard Oil—position papers written by management to solicit shareholder's votes. The statements indicate that the board of directors feel a high degree of responsibility to shareholders, ordinary employes and consumers. Executive pay and perquisites are quite modest compared to those in other companies of similar size.

So far as I can observe, Standard is dominated by engineering executives, and its engineering record is excellent—precisely what I as a citizen desire from the controller of necessary but complex and dangerous assets like gas wells, refineries, pipelines and tankers.

For all these reasons, I don't begrudge Standard its recent 10% annual return on U.S. assets.

The oil business has always been an intensive user of capital; nevertheless, its capital needs will soon increase substantially. Our future energy requirements, particularly in the face of domestic-reserve exhaustion, will demand extensive research and development programs. And investments made in these areas are wise ones.

Consumers stand to suffer more if corporations limit reinvestment in energy development than they would from minor gasoline price increases. I, personally, advocate the higher prices and Standard's higher earnings because I believe that they lead to higher reinvestment and subsequent consumer benefits. There is definitely such a thing as a pro-consumer price increase, when the supplier's long-term vitality is required to support the consumer's long-term vitality. And, as demonstrated by the history of my wife's investment, consumers as yet need not worry that they are causing any unfair bonanza for Standard Oil shareholders.

As a businessman, I have learned (and have some assets and scars to prove it) that what is working well, if nourished and supported, can usually meet additional demands. Conversely, what is working poorly is usually either uncorrectable or 10 times harder to correct than you might think.

My business experience makes me react with horror from proposals by politicians to break up Standard Oil and its counterparts in "Big Oil," or turn many of their functions over to the government. I think we should reserve our tinkering for those institutions which are plainly deteriorating. I, for one, am quite satisfied with the work of the good grey engineers at the Standard Oil Company of California.

Sunday World-Herald OMAHA, NEBRASKA AUGUST 10, 1986
SECTION M, 8 PAGES

Buffett's Right-Hand Man . . .

Charlie Munger Thinks Like Berkshire's Chairman

By Robert Dorr
World-Herald Staff Writer

Los Angeles — Warren Buffett's closest business associate says he and Buffett think so much alike that they usually agree instinctively on whether to go ahead with a major investment.

Decisions involving many millions of dollars sometimes are reached in minutes, said Charles T. Munger, vice-chairman of Omaha-based Berkshire Hathaway Inc.

The tendency to think alike isn't always a plus, he said. "If a mistake goes through one filter, it is likely to go through both."

During an interview in the modest downtown office where he works as Buffett's right-hand man, Munger talked about his longtime association with the Omahan who heads Berkshire Hathaway and is regarded as one of the nation's top investors.

Munger

Buffett

Munger, who grew up in Omaha, worked as a youth at the former Buffett and Son grocery store at 5015 Underwood Ave. operated by Warren Buffett's grandfather and uncle.

But Munger, now 62, didn't meet Buffett until the two were adults. By then, Munger had graduated magna cum laude from Harvard Law School and had started a Los Angeles law practice.

Mutual friends arranged a meeting during a visit by Munger to Omaha in 1959, three years after Buffett began the investment partnership that he operated through the 1960s.

Sun Porch

Buffett and Munger, who had investment interests of his own, had dinner at Johnny's Cafe and talked about securities and the investment process.

Munger said he was amused when Buffett described how he ran his investment business "from the sun porch at his house" with the help of a part-time bookkeeper.

He was quickly impressed "with the way his head worked," Munger said of Buffett. "We hit it off from the very beginning."

In a separate interview in Omaha, Buffett said he first heard Munger's name during a 1957 conversation with an Omaha couple who became early investors in his partnership.

The investors were Dr. and Mrs. Edwin Davis, both now dead. Buffett had gone to the Davis home to explain his investment ideas. Dr. Davis asked few questions during Buffett's presentation, but at the end agreed to invest $100,000.

Buffett said he asked Dr. Davis why he had decided so quickly to invest that amount of money. "Because you remind me of Charlie Munger," he replied.

Even today, Buffett's and Munger's voices sound alike, and although Buffett is the younger man at 55, they even resemble each other somewhat in physical appearance.

Two years after Buffett's investment presentation to the Davises, Mrs. Davis arranged for Buffett to meet Munger.

Investment Expert

The two gradually developed a close working relationship. In 1965, at Buffett's urging, Munger quit his law practice and turned to full-time investing.

Munger invested on behalf of family members and former legal clients, as well as with Buffett.

Although he is a lawyer, Munger contributes investment expertise rather than legal expertise to Berkshire Hathaway, Buffett said.

Like Buffett, Munger is a generalist rather than a specialist in one or two types of investments. "Charlie can analyze and evaluate any kind of deal faster and more accurately than any man alive," said Buffett. "He sees any valid weakness in 60 seconds. He's a perfect partner."

The two partners haven't found it necessary to move to the same city. "Warren is happy where he is and I'm happy where I am," Munger said.

They talk by phone about eight times a week on average. When it comes time to close a deal, they get together in the same place.

When one of the two is unavailable, the other has the authority to act, Buffett said. "We know so much about how each other thinks that we may move pretty far along even if the other isn't available."

Their business relationship isn't spelled out in any contract. "It's more like a brother act," Buffett said.

What You Get

Most of the investment ideas are Buffett's, Munger said.

He described Buffett as the same in private or public — open, pleasant and straightforward. No side of his personality is hidden, he said. "What you see is exactly what you get."

Buffett's natural manner "helps enormously" in business, Munger said.

"When you behave that way, people trust you. They ought to teach that in business school."

Munger said he thinks business schools should require students to read the writings of Benjamin Franklin on human behavior before proceeding to technical courses.

Dealings based on mutual admiration produce good business results and few lawsuits, he said. "Think how much better your life would work if you could do that."

There's no doubt that Buffett has fun while working, Munger said.

"I have fun working, too, but he's off the wall," he said. Buffett's term for his office, Munger said, is "the pleasure palace."

The lawyer said he couldn't recall Buffett getting angry. "Even when I took him fishing in Minnesota and upset the boat and we had to swim to shore, he didn't scream at me."

Munger said he enjoys fishing; Buffett does not. They

Please turn to Page 8, Col. 4

Sunday World-Herald

Charlie Munger Thinks Like Buffett

•Continued from Page 1

have a common love of playing bridge.

Munger owned 22,710 shares of Berkshire Hathaway stock as of last March 18, according to information sent to stockholders before this year's annual meeting. Those shares would be worth $63.8 million at Friday's closing bid price of $2,810 a share.

During the interview, Munger said that more than half his assets consist of Berkshire Hathaway stock.

Munger has eight children and stepchildren from 18 to 38 in age. A sister, Mrs. Robert Estabrook, lives in Omaha.

He is a supporter of the Harvard School, a private secondary school in Los Angeles, and is longtime chief financial officer of Planned Parenthood of Los Angeles.

Berkshire Hathaway's growth is "100 percent certain" to slow after last year's spectacular results, Munger said, echoing a view voiced by Buffett.

The diversified company, with holdings in television, newspapers, insurance and furniture retailing, had a gain of $613.6 million, or 48.2 percent, in net worth during 1985.

Buffett has said that if he were to die suddenly, Munger would take the reins of Berkshire Hathaway until a long-term successor could be found.

If Buffett died now, the relationship between Berkshire Hathaway and the companies it partly or fully owns wouldn't change, Munger said.

"People have sold (their businesses) to us expecting to operate in a certain kind of culture, and that would continue."

Reproduced on this page is a copy of the May 30, 1989 letter of resignation of Mutual Savings and Loan Association from the United States League of Savings Institutions.

MUTUAL SAVINGS
AND LOAN ASSOCIATION
315 EAST COLORADO BLVD. • PASADENA, CALIFORNIA 91101-1954

May 30, 1989

United States League of Savings Institutions,
1709 New York Avenue N. W.,
Washington, D. C. 20006

Gentlemen:

This letter is the formal resignation of Mutual Savings and Loan Association from the United States League of Savings Institutions.

Mutual Savings is a subsidiary of Wesco Financial Corporation, listed ASE, and Berkshire Hathaway Inc., listed NYSE, which are no longer willing to be associated with the League.

Mutual Savings does not lightly resign after belonging to the League for many years. But we believe that the League's current lobbying operations are so flawed, indeed disgraceful, that we are not willing to maintain membership.

Our savings and loan industry has now created the largest mess in the history of U. S. financial institutions. While the mess has many causes, which we tried to summarize fairly in our last annual report to stockholders, it was made much worse by (1) constant and successful inhibition over many years, through League lobbying, of proper regulatory response to operations of a minority of insured institutions dominated by crooks and fools, (2) mickey-mouse accounting which made many insured institutions look sounder than they really were, and (3) inadequate levels of real equity capital underlying insured institutions' promises to holders of savings accounts.

It is not unfair to liken the situation now facing Congress to cancer and to liken the League to a significant carcinogenic agent, And, like cancer, our present troubles will recur if Congress lacks the wisdom and courage to excise elements which helped cause the troubles.

Moreover, despite the obvious need for real legislative reform, involving painful readjustment, the League's recent lobbying efforts regularly resist minimal reform. For instance, the League supports (1) extension of accounting conventions allowing "goodwill" (in the financial institutions' context translate "air") to count as capital in relations with regulators and (2) minimization of the amount of real equity capital required as a condition of maintenance of full scale operations relying on federal deposit insurance.

In the face of a national disaster which League lobbying plainly helped cause, the League obdurately persists in prescribing continuation of loose accounting principles, inadequate capital and, in effect, inadequate management at many insured institutions. The League responds to the savings and loan mess as Exxon would have responded to the oil spill from the Valdez if it had insisted thereafter on liberal use of whiskey by tanker captains.

It would be much better if the League followed the wise example, in another era, of the manufacturer which made a public apology to Congress. Because the League has clearly misled its government for a long time, to the taxpayers' great detriment, a public apology is in order, not redoubled efforts to mislead further.

We know that there is a school of thought that trade associations are to be held to no high standard, that they are supposed to act as the League is acting. In this view, each industry creates a trade association not to proffer truth or reason or normal human courtesy following egregious fault, but merely to furnish self-serving nonsense and political contributions to counterbalance, in the legislative milieu, the self-serving nonsense and political contributions of other industries' trade associations. But the evidence is now before us that this type of trade association conduct, when backed as in the League's case by vocal and affluent constituents in every congressional district, has an immense capacity to do harm to the country. Therefore, the League's public duty is to behave in an entirely different way, much as major-league baseball reformed after the "Black Sox" scandal. Moreover, just as client savings institutions are now worse off because of the increased mess caused by League short-sightedness in the past, client institutions will later prove ill-served by present short-sightedness of the League.

Believing this, Mr. Warren E. Buffett and I are not only causing Mutual Savings to resign from the U.S. League of Savings Institutions; we are also, as one small measure of protest, releasing to the media, for such attention as may ensue, copies of this letter of resignation.

Truly yours,

MUTUAL SAVINGS AND LOAN ASSOCIATION

Charles T. Munger

Charles T. Munger
Chairman of the Board

September 1, 2000

The Washington Post

AN INDEPENDENT NEWSPAPER

Charles T. Munger

A Perverse Use of Antitrust Law

As best I can judge from the Microsoft antitrust case, the Justice Department believes the following: that any seller of an ever-evolving, many-featured product—a product that is constantly being improved by adding new features to every new model—will automatically violate antitrust law if: (1) it regularly sells its product at one all-features-included price; (2) it has a dominant market share and (3) the seller plays "catch-up" by adding an obviously essential feature that has the same function as a product first marketed by someone else.

If appellate courts are foolish enough to go along with the trial court ruling in the Microsoft case, virtually every dominant high-tech business in the United States will be forced to retreat from what is standard competitive practice for firms all over the world when they are threatened by better technology first marketed elsewhere.

No other country so ties the hands of its strongest businesses. We can see why by taking a look at America's own history. Consider the Ford Motor Co. When it was the dominant U.S. automaker in 1912, a small firm—a predecessor of General Motors—invented a self-starter that the driver could use from inside the car instead of getting out to crank the engine. What Ford did in response was to add a self-starter of its own to its cars (its "one-price" package)—thus bolstering its dominant business and limiting the inroads of its small competitor. Do we really want that kind of conduct to be illegal?

Or consider Boeing. Assume Boeing is selling 90 percent of U.S. airliners, always on a one-price basis despite the continuous addition of better features to the planes. Do we really want Boeing to stop trying to make its competitive position stronger—as it also helps travelers and improves safety by adding these desirable features—just because some of these features were first marketed by other manufacturers?

The questions posed by the Microsoft case are (1) What constitutes the impermissible and illegal practice of "tying" a separate new product to a dominant old product and (2) what constitutes the permissible and legal practice of improving an existing one-price product that is dominant in the market.

The solution, to avoid ridiculous results and arguments, is easy. We need a simple, improvement-friendly rule that a new feature is always a permissible improvement if there is any plausible argument whatever that product users are in some way better off.

It is the nature of the modern era that the highest standards of living usually come where we find many super-successful corporations that keep their high market shares mostly through a fanatical devotion to improving one-price products.

The Microsoft prosecution threatens our best high-tech businesses.

In recent years, one microeconomic trend has been crucial in helping the United States play catch-up against foreign manufacturers that had developed better and cheaper products: Our manufacturers learned to buy ever-larger, one-price packages of features from fewer and more-trusted suppliers. This essential modern trend is now threatened by the Justice Department.

Microsoft may have some peculiarities of culture that many people don't like, but it could well be that good software is now best developed within such a culture. Microsoft may have been unwise to deny that it paid attention to the competitive effects of its actions. But this is the course legal advisers often recommend in a case such as this one, where motives within individuals at Microsoft were mixed and differed from person to person. A proper antitrust policy should not materially penalize defendants who make the government prove its case. The incumbent rulers of the Justice Department are not fit to hold in trust the guidance of antitrust policy if they allow such considerations of litigation style to govern the development of antitrust law, a serious business with serious consequences outside the case in question.

While I have never owned a share of Microsoft, I have long watched the improvement of its software from two vantage points. First, I am an officer and part owner of Berkshire Hathaway Inc., publisher of the World Book Encyclopedia, a product I much admire because I know how hard it was to create and because I grew up with it and found that it helped me throughout a long life.

But despite our careful stewardship of World Book, the value of its encyclopedia business was grossly and permanently impaired when Microsoft started including a whole encyclopedia, at virtually no addition in price, in its software package. Moreover, I believe Microsoft did this hoping to improve its strong business and knowing it would hurt ours.

Even so, and despite the huge damage to World Book, I believe Microsoft was entitled to improve its software as it did, and that our society gains greatly—despite some damage to some companies—when its strong businesses are able to improve their products enough to stay strong.

Second, I am chairman and part owner of Daily Journal Corp., publisher of many small newspapers much read by lawyers and judges. Long ago, this corporation was in thrall to IBM for its highly computerized operation. Then it was in thrall to DEC for an even more computerized operation. Now it uses, on a virtually 100 percent basis, amazingly cheap Microsoft software in personal computers, in a still more highly computerized operation including Internet access that makes use of Microsoft's browser.

Given this history of vanished once-dominant suppliers to Daily Journal Corp., Microsoft's business position looks precarious to me. Yet, for a while at least, the pervasiveness of Microsoft products in our business and elsewhere helps us—as well as the courts that make use of our publications—in a huge way.

But Microsoft software would be a lousy product for us and the courts if the company were not always improving it by adding features such as Explorer, the Internet browser Microsoft was forced to add to Windows on a catch-up basis if it didn't want to start moving backward instead of forward.

The Justice Department could hardly have come up with a more harmful set of demands than those it now makes. If it wins, our country will end up hobbling its best-performing high-tech businesses. And this will be done in an attempt to get public benefits that no one can rationally predict.

Andy Grove of Intel, a company that not long ago was forced out of a silicon chip business in which it was once dominant, has been widely quoted as describing his business as one in which "only the paranoid survive." If this is so, as seems likely, then Microsoft should get a medal, not an antitrust prosecution, for being so fearful of being left behind and so passionate about improving its products.

The writer is vice chairman of Berkshire Hathaway Inc.

HARVARD-WESTLAKE

LIFE

SPRING 1995

MUNGER SCIENCE CENTER NEARLY COMPLETE

The Munger Science Center, scheduled for occupancy by the beginning of the 1995-96 school year, has been designed to serve Harvard-Westlake's Upper School science classes for the next century or so.

The state-of-the-art facility, nestled below Seaver on the hillside overlooking Coldwater Canyon, includes a dozen customized laboratory-classrooms, a conference room, a computer center and a theater-style lecture hall with each of the 110 seats wired to accommodate laptop

computers. All of the rooms will have the most up-to-date audiovisual technology and the whole building will be computer-networked.

"The problem with most buildings is that they don't build enough flexibility into them. We tried to assure that it will work, and work well, for the better part of a century. I see no reason why it should become obsolete," says trustee Charles T. Munger, who, with his wife, Nancy, has donated over $7 ½ million to date for the new building.

While the old science classrooms in Harvard Hall were not exactly obsolete, having been updated and remodeled periodically over the years, they were over-crowded and the eventual need to replace them had been obvious for more than a decade.

"We were already short of science facilities before the merger, and then when we doubled up on the advanced grades, we had an enormous need. It was basically a no-brainer," Munger says. "It would have been educational malpractice not to have improved the science facilities."

Munger was involved in every aspect of the planning from the onset, but he and Nancy did not initially expect to be quite so generous, pledging ever larger and larger amounts as plans for the facility became more ambitious.

"We sort of drifted into it," he chuckled,

Continued page 8

FAR RIGHT: East side excavation for the Munger Science Center building. The shoring system allowed for vertical excavation adjacent to the existing building. CENTER RIGHT: Perimeter walls and shear walls were formed and filled with concrete to a height of 30 feet. RIGHT: An extended concrete pump was needed to pump concrete up to the second level of the building. BELOW: Steel members formed a nine-sided polygon. A court below will separate the north and south sections of the building with an elevator from the lower level to the roof level of the south wing leading to the bridge and Seaver Building.

leaning back in his chair in the downtown Los Angeles law offices of Munger, Tolles & Olson, where he no longer practices law, but oversees widespread business and investment interests.

"It is the largest donation that Nancy and I have ever made."

Munger is particularly proud of the participation of the science faculty into the design.

"There is nothing in this building that hasn't been fussed over," he says. "I doubt if any secondary school has ever had more input from the people who are going to do the teaching. They have been intimately involved in the planning."

Munger believes the best buildings result from a collaboration between a great architect and an intelligent owner, and says that Headmaster Thomas C. Hudnut, Director of Financial Affairs Rob Levin and Construction Manager Frank Hedge functioned on behalf of the school as "excellent owners."

"We were also fortunate to have the architect, Ki Suh Park, and the builder, Kurt Franzen, both as school parents," he notes.

In the early planning stages, Upper School Science Chair John Feulner was dispatched to inspect science facilities at public and private secondary schools and colleges across the country. He, Levin and Hedge visited far-flung schools from the state of Washington to New Jersey, but Feulner says they were disappointed by much of what they saw.

"We were seeing a lot of repetition, and the decision was made to stop looking and design our own," Feulner said. "We learned more about the process and what mistakes others had made than discovered anything to copy. Harvard-Westlake has always been a leader, so we decided just to take the best of what we'd seen and incorporate that and use the expertise of our own faculty."

Once the site was chosen, the architect worked with the various ideas to fit them into the available space.

"It is a very difficult construction, on a tight hillside site, and we had to build right in the middle

Charles T. Munger

of a school year," Munger points out. "We had to make some changes during the course of construction, the road access had to be changed."

In the new building, Feulner says, "We will have almost tripled our usable space over what we have now. The laboratory-classroom combos, without counting preparation area, will be 1,700 square feet. Many people's houses aren't that big. The preparation area will be the length of the building and all chemistry labs will open into the same prep space. The same thing goes for all the sub disciplines."

There will be twelve laboratory-classrooms, four more than in Harvard Hall, with four specially equipped for biology, four for chemistry, two for physics and two multidisciplinary labs.

Feulner points out that in Harvard Hall, there is one fume hood. The Munger Science Center will have two double-side fume hoods per chemistry lab.

"Some schools have none," he observed.

The student work areas have been expanded, which is desirable both for efficiency and safety, and every classroom will have a full audiovisual and computer system.

Teachers' desks have been custom designed in an L shape, providing room for each teacher to work with two students. In the fully equipped computer resource center, there will be 29 computers, up from 12 in Harvard Hall.

One laboratory will have reinforced beams to hang 1,000-pound weights for mechanics demonstrations, which Feulner says "is really cool."

Teachers were consulted on such details as where to put the electrical outlets and what kinds of tables they wanted. Different benches were designed for biology than for chemistry and physics.

"We tried to build in flexibility for the future, and I can't say enough positive things about Kurt Franzen. He tried to give us what we wanted and we had absolutely marvelous cooperation from everyone," Feulner says.

"They basically left us alone to design in our way, unlike other schools I saw where the teachers had little to say about what they needed. There were no limitations or constraints. The consideration was always what was right for our needs. On behalf of the science department, we are thrilled."

"We are thrilled to have a donor who wants the best of its kind," Feulner says. "He always pushed to make it right."

He said Munger left the planning of the science facilities to the teachers, but was vehement about first-rate ventilation and heating, and that the building far exceed current earthquake standards.

"We're a school built where there are earthquakes," Munger says. "It is the right way to behave."

Munger himself is a product of public schools in Omaha, Nebraska, where he was born on January 1, 1924. From Omaha Central, he enrolled at the University of Michigan, but dropped out after a year and a half to join the Army Air Force, in January 1943. While in the military, he attended the University of New Mexico and the California Institute of Technology, graduating as a Second Lieutenant, Meteorologist, in June 1944. After his discharge, he earned a law degree *magna cum laude* from Harvard Law School.

He practiced law at Musick, Peeler & Garrett in Los Angeles, where he was a partner until leaving in 1962 to help establish Munger, Tolles, Hills & Rickershauser, now known as Munger, Tolles & Olson.

In 1965 he gave up practicing law to devote more time to his business interests. He is vice chairman of Berkshire Hathaway, the investment firm headed by his longtime personal friend, Warren Buffett. He has been chairman of the board of Blue Chip Stamps, Director of the New America Fund, Chairman of the Board of the *Los Angeles Daily Journal*, and part owner of the *Buffalo News*.

His community involvement also includes serving as Chief Financial Officer and Trustee of Planned Parenthood of Los Angeles, Trustee of the Hospital of the Good Samaritan, and President and Founder of the Alfred C. Munger Foundation.

His and Nancy's interest in education has included her service as a trustee to the Marlborough School and Stanford University, and the Mungers donated a 40 x 80 foot swimming pool and shower/changing facility to the YMCA Camp Whittle near Big Bear. Mrs. Munger is a longtime member of the YMCA's Board of Directors.

Charles and Nancy Munger's involvement with Harvard-Westlake began as parents. Each has two children from prior marriages, and four together, and all five of their sons (Hal Borthwick '66, David Borthwick '70, Charles T. Munger, Jr. '74, Barry A. Munger '80, Philip R. Munger '86) are graduates of Harvard School. Their three daughters attended Marlborough and the Westridge School in Pasadena.

"I like the place, and I think we've made enormous progress," Munger says, comparing his feelings about Harvard-Westlake to a quotation from Daniel Webster, who said of Dartmouth College: "It is a small school, but there are those who love it."

Munger became a trustee in 1969 and served as chairman of the board of trustees from 1974 to 1979. His quarter of a century as a member of the Harvard and Harvard-Westlake board of trustees sets a record for the longest service of any trustee. But it's not out of the ordinary for Munger himself, who has served that long on the board of Planned Parenthood of Los Angeles as well.

"I am very proud of the school in every way. It is outstanding in education and in moral tone. It has improved over the years, the faculty has steadily been upgraded, and there was nothing wrong with it before. I regard it as one of the best institutions of its type in the world.

"Many of the students have never experienced anything else, so they don't know what an unusual privilege they have, but we trustees marvel at it."

Munger says he believes that "the best way to get what you want in life is to deserve what you want, and Harvard-Westlake deserves this building."

The not-so-silent partner

Meet Charlie Munger, the Los Angeles lawyer who converted Warren Buffett from an old-fashioned Graham value investor to the ultimate buy-and-hold value strategist.

By Robert Lenzner
and David S. Fondiller

Berkshire Hathaway Vice Chairman Charles Munger and role model Ben Franklin
"Money can beget money, and its offspring can beget more," wrote Franklin.

78 Forbes ■ January 22, 1996

WARREN BUFFETT, probably the greatest investor in modern American history, did not do it alone. He never claimed he did, but so overwhelming has his public presence become that few people realize that for more than 30 years Buffett has had a not-so-silent partner who is as much the creator of the Berkshire Hathaway investment philosophy as is the master himself.

Charles Munger is a 72-year-old lawyer and investor, a curmudgeon who lives in Los Angeles, 1,300 miles and a two-hour time difference from Buffett's headquarters in Omaha, Neb. Munger and Buffett complement each other beautifully. Munger comes on more arrogant and erudite, while Buffett comes on modest and folksy. But that's the surface in both cases. Underneath, these are two minds in almost uncanny sync.

"I probably haven't talked to anyone on Wall Street one hundredth of the times I speak to Charlie," says Buffett. Charlie Munger is the quintessential realist against whom Buffett tests his ideas. "Charlie has the best 30-second mind in the world. He goes from A to Z in one move. He sees the essence of everything before you even finish the sentence." In 1978 Munger was named vice chairman of Berkshire Hathaway and in 1983 chairman of Wesco Financial Corp., a finance company that's 80% controlled by Berkshire. He is also a director of Salomon Inc.

To understand Munger's influence on Buffett you have to recall the gradual evolution of the latter's investment philosophy. The Omaha phenomenon began as pure Ben Graham—buy cheap stocks at giveaway prices if possible and sell them when they are no longer cheap. You figure out when they are cheap by careful balance sheet analysis. Buffett still follows the Graham precepts of careful analysis, but it's been years since Buffett has bought stocks that, by Graham's standards, are cheap in terms of assets, earnings or cash flow. Nor does he, in classic Graham style, look to sell holdings when they catch up with the market.

Over the years, especially in the 1980s and 1990s, Buffett has moved closer to the concept of one-decision growth stocks—buy 'em and hold 'em forever, or at least until their fundamentals deteriorate.

Coca-Cola wasn't cheap by conventional standards when Berkshire Hathaway first bought it in 1988. On The Street it was regarded as an excellent but fully valued stock. Coca-Cola has since appreciated by close to 600%, or a compound annual rate of return of some 25%, but Berkshire has taken not a penny in profits and has sold not a single share.

What distinguishes Buffett and Munger from the herd that went to its doom in 1974 with the Nifty 50 one-decision growth stocks is this: In true Ben Graham fashion Buffett and Munger do their homework. Berkshire Hathaway's one-decision picks—Coca-Cola, Washington Post Co., Geico, Gillette, Wells Fargo, Buffalo News and Dexter Shoes—were chosen only after exhaustive analysis of balance sheets and of social and economic trends. Where most analysts saw only good but fully valued properties, Buffett saw franchises that were priceless, virtually immune from inflation and capable of continued growth—compound interest machines, in short. None of the flashes in the pan here like Avon Products or Xerox that passed as buy-and-hold-forever stocks 20 years back.

In that gradual synthesis of Graham and one-decision theory, Charlie Munger played the creative role. Buffett says: "Charlie shoved me in the direction of not just buying bargains, as Ben Graham had taught me. This was the real impact he had on me. It took a powerful force to move me on from Graham's limiting views. It was the power of Charlie's mind. He expanded my horizons."

As if completing Buffett's thought—though in a separate interview—Munger explains further: "We realized that some company that was selling at two or three times book value could still be a hell of a bargain because of momentums implicit in its position, sometimes combined with an unusual managerial skill plainly present

Should Berkshire go for all Disney stock? Or choose half stock and half cash? Maybe with the Dow over 5000, it should cash in all its chips.

in some individual or other, or some system or other."

Coca-Cola fits that pattern. So do See's Candies and the Washington Post Co. Munger says: "We intend to hold Coca-Cola forever." Forever? That's a word not to be found in Ben Graham's investment lexicon.

Conventional wisdom says that no one ever went broke taking profits. Munger doesn't think that way. "There are huge advantages for an individual to get into a position where you make a few great investments and just sit back. You're paying less to brokers. You're

The OPM factor

You probably never thought of it this way, but buying Berkshire Hathaway stock is a way of buying on margin a portfolio of investments assembled by Warren Buffett and his longtime partner, Charles Munger. On margin? Yep, even if you pay all cash, with Berkshire Hathaway you get the leverage without the risk of margin calls. Best of all, the borrowed money costs Berkshire next to nothing, so all of the profit made from it accrues to shareholders. Thus Berkshire Hathaway shareholders have working for them all the advantages of leverage without all of the risks. Selling at a premium of 35% over asset value, the stock looks grossly overpriced. But factor in the leverage, and the premium looks a lot less imposing. Says Buffett: "There is less of a premium in the stock than it appears."

Explains Munger: "Warren and I are chicken about buying stocks on margin. There's always a slight chance of catastrophe when you own securities pledged to others. The ideal is to borrow in a way no temporary thing can disturb you."

Which is precisely what Berkshire Hathaway does: It invests not only its shareholders' equity but also $13.4 billion—$11,700 per share—of essentially interest-free, borrowed money.

That's why Buffett can say that the premium on Berkshire stock is less than it appears. By the published figures, this $32,050 stock has a per share book value of $23,780. Roughly speaking, for every $1,000 in Berkshire assets, shareholders get another $500 in OPM as its slave. Add in that Other People's Money *(see chart)*—which works just as hard for shareholders as the assets—and much of the premium vanishes.

Some of the OPM derives from the Buffett-Munger buy-and-rarely-sell strategy: Thus hefty capital gains taxes are accrued but scant few are paid; by October 1995, Berkshire had a $5.1 billion deferred tax liability but paid only $155 million to the IRS.

Munger: "The object is to buy a non-dividend-paying stock that compounds for 30 years at 15% a year and pay only a single tax of 35% at the end of the period. After taxes this works out to a 13.4% annual rate of return."

Next comes the insurance company "float." Float is a technical term referring to the provisions for unpaid claims and the premiums paid in advance by the insured, which are, of course, held and used by the insurance company pending the payment of claims.

This is virtually free money for the insurer, though sometimes it must be dipped into for paying out claims. The Berkshire Hathaway insurance company "float" is $3.8 billion, soon to be $6.8 billion, with the imminent absorption of auto insurer Geico.

Then there's Berkshire Hathaway's debt of $1.5 billion, the only part of OPM that costs any money at all. Big deal: The interest rate is a paltry 6.5%.

"We regard our float as a very significant asset," says Buffett. "We probably have as large an amount of float compared to our premium volume as virtually any property and casualty company there is—and that's intentional."

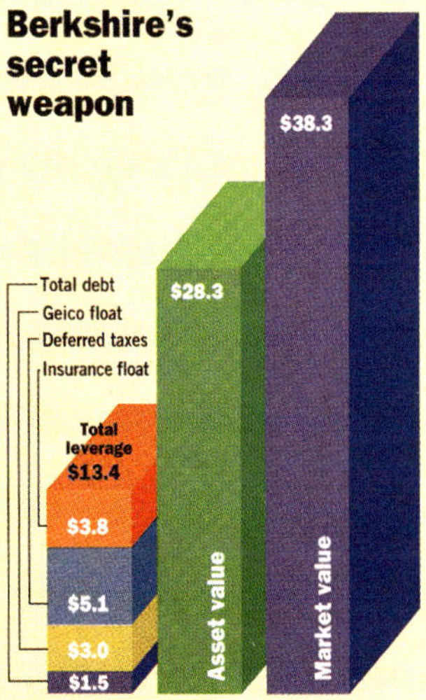

All figures are in billions of dollars.

The Other People's Money headquarters
Berkshire Hathaway acquired its insurance operation for $8.5 million in 1967. Now it has $19 billion in surplus. But the headquarters hasn't changed.

80 Forbes ■ January 22, 1996

listening to less nonsense."

Best of all, Munger says, you don't have to pay off the tax collector every year. "If it works, the governmental tax system gives you an extra one, two or three percentage points per annum with compound effects." Munger is referring to what most investors know in theory but ignore in practice: that the so-called capital gains tax is no capital gains tax at all. It is a transaction tax. No transaction, no tax. Since profit-taking involves transactions it obliges you to take the IRS in as a partner. With profits not taken, there

"Warren and I are chicken about buying stocks on margin. There's always a slight chance of catastrophe when you own securities pledged to others."

Had Berkshire had to borrow that money at prevailing interest rates, the cost would have been close to $800 million a year.

All insurance companies have float. Berkshire Hathaway's is different.

What makes it different is that a portion of it is in so-called super cat policies. It all started back in early 1967, when Berkshire Hathaway paid $8.5 million for two small Omaha insurance companies, National Indemnity and National Fire & Marine. The two tiny underwriters had $17.3 million in so-called float—or double the companies' acquisition cost.

Around this small acquisition, Berkshire developed a big business in writing super catastrophe insurance—which is reinsurance on reinsurance. It works like this: An insurance company is heavily exposed, let's say, to homes in southern California. What if an earthquake devastates the place? The insurance company lays off some of its risk to Berkshire Hathaway or another company, which agrees to pay part of its claims over a certain amount—reinsurance. Sometimes the reinsurer wants to lay off some of its risk. So it buys super cat insurance. Berkshire Hathaway sells it to them, too.

Michael Malone

This is tricky business but immensely profitable. When Berkshire Hathaway writes a super cat policy, it takes the entire premium, say 15% of the face value, as a reserve for the first year. At the end of the year, if the horrendous earthquake or wind storm didn't happen, "we've made the money," says Munger. Berkshire Hathaway then books the full premium as income.

You can view the whole thing as a sophisticated kind of gambling: A hurricane could sweep away much of southern Florida. Berkshire is, in effect, betting that it won't happen, and sets the odds in its favor by charging a premium of 15% of the policy's face value.

If the sky doesn't fall that year, Berkshire wins the entire bet. If it loses? The odds of another major earthquake in the Los Angeles basin in any single year are 20-to-1, in Buffett's opinion. An earthquake causing $30 billion in damage would cost Berkshire up to $1 billion; spread over 20 years that's $50 million a year. The Northridge quake, which cost insurers about $12 billion, cost Berkshire hardly anything.

Munger says that Berkshire's worst-case annual loss from super cat insurance would be $600 million after taxes. This would wipe out a year's premiums, but that's all. The biggest single policy Berkshire has written is $400 million, for 20th Century Insurance, which lost its entire capital because of the destruction of homes during the Northridge earthquake. Usually, though, Berkshire Hathaway spreads the risk among oil platform explosions, wind storms, earthquakes and other disasters. With a diversified book it spreads its risk widely.

Berkshire has done so well because it has avoided the asbestos and environmental hazard policies that sank so many other insurers. Its largest underwriting loss ever was $120 million in 1991.

The bottom line: For the last three years, Berkshire has made underwriting profits. So, its cost of funds is less than zero, which means the return on the float is pure profit.

Investing the float, Buffett and Munger have been able to get a compound rate of return of 23%. Now you know why FORBES calls Berkshire a wonderful compound interest machine.

Meanwhile, the average float grows geometrically. It has more than doubled, from $1.6 billion in 1990 to $3.8 billion in 1995. Berkshire's once tiny insurance operation has become the second-best capitalized insurance company in the U.S. It is an A++-rated company with $19 billion in policyholders' surplus—second only to State Farm, with $24 billion, more than double the size of Allstate or AIG.

But don't bother looking for limousines or antiques in National Indemnity's office. It still operates with a tiny staff out of its nondescript Omaha headquarters.

–R.L. and D.S.F. ■

Forbes ■ January 22, 1996 81

Berkshire Hathaway Chairman Warren Buffett and Munger **"You know the cliché that opposites attract?" asks Munger. "Well, opposites don't attract."**

"I probably haven't talked to anyone on Wall Street one hundredth of the times I speak to Charlie," says Buffett.

remains a theoretical tax liability, but the money is still working for you.

Besides, if you sell stock in a great company, where can you find a comparable investment? As the poet Omar Khayyam put it: "Oft I wonder what the vintner buys half so precious as the stuff he sells."

Buffett and Munger share a deep respect for the awesome, mysterious power of compound interest. Charlie Munger loves to quote his hero, Benjamin Franklin, on the subject. Wrote Franklin of compounding: ". . . 'tis the stone that will turn all your lead into gold. . . . Remember that money is of a prolific generating nature. Money can beget money, and its offspring can beget more."

Munger is rarely without a compound rate of return table. He illustrates its magic by taking an investment of $1 and demonstrating that a return of 13.4% a year, after taxes, over 30 years, will make that $1 worth $43.50. To Munger it's much better to depend on compounding than on market timing.

What few people realize is that Buffett and Munger wring extra power from the compounding principle through use of leverage. Take that $1 compounded for 30 years at 13.4%. Suppose in the first year you borrow 50 cents at 8% and invest that, too. The net effect is to raise your rate of return from 13.4% to 18.8%. Repeat that process every year, and over the full 30 years your $1 will beget its way to $176.

"Understanding both the power of compound return and the difficulty getting it is the heart and soul of understanding a lot of things," says Munger in typically grandiose terms. (To see how Berkshire Hathaway leverages its capital with other people's money, see box, p. 80.)

Munger persuaded Buffett to buy 100% of See's Candies for Berkshire in 1972 for $25 million, net of surplus cash. This was no Ben Graham stock. But it has turned

"Understanding both the power of compound return and the difficulty getting it is the heart and soul of understanding a lot of things."

out to be a compound interest machine. Last year See's made about $50 million pretax, putting a value on the company of $500 million. That's a 13.3% compounded rate of return for 24 years. Add in pretax retained earnings over this period—which were reinvested—and you get a total pretax return of over 23% annually.

At any time in these 24 years Berkshire Hathaway could have cashed in all or part of See's through an initial public offering. Why didn't it? Answers Munger: "The number of acquisitions making 23% pretax is very small in America." Better to leave the money compounding in a relatively sure thing.

In Roger Lowenstein's insightful and highly readable biography, *Buffett: The Making of an American Capitalist*, Munger gets relatively few pages of his own. Yet Buffett would be the first to admit that without Charlie Munger he probably would not have become one of the richest men in the world.

Lowenstein doesn't ignore Munger's role but, perhaps because it is less dramatic than Buffett's, he underplays it. Once a year Warren and Charlie sit side-by-side on the stage of an auditorium in Omaha on the day of the Berkshire Hathway annual meeting. They often meet in New York and California, and recently spent the weekend in Seattle with Buffett's close pal, Microsoft's Bill Gates. But for most of the year they are connected only by the telephone wires.

In the exchanges carried over those wires, Buffett is the stock picker while Munger is the doubter, the skeptic, the devil's advocate, against whom Buffett tests his ideas. The simple fact is that you can't tell whether an idea is likely to work unless you consider all the possible negatives. Not that Munger is a sour puss. Their verbal exchanges are larded with jokes. For all their surface differences, these two men have similar minds. "Everybody engaged in complicated work needs colleagues," explains Munger. "Just the discipline of having to put your thoughts in order with somebody else is a very useful thing."

"You know this cliché that opposites attract? Well, opposites don't attract. Psychological experiments prove that it's people who are alike that are attracted to each other. Our minds work in very much the same way."

Where and how do their minds work together? "On the close calls," Munger replies. Okay, it's a good company. But is the price low enough? Is the management made up of people Munger and Buffett are comfortable with? If it is cheap enough to buy, is it cheap for the wrong reason or the right reason? As Munger puts it: "What's the flip side, what can go wrong that I haven't seen?"

Right now the two men are matching wits about Berkshire Hathaway's 20 million shares, or 13% stake, in Capital Cities/ABC, worth $2.5 billion. By early this year, when shareholders vote on the takeover of Capital Cities by Walt Disney Co., Munger and Buffett will have to decide whether they want to become one of the two largest shareholders in what would be the biggest entertainment concern in the nation.

Should they go for all Walt Disney stock in the deal? Or compromise by choosing half stock and half cash? Maybe with the Dow over 5000, they should cash in all their chips.

Don't be surprised if Buffett and Munger go for a good-sized chunk of cash. "We have huge admiration for what Disney has achieved. But the stock is very high, and the market itself is near record levels," Munger tells FORBES. Disney is selling at 22 times earnings and 5 times book value. It's good but is it that good? Munger and Buffett are keeping the wires burning talking about it.

In a tie vote, Munger says, Buffett wins. After they have kicked around a subject, he is willing to let Buffett make the final decision. "A lot of dominant personalities, like me, can never play the subservient role even to Warren, who is more able and dedicated than I am," Munger says.

That last sentence explains a lot about both men. Munger is immensely opinionated. Yet he is willing to play second fiddle. To subordinate strong views and a powerful personality requires a high degree of self-discipline and objectivity. Objectivity is the key word here. It means stripping decisions of emotions, of hopes and fears, of impatience and self-delusion and all purely subjective elements. Few people have this strength. Munger does. Giving in sometimes to Buffett requires, in Munger's own words, "objectivity about where you rank in the scheme of things."

Another word for objectivity is "cold-blooded." Most of us mere humans get dizzy when a stock we hold goes up and up. Acrophobia sets in. We fear losing our paper profits. So we sell and sometimes we are sorry. At the other extreme, we like an investment but shy away because the consensus says we are wrong. Munger and

"Charlie has the best 30-second mind in the world," says Buffett. "He goes from A to Z in one move. He sees the essence of everything before you even finish the sentence."

Buffett strive to strip out emotion. Likewise, when things start to go wrong, most of us keep hoping they will soon get better. Munger and Buffett try not to hope but to coldly analyze the possibilities. This hard-nosed objectivity had a recent demonstration in the joint decision to redeem $140 million worth of preferred shares in troubled Salomon Inc. rather than convert them into common shares. Emotionally, Buffett and Munger had a lot tied up in Salomon. Objectively, they could find better places to put the money. Salomon just had to go.

Munger backed up Buffett on one of the most cold-blooded decisions at Salomon: to refuse to pay all of the deferred and vested compensation former chairman John Gutfreund claimed he was owed. Contrast this with the rich payoffs recently given to ousted executives at Time Warner. In Munger's view, Gutfreund let the company down and deserved no huge golden handshake.

Gutfreund is bitter toward Munger. For the sake of keeping the peace most executives would have paid Gutfreund off. But in Munger's view that would not be an objective decision.

More often than they disagree, Munger and Buffett see things exactly alike. It took them only about three hours to decide about accumulating a 4% position in the Federal Home Loan Mortgage Corp. for Berkshire Hathaway in 1989. That position, for which Berkshire paid only $72 million, is today worth over half a billion dollars.

It was a no-brainer, says Munger. "Only savings and loans could own it. And nobody could own more than 4%. Here was the perfect inefficient market. You've got something that makes hundreds of millions of dollars. It was obvious."

For Buffett and Munger maybe. But not for everyone.

Buffett is by far the wealthier of the two. Buffett—who got there first—with his wife owns 43.8% of Berkshire Hathaway, worth $17 billion. Munger's 1.6% is currently worth $610 million.

Where Buffett says he can't remember ever selling a share of Berkshire stock, Munger has given away several hundred shares as charitable gifts. He has given heaps of money to Los Angeles' Good Samaritan Hospital. He has contributed liberally to Planned Parenthood and the Stanford University Law School, and was the major donor of a new science center at the Harvard-Westlake School, a private day school in Los Angeles.

It's not a question of relative greed: Buffett does not live an especially lavish life and plans on leaving almost everything to his wife, Susan, who in turn has promised to leave it to the best endowed foundation in the world. It's as if the two men, on this point, have different time spans: Munger wants the satisfaction of seeing his money do good things now; Buffett sees his role as piling up more chips for his heirs to do good things with.

Apparently Buffett figures that the longer he has to work his compound interest magic, the more money his heirs will have to do good with. While a lot of people criticize Buffett for not being more generous, Munger stoutly defends his friend: "It's more useful for Warren to be piling it up than to be giving it away." It was Munger, not Buffett, who initiated the designated contributions plan under which Berkshire shareholders get to donate $13 for each of their shares to their favorite charity.

One thing on which Munger and Buffett do not exactly agree is politics. Munger who, with his second wife Nancy, has eight children, is a registered Republican. Buffett is a Democrat who has enjoyed rubbing elbows with the Clintons. "I'm more conservative but I'm not a typical Colonel Blimp," says Munger.

While he has less passion than Buffett for civil rights, Munger does agree with Buffett on population control and abortion rights. During the 1960s Munger helped California women obtain abortions in Mexico by paying for their trips. Later, he was a driving force in helping persuade the California Supreme Court to make the first decision overturning, on constitutional grounds, a law prohibiting abortions. Recalls Buffett: "Charlie took over the case. He solicited the deans of leading medical and law schools to enter amicus briefs. Charlie did all the work on it night and day, even writing some of the briefs himself."

There must be something in the air or the water in Omaha. Though the pair met only in the late 1950s, the house Munger grew up in is only 200 yards from Buffett's current home. As a young man Munger also worked in Buffett's grandfather's grocery store. After attending the University of Michigan and the California Institute of Technology without getting a degree, Munger served as meteorological officer in the Air Force in World War II. He gained entrance to Harvard Law School without an under-

"I've tried to imitate, in a poor way, the life of Benjamin Franklin. When he was 42, Franklin quit business to focus more on being a writer, statesman, philanthropist, inventor and scientist. That's why I have diverted my interest away from business."

graduate degree, and graduated in 1948.

He was only 22 when he entered Harvard, but even by the standards of that arrogant institution Munger was noted as a brainy but somewhat pompous and conceited fellow. Unprepared for a lesson one day, he calmly told his professor, "Give me the facts and I'll give you the law."

Unlike Buffett, Munger has never devoted full time to investing. After graduation he shunned his home town, plying for the richer prospects in Los Angeles where he joined Musick Peeler & Garrett, the law firm which represented wealthy local entrepreneurs including J. Paul Getty.

Later, Munger formed his own firm, Munger, Tolles & Olson, which still carries his name first. It is one of the leading California firms, representing Southern California Edison and Unocal, as well as Berkshire Hathaway. In 1965 he stepped down as an active partner of the firm, though he keeps his office there and still lectures the partners on the importance of choosing clients like friends, and not going for the last dollar.

Munger began his investment career independent of Buffett. From 1962 until 1975 he managed Wheeler Munger & Co., an investment counseling firm, from a grungy office in the Pacific Coast Stock Exchange building. Munger's investment record did not match Buffett's in those years, but he earned a highly respectable compound return of 19.8% a year before fees and after expenses.

Munger did not become a large Berkshire Hathaway shareholder until the late 1970s when two of his holdings, Diversified Retailing, and later Blue Chip Stamps, were merged into Berkshire. After that, Buffett and Munger got to know each other better—and Buffett moved into his most productive period.

The two live very different lives. Of late Buffett has begun to enjoy his popularity, while not neglecting his investing. Munger, as always, pursues a wide range of activities. "I've tried to imitate, in a poor way, the life of Benjamin Franklin. When he was 42, Franklin quit business to focus more on being a writer, statesman, philanthropist, inventor and scientist. That's why I have diverted my interest away from business."

Remarkably, neither Munger nor Buffett has much regard for Wall Street, though it has made their fortunes. "On a net basis the whole investment management business together gives no value added to all stock portfolio owners combined," Munger says. "That isn't true of plumbing and it isn't true of medicine. Warren agrees with me 100%. We shake our heads at the brains that have been going into money management. What a waste of talent."

Munger likens the market to the race track, where it's notoriously hard to beat the odds because the track takes a 17% cut on each dollar bet. Add in commissions, management charges, underwriting profits, and the whole fee structure, and the financial community's take, while less than that of a race track, can still be quite material.

"Beating the market averages, after paying substantial costs and fees, is an against-the-odds game; yet a few people can do it, particularly those who view it as a game full of craziness with an occasional mispriced something or other," Munger says.

He adds: "Personally, I think that if security trading in America were to go down by 80%, the civilization would work better. And if I were God, I'd change the tax rules so it would go down by 80%—in fact, by more than 80%." Munger once proposed a 100% tax on gains taken in less than a year from securities trading.

Is there a contradiction between this disdain for professional investing and Buffett and Munger's brilliant practice of the art? You can tell by his answer that Munger has given a great deal of thought to that question.

"I join John Maynard Keynes in characterizing investment management as a low calling," he responds, "because most of it is just shifting around a perpetual universe of common stocks. The people doing it just cancel each other out. You will note that none of my children is in investment management. Warren and I are a little different in that we actually run businesses and allocate capital to them.

"Keynes atoned for his 'sins' by making money for his college and serving his nation. I do my outside activities to atone and Warren uses his investment success to be a great teacher. And we love to make money for the people who trusted us early on, when we were young and poor."

In FORBES' view, the social conscience Munger expresses is part and parcel of his investment success, as is Buffett's. And so these complex, aging prodigies carefully tend their compound interest machine, a joint creation of two exceptional personalities. Others may try to duplicate Berkshire Hathaway but they won't be able to duplicate these two exceptional minds. ■

Forbes ■ January 22, 1996 85

The Washington Post

Optimism Has No Place in Accounting

By Charles T. Munger

Thursday, April 4, 2002; Page A17

The fiasco at Enron had two causes: (1) perverted "financial engineering" that portrayed failure as progress and (2) generally accepted accounting principles that practically invited delusion and fraud.

The faults of those who misled now get much attention and create demands for greater criminal penalties. But the faults of generally accepted accounting principles are more important, because changing accounting rules, and the way they are adopted, has a greater potential for preventing Enron-type disasters.

Fools and knaves, like those at Enron, will always be with us and will be particularly active where big money can be made -- for instance, in reporting ever-higher earnings.

Therefore, accounting rules must make it very difficult for fools and knaves to fake profits and net assets. Every retailer knows that his "shrink rate" from stealing depends on his maintaining a system that makes it hard for anyone to get away with theft. Similarly, sound accounting must make it difficult for corporations to get away with presenting failure as success.

A rule-making system that instead makes misuse of numbers *easy* operates like a retailing system without cash registers. Troubles are sure to come in each instance, no matter what the criminal penalties, because neither system insists on the margin of safety demanded by, say, engineering, which seeks to prevent damage from inevitable human foibles. For instance, engineering, reacting to many avoidable deaths in surgery, created anesthesia machines that do not permit operators to reduce oxygen delivery to zero. Wise accounting rules must display similar shrewdness in preventing undesirable accounting.

The way to get maximum safety from accounting rules is to force a pessimistic outlook. In the long term, huge public benefits are to be gained, with almost no public dangers, from pessimistic accounting, while optimistic accounting is a public menace.

Seldom has this been better demonstrated than in the case of Enron, where optimistic accounting of its derivatives trading resulted in a "front-ending" of too much dubious and uncollected revenue into earnings. In the first part of this charade, generally accepted accounting principles allowed "marked to market" valuations, based on defective information about market prices and inadequate allowance for the risks of clearing trades. Later, hundreds of turgid pages of accounting rules were used to justify determining earnings on a "mark to model" basis, in which "model" prices were calculated by the very traders subject to audit while they were paid bonuses based on reported profits.

The system of generally accepted accounting principles is defective because the desires of accounting firms and the wishes of their clients make it so. Moreover, because significant parts of the system are rotten to the core, the trouble will not be limited to firms that engaged in derivatives trading or hired the accounting firm Arthur Andersen. Huge vested interests love misleading accounting. And the Securities and Exchange Commission, even under a would-be reformer like Arthur Levitt, can't bring about much reform because it is deterred by politicians serving the vested interests.

To so state the problem suggests a solution: placing the control of accounting much farther away than it now is from the influence of accounting firms, corporations and politicians.

Thus, our model for accounting rule-making should be, first, some new control body similar to but even more independent than the Federal Reserve System. Second, the SEC must be required to enforce the standards established by the new rule-setters.

These rule-makers should be at least as expert, determined and virtuous as Paul Volcker was when he tamed inflation. They should also be less removable than the head of the Fed. After all, folly often is not appraised as such by those who profit from it, and eliminating it will be painful for some.

Some people think that, to correct accounting, we merely need some new committee or some increase in power for the SEC. But these ideas have failed, time after time, because they are equivalent to trying to influence an elephant with a peashooter. We need a stronger remedy.

The writer is vice chairman of Berkshire Hathaway Inc.

One Final
I Have Nothing to Add...

We conclude with this final question:

Question: "In your Harvard speech on 'The Psychology of Human Misjudgment,' you mention the strange case of the Latin American country, where some very clever reformers used psychology, not economic remedies, to fix an enormously corrupt market system. Can you tell us what country that was and provide more details?"

Answer: "Oh, yes—I ran across that fascinating story not in an Economics book, but in a Psychology paper. I could dig it out of my files for you, but it's too much effort, so I won't ."

Editor's note: Sometimes we remain in the dark....

Index

A

B

E

F

J

K

L

M

N

O

P

Q

R

S

T

U

V

W

X

Y

Z

Other Acknowledgments

We also wish to express our appreciation for document submittal, preparation and editing by the following individuals: Sharon Broggie, Robert Denham, Dick Esbenshade, Elaine Fong, Joseph Hsiung, Sylvia Licup, Stefaan Marien, Pat McGee, Jeff Moore, Nancy Munger, Sandra Shatto, Nancy Stepanovich, Stephen Sweeney, Sherwin Tieng, and Christopher Toomey.

For our abridged and second editions, we wish to recognize the efforts of Russell O. Wiese and KimMarie Zamot of Davis Advisors who were a joy to work with in every respect; writer Steve Goldberg and editor Fred Frailey of *Kiplinger Personal Finance Magazine* for their September 2005 interview of Charlie; Paul DePodesta, Professor Mark Hirschey, Alexis Livanos, John K. Martin, Matt Ouimet, and Ben Smeal for helpful input; and William N. Thorndike, Jr. and Aleem Choudhry's research in connection with the Henry Singleton and Teledyne sidebar.

December 10, 2004, with the first mockup of *Poor Charlie's Almanack.*

And a special thank you from the Editor to Warren Buffett for the encouragement and support that made *Poor Charlie's Almanack* a reality.

Charles T. Munger—Chronology

1924 Charles Thomas Munger born January 1 in Omaha, Nebraska, to Al and Toody Munger.

1941–42 Charlie attends the University of Michigan as a math major. Does not graduate.

1943 Charlie joins the U.S. Army Air Corps and serves as a meteorological officer.

1943–44 While serving in the Army Air Corps, Charlie attends the California Institute of Technology in Pasadena, California.

1946 Charlie marries Nancy Huggins.

1948 Charlie graduates from Harvard Law School, magna cum laude. He begins practicing law in Los Angeles at Wright & Garrett, which later became Musick Peeler & Garrett.

1949 Charlie admitted to the California Bar.

1950 Charlie builds a relationship with Ed Hoskins and eventually joins him in ownership and operation of Transformer Engineers Company.

1953 Charlie and Nancy Huggins divorce.

1955 Charlie's son Teddy dies of leukemia.

1956 Charlie marries Nancy Barry Borthwick, his wife of forty-nine years.

1959 Warren Buffett and Charlie meet at a dinner in Omaha hosted by children of their mutual friend Dr. Edwin Davis.

1960 Charlie demolishes a family mansion on two lots in the Hancock Park area of Los Angeles. He sells one lot to finance the project and moves his family into a house he builds on the other lot.

1961 Charlie and partner Ed Hoskins sell Transformer Engineers Company. Otis Booth and Charlie begin their first real estate development.

1962 On February 1, Wheeler, Munger & Company, a limited partnership, is established in Los Angeles, with Charlie and Jack Wheeler as partners. The law firm of Munger, Tolles is launched with seven attorneys, including Roy Tolles, Roderick Hills, who later became chairman of the SEC, and his wife, Carla Anderson Hills, who among other top government posts, became U.S. Trade Representative. Warren starts buying shares in Berkshire Hathaway, later acquiring control of the beleaguered New Bedford, Massachusetts, textile manufacturer.

1965 Charlie steps down as an active member of Munger, Tolles & Olson, ceasing his practice of law. Charlie, Warren, and Rick Guerin begin buying shares in Blue Chip Stamps. Warren accumulates enough shares of Berkshire to take control of the company.

1967 Charlie and Warren go to New York to buy Associated Cotton Shops. Warren has earlier acquired National Indemnity Company and National Fire and Marine Insurance Company for $8.6 million.

1968 Warren convenes a group of friends and fellow investors, including Charlie, to travel to Coronado, California, to meet with Benjamin Graham and discuss the flagging stock market. Warren starts to liquidate Berkshire's assets and restructure it as a holding company.

1969 Charlie and Warren provide financial and legal support for the appeal to the California Supreme Court of Dr. Belous, a physician who referred a patient to an abortion clinic. Charlie becomes a trustee of Harvard School in Los Angeles, which later merged with Westlake School. The one-hundred-member Buffett Partnership is terminated at the end of the year. Investors had multiple choices—take cash, take shares in Berkshire, or follow Warren's recommendation to invest in the Sequoia Fund. Previously, Berkshire has purchased the Illinois National Bank.

1972 Through Blue Chip Stamps, Warren and Charlie buy See's Candy for $25 million. Rick Guerin and Charlie acquire controlling interest in the New America Fund.

1973 Berkshire's *Omaha Sun* newspaper, under the direction of Stan Lipsey, wins a Pulitzer Prize for its exposé of Boys Town. Berkshire begins investing in The Washington Post Company, becoming the largest shareholder outside the family of Katharine Graham.

1974 Charlie becomes chairman of the board of Harvard School, serving until 1979. Warren and Charlie buy Wesco Financial, the parent company of a Pasadena savings and loan association.

1975 Charlie steps down as head of Wheeler, Munger & Company, and the partnership is liquidated in 1976. Its compounded annual growth rate from 1962 to 1975 was 19.8 percent vs. 5.0 percent for the Dow.

1976 The Securities and Exchange Commission completes an investigation of the relationship of Blue Chip Stamps, Wesco Financial, and Berkshire, Blue Chip Stamps settles. Warren and Charlie settle without claiming innocence or admitting guilt and pays $115,000 to Wesco shareholders who may have been damaged by their business practices. Charlie becomes chairman of Blue Chip Stamps.

1977 Through Blue Chip Stamps, Warren and Charlie purchase the *Buffalo Evening News* for $32 million. Berkshire's equity interest in Blue Chip Stamps increases to 36.5 percent by the end of the year. Berkshire invests $10.9 million in Capital Cities Communications.

1978 Charlie becomes Berkshire's vice chairman. Berkshire's stake in Blue Chip Stamps increases to fifty-eight percent, requiring that the company be fully consolidated into Berkshire's financial statements. Charlie's vision problems begin.

1979 Wesco Financial acquires Precision Steel Warehouse.

1980 Charlie loses vision in his left eye after failed cataract surgery and extremely painful complications. Vision in his right eye